JOHN WILLIS

SCREEN WORLD

1998

VOLUME 49

ASSOCIATE EDITOR
BARRY MONUSH

LIBRARY OF CONGRESS CARD NO. 50-3023
ISBN: 1-55783-341-9 (CLOTH)
ISBN: 1-55783-342-7 (PAPER)

1957

1957

1964

1966

1972

1973

1978

1984

1990

To

JOANNE WOODWARD

one of the most gifted actresses of her generation, who has found truth in a rich collection of characters of edgy intelligence and indomitable spirit.

FILMS:*Count Three and Pray* (1955), *A Kiss Before Dying* (1956), *The Three Faces of Eve* (1957; Academy Award for Best Actress), *No Down Payment* (1957), *The Long Hot Summer* (1958), *Rally 'Round the Flag, Boys!* (1958), *The Sound and the Fury* (1959), *The Fugitive Kind* (1959), *From the Terrace* (1960), *Paris Blues* (1961), *The Stripper* (1963), *A New Kind of Love* (1963), *Signpost to Murder* (1964), *A Fine Madness* (1966), *A Big Hand for the Little Lady* (1966), *Rachel, Rachel* (1968; Academy Award nomination), *Winning* (1969), *King: A Filmed Record...Montgomery to Memphis* (1970), *WUSA* (1970), *They Might Be Giants* (1971), *The Effect of Gamma Rays on Man-in-the-Moon-Marigolds* (1972), *Summer Wishes, Winter Dreams* (1973; Academy Award nomination), *The Drowning Pool* (1975), *The End* (1978) *Harry and Son* (1984), *The Glass Menagerie* (1987), *Mr. and Mrs. Bridge* (1990; Academy Award nomination), *The Age of Innocence* (narrator), *Philadelphia* (1993)

Leonardo DiCaprio, Kate Winslet in *Titanic*
Academy Award Winner for Best Picture of 1997
© Paramount Pictures/Twentieth Century Fox

CONTENTS

EDITOR: John Willis

ASSOCIATE EDITOR: Barry Monush

Staff: Marco Starr Boyajian, William Camp, Jimmie Hollifield, II,

Tom Lynch, John Sala

Acknowledgements: John Alston, Ed Arentz, Arrow Releasing, Artistic License, Castle Hill, Castle Rock Entertainment, Cinepix Films Properties, City Cinemas, Cline & White, Richard D'Attile, Dennis Davidson Associates, Alex Dawson, Samantha Dean, Dream Works, Brian Durnin, The Film Forum, First Look, First Run Features, Fox Serchlight, Adrian Goycoolea, Gramercy Pictures, Khan & Jacobs, Craig Keleman, Kino International, Legacy Releasing, Leisure Time Features, LIVE Entertainment, Mike Maggiore, David Mazor, Robert Milite, Jr., Miramax Films, Jennifer Morgerman, David Munro, New Line Cinema/Fine Line Features, New Yorker Films, Northern Arts Entertainment, October Films, PMK Publicity, Paramount Pictures, Phaedra Films, PolyGram, Quad Cinema, George Scherling, Kimberly Scherling, 7th Art Releasing, Sony Pictures Entertainment, Sheldon Stone, Strand Releasing, Paul Sugarman, Twentieth Century Fox, Universal Pictures, Jen Wallace, Walt Disney Pictures, Glenn Young, Zeitgeist Films.

1. Harrison Ford

2. Julia Roberts

3. Leonardo DiCaprio

4. Will Smith

5. Tom Cruise

6. Jack Nicholson

7. Jim Carrey

8. John Travolta

9. Robin Williams

10. Tommy Lee Jones

11. Brad Pitt

12. Neve Campbell

13. Pierce Brosnan

14. Jodie Foster

15. Nicolas Cage

16. Tim Allen

TOP BOX OFFICE STARS OF 1997

17. Michael Douglas

18. Demi Moore

19. Michelle Pfeiffer

20. Sandra Bullock

1997 RELEASES

January 1 Through December 31, 1997

21. Cameron Diaz

22. Brendan Fraser

23. Denzel Washington

24. Robert De Niro

25. Meg Ryan

Dustin Hoffman

Jamie Lee Curtis

Ethan Hawke

TURBULENCE

(MGM) Producer, Martin Ransohoff, David Valdes; Executive Producer, Keith Samples; Director, Robert Butler; Screenplay, Jonathan Brett; Photography, Lloyd Ahern II; Designer, Mayling Cheng; Editor, John Duffy; Music, Shirley Walker; Costumes, Robert Turturice; Visual Effects Supervisor, Mark Vargo; Casting, Phyllis Huffman; a Rysher Entertainment presentation of a Martin Ransohoff production; Distributed by MGM/UA; Dolby Digital SDDS Stereo; Super 35 Widescreen; Color; Rated R; 103 minutes; January release

CAST

Ryan Weaver .... Ray Liotta
Teri Halloran .... Lauren Holly
Stubbs .... Brendan Gleeson
Detective Aldo Hines .... Hector Elizondo
Rachel Taper .... Rachel Ticotin
Brooks .... Jeffrey DeMunn
Sinclair .... John Finn
Captain Sam Bowen .... Ben Cross
Maggie .... Catherine Hicks
Betty .... Heidi Kling
Carl .... Gordy Owens
Captain Matt Powell .... J. Kenneth Campbell
First Officer Ted Kary .... James MacDonald
Marshal Douglas .... Michael Harney
Marshal Arquette .... Grand L. Bush
Marshal Riordan .... Richard Hoyt Miller
Marshal Green .... Michael F. Kelly
Mr. Kramer .... Alan Bergmann
Mrs. Kramer .... Danna Hansen
Kip .... R.J. Knoll
Career Woman .... Sondra Spriggs
LAX Manager .... Garrett Brown
Limato .... Darryl Theirse
Asian Businessman .... Fritz Mashimo
Mr. Hollywood .... Tom Todoroff

and Jeffrey Joseph (Detective), Dennis Redfield (Desk Sergeant), Malachy McCourt (Ray the Doorman), Gary Rodriguez (Rodriguez), Billy Burton (Port Authority Cop), Callie Thorne (Laura), John Elsen (Stone), Bill Cross (William Harris), Tannis Benedict, Don Dowe, Scott Gurney (Controllers), Cooper Huckabee (Wing Commander), Ken Thatcher II (SWAT Member), Kevin O'Rourke (Mark Pavone), Scott Lawrence (Felix), Ken Mosley (Tower Air Co-Pilot)

During a stormy Christmas Eve flight from New York to Los Angeles, a gun battle errupts killing the pilots and leaving a murderer free of his police escorts, as stewardess Teri Halloran tries to bring the plane safely to the ground.

Lauren Holly, Ray Liotta

Tom Sizemore, Penelope Ann Miller

THE RELIC

(PARAMOUNT) Producers, Sam Mercer, Gale Anne Hurd; Executive Producers, Gary Levinsohn, Mark Gordon; Director/Photography, Peter Hyams; Screenplay, Amy Jones, John Raffo, Rick Jaffa, Amanda Silver; Based upon the novel by Douglas Preston and Lincoln Child; Designer, Philip Harrison; Editor, Steven Kemper; Visual Effects Supervisor, Gregory L. McMurry; Creature Effects, Stan Winston; Costumes, Dan Lester; Music, John Debney; Casting, Penny Perry; a Pacific Western production, presented in association with Cloud Nine Entertainment; Dolby DTS Stereo; Panavision; Deluxe color; Rated R; 110 minutes; January release

CAST

Dr. Margo Green .... Penelope Ann Miller
Lt. Vincent D'Agosta .... Tom Sizemore
Dr. Ann Cuthbert .... Linda Hunt
Dr. Albert Frock .... James Whitmore
Detective Hollingsworth .... Clayton Rohner
Greg Lee .... Chi Muoi Lo
Parkinson .... Thomas Ryan
Mayor Owen .... Robert Lesser
Mayor's Wife .... Diane Robin
John Whitney .... Lewis Van Bergen
Mrs. Blaisedale .... Constance Towers
Mr. Blaisedale .... Francis X. McCarthy
Dr. Zwiezic .... Audra Lindley
McNally .... John Kapelos
Bailey .... Tico Wells
Bradley .... Mike Bacarella

and Gene Davis (Martini), John DiSanti (Wootton), David Proval (Johnson), David Graubart (Eugene), Ronald Joshua Scott (Josh), Jophery C. Brown (Frederick Ford), Thomas Joseph Carroll (Evans), Montrose Hagins (Chanting Woman), Santos Morales (Captain Borne), Ralph Seymour (Sergeant), La Donna Tittle (Teacher), Edward Jemison (Museum Worker), David Hollander (Charlie), Amanda Ingber (Donna), Katharine Mitchell, Candy Coburn, Kurt Naebig, Don MacLellan, Marc P. Shelton (Police Officers), Don Harvey (Spota), Ken Magee (Coroner's Assistant), Aaron Lustig (Dr. Brown), Kent George (Student), Lynn A. Henderson (Perri Masai), Ron Cummins (Dr. Gross), Matthew Daniel Moses Furlin (Crazy Man), Elwood Forbes (Graduate Student), Dina Bair (Reporter), Mark Lake (Swat Team Guy), Ned Schmidtke (Captain Martin), Vincent Hammond, Brian Steele (Kothoga)

A deadly creature, unwittingly brought back from the jungles of South America, breaks loose and creates havoc at the Chicago Natural History Museum.

ALBINO ALIGATOR

(MIRAMAX) Producers, Brad Krevoy, Steve Stabler, Brad Jenkel; Director, Kevin Spacey; Screenplay, Christian Forte; Photography, Mark Plummer; Designer, Nelson Coates; Editor, Jay Cassidy; Music, Michael Brook; Costumes, Isis Mussenden; Casting, David Rubin; a Brad Krevoy & Steve Stabler production presented in association with Motion Picture Corporation of America; Dolby Stereo; Color; Rated R; 105 minutes; January release

CAST

Dova .... Matt Dillon
Janet .... Faye Dunaway
Milo .... Gary Sinise
Law .... William Fichtner
Guy .... Viggo Mortensen
Jack .... John Spencer
Danny .... Skeet Ulrich
Marv .... Frankie Faison
Jenny .... Melinda McGraw
Dino .... M. Emmet Walsh
G.D. Browning .... Joe Mantegna

and Doug Spinuzza, Spencer Garrett, Enrico Colantoni (Agents), Tulsy Ball (ATF Agent), Travis Appel (Another Agent), Brad Koepenick (Browning's Assistant), Jock Worthen (Medic), Willie C. Carpenter, Alexander Smith, Michael Unger (Reporters), Toni Montgomery (Officer), Jeff Hoffman (Jenny's Cameraman)

After their heist goes awry, three criminals take refuge in Dino's Last Chance Bar and find themselves surrounded by the police. This film marked the directorial debut of actor Kevin Spacey.

Matt Dillon, Gary Sinise

Joe Mantegna

Faye Dunaway, Skeet Ulrich, Viggo Mortensen, John Spencer

Eddie Murphy, Michael Rapaport

METRO

(TOUCHSTONE) Producer, Roger Birnbaum; Executive Producers, Mark Lipsky, Riley Kathryn Ellis; Director, Thomas Carter; Screenplay, Randy Feldman; Co-Producers, George W. Perkins, Ray Murphy, Jr., Randy Feldman; Photography, Fred Murphy; Designer, William Elliott; Costumes, Ha Nguyen; Editor, Peter E. Berger; Music, Steve Porcaro; Casting, Ellen Chenoweth; a Roger Birnbaum production, presented in association with Caravan Pictures; Distributed by Buena Vista Pictures; Dolby Digital Stereo; Panavision; Technicolor; Rated R; 117 minutes; January release

CAST

Scott Roper....................Eddie Murphy
Kevin McCall....................Michael Rapaport
Michael Korda....................Michael Wincott
Ronnie Tate....................Carmen Ejogo
Captain Frank Solis....................Denis Arndt
Lieutenant Sam Baffert....................Art Evans
Earl....................Donal Logue
Clarence Teal....................Paul Ben-Victor
Detective Kimura....................Kim Miyori
Officer Forbes....................James Carpenter
Debbie....................Jeni Chua
Bank Manager....................Dick Bright
SWAT Officer Jennings....................David Michael Silverman
Reporters....................Frank Somerville, Malou Nubla
Repoman....................Nino Degennaro
Screaming Lady....................Val Diamond
Ronnie's Boyfriend Greg....................Charleston Pierce
Detective Glass....................Will Marchetti
Racetrack Announcer....................Trevor Denman
SWAT Captain....................Joe Vincent
Jewelry Salesgirls....................Corie Henninger, Karen Kahn
Jewelry Customer Dotson....................Nellie Cravens
Jewelry Manager....................Danny Teal

and Jeff Mosley (Cable Car Brakeman), Ralph Peduto (Bail Bondsman Hawkins), James Cunningham (Postrio Waiter), C.W. Morgan (Jail Laundry Room Guard), Nick Scoggin (Property Room Sergeant Frank), Marie Villatuya (Tahitian Waitress)

Hostage negotiator Scott Roper teams with SWAT team sharp-shooter Kevin McCall to trap a deadly jewel thief.

Eddie Murphy

Carmen Ejogo, Eddie Murphy

Michael Wincott

BEVERLY HILLS NINJA

(TRISTAR) Producers, Brad Krevoy, Steve Stabler, Brad Jenkel; Executive Producers, Jeffrey D. Ivers, John Bertolli, Michael Rotenberg; Director, Dennis Dugan; Screenplay, Mark Feldberg, Mitch Klebanoff; Photography, Arthur Albert; Designer, Ninkey Dalton; Editor, Jeff Gourson; Costumes, Mary Claire Hannan; Music, George S. Clinton; Co-Producers, Marc S. Fischer, Mitch Klebanoff; Casting, Gary M. Zuckerbrod; Stunts, Rick Barker; a Motion Picture Corporation of America production in association with Brad Krevoy & Steve Stabler; Dolby SDDS Stereo; Technicolor; Rated PG-13; 90 minutes; January release

CAST

Haru .... Chris Farley
Alison .... Nicollette Sheridan
Gobei .... Robin Shou
Tanley .... Nathaniel Parker
Sensei .... Soon-Tek Oh
Nobu .... Keith Cooke Hirabayashi
Joey .... Chris Rock
Izumo .... Francois Chau
Old Japanese Man .... Dale Ishimoto
Head Kobudosai .... Da Ming Chan
Mr. Ozaru .... Burt Bulos
Billy .... Curtis Blanck
Billy's Dad .... Tom Bailey
Busboy .... Jason J. Tobin
Driver .... Richard Kline
Traveler .... Anna Mathias
Fisherman .... Nathan Jung
Policemen .... John Farley, Kevin Farley
Porter .... Gerry Del Sol
Reporters .... Cynthia Allison, Francesca Cappucci
Security Person .... Hideo Kimura
Woman .... Saachiko
Guard .... James Laing

and Robbie Thibaut, Jr. (Grandson at Hotel) Michael Cardenas (Patron at Hop Louie's), Brett Golov, Joe Decker (Club Patrons), Charles Dugan (Man with Shoes), Jason Davis (Young Haru), Alexandra Stabler (Girl on Rodeo Drive), Nicolas Stabler (Boy on Rodeo Drive), Tania L. Pearson, Lisa C. Boltanzer, Nancy Howard (Dancers), Conrad Goode, Bryan Hays Currie, Caesar Luisi (Bouncers), Rick Miller (Motorcycle Rider), Eric C. Charmelo (Guy at Plant), Sarah Pierce (Poodle Lady)

Haru, believing himself to be the Great White Ninja, travels to Beverly Hills to save a mysterious and beautiful woman.

Chris Farley, Robin Shou

Roxanne, Kathleen Quinlan

Zeus, Jessica Howell, Majandra Delfino, Miko Hughes

ZEUS AND ROXANNE

(MGM) Producers, Frank Price, Gene Rosow, Ludi Boeken; Executive Producers, Laura Friedman, Hilton Green; Director, George Miller; Screenplay, Tom Benedek; Photography, David Connell; Designer, Bernt Capra; Editor, Harry Hitner; Co-Producer, Frederic W. Brost; Music, Bruce Rowland; Casting, Karen Rea; a Rysher Entertainment presentation of a Frank Price production; Dolby DTS Stereo; Color; Rated PG; 97 minutes; January release

CAST

Terry Barnett .... Steve Guttenberg
Mary Beth Dunhill .... Kathleen Quinlan
Dr. Claude Carver .... Arnold Vosloo
Becky .... Dawn McMillan
Jordan Barnett .... Miko Hughes
Judith Dunhill .... Majandra Delfino
Nora Dunhill .... Jessica Howell
Mrs. Rice .... Duchess Tomasello
Linda .... Shannon K. Foley
Phil .... Jim R. Coleman
Floyd .... Alvin Farmer

and Harri James (Airline Attendant), Justin Humphrey (Craig), James Stone (Security Guard), Maury Covington (Reverend), Michael A. Xynidis (Messenger), Nikki, Tito, Rosa (Zeus), Cayla, Bimini, Stripe (Roxanne), Benjamin Pettijohn (Additional Zeus Vocals), David Nathaniel Hoyte (Lead Steel Pan Performer)

Marine biologist Mary Beth Dunhill is surprised to discover that her neighbor's dog, Zeus, has its own form of communication with a captive dolphin named Roxanne.

FIERCE CREATURES

(UNIVERSAL) Producers, Michael Shamberg, John Cleese; Executive Producer, Steve Abbott; Directors, Robert Young, Fred Schepisi; Screenplay, John Cleese, Iain Johnstone; Co-Producer, Patricia Carr; Photography, Adrian Biddle, Ian Baker; Music, Jerry Goldsmith; Editor, Robert Gibson; Designer, Roger Murray-Leach; Costumes, Hazel Pethig; Chief Animal Trainer, Jim Clubb; Casting, Priscilla John; a Fish Productions/Jersey Films production; Digital DTS Stereo; Panavision; Eastmancolor; Rated PG-13; 93 minutes; January release

Michael Palin, John Cleese, Jamie Lee Curtis, Kevin Kline

CAST

Rollo Lee........John Cleese
Willa Weston........Jamie Lee Curtis
Vince McCain/Rod McCain........Kevin Kline
Bugsy Malone........Michael Palin
Reggie Sealions........Ronnie Corbett
Cub Felines........Carey Lowell
Sydney Small Mammals........Robert Lindsay
Neville Coltrane........Bille Brown
Gerry Ungulates........Derek Griffiths
Pip Small Mammals........Cynthia Cleese
Hugh Primates........Richard Ridings
Di Admin........Maria Aitken
Ant Keeper........Michael Percival
Flamingo Keeper........Fred Evans
Sealion Keeper........Lisa Hogan
Parrot Keeper........Choy-Ling Man
Vulture Keeper........Tim Potter
Aquarium Keeper........Jenny Galloway
Tiger Keeper........Kim Vithana
Buffalo Keeper........Sean Francis
Rodent Keeper........Julie Saunders

and Susie Blake (Woman in Red Dress), Pat Keen (Her Mother), Denis Lill (Her Husband), Gareth Hunt (Inspector Masefield), Ron Donachie (Sergeant Scott), Paul Haigh (Sergeant Irving), Leon Herbert, Stewart Wright (Octopus Security Guards), Kerry Shale (Frightened Executive), Mac McDonald (TV Producer), Amanda Walker (Zoo Secretary), Terence Conoley (Man in Straw Hat), Tom Georgeson, John Bardon, Anthony Pedley (Sealion Spectators), Jennie Goossens, Georgia Reece, Hilary Gish, Kenneth Price, Brian King, Peter Silverleaf (Sponsors), Kevin Moore (Hotel Manager), Leslie Lowe, Iain Mitchell (Assistant Hotel Managers), Valerie Edmond (Hotel Maid), Nick Bartlett (Policeman), Ricco Ross, Kate Harper (TV Journalists), Nicholas Hutchison (TV Reporter), Kate Alderton, Jack Davenport, Jo Ann Geary, William Grove, Francis Pope, Jaqui Thomas, David Wood (Student Zoo Keepers), John Alexander (Gorilla Performer—Jambo), Peter Elliott (Gorilla Performer), Tessa Crockett, Phillip Hill, Holly Hoffman, Mario Kalli, Tina Maskell, Elizabeth O'Brien (Background Gorillas), Ailsa Berk (Panda Performer)

Kevin Kline, Jamie Lee Curtis

Hoping to keep media mogul Rod McCain from closing the floundering Marwood Zoo, Rollo Lee comes up with the marketing idea of stocking the place exclusively with violent, man-eating creatures.

John Cleese

Michael Percival, Carey Lowell, Robert Lindsay, Fred Evans, John Cleese, Richard Ridings

PREFONTAINE

(HOLLYWOOD PICTURES) Producers, Irby Smith, Jon Lutz, Mark Doonan, Peter Gilbert; Director, Steve James; Screenplay, Steve James, Eugene Corr; Co-Producer, Shelly Glasser; Photography, Peter Gilbert; Designer, Carol Winstead Wood; Editor, Peter Frank; Music, Mason Daring; Costumes, Tom Bronson; Casting, Pam Dixon Mickelson; an Irby Smith/Jon Lutz/Mark Doonan production; Distributed by Buena Vista Pictures; Dolby Digital Stereo; Technicolor; Rated PG-13; 106 minutes; January release

CAST

Steve Prefontaine........Jared Leto
Bill Bowerman........R. Lee Ermey
Bill Dellinger........Ed O'Neill
Pat Tyson........Breckin Meyer
Elfriede Prefontaine........Lindsay Crouse
Nancy Alleman........Amy Locane
Elaine Finley........Laurel Holloman
Mac Wilkins........Brian McGovern
Curtis Cunningham........Kurtwood Smith
and Adrian Amadeus (Finnish Teammate), Laurence Ballard (O'Hara), Ryan Brewer (12 Year Old Black), Robert Karl Burke (Young Pre), Gaard Swanson, Kevin Calabro (Airport Reporters), George Catalano, Jim Freeman (Patrons), Wade Clegg (German Security), Wally Dalton (Dick Burke), Adam Fitzhugh (Thomas Becker), Tom Glasgow, David Grosby (NCAA Press), Geoff Haley (German Soldier), Dag Hinrichs (Jeff Galloway), Tracy Hollister (Lasse Viren), Peter Anthony Jacobs (Ray Prefontaine), Eric Johnson (Olympic Trials Reporter), Eric Keenleyside (James Buck), Steve Kelley (U of O Reporter), Stephen J. Lang (Bar Back), Shannon Leto (Bar Patron), Eric Liddell (Gary Powers), Jochen Liesche (German Newscaster), Henry Lubatti (Frank Shorter), Jeff McAtee (Reporter at Village Gate), Michael Patten (Munich Stadium Official), John Charles Pavlich (Husband), Wendy Ray (Himself), Brad Tuinstra (Finnish Runner), Brad Upton (Neighborhood Man), Bruce Walker (Olympic Village Reporter), Hugh P. Wallace (Man on Winding Road), Mac Wilkins (Track Official), Phaedra Wilson (German Security Girl), Pauly Yarnold (Reporter at Trailer Park)

The true story of long distance runner Steve Prefontaine and his participation in the 1972 Munich Olympics. Prefontaine's life was also the basis for the 1998 film Without Limits starring Billy Crudup and Donald Sutherland.

Jared Leto, Ed O'Neill, R. Lee Ermey

Tim Roth, Tupac Shakur

GRIDLOCK'D

(GRAMERCY) Producers, Damian Jones, Paul Webster, Erica Huggins; Executive Producers, Ted Field, Russell Simmons, Scott Kroopf; Co-Executive Producers, Preston Holmes, Stan Lathan; Co-Producers, Michael Bennett, Steven Siebert; Director/Screenplay, Vondie Curtis Hall; Photography, Bill Pope; Designer, Dan Bishop; Editor, Christopher Koefoed; Costumes, Marie France; Music, Stewart Copeland; Casting, Robi Reed-Humes; a PolyGram Filmed Entertainment presentation of an Interscope Communicatios production in association with Def Pictures/Webster/Dragon Pictures; Dolby Digital Stereo; Deluxe Color; Rated R; 90 minutes; January release

CAST

Stretch........Tim Roth
Spoon........Tupac Shakur
Cookie........Thandie Newton
Mr. Woodson........Charles Fleischer
Blind Man........Howard Hesseman
Supervisor........James Pickens, Jr.
Cops........John Sayles, Eric Payne
D-Reper's Henchman........Tom Towles
Koolaid........Tom Wright
Patrolmen........James Shanta, Jim O'Malley
Chuck........George Poulos
Clerk........Debbie Zaricor
Officer #1........Mik Scriba
Cee-Cee........Lucy Alexis Liu
Resident Doctor........Richmond Arquette
Medicaid Women........Billie Neal, Debra Wilson
Nurse........Rusty Schwimmer
Admissions Person........Elizabeth Anne Dickinson
Vendor........Joey Dente
Panhandler........Darryl Jones
and Jasen Govine (Medicaid Security Guard), Tim Truby (Man with Directions), Venssia Valentino (Woman in ER), Ron Cummins (Man in ER), Bradley Jordan Spencer, Rory J. Shoaf (Paramedics), Tracy Vilar (Screaming Woman), Roslyn McKinney (Clerk), Roderick Garr (Welfare Security Guard), William Long, Jr. (Right Wing TV Show Host), Mark Ericson (Bill the Anchor Man), Tonia Rowe (Woman on TV), Lynn Blades (Alexia Cruz), Kasi Lemmons, Henry Hunter Hall (Madonna and Child), Vondie Curtis Hall (D-Reper)

When the singer in their band overdoses and ends up in a coma, Stretch and Spoon decide it is time that they clean up their drug habits.

JOHNS

(FIRST LOOK PICTURES) Producers, Beau Flynn, Stefan Simchowitz; Executive Producer, P. Holt Gardiner; Director/Screenplay, Scott Silver; Photography, Tom Richmond; Editor, Dorian Harris; Co-Executive Producer, Dolly Hall; Line Producer, Elyse Katz; Designer, Amy Beth Silver; Costumes, Sara Jane Slotnick; Music, Charles Brown, Danny Caron; Casting, Mary Vernieu; a Flynn/Simchowitz production, presented in association with Bandeira Entertainment; Dolby Stereo; CFI color; Rated R; 96 minutes; January release

CAST

Donner .... Lukas Haas
John .... David Arquette
John Cardoza .... Arliss Howard
Homeless John .... Keith David
Eli .... Christopher Gartin
David .... Josh Schaefer
Mikey .... Wilson Cruz
Jimmy the Warlock .... Terrence Dashon Howard
Mix .... Nicky Katt
Nikki .... Alanna Ubach
Manny Gould .... Elliott Gould
Paul Truman .... Richard Kind
Old Man .... Harper Roisman
Danny Cohen .... John C. McGinley
Mr. Popper .... Richard Timothy Jones
John Wayne .... Louis Mustillo
Santa Claus .... Tony Epper
Tourist Mom .... Ruth Silver
Young Hustler .... Kurtis Kunzler
Tiffany the Prostitute .... Nina Siemaszko
Christmas Preacher on Radio .... Craig Bierko

As Christmas approaches John, a Hollywood prostitute, hopes to come up with the $300 he needs to spend a night in a luxury hotel.

Lukas Haas

David Arquette

David Arquette, Lukas Haas

MEET WALLY SPARKS

(TRIMARK) Producer, Leslie Greif; Director, Peter Baldwin; Screenplay, Rodney Dangerfield, Harry Basil; Story, Harry Basil; Co-Producers, Harry Basil, Elliot Rosenblatt; Photography, Richard Kline; Designer, Bryan Jones; Costumes, Alexandra Walker; Editor, Raul Davalos; Music, Michel Colombier; Casting, Fern Champion, Mark Paladini; a Leslie Greif production; Dolby DTS Stereo; Color; Rated R; 104 minutes; January release

CAST

Wally Sparks....Rodney Dangerfield
Governor Floyd Preston....David Ogden Stiers
Sandy Gallo....Debi Mazar
Harvey Bishop....Mark L. Taylor
Emily Preston....Cindy Williams
Priscilla Preston....Lisa Thornhill
Dean Sparks....Michael Weatherly
Lola Larue....Cindy Ambuehl
Joey....Lenny Clarke
Judge Randal Williams....Alan Rachins
Helen Williams....Rita McKenzie
Canadian Ambassador....Edmund L. Shaff
Canadian Ambassador's Wife....Kay Gerhard
Alan Miller....Eamonn Roche
Mr. Spencer....Burt Reynolds
Robby Preston....Glenn Walker Harris, Jr.
Butler....Albert Able Eisenmann
Bartender....George Wallace
Mr. Harry Karp....Gilbert Gottfried
Mrs. Martha Karp....Julia Sweeney
Actor....Ron Jeremy
Robby's Friend #1....Ryan Tomlinson
Commercial Director....Sandy Helberg
Bum....Carmen Filpi
Nurse....Lesley-Anne Down
and George Greif, Dee Booher (Guests), Barry Nolan, "Stuttering" John Melendez, Karen Duffy, Bob Saget (Reporters), Connie Danese, Jennifer Koppelman, Michael Stadvec (Fans), Big Nate Kanae, Randy Kiyabo (Sumo Wrestlers), Nils Allen Stewart, Scott L. Schwartz (American Wrestlers), Laura Basil, Patricia Forte (Constituents), Janice Hart (Agnes Farber), Andre Rosey Brown (Teamster), Lewis Arquette (Cardinal), Rochelle Swanson (Dixie), Tim Allen, Morton Downey Jr., Michael Bolton, Jay Leno, John Hensen, Richard Bey, George Hamilton, Sally Jessy Raphael, Geraldo Rivera, Roseanne, Jerry Springer, Alana Stewart, Rolanda Watts (Themselves), Tony Danza (Taxi Driver), Sir Mix-a-Lot (Rapper Announcer), Michael Rooker (Bar Patron), Harry Basil (Stable Boy), Marzia Greif (Miss Bussone), Ron Jeremy (Porn Actor), Thomas Weber (Agent Cameron)

Uncouth talk show host Wally Sparks, told to clean up his program or else, pursues a seemingly safe story on Georgia governor Floyd Preston, only to uncover a scandal.

Rodney Dangerfield

Glenn Walker Harris Jr., David Ogden Stiers, Cindy Williams

Rodney Dangerfield, Cindy Williams

Burt Reynolds

Debi Mazar

Fred Willard, Catherine O'Hara, Christopher Guest, Parker Posey, Eugene Levy

WAITING FOR GUFFMAN

(SONY CLASSICS) Producer, Karen Murphy; Director, Christopher Guest; Screenplay, Christopher Guest, Eugene Levy; Photography, Roberto Schaefer; Designer, Joseph T. Garrity; Editor, Andy Blumenthal; Costumes, Julie Carnahan; Music/Lyrics, Michael McKean, Harry Shearer, Christopher Guest; a Castle Rock Entertainment presentation of a Pale Morning Dun production; Dolby Stereo; Color; Rated R; 84 minutes; January release

CAST

Corky St. Clair .... Christopher Guest
Dr. Allan Pearl .... Eugene Levy
Sheila Albertson .... Catherine O'Hara
Ron Albertson .... Fred Willard
Libby Mae Brown .... Parker Posey
Lloyd Miller .... Bob Balaban
Clifford Wooley .... Lewis Arquette
Johnny Savage .... Matt Keeslar
Gwen Fabin-Blunt, Councilwoman .... Deborah Theaker
Steve Stark, Councilman .... Michael Hitchcock
Tucker Livingston, Councilman .... Scott Williamson
Glenn Welsch, Mayor .... Larry Miller
Phil Burgess, Blaine Historian .... Don Lake
UFO Expert .... David Cross
Singing Auditoner .... Jim McQueen
Ping Pong Ball Juggler .... Turk Pipkin
Raging Bull Auditioner .... Jerry Turman
UFO Abductee .... Paul Dooley
Mrs. Allan Pearl .... Linda Kash
Red Savage .... Brian Doyle-Murray
Costume Designer .... Miriam Flynn
Stage Manager .... Jill Parker-Jones
Costume Dresser .... Margaret Bowman
Not Guffman .... Paul Benedict

Mock-documentary spotlights director Corky St. Clair as he stages a lavish musical revue to commemorate the 150th anniversary of the town of Blaine, Missouri, the Stool Capital of the World.

Bob Balaban

Matt Keeslar

DANTE'S PEAK

Jeremy Foley, Jamie Renée Smith, Pierce Brosnan, Linda Hamilton

(UNIVERSAL) Producers, Gale Anne Hurd, Joseph M. Singer; Executive Producer, Ilona Herzberg; Director, Roger Donaldson; Screenplay, Leslie Bohem; Photography, Andrzej Bartkowiak; Designer, Dennis Washington; Editors, Howard Smith, Conrad Buff, Tina Hirsch; Visual Effects Supervisor, Patrick McClung; Associate Producer, Geoff Murphy; Co-Producer, Marliese Schneider; Costumes, Isis Mussenden; Music, John Frizzell, James Newton Howard; Casting, Mike Fenton, Allison Cowitt; a Pacific Western production; DTS Digital Stereo; Super 35 Widescreen; Deluxe color; Rated PG-13; 112 minutes; February release

CAST

Harry Dalton	Pierce Brosnan
Rachel Wando	Linda Hamilton
Lauren Wando	Jamie Renée Smith
Graham Wando	Jeremy Foley
Ruth	Elizabeth Hoffman
Paul Dreyfus	Charles Hallahan
Greg	Grant Heslov
Terry Furlong	Kirk Trutner
Nancy	Arabella Field
Stan	Tzi Ma
Les Worrell	Brian Reddy
Dr. Jane Fox	Lee Garlington
Sheriff Turner	Bill Bolender
Mary Kelly	Carol Androsky
Norman Gates	Peter Jason
Jack Collins	Jeffrey L. Ward
Elliot Blair	Tim Haldeman
Marianne	Walker Brandt
Warren Cluster	Hansford Rowe
Karen Narlington	Susie Spear
Hot Spring Man	David Lipper
Hot Springs Woman	Heather Stephens

and Ingo Neuhaus (National Guardsman), Patty Raya MacMillan (News Stringer), R.J. Burns (Man at Helicopter), Tammy L. Smith (Town Meeting Woman), Christopher Murray (Pilot), Justin Williams (Paramedic), Donna Deshon, Tom Magnuson (Road Block Newspersons), Marilyn Leubner (Babysitter)

Volcanologist Harry Dalton arrives in the mountain town of Dante's Peak predicting that a sleeping volcano will soon errupt.

Pierce Brosnan, Linda Hamilton

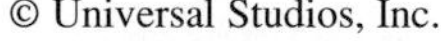

Pierce Brosnan, Linda Hamilton

THE BEAUTICIAN AND THE BEAST

(PARAMOUNT) Producers, Howard W. "Hawk" Koch, Jr., Todd Graff; Executive Producers, Roger Birnbaum, Fran Drescher, Peter Marc Jacobson; Director, Ken Kwapis; Screenplay, Todd Graff; Photography, Peter Lyons Collister; Designer, Rusty Smith; Editor, Jon Poll; Music, Cliff Eidelman; a Koch Company production in association with High School Sweethearts; Dolby Stereo; Color; Rated PG; 105 minutes; February release

CAST

Joy Miller	Fran Drescher
Boris Pochenko	Timothy Dalton
Grushinsky	Ian McNeice
Kleist	Patrick Malahide
Katrina	Lisa Jakub
Jerry Miller	Michael Lerner
Judy Miller	Phyllis Newman
Karl	Adam LaVorgna
Masha	Heather DeLoach
Yuri	Kyle & Tyler Wilkerson
Alek	Timothy Dowling
Stage Manager	Michael Immel
Model	Tonya Watts
Consuela	Tamara Mello
Lupe	Celeste Russi
Hector	Daniel R. Escobar
Fireman	Bill Brown
Photographer	Jorge Noa
Students	Carmela Rappazzo, Clyde Wrenn
Factory Worker	Earl Carroll
Jailer	Vincent Schiavelli
Chef	Marianne Muellerleile
Cousin Doris	R. Sparkle Stillman
Elderly Man	Ed Cambridge
Denny	Todd Graff
Servant	Gene Chronopoulos
Agent	Paul Beringer
Kitchen Worker	David Shackelford
Neighbor at Party	J.J. Chaback

Queens Beautician Joy Miller is mistaken for a school instructor and asked to come to the nation of Slovetzia to teach the children of barbaric dictator Boris Pochenko.

Timothy Dalton, Fran Drescher

Fran Drescher, Timothy Dalton

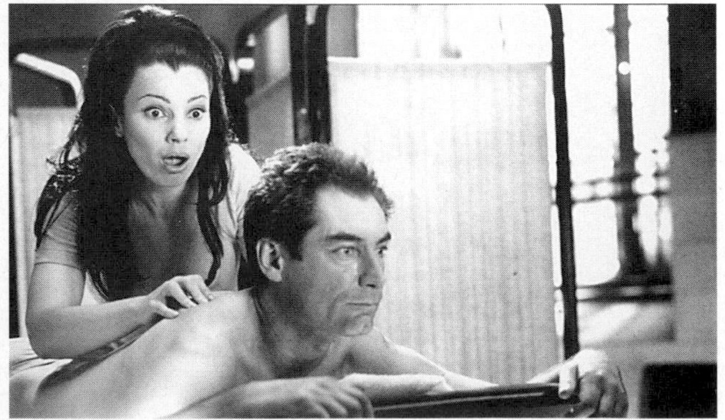

Fran Drescher, Timothy Dalton

Timothy Dalton, Lisa Jakob, Fran Drescher, Heather DeLoach, Adam LaVorgna

Giovanni Ribisi, Nicky Katt

Jayce Bartok, Parker Posey

Steve Zahn, Dina Spybey

SUBURBIA

(SONY CLASSICS) Producer, Anne Walker-McBay; Executive Producer, John Sloss; Director, Richard Linklater; Screenplay, Eric Bogosian, based on his play; Photography, Lee Daniel; Designer, Catherine Hardwicke; Editor, Sandra Adair; Music, Sonic Youth; Casting, Judy Henderson, Alycia Aumuller; a Castle Rock Entertainment presentation of a Detour Film production; Dolby Stereo; Color; Rated R; 118 minutes; February release

CAST

Pony .... Jayce Bartok
Sooze .... Amie Carey
Tim .... Nicky Katt
Nazeer .... Ajay Naidu
Erica .... Parker Posey
Jeff .... Giovanni Ribisi
Pakeesa .... Samia Shoaib
Bee-Bee .... Dina Spybey
Buff .... Steve Zahn

A group of aimless twenty-year-olds hang out at a strip-mall parking lot awaiting the arrival of an old friend who has made it big as a rock singer. Steve Zahn and Samia Shoaib repeat their roles from the 1994 Off-Broadway production.

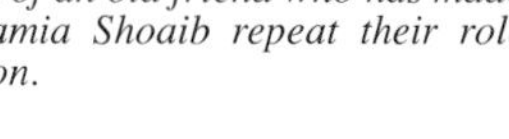

Steve Zahn

Samia Shoaib

THE PEST

(TRISTAR) Producers, Sid Sheinberg, Jon Sheinberg, Bill Sheinberg; Executive Producer, Robert A. Papazian; Director, Paul Miller; Screenplay, David Bar Katz; Story, David Bar Katz, John Leguizamo; Photography, Roy H. Wagner; Designer, Rodger E. Maus; Editors, Ross Albert, David Rawlins; Costumes, Tom McKinley; Co-Producers, John Leguizamo, David Bar Katz; Music, Kevin Kiner; Casting, Wendy Kurtzman; a presentation of The Bubble Factory of a Sheinberg production; Dolby SDDS Stereo; Technicolor; Rated PG-13; 82 minutes; February release

CAST

Pestario "Pest" Vargas .... John Leguizamo
Gustav Shank .... Jeffrey Jones
Himmel Shank .... Edoardo Ballerini
Ninja .... Freddy Rodriguez
Xantha Kent .... Tammy Townsend
Chubby .... Aries Spears
Mr. Kent .... Joe Morton
Angus .... Charles Hallahan
Leo .... Tom McCleister
Gladyz .... Ivonne Coll
Glen Livitt .... Pat Skipper

and Jorge Luis Abrell (Piercer), Jennifer Broughton (Bank Employee), Yau Gene Chan (Cook), Judyann Elder (Mrs. Kent), Paul Harris (Karaoke Singer), Joe Jokubeit (Laphroig), David Bar Katz, Will Potter (White Guys), Les Lannom (Bagpipe Player), Jim Lau (Mr. Cheung), Barrie Mizerski (Host), Hugh Murphy (Emcee), Kristin Norton (Trixy), Yelba Osorio (Malaria), Tony Perez (Felix), Cantor Aviva Rosenbloom (Cantor), Julian Scott Urena (Sergio)

Con-man Pestario "Pest" Vargas agrees to become the target for crazed hunter Gustav Shank, assuming that if he survives for a 24-hour period he will receive $50,000.

John Leguizamo, Tammy Townsend

Freddy Rodriguez, John Leguizamo, Aries Spears

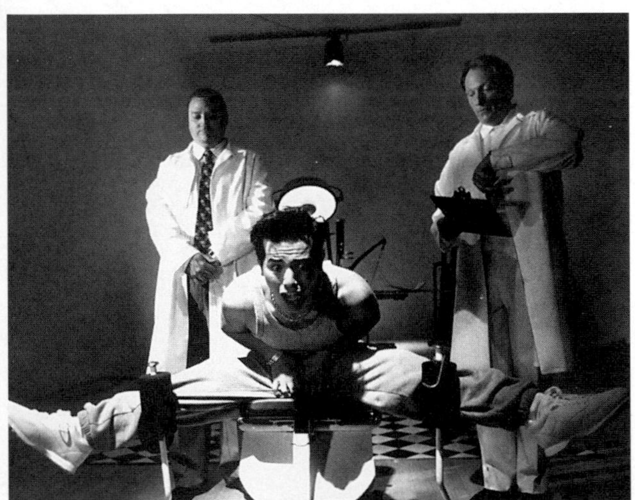

Tom McCleister, John Leguizamo, Jeffrey Jones

Edoardo Ballerini, John Leguizamo

FOOLS RUSH IN

(COLUMBIA) Producer, Doug Draizin; Executive Producer, Michael McDonnell; Director, Andy Tennant; Screenplay, Katherine Reback; Story, Joan Taylor, Katherine Redback; Photography, Robbie Greenberg; Designer, Edward Pisoni; Editor, Roger Bondelli; Costumes, Kimberly A. Tillman; Co-Producer, Anna Maria Davis; Music, Alan Silvestri; Casting, Juel Bestrop; a Doug Draizin production; Dolby SDDS Stereo; Technicolor; Rated PG-13; 106 minutes; February release

CAST

Alex Whitman ....Matthew Perry
Isabel Fuentes ....Salma Hayek
Jeff....................Jon Tenney
Chuy ....Carlos Gomez
Tomas Fuentes ....Tomas Milian
Lanie ....Siobhan Fallon
Richard Whitman....................John Bennett Perry
Judd Marshall....................Stanley DeSantis
Cathy Stewart ....Suzanne Snyder
Amalia....................Anne Betancourt
Nan....................Jill Clayburgh
Great Grandma....................Angelina Calderon Torres
Donna ....Debby Shively
Juan Fuentes ....Mark Adair Rios
Dr. Lisa Barnes....................Annie Combs
Aunt Carmen ....Shelley Morrison
Aunt Yolanda ....Maria Cellario
Aunt Rosa ....Irene Hernandez
Antonio Fuentes....................Josh Cruze
Petra ....Angela Lanza
Dam Policemen ....Randy Sutton, Christopher Michael
Carlos....................Angel Valdez
Enrique ....Cesar Santana
Osha Rep....................Garret Davis
Priest....................Chris O'Neill
Man in Lobby....................John Tripp
Assorted Cheeses....................Andrew Hill Newman
Phil ....Chris Bauer
Hank ....Douglas Weston
and Rupert Baca (Porter), Jan Austell (Bruce Stewart), Cydney Arther (Diane Stewart), Leslie Silva (Process Server), Maryann Plunkett (Heliport Mother), Juel Mendel (Receptionist), Eddie Powers (Elvis), Salvador Saldaña (Mariachi Singer)

Three months after a one night stand, businessman Alex Whitman decides to marry Isabel Fuentes after discovering that she is pregnant.

Jon Tenney, Mathew Perry, Salma Hayek

Bill Pullman, Patricia Arquette

Natasha Gregson Wagner

LOST HIGHWAY

(OCTOBER) Producers, Deepak Nayar, Tom Sternberg, Mary Sweeney; Director, David Lynch; Screenplay, David Lynch, Barry Gifford; Photography, Peter Deming; Designer/Costumes, Patricia Norris; Editor, Mary Sweeney; Music, Angelo Badalamenti, Barry Adamson; Casting, Johanna Ray, Elaine J. Huzzar; a Ciby 2000/Asymmetrical production; Dolby Digital Stereo; Panavision; Color; Rated R; 135 minutes; February release

CAST

Fred Madison ....Bill Pullman
Renee Madison/Alice Wakefield....................Patricia Arquette
Pete Dayton ....Balthazar Getty
Mystery Man ....Robert Blake
Mr. Eddy/Dick Laurent ....Robert Loggia
Arnie ....Richard Pryor
Bill Dayton ....Gary Busey
Candace Dayton ....Lucy Butler
Sheila ....Natasha Gregson Wagner
and John Roselius (Al), Lou Eppolito (Ed), Jenna Maetlind (Party Girl), Michael Massee (Andy), Henry Rollins (Guard Henry), Michael Shamus Wiles (Guard Mike), Mink Stole (Forewoman), Leonard Termo (Judge), Ivory Ocean (Guard Ivor), Jack Kehler (Guard Johnny Mack), David Byrd (Dr. Smordin), Gene Ross (Warden Clements), F. William Parker (Capt. Luneau), Guy Siner, Alexander Folk (Prison Officials), Carl Sundstrom (Hank), John Solari (Lou), Jack (The Dog), Al Garrett (Carl), Heather Stephens (Lanie), Giovanni Ribisi (Steve "V"), Scott Coffey (Teddy), Amanda Anka (Girl #1), Jennifer Syme (Junkie Girl), Matt Sigloch, Gil Combs (Assistants), Greg Travis (Tail Gate Driver), Jack Nance (Phil), Lisa Boyle (Marian), Leslie Bega (Raquel), Marilyn Manson, Twiggy Ramirez (Porno Stars)

A jazz musician, certain his wife is having an affair, is accused of her murder; a garage mechanic becomes involved with a dangerous woman who is cheating on her gangster lover.

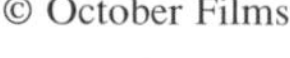

Clint Eastwood, Laura Linney

ABSOLUTE POWER

(COLUMBIA) Producers, Clint Eastwood, Karen Spiegel; Director, Clint Eastwood; Executive Producer, Tom Rooker; Screenplay, William Goldman; Based on the novel by David Baldacci; Photography, Jack N. Green; Designer, Henry Bumstead; Editor, Joel Cox; Music, Lennie Niehaus; Casting, Phyllis Huffman; a Castle Rock Entertainment presentation of a Malpaso production; SDDS Stereo; Panavision; Technicolor; Rated R; 121 minutes; February release

CAST

Luther Whitney .... Clint Eastwood
President Alan Richmond .... Gene Hackman
Seth Frank .... Ed Harris
Kate Whitney .... Laura Linney
Bill Burton .... Scott Glenn
Tim Collin .... Dennis Haysbert
Gloria Russell .... Judy Davis
Walter Sullivan .... E.G. Marshall
Christy Sullivan .... Melora Hardin
Sandy Lord .... Ken Welsh
Laura Simon .... Penny Johnson
Michael McCarty .... Richard Jenkins
Red .... Mark Margolis
Valerie .... Elaine Kagan
Art Student .... Alison Eastwood
Waiter .... Yau-Gene Chan
Airport Bartender .... George Orrison
Medical Examiner .... Charles McDaniel
Repairman .... John Lyle Campbell
White House Tour Guide .... Kimber Eastwood
Oval Office Agent .... Eric Dahlquist, Jr.
Watergate Doorman .... Jack Stewart Taylor
Reporter .... Joy Ehrlich
Cop .... Robert Harvey

While pulling off a heist, master thief Luther Whitney accidentally witnesses the President of the United States involved in the death of his mistress.

Gene Hackman, Judy Davis

Clint Eastwood, Ed Harris

Scott Glenn, Judy Davis

THAT DARN CAT

(WALT DISNEY PICTURES) Producer, Robert Simonds; Executive Producer, Andrew Gottlieb; Director, Bob Spiers; Screenplay, S.M. Alexander, L.A. Karaszweski; Based on the novel *Undercover Cat* by The Gordons, and the screenplay by The Gordons and Bill Walsh; Photography, Jerzy Zielinski; Designer, Jonathan Carlson; Editor, Roger Barton; Costumes, Marie France; Music, Richard Kendall Gibbs; Head Animal Trainer, Larry M. Madrid; Casting, Gary Zuckerbrod; Distributed by Buena Vista Pictures; Dolby Digital Stereo; Technicolor; Rated PG; 89 minutes; February release

CAST

Patti Randall .... Christina Ricci
Zeke Kelso .... Doug E. Doug
Mr. Flint .... Dean Jones
Boetticher .... George Dzundza
Pa .... Peter Boyle
Peter Randall .... Michael McKean
Judy Randall .... Bess Armstrong
Mrs. Flint .... Dyan Cannon
Dusty .... John Ratzenberger
Lu .... Megan Cavanagh
Old Lady McCracken .... Estelle Parsons
Ma .... Rebecca Schull
Melvin .... Tom Wilson
Marvin .... Brian Haley
Rollo .... Mark Christopher Lawrence
D.C. ("That Darn Cat") .... Elvis
Lizzy .... Rebecca Koon
and Ned Bellamy, Brad Sherwood, Rob Cleveland, Jeffrey King (Agents), Tom Turbiville (Field Agent #1), Libby Whittemore (Another Agent), Cassandra Lawton (Newscaster), Margo Moorer (Teacher), Hillary Tolle, Paula Jones, Kinsey McLean (Kids), Jon Kohler (Hollywood Cat Choreographer), Wilbur T. Fitzgerald, Terrence Gibney (Scientists), Harvey Reaves, Michael Genevie (Cops), Bill Coates (Old Ticket Man), Alex Van (Trash Man), Michelle B. Cooper (Nurse), Stephen Michael Ayers (Disbelieving Cop #1), Douglas Myers (Judge), Frank Smith (Announcer), Larue Stanley (Widow), David Wayne Evans, Margaret Ellis (Agents)

Patti Randall's tomcat, D.C., returns home with a watch that turns out to be an important clue in a mysterious kidnapping. Remake of the 1965 Disney film which starred Hayley Mills, Dean Jones, Dorothy Provine, and Roddy McDowall. Jones, who played Kelso in the original film, also appears in this version.

Doug E. Doug, Christina Ricci

Dyan Cannon, Dean Jones

Vivica A. Fox, Jamie Foxx, Tamala Jones, Tommy Davidson

BOOTY CALL

(COLUMBIA) Producer, John Morrissey; Director, Jeff Pollack; Screenplay, Takashi Bufford, Bootsie; Photography, Ron Orieux; Designer, Sandra Kybartas; Editor, Christopher Greenbury; Costumes, Vicki Graef; Music, Robert Folk; Co-Producer, John M. Eckert; Casting, Mary Vernieu, Ronnie Yeskel; a Turman/Morrissey Company production; Dolby SDDS Stereo; Technicolor; Rated R; 77 minutes; February release

CAST

Bunz .... Jamie Foxx
Rushon .... Tommy Davidson
Lysterine .... Vivica A. Fox
Nikki .... Tamala Jones
Singh .... Scott LaRose
Mr. Chiu .... Ric Young
Chan .... Gedde Watanabe
Akmed .... Art Malik
Judge Peabody .... Bernie Mac
Arguing Woman .... Amy Monique Waddell
Arguing Man .... Wiley Moore
Ug Lee .... Kam Ray Chan
Yoyo .... Ammie Sin
Judge's Woman .... Olivia Yap
and Bill MacDonald (Hold Up Man), John Moraitis (Greek Cabbie), Karen Robinson (Admitting Nurse), Donna Preising (Triage Nurse), Johnie Chase (Guard), Amanda Tapping (Dr. Moore), Beatriz Pizano (Pregnant Woman), Bootsie (Older Man), James Mainprize (Another Patient), Pedro Salvin (Male Nurse), Robert Bidaman (Dr. Zevroloski), Julia Paton (Nurse), Valerie Boyle (O.R. Nurse), David Hemblen (Dr. Blade), James Kidnie (Mummified Man), Michael Anthony Joseph, Dominic Marcus, George Ramsey, Derrick Simmons (Dice Players)

Bunz and Rushon find that their dates, Nikki and Lysterine, are so adamant about safe sex, that the two men end up on a frantic pursuit to find condoms.

Paul Mazursky, Lolita Davidovich

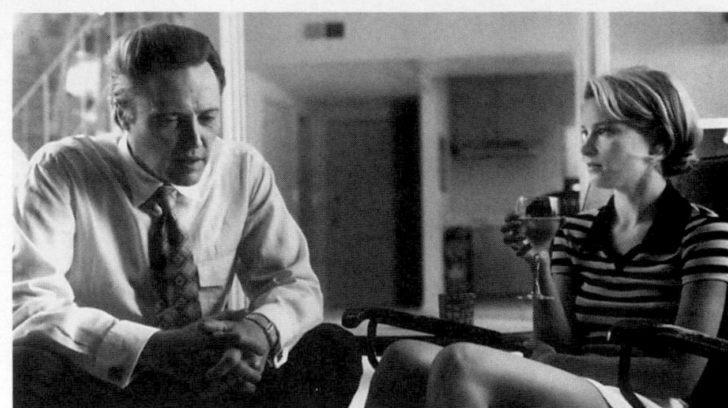

Christopher Walken, Bridget Fonda

Gina Gershon

Janeane Garofalo

Bridget Fonda, Skeet Ulrich

TOUCH

(UNITED ARTISTS) Producers, Lila Cazès, Fida Attieh; Director/Screenplay, Paul Schrader; Based upon the novel by Elmore Leonard; Co-Producer, Llewellyn Wells; Photography, Ed Lachman; Designer, David Wasco; Editor, Cara Silverman; Costumes, Julie Weiss; Music, David Grohl; Casting, Ronnie Yeskel, Mary Vernieu; a Lumiere International presentation of a Lila Cazès production; Distributed by MGM/UA; Dolby Stereo; CFI color; Rated R; 97 minutes; February release

CAST

Lynn Faulkner .... Bridget Fonda
Bill Hill .... Christopher Walken
Juvenal .... Skeet Ulrich
August Murray .... Tom Arnold
Debra Lusanne .... Gina Gershon
Antoinette Baker .... Lolita Davidovich
Artie .... Paul Mazursky
Kathy Worthington .... Janeane Garofalo
Elwin Worrel .... John Doe
Virginia Worrel .... Conchata Ferrell
Father Nestor .... Mason Adams
Greg Czarnicki .... Breckin Meyer
Father Donahue .... Anthony Zerbe
Himself .... LL Cool J
Alisha .... Maria Celedonio
Scruffy Staff Worker .... Chris Hogan
Court Clerk .... William Newman
Bailiff .... Matt O'Toole
Judge .... Richard Fancy
Prosecutor .... Tamlyn Tomita
Father Navaroli .... Don Novello
Jerry .... Richard Schiff
Bib Overalls .... O-Lan Jones
Arnold .... Brent Hinkley
Song Leader .... Diana Georger
Richie Baker .... Theo Greenly
Roman Governor .... Richard Coe
Shelly .... Julie Condra
Palsied Man .... John Gay
Waitress .... Missy Hargraves
Stripper .... Casey Gray
Edith .... Kate Williamson
Hillbilly .... Dennis Burkley

A young man whose touch can heal, arrives in Los Angeles to work at a rehab center and finds himself being exploited by a pair of con-men.

BLOOD AND WINE

(FOX SEARCHLIGHT) Producer, Jeremy Thomas; Executive Producers, Chris Auty, Bernie Williams; Director, Bob Rafelson; Screenplay, Nick Villiers, Alison Cross; Story, Nick Villiers, Bob Rafelson; Photography, Newton Thomas Sigel; Designer, Richard Sylbert; Editor, Steven Cohen; Costumes, Lindy Hemming; Co-Producers, Hercules Bellville, Noah Golden; Music, Michal Lorenc; a Recorded Picture Company presentation of a Jeremy Thomas production; Dolby Stereo; Deluxe color; Rated R; 98 minutes; February release

CAST

Alex Gates .... Jack Nicholson
Jason .... Stephen Dorff
Gabriela .... Jennifer Lopez
Suzanne Gates .... Judy Davis
Victor Spansky .... Michael Caine
Henry .... Harold Perrineau, Jr.
Dina .... Robyn Peterson
Mike .... Mike Starr
Frank .... John Seitz
Guard .... Marc Macaulay
Todd .... Dan Daily
Gabriela's Cousin .... Marta Velasco
Jeweler #2 .... Thom Christopher

and Mario Ernesto Sanchez (Artie—Fishing Ace), John Hackett (Gas Station Attendant), Hector Montano (Gabriela's Grandfather), Vanessa L. Hernandez (Cuban Little Girl), Carmen Lopez (Head Nurse), Antoni Corone (Caribbean Club Bartender), Jim Torres Towers (Father of Gabriela's Cousin), Glice Montano (Gabriela's Grandmother)

Wine merchant Alex Gates creates further friction between himself, his wife Suzanne and his stepson Jason when he helps his safe-cracker buddy Victor steal a valuable diamond necklace.

Jennifer Lopez, Jack Nicholson

Stephen Dorff, Jack Nicholson

Jack Nicholson, Michael Caine

Jack Nicholson, Michael Caine

Al Pacino, James Russo, Bruno Kirby, Michael Madsen, Johnny Depp

Johnny Depp

Al Pacino, Johnny Depp

Johnny Depp, Anne Heche

DONNIE BRASCO

(TRISTAR) Producers, Mark Johnson, Barry Levinson, Louis DiGiaimo, Gail Mutrux; Executive Producers, Patrick McCormick, Alan Greenspan; Director, Mike Newell; Screenplay, Paul Attanasio; Based on the book *Donnie Brasco: My Undercover Life in the Mafia* by Joseph D. Pistone, with Richard Woodley; Photography, Peter Sova; Designer, Donald Graham Burt; Editor, Jon Gregory; Costumes, Aude Bronson-Howard, David Robinson; Music, Patrick Doyle; Casting, Louis DiGiaimo, Brett Goldstein; a Mandalay Entertainment presentation of a Baltimore Pictures/Mark Johnson production; Dolby SDDS Stereo; Super 35 Widescreen; Technicolor; Rated R; 121 minutes; February release

CAST

Lefty Ruggiero .... Al Pacino
Joe Pistone (Donnie Brasco) .... Johnny Depp
Sonny Black .... Michael Madsen
Nicky .... Bruno Kirby
Paulie .... James Russo
Maggie Pistone .... Anne Heche
Tim Curley .... Zeljko Ivanek
Dean Blandford .... Gerry Becker
Sonny Red .... Robert Miano
Bruno .... Brian Tarantina
Richie Gazzo .... Rocco Sisto
Dr. Berger .... Zach Grenier
Sheriff .... Walt MacPherson
Annette .... Ronnie Farer
Strip Club Owner .... Terry Serpico
Sonny's Girlfriend .... Gretchen Mol
Philly Lucky .... Tony Lip
Big Trin .... George Angelica
Trafficante .... Val Avery
Jilly .... Madison Arnold
Daughters .... Delanie Fitzpatrick, Katie Sagona, Sara Gold
Tommy .... Larry Romano
FBI Technicians .... Tim Blake Nelson, Paul Giamatti
FBI Agent .... James Michael McCauley
U.S. Attorney .... Jim Bulleit
Hollman .... Andrew Parks
Japanese Maitre D' .... Keenan Shimizu
Trafficante's Men .... Rocco Musacchia, Joe Francis
Mare Chiaro Bartender .... Sal Jenco

and Billy Capucilli, Laura Cahill (Communion Party Couple), Doreen Murphy, Elle Alexander, Denise Faye, Elaine Del Valle (Mob Girlfriends), John Horton (FBI Director), Dan Brennan (FBI Photographer), LaJuan Carter, Sandy Barber, Joyce Stovall (Singers), Frank Pesce, Randy Jurgensen, John DiBenedetto, Richard Zavaglia, Tony Ray Rossi, Edward Black, Gaetano LoGiudice, Carmelo Musacchia, Pat Vecchio (Wiseguys)

True story of how FBI agent Joe Pistone, under the identity of Donnie Brasco, gained the confidence of hit-man Lefty Ruggerio and infiltrated the Mafia. This film received an Oscar nomination for screenplay adaptation.

Johnny Depp, Al Pacino

Al Pacino

Terry Serpico, Johnny Depp

HARD EIGHT

Samuel L. Jackson

(GOLDWYN) Producers, Robert Jones, John Lyons; Executive Producers, Keith Samples, Hans Brockmann, Francois Duplat; Director/Screenplay, Paul Thomas Anderson; Photography, Robert Elswitt; Designer, Nancy Deren; Editor, Barbara Tulliver; Co-Producer, Daniel Lupi; Music, Michael Penn, Jon Brion; Costumes, Mark Bridges; Casting, Christine Sheaks; a Rysher Entertainment presentation of a Green Parrot production in association with Trinity of a P.T. Anderson Picture; Dolby Stereo; Super 35 Widescreen; Color; Rated R; 101 minutes; February release

CAST

Sydney .... Philip Baker Hall
John .... John C. Reilly
Clementine .... Gwyneth Paltrow
Jimmy .... Samuel L. Jackson
Hostage .... F. William Parker
Young Craps Player .... Philip Seymour Hoffman
Restroom Attendant .... Nathanael Cooper
Waitress .... Wynn White
Keno Bar Manager .... Robert Ridgely
Keno Girl .... Kathleen Campbell
Pitt Boss .... Michael J. Rowe
Bartender .... Peter D'Allessandro
Stickman .... Steve Blane

and Xaleese (Cocktail Waitress), Melora Walters (Jimmy's Girl), Jean Langer (Cashier), Andy Breen (Groom), Renee Breen (Bride), Jane W. Brimmer (Aladdin Cashier), Mark Finizza (Desk Clerk), Richard Gross (Floorman), Cliff Keeley (Aladdin Change Booth Attendant), Carrie McVey (El Dorado Cashier), Pastor Truman Robbins (Pastor), Ernie Anderson, Wendy Weidman, Jason "Jake" Cross (Pants on Fire People)

Sydney, a professional gambler, takes young John under his wing and teaches him the art of gambling. Two years later their bond is challenged by a small-time crook, Jimmy, and a cocktail waitress named Clementine.

Gwyneth Paltrow

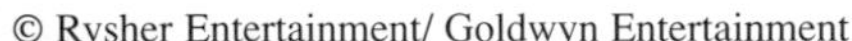

John C. Riley, Philip Baker Hall

JUNGLE 2 JUNGLE

(WALT DISNEY PICTURES) Producer, Brian Reilly; Executive Producers, Richard Baker, Rick Messina, Brad Krevoy; Director, John Pasquin; Screenplay, Bruce A. Evans, Raynold Gideon; Based on the film *Un Indien Dans La Ville (Little Indian, Big City)* written by Herve Palud, Thierry Lhermitte, Igor Aptekman, Philippe Bruneau de la Salle; Co-Producer, William W. Wilson III; Associate Producers, Thierry Lhermitte, Louis Becker, Kimberly Brent, Bruce Economou; Photography, Tony Pierce-Roberts; Designer, Stuart Wurtzel; Editor, Michael A. Stevenson; Costumes, Carol Ramsey; Music, Michael Convertino; Casting, Renee Rousselot; Stunts, Danny Aiello III; Dolby Digital Stereo; Technicolor; Rated PG; 105 minutes; March release

Tim Allen, Martin Short

CAST

Michael Cromwell .... Tim Allen
Mimi-Siku .... Sam Huntington
Dr. Patricia Cromwell .... JoBeth Williams
Charlotte .... Lolita Davidovich
Richard .... Martin Short
Jan .... Valerie Mahaffey
Karen .... LeeLee Sobiesky
Andrew .... Frankie Galasso
Abe .... Luis Avalos
Langston .... Bob Dishy
Sarah .... Rondi Reed
Madeleine .... Oni Faida Lampley
Ian .... Dominic Keating
Fiona .... Carole Shelley
Gino .... Michael Mastro
Mrs. Prelot .... Joan Copeland
Mr. Uhley .... Jack McGee
Jovanovic .... David Ogden Stiers
Jovanovic Thugs .... Nicholas J. Giangiulio, Don Picard
Stewardess .... Christine Toy
Homeless Person .... Jack O'Connell
Benjamin .... Jake Cooper
Ride Operator .... Ken Larsen
Broker .... Lowell Sanders
Morrison .... Adam LeFevre
Deli Clerk .... John Tormey

and Diana Roberts ("Hello You" Girl), Derek Smith (Louis), Tanya Memme (Trader's Assistant), R.M. Haley (Hot Dog Vendor), Glen Trotiner (Dart Booth Attendant), Eva Veronika (Jovanovic's Mother), Georgina Kess (Fish Market Employee), Maureen Beitler (Nurse), Shthd Right-Turn Clyde (Matitika), Brian M. Reilly (Fingerless Hand), John Pasquin (Bearded Man in Times Square)

Tim Allen, Sam Huntington

New York commodities trader Michael Cromwell travels to the Amazon jungle to finalize a divorce with his wife only to find that he has a 13 year old son, raised in the ways of the jungle tribesmen. Remake of the film Little Indian, Big City which was released in the U.S. in 1996 by the Walt Disney Company.

Lolita Davidovich, Tim Allen

Howard Stern, Fred Norris

Mary McCormack, Howard Stern

Robin Quivers

PRIVATE PARTS

(PARAMOUNT) Producer, Ivan Reitman; Executive Producers, Daniel Goldberg, Joe Medjuck, Keith Samples; Director, Betty Thomas; Screenplay, Len Blum, Michael Kalesniko; Based on the book by Howard Stern; Photography, Walt Lloyd; Designer, Charles Rosen; Editor, Peter Teschner; Co-Producer, Celia Costas; Music Supervisor, Peter Afterman; Costumes, Joseph G. Aulisi; Casting, Phyllis Huffman, Olivia Harris; a Rysher Entertainment presentation of an Ivan Reitman production; Dolby Stereo; DuArt color; Rated R; 109 minutes; March release

CAST

Himself....................Howard Stern
Herself....................Robin Quivers
Alison Stern....................Mary McCormack
Himself....................Fred Norris
Kenny....................Paul Giamatti
Himself....................Gary Dell'Abate
Himself....................Jackie Martling
Gloria....................Carol Alt
Ben Stern....................Richard Portnow
Ray Stern....................Kelly Bishop
Moti....................Henry Goodman
Griff....................Jonathan Hadary
Ross Buckingham....................Paul Hecht
Dee Dee....................Allison Janney
Roger Erlick....................Michael Murphy
Payton....................James Murtaugh
Vallesecca....................Reni Santoni
Marvin Mamoulian....................Lee Wilkof
Brittany....................Melanie Good
Orgasm Woman....................Theresa Lynn
Julie....................Amber Smith
The Kielbasa Queen....................Althea Cassidy
Mandy....................Jenna Jameson
Seven-year-old Howard....................Bobby Borriello
12-year-old Howard....................Michael Maccarone
16-year-old Howard....................Matthew Friedman
Music Awards Technician....................John Michael Bolger
Howard's Agent....................Steven Gilborn
Airline Representative....................Curtis McClarin
Symphony Sid....................Richard B. Shull
Elliot....................Evan Roberts
Herbie....................Gabriel De Silva
Coeds....................Jennifer Gareis, Mandy Steckelberg
Blind Coed....................Ali Marsh
Friends....................Scott Cohen, James Villemaire
Elyse....................Wendy Hoopes
Film Professor....................Richard Russell Ramos
Unshaven Deejay....................Gordon Joseph Weiss
Barb....................Allison Furman
Patricia Fonfara....................Julie Gawkowksi
Nurse....................Davenia McFadden
Duke of Rock....................Michael Gwynne
The Leather Weather Lady....................Irene DeCook
Rubberbound Man....................Jordan Derwin
Trembling Patient....................Stuart Rudin

and John Stamos, Chris Barron, Flava Flav, Hammer, Ted Nugent, Ozzy Osbourne, John Popper, Slash, Dee Snider, Renee Suran, Tiny Tim, David Letterman, "Stuttering" John Melendez, George "Crackhead Bob" Harvey, Nicole Bass (Themselves), Richard Ziman (Salesman), Adam LeFevre (Sales Manager), Janine Lindemulder (Camp Director's Wife), Scott Lawrence (News Guy), Christine Tucci (Doctor), Kim Chan (Waiter), Nick Wyman (Douglas Kiker), Stephen Pearlman (Husband), Catherine Wolf (Wife), Luke Reilly (Imus), Rick Levi, Peter Jacobson (Lawyers), Leslie Bibb (NBC Tour Guide), Joanne Camp (Reenie), Peter Maloney (Researcher), Sarah Zinsser (Kenny's Secretary), Barry Papick (Engineer), Christine Toy, Alison Stern (NBC Switchboard Operators), Brian Johnson, Angus Young, Malcolm Young, Phil Rudd, Cliff Williams (AC/DC), Susan Pratt (Stewardess), Sasha Martin, Sarah Jane Hyland (Howard's Daughters), Larry Grey (Dr. Larry), Camille Donatacci (Bikini Girl in Westchester), Danna Bradley, Seth Silver (Transvestites), Carrie Flaska (Wife in Car), Steve Ballot (Husband), Brian Constantini, Barnett Milton Lloyd (DC Cops), Aimee Luzier (Betty Jean Rushton)

The true story of how Howard Stern rose from obscurity to become the number one rated nationally syndicated radio disc jockey.

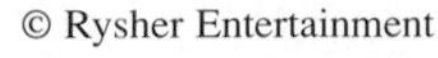

Liev Schreiber, Parker Posey, Anne Meara, Hope Davis, Pat McNamara

Hope Davis, Liev Schreiber, Parker Posey

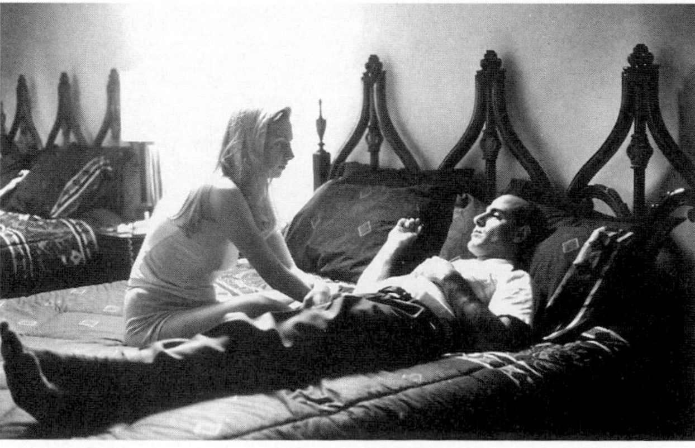

Hope Davis, Stanley Tucci

THE DAYTRIPPERS

(CFP) Producers, Nancy Tenenbaum, Steven Soderbergh; Executive Producers, Lawrence S. Kamerman, David Heyman, Campbell Scott; Director/Screenplay, Greg Mottola; Photography, John Inwood; Designer, Bonnie J. Brinkley; Editor, Anne McCabe; Costumes, Barbara Presar; Music, Richard Martinez; Casting, Sheila Jaffe, Georgianne Walken; a Nancy Tenenbaum Films presentation; Dolby DTS Stereo; Color; Not rated; 87 minutes; March release

CAST

Eliza D'Amico .... Hope Davis
Louis D'Amico............ Stanley Tucci
Jo Malone .... Parker Posey
Carl .... Liev Schreiber
Rita Malone .... Anne Meara
Jim Malone............ Pat McNamara
Eddie, The Author .... Campbell Scott
Ronnie............ Andy Brown
Leon, Ronnie's Father .... Paul Herman
Aaron, Book Publicist............ Marc Grapey
Libby .... Marcia Gay Harden
Molly............ Marcia Haufrecht
Doris .... Carol Locatell
Chap, Louis' Boss............ Douglas McGrath
Amy Corinne Fairbright-Lebow............ Amy Stiller
Cassandra, the Receptionist .... Stephanie Venditto
Nick Woodman .... Peter Askin
Libby's Ex-Boyfriend .... Adam Davidson
Monica .... Jill Rowe
Monica's Friend .... Tracey Barry
Sandy .... F. Evanson

After Eliza finds a love letter written to her husband, she collects together her family to venture into New York City for a confrontation.

CITY OF INDUSTRY

(ORION) Producers, Evzen Kolar, Ken Solarz; Executive Producer, Barr Potter; Director, John Irvin; Screenplay, Ken Solarz; Co-Producers, Matthew Gayne, Frank K. Isaac; Photography, Thomas Burstyn; Designer, Michael Novotny; Music, Stephen Endelman; Editor, Mark Conte; Costumes, Eduardo Castro; Casting, Henderson/Zuckerman; from Largo Entertainment; Dolby Stereo; Deluxe Color; Rated R; 97 minutes; March release

CAST

Roy Egan .... Harvey Keitel
Skip Kovich .... Stephen Dorff
Lee Egan .... Timothy Hutton
Rachel Montana .... Famke Janssen
Jorge Montana .... Wade Dominguez
Odell Williams .... Michael Jai White
Cathi Rose .... Lucy Alexis Liu
Keshaun Brown .... Reno Wilson
Gena .... Dana Barron
Sunny .... Tamara Clatterbuck
Backus .... Brian Brophy
Uncle Like .... Francois Chau
A Roc .... Flex
Pai-Gow Dealer .... Brian Shen
Gwen .... Ai Wan
Steady .... Cyrus Farmer
Henry Montana .... Eli Ruiz
Gingerhead .... Vien Hong
Shrimp Boy .... Michael Trac
Droutzkoy .... Evzen Kolar
Jewelry Manager .... Jonathan Schmock

and Raymond Ma (Paradise Hotel Clerk), Georg D. Rice (Royal Sentry Security Guard), Brian Habicht (Phone Company Employee), Arthus Louis Fuller (Bouncer), Sarah Sullivan (Nurse), Jane Crawley (Waitress), Antonio Molina (Mailman), Philip Tan (Jimmie), Stuart Quan (Onion Head), Anthony James DeJesus (Jorge, Jr.), John Koyama (Two Gun), Steven Ho (Gang Member), Brian Imada (Sweet Plum), Leo Lee (Redman), William Leong (Jesse), Andrew Markell (Kangol), Eddie Yansick, Eddie Mathews, Tim Rigby (Bodyguards), Fred Lerner (Security Guard), Elliott Gould

Lee Egan talks his brother Roy into joining him in a heist which goes terribly wrong when one of the other participants decides to take the haul for himself.

Timothy Hutton, Harvey Keitel

Famke Janssen

Stephen Dorff

MANDELA

(ISLAND) Producers, Jonathan Demme, Edward Saxon, Jo Menell; Executive Producers, Chris Blackwell, Dan Genetti; Co-Producer, Peter Saraf; Photography, Dewald Aukema, Peter Tischhauser; Music, Cedric Gradus Samson, Hugh Masekela; Editor, Andy Keir; a Clinica Estetico production; Dolby Stereo; Color; Not rated; 120 minutes; March release. Documentary on Nelson Mandela and his journey from childhood to presidency of a reborn South Africa.

This film received a 1996 Oscar nomination for feature documentary.

BOYS LIFE 2

(STRAND) Color; Not rated; 74 minutes.

MUST BE THE MUSIC

Producer, Rafi Stephan; Director/Screenplay, Nickolas Perry; Photography, Steve Adcock; Editor, Craig A. Colton; Casting, Aaron Griffith.

CAST

Eric....................Michael Saucedo
Kevin....................Justin Urich
Dave....................Travis Sher
Jason....................Milo Ventimiglia
and Germane Montel (Eric's Friend/Lead Dancer), Gabriel Fuller, Ryan Vernotico (Kissing Boys), Grant Swanson (Matt), Eddie Mui (Gregg), Jason Adelman (Michael), David Ko (Michael's Friend), Chris Fuentes (D.J.)

NUNZIO'S SECOND COUSIN

Executive Producer, Camille Taylor; Director/Screenplay, Tom DeCerchio; Photography, Steve Poster; Editor, Mike Murphy; Line Producer, Gayle S. Newborn; Music, Robert Folk; Casting, Ferne Cassel.

CAST

Sgt. Tony Randozza....................Vincent D'Onofrio
Jimmy....................Miles Perlich
Mrs. Randozza....................Eileen Brennan
and David Fresco (Mr. Perlin), Harry Walters, Jr. (Tony's Date), Christian Meoli, Seth Green, Jarred Blancard, Josh Scheafer (Homophobes)

ALKALI, IOWA

Producer, Ann Ruark; Director/Screenplay, Mark Christopher; Photography, Jamie Silverstein; Editor, Gloria Whittemore; Music, Julian Harris.

CAST

June Gudmanson....................Mary Beth Hurt
Jack Gudmanson....................J.D. Cerna
Blondie....................Kent Broadhurst
and Ellen Hamilton-Latzen (Carol), Ed Seamon (Bill Gudmanson), Greg Villepique (Jacko)

TREVOR

Producers, Peggy Rajski, Randy Stone; Director, Peggy Rajski; Screenplay, James Lecesne; Photography, Marc Reshovsky; Editor, John Tintori; Music, Danny Troob; Casting, Avy Kaufman.

CAST

Trevor....................Brett Barsky
Father Joe....................Stephen Tobolowsky
Trevor's Mom....................Judy Kain
Trevor's Dad....................John Lizzi
Pinky....................Jonah Rooney
Walter....................Allen Doraine

Four short films dealing with gay young men and their different journeys from adolesence to manhood. Trevor was the recipient of the 1994 Academy Award for Best Live Action Short Subject.

Travis Sher, Gabriel Fuller, Ryan Vernotico in *Must Be the Music*

Jonah Rooney, Brett Barsky in *Trevor*

Miles Perlich, Vincent D'Onofrio in *Nunzio's Second Cousin*

Larenz Tate, Nia Long

LOVE JONES

(NEW LINE CINEMA) Producers, Nick Wechsler, Jeremiah Samuels; Executive Producers, Julia Chasman, Jay Stern, Amy Henkels, Helena Echegoyen; Director/Screenplay, Theodore Witcher; Photography, Ernest Holzman; Editor, Maysie Hoy; Designer, Roger Fortune; Music, Darryl Jones; Costumes, Shawn Barton; Casting, Jane Alderman, Robi Reed-Humes; an Addis-Wechsler production; Dolby Stereo; Deluxe color; Rated R; 110 minutes; March release

CAST

Darius Lovehall .... Larenz Tate
Nina Mosley .... Nia Long
Savon Garrison .... Isaiah Washington
Josie Nichols .... Lisa Nicole Carson
Hollywood .... Bill Bellamy
Eddie Coles .... Leonard Roberts
Sheila Downes .... Bernadette L. Clarke
Marvin Cox .... Khalil Kain
Troy Garrison .... Cerall Duncan
Publisher .... David Nisbet
Roger Lievsey .... Simon James
Model (Lievsey Studio) .... Oona Hart
Lisa Martin .... Jacqueline Fleming
Nina's Assistant .... Manao DeMuth
Tracey Powell .... Marie-Francoise Theodore
Themselves .... Reginald Gibson, Malik Yosef

and Kahil El Zabar (Percussionist), Darryl "Munch" Jones (Bassist), Teodross Avery (Saxophonist), Everette Dean (Porter), Benjamin LeVert (Savon's Son), John M. Watson, Sr. (Tiki Room Bartender), William Yancey (Sanctuary Bartender), Ernest Perry (Model), Helena Echegoyen (Woman on Train), Troy Borisy (Taxi Driver), Michelle Poole, Kevin Bell (Kissing Couple)

Darius, a struggling writer, and Nina, a disillusioned photographer's assistant, begin a relationship which is tested when Nina's former fiancee shows up wanting her back.

Lisa Nicole Carson, Nia Long

Nia Long, Larenz Tate

THE DEVIL'S OWN

(COLUMBIA) Producers, Lawrence Gordon, Robert F. Colesberry; Executive Producers, Lloyd Levin, Donald Laventhall; Director, Alan J. Pakula; Screenplay, David Aaron Cohen, Vincent Patrick, Kevin Jarre; Story, Kevin Jarre; Photography, Gordon Willis; Designer, Jane Musky; Editors, Tom Rolf, Dennis Virkler; Costumes, Bernie Pollack; Music, James Horner; Casting, Alixe Gordin; a Lawrence Gordon presentation; Dolby SDDS Stereo; Panavision; Technicolor; Rated R; 110 minutes; March release

CAST

Tom O'Meara....Harrison Ford
Rory Devaney (Frankie McGuire)....Brad Pitt
Sheila O'Meara....Margaret Colin
Edwin Diaz....Ruben Blades
Billy Burke....Treat Williams
Peter Fitzsimmons....George Hearn
Chief Jim Kelly....Mitchell Ryan
Megan Doherty....Natascha McElhone
Sean Phelan....Paul Ronan
Harry Sloan....Simon Jones
Bridget O'Meara....Julia Stiles
Morgan O'Meara....Ashley Carin
Annie O'Meara....Kelly Singer
Martin MacDuff....David O'Hara
Dessie....David Wilmot
Gerard....Athony Brophy
Young Frankie....Shane Dunne
Frankie's Father....Martin Dunne
Frankie's Mother....Gabrielle Reidy
Frankie's Sister....Samantha Conroy
Customs Agent....Baxter Harris
Teenager....Hassan Johnson
Rookie Cop....Scott Nicholson
Jerry....Jonathan Earl Peck
Hispanic Man....Sixto Ramos
Hispanic Woman....Mya Michaels
Hispanic Girl....Jessica Marie Kavanagh
Teddy....Brendan Kelly
Thug....Kevin Nagle
Tony....Greg Salata
Joey the Bartender....Joseph Dandry
Jack Fitzsimmons....Jack McKillop

and Mac Orange (The Maid), Malachy McCourt (Bishop), Marian Tomas Griffin (Cousin Eileen), Peggy Shay (Aunt Birdie), Danielle McGovern (Brooke), Ciaran O'Reilly (Father Canlon), Rob McElhenny (Kevin), Donald J. Meade, Patrick Reynolds, Peter Rufli (Irish Musicians), Debbon Ayer (Tour Guide), Mario Polit (Young Domincian), Chance Kelly (Masked Burglar), Greg Stebner (Uniformed Cop), William Paulson (Detective), Bill Hoag (Trucker), Victor Slezak (Evan Stanley, FBI), Damien Leake (Art Fisher, FBI)

New York cop Tom O'Meara allows a young Irishman, Rory Devaney, to take room and board in his home, unaware that he is in actuality a terrorist sent to the United States to buy weapons.

Harrison Ford, Brad Pitt

Brad Pitt, Natascha McElhone

Harrison Ford, Margaret Colin, Julia Stiles, Brad Pitt, Kelly Singer

Jim Carrey, Jennifer Tilly

Swoosie Kurtz, Eric Pierpont, Jennifer Tilly, Jim Carrey

LIAR LIAR

(UNIVERSAL) Producer, Brian Grazer; Executive Producers, James D. Brubaker, Michael Bostick; Director, Tom Shadyac; Screenplay, Paul Guay, Stephen Mazur; Photography, Russell Boyd; Designer, Linda DeScenna; Editor, Don Zimmerman; Costumes, Judy L. Ruskin; Music, John Debney; Casting, Junie Lowry Johnson, Ron Surma; an Imagine Entertainment presentation of a Brian Grazer production; DTS Stereo; Deluxe color; Rated PG-13; 86 minutes; March release

CAST

Fletcher Reede .... Jim Carrey
Audrey Reede .... Maura Tierney
Max Reede .... Justin Cooper
Jerry .... Cary Elwes
Greta .... Anne Haney
Samantha Cole .... Jennifer Tilly
Miranda .... Amanda Donohoe
Judge Marshall Stevens .... Jason Bernard
Dana Appleton .... Swoosie Kurtz
Mr. Allan .... Mitchell Ryan
Kenneth Falk .... Chip Mayer
Richard Cole .... Eric Pierpoint
Skull .... Randall "Tex" Cobb
Jane .... Cheri Oteri
Pete .... SW Fisher
Randy .... Ben Lemon
Zit Boy .... Jarrad Paul
Ms. Berry .... Marianne Muellerleile
Lady in Elevator .... Krista Allen
Police Officer .... Stephen James Carver
Beggar at Courthouse .... Don Keefer
Beggar at Office .... Paul Roache
Detective Bryson .... Randy Oglesby
Restroom Man .... Charlie Dell
Pilot .... Jim Hansen
Co-Pilot .... Terry Rhoads
Tow Yard Employee .... Michael Leopard
Skycap .... Charles Walker
Mechanic .... Ed Trotta
Bailiff .... Ernest Perry, Jr.
Court Guard .... Skip O'Brien
Cop .... Tony Carreiro
Publicist .... Amanda Carlin
Cole Children .... Matthew Michael Goodall, Samantha Heyman
Fred .... Anthony Lee
Sharpo the Clown .... Eric Sharp
Lupe .... Christine Avila
Playground Teacher .... Hope Allen
Stenographer .... Carrie Armstrong
Deputy .... Craig Barnett
Flight Attendant .... Brandi Burkett
Macho Attorney .... Charles Emmett
Driver .... Mike Grief
Colleague .... Matthew Arkin

and Steven M. Gagnon, Moon Jones, Rick Hill (Jail Guards), Kelly Anne Conroy, Richard Jones (Passengers on Plane), Dennis Napolitano (Piano Player), Michael Adler, Joe Barnaba, Ben Brown, Mark Chaet, Catherine Evans, Colleen Fitzpatrick, David Fresco, Sue Goodman, Michael Kostroff, Howard S. Miller (Conference Room Attorneys), Edward Amuwa, Ashley Monique Clark, Derrick Friedman, David Kikuta, Oliver Kindred, Patrick Lawrence McTavish, Sara Paxton, Ashley Rumph, Jacob Stein, Mercedes Villamil (Children at Party and School)

Max Reede, tired of the undependability of his slick lawyer dad, makes a birthday wish that his father not be able to lie, a wish that comes true for a twenty-four hour period.

Jim Carrey, Justin Cooper

Cary Elwes

Maura Tierney

Jim Carrey, Maura Tierney

THE SIXTH MAN

(TOUCHSTONE) Producer, David Hoberman; Executive Producer, Jody Savin; Director, Randall Miller; Screenplay, Christopher Reed, Cynthia Carle; Photography, Michael Ozier; Designer, Michael Bolton; Editor, Eric Sears; Music, Marcus Miller; Co-Producer, Justis Greene; Costumes, Grania Preston; Special Effects Coordinator, Stewart Bradley; Casting, Dan Parada; a Mandeville Films production; Distributed by Buena Vista Pictures; Dolby Digital Stereo; Technicolor; Rated PG-13; 107 minutes; March release

CAST

Kenny Tyler....................Marlon Wayans
Antoine Tyler....................Kadeem Hardison
Coach Pederson....................David Paymer
R.C. St. John....................Michael Michele
Mikulski....................Kevin Dunn
Gertz....................Gary Jones
Malik Major....................Lorenzo Orr
Zigi Hrbacek....................Vladimir Cuk
Danny O'Grady....................Travis Ford
Luther LaSalle....................Jack Karuletwa
Jimmy Stubbs....................Chris Spencer
Coach Nichols....................Kirk Baily
Camille Tyler....................Saundra McClain
James Tyler....................Harold Sylvester
Nativity Watson....................Octavia L. Spencer
Cheryl....................Danielle Saklofsky
Jordy....................Christopher Turner
Ernie....................Scott LaRose
Bernie....................Paul Ben-Victor

and Emil Pinnock (Young Antoine), Allan Lindo (Young Kenny), Tyronne L'Hirondelle (Doctor), Tony Marr (Paramedic), Rod Crawford (Man in Bathroom), Jody Savin, Dave Young (Reporters), Randall Miller (Booster), Lauro Chartrand (Husky Mascot), William Sasso (Guy in Bar), Flex (Jerrod Smith), Brent Kerray (Wilson), Greg Collins, Kevin Benton, Howard Storey (Refs), Keith Gibbs (O'Neil), Brad Nessler, James "Bruiser" Flint, Jerry Tarkanian, Billy Packer, John Thompson, Nolan Richardson, George Raveling, Todd Bozeman (Themselves), Chris Reimer, Mark Poyser, Brady Ibbetson, Dave Nelson, Craig Wayans, Shaun Hawke, Mark Lewis (Husky Players)

The ghost of former college basketball star Antoine Tyler materializes to help his younger brother Kenny and his last place team to victory.

Kadeem Hardison, Marlon Wayans

Paulina Porizkova, Tilda Swinton

FEMALE PERVERSIONS

(OCTOBER) Producer, Mindy Affrime; Executive Producers, Zalman King, Gina Resnick, Rena Ronson; Director, Susan Streitfeld; Screenplay, Julie Hebert, Susan Streitfeld; Based upon the book Female Perversions: The Temptation of Emma Bovary by Dr. Louise J. Kaplan; Photography, Teresa Medina; Designer, Missy Stewart; Costumes, Angela Billows; Editors, Curtiss Clayton, Leo Trombetta; Music, Debbie Wiseman; Associate Producer, Janine Gold; Line Producer, Rana Joy Glickman; Casting, Christine Sheaks; a Trans Atlantic Entertaiment and Mindy Affrime Productions presentation; Dolby Stereo; Color; Rated R; 119 minutes; March release

CAST

Eve Stephens....................Tilda Swinton
Madelyn Stephens....................Amy Madigan
Renee....................Karen Sillas
Langley Flynn....................Paulina Porizkova
John....................Clancy Brown
Annunciata....................Frances Fisher
Margot Fuchs....................Lisa Jane Persky
Edwina....................Dale Shuger
Emma....................Laila Robins
Jake Rock....................John Diehl
Make-up Salesgirl....................Shawnee Smith
Lingerie Saleswoman....................Nina Wise
Boutique Saleswoman....................Judy Jean Berns
Wallace Leishman....................J. Patrick McCormack
Homeless Man....................Abdul Salaam el Razzac
Trudy (License to Flirt)....................Sandy Martin

and Elizabeth Cava (Jail Guard), Scotch Ellis Loring (Joey—Cab Driver), John Cassini (Gas Station Attendant), Rick Zieff (Office Boy), Marcia Cross (Eve's Mother), Don Gettinger (Eve's Father), Marra Racz (Earthwoman), Ruben Knight (Judge), Russ Gething (Courthouse Guard), Bailee Bileschi (Young Eve), Kim Blank (Mother in Boutique), Robert Rider (Old Man in Boutique), Bea Marcus (Old Lady on Bus Bench), Jim James (Detective), Evangelina Rodriguez (Latina Corn Seller), Kirstie Tyrone (Young Madelyn), Tere Wierson, Rana Joy Glickman, Viktor Manoel, Torry Pendergrass (Caryatids in Fantasy), Wade Durbin (King), Azalea Davila (Queen)

A drama exploring the erotic fantasies, nightmares and memories of various women.

THAT OLD FEELING

(UNIVERSAL) Producers, Leslie Dixon, Bonnie Bruckheimer; Executive Producer, Tom Joyner; Director, Carl Reiner; Screenplay, Leslie Dixon; Photography, Steve Mason; Designer, Sandy Veneziano; Editor, Richard Halsey; Music, Patrick Williams; Song: "Somewhere Along the Way" by Sammy Gallop and Ada Kurtz/performed by Bette Midler; Costumes, Robert De Mora; Casting, Nancy Nayor; The Bubble Factory presentation of a Sheinberg production in association with Boy of the Year and All Girl Productions; DTS Digital Stereo; Deluxe color; Rated PG-13; 105 minutes; April release

CAST

Lilly....Bette Midler
Dan....Dennis Farina
Molly....Paula Marshall
Rowena....Gail O'Grady
Alan....David Rasche
Keith....Jamie Denton
Joey....Danny Nucci
Bar Pianist....Blu Mankuma
Aunt Iris....Jayne Eastwood
Senator Marks....Michael J. Reynolds
Senator Marks' Wife....Joan Luchak
Man at Wedding....Mike Wilmot
Granny Tapper....Lula Franklin
Bandleader....George Hevenor
Inn Proprietress....Arlene Meadows
Desk Clerk....Don Allison
Rufus....Ian Clark
Cops....David Huband, Tony Craig
Waitresses....Kim Bourne, Cara Chisholm
Waiter....Pedro Salvin
Best Man....Doug Murray
Sanford (Usher)....John Nightingale
Gordon (Usher)....Scott Gibson
Girl at Tabloid....Mary Jo Eustace
Busboy....Simon Barry
Minister....Ian Downie

and Marjorie Lowe, Michelle Carberry, Justina Taglialatela (Bridesmaids), Tabitha Lupien, Brittney Kuczynski, Alexandra Longo (Flower Girls), Gerry Mendicino (Maitre d'), Jerry Schaeffer (Fan), Madeline Lee (Woman at Sidewalk Cafe)

At their daughter's wedding Lily and Dan, happily divorced for 12 years, find their passions for one another being unexpectedly reignited.

Bette Midler, David Rasche

Dennis Farina, Bette Midler

Dennis Farina, Gail O'Grady

Danny Nucci, Paula Marshall

Dwight Ewell, Ben Affleck, Jason Lee

Jason Mewes, Kevin Smith

CHASING AMY

(MIRAMAX) Producer, Scott Mosier; Executive Producer, John Pierson; Director/Screenplay, Kevin Smith; Photography, David Klein; Associate Producer, Robert Hawk; Designer, Robert "Ratface" Holtzman; Editors, Kevin Smith, Scott Mosier; Line Producer, Derrick Tseng; Costumes, Christopher Del Coro; "Bluntman & Chronic/Chasing Amy" Artwork, Mike Allred; Music, David Pirner; Casting, Shan Lory; a View Askew production; Dolby Stereo; Color; Rated R; 111 minutes; April release

CAST

Holden McNeil .... Ben Affleck
Alyssa Jones .... Joey Lauren Adams
Banky Edwards .... Jason Lee
Hooper........ Dwight Ewell
Jay .... Jason Mewes
Silent Bob .... Kevin Smith
Fan........ Ethan Suplee
Collector .... Scott Mosier
Little Kid .... Casey Affleck
Singer .... Guinevere Turner
Kim .... Carmen Lee
Executives........ Brian O'Halloran, Matt Damon
Train Attendant........ Dan Lunney
Cashier........ Tony Torin
Dalia........ Rebecca Waxman
Tory .... Paris Petrick
Jane........ Welker White
Nica .... Kelli Simpkins
Cohee Lundin........ John Willyung
Young Black Kid........ Tsemach Washington
Bystander........ Ernie O'Donnell
Waitress........ Kristin Mosier
Con Woman .... Virginia Smith

Comic book creator Holden McNeil finds himself falling in love with fellow artist Alyssa Jones though her preference for women dictates the two function strictly as friends.

Ben Affleck, Joey Lauren Adams

Joey Lauren Adams, Ben Affleck

Ben Affleck, Joey Lauren Adams, Jason Lee

Joey Lauren Adams, Dwight Ewell

THE SAINT

(PARAMOUNT) Producers, David Brown, Robert Evans, William J. MacDonald, Mace Neufeld; Executive Producers, Paul Hitchcock, Robert S. Baker; Director, Phillip Noyce; Screenplay, Jonathan Hensleigh, Wesley Strick; Story, Jonathan Hensleigh; Based on the character created by Leslie Charteris; Photography, Phil Meheux; Designer, Joseph Nemec III; Editor, Terry Rawlings; Associate Producer, Lis Kern; Music, Graeme Revell; Costumes, Marlene Stewart; Casting, Patsy Pollock, Elisabeth Leustig; a David Brown and Robert Evans production, presented in association with Rysher Entertainment; Dolby Stereo; Panavision; Rated PG-13; 116 minutes; April release

Elisabeth Shue, Val Kilmer

CAST

Simon Templar .... Val Kilmer
Dr. Emma Russell .... Elisabeth Shue
Ivan Tretiak .... Rade Serbedzija
Ilya Tretiak .... Valery Nikolaev
Dr. Lev Botvin .... Henry Goodman
Chief Inspector Teal .... Alun Armstrong
Tretiak's Aide—Vereshagin .... Michael Byrne
President Karpov .... Evgeny Lazarev
Frankie .... Irina Apeximova
General Sklarov .... Lev Prigunov
Inspector Rabineau .... Charlotte Cornwell
Woman on Plane .... Emily Mortimer
Russian Prostitute .... Lucija Serbedzija
Skinhead .... Velibor Topic
Scarface .... Tommy Flanagan
Scratchface .... Yegor Pozenko
Young Simon Templar .... Adam Smith
Catholic Priest .... Pat Laffan
Agnes .... Verity Dearsley

and Michael Marquez (Boy in Orphanage), Lorelei King (TV Reporter), Alla A. Kazanskaya (Old Russian Lady), Ronnie Letham (Old Russian Man), Tusse Silberg (Prostitute's Mother), Peter Guinness (Frankie's Curator), Stefan Gryff (President's Aide), Malcolm Tierney (Russian Doctor), Stephen Tiller (Russian Policeman), Christopher Rozycki (Russian Chief of Police), Etela Pardo (President Karpov's Wife), Nikolai Veselov (Red Square Tramp), David Schneider (Rat Club Comedian), Oxana Popkova (Ilya's Girlfriend), Agnieszka Liggett (Rat Club Party Girl), Lydia Zovkic (Rat Club Beauty), Alexander Tutin (Russian Colonel), Vadim Stepashkin (Russian Soldier), Ravil Isyanov (Tretiak Guard), Alexander Kadanyov (Tretiak Security Guard), Petar Vidovic (Tretiak's Builder), Susan Porrett (Orphanage Nun), Cliff Parisi (Pub Waiter), Richard Cubison, Tony Armatrading (Customs Officers), Benjamin Whitrow (Chairman at Oxford), Julian Rhind-Tutt (Young Student), Kate Isitt (Second Student), Barbara Jefford (Academic Woman), Sean O'Kane (Running Student), Lucy Akhurst (Policewoman), Nigel Clauzel (Marine Guard), Eric Loren (Embassy Official), William Hope (State Department Official), Michael Cochrane (Cold Fusion Broker), Ginny Holder (Jamaican Video Girlfriend), Akiko (Japanese Video Girlfriend), Melissa Knatchbull (English Video Girlfriend), Caroline Lee Johnson (Private Hotel Receptionist), Roger Moore (Voice on Radio)

Elisabeth Shue, Val Kilmer

Spy Simon Templar is hired to steal a valuable formula for cold fusion and winds up in love with the scientist responsible for its development. The character of "The Saint" first appeared on screen in the 1938 RKO film The Saint in New York, starring Louis Hayward; he was subsequently played by George Sanders(The Saint Strikes Back, The Saint in London, The Saint's Double Trouble, The Saint Takes Over, and The Saint in Palm Springs), Hugh Sinclair (The Saint's Vacation and The Saint Meets the Tiger), again by Louis Hayward (The Saint's Girl Friday)and on tv by Roger Moore in the series "The Saint" (syndication: 1963-66; NBC: 1967-68), and Ian Ogilvy in the CBS series "Return of the Saint" (1979-80).

Elisabeth Shue

INVENTING THE ABBOTTS

(20TH CENTURY FOX) Producers, Ron Howard, Brian Grazer, Janet Meyers; Executive Producers, Karen Kehela, Jack Cummins; Director, Pat O'Connor; Screenplay, Ken Hixon; Based on the story by Sue Miller; Photography, Kenneth MacMillan; Designer, Gary Frutkoff; Editor, Ray Lovejoy; Music, Michael Kamen; Costumes, Aggie Guerard Rodgers; an Imagine Entertainment production; Dolby Stereo; Deluxe color; Rated R; 110 minutes; April release

CAST

Doug Holt .... Joaquin Phoenix
Jacey Holt .... Billy Crudup
Lloyd Abbott .... Will Patton
Helen Holt .... Kathy Baker
Eleanor Abbott .... Jennifer Connelly
Steve .... Michael Sutton
Pamela Abbott .... Liv Tyler
Alice Abbott .... Joanna Going
Joan Abbott .... Barbara Williams
Peter Vanlaningham .... Alessandro Nivola
Giggling Girls .... Nicole M. Vassallo, Amanda Sherman
Victor .... Shawn Hatosy
Webb Crosby .... Garrett M. Brown
Co-ed .... Julie Benz
Sandy .... Zoe McLellan
Ted .... David Frazier
Store Clerk .... Margaret Ash
Principal .... Clive Rosengren
Mrs. Porter .... Susan Barnes
Waitress .... Andrea Post
Funeral Director .... Jack Cummins
Pre-Record Singer .... David Heckendorn
Narrator .... Michael Keaton

In a Midwestern town during the 1950s, the working class Holt Brothers find themselves becoming involved with the three Abbott sisters from the wealthy side of town.

Billy Crudup, Liv Tyler, Joaquin Phoenix

Liv Tyler, Joaquin Phoenix

Joaquin Phoenix, Billy Crudup

Kathy Baker, Joaquin Phoenix, Billy Crudup

8 HEADS IN A DUFFEL BAG

(ORION) Producers, Brad Krevoy, Steve Stabler, John Bertolli; Director/Screenplay, Tom Schulman; Co-Producer, Tim Foster; Photography, Adam Holender; Designer, Paul Peters; Editor, David Holden; Costumes, Sanja Milkovic Hays; Music, Andrew Gross; Executive Producer, Jeffrey D. Ivers; Line Producer, Andrew G. Lamarca; Special Makeup Effects Creator, Greg Cannom; Casting, Janet Hirshenson, Jane Jenkins, Amy IcIntyre Britt; a Brad Krevoy & Steve Stabler production, presented in association with Rank Film Distributors; Dolby Digital Stereo; Deluxe color; Rated R; 93 minutes; April release

CAST

Tommy Spinelli .... Joe Pesci
Charlie .... Andy Comeau
Laurie Bennett .... Kristy Swanson
Steve .... Todd Louiso
Dick Bennett .... George Hamilton
Annette Bennett .... Dyan Cannon
Ernie .... David Spade
Rico .... Anthony Mangano
Benny .... Joe Basile
Paco .... Frank Roman
Big Sep .... Howard George
Hugo .... Tom Platz
Marty .... Endre Hules
Jamal .... Calvin Levels

and John Zurlo (Little Joey), Roger Cobra (Frank), Jeff Sanders (Isaiah), Ric Sarabia (Benito), Tony Montero (So-So Stu), Michael Groh (Bad Frank), Wendy Clifford (Woman with Baby), Matthew Fonda (Organ Carrier), Michael Nickles (Juan the Bandito), Suzanne Krull (Woman at Phone), Miguel Perez (Customs Inspector), John Webber (Airline Ticket Agent), Eduardo Ricard (Hotel Doctor), Sally Colon, Irene Olga Lopez (Maids), Charles Martiniz (Airport Security Guard), Glenn Taranto (Mr. Escobedo), Bart Braverman (Rental Dealer), Phillip Suriano (Gangster), Ellis E. Williams (Newark Porter), Horacio LeDon (Airport Customs Inspector), Joe Xavier Rodriguez (La Purisima Police Officer), Darius Anderson (Mexican Man)

Mob courier Tommy Spinelli, transporting the heads of eight slain gangsters, finds that he has accidentally swapped his bag at the airport with that of an innocent graduate student.

David Spade, Todd Louiso, Joe Pesci

Jean-Claude Van Damme, Dennis Rodman

DOUBLE TEAM

(COLUMBIA) Producer, Moshe Diamant; Executive Producers, Don Jakoby, David Rodgers; Director, Tsui Hark; Screenplay, Don Jakoby, Paul Mones; Story, Don Jakoby; Photography, Peter Pau; Editor, Bill Pankow; Designer, Marek Dobrowolski; Music, Gary Chang; Costumes, Magali Guidasci; Co-Producers, Rick Nathanson, Nansun Shi; Casting, Penny Perry, Illana Diamant; Stunts, Charles Picerni; a Mandalay Entertainment presentation of a Moshe Diamant production/a One Story Pictures production; Dolby SDDS Stereo; Super 35 Widescreen; Technicolor; Rated R; 91 minutes; April release

CAST

Jack Quinn .... Jean-Claude Van Damme
Yaz .... Dennis Rodman
Stavros .... Mickey Rourke
Goldsmythe .... Paul Freeman
Kath .... Natacha Lindinger
Dr. Maria Trifioli .... Valeria Cavalli
Brandon .... Jay Benedict
Stavros' Girlfriend .... Joelle Devaux-Vullion
Kofi .... Bruno Bilotta
James .... Mario Opinato
Carney .... Grant Russell
Roger .... William Dunn
Moishe .... Asher Tzarfati
Dieter Staal .... Rob Diem
Stevenson .... Ken Samuels
Delta Two .... Sandy Welch
Delta Three .... Jessica Forde
Delta Four .... Malick Bowens
Delta Five .... Dominic Gould
Delta Six .... Frederick Renard
Bravo One .... Dufaut Cyrille
Bravo Two .... Eric Gauchy
Bravo Three .... Patrick Gauderlier

and Orso Maria Guerrini (Colony Resident), Alexander Koumpaan (Russian Man), Hans Meyer (British Man), Jesse Joe Walsh (Jacseck), Peter Nelson (American CIA Agent), Paolo Calissano (Rome CIA Agent), Pascal Lopez, Dominique Fouassier (Stavros' Men), Paolo Paoloni (Old Monk), Jean-Pierre Stewart (Yamir), Ted Russof (Brother Ramulu), Umberto Raho (Brother Regulo), Adam Kaci (Cyrus), Xin Xin Xiong (Stavros' Man—Hotel), Pascaline Girardot (Domestic), Nathalie Grac (Mermaid), M. Benabiles (Pilot), M. Szkolnic (Co-Pilot), Sigal Diamant (Giada), Angelo Ragusa (Stavros Goon), Gabriella D'Olive (Nurse), Nick Brett (Hospital Guard)

On his final mission counter-terrorist Jack Quinn fails to dispose of Stavros and winds up the target of his evil vengeance.

GROSSE POINTE BLANK

(HOLLYWOOD PICTURES) Producers, Susan Arnold, Donna Arkoff Roth, Roger Birnbaum; Executive Producers, Jonathan Glickman, Lata Ryan; Director, George Armitage; Screenplay, Tom Jankiewicz, D.V. DeVincentis, Steve Pink, John Cusack; Story, Tom Jankiewicz; Co-Producers, John Cusack, Steve Pink; Photography, Jamie Anderson; Designer, Stephen Altman; Editor, Brian Berdan; Costumes, Eugenie Bafaloukos; Music, Joe Strummer; Casting, Junie Lowry Johnson, Ron Surma; a Roger Birnbaum & Roth/Arnold production in association with New Crime Production, presented in association with Caravan Pictures; Dolby Digital Stereo; Technicolor; Rated R; 107 minutes; April release

Dan Aykroyd, John Cusack

CAST

Martin Q. Blank .... John Cusack
Debi Newberry .... Minnie Driver
Dr. Oatman .... Alan Arkin
Grocer .... Dan Aykroyd
Marcella .... Joan Cusack
Lardner .... Hank Azaria
McCullers .... K. Todd Freeman
Mr. Newberry .... Mitchell Ryan
Paul Spericki .... Jeremy Piven
Bob Destepello .... Michael Cudlitz
Felix .... Benny Urquidez
Ultimart Carl .... Duffy Taylor
Arlene .... Audrey Kissel
Ken .... Caros Jacott
Husky Man .... Brian Powell
Amy .... Ann Cusack
Dan Koretzky .... D.V. DeVincentis
Mary Blank .... Barbara Harris
Melanie the Waitress .... Wendy Thorlakson
Mrs. Kinetta .... Belita Moreno
Nathaniel .... Pat O'Neill
Tanya .... Jenna Elfman
Terry Rostand .... Steve Pink
Tracy .... K.K. Dodds
Waiter .... Bill Cusack

and Traci Dority (Jenny Slater), Doug Dearth (Eckhart), Colby French (Bartender), Brent Armitage (Cosmo), Jackie Rubin (Marie), Sarah DeVincentis (Dr. Oatman's Patient), Eva Rodriguez (Nurse), David Barrett (Bicycle Messenger), Bobby Bass, Lance Gilbert, Pete Antico, Laurence Bilzerian (Assassins)

Jeremy Piven

Alan Arkin

Hoping to find some meaning to his empty life as a professional hit man, Martin Blank returns to his home town for his high school reunion, unaware that his rival, Grocer, is on his trail intending to exterminate him.

Minnie Driver, John Cusack

John Cusack, Joan Cusack

ANACONDA

(COLUMBIA) Producers, Verna Harrah, Leonard Rabinowitz, Carole Little; Executive Producer, Susan Ruskin; Director, Luis Llosa; Screenplay, Hans Bauer, Jim Cash, Jack Epps Jr.; Photography, Bill Butler; Designer, Kirk M. Petruccelli; Editor, Michael R. Miller; Music, Randy Edelman; Co-Producer, Beau Marks; Visual Effects, John Nelson; Animatronic Effects, Walt Conti; Casting, Mindy Marin; a CL Cinema Line Films Corporation Production; Dolby SDDS Stereo; Super 35 Widescreen; Color; Rated PG-13; 90 minutes; April release

CAST

Terri Flores .... Jennifer Lopez
Danny Rich .... Ice Cube
Paul Sarone .... Jon Voight
Dr. Steven Cale .... Eric Stoltz
Warren Westridge .... Jonathan Hyde
Gary Dixon .... Owen Wilson
Denise Kalberg .... Kari Wuhrer
Mateo .... Vincent Castellanos
Poacher .... Danny Trejo

A film crew's expedition down the Amazon is sidetracked by a mysterious loner who leads them into dangerous waters in his attempt to track a deadly 40-foot Anaconda.

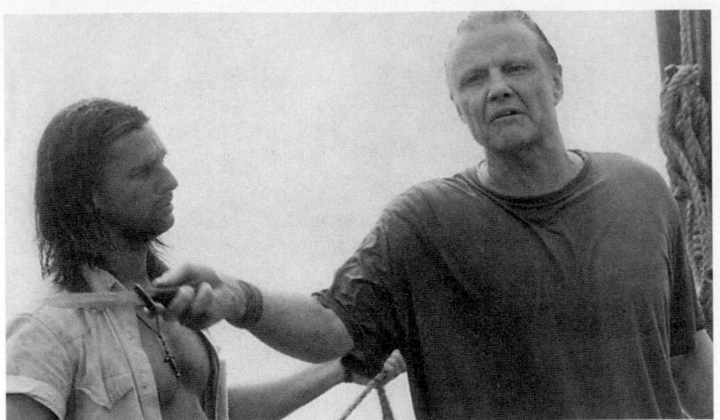

Vincent Castellanos, Jon Voight

Kari Wuhrer, Owen Wilson, Jennifer Lopez

Jennifer Lopez, Eric Stoltz

Jennifer Lopez, Ice Cube

Mark Wahlberg, Bill Paxton

TRAVELLER

(OCTOBER) Producers, Bill Paxton, Brian Swardstrom, Mickey Liddell, David Blocker; Executive Producers, Robert Mickelson, Rick King; Director, Jack Green; Screenplay, Jim McGlynn; Designer, Michael Helmy; Music, Andy Paley; Editor, Michael Ruscio; Casting, Joseph Middleton; a Banner Entertainment production; Dolby Stereo; Color; Rated R; 100 minutes; April release

CAST

Bokky .... Bill Paxton
Pat O'Hara .... Mark Wahlberg
Jean .... Julianna Margulies
Double D .... James Gammon
Boss Jack .... Luke Askew
Kate .... Nikki Deloach
Shane .... Danielle Wiener
Lip .... Michael Shaner
Bimbo .... Vincent Chase
Pincher .... Andrew Porter
Bokky's Grandmother .... Jean Howard
Farmer .... Rance Howard
Farmer's Son .... Robert Peters
Boss Jack's Wife .... Jo Ann Pflug
Snipe .... Scott Schultz

and John Bennes (Hearse Driver), Barbara Rowan (Pregnant Wife), Trenton McDevitt (Pregnant Wife's Husband), Moses Gibson (Porter), Bonnie Cook (Cashier), John Paxton (Financial Planner), Jim Flowers, Frederick E. Dann (Bar Regulars), Walter Cobb (Priest), Joanne Pankow (Elderly Woman), Chuck Kinlaw (Elderly Woman's Son), Blaque Fowler (Gas Station Owner), Ted Manson (First Trailer Buyer), Kerry Maher (Bartender), John Easterbrook (Trailer Salesman), Paddy Keenan, John Williams, Nigel Stevens, Jackie Moran (Traveller Musicians), Mary K. Heneghan (Traveller Camp Dancer)

A young man, cast out of a band of Irish grifters for marrying an outsider, returns to the group and is taken under the wing of Bokky who intends to teach him the way of their forefathers.

Julianna Margulies

Scott Schultz, Mark Wahlberg

Don Cheadle

Tommy Lee Jones, Gaby Hoffman

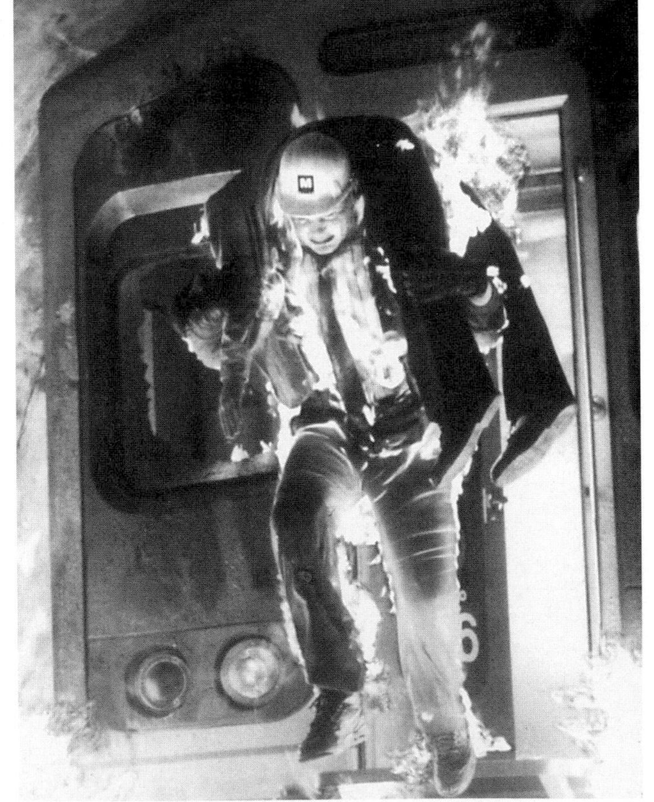

VOLCANO

(20TH CENTURY FOX) Producers, Neal H. Moritz, Andrew Z. Davis; Executive Producer, Lauren Shuler Donner; Director, Mick Jackson; Screenplay, Jerome Armstrong, Billy Ray; Story, Jerome Armstrong; Photography, Theo van de Sande; Designer, Jackson DeGovia; Editors, Michael Tronick, Don Brochu; Costumes, Kirsten Everberg; Music, Alan Silvestri; Stunts, Mic Rodgers; Special Effects Supervisor, Dale Ettema; Special/Mechanical Effects Coordinators, Clay Pinney, Marty Bresin; a Shuler Donner/Donner and Moritz Original production; Dolby Stereo; Deluxe color; Rated PG-13; 102 minutes; April release

CAST

Mike Roark ....Tommy Lee Jones
Dr. Amy Barnes ....Anne Heche
Kelly Roark ....Gaby Hoffmann
Emmit Reese ....Don Cheadle
Dr. Jaye Calder ....Jacqueline Kim
Lt. Ed Fox ....Keith David
Norman Calder ....John Corbett
Gator Harris ....Michael Rispoli
Stan Olber ....John Carroll Lynch
Kevin ....Marcello Thedford
Rachel ....Laurie Lathem
and Bert Kramer (Fire Chief), Bo Eason (Bud McVie), James G. MacDonald (Terry Jasper), Dayton Callie (Roger Lapher), Michael Cutt (Armstrong), Kevin Bourland (Bob Davis), Valente Rodriguez (Train Driver), Sheila Howard (Panicked Woman/Nanny), Gerry Black (Train Passenger), Susie Essman (Anita), Lou Myers (Pastor Lake), Gareth Williams (Pete), Juan Gabriel Reynoso (Carlos), Angela Albarez (Lydia Perez), Richard Penn (Middle Aged Man), Jennifer Bill (Nurse Fran), Mickey Cottrell (Councilman Gates), M. Darnell Suttles (Chief Sindelar), Ken Kerman (Museum Guard), Sal Rendino (Chuck), Michael Manuel (Del), Jared Thorne, Taylor Thorne (Tommy), Richard Schiff (Haskins), Brad Parker (Ken Woods), Pete Kasper (Kenny Lopez), Brian Markinson, Robert Wisdom, Katie Rich, Ceal Coleman, Phil Nee, Carlos Cervantes, George Zaver, Marty Levy, Wayne Grace (OEM Staffers), Mother Love (Traffic Cop), Kayli DeGregorio, Kelsi DeGregorio (5 Year Old Chuckie), Steven Mainz (K-Rail Driver), Josie Dapar, Joy Baggish (Survivors), Ron Perkins (Fire Chief), Todd Sible (Scott), Joshua Fardon (Medic), Catherine Schreiber (Displeased Protestor), David Pressman (Second Protestor), Danny Comden (Ascending Cop), Michael McGrady (Policeman), Michole Briana White (ER Nurse #1), Steve MacLaughlin (Construction Supervisor), Howard DuVall, Sam Alejan, Gary Kent James, Robert Tittot, John Perry Edson, Jr., David T. Mabowe, Ken Thomas, Eddie J. Low (Engineers), Georganna Barry (Java Lady), Tom Crabson (Passenger on Train), Rick Rogers (Sgt. Riley), Terry Anzur, Kerry Kilbride, Jennifer Bjorklund, Lonnie Lardner, Frank Buckley, Harvey Levin, Larry Carroll, Chris Myers, Angie Crouch, Shepard Smith, Steve Edwards, Christopher Spinder, Sasha Foo, Jeremy Thompson, Rick Garcia, Peter Trunk, Penny Griego, Michael Louis Villani, Pat Lalama, Bruce Orchid, Paula Bond, Charles Perez, Sandra Clark, Teresa Quevedo-Stoll, Rich Goldner, Leo Quinones, Juan Carlos Gonzalez, Alina Recasens, James Scott Hodson, Walter Richards, Jere Laird, Richard L.D. Saxton, Luann Lee, Sergio Urquidi, D. Lucey, Jane Velez-Mitchell, Jean Martirez, Jillian Warry, Chris McWatt, Jane Wells, Al Naipo, Karl T. Wright, Warren Olney, Andrea Wynn, Takayuki Yamauchi (The Media—Themselves)

A volcano errupts in the La Brea Tar Pits in the middle of downtown Los Angeles causing a lava flow that threatens to destroy the city.

Tommy Lee Jones, Anne Heche

Tommy Lee Jones, Anne Heche

A BROTHER'S KISS

(FIRST LOOK PICTURES) Producers, Bob Potter, E. Bennett Walsh; Executive Producer, Jim Walton; Director/Screenplay, Seth Zvi Rosenfeld; Based on his play; Co-Producers, Al Corley, Bart Rosenblatt; Photography, Fortunato Procopio; Designer, Roger Fortune; Music, Frank London; Editor, Donna Stern; Casting, Francine Maisler, Tracey Marable Moore; a Rosefunk Pictures Ltd. production; Ultra-Stereo; Color; Rated R; 92 minutes; April release

CAST

Lex ... Nick Chinlund
Mick ... Michael Raynor
Young Lex ... Justin Pierce
Doreen ... Cathy Moriarty
Young Mick ... Joshua Danowsky
Debbie ... Rosie Perez
Missy ... Marisa Tomei
Jimmy ... Richard Palmer
Lefty ... John Leguizamo
Nancy ... Erica Nicole Grier
Referee ... Andre Blake
Dope Fiend ... Adrian Pasdar
Junita ... Anjeanette Dejesus
Reefer Kid ... Rafael Nunez
Lucy ... Jennifer Esposito

and Scott Cohen (Rapist), Arthur Nascarella (Lex's Father), Michael Rapaport (Stingy), Jason Andrews, Kevin Thigpen (Cops), Talent Harris (Vic), Frank Minucci (Uncle Mac), Maurice Ballard (Ball Player), Aesha (Young Lex's Girlfriend), Ulysses Torrero, Ian Kelly (Variety Boys), Cameron Lucente (Baby), Blaze (Gunman), Pitzly You (Dealer), Seth Zvi Rosenfeld (Spam Man)

Two brothers, raised in a tough East Harlem neighborhood, vow to live a clean life and realize their dreams. Years later Mick becomes a cop while his younger, sensitive brother Lex gets lost in the world of drug dealing and addiction.

Michael Raynor, Nick Chinlund

Joshua Danowsky, Cathy Moriarty, Justin Pierce

Shiloh, Blake Heron

SHILOH

(LEGACY) Producers, Zane W. Levitt, Dale Rosenbloom; Executive Producers, Carl Borack, Mark Yellen; Director/Screenplay, Dale Rosenbloom; Based on the novel by Phyllis Reynolds Naylor; Photography, Frank Byers; Editor, Mark Westmore; Music, Joel Goldsmith; Designer, Amy Ancona; Costumes, Charmain Schreiner; Casting, Laura Schiff; a Utopia Pictures/Carl Borack production in association with Zeta Entertainment; Dolby Digital Stereo; Color; Rated PG; 93 minutes; April release

CAST

Ray Preston ... Michael Moriarty
Doc Wallace ... Rod Steiger
Marty Preston ... Blake Heron
Judd Travers ... Scott Wilson
Mrs. Wallace ... Bonnie Bartlett
Louise Preston ... Ann Dowd
Becky Preston ... Tori Wright
Dara Lynn Preston ... Shira Roth
Samantha ... J. Madison Wright
Sue ... Rachel Winfree
Mrs. McCallister ... Montrose Hagins
Mrs. Young ... Amzie Strickland

A beagle, abused by its cantankerous owner, runs away and finds a friend in young Marty Preston who hopes to keep the dog for his own.

ROMY AND MICHELE'S HIGH SCHOOL REUNION

(TOUCHSTONE) Producer, Laurence Mark; Executive Producers, Barry Kemp, Robin Schiff; Director, David Mirkin; Screenplay, Robin Schiff, based on characters from her play *Ladies' Room*; Co-Producer, Richard Luke Rothschild; Photography, Reynaldo Villalobos; Designer, Mayne Berke; Editor, David Finfer; Costumes, Mona May; Music, Steve Bartek; Character Makeup Designer/Supervisor, Kevin Haney; Choreographer, Smith Wordes; Casting, Marcia Ross; a Laurence Mark production in association with Bungalow 78 productions; Distributed by Buena Vista Pictures; Dolby Digital Stereo; Technicolor; Rated R; 91 minutes; April release

CAST

Romy	Mira Sorvino
Michele	Lisa Kudrow
Heather Mooney	Janeane Garofalo
Sandy Frink	Alan Cumming
Christie	Julia Campbell
Cheryl	Mia Cottet
Kelly	Kristin Bauer
Lisa	Elaine Hendrix
Billy	Vincent Ventresca
Toby	Camryn Manheim
Cowboy	Justin Theroux
Ramon	Jacob Vargas
Receptionist at "Singled Out"	Tami-Adrian George
Boutique Manager	Neil Dickson
Mr. Lish	E.J. Callahan
Kick Boxing Instructor	Kathy Long
Spinning Instructor	Betsy Folsom
Head of Personnel	Zack Phifer
Guy at Rehab Meeting	Ricky Paull Goldin
Creepy Manager	Robb Skyler
Service Guys	Deezer D, Kivi Rogers
Brat	Brian McGregor
Truck Stop Waitress	Pat Crawford Brown
Bartender Vic	Victor Wilson
Suit Salesman	Paul Keeley

and Amelinda Smith, Keana Hall, Alison Gale, Anne Jensen (Reunion Guests), Elizabeth Norment (Irate Customer), Rick Pasqualone (Mark), Tate Taylor (Casey), Linda Clements (Beverly Hills Lady), Alan Purwin (Helicopter Pilot)

Best friends Romy and Michele decide they must revamp themselves and their lives in order to make an impression at their ten-year high school reunion. Lisa Kudrow repeats her role from the original L.A. stage production.

Lisa Kudrow, Mira Sorvino

Alan Cumming, Julia Campbell

Lisa Kudrow, Janeane Garofalo, Mira Sorvino

Vincent Ventresca, Mira Sorvino

ALL OVER ME

(FINE LINE FEATURES) Producer, Dolly Hall; Executive Producers, Andreas Buhler, Stephen X. Graham, Nina M. Benton; Director, Alex Sichel; Screenplay, Sylvia Sichel; Photography, Joe DeSalvo; Designer, Amy Beth Silver; Editor, Sabine Hoffmann; Music, Miki Navazio; Costumes, Victoria Farrell; Casting, Lina Todd; a Medusa Pictures presentation in association with Baldini Pictures and Slam Pictures; Ultra-Stereo; Color; Rated R; 90 minutes; April release

CAST

Claude .... Alison Folland
Ellen .... Tara Subkoff
Mark .... Cole Hauser
Jesse .... Wilson Cruz
Claude's Mom .... Ann Dowd
Lucy .... Leisha Hailey
Luke .... Pat Briggs
Gus .... Shawn Hatosy
Don .... Vincent Pastore

Claude, a fifteen year-old girl living in New York's Hell's Kitchen, becomes jealous when her best friend Ellen begins showing interest in a guy, bringing her to the realization that she herself is in love with Ellen.

Tara Subkoff, Alison Folland

Tara Subkoff, Pat Briggs

Anthony LaPaglia, Courteney Cox, Aidan Quinn

Courteney Cox, Aidan Quinn

COMMANDMENTS

(GRAMERCY) Producers, Michael Chinich, Joe Medjuck, Daniel Goldberg; Executive Producer, Ivan Reitman; Director/Screenplay, Daniel Taplitz; Photography, Slawomir Idziak; Designer, Robin Standefer; Editor, Michael Jablow; Music, Joseph Vitarelli; Costumes, John Dunn; Co-Producer, Nellie Nugiel; Casting, Lynn Kressel; a Northern Lights Entertainment production; DTS Stereo; Deluxe color; Rated R; 87 minutes; May release

CAST

Seth Warner .... Aidan Quinn
Rachel Luce .... Courteney Cox
Harry Luce .... Anthony LaPaglia
Sylvia .... Shirl Bernheim
Melissa Murphy .... Pamela Gray
Rudy Warner .... Louis Zorich
Detective Mahoney .... Scott Sowers
Police Chief Warren .... Pat McNamara
Gordon Bloom .... Jack Gilpin
Mr. Mann .... Tom Aldredge
Mrs. Mann .... Alice Drummond
Mr. Neer .... Stephen Singer

and Peter Jacobson, Patrick Garner (Bankers), Marcia Debonis (Receptionist), Lisa Louise Langford (Paramedic), Chris McGinn (Nurse), Amy Sedaris (Scholar), Stephen Pearlman (Rabbi), Frank Girardeau (Bartender), John Tormey (Desk Sergeant), Michael Badalucco (Detective), Stu "Large" Riley (Inmate), Tom Riis Farrell (Marine Biologist)

When one unspeakable tragedy after another strikes Seth Warner he decides to challenge God by breaking all of the Ten Commandments.

NIGHT FALLS ON MANHATTAN

(PARAMOUNT) Producers, Thom Mount, Josh Kramer; Director/Screenplay, Sidney Lumet; Based upon the book Tainted Evidence by Robert Daley; Co-Producer, John H. Starke; Photography, David Watkin; Designer, Philip Rosenberg; Editor, Sam O'Steen; Costumes, Joseph G. Aulisi; Music, Mark Isham; Casting, Billy Hopkins, Suzanne Smith, Kerry Barden; a Spelling Films presentation of a Mount/Kramer production; Dolby Stereo; Deluxe color; Rated R; 113 minutes; May release

Andy Garcia, Richard Dreyfuss, Dominic Chianese

CAST

Sean Casey....Andy Garcia
Liam Casey....Ian Holm
Joey Allegretto....James Gandolfini
Peggy Lindstrom....Lena Olin
Jordan Washington....Shiek Mahmud-Bey
Elihu Harrison....Colm Feore
District Attorney Morgenstern....Ron Leibman
Sam Vigoda....Richard Dreyfuss
Judge Impelliteri....Dominic Chianese
McGovern....Paul Guilfoyle
Instructor....Bonnie Rose
Detective....Norman Matlock
Judge....Sidney Armus
Man in Asylum....Jim Murtaugh
Legal Aid Attorney....Melba Martinez
Eduardo....Santo Fazio
Shmuel....Anthony Alessandro
Half-Naked Girl....Nafisah Sayyed
Eileen....Marcia J. Kurtz
Lieutenant Wilson....Jude Ciccolella

and David Wolos-Fonteno, John Seitz, Robert Sean Miller (Captains), John Randolph Jones (Captain Lawrence), Chuck Pfeiffer (Captain Gentile), Stephen Beach, Vincent Pastore, Allen Collodow, Dennis Paladino, Salvatore Paul Piro (Cops), Clark D. Williams, Tamara Phillips, Bill Boggs (News), Louis Guss (Court Clerk), Richard Bright (64 Precinct Lieutenant), Ronald von Klaussen (65 Precinct Sergeant), John DiBenedetto (Patrolman #2), Kevin Ramsey (Sean's Assistant), Kermit Frazier (Jury Foreman), Vernica Hall (Pier Cop), Vic Noto (Diver), Jim Moody (Mayor Williams), Socorro Santiago (Lab Assistant), Fran Anthony (Moderator), Donna Hanover, Jack Cafferty, Kaity Tong (TV Newsperson), Mike Cammallere, Mike Sheehan (Sergeants), Jim Mauro, Joe Mosso (Lieutenants), Frank Vincent (Captain), Teddy Coluca, Roslyn Coh, Elliot Cuker (Reporters), Yvette Mercedes (Meter Maid), Kristina Lear (Girl in Restaurant), Joe Drago (D.A. Driver), Catherine Schreiber (Sean's Assistant #2), Bobby Cannavale (Vigoda Assistant #1)

A young Manhattan District Attorney, Sean Casey, is assigned to a high profile case in which his father, a cop, has been wounded in a shoot out with a drug dealer.

Lena Olin, Andy Garcia

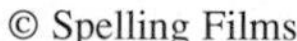

Ian Holm, Andy Garcia

Ron Liebman, Colm Feore, Andy Garcia

Kathleen Quinlan, Kurt Russell

Kurt Russell

J.T. Walsh, Kurt Russell, Kathleen Quinlan

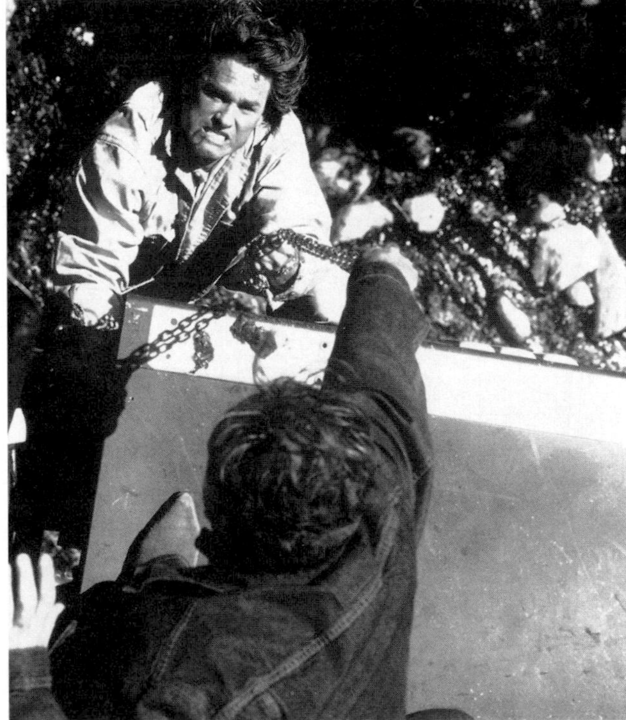

Kurt Russell, J.T. Walsh

BREAKDOWN

Kurt Russell

(PARAMOUNT) Producers, Martha De Laurentiis, Dino De Laurentiis; Executive Producers, Jonathan Fernandez, Harry Colomby; Director/Story, Jonathan Mostow; Screenplay, Jonathan Mostow, Sam Montgomery; Line Producer, Jeffrey Sudzin; Photography, Doug Milsome; Designer, Victoria Paul; Editors, Derek Brechin, Kevin Stitt; Costumes, Terry Dresbach; Music, Basil Poledouris; Casting, Carol Lewis; Presented in association with Dino De Laurentiis and Spelling Films; Dolby Digital Stereo; Super 35 Widescreen; Deluxe color; Rated R; 95 minutes; May release

CAST

Jeff Taylor	Kurt Russell
Red Barr	J.T. Walsh
Amy Taylor	Kathleen Quinlan
Earl	M.C. Gainey
Billy	Jack Noseworthy
Sheriff Boyd	Rex Linn
Al	Ritch Brinkley
Arleen	Moira Harris
Deputy Len Carver	Kim Robillard
Calhoun	Thomas Kopache
Bartender	Jack McGee
Deke	Vincent Berry
Flo	Helen Duffy
Barfly	Ancel Cook
Tow Truck Driver	Gene Hartline
Cowboy in Bank	Steve Waddington
Truck Stop Trucker	Rick Sanders

After their jeep breaks down in the desert, Jeff Taylor stays with the vehicle while his wife accepts a lift from a trucker. Hours later Jack discovers that she has disappeared without a trace.

Kathleen Quinlan, Kurt Russell

Kurt Russell, J.T. Walsh, Rex Linn

AUSTIN POWERS:
INTERNATIONAL MAN OF MYSTERY

(NEW LINE CINEMA) Producers, Suzanne Todd, Demi Moore, Jennifer Todd, Mike Myers; Executive Producers, Eric McLeod, Claire Rudnick Polstein; Director, Jay Roach; Screenplay, Mike Myers; Photography, Peter Deming; Designer, Cynthia Charette; Editor, Debra Neil-Fisher; Costumes, Deena Appel; Music, George S. Clinton; Casting, John Papsidera; a Moving Pictures/Eric's Boy production, presented in association with Capella International/KC Medien; Dolby Digital Stereo; Super 35 Widescreen; CFI color; Rated PG-13; 89 minutes; May release

Mike Myers, Elizabeth Hurley

CAST

Austin Powers/Dr. Evil .... Mike Myers
Vanessa Kensington .... Elizabeth Hurley
Basil Exposition .... Michael York
Mrs. Kensington .... Mimi Rogers
Number Two .... Robert Wagner
Scott Evil .... Seth Green
Alotta Fagina .... Fabiana Udenio
Frau Farbissina .... Mindy Sterling
Patty O'Brien .... Paul Dillon
Commander Gilmour .... Charles Napier
Mustafa .... Will Ferrell
'60s Models........Joann Richter, Anastasia Nicole Sakelaris, Afifi Alaouie
Mod Girl .... Monet Mazur
Andy Warhol .... Mark Bringelson
Radar Operator .... Clint Howard
Borschevsky .... Elya Baskin
Gary Coleman .... Carlton Lee Russell
Vanilla Ice .... Daniel Weaver
Quartermaster Clerk .... Neil Mullarkey
Random Task .... Joe Son
Las Vegas Tourist .... Tyde Kierny
Casino Dealer .... Larry Thomas
Himself .... Burt Bacharach
UN Secretary .... Brian George
Mrs. Exposition .... Kay Wade

and Lea Sullivan, Chekesha Van Putten, Heather Marie, Sara Smith, Laura Payne-Gabriel (Go-Go Dancers), Cheryl Bartel, Cindy Margolis, Donna W. Scott, Barbara Ann Moore, Cynthia Lamontagne (Fembots), Steve Monroe (Son), Vince Melocchi (Dad), Patrick Bristow (Virtucon Tour Guide), Jim McMullan (American UN Representative), Robin Gammell (British UN Representative), Ted Kairys (Eastern European Technician), Carrie Fisher (Session Leader), Tom Arnold (Man in Toilet)

Swingin' sixties secret agent Austin Powers is put into deep freeze in order to trap his nemesis Dr. Evil, both men finding themselves hopelessly out-of-date when they are defrosted in the 1990s.

Mike Myers

Robert Wagner

Mike Myers

Robert Wagner

Elizabeth Hurley

Mike Myers

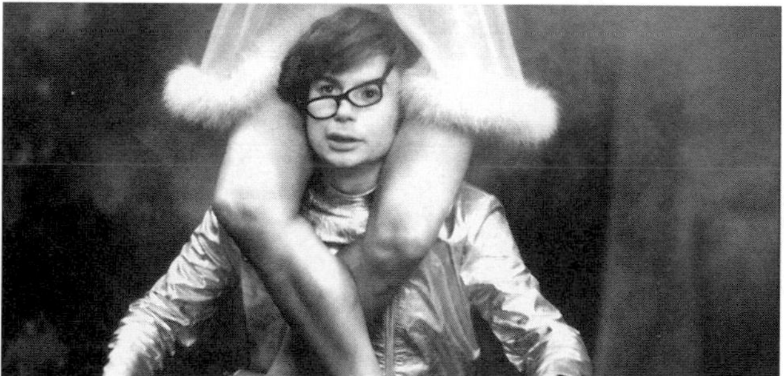

Mike Myers

Mike Myers, Elizabeth Hurley

John Glover, Stephen Bogardus, Jason Alexander, Justin Kirk, Randy Becker, Stephen Spinella, John Benjamin Hickey

Stephen Bogardus, Jason Alexander

Stephen Bogardus, Randy Becker

John Benjamin Hickey, Stephen Spinella

Jason Alexander

LOVE! VALOUR! COMPASSION!

(FINE LINE FEATURES) Producers, Doug Chapin, Barry Krost; Executive Producers, Ruth Vitale, Jonathan Weisgal, Amy Labowitz; Director, Joe Mantello; Screenplay, Terrence McNally, based on his play; Line Producer, Diane Conn; Photography, Alik Sakharov; Editor, Colleen Sharp; Designer, François Seguin; Music, Harold Wheeler; Costumes, Jess Goldstein; Choreographer, John Carrafa; a Krost/Chapin production; Dolby Stereo; Color; Rated R; 110 minutes; May release

CAST

John Jekyll/James Jekyll ....John Glover
Perry Sellars ....Stephen Spinella
Gregory Mitchell..Stephen Bogardus
Arthur Pape..John Benjamin Hickey
Bobby Brahms ....Justin Kirk
Ramon Fornos ....Randy Becker
Buzz Hauser ....Jason Alexander

A look at the lives, loves and relationships of eight gay friends as they spend three separate weekends together during the course of a summer. All of the principles (except Jason Alexander) repeat their roles from the original 1994 Off-Broadway production. The 1995 Tony Award-winning Broadway production featured Anthony Heald in the role of Perry. Nathan Lane played the role of Buzz in both productions.

Stephen Spinella, John Benjamin Hickey

Randy Becker

Stephen Bogardus, Justin Kirk, John Glover, John Benjamin Hickey, Jason Alexander, Randy Becker

NOWHERE

(FINE LINE FEATURES) Producers, Gregg Araki, Andrea Sperling, Why Not Productions; Director/Screenplay/Editor, Gregg Araki; Photography, Arturo Smith; Designer, Patti Podesta; Costumes, Sara Jane Slotnick; Casting, Rick Montgomery, Dan Parada, Mary Margiotta, Karen Margiotta; from Desperate Pictures/Blurco/Why Not Productions (France); U.S.-French; Color; Rated R; 85 minutes; May release

CAST

Dark .... James Duval
Mel .... Rachel True
Montgomery .... Nathan Bexton
Kriss .... Chiara Mastroianni
Kozy .... Debi Mazar
Lucifer .... Kathleen Robertson
Zero .... Joshua Gibran Mayweather
Alyssa .... Jordan Ladd
Dingbat .... Christina Applegate
Egg .... Sarah Lassez
Cowboy .... Guillermo Diaz
Bart .... Jeremy Jordan
Handjob .... Alan Boyce
The Teen Idol .... Jaason Simmons
Shad .... Ryan Phillippe
Lilith .... Heather Graham

and Scott Caan (Ducky), Thyme Lewis (Elvis), Mena Suvari (Zoe), Beverly D'Angelo (Dark's Mom), Charlotte Rae (Fortune Teller), Denise Richards (Jana), Teresa Hill (Shannon), Kevin Light (Noah), Traci Lords, Shannen Doherty, Rose McGowan (Val Chicks), John Ritter (Moses Helper), Christopher Knight (Mr. Sigvatssohn), Eve Plumb (Mrs. Sigvatssohn), Lauren Tewes (Julie, the Newscaster), David Leisure (Egg & Ducky's Dad), John Enos III, Nicolette Gato, Brian Buzzini (The Scary Drag Queens), Aaron Smith, Tres Trash Temperilli, Sara Jane (The Atari Gang), Devon Odessa (What), Stacy Keanan (Ever), Gibby Haynes (Jujyfruit), Keith Brewer (Surf), Derek Brewer (Ski), Roscoe (The Alien)

A look at the lives of various aimless L.A. teenagers and their experiences with love, sex, crime, and drugs.

James Duval

Joe Torry, Rusty Cundieff, Tisha Campbell, Paula Jai Parker

SPRUNG

(TRIMARK) Producer, Darin Scott; Executive Producer, Mark Amin; Director, Rusty Cundieff; Screenplay, Rusty Cundieff, Darin Scott; Co-Producer, Jonathan Komack Martin; Photography, Joao Fernandes; Designer, Terrence Foster; Editor, Lisa Bromwell; Associate Producer, Andrew Hersh; Line Producer, Elaine Dysinger; Music, Stanley Clarke; Costumes, Tracey White; Casting, Tony Lee; a Darin Scott production; Dolby Stereo; Color; Rated R; 105 minutes; May release

CAST

Brandy .... Tisha Campbell
Montel .... Rusty Cundieff
Adina .... Paula Jai Parker
Clyde .... Joe Torry
Detective .... John Witherspoon
Veronica .... Jennifer Lee
Grand Daddy .... Clarence Williams III
Bride's Mother .... Loretta Jean
Party Guard .... Ronny Willis
Watch Commander .... Ron Brooks

and John Ganun, David McKnight (Patrol Officers), Bobby McGee (First Suspect), Moon Jones (Godzilla Nuts Suspect), Bobby Mardis (Foreign Suspect), J.P. Stevenson (Flaming Suspect), Maryn Tasco (Cute Older Lady), Rai Tasco (Cute Older Man), Jeri Gray (Dancing Older Lady), Nick LaTour (Dancing Older Man), Angela Dickerson (Consuela), Darin Scott (Inconsiderate "Husband"), Isabel Sanford, Angela Means, Yolanda Whitaker, Homselle Joy (Sistas), Sherman Hemsley, Reynaldo Rey, Mark Christopher Lawrence, Tim Hutchinson (Brothas), Freda Payne (Vocalist), Shari Randolph, Karlotta Nelson, Trina Davis, Robyn Lattaker (Restaurants)

Montel, looking for a serious relationship, and his sex-hungry friend Clyde go to a sorority alumni jam where they meet and pair up with the jaded Brandy and her money-obsessed friend Adina.

THE LOST WORLD: JURASSIC PARK

(UNIVERSAL) Producers, Gerald R. Molen, Colin Wilson; Executive Producer, Kathleen Kennedy; Director, Steven Spielberg; Screenplay, David Koepp; Based on the novel The Lost World by Michael Crichton; Photography, Janusz Kaminski; Designer, Rick Carter; Editor, Michael Kahn; Music, John Williams; Associate Producers, Bonnie Curtis; Full Motion Dinosaurs, Dennis Muren; Live Action Dinosaurs, Stan Winston; Special Dinosaur Effects, Michael Lantieri; Visual Effects Producer, Ned Gorman; Casting, Janet Hirshenson, Jane Jenkins; an Amblin Entertainment production; Dolby DTS Stereo; Deluxe color; Rated PG-13; 134 minutes; May release

CAST

Ian Malcolm....Jeff Goldblum
Sarah Harding....Julianne Moore
Roland Tembo....Pete Postlethwaite
Peter Ludlow....Arliss Howard
John Hammond....Richard Attenborough
Nick Van Owen....Vince Vaughn
Kelly Curtis....Vanessa Lee Chester
Dieter Stark....Peter Stormare
Ajay Sidhu....Harvey Jason
Eddie Carr....Richard Schiff
Dr. Robert Burke....Thomas F. Duffy
Tim....Joseph Mazzello
Lex....Ariana Richards
Carter....Thomsa Rosales
Cathy Bowman....Camilla Belle
Mrs. Bowman....Cyd Strittmatter
Mr. Bowman....Robin Sachs
Senior Board Member....Elliott Goldwag
Board Member....J. Patrick McCormack
Curious Man....Ross Partridge
Butler....Ian Abercrombie
Workman....David Sawyer
Barge Captain....Geno Silva

and Alex Miranda (Barge Captain's Son), Robert "Bobby Z" Zajonc (Ingen Helicopter Pilot), Bob Boehm, Bradley Jensen, Alan Purwin, Ben Skorstad, Rick Wheeler, Kenyon Williams (Cargo Helicopter Pilots), Gordon Michaels, J. Scott Shonka, Harry Hutchinson, Bill Brown, Brian Turk (Ingen Workers), Jim Harley (Harbor Master), Colton James (Benjamin), Carey Eidel (Benjamin's Dad), Katy Boyer (Benjamin's Mom), David Koepp (Unlucky Bastard), Eugene Bass, Jr. (Attorney), Bari Buckner (Screaming Woman), P.B. Hutton, David St. James, Mark Brady, Marjean Holden, Jacqueline Schultz, Domini Hofmann De Salgado, Thomas Stuart (Screamers), Ransom Walrod (Ship Driver), David Gene Gibbs (Police Helicopter Pilot), Michael N. Fujimoto, Paul Fujimoto, Darryl A. Imai, Darryl Oumi (Asian Tourists), Vincent Dee Miles (Screaming Hunter), Bernard Shaw (CNN Reporter/Himself)

Chaos theorist Ian Malcolm arrives on the dinosaur manufacturing facility for Jurassic Park where his girlfriend Dr. Sarah Harding has gone to study the surviving dinosaurs. Meanwhile Peter Ludlow dispatches a team of hunters to capture the creatures and bring them back to the mainland. Sequel to the 1993 Universal release Jurassic Park with Jeff Goldblum, Richard Attenborough, Joseph Mazzello, and Ariana Richards repeating their roles from that film. This film received an Oscar nomination for visual effects.

Jeff Goldblum, Vanessa Lee Chester, Vince Vaughn, Julianne Moore, Richard Schiff

Richard Schiff, Julianne Moore, Jeff Goldblum, Vince Vaughn

Jeff Goldblum, Richard Schiff, Vince Vaughn

Dylan McDermott, Sarah Jessica Parker, Jeanne Tripplehorn

Jeanne Tripplehorn, Dylan McDermott

Jennifer Aniston, Jeanne Tripplehorn

'TIL THERE WAS YOU

(PARAMOUNT) Producers, Penney Finkelman Cox, Tom Rosenberg, Alan Poul; Executive Producers, Sigurjon Sighvatsson, Ted Tannebaum; Director, Scott Winant; Screenplay, Winnie Holzman; Photography, Bobby Bukowski; Designer, Craig Stearns; Editors, Richard Marks, Joanna Cappuccilli; Music, Miles Goodman, Terence Blanchard; Costumes, Enid Harris, Rita Salazar; Co-Producers, Richard S. Wright, Julie Golden; Associate Producers, Karen Montgomery, James McQuaide; Casting, Amanda Mackey Johnson, Cathy Sandrich; a Lakeshore Entertainment presentation of a Penney Finkelman Cox production; Dolby Stereo; Deluxe color; Rated PG-13; 113 minutes; May release

CAST

Gwen Moss....Jeanne Tripplehorn
Nick Dawkan....Dylan McDermott
Francesca Lansfield....Sarah Jessica Parker
Debbie....Jennifer Aniston
Jon Haas....Craig Bierko
Sophia Monroe....Nina Foch
Harriet....Alice Drummond
Beebee Moss....Christine Ebersole
Saul Moss....Michael Tucker
Bob....Reg Rogers
Angenelle....Kasi Lemmons
Timo....Patrick Malahide
Kevin....Steven Antin
Robin....Susan Walters
Vince....Kale Browne
Saul (age 25)....John Plumpis
Beebee (age 25)....Janel Moloney
Gwen (age 7)....Yvonne Zima
Nick (age 7)....Kellen Fink
Betty....Karen Allen
Taffy (age 7)....Alexandra Theriault
Taffy (age 12)....Kimberly Paige
TV Dad....Jim Jansen
Gregory....Ken Olin
Jonny (age 8)....Andrew Armbruster
Debbie (age 13)....Amanda Fuller
Gwen (age 12)....Madeline Zima
Nick (age 12)....Joshua Rubin
Gwen's Prom Date....Matt Alexander

and John Mascaro (Gwen's College Date), Michael Moertl (Dean), Richard Fancy (Murdstone), Earl Carroll (Heep), Ian Gomez (Scott), Matt Roth (Todd), Karen Mayo Chandler (Awful Truth Woman), Anthony Guidera (Maitre' D), Alexa Jago (Suzanne), John Hawkes (Gawayne), Jack Kruschen (Mr. Katz), Danielle Wiener (Chelsea), Julio Oscar Mechoso, Bruce Winant (Movers), Cinders (Himself), David C. Miller (Man with Flyer), Tiffany Paulsen (Tiffany), William Utay (Paul Pullman), William Forward (Chairman), David Elliot (Waiter with Tray), Kelly McCarthy (Waitress), Annabelle Gurwitch (Woman in Bathroom), Marina Malota (Gwen's Daughter)

Gwen Moss and Nick Dawkan literally bump into one another as children then spend their lives going their separate ways, searching for perfect relationships, always just missing one another despite the fact that they share common friends and acquaintances.

TRIAL AND ERROR

(NEW LINE CINEMA) Producers, Gary Ross, Jonathan Lynn; Executive Producers, Mary Parent, Allen Alsobrook; Director, Jonathan Lynn; Screenplay, Sara Bernstein, Gregory Bernstein; Story, Sara Bernstein, Gregory Bernstein, Cliff Gardner; Photography, Gabriel Beristain; Designer, Victoria Paul; Editor, Tony Lombardo; Music, Phil Marshall; Costumes, Shay Cunliffe; Associate Producers, Jane DeVries Cooper, Edward Lynn; Casting, Terry Liebling; a Larger Than Life production; Dolby Digital; Super 35 Widescreen; CFI Color; Rated PG-13; 98 minutes; May release

CAST

Richard Rietti....Michael Richards
Charles Tuttle....Jeff Daniels
Billie Tyler....Charlize Theron
Elizabeth Gardner....Jessica Steen
Judge Paul Z. Graff....Austin Pendleton
Benny Gibbs....Rip Torn
Tiffany....Alexandra Wentworth
Jacqueline....Jennifer Coolidge
Whitfield....Lawrence Pressman
Dr. Stone....Dale Dye
Dr. Brown....Max Casella
Charles' Assistant....McNally Sagal
Hank Crabbit....Kenneth White
Buck Norman....Keith Mills
Bailiff....Zaid Farid
Mrs. Sussex....Rachel Winfree
Clerk....Ken Magee
Court Reporter....Michelle Bonilla
Eric....Mark Davenport
Kurt....Kelly Perine
Phil....Rick La Fond
and Paul Joseph Dworkin, John Bigham (Bartenders), Nancy Linehan Charles (Witness), Jim Cody Williams (Tattooed Lowlife), Jodi Faith Cahn (Elizabeth's Secretary), Brian Mahoney (Man in Bar), Gerry Spence (Himself), Norman Brennar (Courtroom Janitor)

When lawyer Charles Tuttle is unable to make a court appearance his best friend, Richard, an actor, fills in for him, little realizing that he will have to go on posing as Charles for the remainder of the trial.

Danny Glover, Joe Pesci

Michael Richards, Jeff Daniels

GONE FISHIN'

(HOLLYWOOD PICTURES) Producers, Roger Birnbaum, Julie Bergman Sender; Executive Producer, Jill Mazursky Cody; Director, Christopher Cain; Screenplay, Jill Mazursky Cody, Jeffrey Abrams; Photography, Dean Semler; Designer, Lawrence Miller; Editor, Jack Hofstra; Co-Producers, Richard H. Prince, Lou Arkoff; Music, Randy Edelman; Costumes, Lizzy Gardiner; Casting, Rick Montgomery, Dan Parada; Stunts, Shane Dixon; a Roger Birnbaum production, presented in association with Caravan Pictures; Dolby Digital Stereo; Technicolor; Rated PG; 94 minutes; May release

CAST

Joe Waters....Joe Pesci
Gus Green....Danny Glover
Rita....Rosanna Arquette
Angie....Lynn Whitfield
Billy "Catch" Pooler....Willie Nelson
Dekker Massey....Nick Brimble
Phil Beasly....Gary Grubbs
Donna Waters....Carol Kane
Cookie Green....Edythe Davis
Gina Waters....Jenna Bari
Tracy Green....Samantha Brown
Mack Waters....Jeff DiLucca
Gregory Green....Jamil Akim O'Quinn
Young Joe....Frank Nasso
and Raynor Scheine (Glenn), Robyn Hackett (Nicky), James R. Greene (Bubba), Steve Wise (JP), Claudia Haro (Julie), Jonathan Avildsen (Parking Valet), Bob Noble (Manager), Jeff Prettyman (Maitre D'), Judy Clayton (Deana Bernini), Antoni Corone (Front Desk Clerk), Dana Adamstein, Valerie J. Boey (Reporters), Joseph Scalora (Officer), Tommy DeVito (Construction Foreman), Leonard Termo, Alfred Nittoli (Vending Workers), Gary Morgan (Bergman), Lisa Hewlett Keen (Dining Room Guest), Dave Corey (Actor), Baynor Foy Crane (Actress), Mark Futch (Seaplane Pilot), John Griffen (Blind Driver), Louise Fletcher, Maury Chaykin

Gus and Joe, on their way to the Florida Everglades for a fishing vacation, have their car stolen by a mysterious man on his way to recover some stolen cash.

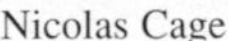
Nicolas Cage

Rachel Ticotin

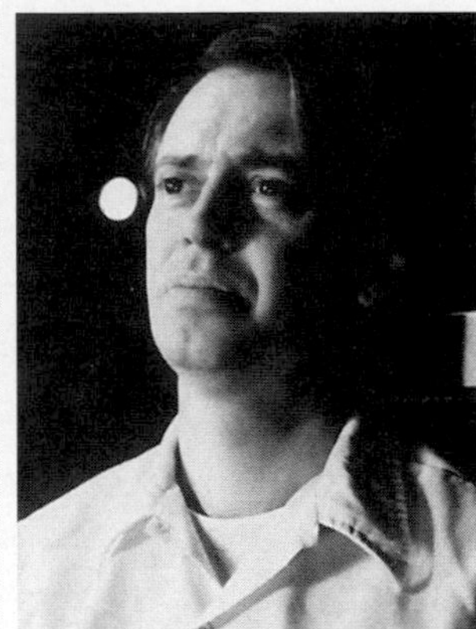
Steve Buscemi

Ving Rhames

Danny Trejo

Nicolas Cage, Mykelti Williamson

CON AIR

(TOUCHSTONE) Producer, Jerry Bruckheimer; Executive Producers, Chad Oman, Jonathan Hengsleigh, Peter Bogart, Jim Kouf, Lynn Bigelow; Director, Simon West; Screenplay, Scott Rosenberg; Photography, David Tattersall; Art Director, Edward T. McAvoy; Editors, Chris Lebenzon, Steve Mirkovich, Glen Scantlebury; Music, Mark Mancina, Trevor Rabin; Costumes, Bobbie Read; Visual Effects Supervisor, David Goldberg; Visual Effects, Dream Quest Images; Stunts, Kenny Bates; Casting, Victoria Thomas; a Jerry Bruckheimer production; Distributed by Buena Vista Pictures; Dolby Digital Stereo; Panavision; Technicolor; Rated R; 115 minutes; June release

John Cusack, Colm Meaney, John Roselius

CAST

Cameron Poe........Nicolas Cage
U.S. Marshal Vince Larkin........John Cusack
Cyrus "The Virus" Grissom........John Malkovich
Garland Greene........Steve Buscemi
Billy Bedlam........Nick Chinlund
U.S. Marshal Guard Sally Bishop........Rachel Ticotin
Duncan Malloy........Colm Meaney
Swamp Thing........M.C. Gainey
Diamond Dog (Nathan Jones)........Ving Rhames
Conrad........Brendan Kelly
Baby-O........Mykelti Williamson
Johnny 23........Danny Trejo
Sally Can't Dance........Renoly
Francisco Cindino........Jesse Borrego
"Pinball" Parker........Dave Chappelle
Con #1........Carl N. Ciarfalio
Ajax........Jerry Mongo Brownlee
Falzon........Steve Eastin
Sims........Jose Zuniga
Chopper Pilot........Ned Bellamy
Gator........John Marshall Jones
Devers........John Roselius
Pilot........Fredric Lane
Co-Pilot........Martin McSorley
Starkey........Dylan Haggerty
Chambers........Matt Barry
Tricia Poe........Monica Potte
Casey Poe........Landry Allbright
Fuel Jockey........Dan Bell
Ted, the Pilot........Robert Stephenson
Bus Guard........Scott Ditty
Sheriff........Tommy Bush

and Lauren Pratt (Debbie 6yrs. old), Steve Hulin (Ronnie), Don Charles McGovern (Smoke), Angela Featherstone (Ginny), Doug Hutchinson (Donald), Jeris Poindexter (Watts), David Ramsey (Londell), Conrad Goode (Viking), Emillio Rivera (Carlos), Tyrone Granderson Jones (Blade), Mario Roberts (Mongoose—Stunt), Earl Billings, Greg Collins, Billy Devlin, Mark Ginther, Joseph Patrick Kelly (Guards), Jeff Olson (Uncle Bob), Dawn Bluford (Baggage Handler), Charlie Paddock (Transportation Officer #1), Randee Barnes (Stickman), Don Davis (Man in Car), Barbara Sharma (Woman in Car), Tommy Rosales, Eddie Perez, Scott McCoy (Cindino Gunmen—Stunts), Brian Hayes Currie (Cop in Vegas), Ashley Smock (Huey Pilot), Charles Lynn Frost (DEA Agent), Joey Miyashima (Tech Guy), Scott Burkholder (Air Traffic Controller), Kevin Cooney (Judge), Gerard L'Heureux (Guard Renfro), Peter Antico (Guard Garner), John Robotham (Guard Ryan), Gilbert Rosales (Ramirez—Stunt), Richard Duran (Warlock—Stunt), George Randall (Old Con on Plane), James Bozian, Harley Zumbrum, Doug Dearth (Cons), David Roberson (Supervisor), Alexandra Balahoutis (Waitress), Dick "Skip" Evans (Airplane Pilot), Sheldon Worthington (Co-Pilot), Robert Taft, Robert White (Soldiers), Chris Ellis (BOP Official Grant), John Campbell (BOP Bus Driver), Brian Willems, Bill Cusack (Paramedics), Dabbs Greer (Old Man under Truck), Marco Kyris (Cindino's Pilot)

John Malkovich

Eager to get home to his wife and child, recently paroled Cameron Poe takes passage on a plane transporting a group of dangerous criminals only to find that it is up to him to save the day when the convicts take over the vehicle. This film received Oscar nominations for song ("How Do I Live") and sound.

Mykelti Williamson, Nicolas Cage, Rachel Ticotin

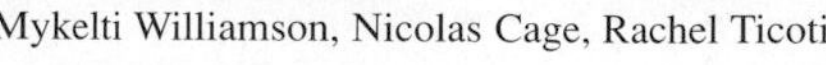

BUDDY

(COLUMBIA) Producers, Steve Nicolaides, Fred Fuchs; Executive Producers, Francis Ford Coppola, Stephanie Allain, Brian Henson; Director/Screenplay, Caroline Thompson; Based upon the book Animals Are My Hobby by Gertrude Davies Lintz; Screen Story, William Joyce, Caroline Thompson; Photography, Steve Mason; Designers, David Nichols, Daniel Lomino; Editor, Jonathan Shaw; Music, Elmer Bernstein; Costumes, Colleen Atwood; Creature Effects, Jim Henson's Creature Shop; Casting, Carrie Frazier; a Jim Henson Pictures presentation of an American Zoetrope production; Dolby SDDS Stereo; Panavision; Technicolor; Rated PG; 84 minutes; June release

CAST

Trudy Lintz....Rene Russo
Dr. Bill Lintz....Robbie Coltrane
Dick Kroener....Alan Cumming
Emma....Irma P. Hall
Buddy....Peter Elliott, Mak Wilson
(and Lynn Robertson Bruce, Mark Sealey, Rob Tygner, Michelan Sisti, Peter Hurst, Leif Tilden, Star Townshend)
Professor Spatz....Paul Reubens
Mr. Bowman....John Aylward
Mrs. Bowman....Mimi Kennedy
Theater-goer....Jon Simmons
Movie Woman....Kathleen Klein
Usher....Russell Young
Zoo Keeper....Frank Collison
Barker....Al Weber
Minister....Philip Baker Hall
Bellowing Man....Kyle Galyean
Fair Cop....Dane Cook
Skinny Man....Michael Reid Mackay
Policemen....John Ennis, Jeff Hatz
Ali Baba....Bradley J. Lesley
Cornered Woman....Julianna Wheeler
Buddy Vocals....Frank Welker, Gary Hecker, Hector C. Gika

The true story of eccentric socialite Gertrude "Trudy" Lintz who kept a menagerie of wild animals on her New York estate, most notably a gorilla named "Buddy" that she raised since he was a baby.

Buddy, Rene Russo

Alan Cumming

Rene Russo

Mimi Kennedy, John Aylward, Buddy

Vanessa Zima, Peter Fonda

Patricia Richardson

Jessica Biel, Peter Fonda, Vanessa Zima

ULEE'S GOLD

(ORION) Co-Producers, Sam Gowan, Peter Saraf; Executive Producers, Edward Saxon, John Sloss, Valerie Thomas; Director/Screenplay, Victor Nunez; Photography, Virgil Mirano; Designer, Pat Garner; Music, Charles Engstrom; Costumes, Marilyn Wall-Asse; Casting, Judy Courtney; a Jonathan Demme presentation of a Nunez-Gowan/Clinica Estetico production; Dolby Stereo; Deluxe color; Rated R; 111 minutes; June release

CAST

Ulee Jackson ....Peter Fonda
Connie Hope ....Patricia Richardson
Helen Jackson ....Christine Dunford
Jimmy Jackson....................Tom Wood
Casey Jackson....................Jessica Biel
Penny Jackson....................Vanessa Zima
Eddie Flowers ....Steven Flynn
Ferris Dooley ....Dewey Weber
Sheriff Bill Floyd....................J. Kenneth Campbell
Chance Barrow....................Traber Burns
Charley Myers ....Ryan Marshall
Markie....................Chad Fish
Child at Rest Stop ....Will Sexton
Beekeeper Assistants....................Dale C. Marshall, James Whitehurst, Charles Branner

Florida beekeeper Ulee Jackson, raising his two granddaughters, must cope again with the girls' irresponsible, drug-addicted mother when he is asked by his son to retrieve the woman from a pair of dangerous criminals. This film received an Oscar nomination for actor (Peter Fonda).

Christine Dunford

Tom Wood

J. Kenneth Campbell

SPEED 2: CRUISE CONTROL

(20TH CENTURY FOX) Producers, Jan De Bont, Steve Perry, Michael Peyser; Director, Jan De Bont; Screenplay, Randall McCormick, Jeff Nathanson; Story, Jan De Bont, Randall McCormick; Based on characters created by Graham Yost; Executive Producer, Mark Gordon; Photography, Jack N. Green; Designers, Joseph Nemec III, Bill Kenney; Editor, Alan Cody; Music, Mark Mancina; Special Effects Supervisors, Stefen Fangmeier (ILM), Bert Terreri (Rhythm & Hues, Inc.); Costumes, Louise Frogley; Stunts, Dick Ziker; Casting, Risa Bramon Garcia, Randi Hiller; a Blue Tulip production; Dolby Digital Stereo; Panavision; Deluxe color; Rated PG-13; 121 minutes

CAST

Annie Porter ....Sandra Bullock
Alex Shaw ....Jason Patric
John Geiger ....Willem Dafoe
Juliano ....Temuera Morrison
Merced ....Brian McCardie
Drew ....Christine Firkins
Harvey ....Michael G. Hagerty
Debbie ....Colleen Camp
Celeste ....Lois Chiles
Rupert ....Francis Guinan
Sheri ....Tamia
Ashton ....Jeremy Hotz
Alejandro ....Enrique Murciano, Jr.
Isabel ....Jessica Diz
Fran ....Connie Ray
Ruby ....Patrika Darbo

and Kimmy Robertson (Liza the Cruise Director), Charles Parks (Frank), Susan Barnes (Constance), Bo Svenson (Captain Pollard), Royale Watkins (Dante), Alex Montesino (Control Room Chief Engineer), Glenn Plummer (Maurice), Allison Dean (Marifa), Joe Foster (Pool Officer), Richard Speight, Jr. ("C" Deck Officer), Tim Conway (Mr. Kenter), Mark Adair-Rios, Xavier Coronel, Tyler Patton, Craig A. Pinckes (Engine Room Crew Members), Michael Robinson, Joe d'Angerio (Muster Deck Officers), Michael O'Hagan (Supertanker Captain), Christopher Wynne, Robert Herrick (Supertanker Officers), Ivory Broome (Supertanker Crew Member #1), Thomas J. Huff (Diaper Van Driver), Jay Lacopo (Real Estate Salesman), Alexander De Bont (Little Boy—Condo), Kathryn Rossetter (Mother at Condo), Mark Beltzman (Convertible Owner), Mark Kriski (News Reporter), Ben Meyerson, Gustavo Laborie (Bridge Officers), Ben Siegler (Policeman), Jennifer S. Badger, Cheryl Bermeo, Jeff Brockton, Don Pulford, Cliff McLaughlin, Matthew Taylor, PJ Wagner, May R. Boss, Nancy Collet (Passengers), Wilma Edward (Woman on phone)

Annie and Alex take a Caribbean cruise only to discover that the ship they are sailing on has been hijacked by a crazed terrorist. Sequel to the 1994 20th Century Fox release Speed with Sandra Bullock and Glenn Plummer repeating their roles from that film.

Jason Patric, Sandra Bullock

Sandra Bullock, Willem Dafoe

Illeana Douglas, Paulina Porizkova, Julie Warner

WEDDING BELL BLUES

(LEGACY/BMG) Producers, Ram Bergman, Dana Lustig, Mike Curb, Carole Curb Nemoy; Director, Dana Lustig; Screenplay, Annette Goliti Gutierrez; Story, Dana Lustig, Annette Goliti Gutierrez; Photography, Kent Wakeford; Editor, Caroline Ross; Designer, Shay Austin; Costumes, Dana Allyson; Music, Paul Christian Gordon, Tal Bergman; Casting, Margiotta Casting; from Bergman Lustig productions/Curb Entertainment International Corp.; Color; Rated R; 100 minutes; June release

CAST

Jasmine ....Illeana Douglas
Tanya ....Paulina Porizkova
Micki ....Julie Warner
Cary ....John Corbett
Matt ....Jonathan Penner
Oliver ....Charles Martin Smith
Tom ....Richard Edson
Jeff ....Joseph Urla
Tanya's Mother ....Stephanie Beacham
Violet ....Carla Gugino
Robert ....Leo Rossi
Herself ....Debbie Reynolds

and John Capodice (Jasmine's Father), Liz Sheridan (Micki's Mother), Stephen Gilborn (Micki's Father), Jeff Seymour (Jan), Victoria Jackson (Boutique Customer), Kamala Dawson (Pregnant Woman), Carol Ann Susi (Aunt Anash), Andrew Heckler (Zane), Marcy Lafferty Shatner (Sonya), Bill Elliot (Anxious Husband), Carlos Montilla (Gustavo), David Wilbur (Priest), Kate Asner (Alice), Danny Koker (Beautiful Groom), Kevin Hunt (All-American Man), Brendan "Reno" Duffy (Elvis Impersonator)

Three women drive to Las Vegas where they hope to find husbands, marry them and divorce them within 24 hours, in order to say they were wed before they reached the age of thirty.

DREAM WITH THE FISHES

(SONY CLASSICS) Producers, Johnny Wow, Mitchell Stein; Co-Producers, David Arquette, Laurie A. Miller, Jeffrey Brown; Executive Producers, John Sideropoulos, Charles Hsiao; Director/Screenplay, Finn Taylor; Story, Finn Taylor, Jeffrey Brown; Photography, Barry Stone; Editor, Rick Le Compte; Designer, Justin McCartney; Costumes, Amy Brownson; Casting, Joseph Middleton; a 3 Ring Circus Films presentation; Dolby Stereo; Color; Rated R; 96 minutes; June release

CAST

Terry .... David Arquette
Nick .... Brad Hunt
Aunt Elise .... Cathy Moriarty
Liz .... Kathryn Erbe
Don .... Patrick McGaw
Joe, Nick's Father .... J.E. Freeman
Michelle .... Timi Prulhiere
Mary .... Anita Barone
Sophia .... Allyce Beasley
Pharmacist .... Peter Gregory
Sheriff .... Richmond Arquette
Funeral Director .... George Maguire
Terry's Bowling "Date" .... Kristina Robbins
Nick's Bowling "Date" .... Katherine Copenhaver
Drug Dealer .... Gary Brickman
Psychic .... Nina Peschcke-Koedt
Priest .... Orril Fluharty
and Michael Halton (Liquor Store Clerk), Mike Por (Donut Shop Clerk), Chris Pay (Emergency Room Doctor), Felix Justice, James Carraway (Nick's Doctors), Michael Vaughn (Bank Security Guard), Beth Daly (Librarian), Banda El Rincon (Band in Bar), Michael Hsiao (Restaurant Pianist), Alec Ingalls (Bartender), Jack A. Roe (Angry Taxi Passenger), Xris (Convenience Store Clerk), Capt. Greg Love, Officer Ken Cunningham, Officer Mike Price (Cops at Funeral/Pharmacy), Roland Absolo (Aquarium Security Guard), Sophia Stefanek (Mary's Daughter), Mark Hager (Garbage Man), Peaches (Nick's Ashes)

Terry, determined to commit suicide, hooks up with terminally ill Nick and the two decide to drop out of society to live life on the edge.

Brad Hunt, David Arquette

Phuong Duong, Eddie Cutanda, Tyrone Burton

SQUEEZE

(MIRAMAX) Producers, Ari Newman, Garen Topalian, Stephanie Danan, Patricia Moreno; Executive Producer, Mitchell B. Robbins; Director/Screenplay, Robert Patton-Spruill; Photography/Editor, Richard Moos; Associate Producers, Emmett Folgert, Laura Bernieri, H. Forrest Logan; Designer, Maximilian Cutler; Line Producer, Lee Beckett; a Robbins Entertainment presentation of a ca*thar*tic film Works and Danan/Moreno Films production in association with the Dorcester Youth Collaborative Extreme Close-Up; Dolby Stereo; Color; Rated R; 89 minutes; June release

CAST

Tyson .... Tyrone Burton
Hector .... Eddie Cutanda
Bao .... Phuong Duong
JJ .... Geoffrey Rhue
Tommy .... Russell G. Jones
Marcus .... Leigh Williams
Uzi .... Robert Agredo
Derick .... Beresford Bennett
Lisa .... Jennifer Maxcy
Fiend .... Harlem Logan
Aunt C. .... Diane Beckett
Pearl .... Ingrid Askew
Psychiatrist/Homelessman .... James Spruill
Jason .... William Butler
Mason .... Daryl Bugg
Tisha .... Maleah Liggins
Pinky .... Pinky Lugo
Angela .... Milagros Jones
and Catherine Oberg, Patrick Ruth (Cat Fighters), Sean Henderson, Johnny Henderson (Bad Kids), Lynda Patton, Georgette Leslie (Women in Car), Bruce Serefin (Police Officer), Gerry Nuzollo (Gas Station Attendant), Jessica Edwards (Marrisa), Victor Nunez (Julio), Alfredo Rivera (Doorman), John Bonaparte (Man with Burning Book), Juanita Rodriguez (Youth Center Receptionist), Monique Douglas (Youth Worker), Sparkle Henderson, Nicole Kelly, Melissa Khomblassen (Girls with Rakes), Aaron Stewart, Roy J. Lynch (Barbers), Max Cutler (Hospital Patient)

Three Boston teens are faced with the decision of helping out at a local youth center or taking the dangerous road of gangs and drug dealing.

Pegasus, Phil, Hercules

Hades, Meg

Hercules, Hydra

Hercules, Nessus

Panic, Pain

HERCULES

(WALT DISNEY PICTURES) Producers, Alice Dewey, John Musker, Ron Clements; Directors, John Musker, Ron Clements; Animation Screenplay, Ron Clements, John Musker, Donald McEnery, Bob Shaw, Irene Mecchi; Art Director, Andy Gaskill; Designer, Gerald Scarfe; Editor, Tom Finan; Associate Producer, Kendra Haaland; Music, Alan Menken; Lyrics, David Zippel; Artistic Supervisors: Story, Barry Johnson; Production Stylist, Sue C. Nichols; Layout, Rasoul Azadani; Background, Thomas Cardone; Visual Effects, Mauro Maressa; Computer Graphics Imagery, Roger L. Gould; Clean-Up, Nancy Kniep; Artistic Coordinator, Dan Hansen; Distributed by Buena Vista Pictures; Dolby Digital Stereo; Technicolor; Rated G; 92 minutes; June release

VOICE CAST

Alemene....Barbara Barrie
Young Hercules (singing)....Roger Bart
Earthquake Lady....Mary Kay Bergman
Burnt Man....Corey Burton
Nessus....Jim Cummings
Apollo....Keith David
Phil....Danny DeVito
Hercules....Tate Donovan
Fate....Paddi Edwards
Meg....Susan Egan
Hera....Samantha Eggar
Heavyset Woman....Kathleen Freeman
Muse (Melpomene)....Cheryl Freeman
Panic....Matt Frewer
Pain....Bobcat Goldthwait
Little Boys....Bug Hall, Kellen Hathaway
Narrator....Charlton Heston
Amphitryon....Hal Holbrook
Young Hercules (speaking)....Joshua Keaton
Demetrius....Wayne Knight
Muse (Terpsichore)....LaChanze
Ithicles....Aaron Michael Metchik
Cyclops....Patrick Pinney
Fate....Amanda Plummer
Muse (Thalia)....Roz Ryan
Hermes....Paul Shaffer
Fate....Carole Shelley
Muse (Clio)....Vaneese Thomas
Zeus....Rip Torn
Lead Muse (Calliope)....Lillias White
Hades....James Woods

and Tawatha Agee, Jack Angel, Shelton Becton, Bob Bergen, Rodger Bumpass, Jennifer Darling, Debi Derryberry, Bill Farmer, Milt Grayson, Sherry Lynn, Mickie McGowan, Denise Pickering, Phil Proctor, Jan Rabson, Riley Steiner, Fonzi Thorton, Erik Von Detten, Ken Williams (Additional Voices)

Hoping to rule the Universe the evil god of the Underworld, Hades, has Zeus's son Hercules abducted from Mount Olympus and taken to earth. There the boy is raised as mortal despite having retained his super-human strength. Previous film versions of Hercules include the 1957 release starring Steve Reeves and the 1983 MGM production with Lou Ferrigno. This film received an Oscar nomination for song ("Go the Distance").

Hades, Hercules

Phil, Hercules

Meg, Hercules, Pegasus

MY BEST FRIEND'S WEDDING

(TRISTAR) Producers, Jerry Zucker, Ronald Bass; Executive Producers, Gil Netter, Patricia Whitcher; Director, P.J. Hogan; Screenplay, Ronald Bass; Photography, Laszlo Kovacs; Designer, Richard Sylbert; Editors, Garth Craven, Lisa Fruchtman; Costumes, Jeffrey Kurland; Music, James Newton Howard; Casting, David Rubin; a Jerry Zucker/Predawn production; Dolby SDDS Stereo; Panavision; Technicolor; Rated PG-13; 105 minutes; June release

Julia Roberts, Cameron Diaz

CAST

Julianne Potter....................Julia Roberts
Michael O'Neal....................Dermot Mulroney
Kimmy Wallace....................Cameron Diaz
George Downes....................Rupert Everett
Walter Wallace....................Philip Bosco
Joe O'Neal....................M. Emmet Walsh
Samantha Newhouse....................Rachel Griffiths
Amanda Newhouse....................Carrie Preston
Isabelle Wallace....................Susan Sullivan
Scott O'Neal....................Chris Masterson
Title Sequence Performers....................Raci Alexander, Jennifer Garrett, Kelly Sheerin, Bree Turner
Flower Girl....................Cassie Creasy
Kimmy's Grandma....................Lucina Paquet
Old Woman #2....................Aida Baggio
Oldest Lady....................Shirley Kelly
Party Guests....................George Bozonelos, Loretta Paoletti
Stoner Guys....................Joseph Sikora, Shale Marks
Wedding Singer....................Phillip Ingram
Seamstress....................Rose Abdoo
Tailor....................JoBe Cerny
Bellman....................Paul Giamatti
Himself....................Chef Charlie Trotter
Chef....................Guillermo Tellez
Captain....................Ned Schmidtke
Karaoke Singer....................Mark Swenson

and Mara Casey (Karaoke Girl), Tonray Ho (Karaoke Waitress), Michelle Hutchison (Drunken Trashy Girl), Robert Sutter (Crabhouse Pianist), Charlotte Zucker, Susan Breslau, Burton Zucker, Sharon Haight (Customers), Nydia Rodriguez Terracina (Walter's Secretary), Mike Bacarella (Office Janitor), Larry Santori (Conductor), Gene Janson, Kevin Michael Doyle (Sport Magazine Guys), Scott Kuhagen (Werner), Sid Hillman, Norman Merrill, Renata Scott, Anh Duong (Dining Guests), Harry Shearer (Jonathan P.E. Rice), Jennifer McComb (Excited Woman), Mary-Pat Green (Angry Woman), Davenia McFadden (Angrier Woman), Jo Farkas (Loony Woman), The Morning Choir of the 4th Presbyterian Church of Chicago (Wedding Choir)

Julia Roberts, Rupert Everett

Julianne, realizing she still has very strong feelings for her best friend Michael, tries to break up his relationship with his fiancee in the four days leading up to their wedding. This film received an Oscar nomination for original music or comedy score.

Cameron Diaz, Dermot Mulroney, Julia Roberts

Philip Bosco, Susan Sullivan

Chris Masterson, Dermot Mulroney

Julia Roberts, Cameron Diaz

Julia Roberts, Dermot Mulroney, Rupert Everett

Nicolas Cage, John Travolta

Joan Allen, John Travolta

Dominique Swain

Nicolas Cage, Alessandro Nivola

FACE/OFF

(PARAMOUNT) Producers, David Permut, Barrie M. Osborne, Terence Chang, Christopher Godsick; Executive Producers, Jonathan D. Krane, Michael Douglas, Steven Reuther; Director, John Woo; Screenplay/Co-Producers, Mike Werb, Michael Colleary; Photography, Oliver Wood; Designer, Neil Spisak; Editors, Christian Wagner, Steven Kemper; Costumes, Ellen Mirojnick; Music, John Powell; Associate Producer, Jeff Levine; Visual Effects Supervisors, Richard Hollander, Boyd Shermis; Special Makeup Effects Creator, Kevin Yagher; Stunts, Brian Smrz; Casting, Mindy Marin; a Douglas/Reuther—WCG Entertainment — David Permut production; Dolby Stereo; Panavision; Deluxe color; Rated R; 138 minutes; June release

John Travolta, Nicolas Cage

CAST

Sean Archer .... John Travolta
Castor Troy .... Nicolas Cage
Eve Archer .... Joan Allen
Pollux Troy .... Alessandro Nivola
Sasha Hassler .... Gina Gershon
Jamie Archer .... Dominique Swain
Dietrich Hassler .... Nick Cassavetes
Lazzaro .... Harve Presnell
Dr. Malcolm Walsh .... Colm Feore
Prison Guard Walton .... John Carroll Lynch
Hollis Miller .... CCH Pounder
Tito .... Robert Wisdom
Wanda .... Margaret Cho
Buzz .... Jamie Denton
Loomis .... Matt Ross
Leo Fry .... Tommy J. Flanagan
Lars .... Dana Smith
Kimberly .... Romy Walthall
Fitch .... Paul Hipp
Aldo Adino .... Kirk Baltz
Dubov .... Chris Bauer
Burke Hicks .... Thomas Jane
Agent Winters .... Lauren Sinclair
Pilot .... Ben Reed
Janitor .... Del Zamora
Cindee .... Lisa Boyle
Livia .... Linda Hoffman
Karl .... Danny Masterson
Priest .... Father Michael Rocha
Adolescent Girl .... Megan Paul
Iris' Dad .... Mike Werb
LAPD Cop .... Tom Reynolds
Interrogating Agent .... Steve Hytner

and Myles Jeffrey (Michael Archer), Carmen Thomas (Reporter Valerie), John Bloom (Prison Medical Technician), Walter Scott (Port Police Commander), Brooke Leslie (ER Nurse), David McCurley (Adam Hassler), Cam Brainard (Dispatcher), David Warshofsky (Bomb Leader), John Neidlinger (Bomb Technician), Norm Compton (Cigarette Guard), Gregg Shawzin (Lock Down Guard), Clifford Einstein (Restorative Surgeon), Marco Kyris (Recreation Guard), Tom Fridley (Prison Guard), Andrew Wallace (Altar Boy), Jacinto Rodriguez (Prisoner), Chic Daniel (FBI Squad Leader), Laurence Walsh (Walsh Clinic Nurse)

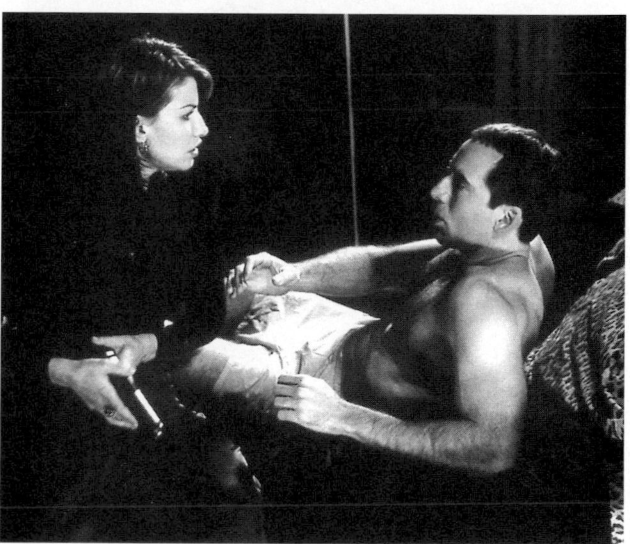

Gina Gershon, Nicolas Cage

Having captured Castor Troy, the crazed terrorist who killed his son, FBI agent Sean Archer agrees to a bizarre experiment wherein he will swap faces with Troy in order information from Troy's brother, a plan which goes terribly awry. This film received an Oscar nomination for sound effects editing.

Nicolas Cage, John Travolta

Will Smith, Tommy Lee Jones

Will Smith, Tony Shalhoub

Mikey

Rip Torn

Tommy Lee Jones, Will Smith, Linda Fiorentino

MEN IN BLACK

(COLUMBIA) Producers, Walter F. Parkes, Laurie MacDonald; Executive Producer, Steven Spielberg; Director, Barry Sonnenfeld; Screenplay/Story, Ed Solomon; Based on the Malibu Comic by Lowell Cunningham; Co-Producer, Graham Place; Photography, Don Peterman; Designer, Bo Welch; Editor, Jim Miller; Costumes, Mary E. Vogt; Music, Danny Elfman; Visual Effects Supervisor, Eric Brevig; Visual Effects, Industrial Light & Magic; Alien Make-up Effects, Rick Baker; Casting, David Rubin, Debra Zane; an Amblin Entertainment production in association with MacDonald/Parkes productions; Dolby DTS Stereo; Technicolor; Rated PG-13; 98 minutes; July release

Baby Redgick, Will Smith

CAST

K....................Tommy Lee Jones
J....................Will Smith
Dr. Laurel Weaver....................Linda Fiorentino
Edgar....................Vincent D'Onofrio
Zed....................Rip Torn
Jeebs....................Tony Shalhoub
Beatrice....................Siobhan Fallon
Gentle Rosenberg....................Mike Nussbaum
Van Driver....................Jon Gries
Jose....................Sergio Calderon
Arquillian....................Carel Struycken
INS Agent Janus....................Fredric Lane
D....................Richard Hamilton
1st Lt. Jake Jensen....................Kent Faulcon
Mikey....................John Alexander
Perp....................Keith Campbell
Orkin Man....................Ken Thorley
Mr. Redgick....................Patrick Breen
Mrs. Redgick....................Becky Ann Baker
Passport Officer....................Sean Whalen
News Vendor....................Harsh Nayyar
Cop in Morgue....................Michael Willis
Police Inspector....................Willie C. Carpenter
Tow Truck Driver....................Peter Linari
Morgue Attendant....................David Cross
MIB Agent Bee....................Charles C. Stevenson, Jr.
Cook....................Boris Leskin

and Steve Rankin, Andy Prosky (INS Agents), Michael Goldfinger (NYPD Sergeant), Alpheus Merchant (Security Guard), Norma Jean Groh (Mrs. Edelson), Bernard Gilkey (Baseball Player), Sean Plummer, Michael Kaliski (First Contact Aliens), Richard Arthur (2nd First Contact Alien), Debbie Lee Carrington (Alien Father), Verne Troyer (Alien Son), Mykal Wayne Williams (Scared Guy), Tim Blaney (Frank the Pug), Mark Setrakian (Rosenberg Alien), Brad Abrell, Thom Fountain, Carl J. Johnson, Drew Massey (Worm Guys)

Vincent D'Onofrio

J joins the goverment agency known as Men in Black whose mission it is to regulate all alien immigration from other planets. 1997 Academy Award-winner for Best Makeup. This film received additional Oscar nominations for art direction and original musical or comedy score.

Tommy Lee Jones, Will Smith

OUT TO SEA

(20TH CENTURY FOX) Producers, John Davis, David T. Friendly; Executive Producers, Dylan Sellers, Barry Berg; Director, Martha Coolidge; Screenplay, Robert Nelson Jacobs; Photography, Lajos Koltai; Designer, James Spencer; Editor, Anne V. Coates; Music, David Newman; Choreography, Kim Blank; Costumes, Jane Robinson; Casting, Jackie Burch; a Davis Entertainment Company production; Dolby Stereo; Deluxe color; Rated PG-13; 109 minutes; July release

CAST

Herb Sullivan .... Jack Lemmon
Charlie Gordon .... Walter Matthau
Liz LaBreche .... Dyan Cannon
Vivian .... Gloria DeHaven
Gil Godwyn .... Brent Spiner
Mavis .... Elaine Stritch
Mac .... Hal Linden
Jonathan .... Donald O'Connor
Mrs. Carruthers .... Rue McClanahan
Cullen Carswell .... Edward Mulhare
Shelly .... Alexandra Powers
Alan .... Sean O'Bryan
Maria .... Esther Scott
Sebastian .... Allan Rich
Bridget .... Estelle Harris
Willie .... Leon Singer
Madge .... Concetta Tomei
Tanaka .... Goh Misawa
Dance Instructor .... Kim Blank
Edie .... Louisa Abernathy
Purser .... Michael Laskin
Parrot .... Hector Mercado
Flight Attendant .... Carol Barbee
Sylvia .... Dale Raoul
Shapiro .... Lomax Study
Pearl .... Beverly Polcyn
Bettor in Front .... Shaun Troub

and Bert Rosario (Cab Driver), Paul Kievit (Ship Captain), Henk Ijdens (Ship Officer), Frank Patton (Dealer), Natalia Momtchilova (Shopgirl), Rod Phillips (Julian), P.D. Mani (Floor Person), Trevor Denman (Track Announcer), Bubba Dean Rambo, Allen Walls (Dance Hosts), Laura Canellias, Cindera Che, Leslie Cook, Andre Fortin, Dotti Karlstein, Albert Torres (Ballroom Dancers), Michelle Elkin, Sharon Ferguson, Diane Mizota, Andrea Paige Wilson (Showgirls), Bubba Carr, Ronnie Willis (Showguys), Ungela Brockman, John R. Corella, Joaquin Escamilla, Eddie Garcia, Sal Lorez, U. Lucero, Rosero, Darrell W. Wright (Mexican Dancers), Thomas DeLuca (Piano Player)

Charlie cons his brother-in-law Herb into joining him on a luxury cruise where the two will get free passage under the guise of dance instructors. This was the last film of actor Edward Mulhare who died on May 24, 1997.

Jack Lemmon, Brent Spiner, Walter Matthau

Walter Matthau, Dyan Cannon, Edward Mulhare

Gloria DeHaven, Jack Lemmon

Donald O'Connor, Rue McClanahan, Hal Linden

THIS WORLD, THEN THE FIREWORKS

Gina Gershon, Billy Zane

(ORION CLASSICS) Producers, Chris Hanley, Brad Wyman, Larry Gross; Executive Producer, Barr Potter; Co-Executive Producer, Billy Zane; Director, Michael Oblowitz; Screenplay, Larry Gross; Based on the story by Jim Thompson; Photography, Tom Priestley, Jr.; Designer, Maia Javan; Music, Pete Rugolo; Costumes, Dan Moore; Special Effects, Michael Schorr; Casting, Mary Vernieu; a Largo Entertainment presentation of a Muse, Balzac's Shirt, Wyman Production; Dolby Stereo; Color; Rated R; 100 minutes; July release

CAST

Marty Lakewood .... Billy Zane
Carol Lakewood .... Gina Gershon
Lois Archer .... Sheryl Lee
Mrs. Lakewood .... Rue McClanahan
Police Lt. Morgan .... Will Patton
Joe .... Richard Edson
Police Detective Harris .... Seymour Cassel
Marty's Father .... Philip Loch
Little Marty .... Christian Durango
Little Carol .... Sloan Cobb
Young Carol .... Megan Leigh Brown
Young Marty .... Christopher Jones

and Elizabeth Imboden (Neighbor's Wife), Roberta Hanley (Younger Mom Lakewood), Robert Pentz (Lou), Marianna Alacchi (Glenda), Orson Oblowitz (Eugene), Willy Cobbs (Blues Musician), Max Maxwell, Max O'Toole (Thugs in Bar), Mert Hatfield (Bus Driver), Tom Keeley (Cousin Lyle), Thad Mace (Tim), Jonathan Taylor Luthren (Ben), Stephanie Fisher (Claire), Mark Jeffrey Miller (Lloyd), Vincent Schilling (Patron), Lou Criscuolo (McCloud), Jeffrey Pillars (Galloway), Paul Allan Sincoff (Assistant), William Hootkins (Jake Krutz), Barry Bell (Barnett Gibons), David Lenthall (Doctor), Brian Gamble (Undertaker), Terry Nienhuis (Minister), Val DeVargas (Mexican Doctor), Dean Mumford (Capt. Miles Archer), Rick Warner (Real Estate Guy)

The incestuous Marty and Carol Lakewood, a con man and a hooker, team up to fleece a repressed police woman who has been seduced by Marty.

Billy Zane, Rue McClanahan

Billy Zane, Sheryl Lee

A SIMPLE WISH

(UNIVERSAL) Producers, Sid, Bill and Jon Sheinberg; Director, Michael Ritchie; Screenplay, Jeff Rothberg; Photography, Ralf Bode; Designer, Stephen Hendrickson; Editor, William Scharf; Co-Producers, Michael S. Glick, Jeff Rothberg; Costumes, Luke Reichle; Music, Bruce Broughton; Computer Generated Visual Effects, Blue Sky Studios Inc; Special Visual Effects, Matte World Digital, Pacific Data Images; Casting, Rick Pagano; DTS Stereo; Deluxe color; Rated PG; 89 minutes; July release

CAST

Murray .... Martin Short
Claudia .... Kathleen Turner
Anabel Greening .... Mara Wilson
Oliver Greening .... Robert Pastorelli
Boots .... Amanda Plummer
Charlie Greening .... Francis Capra
Hortense .... Ruby Dee
Rena .... Teri Garr
Tony Sable .... Alan Campbell
Lord Richard .... Jonathan Hadary
Jeri .... Deborah Odell
Duane .... Lanny Flaherty
Ms. Bramble .... Clare Coulter
Manny .... Neil Foster
Joe .... Jaime Tirelli
Officer O'York .... Jack McGee
Schoolgirls .... Lillian Ritchie, Miriam Ritchie
Tony's Agent .... David Crean
Grocer .... Kwok-Wing Leung

and H.D. Trayer, Sabine Thomson, Peter Linari, Maja Niles (German Tourists), Bunty Webb, Valerie Boyle, Barbara Stewart, Kathryn Kirkpatrick (Fairy Godmothers), Adam David (Sable's Chauffeur), Rick Fox (Pianist), Derek Carkner (Shaw's Assistant), Henry Gomez (Investor), Frank Cee (Vendor), John Douglas Williams (Paperboy)

Anabel Greening, desperate to help her father land a part in a Broadway musical, calls on her fairy godmother for help and ends up with a bumbler named Murray.

Kathleen Turner, Mara Wilson, Martin Short

Shirley Wesley King

4 LITTLE GIRLS

(HBO/40 ACRES AND A MULE) Producers, Spike Lee, Sam Pollard; Director, Spike Lee; Photography, Ellen Kuras; Music, Terence Blanchard; Editor, Sam Pollard; Associate Producer, Michele Forman; Color; Not rated; 102 minutes; July release.

A documentary on four Birmingham, Alabama school girls who, in September of 1963, were killed when a terrorist bomb exploded in the basement of a Baptist church. This film received an Oscar nomination for feature documentary.

WITNESSES

Chris McNair, Maxine McNair, Helen Pegues, Queen Nunn, Arthur Hanes Jr., Bill Baxley, Howell Raines, Alpha Robertson, Wamo Reed Robertson, Harold McNair, Carole C. Smitherman Esq., Diane Braddock, Carolyn Lee Brown, Reverend Fred Shuttlesworth, Wyatt Tee Walker, Florence Terrell, Gwendolyn White, Doris Lockhart, Gerald Colbert, Dr. Freeman Hrabowski III, Nadean S. Williams, Shirley Wesley King, Carolyn M. McKinstry, David J. Vann, Reverened Andrew Young, Taylor Branch, Janie Gaines, Rhonda Nunn Thomas, Barbara Nunn, Reverend James Bevel, Tommy Wrenn, George Wallace, Nicholas Katzenbach, Lillie Brown, Billie Harris, Rickey Powell, Ossie Davis, Reverend John Cross, Barbara Cross, Morris Marshall, Junie Collins, Diane Nash, Faye Davis, Coretta Scott King, Walter Cronkite, Bill Cosby, Reverend Jesse L. Jackson Sr., Reverend Reggie White

GEORGE OF THE JUNGLE

(WALT DISNEY PICTURES) Producers, David Hoberman, Jordan Kerner, Jon Avnet; Executive Producer, C. Tad Devlin; Director, Sam Weisman; Screenplay, Dana Olsen, Audrey Wells; Story, Dana Olsen; Based upon Characters Developed by Jay Ward; Photography, Tom Ackerman; Designer, Stephen Marsh; Editors, Stuart Pappé Roger Bondelli; Visual Effects, Dream Quest Images; Special Creature Effects, Jim Henson's Creature Shop; Co-Producer, Lou Arkoff; Music, Marc Shaiman; Title song by Stan Worth and Sheldon Allman/Performed by the Presidents of the United States of America; Costumes, Lisa Jensen; Casting, Amanda Mackey Johnson, Cathy Sandrich; a Mandeville Films, Avnet/Kerner production; Distributed by Buena Vista Pictures; Dolby Digital Stereo; Color; Rated PG; 89 minutes; July release

CAST

George....Brendan Fraser
Ursula Stanhope....Leslie Mann
Lyle Van de Groot....Thomas Haden Church
Kwame....Richard Roundtree
Max....Greg Cruttwell
Thor....Abraham Benrubi
Beatrice Stanhope....Holland Taylor
Betsy....Kelly Miller
Arthur Stanhope....John Bennett Perry
Voice of an Ape Named "Ape"....John Cleese
N'Dugu....Michael Chinyamurindi
Kip....Abdoulaye N'Gom
Bateke....Lydell Cheshier
The Narrator....Keith Scott
Guests at Party....Spencer Garrett, Jon Pennell
Ursula's Friends....Lauren Bowles, Afton Smith, Samantha Harris
Lion....Joseph, Kaleb, Bongo
Shep....Tai
Tookie....Tookie, Scooper, Hopper
Little Monkey....Binx, Zachery, Emely
Ape Body Actor....Nameer El-Kadi
Jailer....Rodney Johnson

and Hans Schoeber, Alexander Denk, Sven-Ole-Thorsen (Mercenaries), Peter F. Giddings, C.C.M. (TV Weatherman), Terilyn Joe (TV Anchor), Michel Camus (Cameraman), Valerie Perri (TV Reporter), Mayor Willie L. Brown, Jr. (Himself), Carrie Zanoline (Perfume Lady), Garrett Griffin (Fireboat Captain), Harve Cook, Aristide Sumatra (Bongo Drummers at Dance Studio), Noah John Cardoza, Benjamin John Cardoza (George, Jr.), Tom Fisher, Philip Tan, Jody St. Michael, Leif Tilden (Gorilla Body Actors)

George, a young man raised in the jungle by animals, falls in love with career woman Ursula on an expedition with her fiancee to capture the "great white ape." Based on the animated series on ABC from 1967 to 1970.

Thomas Haden Church, Greg Cruttwell, Abraham Benrubi

Brendan Fraser, Leslie Mann

Brendan Fraser

Brendan Fraser, Ape

Tim Robbins, Martin Lawrence

NOTHING TO LOSE

(TOUCHSTONE) Producers, Martin Bregman, Dan Jinks, Michael Bregman; Executive Producer, Louis A. Stroller; Director/Screenplay, Steve Oedekerk; Photography, Donald E. Thorin; Designer, Maria Caso; Editor, Malcolm Campbell; Music, Robert Folk; Casting, Gretchen Rennell Court; a Bergman production; Distributed by Buena Vista Pictures; Dolby Digital Stereo; Panavision; Technicolor; Rated R; 97 minutes; July release

Kelly Preston, Tim Robbins

CAST

T. Paul .... Martin Lawrence
Nick Beam .... Tim Robbins
Davis "Rig" Lanlow .... John C. McGinley
Charlie Dunt .... Giancarlo Esposito
Ann .... Kelly Preston
Phillip Barrow .... Michael McKean
Danielle .... Rebecca Gayheart
Delores .... Susan Barnes
Bertha .... Irma P. Hall
Lisa .... Samaria Graham
Joey .... Marcus Paulk
Tonya .... Penny Bae Bridges
Security Guard Baxter .... Steve Oedekerk
Grace .... Mary Jo Keenen
Emma .... Lisa Mende
Alan .... Clark Reiner
Zach .... Ned Gill
Henry .... Patrick Cranshaw
Sheriff .... Randy Oglesby
Sheriff Officer #1 .... Steven M. Porter
Hillbilly Attendant .... Robert Louis Kempf
English Driver .... Dave Lea
LAPD Sergeant .... Dan Martin
LAPD Officer .... Lance August
Security Guard .... Joe Minjares
Overweight Security Guard .... Carl Sundstrom
Manny .... Hank Garrett

and Selma Stern (Old Woman in Elevator), Caroline Keenan (Ann's Sister), Jim Meskimen (Business Suit Man), J.J. Boone (Ginger), Kim Kim (Mary Ann), Jodi Jinks (Girl at Checkout), Willy Parsons (Truck Driver), Victoria Redstall (Woman in Bar)

Giancarlo Esposito, Martin Lawrence, John C. McGinley

Nick Beam, at the end of his rope after finding his wife carrying on with his boss, meets up with a would-be carjacker, T. Paul, and promptly takes his attacker hostage.

STAR MAPS

(FOX SEARCHLIGHT) Producer, Matthew Greenfield; Executive Producers, Esther Shapiro, Chris Iovenko, Scott King, Mitchell Kelly, Beth Colt; Co-Producers, Eden J. Shapiro, Ron Nyswaner, Kathleen Brown Corbin; Director/Screenplay, Miguel Arteta; Story, Miguel Arteta, Matthew Greenfield; Photography, Chuy Chavez; Editors, Jeff Betancourt, Tom McArdle, Tony Selzer; Designer, Carol Strober; Casting, Belinda Gardea; a Flan de Coco Films production in association with King Pictures; Dolby Stereo; Color; Rated R; 95 minutes; July release

CAST

Carlos .... Douglas Spain
Pepe .... Efrain Figueroa
Jennifer .... Kandeyce Jorden
Teresa .... Martha Velez
Maria .... Lysa Flores
Letti .... Annette Murphy
Martin .... Robin Thomas
Juancito .... Vincent Chandler
Fred .... Al Vicente
Cantinflas' Ghost .... Herbert Siguenza
Frank Rivers .... Jeff Sanna
Bartender .... Jeff Michalski
Carmel County Stage Manager .... Beth Colt
Carmel County Writers .... Zak Penn, Michael White
Star Map Boys .... Luis Fernando Guizar, Alejandro Parra, Caesar Garcia, Elvis Saint Hilaire, Michael Peña
Carmel County Casting Director .... Alisa Steen
Nanny .... Anna Padgett
Hotel Guard .... Danny De La Paz
Angry Customer .... Mark Beltzman
Bel Air Woman .... Hana Delaney
Bel Air Man .... Bill Gordon
Young Carlos .... Andrew Garcia
Jennifer's Son .... T.J. Forster

and Kate Movius (Carmel County Actress), Joshua Fardon (Carmel County Actor), Adam Parker (Man Mistaken for Customer), Joe Mayesh (Guard at Gate), Michael Caldwell, Rachel Winfree (Tourists), Doug Kieffer (Waiter)

Young Carlos joins his family in Los Angeles where he is immediately forced by his father to work on the streets, using the cover of selling maps to the stars' homes while actually working as a prostitute.

Douglas Spain

GOOD BURGER

(PARAMOUNT) Producers, Mike Tollin, Brian Robbins; Executive Producer, Julia Pistor; Director, Brian Robbins; Screenplay, Dan Schneider, Kevin Kopelow, Heath Seifert, based on their characters created for Nickelodeon's tv series "All That;" Photography, Mac Ahlberg; Designer, Steven Jordan; Editor, Anita Brandt-Burgoyne; Co-Producers, Diane Batson-Smith, Dan Schneider; Music, Stewart Copeland; Casting, Jaki Brown-Karman, Robyn M. Mitchell; a Tollin/Robbins production; Presented in association with Nickelodeon Movies; Dolby Stereo; Deluxe color; Rated PG; 97 minutes; July release

CAST

Ed .... Kel Mitchell
Dexter Reed .... Kenan Thompson
Mr. Wheat .... Sinbad
Otis .... Abe Vigoda
Monique .... Shar Jackson
Mr. Bailey .... Dan Schneider
Kurt Bozwell .... Jan Schwieterman
Spatch .... Ron Lester
Fizz .... Josh Server
Deedee .... Ginny Schreiber
Heather .... Linda Cardellini
Himself .... Shaquille O'Neal
Dancing Crazy .... George Clinton
Huge Scary Man .... Richard Haje
Angry Customer .... Robert Wuhl
Corey .... Corrie Harris
Connie Muldoon .... Lori Beth Denberg
Jake .... Marques Houston
News Reporter .... Matthew Gallant
Customer .... Teresa Ganzel
Upset Customer .... Brian Peck
Troy .... Hamilton Von Watts
Griffen .... J. August Richards

and Kevin Kopelow (Sad Clown), Floyd Levine (Ice Cream Man), Brett Jones (Driving Attendant), Brad Wilson (Scared Customer), Melissa Spell (Frightened Customer), Andrew Aybar (Mondo Worker), Eve Sigall, Jo Farkas (Elderly Ladies), Paul Parducci, Kim Delgado (Police Officers), Wendy Worthington (Demented Hills Nurse), Chet Nichols, Carl A. McGee (Guards), David Shackelford, Rob Elk (Attendants), Carmit Bachar, Stella Choe, John Corella, Kelly Devine, Cindy Leos, Courtney Miller, Nezester Ponder, Chonique Sneed, Miranda Stamatelatos (Demented Hills Dancers)

Two high schoolers get jobs at a failing burger joint, Good Burger, causing a competitor at Mondo Burger to hound them for the recipe for their secret sauce.

Kenan Thompson, Shaquille O'Neal, Kel Mitchell

AIR FORCE ONE

(COLUMBIA) Producers, Armyan Bernstein, Jon Shestack, Wolfgang Petersen, Gail Katz; Executive Producers, Thomas A. Bliss, Marc Abraham, David Lester; Director, Wolfgang Petersen; Screenplay, Andrew W. Marlowe; Photography, Michael Ballhaus; Designer, William Sandell; Editor, Richard Francis-Bruce; Visual Effects Supervisor, Richard Edlund; Costumes, Erica Edell Phillips; Music, Jerry Goldsmith; Casting, Janet Hirshenson, Jane Jenkins; a Beacon Pictures presentation of a Radiant Production; Dolby SDDS Stereo; Super 35 Widescreen; Technicolor; Rated R; 118 minutes; July release

Gary Oldman, Harrison Ford

CAST

President James Marshall ....Harrison Ford
Ivan Korshunov ....Gary Oldman
Vice President Kathryn Bennett ....Glenn Close
Grace Marshall ....Wendy Crewson
Alice Marshall ....Liesel Matthews
Chief of Staff Lloyd Shepherd ....Paul Guilfoyle
Agent Gibbs ....Xander Berkeley
Major Caldwell ....William H. Macy
Defense Secretary Walter Dean ....Dean Stockwell
NSA Advisor Jack Doherty ....Tom Everett
General Alexander Radek ....Jurgen Prochnow
Press Secretary Melanie Mitchell ....Donna Bullock
AFO Pilot Colonel Axelrod ....Michael Ray Miller
AFO Co-Pilot Lt. Col. Ingrahams ....Carl Weintraub
AFO Navigator ....Elester Latham
Andrei Kolchak ....Elaya Baskin
Sergei Lenski ....Levani
Igor Nevsky ....David Vadim
Boris Bazylev ....Andrew Divoff
Vladimir Krasin ....Ilia Volokh
Major Perkins ....Chris Howell
White House Aide Thomas Lee ....Spencer Garrett
General Northwood ....Bill Smitrovich
U.S. Attorney General Ward ....Philip Baker Hall
"Football" Colonel ....Albert Owens
White House Comm. Officer ....Willard Pugh
Assistant Press Secretary ....Michael Monks
Russian President Petrov ....Alan Woolf
Future Postmaster General ....Messiri Freeman
Steward Mike ....Thomas Crawford
Steward Joey ....Fenton Lawless
Notre Dame Aide ....Dan Shor
Agent Johnson ....David Gianopolous
Agent Walters ....Glenn Morshower
AFO Back-up Pilot ....Richard Doyle
F-15 Leader Colonel Carlton ....Don R. McManus
F-15 "Halo 2" Fighter Pilot ....Duk Miglin

and Pavel D. Lychnikoff, Oleg Taktarov (Prison Guards), Mario Roberts, Keith Woulard, J. Mark Donaldson, Bruce Holman (Special Service Agents), Brian Libby (Chief Mechanic), Diana Bellamy (Switchboard Operator), Thom Barry (Ramstein S.O.F. Watch Officer), Harry Hutchinson (Ramstein Airbase Controller), E.E. Bell, Mark Thomson, Marciarose Shestack, Ren Hanami (Reporters), Suzanne Michaels (CNN Anchor), Boris Krutonog (MiG Leader), Alex Veadov (MiG Pilot), Allan Kolman (Kazak Soldier), Dan Barringer (USAF Jump Master), Jim Harley (Willis), Aleks Shaklin (Government Official), Igor N. Lobotsky (Russian Official), Koko Kiledjian (Russian Speaker), Gordon Michaels, Robert Peters, Kristian Sorensen (USAF Radio Specialists), Stuart Nixon (USAF Security), Marty Rosen (CIA Director), Lee Faranda (Russian Bad Guy), Mike Hambrick (CNN Reporter), Catherine T. Yang (Foreign TV Reporter), David MacIsaac (MC-130 Pilot), J. Scott Shonka, Paul Sklar (Pararescue Jumpers), David Permenter (Winch Recovery Master), David O'Donnell (Young Airman)

Harrison Ford

A terrorist group, demanding the release of a tyrannical Russian general, take the crew and passengers of Air Force One hostage, including the President of the United States. This film received Oscar nominations for film editing and sound.

Glenn Close

Levani, Harrison Ford

Elaya Baskin

Jurgen Prochnow

Alan Woolf

Dean Stockwell

Wendy Crewson, Harrison Ford, Liesel Matthews

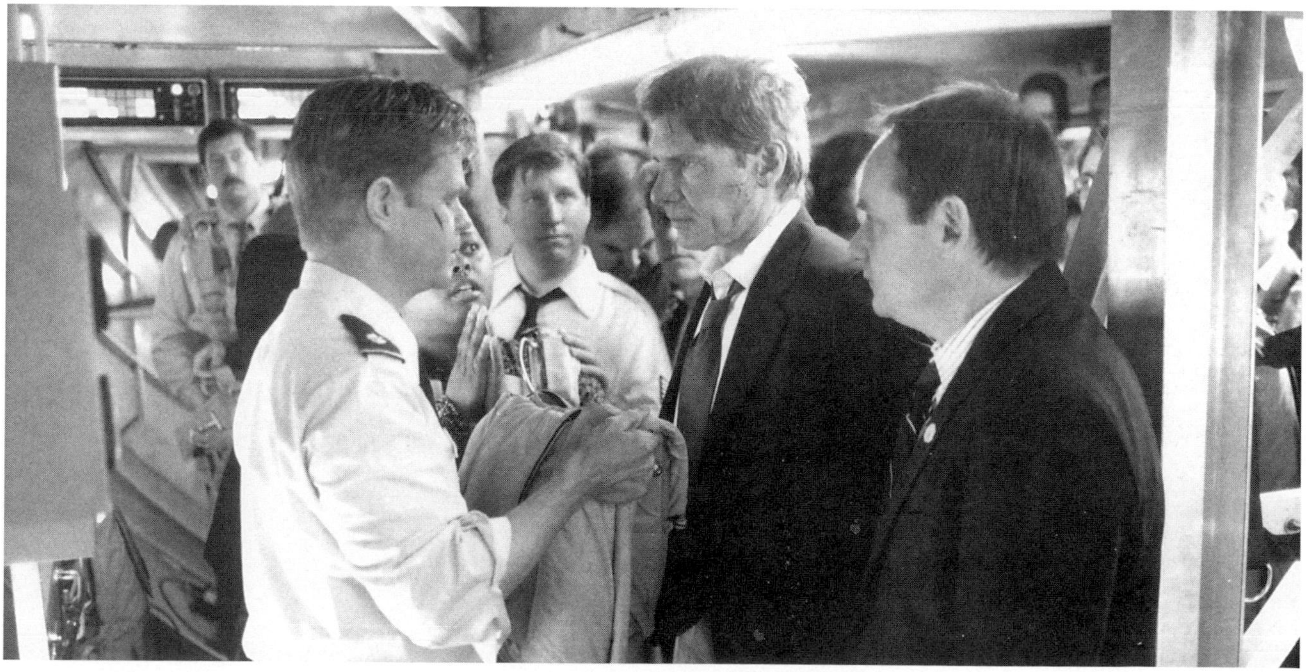

William H. Macy, Harrison Ford, Paul Guilfoyle

BOX OF MOONLIGHT

(TRIMARK) Producers, Marcus Viscidi, Thomas A. Bliss; Executive Producers, Michael Mendelsohn, Tom Rosenberg, Sigurjon Sighvatsson, Steven Sherman; Director/Screenplay, Tom DiCillo; Co-Producers, Meredith Zamsky, Taylor MacCrae; Photography, Paul Ryan; Designer, Therese DePrez; Editor, Camilla Toniolo; Costumes, Ellen Lutter; Music, Jim Farmer; Casting, Marcia Shulman; a Lakeshore Entertainment presentation of a Lemon Sky production; Dolby Stereo; Color; Rated R; 107 minutes; July release

CAST

Al Fountain	John Turturro
The Kid	Sam Rockwell
Floatie Dupre	Catherine Keener
Purlene Dupre	Lisa Blount
Deb Fountain	Annie Corley
Bobby Fountain	Alexander Goodwin
Wick	Dermot Mulroney
Doob	Mike Stanley
Doris	Rica Martens
Soapy	Ray Aranha
Dex	Robert Wightman
Taco	James Richardson
Elwood	Stephen Dupree
Lyle	Eugene Wolf
Luvven Coddle	Reathel Bean
Wynelle Coddle	Betty Wills Stephens
Curious Waitress	Linda Libby
Motel Clerk	Ernest R. Ogg
Earl Sykes	Gary Lowery
Willard Snarp	Bodi Soham
Barnett	Horace E. Smith
Stinky	Stuart Greer
Sheriff	John E. Davis
Newscasters	Gene Patterson, Kristin Hoke
Uncle Samson	Buddy Landel
Castroater	Chaz Warrington
Saddam Insane	Glenn Ruth

Questioning his life, electrical engineer Al Fountaine takes off on a journey of self-discovery where he befriends an offbeat dreamer named "The Kid" who lives by his own means in a trailer in the woods.

John Turturro, Sam Rockwell

Alexander Goodwin, John Turturro

Mike Stanley, Dermot Mulroney, Sam Rockwell,

Lisa Blount, Catherine Keener

AIR BUD

(WALT DISNEY PICTURES) Producers, William Vince, Robert Vince; Executive Producers, Michael Strange, Anne Vince, Bob Weinstein, Harvey Weinstein; Director, Charles Martin Smith; Screenplay, Paul Tamasy, Aaron Mendelsohn; Based on the character "Air Bud" created by Kevin DiCicco; Photography, Mike Southon; Designer, Elizabeth Wilcox; Music, Brahm Wenger; Editor, Alison Grace; Associate Producer, James A. Jusko; Line Producer, Michael Potkins; Buddy's Trainer, Kevin DiCicco; Casting, Abra Edelman, Elisa Goodman; a Robert Vince production presented in association with Keystone Pictures; Distributed by Buena Vista Pictures; Dolby Digital Stereo; Technicolor; Rated PG; 97 minutes; August release

Kevin Zegers, Buddy

CAST

Norm Snively..........Michael Jeter
Josh Framm..........Kevin Zegers
Jackie Framm..........Wendy Makkena
Arthur Chaney..........Bill Cobbs
Judge Cranfield..........Eric Christmas
Referee 1..........Jay Brazeau
Principal Pepper..........Nicola Cavendish
Larry Willingham..........Brendan Fletcher
Buck Willingham..........Norman Browning
Coach Barker..........Stephen E. Miller
Tom..........Shayn Solberg
Greg..........Chris Turner
Melissa..........Christine Kennedy
Bailiff..........Frank C. Turner
Reporter..........Marian Dodd
Party Mom..........Ursula Martin
Referee 2..........Kevin DiCicco
Andrea Framm..........Jessebel Mather, Kati Mather
Buddy/Air Bud..........Buddy

A shy 12-year-old boy befriends a runaway dog who turns out to have an uncanny ability to play basketball. Sequel Air Bud: Golden Receiver was released in 1998 by Miramax with Kevin Zegers repeating his role.

Michael Jeter

Wendy Makkena

Kevin Zegers, Buddy

Kevin Zegers, Buddy

Jay Mohr, Jennifer Aniston

PICTURE PERFECT

(20TH CENTURY FOX) Producer, Erwin Stoff; Executive Producers, Williem Teitler, Molly Madden; Director, Glenn Gordon Caron; Screenplay, Arleen Sorkin, Paul Slansky, Glenn Gordon Caron; Story, Arleen Sorkin, Paul Slansky, May Quigley; Photography, Paul Sarossy; Designer, Larry Fulton; Editor, Robert Reitano; Costumes, Jane Robinson; Music, Carter Burwell; Casting, Mary Colquhoun; a 3 Arts production; Dolby Digital Stereo; Color; Rated PG-13; 100 minutes; August release

CAST

Kate Mosley	Jennifer Aniston
Nick	Jay Mohr
Sam Mayfair	Kevin Bacon
Rita Mosley	Olympia Dukakis
Darcy O'Neal	Illeana Douglas
Mr. Mercer	Kevin Dunn
Sela	Anne Twomey
Mrs. Mercer	Faith Prince
Jim Davenport	John Rothman
Mrs. Davenport	Margaret Gibson
Brad	Paul Cassell
Ad Executives	Ivar Brogger, Peter McRobbie, Bray Poor, Daryl Edwards, Jenna Stern
Ad Agency Receptionist	Bellina Logan
Ad Agency Researcher	Sean Patrick Thomas
Pregnant Friend	Andrea Bendewald
Rosie	Marcia DeBonis
Darcy's Husband	Matthew Sussman
Anchor Person	Jim Ryan
Maitre D'	Doug Easley
Snack Lady	Ali Marsh
Watch Seller	Richard Spore
Susan	Amelia Campbell
The Maharishi	Vimesh Thakar
Sajit	Faran Tahir
Minister	David Cromwell
Bride	Jessica Cushman
Groom	Barry Del Sherman
Little Girl	Kaley Cuoco

When her friend invents a fiancee for Kate in order to impress her boss, Kate asks a wedding photographer named Nick to pose as her boyfriend to carry on the deception.

Kevin Bacon, Jennifer Aniston

Illeana Douglas, Jennifer Aniston

Olympia Dukakis, Jennifer Aniston

IN THE COMPANY OF MEN

(SONY CLASSICS) Producers, Mark Archer, Stephen Pevner; Director/Screenplay, Neil LaBute; Photography, Tony Hettinger; Editor, Joel Plotch; Music, Ken Williams, Karel Roessingh; Executive Producers, Toby Gaff, Mark Hart, Matt Malloy; Line Producer, Lisa Bartels; Designer, Julia Henkel; a Stephen Pevner/Atlantis Entertainment production in association with Fair and Square productions; Color; Rated R; 93 minutes; August release

CAST

Chad .... Aaron Eckhart
Christine .... Stacy Edwards
Howard .... Matt Malloy
Co-Workers .... Michael Martin, Chris Hayes
John .... Mark Rector
Intern .... Jason Dixie
Suzanne .... Emily Cline

Two businessmen, frustrated at their recent failed relationships with women, decide to get revenge by romancing and then dumping a deaf temp in their office.

Aaron Eckhart, Matt Malloy

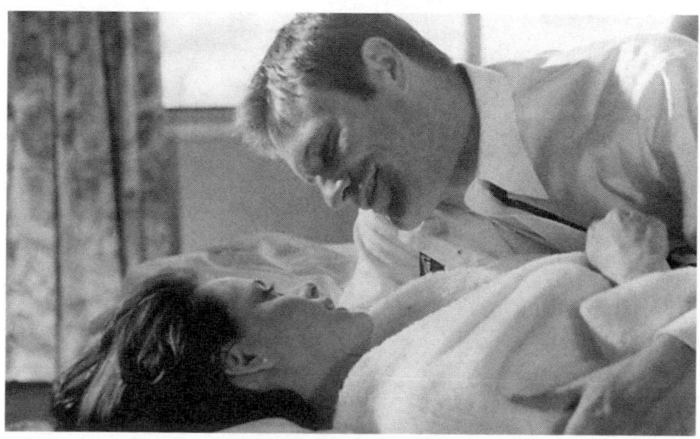

Stacy Edwards, Aaron Eckhart

Matt Malloy, Aaron Eckhart

Jason Dixie, Aaron Eckhart

Aaron Eckhart, Stacy Edwards

John Leguizamo, Martin Sheen

Michael Jai White

SPAWN

(NEW LINE CINEMA) Producer, Clint Goldman; Executive Producers, Todd McFarlane, Alan C. Blomquist; Director, Mark A.Z. Dippé Screenplay, Alan McElroy; Screen Story, Alan McElroy, Mark A.Z. Dippé Based on the comic book by Todd McFarlane; Co-Executive Producers, Brian Witten, Adrianna AJ Cohen; Photography, Guillermo Navarro; Designer, Philip Harrison; Costumes, Dan Lester; Editor, Michael N. Knue; Visual Effects Supervisor, Steve "Spaz" Williams; ILM Animation Supervisor, Dennis Turner; Special Make-Up and Animatronic Creature Effects, Robert Kurtzman, Gregory Nicotero, Howard Berger; a Dippé Goldman Williams production, presented in association with Todd McFarlane Entertainment; SDDS Stereo; Fujicolor; Rated PG-13; 97 minutes; August release

CAST

Al Simmons/Spawn ....Michael Jai White
Clown...John Leguizamo
Jason Wynn...Martin Sheen
Wanda..Theresa Randle
Cogliostro..Nicol Williamson
Terry Fitzgerald..D.B. Sweeney
Jessica Priest...Melinda Clarke
Zack...Miko Hughes
Cyan...Sydni Beaudoin
Zack's Dad ....Michael Papajohn
Voice of The Devil Malebolgia ....Frank Welker
XNN Reporter...Robia LaMorte
News Anchor...Caroline Gibson
African Liaisons ....John Cothran, Jr., Tony Haney
Punks.....................................Marc Robinson, Chris Coppola, Jay Caputo
Security Guard ....Darryl Warren
Foreign Dignitaries.....................................Mike Akrawi, Romeo Akrawi
Doctor ....Jack Coleman
Angela...Laura Stepp
Anesthesiologist...Garrison Singer
Alley Bum...Todd McFarlane

Five years after his murder Al Simmons makes a pact with the devil to return from the dead as the leader of Hell's Army in order that he might see his wife. Once on Earth he is torn between two different mysterious figures, one encouraging him to rebel against the devil and fight evil, the other prodding him to lead the Armageddon.

Nicol Williamson

Michael Jai White

D.B. Sweeney

EVENT HORIZON

(PARAMOUNT) Producers, Lawrence Gordon, Lloyd Levin, Jeremy Bolt; Executive Producer, Nick Gillott; Director, Paul Anderson; Screenplay, Philip Eisner; Photography, Adrian Biddle; Designer, Joseph Bennett; Editor, Martin Hunter; Visual Effects Supervisor, Richard Yuricich; Costumes, John Mollo; Music, Michael Kamen; Casting, Deborah Aquila, Jane Shannon-Smith (US), John and Ros Hubbard (UK); a Lawrence Gordon presentation of a Golar production, in association with Impact Pictures; Dolby Digital Stereo; Panavision; Rank color; Rated R; 95 minutes; August release

CAST

Captain Miller .... Laurence Fishburne
Dr. William Weir .... Sam Neill
Peters .... Kathleen Quinlan
Starck .... Joely Richardson
Cooper .... Richard T. Jones
Justin .... Jack Noseworthy
D.J. .... Jason Isaacs
Smith .... Sean Pertwee
Kilpack .... Peter Marinker
Claire .... Holley Chant
Denny .... Barclay Wright
Burning Man .... Noah Huntley
Rescue Technician .... Robert Jezek

When Event Horizon, a prototype spaceship that had mysteriously disappeared, abruptly reappears seven years later, a USAC rescue team is sent to find out who is sending a signal from the ship.

Kathleen Quinlan, Laurence Fishburne

Jack Noseworthy

Laurence Fishburne, Sam Neill, Kathleen Quinlan, Jason Isaacs

Robert De Niro, Sylvester Stallone, Harvey Keitel

Peter Berg, Arthur J. Nascarella

Arthur J. Nascarella, Michael Rapaport

Robert De Niro, Sylvester Stallone

Janeane Garofalo, Sylvester Stallone

COP LAND

(MIRAMAX) Producers, Cary Woods, Cathy Konrad, Ezra Swerdlow; Executive Producers, Bob Weinstein, Harvey Weinstein, Meryl Poster; Co-Producer, Kerry Orent; Director/Screenplay, James Mangold; Associate Producers, Christopher Goode, Kevin King, Richard Miller; Photography, Eric Edwards; Editor, Craig McKay; Designer, Lester Cohen; Costumes, Ellen Lutter; Music, Howard Shore; Casting, Todd Thaler; a Wood Entertainment production; Dolby Stereo; Color; Rated R: 105 minutes; August release

CAST

Freddy Heflin .... Sylvester Stallone
Ray Donlan .... Harvey Keitel
Gary Figgis .... Ray Liotta
Moe Tilden .... Robert De Niro
Joey Randone .... Peter Berg
Deputy Cindy Betts .... Janeane Garofalo
Jack Rucker .... Robert Patrick
Murray Babitch .... Michael Rapaport
Liz Randone .... Annabella Sciorra
Deputy Bill Geisler .... Noah Emmerich
Rose Donlan .... Cathy Moriarty
Leo Crasky .... John Spencer
PDA President Lassaro .... Frank Vincent
Detective Carson .... Malik Yoba
Frank Lagonda .... Arthur J. Nascarella
Berta .... Edie Falco
Russell .... Victor J. Williams
Hector (Medic) .... Paul Calderon
Lassaro's Aide .... John Doman
Delores .... Deborah Harry
Medic #2 .... Vincent Larseca
Black Man .... Oliver Solomon
Black Woman .... Terri Towns
Thin Cop .... David Butler
Young Cop .... Brad Beyer
TV Cyril Johns .... Charles Dumas
News Anchor .... John Johnson
Mayor .... Frank Pellegrino
Officer B .... Robert John Burke
Officer V .... John Ventimiglia
Tony (Wincing Cop) .... Terry Serpico
Shondel .... Method Man
Other Cop .... Sean Cullen
Game Operator .... Paul Herman
Monica .... Mel Gorham
Spanish Woman .... Graciela Lecube
Gordon .... Chris Conte
Young Freddy .... Anthony Citro
Young Liz .... Alexandra Adi

and Mark Cassella (Fireman), Timothy Stickney (Window Yeller), Father William Kalaidjian (Police Chaplain), Sean Runnette, Michael Gaston (IA Detectives), BEn Ellerni (Little Kid with Gordon), David Diaz (Funeral Reporter), Tracy O, Emory (Video Canera OP (News Segment)) Robert Castle (Chaplain at Joey's funeral), Bruce Altman (Counsel Burt Kandel), Carly Fordham (Liz'z Daughter), Tony Giorgio (Ceremonial Officer), Kevin O'Sullivan (Head Pall Bearer/Flag Holder), Louis D'Alto (Exiting Cop), Sylvia Khan (Deli Lady), Ronn Munro (Chief of Police), John Henry (Officer in Alleyway), Richard Lisi (Officer in Alleyway "Charlie"), Hans Moody (Sergeant in Alleyway), Garry Pastore (Core Cop "Johnny B"), Tony Sirico (Toy Torillo), Peter Wise, P.J. Brown, Manuel Corrado, Jeffrey Kaufman, Europe Harmon, Rene Ojeda (Plaza Cops)

Across the river from New York in the quiet New Jersey town of Garrison, sheriff Freddy Heflin discovers that a young NYPD officer, involved in a cover-up scandal and thought to be dead, is actually being hidden by his uncle, Ray Donlan, one of the many cops residing in Freddy's jurisdiction.

Sylvester Stallone, Ray Liotta

Annabella Sciorra, Sylvester Stallone

Harvey Keitel, Robert Patrick, Arthur J. Nascarella

Angel David, Demi Moore, Gregg Bello

Anne Bancroft, Demi Moore

Viggo Mortensen, Demi Moore

G.I. JANE

(HOLLYWOOD PICTURES) Producers, Ridley Scott, Roger Birnbaum, Demi Moore, Suzanne Todd; Executive Producers, Danielle Alexandra, Julie Bergman Sender; Co-Producer, Nigel Wooll; Director, Ridley Scott; Screenplay, David Twohy, Danielle Alexandra; Story, Danielle Alexandra; Photography, Hugh Johnson; Designer, Arthur Max; Editor, Pietro Scalia; Costumes, Marilyn Vance; Music, Trevor Jones; Casting, Louis Di Giaimo, Brett Goldstein; a Roger Birnbaum/Scott Free/Moving Pictures production, presented in association with Scott Free and Largo Entertainment; Dolby Digital Stereo; Panavision; Technicolor; Rated R; 125 minutes; August release

CAST

Lt. Jordan O'Neil....................Demi Moore
Command Master Chief John Urgayle....................Viggo Mortensen
Lillian DeHaven....................Anne Bancroft
Royce....................Jason Beghe
Theodore Hayes....................Daniel Von Bargen
Chief of Staff....................John Michael Higgins
Instructor Pyro....................Kevin Gage
Instructor Johns....................David Warshofsky
Cortez....................David Vadim
McCool....................Morris Chestnut
Flea....................Josh Hopkins
Slovnik....................Jim Caviezel
Wickwire....................Boyd Kestner
Newberry....................Angel David
Stamm....................Stephen Ramsey
Miller....................Gregg Bello
C.O. Salem....................Scott Wilson
Blondell....................Lucinda Jenney
Flag Officers....................Ted Sutton, Gary Wheeler
Yeoman Davis....................Donn Swaby
Goldstein....................Jack Gwaltney
Duty Officer....................Neal Jones
and Rhonda Overby (Civilian Secretary), Stephen Mendillo (Admiral O'Connor), Dan DePaola (Cook Compliments), Susan Aston (Civilian Girl), John Seitz, Kent Lindsey (JAGS), Bob Moore (WNM Reporter), Harry Humphries (Artillery Instructor), Michael Currie (Commission Speaker), Steve Gonzales (Press Hound), Arthur Max (Barber), Billy Dowd (Photographer), Duffy Gaver, Scott Helvenston (Instructors), Phil Neilson (Hostile Rat), Dimitri Diatchenko, David Bruce, David Overton, Hashem Shaalan, Chris Soule (Trainees), Joseph Merzak Makkar (Libyan Sentry)

Lt. Jordan O'Neil is recruited as a test case to be the first woman to train for the Navy SEALs.

Demi Moore, Jason Beghe

Chris Tucker, Paul Sorvino, Charlie Sheen

MONEY TALKS

(NEW LINE CINEMA) Producers, Walter Coblenz, Tracy Kramer; Executive Producer, Chris Tucker; Co-Producer, Art Schaefer; Director, Brett Ratner; Screenplay, Joel Cohen, Alec Sokolow; Co-Executive Producers, Jay Stern, Amy Henkels; Photography, Russell Carpenter, Robert Primes; Designer, Robb Wilson King; Editor, Mark Helfrich; Costumes, Sharen Davis; Music, Lalo Schifrin; Casting, Valerie McCaffrey; Dolby SDDS Stereo; Super 35 Widescreen; Deluxe color; Rated R; 95 minutes; August release

Chris Tucker

CAST

Franklin Hatchett....Chris Tucker
James Russell....Charlie Sheen
Guy Cipriani....Paul Sorvino
Grace Cipriani....Heather Locklear
Pickett....Paul Gleason
Paula....Elise Neal
Barklay....David Warner
Connie Cipriani....Veronica Cartwright
Roland....Larry Hankin
Mercedes Owner....Robertson Dean
News Cameraman....Nathan Anderson
Carmine....Damian Chapa
Detective at Carwash....Richard Noyce
Cellmate....Faizon Love
Raymond Villard....Gerard Ismael
Prison Bus Guard....Ralph Odum
Debray....Frank Bruynbroek
News Anchor....Doug Llewelyn
Diner Cops....Jeff Brockton, Gary Price
Officer Williams....Dan Roebuck
Cabby at Pier....Vahe Berberian
Red Camel Doorman....Jon Chardiet
Store Owner....Tom Huff
Aaron's Bodyguard....Rosey Brown
Aaron....Michael Wright
Detective at Precinct....Kevin Lowe

and Marty Levy, Mark Benninghofen, David McLain (Ticket Customers), Tawny Little (News Reporter), Viveca Paulin (Auctioneer), Mojoe Nicosia (Carmine's Driver), Dexter Tucker, Norris Tucker (Aaron's Boys), Matthew G. Brandstein (Cameraman #2), Rance Howard (Reverend)

Chris Tucker, Heather Locklear, Charlie Sheen

A headline-grabbing newsman draws attention to a con artist who has been wrongly accused of killing police officers during a prison break.

SUNDAY

(CFP) Producers, Jonathan Nossiter, Alix Madigan, Jed Alpert; Executive Producers, D.J. Paul, George Pezyos; Director, Jonathan Nossiter; Screenplay, James Lasdun, Jonathan Nossiter; Photography, Michael Barrow, John Foster; Editor, Madeleine Gavin; Designer, Deana Sidney; Casting, Mali Finn; from Goatworks Films; Ultra-Stereo; Color; Not rated; 93 minutes; August release

CAST

Matthew/Oliver....David Suchet
Madeleine Vesey....Lisa Harrow
Ray....Jared Harris
Ben Vesey....Larry Pine
Scotti Elster....Joe Grifasi
Andy....Arnold Barkus
Abram....Bahman Soltani
Selwyn....Willis Burks
Subalowsky....Joe Sirola
Sam....Henry Hayward
David....Kevin Thigpen
and Chen Tsun Kit, Jimmy Broadway (Themselves), Young Joo Kim (Suky Vesey), Fran Capo (Judy, Madeleine's Friend), Spencer Paterson (Johnnie O)

A struggling British actress living in Queens, and a recently laid off accountant living in a homeless shelter, meet when she mistakes him for a famous film director.

David Suchet, Lisa Harrow

John Travolta, Robin Wright Penn

Harry Dean Stanton, Sean Penn

SHE'S SO LOVELY

(MIRAMAX) formerly *She's De Lovely*; Producer, Rene Cleitman; Executive Producers, John Travolta, Gerard Depardieu, Sean Penn, Bernard Bouix; Co-Executive Producers, Bob Weinstein, Harvey Weinstein; Director, Nick Cassavetes; Screenplay, John Cassavetes; Co-Producer, Avram Butch Kaplan; Photography, Thierry Arbogast; Designer, David Wasco; Costumes, Beatrix Aruna Pasztor; Editor, Petra Von Oelffen; Music, Joseph Vitarelli; Casting, Matthew Barry; a Hachette Premiere & Cie production, in association with Clyde Is Hungry Films; U.S.- French; Dolby Digital Stereo; Research PLC Widescreen; Color; Rated R; 100 minutes; August release

CAST

Eddie....Sean Penn
Maureen....Robin Wright Penn
Joey....John Travolta
Shorty....Harry Dean Stanton
Georgie....Debi Mazar
Miss Green....Gena Rowlands
Kiefer....James Gandolfini
Saul....David Thornton
Jeanie....Kelsey Mulrooney
Lucinda....Susan Traylor
Cooper....Bobby Cooper
Leonard....John Marshall Jones
Nancy Swearingen....Chloe Webb
Avi....James Soravilla
Interns....James Bozian, Paul Johansson
Ticket Taker....Justina Machado
Lead Singer....Tito Larriva
Band Member....Tony Marsico
Taxi Driver....Ilya Brodsky
Lorenzo....Burt Young
Mario....Neill Barry
Attendants....Clayton Landey, Jason O'Malley
and Dennis Fanning, John Cundari, Noon Orsatti (Cops), Nina Barry (Helen Caldwell), Chris Kinkade (Security Guard), Kristina Malota (Rosie), Nicollette Little (Dolly), Lester Matthews (Black Dude), and Talia Shire

A wild and unstable married couple, Eddie and Maureen, lead a life on the edge until Eddie is arrested and put away. When he is released years later he is stunned to find that Maureen has remarried. Based on a script by the late John Cassavetes, the father of the director, Nick Cassavetes. Nick's mother, Gena Rowlands, also appears in the film.

HOODLUM

(UNITED ARTISTS) Producer, Frank Mancuso, Jr.; Executive Producers, Bill Duke, Laurence Fishburne, Helen Sugland; Co-Producers, Paul Eckstein, Chris Brancato; Director, Bill Duke; Screenplay, Chris Brancato; Line Producer, Vikki Williams; Photography, Frank Tidy; Designer, Charles Bennett; Music, Elmer Bernstein; Editor, Harry Keramidas; Costumes, Richard Bruno; Casting, Amanda Mackey Johnson, Cathy Sandrich; a Frank Mancuso, Jr. production; Distributed by MGM Distribution; DTS Stereo; Deluxe color; Rated R; 130 minutes; August release

Laurence Fishburne, Andy Garcia

CAST

Ellsworth "Bumpy" Johnson........Laurence Fishburne
Dutch Schultz........Tim Roth
Francine Hughes........Vanessa L. Williams
Lucky Luciano........Andy Garcia
Stephanie St. Clair........Cicely Tyson
Illinois Gordon........Chi McBride
Bub Hewlett........Clarence Williams III
Captain Foley........Richard Bradford
Thomas Dewey........William Atherton
Pigfoot Mary........Loretta Devine
Sulie........Queen Latifah
Albert Salke........Mike Starr
Jules Salke........Beau Starr
Whispers........Paul Benjamin
Bo Weinberg........Joe Guzaldo
Lulu Rosenkrantz........Ed O'Ross
Calvin........J.W. Smith
Tee-Ninchy........Eddie "Bo" Smith, Jr.
Vallie........John Toles-Bey
Johnny "Figures" DiPalmero........David Darlow
Lucky's Henchman........Steve Pickering
Undertaker........Ellis Foster
Mr. Redmond........Bill Henderson
Enrique "Henry" Miro........Juan A. Ramirez
Waldo........Kevin Morrow
Dutch's Driver........Tony Fitzpatrick
Hobo........Robert Cornelius
Willie Brunder........Tab Baker

and Joe Van Slyke (Warden), Daniel Bryant (Hep-Cat Man), Don James (Piano Man), Sulanya "Sue" Conway (Miss Philmore), Paul Eckstein (Dutch's Thug), Christian Payton (Jimmy), Jackie Taylor (Mrs. Andrews), Dick Gjonola (Owney Madden), David Nisbet (Man in Cotton Club), Nancy Nickel (Woman in Cotton Club), Ted Love, Kenya Cagle (Runners), Jim Saltouros (Lieutenant), Marc Vann (Dutch's Liquor Henchman), Cheridah Best (Prostitute), Colin Bradley Sylvester (Chee Chee), Iris Lieberman (Prison Guard), Leonard Roberts (Tyrone), John Watson, Sr. (Manager of Pool Hall), Lisa Botauzer (Dancer), Michael McCary (Osgood), Eric Kilpatrick (Security Guard), Demetrice O'Neal (Singer), Tony Powell (Rent Party Singer), Kevin Morrow (Church Conductor), Louis Price, Vernon Oliver Price (Church Singers), Laurnea Wilkerson (Cotton Club Singer), Tony Rich (Duke Ellington), Kim Adams (Show Girl), David A. Jansen (Doorman), Fred Nelson (Sideline Musician), Robert Keating, Charles Koysta, Joe Testa, Rocky McCord (Luciano's Mob Bosses)

Laurence Fishburne, Vanessa L. Williams

Fictional look at the life of gangster Ellsworth "Bumpy" Johnson, who became king of the Harlem numbers racket during the 1930s.

Laurence Fishburne, Cicely Tyson, Paul Benjamin, Eddie "Bo" Smith

EXCESS BAGGAGE

(COLUMBIA) Producers, Bill Borden, Carolyn Kessler; Director, Marco Brambilla; Screenplay, Max D. Adams, Dick Clement, Ian La Frenais; Photography, Jean Yves Escoffier; Designer, Missy Stewart; Editor, Stephen Rivkin; Co-Producer, B. Casey Grant; Music, John Lurie; Costumes, Beatrix Aruna Pasztor; Casting, Mike Fenton, Allison Cowitt; a First Kiss production; Dolby SDDS Stereo; Technicolor; Rated PG-13; 101 minutes; August release

CAST

Emily T. Hope .... Alicia Silverstone
Vincent Roche .... Benicio Del Toro
"Uncle" Ray Perkins .... Christopher Walken
Alexander Hope .... Jack Thompson
Greg Kistler .... Harry Connick, Jr.
Stick .... Nicholas Turturro
Gus .... Michael Bowen
Detective Sims .... Robert Wisden
Detective Barnaby .... Leland Orser
Louise .... Sally Kirkland
Jon .... Hiro Kanagawa
Man on Pay Phone .... Brendan Beiser
Surveillance Van Cop .... Demetri Goritsas
Mini Mart Clerk .... Jorge Vargas
Monique .... Danielle Saklofsky
Car Showroom Receptionist .... Stacy Grant
Motel Manager .... Callum Rennie
Waitress at Diner .... Carrie Cain Sparks
Waitress at Knotty Pines .... Nicole Parker
and Bill Croft, C. Ernst Harth, Adrien Derval (Truckers), Claire Riley (Dream Reporter), Dean Wray (Barge Mate), Fulvio Cecere (Sharp Shooter), David Longworth (RV Gas Pumper)

Feeling neglected by her father, Emily Hope intends to fake her own kidnapping, only to be inadvertently abducted by professional car thief Vincent Roche.

Benicio Del Toro, Alicia Silverstone

LEAVE IT TO BEAVER

(UNIVERSAL) Producer, Robert Simonds; Executive Producers, Ben Myron, David Helpern, Lynn Arost; Director, Andy Cadiff; Screenplay, Brian Levant, Lon Diamond; Based on the tv series created by Bob Mosher and Joe Connelly; Photography, Thomas Del Ruth; Designer, Perry Andelin Blake; Editor, Alan Heim; Co-Producer, Kelly Van Horn; Associate Producer, Rita Smith; Costumes, Jean Pierre Dorleac; Music, Randy Edelman; Leave It to Beaver Theme (Toy Parade) by Dave Kahn and Melvyn Lenard; Casting, Joanna Colbert; a Robert Simonds production; DTS Stereo; Eastman color; Rated PG; 88 minutes; August release

CAST

Ward Cleaver .... Christopher McDonald
June Cleaver .... Janine Turner
Theodore "Beaver" Cleaver .... Cameron Finley
Wally Cleaver .... Erik von Detten
Eddie Haskell .... Adam Zolotin
Aunt Martha .... Barbara Billingsley
Eddie Haskell, Sr. .... Ken Osmond
Karen Connelly .... Erika Christensen
Frank .... Frank Bank
Fred Rutherford .... Alan Rachins
Larry Mondello .... E.J. De La Pena
Lumpy .... Justin Restivo
Coach Gordon .... Geoff Pierson
Gilbert Bates .... Louis Martin Braga III
Punk .... Glenn Harris, Jr.
Miss Landers .... Grace Phillips
Richard Rickover .... Sam Gifaldi
and Brighton Hertford (Judy Hensler), Shirley Prestia (Claire Hensler), Brenda Song (Susan), Fran Bennett (Dr. Beaumont), Wendy Walsh (Reporter), Lindsay Boyd (Lusty Girl), Heather Lauren Olson (Tamara), Matthew Thomas Carey (Kyle), George Fisher (Bert the Pie Man), Kate C. Sklar (Cute Girl), Darryl Smith (Referee)

Beaver Cleaver sets his sights on getting a bicycle for his eighth birthday. Based on the ABC tv series that ran from 1958 to 1963 and starred Hugh Beaumont (Ward), Barbara Billingsley (June), Tony Dow (Wally), and Jerry Mathers (Beaver). The follow-up series, Still the Beaver/The New Leave It to Beaver ran on cable stations from 1986 to 1989 and was created by this film's writer, Brian Levant. Billingsley, Ken Osmond (the original Eddie Haskell), and Frank Bank (Lumpy Rutherford) from the original series also appear in this film.

Erik von Detten, Cameron Finley, Christopher McDonald, Janine Turner

MIMIC

(MIRAMAX) Producers, Bob Weinstein, B.J. Rack, Ole Bornedal; Executive Producer, Michael Phillips; Director, Guillermo Del Toro; Screenplay/Screen Story, Matthew Robbins, Guillermo Del Toro; Based on the short story by Donald A. Wolheim; Co-Producers, Gary Granat, Richard Potter, Andrew Rona, Scott Shiffman, Michael Zoumas; Photography, Dan Laustsen; Designer, Carol Spier; Editor, Patrick Lussier; Music, Marco Beltrami; Visual Effects Supervisor, Brian M. Jennings; Creatures Created by Rick Lazzarini/The Character Shop; Creature Designers, Rob Bottin, Tyruben Ellingson; Costumes, Marie-Sylvie Deveau; Casting, Billy Hopkins, Suzanne Smith, Kerry Barden; a Dimension Films presentation; Dolby Digital Stereo; Color; Rated R: 105 minutes; August release

CAST

Susan Tyler .... Mira Sorvino
Peter Mann .... Jeremy Northam
Chuy .... Alexander Goodwin
Manny .... Giancarlo Giannini
Leonard .... Charles S. Dutton
Josh .... Josh Brolin
Remy .... Alix Koromzay
Dr. Gates .... F. Murray Abraham
Ricky .... James Costa
Davis .... Javon Barnwell
Jeremy .... Norman Reedus
Preacher .... Pak-Kwong Ho
Yang .... Glen Bang
Chinese Woman .... Margaret Ma
Bag Lady .... Warna Fisher
Skeletal Bum .... Alan Argue
Homeless Man .... Charles Hayter
Workman .... Julian Richings
Subway Repairman .... James Kidnie
Homeless Woman .... Eve English
Long John .... Bill Lasovich, Doug Jones, Roger Clown

A pair of scientists, Susan Tyler and Peter Mann, successfully eradicate a life-threatening epidemic by coming up with a biological counteragent to the carrier of the disease. Years later they realize that they have inadvertently created a breed of giant insect-like creatures that are living under New York City.

Charles S. Dutton, Giancarlo Giannini, Mira Sorvino, Jeremy Northam

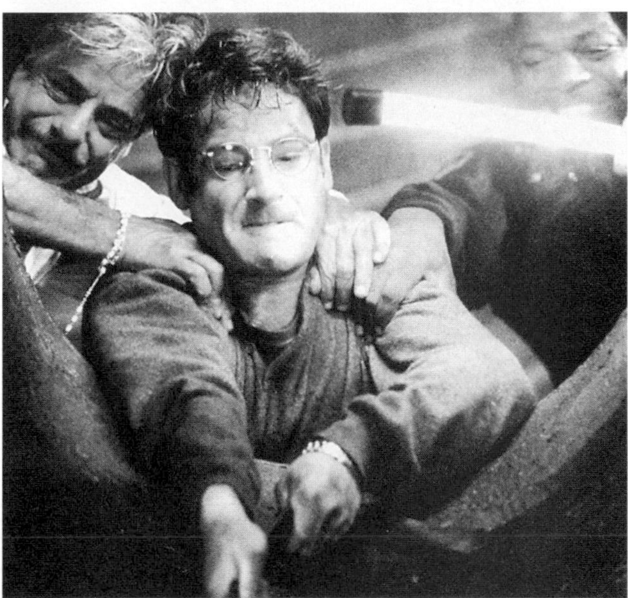

Giancarlo Giannini, Jeremy Northam, Charles S. Dutton

Josh Brolin

Mira Sorvino

THE KEEPER

(KINO INTERNATIONAL) Producer, Jordi Torrent, Joe Brewster; Director/Screenplay, Joe Brewster; Co-Producer, Giancarlo Esposito; Executive Producers, Juan Amalbert, Forrest Murray; Co-Executive Producer, Marcia Shulman; Photography, Igor Sunara; Designer, Flavia Galuppo; Art Director, Tom Jarmusch; Music, John Petersen; Editor, Tom McArdle; a Rada Films production; Color; Not rated; 90 minutes; September release

CAST

Paul Lamont....Giancarlo Esposito
Angela Lamont....Regina Taylor
Jean Baptiste....Isaach De Bankole
Clarence Ross....Ron Brice
Ron Baker....O.L. Duke
Officer Jones....Alvaleta Guess
Officer Santana....Sam E. Wright
Majhid....Shiek Mahmud-Bey
Officer Corvino....Victor Colicchio
Jimmy Johnson....Arthur French
Captain Walker....Jude Ciccolella
Officer Melendez....Liza Colon
and Cory Glover (Martin), Sixto Ramos (Wilson), Curtis McClarin (Joseph), Laurence Mason (Tony), Michael Kirby (Michael), Mitchell Marchand (Horton), Kenshaka Ali (Officer Williams), Gordon Joseph Weiss (Police Officer Guido), Oni F. Lampley (Mrs. Grant), Novella Nelson (Mrs. Lamont), Emile St. Lot (Mr. Lamont), Aaron Griffin (Young Paul), Diego Lopez (Jose), Jewdyer Osborne (Officer Smith), Lionel Bernard, Constance Bernard (Haitian Musicians), Rocco Iacovone (Hospital Doctor)

A prison guard, moved by the plight of a Haitian immigrant wrongly accused of rape, invites the man to move in with him and his wife.

Giancarlo Esposito

Isaach De Bankole

THE END OF VIOLENCE

(MGM) Producers, Deepak Nayar, Wim Wenders, Nicholas Klein; Executive Producers, Jean François Fonlupt, Ulrich Felsberg; Director, Wim Wenders; Screenplay, Nicholas Klein; Story, Nicholas Klein, Wim Wenders; Photography, Pascal Rabaud; Designer/Costumes, Patricia Norris; Editor, Peter Przygodda; Music, Ry Cooder; Casting, Heidi Levitt, Monika Mikkelsen; a Ciby 2000 presentation of a Ciby Pictures/Road Movies/Kintop Pictures co-production; Dolby Stereo; Super 35 Widescreen; Deluxe color; Rated R; 122 minutes; September release

CAST

Mike Max....Bill Pullman
Paige....Andie MacDowell
Ray Bering....Gabriel Byrne
Doc....Loren Dean
Cat....Traci Lind
Phelps....Daniel Benzali
Six O One....K. Todd Freeman
Lowell....John Diehl
Frank....Pruitt Taylor-Vince
Brian....Peter Horton
Zoltan....Udo Kier
Ramon....Enrique Castillo
Kenya....Nicole Parker
Claire....Rosalind Chao
Mathilda....Marisol Padilla Sanchez
Call....Marshall Bell
MacDermot....Frederic Forrest
and Chris Douridas (Technician), Richard Cummings (Tyler), Soledad St. Hilaire (Anita), Sam Fuller (Louis), Sal Lopez (Tito), Ulises Cuadra (Jose), Aymara De Llano (Florinda), Mili Avital, Kevin Chesley, Teresa De La Riva, Rick Edwards, Russell Gethering, Mark Hardisty, Daryl Hemmrich, Irene Hilleary, Chris Howell, Anne Nielsen, Ailinda Camile Pena, Kerry Rossal, Virgil Smith, Krist Thompson (Featured Background Performers)

Surveillance expert Ray Bering, testing a network of hidden cameras to cut down crime in Los Angeles, witnesses the abduction of successful film producer Mike Max who has made millions from movies that dwell on violence. This was the last film credit of director-actor Samuel Fuller who died on Oct. 30, 1997.

Bill Pullman, Andie MacDowell

Loren Dean, Traci Lind

THE GAME

(POLYGRAM) Producers, Steve Golin, Céan Chaffin; Director, David Fincher; Screenplay/Co-Producers, John Brancato, Michael Ferris; Photography, Harris Savides; Designer, Jeffrey Beecroft; Editor, James Haygood; Music, Howard Shore; Costumes, Michael Kaplan; Executive Producer, Jonathan Mostow; Casting, Don Phillips; a Propaganda Films production; Dolby DTS Digital Stereo; Super 35 Widescreen; Technicolor; Rated R; 128 minutes; September release

CAST

Nicholas Van Orton	Michael Douglas
Conrad Van Orton	Sean Penn
Christine	Deborah Kara Unger
Jim Feingold	James Rebhorn
Samuel Sutherland	Peter Donat
Ilsa	Carroll Baker
Elizabeth	Anna Katarina
Anson Baer	Armin Mueller-Stahl
Nicholas' Father	Charles Martinet
Young Nicholas	Scott Hunter McGuire
Nicholas' Mother	Florentine Mocanu
Maria	Elizabeth Dennehy
Maggie	Caroline Barclay
Himself	Daniel Schorr
Power Executive	John Aprea
Obsequious Executive	Harrison Young
Cynthia, CRS Receptionist	Kimberly Russell
CRS Data Collecting Technician	Joe Frank
James the Bartender	James Brooks
New Member Ted	Gerry Becker
New Member Victor	Jarlon Monroe
Solicitor/Taxi Driver	Tommy Flanagan
Tubercular Commuter	Bill Flannery
Rattle Gatherer	Kathryn Jean Harris
Man in Airport	John Cassini
Ankles	Harris Savides
City Club Waiter	Aaron Thomas Luchich
City Club Maitre D'	Victor Talmadge
City Club Waiter	Marc Siegler
Heart Attack Performer	André Brazeau
Officer Hicks	Keena Turner
Paramedic Graves	Carlos Hoy
Paramedic Stern	Edward Campbell
Paramedic Kirkland	Sean Lanthier
Ambulance EMT	Curtis Vanterpool
Triage Doctor	Jay Gordon
Officer Walker	Jeffrey Michael Young
Pickpocket	Owen Masterson

and Yuji Okumoto (Nikko Hotel Manager), Hideo Kimura (Nikko Hotel Bellhop), Rachel Schadt (Nikko Hotel Maid), Mark Boone Junior (Shady Private Investigator), Joy Ann Ryan (Kaleigh Baer), Peter Davidian (Mr. Garcia), Jack Kehoe (Lt. Sullivan), Christopher John Fields (Detective Boyle), Linda Manz (Christine's Roommate Amy), Victor Ferrerira (Assassin Mobubbi), Duffy Gaver (Assassin Brodi), Robert J. Stephenson (Assassin Kartmann), Sean Moloney (Assassin Rankin), John Hammil (U.S. Embassy Counselor), Rachel Steinberg (Sheraton Desk Clerk), George Maguire (Sheraton Manager), Trish Sommerville (Hot Waitress), Jason Kristopher (Teen Thug), Lily Soh Froelich (New Moon Cafe Manager), Tammy Koehler (Tammy Fisher), Michael Lynwood (Michael Fisher), Alex Lynwood (Alex Fisher), Charles Branklyn (CRS Guard), Spike Jonze (Airbag EMT Beltran), Michael Massee (Airbag EMT Galliano), Sara Davallou (Rachel), Stephen Cowee (Mel)

Successful but stuffy businessman Nicholas Van Orton is signed up to be part of a "game" conducted by a mysterious organization and soon finds that his life is thrown into an uproar from which there appears to be no escape.

Michael Douglas, Deborah Kara Unger

Sean Penn

Michael Douglas

Joan Cusack, Kevin Kline

Kevin Kline

Tom Selleck, Shalom Harlow, Matt Dillon

IN & OUT

(PARAMOUNT) Producer, Scott Rudin; Executive Producer, Adam Schroeder; Director, Frank Oz; Screenplay, Paul Rudnick; Co-Producer, G. Mac Brown; Photography, Rob Hahn; Designer, Ken Adam; Editors, Dan Hanley, John Jympson; Costumes, Ann Roth; Music, Marc Shaiman; Casting, Margery Simkin; a Scott Rudin production, presented in association with Spelling Films; Dolby Digital Stereo; Deluxe color; Rated PG-13; 90 minutes; September release

CAST

Howard Brackett........Kevin Kline
Emily Montgomery........Joan Cusack
Peter Malloy........Tom Selleck
Cameron Drake........Matt Dillon
Berniece Brackett........Debbie Reynolds
Frank Brackett........Wilford Brimley
Tom Halliwell........Bob Newhart
Walter Brackett........Gregory Jbara
Sonya........Shalom Harlow
Jack........Shawn Hatosy
Mike........Zak Orth
Vicky........Lauren Ambrose
Meredith........Alexandra Holden
Ed Kenrow........Lewis J. Stadlen
Ava Blazer........Deborah Rush
Trina Paxton........J. Smith-Cameron
Aunt Becky........Kate McGregor Stewart
Mrs. Lester........Debra Monk
Aldo Hooper........Ernie Sabella
Voice on "Be a Man" Tape........John Cunningham
Danny........Gus Rogerson
Military Attorney........Dan Hedaya
Father Tim........Joseph Maher
Fred Mooney........William Parry
Emmett Wilson........William Duell
Reverend Morgan........Richard Woods
Carl Mickley........Kevin Chamberlin

and Wally Dunn (Cousin Lenny), Larry Clarke (Cousin Ernie), June Squibb (Cousin Gretchen), Alice Drummond (Aunt Susan), Mary Diveny (Cousin Ellen), Anne Russell (Aunt Marge), Patrick Garner (Stan Forrest), Adam LeFevre, Bill Camp, Scott Robertson, John Christopher Jones, MacIntyre Dixon (Bachelor Party Guests), Joanna Wolff (Jennifer the Flower Girl), Chris I. McKenna, Mark Ballou, Charles Newmark, Andrew Levitas, Jonathan Michael Hershfield, Daniel Joseph, Seth Ullian, Greg Siff, Ryan Janis (Locker Room Guys), Jane Hoffman (Mrs. Baxter), Becky Ann Baker (Darlene), William P. Hoag (Bartender), Danny Canton (Cameraman), Selma Blair (Cousin Linda), Patricia Guinan (Billy's Mom), Nesbitt Blaisdell (Billy's Dad), Samantha Buck, Lauren Fox, Lizzy Mahon, Simone Marean, Michael McGruther, Niki Roma, Jacqueline Maloney, Patrick Mylod, Ginger R. Williams (Classroom Students), Joshua Wade Miller, Jill Horner, Lauren Ward, Julie Entwisle, Clare Kramer, Miranda Kent, Tara Carnes, Arden Myrin, Ian Sherwood, Kevin Keating, Kathy Lyn Cavanaugh (Students), Jo-Jo Lowe (Awards Event Model), Lisa Emery, Gary Dewitt Marshall (Classroom Reporters), Marla Sucharetza, Ronald Rand, Ross de Marco, Joanne DiMauro, Tony Jones, Grace DeSena, Bruce Bennetts, Tracy Appleton, Jim Taylor McNickle, Laura Caufield, Mimi Stuart, Dinah Gravel (School Reporters), Peter Barmonde (Wedding Photographer), Glenn Close, Whoopi Goldberg, Jay Leno (Themselves)

On the eve of his wedding, small town English teacher Howard Brackett finds himself the center of media attention when a former student "outs" him on national television at the Academy Awards ceremony. This film received an Oscar nomination for supporting actress (Joan Cusack).

Kevin Kline, Bob Newhart

Kevin Kline

Kevin Kline

Kevin Kline, Tom Selleck

Wilford Brimley, Debbie Reynolds, Joan Cusack, Kevin Kline

GOING ALL THE WAY

(GRAMERCY) Producers, Tom Gorai, Sigurjon Sighvatsson; Executive Producers, Tom Rosenberg, Ted Tannebaum, Michael Mendelsohn; Director, Mark Pellington; Screenplay, Dan Wakefield, based upon his novel; Photography, Bobby Bukowski; Editor, Leo Trombetta; Designer, Therese Deprez; Costumes, Arianne Phillips; Music, Tomandandy; Line Producer, Mark Lipson; Casting, Ellen Chenoweth; a PolyGram Filmed Entertainment presentation of a Tom Gorai/Lakeshore Entertainment production; Dolby Stereo; Foto-Kem color; Rated R; 110 minutes; September release

CAST

Sonny Burns .... Jeremy Davies
Gunner Casselman .... Ben Affleck
Buddy Porter .... Amy Locane
Gale Ann Thayer .... Rose McGowan
Marty Pilcher .... Rachel Weisz
Elwood Burns .... John Lordan
Luke .... Bob Swan
Alma Burns .... Jill Clayburgh
Nina Casselman .... Lesley Ann Warren
Conducter/Ticket Taker .... Richard Gaeckle
Beautiful Young Girl .... Teri Beitel
Wiater .... Everett Greene
Religious Man .... Jerry Panatieri
Blow Mahoney .... Jeff Buelterman
Wilks .... Nick Offerman
and Pat Daley, Charlie Webb (Meadowlark Residents), Wendy Carter (Deedee), Dave Webster (Crooner), Ted Steeg (Minister), Adrienne Reiswerg (Farmer's Wife), David Aikens, Dan Wakefield (Farmers), John Craig (Doctor), Cup a' Joe (Winkie the Dog)

Following military service, Sonny and Gunner, two decidely different young men, form an unlikely friendship as they begin to question the limitations life in Indianapolis has to offer them.

Jeremy Davies, Ben Affleck

Rose McGowan, Jeremy Davies

Ben Affleck, Rachel Weisz

THE LONG WAY HOME

(SEVENTH ART) Producers, Rabbi Marvin Hier, Richard Trank; Director/Screenplay, Mark Jonathan Harris; Photography, Don Lenzer; Editor, Kate Amend; Music, Lee Holdridge; Associate Producer, Christo Brock; a Moriah Films of the Simon Wiesenthal Center presentation; Color; Not rated; 119 minutes; September release. Documentary the plight of the tens of thousands of Jewish refugees who survived the Holocaust; Narrated by Morgan Freeman; and featuring the voices of Edward Asner, Sean Astin, Martin Landau, Miriam Margolyes, David Paymer, Nina Siemaszko, Helen Slater, Michael York.

1997 Academy Award-winner for Best Feature Documentary.

THE MYTH OF FINGERPRINTS

(SONY PICTURES CLASSICS) Producers, Mary Jane Skalski, Tim Perell, Bart Freundlich; Executive Producers, James Schamus, Ted Hope; Director/Screenplay, Bart Freundlich; Photography, Stephen Kazmierski; Designer, Susan Bolles; Editors, Kate Williams, Ken J. Sackheim; Music, David Bridie, John Phillips; Associate Producers, Howard Bernstein, Anthony Bergman, Noah Wyle; Line Producer, Victoria McGarry; Costumes, Lucy W. Corrigan; Casting, Douglas Aibel, Christine Sheaks; a Good Machine production in association with Eureka Pictures; Dolby Stereo; Color; Rated R; 90 minutes; September release

CAST

Daphne .... Arija Bareikis
Lena .... Blythe Danner
Margaret .... Hope Davis
Leigh .... Laurel Holloman
Elliot .... Brian Kerwin
Cezanne .... James LeGros
Mia .... Julianne Moore
Hal .... Roy Scheider
Jake .... Michael Vartan
Warren .... Noah Wyle
and Randee Allen (Waitress), Justin Barreto (Young Jake), Chris Bauer (Jerry), Nicholas Bourgeois (Young Warren), Tom Cumler (Man at Train Station), Christopher Duva (Tom), Kelsey Gunn (Young Leigh), Polly Pelletier (Young Mia), Pamela Polhemus (Bookstore Woman), Michael Rupert (Warren's Psychiatrist)

Hal and Lena's grown-up children return home with their various partners for an uncomfortable Thanksgiving gathering that opens some old wounds.

Roy Scheider, Blythe Danner

Julianne Moore, Noah Wyle, Laurel Holloman, Michael Vartan

Donald Sutherland, Ben Kingsley, Aidan Quinn

THE ASSIGNMENT

(TRIUMPH) Producers, Tom Berry, Franco Battista; Executive Producers, David Saunders, Joseph Newton Cohen; Co-Producer, Stefan Wodoslawsky; Director, Christian Duguay; Screenplay, Dan Gordon, Sabi H. Shabtai; Photography, David Franco; Designer, Michael Joy; Editor, Yves Langlois; Music, Normand Corbeil; Digital Effects Supervisor, Richard Ostiguy; Casting, Mary Margiotta, Karen Margiotta, Lucie Robitaille; an Allegro Films production; Dolby SDDS Stereo; Color; Rated R; 115 minutes; September release

CAST

Annibal Ramirez/Carlos "The Jackal" Sanchez .... Aidan Quinn
Jack Shaw (Henry Fields) .... Donald Sutherland
Amos .... Ben Kingsley
Maura Ramirez .... Claudia Ferri
Carla .... Céline Bonnier
KGB Head Officer .... Vlasta Vrana
Agnieska .... Liliana Komorowska
Koj .... Von Flores
Carl Mickens—CIA .... Al Waxman
Joey Ramirez .... Mitchell David Rothpan
KGB Aide .... Grégory Hlady
KGB Agents .... Gabriel Marian Oseciuc, Frederic Desager
KGB Technician .... Kliment Denchev
and Yonathan Gordon (Yoni), Ndiouga Sarr (Nigerian Oil Minister), Manuel Aranguiz (Venezuelan Oil Minister), Leni Parker (OPEC Receptionist), Jacques Lavallée (Du Foltiere—DST), David Francis (Naval Aide), Gouchy Boy, Tim Post (CIA Aides), Daniel Pilon (Admiral Crawford), Richard Jutras (Commander Scowcroft), Hisham Zayed (Libyan Customs Official), Ted Whittal (Norfolk Police Captain), Francis Delvecchio (Injured Paris Boy), Lisa Wegner (Berlin Lover), Lucie Laurier (Paris Lover), Neil Kroetsch (Ramirez' Father), Matthew Dupuis (Young Ramirez), Paul Stewart (Hospital Father), Claude Genest (Baseball Dad), Michael Caloz (Baseball Kid), David Franco (St. Martin Postman), Heinz Becker, Louis Bouchard, Mark Knoeffel, Andres Lange, Martin Morf (German Beerhall Singers)

Annibal Ramirez, a dead ringer for an illusive international terrorist called "The Jackal," is persuaded by two intelligence agents to impersonate his twin so that they can lay a trap and bring the killer out of hiding.

Jessica Lange, Michelle Pfeiffer, Jennifer Jason Leigh

Keith Carradine, Jessica Lange, Colin Firth

Jennifer Jason Leigh, Jason Robards, Keith Carradine

A THOUSAND ACRES

(TOUCHSTONE) Producers, Marc Abraham, Lynn Arost, Steve Golin, Kate Guinzburg, Sigurjon Sighvatsson; Executive Producers, Armyan Bernstein, Thomas A. Bliss; Co-Producer, Diana Pokorny; Director, Jocelyn Moorhouse; Screenplay, Laura Jones; Based on the novel by Jane Smiley; Photography, Tak Fujimoto; Designer, Dan Davis; Editor, Maryann Brandon; Costumes, Ruth Myers; Music, Richard Hartley; Casting, Nancy Klopper; a Via Rosa/Prairie Films production, presented in association with Beacon Pictures and Propaganda Films; Distributed by Buena Vista Pictures; Dolby Digital Stereo; Panavision; Technicolor; Rated R; 104 minutes; September release

CAST

Rose Cook Lewis .... Michelle Pfeiffer
Ginny Cook Smith .... Jessica Lange
Larry Cook .... Jason Robards
Caroline Cook .... Jennifer Jason Leigh
Jess Clark .... Colin Firth
Ty Smith .... Keith Carradine
Peter Lewis .... Kevin Anderson
Harold Clark .... Pat Hingle
Ken LaSalle .... John Carroll Lynch
Mary Livingstone .... Anne Pitoniak
Charles Carter .... Vyto Ruginis
Pammy .... Michelle Williams
Linda .... Elizabeth Moss
Marv Carson .... Ray Toler
Doctor .... Kenneth Tigar
Laren Clark .... Steve Key
Henry Dodge .... Dan Conway
Frank .... Stan Cahill
Wallace Crockett .... Ray Baker
Roberta .... Beth Grant
Waitress .... Andrea Nittoli

Larry Cook's decision to divide his thousand acre farm between his three daughters causes animosity within the family and brings some terrible past secrets to light.

THE EDGE

(20TH CENTURY FOX) Producer, Art Linson; Executive Producer, Lloyd Phillips; Director, Lee Tamahori; Screenplay, David Mamet; Photography, Donald M. McAlpine; Deisgner, Wolf Kroeger; Editor, Neil Travis; Music, Jerry Goldsmith; Costumes, Julie Weiss; Casting, Donna Isaacson; Bear Trainer, Doug Seus; an Art Linson production; Dolby Digital Stereo; Panavision; Deluxe color; Rated R; 117 minutes; September release

CAST

Charles Morse....Anthony Hopkins
Robert Green....Alec Baldwin
Mickey Morse....Elle Macpherson
Stephen....Harold Perrineau
Styles....L.Q. Jones
Ginny....Kathleen Wilhoite
James....David Lindstedt
Mechanic....Mark Kiely
Jet Pilot....Eli Gabay
Amphibian Pilot....Larry Musser
Reporters....Brian Arnold, Kelsa Kinsly, Bob Boyd
Jack Hawk....Gordon Tootoosis
Bear....Bart the Bear

Following a plane crash, billionaire Charles Morse finds himself stuck in the mountain wilderness with the man who has been carrying on with Morse's beautiful wife.

Anthony Hopkins, Bart

Alec Baldwin, Anthony Hopkins

Harold Perrineau, Alec Baldwin, Anthony Hopkins

Alec Baldwin, Elle Macpherson

(Standing) Vanessa L. Williams, Michael Beach, Jeffrey D. Sams, Vivica A. Fox, Morgan Méchelle Smith; (Seated) Irma P. Hall, Nia Long, Brandon Hammond, Mekhi Phifer

SOUL FOOD

(20TH CENTURY FOX) Producers, Tracey E. Edmonds; Executive Producer, Kenneth "Babyface" Edmonds; Director/Screenplay, George Tillman, Jr.; Photography, Paul Elliott; Designer, Maxine Shepard; Editor, John Carter; Music, Wendy Melvoin, Lisa Coleman; Co-Producer, Michael McQuarn; Line Producer, Llewellyn Wells; Costumes, Salvador Perez; Casting, Robi Reed-Humes; a Fox 2000 Pictures presentation of an Edmonds Entertainment production; Dolby Stereo; Deluxe color; Rated R; 114 minutes; September release

CAST

Teri....Vanessa L. Williams
Maxine....Vivica A. Fox
Bird....Nia Long
Miles....Michael Beach
Lem....Mekhi Phifer
Ahmad....Brandon Hammond
Kenny....Jeffrey D. Sams
Faith....Gina Ravera
Mother Joe....Irma P. Hall
Reverend Williams....Carl Wright
Simuel....Mel Jackson
Kelly....Morgan Méchelle Smith
Uncle Pete....John M. Watson, Sr.
Jada....M.T. Alexander
Harome....Lawrence Petty
Nicole....Marcia Wright
Dr. Benson....Bernard Mixon
Hamp....Hamp Clemons
Blimp....Theron Touché Lykes
Ahmad (age 4)....Martell Hill Edmond
Dread Man....Ras Majah Couzan

and James W. Boinski (Foreman), Mike Bacarella (Printing Company Owner), Joan Collaso (Choir Member #1), Donn C. Harper (Funeral Minister), George Brashear, Larry C. Tankson (Blimp's Henchmen), Austin Curtis (Family Member), Sylvester Phifer (Bartender), Malik Yoda (Studio Engineer), Kenneth "Babyface" Edmonds, Kevon Edmonds, Melvin Edmonds, Jo Jo Hailey, K-Ci Hailey, Simon Horrocks, Randy Walker (Band Members), Tamara Braun (Teri's Secretary)

The relationships of three sisters and their families are tested when their mother, who is instrumental in keeping them together, becomes ill.

Vanessa L. Williams, Michael Beach

Vanessa L. Williams, Nia Long, Vivica A. Fox

Nia Long, Mekhi Phifer

Irma P. Hall, Brandon Hammond

Kevin Kline, Joan Allen

Elijah Wood

Christina Ricci, Tobey Maguire

THE ICE STORM

(FOX SEARCHLIGHT) Producers, Ted Hope, James Schamus, Ang Lee; Director, Ang Lee; Screenplay, James Schamus; Based on the novel by Rick Moody; Photography, Frederick Elmes; Designer, Mark Friedberg; Editor, Tim Squyres; Music, Mychael Danna; Costumes, Carol Oditz; Associate Producers, Alysse Bezahler, Anthony Bregman; Casting, Avy Kaufman; a Good Machine production; Dolby Stereo; Color; Rated R; 113 minutes; September release

CAST

Ben Hood	Kevin Kline
Elena Hood	Joan Allen
George Clair	Henry Czerny
Sandy Carver	Adam Hann-Byrd
Francis Davenport	David Krumholtz
Paul Hood	Tobey Maguire
Wendy Hood	Christina Ricci
Jim Carver	Jamey Sheridan
Mikey Carver	Elijah Wood
Janey Carver	Sigourney Weaver
Dorothy Franklin	Kate Burton
Ted Shackley	William Cain
Philip Edwards	Michael Cumpsty
Mrs. Gadd	Maia Danziger
Pharmacist	Michael Egerman
Marie Earle	Christine Farrell
Neil Conrad	Glenn Fitzgerald
Train Conductor	Tom Flagg
Ted Franklin	Jonathan Freeman
Weather Reporter	Babara Garrick
Stephen Earle	Dennis Gazomiros
Mark Boland	John Benjamin Hickey
Libbets Casey	Katie Holmes
Dot Halford	Allison Janney
Pierce Sawyer	Byron Jennings
Sari Steele	Colette Kilroy
Jack Moellering	Ivan Kronenfeld
Weatherman	Daniel McDonald
Mr. Gadd	Miles Marek
Maria Conrad	Donna Mitchell
Helen Wentworth	Barbara Neal
Claudia White	Nancy Opel
Dave Gorman	Larry Pine
Mikey's Teacher	Marcell Rosenblatt
Pharmacy Attendant	Wendy Scott
Woman in Pharmacy	Evelyn Solann
Marge	Jessica Stone
Beth	Sarah Thompson
Paul's Teacher	Scott Wentworth
Rob Halford	Rob Westenberg

In November of 1973 two families in suburban New Canaan, Connecticut experience the alienation and confusion of the sexual revolution as they loose communication with each other during an ice storm.

Adam Hann-Byrd

Kevin Kline, Sigourney Weaver

Joan Allen, Jamey Sheridan

Tobey Maguire, Joan Allen

Christina Ricci, Kevin Kline

Sigourney Weaver

Nicole Kidman, George Clooney

Marcel Iures

Armin Mueller-Stahl

George Clooney, Nicole Kidman

THE PEACEMAKER

(DREAMWORKS) Producers, Walter Parkes, Branko Lustig; Executive Producers, Michael Grillo, Laurie MacDonald; Director, Mimi Leder; Screenplay, Michael Schiffer; Photography, Dietrich Lohmann; Designer, Leslie Dilley; Editor, David Rosenbloom; Co-Executive Producer, John Wells; Costumes, Shelley Komarov; Music, Hans Zimmer; Co-Producers, Pat Kehoe, Leslie Cockburn, Andrew Cockburn; Casting, Risa Bramon Garcia, Randi Hiller; Dolby DTS Stereo; Super 35 Widescreen; Technicolor; Rated R; 122 minutes; September release

CAST

Thomas Devoe .... George Clooney
Julia Kelly .... Nicole Kidman
Dusan Gavrich .... Marcel Iures
Alexsander Kodoroff .... Alexander Baluev
Vlado Mirich .... Rene Medvesek
Hamilton .... Gary Werntz
Ken .... Randall Batinkoff
General Garnett .... Jim Haynie
Shummaker .... Alexander Strobele
Appleton .... Holt McCallany
CPN Beach .... Michael Boatman
Senator Bevens .... Joan Copeland
Santiago .... Carlos Gomez
Dimitri Vertikoff .... Armin Mueller-Stahl
Stevo .... Slavko Juraga
Vassily .... Alexander Peskov
Driver .... Dejan Acimovic
Dr. Taraki .... Harsh Nayyar
Alan .... Matt Adler
Jody .... Tamara Tunie
Russian Corporal .... Alexander Yatsko
DOE Helo Tech .... Bruce MacVittie
Pockman .... Lubomir Paulovic
Branigan .... Charles Dumas

and Ramsey Faragallah (Cabbie), Murphy Guyer (INS Agent), Leslie Dilley (Priest—NY), David Lomax, Blaise Corrigan, John Ottavio (FBI Agents), Adina Porter (NY Cop), Hubert Kramar (Kordech Guard), Alma Cuervo (UN Representative), Sabastian Roche (German Backpacker), Gordon Catlin (Gunner), Goran Visnjic (Bazta Sgt.), Jay Acovone (Cop), Hannah Werntz (Piano Student), James Colby (Limo Driver), Jean Rogers (CNN Rep—Sarajevo), Matt Winston (UN Official), Terry Serpico, Jerry Dixon (Snipers), Thom Mathews (Maj. Rich Numbers), David Lagle, Jerome Hardeman (Pilots), Lou Mustillo (Costello), Bozidar Smiljanic (Serb Minister), Michael Potts, Richard Poe (DOE Haz-mat Techs), Slobodan Dimitrijevic (Serb Official), Martin Nikodym (Polish IFOR Soldier), Charles Cavalier (Angry Motorist), David Hamilton Simonds (Philly Agent), Irmelin Mai Hoffer (Vienna Cafe Singer), Chuck Cooper (NYPD Cop), Jono Kouzouyan (Bazta Merchant), Jared Chandler (Marine), Evert Sooster (Praporshik), Branko Lustig (Man with Poodle), Matthew Sussman (National Guard Captain), Bill Christ (DOE Agent), William Hill (Agent), Bernie McInerney (Carey), Andrea Doven (Kelly Girl), James Dumont (Young Sniper), Mark Johnson (CIA Agent), Alexander Kuznetsov (Russian Controller), Ed Semenov (Radio Officer), Bruce Gray (CNN Newscaster), Endre Hules (Older Major)

A nuclear scientist and an army intelligence officer team up to track down the terrorists who have hijacked a nuclear weapon during a train crash. This film was the first release from DreamWorks Pictures.

U TURN

(TRISTAR) Producers, Dan Halsted, Clayton Townsend; Director, Oliver Stone; Executive Producer/Screenplay, John Ridley, based on his book *Stray Dogs*; Photography, Robert Richardson; Designer, Victor Kempster; Editors, Hank Corwin, Thomas J. Nordberg; Music, Ennio Morricone; Costumes, Beatrix Aruna Pasztor; Co-Producer, Richard Rutowski; Casting, Mary Vernieu; a Phoenix Pictures presentation of an Illusion Entertainment Group production in association with Clyde is Hungry Films; Dolby SDDS Stereo; Technicolor; Rated R; 125 minutes; October release

CAST

Bobby Cooper............Sean Penn
Jake McKenna............Nick Nolte
Grace McKenna............Jennifer Lopez
Darrell............Billy Bob Thornton
Sheriff Virgil Potter............Powers Boothe
Jenny............Claire Danes
Toby N. Tucker............Joaquin Phoenix
Blind Man............Jon Voight
Bikers............Abraham Benrubi, Richard Rutowski
Jamilla............Aida Linares
Boy in Grocery Store............Sean Stone
Sergi............Ilia Volokh
Mr. Arkady............Valery Nikolaev
Boyd............Brent Briscoe
Ed............Bo Hopkins
Flo............Julie Hagerty
Short Order Cook............Annie Mei-Ling Tien
Grace's Mother............Sheri Foster
Bus Station Clerk............Laurie Metcalf
Girl in Bus Station............Liv Tyler

On his way to Vegas to pay off his gambling debts, Bobby Cooper's car breaks down in a dead end town called Superior, Arizona, where he unwittingly becomes involved with several of its strange inhabitants.

Jennifer Lopez, Sean Penn

Billy Bob Thornton

Nick Nolte

Jon Voight, Sean Penn

Joaquin Phoenix, Claire Danes

Cary Elwes, Alex McArthur, Morgan Freeman

Morgan Freeman

Brian Cox, Cary Elwes, Morgan Freeman

KISS THE GIRLS

(PARAMOUNT) Producers, David Brown, Joe Wizan; Executive Producer, C.O. Erickson; Director, Gary Fleder; Screenplay, David Klass; Based on the novel by James Patterson; Photography, Aaron Schneider; Designer, Nelson Coates; Editors, William Steinkamp, Harvey Rosenstock; Costumes, Abigail Murray; Music, Mark Isham; Casting, Deborah Aquila, Jane Shannon-Smith; a David Brown/Joe Wizan production, presented in association with Rysher Entertainment; Dolby Digital Stereo; Panavision; Deluxe color; Rated R; 119 minutes; October release

CAST

Alex Cross .... Morgan Freeman
Kate Mctiernan .... Ashley Judd
Nick Ruskin .... Cary Elwes
Sikes .... Alex McArthur
Will Rudolph .... Tony Goldwyn
Kyle Craig .... Jay O. Sanders
Sampson .... Bill Nunn
Chief Hatfield .... Brian Cox
Seth Samuel .... Richard T. Jones
Dr. Ruocco .... Roma Maffia
Henry Castillo .... Jeremy Piven
Naomi Cross .... Gina Ravera
Dr. Wick Sachs .... William Converse-Roberts
Nana Cross .... Helen Martin
Janell Cross .... Tatyana M. Ali
Coty Pierce .... Mena A. Suvari
Megan Murphy .... Heidi Schanz
Sgt. Willard .... Rick Warner
Instructor .... Billy Blanks
Jennifer .... Dianna Miranda
and Mary Major, Melinda Renna (TV Reporters), Angel Harper, Alan Wilder, Dan Cashman, Patrick T. O'Brien, Brenda Kincaid, Lonnie McCullough, Larry Cedar, Tresha Rodriguez, Caroline Case (Reporters), Loanne Bishop (Kate's Nurse), Tim Ahern (LAPD Sergeant), W. Earl Brown (Locksmith), Brian Brophy (Swim Team Manager), Michael J. Cutt (FBI Agent—Hospital), Meta Golding, Sadie Kratzig, Brandi Andres, Dana Atwood, Justina Vail, Nichole McAuley (Beautiful Girls), Tricia Vessey (Woman at Nepenthe Bar), John Cothran, Jr. (FBI Agent at Lair), Robert Peters (Agent on Robe), Jill Callaham (Reporter in Durham), Nancy Yee (Chinese Grandmother), Christina Ma (Chinese Mother), David Cowgill (Chief Resident), Weston Blakesley (Bellman), Joe Inscoe (Large Cop), Deborah Strang (Dianne Wainford), Robert Overmyer (Competitive Swimmer), Boise Holmes (Basketball Player)

When detective Alex Cross discovers that his niece has been abducted, he teams with Kate Mctiernan, who has escaped from the same kidnapper, to solve the mystery of the other victims' whereabouts.

Morgan Freeman, Ashley Judd

Jennifer Jason Leigh, Albert Finney

WASHINGTON SQUARE

(HOLLYWOOD PICTURES) Producers, Roger Birnbaum, Julie Bergman Sender; Director, Agnieszka Holland; Screenplay, Carol Doyle; Based on the novel by Henry James; Executive Producer, Randy Ostrow; Photography, Jerzy Zielinski; Designer, Allan Starski; Editor, David Siegel; Costumes, Anna Sheppard; Music, Jan A.P. Kaczmarek; Casting, Debra Zane; a Roger Birnbaum production in association with Ann Dubinet; Presented in association with Caravan Pictures; Distributed by Buena Vista Pictures; Dolby Digital Stereo; Technicolor; Rated PG; 115 minutes; October release

CAST

Catherine Sloper....................Jennifer Jason Leigh
Dr. Austin Sloper....................Albert Finney
Aunt Lavinia Penniman....................Maggie Smith
Morris Townsend....................Ben Chaplin
Mrs. Elizabeth Almond....................Judith Ivey
Mr. Almond....................Arthur Laupus
Marian Almond....................Jennifer Garner
Arthur Townsend....................Robert Stanton
Mrs. Montgomery....................Betsy Brantley
Maureen (Maid)....................Nancy Daly
Catherine Sloper (age 11)....................Sara Ruzicka
Sarah Almond (age 16)....................Rachel Layne Sacrey
Alice Almond (age 17)....................Rachel Osborne
John Ludlow....................Scott Jaeck
Jacob Webber/Notary....................Peter Maloney
Edith....................Lauren Hulsey
Therese (Maid)....................Sara Constance Marshall
Paris Singer....................Marissa Anna Muro
Midwife....................Loretto McNally
Sloper's Cook....................Eva Jean Berg
Engagement Party Pianist....................David Hildebrand
Engagement Party Singer....................James J. Waltz
Engagement Party Guest....................Peter Klaus

Catherine Sloper, the plain and unpopular daughter of a wealthy physician, suddenly finds herself being courted by the handsome Morris Townsend who may or may not be wooing her for her fortune. Henry James' story was previously filmed by Paramount in 1949 as The Heiress (based on the stage play) and starred Olivia de Havilland (Catherine), Montgomery Clift (Morris), and Ralph Richardson (Dr. Sloper).

Ben Chaplin, Jennifer Jason Leigh

Ben Chaplin, Albert Finney

Ben Chaplin, Jennifer Jason Leigh, Maggie Smith

FAST, CHEAP & OUT OF CONTROL

(SONY PICTURES CLASSICS) Producer/Director, Errol Morris; Co-Producers, Julia Sheehan, Mark Lipson, Kathy Trustman; Executive Producer, Lindsay Law; Photography, Robert Richardson; Editors, Shondra Merrill, Karen Schmeer; Designer, Ted Bafaloukos; Music, Caleb Sampson; a Fourth Floor Productions, Inc. production in association with American Playhouse; Color/Black and White; Rated PG; 82 minutes; October release

CAST

Wild Animal Trainer....................Dave Hoover
Topiary Gardner....................George Mendonça
Mole-Rat Specialist....................Ray Mendez
Robot Scientist....................Rodney Brooks

A documentary that looks at the oddball pursuits and professions of four different men.

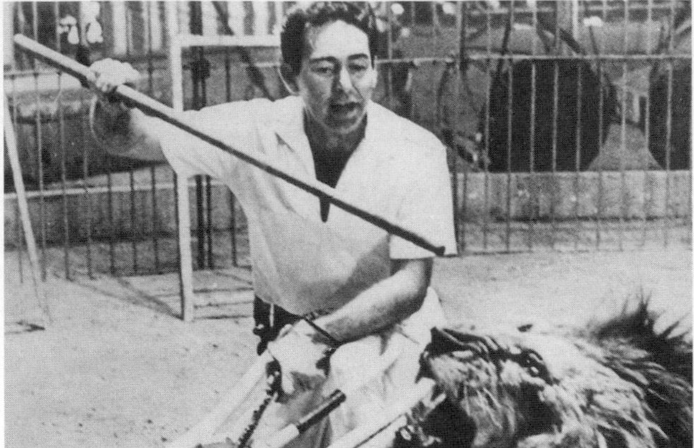

Dave Hoover

George Mendoça

Kate Capshaw, Vince Vaughn

Jeremy Davies, Ashley Judd

THE LOCUSTS

(ORION) Producers, Brad Krevoy, Steve Stabler, Bradley Thomas; Director/Screenplay, John Patrick Kelley; Executive Producers, Adam Duritz, Beth Holden, Charles B. Wessler, Cynthia Guidry; Photography, Phedon Papamichael; Designer, Sherman Williams; Editors, Kathryn Himoff, Erica Flaum; Music, Carter Burwell; Costumes, Gail McMullen; Co-Producers, Bruce Franklin, Marc Ezralow; Line Producer, Garrett Grant; a Brad Krevoy & Steve Stabler production; Dolby Digital Stereo; Super 35 Widescreen; Deluxe color; Rated R; 124 minutes; October release

CAST

Delilah Ashford Potts....................Kate Capshaw
Flyboy....................Jeremy Davies
Clay Hewitt....................Vince Vaughn
Kitty....................Ashley Judd
Earl....................Paul Rudd
Joel....................Daniel Meyer
Patsy....................Jessica Capshaw
Ellen....................Jessie Robertson
Cameron....................Jimmy Pickens
Harlan....................Jerry Haynes
Wrangler....................Jason Davis

Clay Hewitt, a drifter trying to escape from his past, takes a job on a cattle ranch run by the dominant and sensual Mrs. Potts who is responsible for the state of her emotionally crippled son, Flyboy.

SEVEN YEARS IN TIBET

(TRISTAR) Producers, Jean-Jacques Annaud, John H. Williams, Iain Smith; Executive Producers, Richard Goodwin, Michael Besman, David Nichols; Director, Jean-Jacques Annaud; Screenplay, Becky Johnston; Based on the book by Heinrich Harrer; Photography, Robert Fraisse; Designer, At Hoang; Editor, Noële Boisson; Costumes, Enrico Sabbatini; Music, John Williams; Cello Solos by Yo-Yo Ma; Casting, Priscilla John, Francine Maisler; a Mandalay Entertainment presentation of a Reperage and Vanguard Films/Applecross production; Dolby SDDS Stereo; Panavision; Technicolor; Rated PG-13; 131 minutes; October release

CAST

Heinrich Harrer....................Brad Pitt
Peter Aufschnaiter....................David Thewlis
Ngawang Jigme....................B.D. Wong
Kungo Tsarong....................Mako
Regent....................Danny Denzongpa
Chinese "Amban"....................Victor Wong
Ingrid Harrer....................Ingeborga Dapkunaite
Dalai Lama (14 years)....................Jamyang Jamtsho Wangchuk
Pema Lhaki....................Lhakpa Tsamchoe
Great Mother....................Jetsun Pema
Tashi....................Ama Ashe Dongtse
Dalai Lama (8 years)....................Sonam Wangchuk
Dalai Lama (4 years)....................Dorjee Tsering
General Chang Jing Wu....................Ric Young
Lord Chamberlain....................Ven. Ngawang Chojor
British Officer....................Duncan Fraser
Nazi Official....................Benedick Blythe
Lutz Chicken....................Tom Raudaschl
Hans Lobenhoffer....................Wolfgang Tonninger
The Garpon....................Samdup Dhargyal
Garpon's Agent....................Chemchok
Declaration Monk Official....................Ven. Tenzin Jangchub
Tibetan General....................Major Angphurba Sherpa

and Tsering Wangdue, Yama Nugdup Cheshatsang (Burly Guides), Kalsang Dhundop Lungtok (Vendor Ice Skates), Sonam Bidhartsang (Jacket Vendor), Lama Champa Tsondu (Watch Vendor), Geshe Lobsang Nyma (Ling Rinpoche), Geshe Yeshi Tsultrim (Trijang Rinpoche), Lama Champa Chandu (Dalai Lama's Room Attendant), Pemba Norbu Sherpa (Young Sherpa), Karma Apo-Tsang (Messenger to Great Mother), Ven. Ngawang Tenzin Gyatso (Jokhang Monk Official), Choeden Tsering (Military Instructor), Lama Jampa Lekshe (Monk Head of Security), Lama Thupten Nugdup (Head of Security's Aide), Daniel Tedeschi (Marchese), Gerardo Ebert (Horst Immendorf), Sebastian Zevalia (Rolf Harrer—younger), Philipp Kriechbaum (Rolf Harrer—older), Lobsang Gendun Rinpoche, Tenzin Gyaltsen Rinpoche, Sharpa Tulku Rinpoche, Zongra Tulku Rinpoche (Additional Tibetan Roles)

The true story of how Austrian mountaineer Heinrich Harrer escaped from a British prisoner-of-war camp and ended up befriending the young Dalai Lama in the Tibetan city of Lhasa.

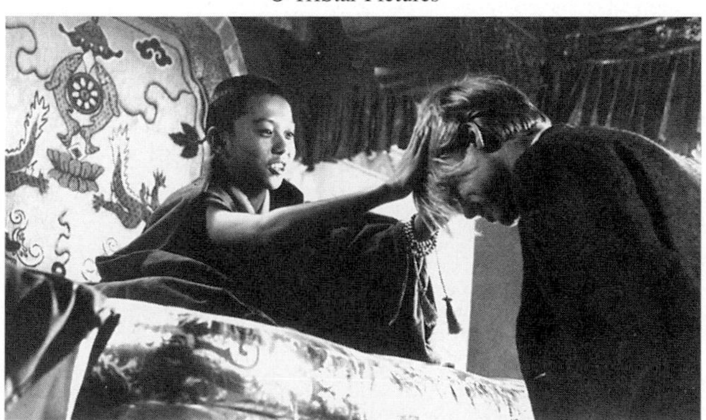

Jamyang Jamtsho Wangchuk, Brad Pitt

David Thewlis, Lhakpa Tsamchoe, Brad Pitt

B.D. Wong

David Thewlis, Brad Pitt

THE HOUSE OF YES

(MIRAMAX) Producers, Beau Flynn, Stefan Simchowitz; Executive Producer, Robert Berger; Director/Screenplay, Mark Waters; Based on the play by Wendy MacLeod; Co-Producers, Ron Wechsler, Jeffrey L. Davidson; Photography, Michael Spiller; Designer, Patrick Sherman; Editor, Pamela Martin; Costumes, Edi Giguere; Music, Rolfe Kent; Co-Executive Producer, Scott Silver; Associate Producer/Casting, Mary Vernieu; a Spelling Films presentation of a Bandeira Entertainment production; Dolby Digital Stereo; CFI color; Rated R; 89 minutes; October release

CAST

Jackie-O Pascal .... Parker Posey
Marty Pascal .... Josh Hamilton
Lesly .... Tori Spelling
Anthony Pascal .... Freddie Prinze, Jr.
Mrs. Pascal .... Genevieve Bujold
Young Jackie-O .... Rachael Leigh Cook
Voice of Young Marty .... David Love

Marty Pascal brings his fiancee Lesly to meet his wildly unconventional family, including his disturbed sister Jackie-O who is obsessed with the Kennedy assassination.

Genevieve Bujold, Tori Spelling

Tori Spelling, Parker Posey, Josh Hamilton, Freddie Prinze Jr.

Keenen Ivory Wayans, Jon Voight

MOST WANTED

(NEW LINE CINEMA) Producer, Eric L. Gold; Executive Producers, Keenen Ivory Wayans, Tony Mark; Director, David Glenn Hogan; Screenplay, Keenen Ivory Wayans; Photography, Marc Reshovsky; Designer, Jean-Philippe Carp; Editors, Michael J. Duthie, Mark Helfrich; Costumes, Ileane Meltzer; Music, Paul Buckmaster; Casting, Valerie McCaffrey; an Ivory Way production; Dolby SDDS Stereo; Super 35 Widescreen; Deluxe color; Rated R; 99 minutes; October release

CAST

Sgt. James Dunn .... Keenen Ivory Wayans
Gen. Adam Woodward/Lt. Col. Grant Casey .... Jon Voight
Dr. Victoria Constantini .... Jill Hennessy
CIA Deputy Director Rackmill .... Paul Sorvino
Asst. Deputy Director Spencer .... Eric Roberts
Donald Bickhart .... Robert Culp
Capt. Steve Braddock .... Wolfgang Bodison
Stephen Barnes .... Simon Baker Denny
SWAT Leader .... Michael Milhoan
Commander Goldstein .... Lee DeBroux
TV Station Manager .... David Groh
Police Captain .... John Diehl
Sergeant .... Thomas G. Waites
Omega 3 .... Michael Marich
Lt. Scruggs .... Dave Oliver
Sgt. Peyton .... Eddie Velez

and Robert Kotecki (Marine Lieutenant), Rick Cramer, Kenn Whitaker (Bus Guards), Donna Cherry (First Lady), Tucker Smallwood (Police Chief William Watson), Amanda Kravat (Charlie), Mario Vitale (Bartender), Ping Wu (Patrolman), Andy Hogan (Video Tech), Casey Lee (Randy), Richard Noyce, Jerry Rector (Policemen in Hospital), Chris Geier (Laundry Orderly), Sasha Foo (Newscaster), Karen Folkes (Checkpoint Officer), Martin Grimes (Hot Dog Vendor), Benny Moore (Man on Street), Kaye Wade (Grocery Woman), L.V. Sanders, Tito Larriva (Gangbangers), Michael D. Roberts (Homeless Man), Vernon P. Thompson (Homeless Camp Police Officer), David Basulto (Library Security Guard), Melanie Van Betten (VA Hospital Clerk), Mitchell Marchand, Antonio T. Arnold, Jr., Ernie Lee Banks (Card Players), Brian Macon (C.I.A. Agent), Christine Devine (Hearing's Reporter)

Awaiting execution for killing an officer in self-defense, Gulf War veteran James Dunn is recruited by a secret government assassination squad called the "Black Sheep" and made to particpate in the killing of a black market industrialist.

I KNOW WHAT YOU DID LAST SUMMER

(COLUMBIA) Producers, Neal H. Moritz, Erik Feig, Stokely Chaffin; Executive Producer, William S. Beasley; Director, Jim Gillespie; Screenplay, Kevin Williamson; Based on the novel by Lois Duncan; Photography, Denis Crossan; Designer, Gary Wissner; Editor, Steve Mirkovich; Music, John Debney; Costumes, Catherine Adair; Casting, Mary Vernieu; a Mandalay Entertainment presentation of a Neal H. Moritz production; Dolby SDDS Stereo; Panavision; Technicolor; Rated R; 100 minutes; October release

CAST

Julie James .... Jennifer Love Hewitt
Helen Shivers .... Sarah Michelle Gellar
Barry Cox .... Ryan Phillippe
Ray Bronson .... Freddie Prinze, Jr.
Benjamin Willis/Fisherman .... Muse Watson
Elsa Shivers .... Bridgette Wilson
Melissa Egan .... Anne Heche
Max .... Johnny Galecki
Officer .... Stuart Greer
MC .... J. Don Ferguson
Mrs. James .... Deborah Hobart
Mrs. Cox .... Mary McMillan
Deb .... Rasool J'Han
Sheriff .... Dan Albright
Pageant Official .... Lynda Clark
Contestants .... Shea Broom, Jennifer Bland
Old Man .... John Bennes
Hank .... William Neely
David Egan .... Jonathan Quint
Band Members .... Richard Dale Miller, Mary Neva Huff, David Lee Hartman

A year after four teenagers secretly dispose of the body of a man they hit during a driving accident, they are taunted and stalked by someone who knows about their dirty deed. 1998 sequel I Still Know What You Did Last Summer also featured Jennifer Love Hewitt and Freddie Prinze, Jr.

Freddie Prinze Jr., Jennifer Love Hewitt, Sarah Michelle Gellar, Ryan Phillippe

Sarah Michelle Gellar, Bridgette Wilson

Sarah Michelle Gellar, Ryan Phillippe, Jennifer Love Hewitt

Sarah Michelle Gellar, Ryan Phillippe, Jennifer Love Hewitt, Freddie Prinze Jr.

Jack Wallace, Ricky Jay, Nicole Ari Parker, Burt Reynolds, William H. Macy, Mark Wahlberg, Julianne Moore, John C. Reilly, Philip Seymour Hoffman

Burt Reynolds, William H. Macy

Mark Wahlberg

Julianne Moore, Mark Wahlberg

John C. Reilly, Mark Wahlberg

BOOGIE NIGHTS

(NEW LINE CINEMA) Producers, Lloyd Levin, Paul Thomas Anderson, John Lyons, Joanne Sellar; Executive Producer, Lawrence Gordon; Director/Screenplay, Paul Thomas Anderson; Co-Producer, Daniel Lupi; Photography, Robert Elswit; Designer, Bob Ziembicki; Editor, Dylan Tichenor; Costumes, Mark Bridges; Music, Michael Penn; Casting, Christine Sheaks; a Lawrence Gordon production in associatiowith Ghoulardi Film Company of a P.T. Anderson Picture; Dolby SDDS Stereo; Panavision; Deluxe color; Rated R; 152 minutes,October Realease

CAST

Buck Swope ....Don Cheadle
Rollergirl ....Heather Graham
Maurice TT Rodriguez ....Luis Guzman
Floyd Gondolli ....Philip Baker Hall
Scotty J. ....Philip Seymour Hoffman
Kurt Longjohn ....Ricky Jay
Little Bill ....William H. Macy
Rahad Jackson ....Alfred Molina
Amber Waves ....Julianne Moore
Becky Barnett ....Nicole Ari Parker
Reed Rothchild ....John C. Reilly
Jack Horner ....Burt Reynolds
The Colonel ....Robert Ridgely
Dirk Diggler (Eddie Adams) ....Mark Wahlberg
Jessie St. Vincent ....Melora Walters
Jerry ....Stanley DeSantis
Eddie's Mother ....Joanna Gleason
Little Bill's Wife ....Nina Hartley
Sheryl Lynn ....Laurel Holloman
Jerome ....Michael Jace
Todd Parker ....Thomas Jane
Mr. Brown ....Howard Morris
Rocky ....Jack Wallace
Bank Worker ....Don Amendolia
Colonel's Limo Driver ....Jason Andrews
Hot Traxx Chef ....Samson Barkhordarian
Big Stud ....Brad Braeden
Sheryl Lynn's Husband ....Kevin Breznahan
Hot Traxx Waiter ....Rico Bueno
Puerto Rican Kid ....Jose Chaidez
Rahad's Asian Kid or Cosmo ....Joe GM Chan
Donut Boy ....Dustin Courtney
Watchers ....Tom Dorfmeister, Jake Cross
Minister ....Gregory Daniel
Thomas ....John Doe
Recording Studio Manager ....Robert Downey, Sr.

and Patricia Forte (Teacher), Jamielyn Gamboa (Colonel's Girflfriend at Hot Traxx), Goliath (Tyrone), Allan Graf (Man with Gun), Laura Greenwood (Angie), Vernon Guichard II (Jack's Bartender), Michael Raye Smith, Mike Gunther, Michael Scott Stencil (Surfer Punks), Veronica Hart (Judge), Lawrence Hudd (Eddie's Father), Amber Hunter (Colonel's O.D. Girlfriend), Ron Hyatt (Jail Guard), B. Philly Johnson (Rahad's Bodyguard), Israel Juarbe, George Anthony Rae (Maurice's Brothers), Raymond Laboriel (Hot Traxx Patron), Greg Lauren (Young Stud), Loren Lazerine (Police Officer), Henry Lee (Tailor), Lexi Leigh (Amateur Actress), Thomas Lenk (Tommy), Kai Lennox (High School Kid), Selwyn Emerson Miller (Hot Traxx DJ), Michael Penn (Recording Studio Engineer), Jonathan Quint (Johnny Doe), George Anthony Rae (Maurice's Brother #2), Leslie Redden (KC Sunshine), Jack Riley (Lawyer), Channon Roe (Surfer), Skye, Summer (Jacuzzi Girls), Alexander D. Slanger (Pete), Melissa Spell (Becky's Friend in Hot Traxx), Mike Stein (Super-Duper Customer), Tony Tedeschi (New Year's Eve Young Stud), Eric Winzenried (Doctor), Jody Wood (Pedestrian), Sharon Ferrol, Anne Fletcher, Scott Fowler, Melanie A. Gage, Eddie Garcia, Sebastian LaCause, Lance MacDonald, Diane Mizota, Nathan Frederic Prevost, Lisa E. Ratzin, Dee Dee Weathers, Darrel W. Wright (Hot Traxx Dancers)

In the late 1970's, during the height of the disco and drug era, naive Eddie Adams rises to the top as male porn star Dirk Diggler, helped by his unusually large physical endowment. This film received Oscar nominations for supporting actor (Burt Reynolds), supporting actress (Julianne Moore), and original screenplay.

Mark Wahlberg, Burt Reynolds

Heather Graham

Don Cheadle

PLAYING GOD

(TOUCHSTONE) Producers, Marc Abraham, Laura Bickford; Executive Producers, Armyan Bernstein, Thomas A. Bliss; Co-Producers, Melanie Greene, Nancy Rae Stone; Director, Andy Wilson; Screenplay, Mark Haskell Smith; Photography, Anthony B. Richmond; Designer, Naomi Shohan; Editor, Louise Rubacky; Music, Richard Hartley; Costumes, Mary Zophres; Casting, Johanna Ray, Elaine J. Huzzar; Presented in association with Beacon Pictures; Distributed by Buena Vista Pictures; Dolby Digital Stereo; Technicolor; Rated R: 93 minutes; October release

CAST

Dr. Eugene Sands....David Duchovny
Raymond Blossom....Timothy Hutton
Claire....Angelina Jolie
Gage....Michael Massee
Vladimir....Peter Stormare
Cyril....Andrew Tiernan
Yates....Gary Dourdan
Flick....John Hawkes
Perry....Will Foster Stewart
Casey....Philip Moon
Andrei....Pavel D. Lynchnikoff
Jim....Tracey Walter
Sue....Sandra Kinder
Jerry....Bill Rosier
Mr. Hsi....Keone Young
Digiacomo....Eric DaRe
Phelps....Gareth Williams
Adonis....Teo

and Stacey Travis (Nurse), Max Lazar (Dimitri), Frank Ensign (Len), Bob A. Jennings (Dr. Clifford), Ross Kettle (Resident Surgeon), Nikki Lee (Anaesthesiologist), John Roselius (Surgeon #1), Damon White (Winston), Dan Hildebrand, J.P. Jones, Jerry Sloan (Russian Thugs), Alphonse V. Walter (Isaac), Melvin Jones (Rasta Doorman), Mara Duronslet (Jessica), Ernest Garcia (Burt), Alex Desert (Bartender), Sarah Stavrou (Woman), Jesse Perez (Crack Dealer), Daniel Rey Silvas (Basketball Player), Michael Chong (Chinese Security Guard #2), Alexander Folk (South African Businessman), Stella Garcia (South American Businesswoman), Guy Siner (Dutch Businessman), Al Ahlf (FBI Agent)

A surgeon, stripped of his medical license, becomes the personal doctor of a ruthless criminal, treating associates of his who cannot risk being taken to a hospital.

David Duchovny

Angelina Jolie, Timothy Hutton

Nick Stahl, Martha Plimpton

EYE OF GOD

(CASTLE HILL) Producers, Wendy Ettinger, Michael Nelson; Director/Screenplay, Tim Blake Nelson; Photography, Russell Lee Fine; Designer, Patrick Geary; Editor, Kate Sanford; Music, David Van Tieghem; a Minnow Pictures presentation; Color; Not rated; 84 minutes; October release

CAST

Ainsley Dupree....Martha Plimpton
Jack Stillings....Kevin Anderson
Sheriff Rogers....Hal Holbrook
Tom Spencer....Nick Stahl
Willard Sprague....Richard Jenkins
Claire Spencer....Mary Kay Place
Les Hector....Chris Freihofer
Glen Briggs....Woody Watson
Dorothy....Margo Martindale
R.J. Prichard....Wally Welch
Jim Nutter....Larry Flynn
Janice....Maggie Moore
Fast Food Customer....Vernon Grote
Lee....Gary Ragland
Mrs. Rogers....Caroline Wickwire

and Toby Metcalf, Darryl Cox (Officers), Karen Carney (Mrs. Sprague), Robert Peters (Del), Lisa Benavides (Nurse), Gail Peister (Doctor)

Short order cook Ainsley Dupree agrees to marry ex-con Jack Stillings who has converted to Christianity while serving time in jail. In a parallel storyline, 14-year-old Tom Spencer has been discovered by the police wandering about in a state of shock after witnessing a violent crime.

TELLING LIES IN AMERICA

(BANNER ENTERTAINMENT) Producers, Ben Myron, Fran Kuzui; Executive Producers, Brian Swardstrom, Mickey Liddell, Naomi Eszterhas; Director, Guy Ferland; Screenplay, Joe Eszterhas; Co-Producer, Fred Caruso; Co-Executive Producer, Kaz Kazui; Photography, Reynaldo Villalobos; Designer, James Gelarden; Music, Nicholas Pike; Editor, Jill Savitt; Costumes, Laura Cunningham; Casting, Emily Schweber, Susan Brown; a Joe Eszterhas presentation in association with Kuzui Enterprises and Ben Myron productions; Dolby Stereo; Super 35 Widescreen; Color; Rated PG-13; 101 minutes; October release

CAST

Billy Magic....Kevin Bacon
Karchy Jonas....Brad Renfro
Dr. Istvan Jonas....Maximilian Schell
Diney Majeski....Calista Flockhart
Father Norton....Paul Dooley
Kevin Boyle....Jonathan Rhys Meyers
Henry....Luke Wilson
Amos....Damen Fletcher
Andy "Croak" Stas....Jerry Swindall
Justine....K.K. Dodds
Cecil Simms....James Kisicki
The Blind Kid....J.J. Horna
Timmy Morelli....Ben Saypol
Danny Hogan....Tony Devon
Sgt. Disapri....Rohn Thomas
Det. Carpenter....Joe Baka
WHK Receptionist....Tuesday Knight
WHK Newscaster....Dave Buckel
Assistant D.A.....Matt Miller
Immigration Judge....Jack Skelley
Groupies....Jane Jean Miller, Wendy Waltz
Giggly Girl....Angelique Osborne
Old Man....Abdullah Bey
Driver....Kevin Willigham
School Kid....Patrick White

In early 1960's Cleveland, struggling high school student Karchy Jonas becomes the friend and protege of smooth radio DJ Billy Magic who introduces the impressionable young lad to the highly desirable world of music, cars, and women.

Brad Renfro, Kevin Bacon

Brad Renfro, Calista Flockhart

Brad Renfro, Maximilian Schell

Kevin Bacon

GATTACA

(COLUMBIA) Producers, Danny DeVito, Michael Shamberg, Stacey Sher; Director/Screenplay, Andrew Niccol; Photography, Slawomir Idziak; Designer, Jan Roelfs; Editor, Lisa Zeno Churgin; Costumes, Colleen Atwood; Music, Michael Nyman; Co-Producer, Gail Lyon; Casting, Francine Maisler; a Jersey Films production; Dolby SDDS Stereo; Super 35 Widescreen; Technicolor; Rated PG-13; 112 minutes; October release

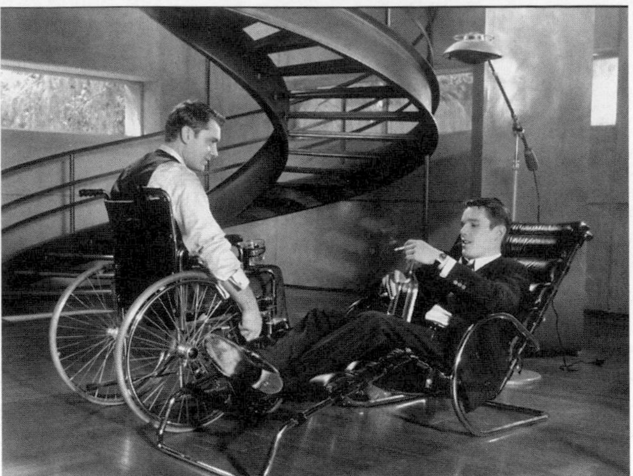

Jude Law, Ethan Hawke

CAST

Vincent Freeman (Jerome) .... Ethan Hawke
Irene .... Uma Thurman
Detective Hugo .... Alan Arkin
Jerome Eugene Morrow (Eugene) .... Jude Law
Anton .... Loren Dean
Director Josef .... Gore Vidal
Caesar .... Ernest Borgnine
Geneticist .... Blair Underwood
Lamar .... Xander Berkeley
German .... Tony Shalhoub
Marie .... Jayne Brook
Antonio .... Elias Koteas
Delivery Nurse .... Maya Rudolph
Head Nurse .... Una Damon
Pre-School Teacher .... Elizabeth Dennehy
Younger Vincent .... Mason Gamble
Younger Anton .... Vincent Nielson
Young Vincent .... Chad Christ
Young Anton .... William Lee Scott
Personnel Officer .... Clarence Graham
Gattaca Hoover .... Carlton Benbry

and Grace Sullivan (Sequencing Customer), Ken Marino (Sequencing Technician), Cynthia Martells (Cavendish), Gabrielle Reece (Gattaca Trainer), Ryan Dorin (Twelve Fingered Pianist), Dean Norris (Cop on the Beat), Russell Milton (Gattaca Detective), George Marshall Ruge (Beaten Detective), Steve Bessen (Blood Test Detective), Lindsey Lee Ginter (Mission Commander)

In the 21st Century, where people who were genetically designed are considered superior, Vincent Freeman, an "In-Valid" who was conceived in love, tries to hide his identity in order to become an astronaut. This film received an Oscar nomination for art direction.

Uma Thurman

Ethan Hawke, Gore Vidal

Loren Dean, Alan Arkin

FAIRY TALE: A TRUE STORY

(PARAMOUNT) Producers, Wendy Finerman, Bruce Davey; Executive Producer, Paul Tucker; Director, Charles Sturridge; Screenplay, Ernie Contreras; Story, Albert Ash, Tom McLoughlin, Ernie Contreras; Photography, Michael Coulter; Designer, Michael Howells; Editor, Peter Coulson; Co-Producers, Selwyn Roberts, Tom McLouglin, Albert Ash; Visual Effects Supervisor, Tim Webber; Music, Zbigniew Preisner; Costumes, Shirley Russell; Casting, Mary Selway, Sarah Trevis; an Icon Productions/Wendy Finerman production; U.S.-British; Dolby Stereo; Deluxe color; Rated PG-13; 99 minutes; October release

CAST

Elsie Wright .... Florence Hoath
Frances Griffiths .... Elizabeth Earl
Arthur Wright .... Paul McGann
Polly Wright .... Phoebe Nicholls
Sir Arthur Conan Doyle .... Peter O'Toole
Harry Houdini .... Harvey Keitel
James Collins .... Jason Salkey
Jean Doyle .... Lara Morgan
Adrian Doyle .... Adam Franks
Denis Doyle .... Guy Witcher
Houdini's Assistant .... Joseph May
Portly Gentleman .... John Bradley
Peter Pan .... Anna Chancellor
Stage Manager .... Leonard Kavanagh
Wounded Corporal .... Anton Lesser
Harry Briggs .... Bob Peck
Mrs. Thornton .... Lynn Farleigh
Lucy .... Sarah Marsden
Judith .... Tara Marie
Margie .... Alannah McGahan
Edward Gardner .... Bill Nighy
John Ferret .... Tim McInnerny
Sergeant Farmer .... Peter Mullan
Albert, the Postman .... Jim Wiggins
Harold Snelling .... David Calder
Geoffrey Hodson .... Anthony Calf

and John Grillo (Mr. West), Benjamin Whitrow (Mr. Binley), Dick Brannick (News Vendor), Barbara Hicks (City Woman), Christopher Godwin (City Businessman), Andrew Cryer, Paul Popperwell (Soldiers), David Norman (O'Neill), Matilda Sturridge (Dorothy), Charlotte Champness (Alice), Anna Ramsey (Charlotte), Peter Wright (Newspaper Editor), Willie Ross (Old Print Worker), Ina Clough (Lady calling to Fairies), Carol Noakes (Station Photographer), Stephen Chapman (Boy in Hospital), Bill Stewart (Chess MC), Don Henderson (Sydney Chalker), Stewart Howson (Red-Faced Man), James Danaher (Joseph Wright), Martin Gent (Pushy Photographer), Anthony Collin (Older Photographer), Tom Georgeson, Angus Barnett (Reporters), Mel Gibson (Frances' Father); The Fairies: Suzy Barton (Lutey), Ali Bastian (Lull), Anna Brecon (Elabigathe), Sean Buckley (Mr. Bandylegs), Lindsey Butcher (Tib), Norma Cohen (Nanny Button Cap), Matt Costain (Prince Malekin), Philip Fowler (Fenoderee), Katie Gibbon (Pinket), Sophy Griffiths (Sib), Sara Li Gustafsson (Loireag), Tara Kemp (Gull), William Lawrance (Tom Cockle), Caleb Lloyd (Lob), Marianne Melhus (Florella), Genevieve Monastesse (Morgana), Simon Penman (Peerifool), Briony Plant (Yarthkins), Anna-Louise Plowman (Shellycoat), Jane Read-Wilson (Asrai), Isabel Rocamora (Queen Mab), Thomas Sturridge (Hob), Mark Tate (Habetrot), Hayley Tibbins (Patch)

In 1917 England cousins Frances Griffiths and Elsie Wright become the center of controversy after insisting that they have photographed actual fairies.

Florence Hoath, Harvey Keitel

Elizabeth Earl

Elizabeth Earl, Florence Hoath, Peter O'Toole

RED CORNER

(MGM) Producers, Jon Avnet, Jordan Kerner, Charles B. Mulvehill, Rosalie Swedlin; Executive Producers, Wolfgang Petersen, Gail Katz; Director, Jon Avent; Screenplay, Robert King; Photography, Karl Walter Lindenlaub; Designer, Richard Sylbert; Editor, Peter E. Berger; Costumes, Albert Wolsky; Music, Thomas Newman; Co-Producers, Martin Huberty, Lisa Lindstrom; Casting, David Rubin; an Avnet/Kerner production; Dolby DTS Stereo; Deluxe color; Rated R; 122 minutes; October release

CAST

Jack Moore....Richard Gere
Shen Yuelin....Bai Ling
Bob Ghery....Bradley Whitford
Lin Dan....Byron Mann
David McAndrews....Peter Donat
Ed Pratt....Robert Stanton
Chariman Xu....Tsai Chin
Lin Shou....James Hong
Li Cheng....Tzi Ma
Gerhardt Hoffman....Ulrich Matschoss
Ambassador Reed....Richard Venture
Hong Ling....Jessey Meng
Huan Minglu....Roger Yuan
General Hong....Li Chi Yu

and Henry O. (Procurator General Yang), Li Jia Yao (Director Liu), Lu Yukun (Director Liu's Associate), Robert Lin (Director Liu's Interpreter), Steve Beebe (Disco DJ), Wei De Zhong, Grace Zhan (Beijing Opera Performers), Yvonne Wang (Disco Waitress), Gao Qiang (PSB Captain), Gao Xiao-Hua, Yao Wang (PSB Arresting Officers), Gu Xiao Yang, Hans Hanbo Cui (Prison Guards), Zong Ping (Captain Feng), Lei Yin (Feng's Assistant), Paul Chen (Visitor's Room Official), Jeffrey Dong (Prison Doctor), Jian Rui Chao (Yuelin's Aide), Daxing Zhang (Procurator Ma), Ding Yi Wang (Procurator Ma's Assistant), Lily L. Lin (People's Housewife Assessor), Mike Wu (People's Accountant Assessor), Bing Yang, Hua Wahrman (Court Interpreters), Ming Lo (Medical Examiner), Ken Leung (Peng), Liu Baifang (Chinese TV Reporter), Danny Wang (PSB Escort), Kenny Ki (Guard at Hotel Door), Jack C. Huang (Guard at Phone Center), Mei-Juin Chen (Phone Clerk), Jin Zheng Hui (Phone Center Supervisor), Kent Faulcon (Marine Guard)

Attorney Jack Moore, in China to close a deal for a large entertainment conglomerate, spends a night with a beautiful woman only to wake up accused of her murder.

Richard Gere, Bai Ling

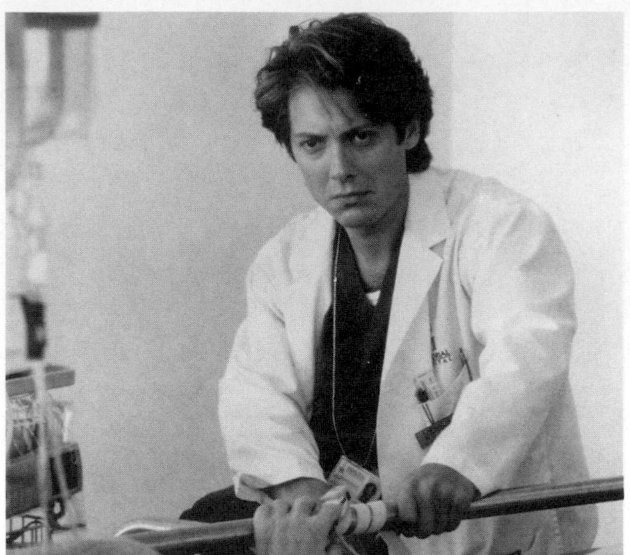

James Spader

CRITICAL CARE

(LIVE ENTERTAINMENT) Producers, Steven Schwartz, Sidney Lumet; Executive Producer, Don Carmody; Director, Sidney Lumet; Screenplay, Steven Schwartz; Based on the book by Richard Dooling; Executive in Charge of Production, Yalda Tehranian; Photography, David Watkin; Designer, Philip Rosenberg; Costumes, Dona Granata; Editor, Tom Swartwout; Music, Michael Convertino; Casting, Avy Kaufman; a LIVE Film and Mediaworks production, presented in association with Village Roadshow-ASQA Film Partnership; Dolby Digital Stereo; Color; Rated R; 109 minutes; October release

CAST

Dr. Werner Ernst....James Spader
Felicia Potter....Kyra Sedgwick
Stella....Helen Mirren
Nun....Anne Bancroft
Dr. Butz....Albert Brooks
Bed Two....Jeffrey Wright
Connie Potter....Margo Martindale
Furnaceman....Wallace Shawn
Dr. Hofstader....Philip Bosco
Wilson....Colm Feore
Robert Payne....Edward Herrmann
Poindexter....James Lally
Judge Fatale....Harvey Atkin
Sheldon Hatchett....Al Waxman
Hansen....Hamish McEwan
Mrs. Steckler....Jackie Richardson

and Barbara Eve Harris (E.R. Nurse), Conrad Coates (Dr. Miller), Bruno Dessler (Potter), Caroline Nielson (Luscious Nurse), Gladys O'Conner (Bed One), Kay Hawtry (Dr. Butz's Secretary), Don Carmody (Matire D'), Kim Roberts, Naomi Blicker (Interns), Merwin Mondesir (Head Injury), Bruce Hemmings (Orderly), Paul Brown (Insurance Man), Michael Colton (The Boy)

A young second-resident assigned to the Intensive Care Unit finds himself in the middle of a battle between two sisters over whether their father should be disconnected from his life support unit.

SWITCHBACK

(PARAMOUNT) Producer, Gale Anne Hurd; Executive Producers, Keith Samples, Mel Efros, Jeb Stuart; Director/Screenplay, Jeb Stuart; Photography, Oliver Wood; Designer, Jeff Howard; Editor, Conrad Buff; Music, Basil Poledouris; Costumes, Betsy Heimann; Stunts, Jeff Habberstad; Casting, Pam Dixon Mickelson; a Rysher Entertainment presentation of a Pacific Western Production; Dolby Digital Stereo; Panavision; Deluxe color; Rated R; 121 minutes; October release

Jared Leto, Danny Glover

CAST

Bob Goodall .... Danny Glover
Frank LaCrosse .... Dennis Quaid
Lane Dixon .... Jared Leto
Sheriff Buck Olmstead .... R. Lee Ermey
Police Chief Jack McGinnis .... William Fichtner
Deputy Sheriff Nate Booker .... Ted Levine
Babysitter .... Claudia Stedelin
Andy LaCrosse .... Ian Nelson
Man on Porch .... Brent Hinkley
Bud .... Walt Goggins
Sim .... Louis Schaefer
Rancher .... Robert L. Somers
Rancher's Daughter .... Lexie Stuart
Bartender .... Ted Markland
Rick .... Gregory Scott Cummins
Ben .... Tommy Puett
Luke .... Stuart Grant
Morgue Attendant .... Ken Thorley
Highway Patrol Captain .... Pat Mahoney
Deputy .... Michael K. Osborn
Sally .... Wendelin Harston
SWAT Leader .... Dean Hallo
Saldez .... Orville Stoeber
Police Captain .... Robert Himber
Cook .... Bill Rodgers

and Roy Yearby (Truck Driver), Allorah Creevay (Wiatress), Maggie Roswell (Fae), Gil Colon (Deputy), Allison Smith (Becky), Julio Oscar Mechoso (Jorge Martinez), Kevin Cooney (Montgomery), Leo Burmester (Shorty), Merle Kennedy (Betty), Donnie L. Betts (Patrolman), Stan Parks (FBI Agent), Ben Fuhrman (Captain Heber), Lois Hicks (Ruth), Gary Giem (Al), Mark Curry (Robby), Martin David Boyd (Hank), Kevin Bartlett (Tate), Vern Porter (Cubby), Leigh Reyburn (Woman in Bar), Lionel Douglas, Paul Parducci (Men in Shower), Kristin McCloskey (News Anchor), Trishia Springer (Reporter), Keith Hatten (Brakeman Ray), Sandy Ward (Tex), Silan Smith, Jim Clark (Engineers), Christopher Michael, Robert Peters (Colorado Troopers), Joe Alphasa (Small Mexican Man)

FBI agent Frank LaCrosse becomes determined to catch the person responsible for a cross-country murder spree after the suspect kidnaps LaCrosse's young son.

Dennis Quaid

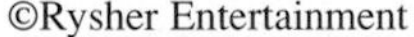

Danny Glover, Jared Leto

Dennis Quaid

Casper Van Dien

Patrick Muldoon

Casper Van Dien, Denise Richards, Neil Patrick Harris

STARSHIP TROOPERS

(TRISTAR) Producers, Jon Davison, Alan Marshall; Co-Producers, Phil Tippett, Ed Neumeier, Frances Doel, Stacy Lumbrezer; Director, Paul Verhoeven; Screenplay, Ed Neumeier; Based on the novel by Robert A. Heinlein; Designer, Allan Cameron; Editors, Mark Goldblatt, Caroline Ross; Costumes, Ellen Mirojnick; Music, Basil Poledouris; Special Visual Effects, Industrial Light & Magic; Spaceship Visual Effects Supervisor, Scott E. Anderson; ILM Visual Effects Supervisor, Scott Squires; Visual Effects Director of Photography, Alex Funke; Creature Visual Effects, The Tippet Studio; Spaceship Visual Effects, Sony Pictures Imageworks Inc.; Full Scale Creature Effects, Alec Gillis, Tom Woodruff Jr./Amalgamated Dynamics Inc.; Casting, Johanna Ray, Elaine J. Huzzar; a co-presentation of Touchstone Pictures, of a Jon Davison production; Dolby SDDS Stereo; Technicolor; Rated R; 129 minutes; November release

CAST

Johnny Rico....................Casper Van Dien
Dizzy Flores....................Dina Meyer
Carmen Ibanez....................Denise Richards
Ace Levy....................Jake Busey
Carl Jenkins....................Neil Patrick Harris
Sgt. Zim....................Clancy Brown
Sugar Watkins....................Seth Gilliam
Zander Barcalow....................Patrick Muldoon
Jean Rasczak....................Michael Ironside
Biology Teacher....................Rue McClanahan
General Owen....................Marshall Bell
Breckinridge....................Eric Bruskotter
Kitten Smith....................Matt Levin
Katrina....................Blake Lindsley
Shujimi....................Anthony Ruivivar
Captain Deladier....................Brenda Strong
Commanding Officer....................Dean Norris
Mr. Rico....................Christopher Curry
Mrs. Rico....................Lenore Kasdorf
Djana'D....................Tami-Adrian George
Corporal Bronski....................Teo
Lt. Willy....................Steven Ford
Corporal Birdie....................Ungela Brockman
Sgt. Gillespie....................Curnal Aulisio

and Greg Travis (Net Correspondent), Bruce Gray (Sky Marshall Dienes), Denise Dowse (Sky Marshall Meru), John Cunningham (Fed Net Announcer), Julianna McCarthy, Timothy McNeil (Experts), Robert David Hall (Recruiting Sergeant), Brad Kane (Lanny), Amy Smart (Pilot Cadet), Timothy Omundson (Psychic), Patrick Bishop (Engineering Officer), Hunter Bodine (Young Cap Trooper), Travis Lowen (Little Boy Trooper), Patrick Wolff (Late Cadet), Mara Duronslet (Communications Officer), Dale A. Dye (General), Michael Stokey (Officer with Morita), Tyrone Tann (Student), Matt Entriken (Marco), Eric Dare (Medic), Ronald L. Botchan (Jumpball Referee), Walter Adrian (Judge), Stephanie Erb (Young Mother), Alexi Lakatos, Nathaniel Marshall, Austin Sanderford, Rhiannon Vigil (Stomping Kids), Mylin Brooks, Armand Darius, Kai Lennox (Troopers)

In the distant future a group of young soldiers are trained to do battle with gigantic alien bugs, intent on wiping out the human race. This film received an Oscar nomination for visual effects.

Lynn Whitfield, Debbi Morgan

Jake Smollett, Meagan Good, Lynn Whitfield, Jurnee Smollett

Jurnee Smollett, Samuel L. Jackson

Jurnee Smollett, Diahann Carroll

EVE'S BAYOU

(TRIMARK) Producers, Caldecot Chubb, Samuel L. Jackson; Executive Producers, Eli Selden, Nick Wechsler, Julie Silverman Yorn; Director/Screenplay, Kasi Lemmons; Co-Executive Producers, Michael Bennett, Margaret Matheson; Co-Producers, Cevin Cathell, Jay Polstein, Cami Winikoff; Photography, Amy Vincent; Designer, Jeff Howard; Editor, Terilyn A. Shropshire; Costumes, Karyn Wagner; Music, Terence Blanchard; Casting, Jaki Brown-Karman, Robyn M. Mitchell; a Chubbco/Addis Wechsler production; Dolby SDDS Stereo; Color; Rated R; 109 minutes; November release

CAST

Eve Batiste .... Jurnee Smollett
Cisely Batiste .... Meagan Good
Louis Batiste .... Samuel L. Jackson
Roz Batiste .... Lynn Whitfield
Mozelle Batiste Delacroix .... Debbi Morgan
Poe Batiste .... Jake Smollett
Gran Mere .... Ethel Ayler
Elzora .... Diahann Carroll
Julian Grayraven .... Vondie Curtis Hall
Lenny Mereaux .... Roger Guenveur Smith
Matty Mereaux .... Lisa Nicole Carson
Harry Delacroix .... Branford Marsalis
Henrietta .... Afonda Colbert
Lynette .... Lola Dalferes
Hosea .... Marcus Lyle Brown
Paige .... Alverta Perkins Dunigan
Vendor .... Ron Flagge
Hilary .... Sharon K. London
Madame Renard .... Carol Sutton
Stevie Hobbs .... Victoria Rowell
Bus Driver .... Oneal A. Isaac
Bartender .... Julian Dalcour
Maynard .... Leonard Thomas
Proprietor .... Allen Toussaint
Ghost of Original Eve .... Billie Neal
Narrator .... Tamara Tunie

In a Louisiana backwater town of the 1960s, ten-year-old Eve Batiste sees her family being torn apart by her father's infidelities.

ANASTASIA

(20TH CENTURY FOX) Producers/Directors, Don Bluth, Gary Goldman; Executive Producer, Maureen Donley; Screenplay, Susan Gauthier, Bruce Graham, Bob Tzudiker, Noni White; Based on the play by Marcelle Maurette as adapted by Guy Bolton and the screenplay by Arthur Laurents; Animation Adaptation, Eric Tuchman; Music Score, David Newman; Songs by Lynn Ahrens (lyrics) and Stephen Flaherty (music); Casting, Brian Chavanne; Directing Animators, Len Simon, John Hill, Troy Saliba, Fernando Moro, Sandro Cleuzo, Paul Newberry; Color Key Styling, Richard C. Bentham, Kenneth Valentine Slevin; Character Layout & Design, Chris Schouten; Production Designer, Mike Peraza; Conceptual Artis, Suzanne Lemieux Wilson; Pre Production Design, John Lakey; Storyboard Artists, Larry Leker, Joe Oranntia, Chip Pace, Jay Schultz, Ferran Xalabarder; a Fox Family Films presentation; Dolby Digital Stereo; Cinemascope; Technicolor; Rated G; 90 minutes; November release

VOICE CAST

Anastasia....Meg Ryan
Dimitri....John Cusack
Vladimir....Kelsey Grammer
Rasputin....Christopher Lloyd
Bartok....Hank Azaria
Sophie....Bernadette Peters
Young Anastasia....Kirsten Dunst
Dowager Empress Marie....Angela Lansbury
Singing Voice of Anastasia....Liz Callaway
Singing Voice of Young Anastasia....Lacey Chabert
Singing Voice of Rasputin....Jim Cummings
Singing Voice of Dimitri....Jonathan Dokuchitz
Czar Nicholas/Servant/ Revolutionary
Soldier/Ticket Agent....Rick Jones
Phlegmenkoff/Old Woman....Andrea Martin
Actress....Debra Mooney
Travelling Man/Major Domo....Arthur Malet
Anastasia Impostor....Charity Jones

In 1920s Russia a pair of con-men hope to pass off a young girl as Anastasia, the surviving child of the murdered royal family. Previous film version was released by 20th Century-Fox in 1956 and starred Ingrid Bergman, Yul Brynner and Helen Hayes. This film received Oscar nominations for song ("Journey to the Past") and original musical or comedy score.

Dimitri, Anastasia, Vladimir

Rasputin, Bartok

Dimitri, Anastasia

THE JACKAL

(UNIVERSAL) Producers, James Jacks, Sean Daniel, Michael Caton-Jones, Kevin Jarre; Executive Producers, Terence Clegg, Hal Lieberman, Gary Levinsohn, Mark Gordon; Director, Michael Caton-Jones; Screen Story and Screenplay, Chuck Pfarrer; Based on the motion picture screenplay *The Day of the Jackal* by Kenneth Ross, from the novel by Frederick Forsythe; Photography, Karl Walter Lindenlaub; Designer, Michael White; Editor, Jim Clark; Costumes, Albert Wolsky; Music, Carter Burwell; Casting, Ellen Chenoweth; a Mutual Film Company presentation of an Alphaville production; Dolby DTS Stereo; Panavision; Deluxe color; Rated R; 123 minutes; November release

CAST

The Jackal .... Bruce Willis
Declan Mulqueen .... Richard Gere
Carter Preston .... Sidney Poitier
Valentina Koslova .... Diane Venora
Isabella .... Mathilda May
Witherspoon .... J.K. Simmons
McMurphy .... Richard Lineback
Donald Brown .... John Cunningham
Lamont .... Jack Black
The First Lady .... Tess Harper
Woolburton .... Leslie Phillips
Douglas .... Stephen Spinella
Jamaican Girl .... Sophie Okonedo
Terek Murad .... David Hayman
George Decker .... Steve Bassett
Politovsky .... Yuri Stepanov
Dennehey .... Walt MacPherson
Ghazzi Murad .... Ravil Isyanov
13 Year Old Girl .... Maggie Castle
Speaker .... Karen Kirschenbauer
Surgeon General .... Terrence Currier
Akashi .... Daniel Dae Kim
Man in Video .... Michael Caton-Jones
Woman in Video .... Laura Viederman
Vasilov .... Peter Sullivan
General Belinko .... Richard Cubison
Green Beret Colonel .... Jim Grimshaw
Paramedic .... Greg Miller
Ambassador Koldin .... Bob Kingdom
NSC Rep .... Murphy Guyer
Bored Teenage Clerk .... Philip Le Maistre
Beaufres .... Serge Houde

and James McCauley, Daniel Ziskie (CIA Reps), Terry Loughlin (Davis), Victor Sobchak (Doctor), Serge Christiaenssens (Immigration Officer), Boris Boscovic (Interrogator), Ewan Bailey (Prison Guard), Danette Alberico, Debra Gano (Women with Champagne), John Bland (Dave), Pamela Poitier (Law Clerk), Jonathan Aris (Alexander Radzinski), Eddie "Bo" Smith, Jr. (Washington Cop), Larry King (Himself), Gayle Jessup (Reporter), Bill Collins (Medic), David Gene Gibbs (Pilot), James M. Helkey (Co-Pilot)

The FBI enlists the aide of imprisoned underground operative Declan Mulqueen to help them track down a cold-blooded assassin named "The Jackal" and find out his intended target before it is too late. Previous version was the 1973 Universal release The Day of the Jackal which starred Edward Fox.

Richard Gere

Bruce Willis

Sidney Poitier, Richard Gere

ONE NIGHT STAND

(NEW LINE CINEMA) Producers, Mike Figgis, Annie Stewart, Ben Myron; Executive Producer, Robert Engelman; Co-Executive Producers, Michael DeLuca, Richard Saperstein; Director/Screenplay/Music, Mike Figgis; Photography, Declan Quinn; Designer, Waldemar Kalinowski; Editor, John Smith; Costumes, Laura Goldsmith, Enid Harris; Casting, Nancy Foy; a Red Mullet production; Dolby SDDS Stereo; Deluxe color; Rated R; 103 minutes; November release

CAST

Max Carlyle .... Wesley Snipes
Karen .... Nastassja Kinski
Mimi .... Ming-Na Wen
Charlie .... Robert Downey, Jr.
Vernon .... Kyle MacLachlan
Young Charlie .... Marcus Paulk
Saffron .... Natalie Trott
Charlie's Father .... John Calley
George .... Glenn Plummer
Margaux .... Amanda Donohoe
Mickey .... Zoe Nathenson
Don .... Thomas Haden Church
Nathan .... Vincent Ward
Phil .... John Ratzenberger
Merv .... Thomas Kopache
Marie .... Annabelle Gurwitch
Malinda .... Susan Barnes
Malissa .... Michelle Jonas
Receptionist .... Margaret Makinen
Hotel Clerk .... Mike Figgis
Nurse Chris .... Julian Sands
Kevin .... Donovan Leitch

and Edita Brychta, Hans Tester, Richard Paradise, Joe Drago (Karen's Business Associates), Johanna Torell (Doctor Olsson), Ione Skye, Xander Berkeley, Greta Gaines (Charlie's Friends), Crystal Pite (Title Dance Sequence and Featured Dancer), Christopher Bauer (Bartender), Anne Lambton, Nick Sandow (Muggers), Michela Zanchi, Tiffany Hecht (Armani Women), Bill Raymond (Gridlock Taxi Driver), Tracy Thorne (Helicopter Traffic Woman), Oscar Conlon, Ahmed Ben Larby (Delegates in Line), Saffron Burrows (Supermodel), Robie Yamamoto (Featured Male Model), Tracey Stockwell, Caroline Hepburn, Sheetel Bhagat, Jesus Yinh, Emily Hseih, Sabrina Van Tassel, Cleveland Mitchell, Lisa Ann Cabasa, Kort Anderson, Michael Pauldine, Karis Jagger, Johanna Torrel, Freeman White (Armani Models), Stacey Elder, Heidi Komarek, Nelle Dreyer, Michelle Merkin (Agency Models), Chris Edwards, Richard Caselnova, Jeffrey Howard Kaufman (Policemen), Joseph John Scott (Flower Vendor), Trula Marcus (Party Guest), Tava Smiley (Hotel Receptionist), David Acosta (Caterer), Aixa Maldonado (Caterer's Assistant), Nadira Hall (Middle Eastern Musician), Daniel Hawk Hicks, Lee Wells (Doormen), Xavier Urquieta (Pakastani Diplomat), Rachel Escalera (Nanny)

Max Carlyle tries to forget his adulterous one night stand with Karen until a return trip to New York to visit a dying friend brings the two together again.

Natassja Kinski, Wesley Snipes

Kyle MacLachlan, Natassja Kinski, Wesley Snipes, Ming-Na Wen

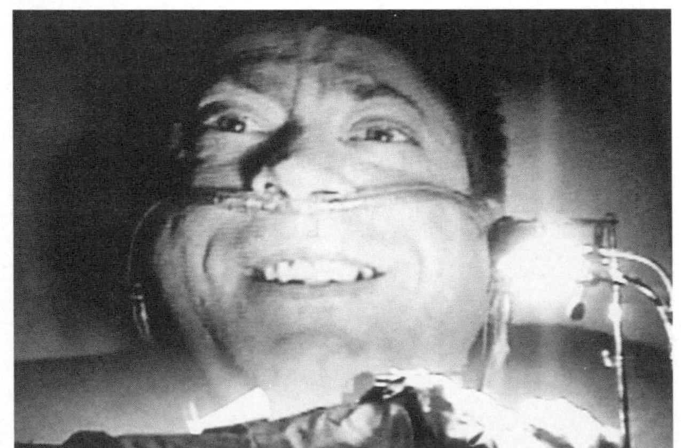

Bob Flanagan

SICK: THE LIFE AND DEATH OF BOB FLANAGAN, SUPERMASOCHIST

(CFP) Producer/Director, Kirby Dick; Photography, Jonathan Dayton, Kirby Dick, Sheree Rose, Geza Sinkovics; Editors, Kirby Dick, Dody Dorn; Co-Producer, Sheree Rose; Music, Blake Leyh; Interviewers, Kathe Burkhart, Kirby Dick, Rita Valencia; a Cinepix Film Properties presentation; Dolby Stereo; Color; Not rated; 89 minutes; November release. Documentary on performance artist Bob Flanagan who dealt in sadomasochism in order to cope with Cystic Fibrosis.

ALIEN RESURRECTION

(20TH CENTURY FOX) Producers, Bill Badalato, Gordon Carroll, David Giler, Walter Hill; Director, Jean-Pierre Jeunet; Screenplay, Joss Whedon; Based on characters created by Dan O'Bannon and Ronald Shusett; Photography, Darius Khondji; Designer, Nigel Phelps; Editor, Herve Schneid; Visual Effects Supervisors, Pitof and Erik Henry; Alien Effects Designers/Creators, Alec Gillis, Tom Woodruff, Jr.; Costumes, Bob Ringwood; Music, John Frizzell; Casting, Rick Pagano; a Brandywine production; Dolby Digital Stereo; Super 35 Widescreen; Deluxe color; Rated R; 108 minutes; November release

CAST

Ripley....Sigourney Weaver
Call....Winona Ryder
Vriess....Dominique Pinon
Johner....Ron Perlman
Christie....Gary Dourdan
Elgyn....Michael Wincott
Hillard....Kim Flowers
General Perez....Dan Hedaya
Dr. Wren....J.E. Freeman
Gediman....Brad Dourif
Distephano....Raymond Cruz
Purvis....Leland Orser
Anesthesiologist....Carolyn Campbell
Scientist....Marlene Bush
Surgeon....David St. James

and Rodney Mitchell (Soldier with Glove), Robert Faltisco (Soldier Shot through Helmet), David Rowe (Frozen Soldier), Garrett House, Rod Damer, Mark Mansfield, Daniel Raymont, Chip Nuzzo (Soldiers), Steven Gilborn (Voice of "Father"), Robert Bastens, Rico Bueno, Alex Lorre, Ron Ramessar (Sleepers), Nicole Fellows (Young Ripley), Tom Woodruff, Jr. (Lead Alien), Joan LaBarbara, Archie Hahn (Newborn Vocals)

A team of scientists, interested in bringing together human and alien genes, resurrects Ripley in order to remove the alien embryo she is carrying inside of her. This is the fourth film in the series of 20th Century-Fox releases, following Alien (1979), Aliens (1986), and Alien3 (1992), all of which starred Sigourney Weaver.

Sigourney Weaver, Winona Ryder

Winona Ryder, Ron Perlman

Sigourney Weaver

Brad Dourif, Sigourney Weaver

Danny DeVito, Matt Damon

Mary Kay Place, Jon Voight

Claire Danes, Matt Damon

Matt Damon, Danny DeVito

John Grisham's THE RAINMAKER

(PARAMOUNT) Producers, Michael Douglas, Steven Reuther, Fred Fuchs; Director/Screenplay, Francis Ford Coppola; Narration, Michael Herr; Based on the novel by John Grisham; Photography, John Toll; Designer, Howard Cummings; Editor, Barry Malkin; Costumes, Aggie Guerard Rodgers; Co-Producer, Georgia Kacandes; Casting, Linda Phillips-Palo; a Constellation Films presentation of a Douglas/Reuther production in association with American Zoetrope; Dolby Stereo; Panavision; Deluxe color; Rated PG-13; 134 minutes; November release

CAST

Rudy Baylor	Matt Damon
Deck Schifflet	Danny DeVito
Kelly Riker	Claire Danes
Leo F. Drummond	Jon Voight
Dot Black	Mary Kay Place
Judge Harvey Hale	Dean Stockwell
Miss Birdie	Teresa Wright
Jackie Lemancyzk	Virginia Madsen
Bruiser Stone	Mickey Rourke
Cliff Riker	Andrew Shue
Buddy Black	Red West
Donny Ray Black	Johnny Whitworth
Judge Tyrone Kipler	Danny Glover
Wilfred Keeley	Roy Scheider
Billy Porter	Randy Travis
Prince Thomas	Wayne Emmons
Butch	Adrian Roberts
Everett Lufkin	Michael Girardin
Jack Underhall	Randall King
F. Franklin Donaldson	Justin Ashforth
B. Bobby Shaw	Michael Keys Hall
J. Michael Floquet	James Cunningham
Mr. Van Landel	Frank Clem
Kermit Aldy	Alan Woolf
Delbert Birdsong	Sonny Shroyer
Vera Birdsong	Pamela Tice Chapman
Jewelry Saleswoman	Trula Marcus
Bruiser's Driver	Tony Dingman
Carl	Daniel O'Callaghan
Homicide Detectives	Tom Kagy, John Yancey
Jailer	Chris Gray
Jury Foreman	Verda Davenport
Courtroom Clerk	Johnetta Shearer
Court Reporter	Tammy Wendel
Mr. McKenzie	Nate Bynum

and James W. Redmond (CNN Reporter), John Gray (Hospital Volunteer), Sherry Sanford (Nurse), Billy Ray Reynolds, Mary Lester (Murder Scene Bystanders), Deborah Frazier (St. Peter's Receptionist), Vernon Newman (Great Benefit Salesman), Lynn Carthane (Newscaster), Rodney Peck (Rehab Center Desk Clerk), Bill Lunn (Himself), Terrance Stewart (Boy with Broken Arm), Bridget Brunner (Bruiser's Receptionist), Mike Cody (Tinley Britt Lawyer), Donald Polden (Legal Commentator), Eloise Dukes (Court Clerk), Katherine Morrow (Deposition Court Reporter), Alex Harvey (Bar Exam Proctor), Melissa Hurst (Waitress at Bar), Anasa Briggs-Graves, Ronnie Dee Blaire (Bailiffs)

While working for a sleazy Memphis lawyer, idealistic Rudy Baylor agrees to help a grief-stricken mother sue the insurance company that rejected the claim for her son who is dying of leukemia.

Matt Damon

Matt Damon, Mickey Rourke

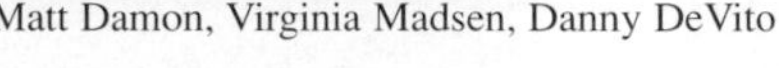

Matt Damon, Virginia Madsen, Danny DeVito

FLUBBER

(WALT DISNEY PICTURES) Producers, John Hughes, Ricardo Mestres; Executive Producer, David Nicksay; Director, Les Mayfield; Screenplay, John Hughes, Bill Walsh; From the screenplay for The Absent Minded Professor by Bill Walsh, based on a story by Samuel W. Taylor; Photography, Dean Cundey; Designer, Andrew McAlpine; Editors, Harvey Rosenstock, Michael A. Stevenson; Costumes, April Ferry; Music (including The Flubber Mambo), Danny Elfman; Co-Producer, Michael Polaire; Visual Effects Supervisors, Peter Crosman, Tom Bertino, Douglas Hans Smith; Casting, Nancy Foy; Stunts, Freddie Hice; a Great Oaks production; Dolby SDDS Stereo; Panavision; Technicolor; Rated PG; 92 minutes; November release

CAST

Prof. Phillip Brainard .... Robin Williams
Sara Jean Reynolds .... Marcia Gay Harden
Wilson Croft .... Christopher McDonald
Chester Hoenicker .... Raymond Barry
Smith .... Clancy Brown
Wesson .... Ted Levine
Bennett Hoenicker .... Wil Wheaton
Martha George .... Edie McClurg
Voice of Weebo .... Jodi Benson
Sylvia .... Leslie Stefanson
Father .... Malcolm Brownson
Window Boy .... Benjamin Brock
Minister .... Dakin Matthews
Teenage Boy .... Zack Zeigler
Willy Barker .... Samuel Lloyd
Dale Jepner .... Scott Michael Campbell
Rutland Coach .... Bob Sarlatte
Referee .... Bob Greene
Medfield Basketball Player .... Tom Barlow
Voice of Flubber .... Scott Martin Gershin
Voice of Weebette .... Julie Morrison
Secretary .... Nancy Olsen

Absent-minded university professor Phillip Brainard creates a revolutionary substance, a flying rubber, that he dubs "flubber," and hopes to use to save his financially troubled school. Remake of the 1961 Disney film The Absent Minded Professor which starred Fred MacMurray, Nancy Olsen, Keenan Wynn, and Tommy Kirk.

Robin Williams

Wil Wheaton, Robin Williams, Raymond Barry, Marcia Gay Harden, Christopher McDonald

Robin Williams

Marcia Gay Harden, Robin Williams

OTHER VOICES, OTHER ROOMS

(ARTISTIC LICENSE) Producers, Peter Wentworth, David Rocksavage; Director, David Rocksavage; Screenplay, Sara Flanigan, David Rocksavage; Based on the novel by Truman Capote; Executive Producers, Robert C. Stigwood, Lili Mahtani; Photography, Paul Ryan; Designer, Amy McGary; Editor, Cynthia Scheider; Costumes, Jane Greenwood; Music, Chris Hajian; Casting, Hopkins, Barden, Smith; a Golden Eye Films presentation;U.S.-British; Color; Not rated; 98 minutes; December release

CAST

Randolph Skully .... Lothaire Bluteau
Amy Skully .... Anna Thomson
Joel Sansom .... David Speck
Zoo .... April Turner
Ed Sansom .... Frank Taylor
Idabell Tompkins .... Aubrey Dollar
Narrator .... Robert Kingdom

13-year-old Joel, sent to a decaying plantation to be with his father, meets up with the house's mistress, Amy Skully, and her debauched cousin Randolph.

Lothaire Bluteau, David Speck

Kirstie Alley, Tim Allen

Tim Allen

FOR RICHER OR POORER

(UNIVERSAL) Producers, Sid, Bill and Jon Sheinberg; Executive Producers, Richard Baker, Rick Messina, Gayle Fraser Baigelman; Director, Bryan Spicer; Screenplay, Jana Howington, Steve Lukanic; Photography, Buzz Feitshans IV; Designer, Stephen Hendrickson; Editor, Russell Denove; Co-Producers, Michael S. Glick, Bruce Economou; Music, Randy Edelman; Costumes, Abigail Murray; Casting, Victoria Burrows; a co-presentation of The Bubble Factory of a Sheinberg production in association with Yorktown Productions; Dolby DTS Stereo; Super 35 Widescreen; Deluxe color; Rated PG-13; 115 minutes; December release

CAST

Brad Sexton .... Tim Allen
Caroline Sexton .... Kirstie Alley
Samuel Yoder .... Jay O. Sanders
Phil Kleinman .... Michael Lerner
Bob Lachman .... Wayne Knight
Derek Lester .... Larry Miller
Frank Hall .... Miguel A. Nunez, Jr.
Levinia Yoder .... Megan Cavanagh
Henner Lapp .... John Pyper-Ferguson
Rebecca Yoder .... Carrie Preston
Jerry .... Ethan Phillips
Dave .... John Caponera
Anna Yoder .... Katie Moore
Samuel, Jr. .... Bobby Steggert
Sammy .... Michael Angarano
Grandma Yoder .... Rosemary Knower
Grandpa Yoder .... David Harscheid

and Hunter and Scout Stover (Baby Yoder), June Claman (Judge Northcutt), Marla Maples (Cynthia), Holly Rudkin (Mary), Crystal Bock (Penny), Monica Deeter (Hanna Yoder), Richard Pelzman (Jonathan Yoder), Madeline Mager (Sarah), Terrence Currier (Elder Joseph), Hal Handerson (Elder Thomas), Michael Howell (Bailiff), Johanna Cox (Emma Yoder), Stefan Aleksander (Jacob Yoder), Holly Atkinson (Teller), Emily Chamberlain (Evelyn), Anthony Azizi (Taxi Driver), David Maples (IRS Agent), Markus Flanagan (George), Wes Johnson (Tourist Man), Rick Foucheux (Tom), Drenda Spohnholtz (Waitress), Marla Sucharetza (Stacy)

A pair of bickering Manhattan socialites, on the run from the IRS, hide out in Amish country, passing themselves off as the long-lost relatives of a local farming family.

GOOD WILL HUNTING

(MIRAMAX) Producer, Lawrence Bender; Executive Producers, Bob Weinstein, Harvey Weinstein, Jonathan Gordon, Su Armstrong; Co-Executive Producers, Kevin Smith, Scott Mosier; Director, Gus Van Sant; Screenplay, Ben Affleck, Matt Damon; Co-Producer, Chris Moore; Photography, Jean Yves Escoffier; Designer, Melissa Stewart; Editor, Pietro Scalia; Music, Danny Elfman; Song: Miss Misery by Elliott Smith; Costumes, Beatrix Aruna Pasztor; Casting, Billy Hopkins, Suzanne Smith, Kerry Barden; a Lawrence Bender production; Dolby Digital Stereo; Color; Rated R; 126 minutes; December release

Robin Williams, Matt Damon

CAST

Sean McGuire .... Robin Williams
Will Hunting .... Matt Damon
Chuckie .... Ben Affleck
Skylar .... Minnie Driver
Lambeau .... Stellan Skarsgard
Morgan .... Casey Affleck
Billy .... Cole Hauser
Tom .... John Mighton
Krystyn .... Rachel Majowski
Cathy .... Colleen McCauley
Girl on Street .... Shannon Egleson
Carmine Scarpaglia .... Rob Lyons
Carmine Friend #1 .... Steven Kozlowski
Lydia .... Jennifer Deathe
Clark .... Scott Williams Winters
Head Custodian .... Philip Williams
Assistant Custodian .... Patrick O'Donnell
Courtroom Guard .... Kevin Rushton
Judge Malone .... Jimmy Flynn
Prosecutor .... Joe Cannons
Court Officer .... Ann Matacunas
Psychologist .... George Plimpton
Hypnotist .... Francesco Clemente
Bunker Hill College Students .... Jessica Morton, Barna Moricz
Toy Store Cashier .... Libby Geller
M.I.T. Professor .... Chas Lawther
Timmy .... Richard Fitzpatrick
Marty .... Patrick O'Donnell
NSA Agents .... Bruce Hunter, Robert Talvano
Security Guard .... James Allodi

and Matt Mercier, Ralph St. George, Bob Lynds, Dan Washington (Barbershop Quartet), Alison Folland, Derrick Bridgeman, Vic Sahay (M.I.T. Students), Frank Nakashima, Chris Britton, David Eisner (Executives)

Minnie Driver, Matt Damon

Will Hunting, an M.I.T. janitor with exceptional mathematical abilities, is reluctant to accept a professor's suggestion that the boy seek a life beyond hanging out in Boston with his drinking buddies. 1997 Academy Award-winner for Best Supporting Actor (Robin Williams) and Original Screenplay. This film received additional Oscar nominations for picture, actor (Matt Damon), supporting actress (Minnie Driver), director, film editing, original dramatic score, and song ("Miss Misery").

Ben Affleck, Matt Damon

Ben Affleck, Matt Damon

Matt Damon, Robin Williams

Robin Williams, Stellan Skarsgard

Minnie Driver, Matt Damon, Ben Affleck

Cole Hauser, Casey Affleck, Matt Damon, Ben Affleck

Morgan Freeman, Chiwetel Ejiofor, Matthew McConaughey, Daniel Von Bargen

Djimon Hounsou (c)

AMISTAD

(DREAMWORKS) Producers, Steven Spielberg, Debbie Allen, Colin Wilson; Executive Producers, Walter Parkes; Director, Steven Spielberg; Screenplay, David Franzoni; Photography, Janusz Kaminski; Designer, Rick Carter; Editor, Michael Kahn; Music, John Williams; Costumes, Ruth E. Carter; Associate Producers, Bonnie Curtis, Paul Deason; Co-Producer, Tim Shriver; Co-Executive Producer, Robert Cooper; Casting, Victoria Thomas; Presented in association with HBO Pictures; Dolby Digital Stereo; Widescreen; Technicolor; Rated R; 152 minutes; December release

CAST

Theodore Joadson....................Morgan Freeman
Martin Van Buren....................Nigel Hawthorne
John Quincy Adams....................Anthony Hopkins
Cinque....................Djimon Hounsou
Roger Baldwin....................Matthew McConaughey
Secretary Forsyth....................David Paymer
Holabird....................Pete Postlethwaite
Lewis Tappan....................Stellan Skarsgård
Yamba....................Razaaq Adoti
Fala....................Abu Bakaar Fofanah
Queen Isabella....................Anna Paquin
Calderon....................Tomas Milian
Ensign Covey....................Chiwetel Ejiofor
Buakei....................Derrick N. Ashong
Ruiz....................Geno Silva
Montes....................John Ortiz
Lieutenant Gedney....................Ralph Brown
Lieutenant Meade....................Darren Burrows
Judge Juttson....................Allan Rich
Attorney....................Paul Guilfoyle
Captain Fitzgerald....................Peter Firth
Hammond....................Xander Berkeley
Judge Coglin....................Jeremy Northam
John C. Calhoun....................Arliss Howard
Professor Gibbs....................Austin Pendleton
Warden Pendelton....................Daniel Von Bargen
Mrs. Pendelton....................Rusty Schwimmer
General Espatero....................Pedro Armendariz

and Frank T. Wells (Crier), Miles Herter (Sailor), Michael Massee (Pickney), Jake Weber (Mr. Wright), Victor Rivers (Captain Ferrar), Fay Masterson (Queen Victoria), Joseph Kosseh (Birmaja), Steve Passewe (Cinque's In-Law), Sherly Acosta Williams (Cinque's Wife), Amistad Africans: Willie Amakye (Folowa), Luc Assogba (Gbatui), Mariah Campbell (Masery), Habib Conteh (Bai), Stephen Conteh (Morlai), Monguehy Fanzy (Fabanna), Jimmy Fotso (Kwong), Adekunle Ilori (Kahei), Sheriff Kargbo (Almamy), Saye Lah (Kessebe), Sylvestre Massaquoi (Santigiie), Samson Odede (Kpona), Chike Okpala (Sorie), Willie Onafesso (Jina), Samuel Pieh (Suuleh), Lansana Sawi (Morlu), Abu Sidique (Tsukama), Elhadju Malik Sow (Golabu), Lamine Thiam (Mahmud); Matthew Sarles (Young Aide), John Sapiel (Old Abnaki Indian), George Gerdes (Marshal), Jerry Molen (Magistrate), Kevin J. O'Connor (Missionary), Robert Walsh (Guardsman), Sean McGuirk (Courier), Tony Owen (Farmer), William Young (Businessman), Michael Riley (British Officer), Frederic Kimball (William Harrison), James Warwick, Zanne Shaw (Aristocrats), Leon Singer (Don Pablo), Castulo Guerra (Spanish Priest), Jonathan Epstein (Second Lieutenant), Brian Smiar (Lieutenant Paine), Harry Groener (Tecora Captain), Father Ellwood Kieser C.S.P. (Priest), Hawthorne James (Creole Cook), Ingrid Walters (Woman Overboard with Baby), Harry A. Blackmun (Associate Justice Joseph Story); Additional Amistad Africans: Curtis Shields (Bassie), Charles Udoma (Kessebe), Tony Onafesso (Baa), Clarence Mobley (Kenei), Edward Appiah (Followolo), Paul Mwakutuya (Sessi), Samuel Orekhio (Fawni), Ransford Thomas (Alkali), Issac Mayanja (Sanpha), Roosevelt Flenoury (Njaooni), Carlos Spivey (Chike), Andrew L. Josiah (Tamba), Peter Mansaray (Kapr), Brian Macon (Yauai), Denver Dowridge (Kpau), Rory Burton (Vakina), Omo Lara Tosin (Kula), Juliette Darko (Teme), Charlean Isata Bangalie (Margru), M.S. Kaleiwo (Kaleiwo)

Off the coast of Cuba, a group of Africans aboard the slaveship Amistad reclaim their freedom only to discover that they must stand trial when they end up in American waters. This film received Oscar nominations for supporting actor (Anthony Hopkins), cinematography, costume design, and original dramatic score.

Morgan Freeman

Anthony Hopkins

Matthew McConaughey

DECONSTRUCTING HARRY

(FINE LINE FEATURES) Producer, Jean Doumanian; Executive Producer, J.E. Beaucaire; Director/Screenplay, Woody Allen; Co-Executive Producers, Jack Rollins, Charles H. Joffe, Letty Aronson; Co-Producer, Richard Brick; Photography, Carlo DiPalma; Designer, Santo Loquasto; Editor, Susan E. Morse; Costumes, Suzy Benzinger; Casting, Juliet Taylor; a Sweetland Films presentation of a Jean Doumanian production; Dolby Stereo; Color; Rated R: 93 minutes; December release

CAST

Doris .... Caroline Aaron
Harry Block .... Woody Allen
Joan .... Kirstie Alley
Richard .... Bob Balaban
Ken .... Richard Benjamin
Burt .... Eric Bogosian
Larry .... Billy Crystal
Lucy .... Judy Davis
Cookie .... Hazelle Goodman
Beth Kramer .... Mariel Hemingway
Jane .... Amy Irving
Grace .... Julie Kavner
Hilly .... Eric Lloyd
Leslie .... Julia Louis-Dreyfus
Harvey Stern .... Tobey Maguire
Helen .... Demi Moore
Fay .... Elisabeth Shue
Paul Epstein .... Stanley Tucci
Mel .... Robin Williams
Max .... Hy Anzel
Ms. Paley .... Scotty Bloch
Professor Clark .... Philip Bosco
Dolly .... Shifra Lerer
Harry's Father .... Gene Saks

and Judy Bauerlein (Actress), Joseph Reidy (First Assistant Director), Phyllis Burdoe (Script Supervisor), Barbara Hollander (Mel's Daughter), Adam Rose (Mel's Son), David S. Howard (Mel's Doctor), Amanda Barudin (Beth Kramer's Daughter), Juliet Gelfman-Randazzo (Baby Hilly), Floyd Resnick (Israeli Patient), Brian McConnachie (Dr. Reese), Peter Jacobson (Goldberg), Tracey Lynne Miller (Goldberg's Girlfriend), Jennifer Garner (Woman in Elevator), Irwin Charone (Bar Mitzvah Host), John Doumanian, Alexa Aronson, Kenneth Edelson (Bar Mitzvah Guests), Viola Harris (Elsie), Si Picker (Wolf Fishbein), Howard Spiegel (Mr. Farber), Eugene Troobnick (Professor Wiggins), Ray Aranha (Professor Aranha), Paul Giamatti (Professor Abbot), Marvin Chatinover (Professor Cole), Daniel Wolf (Professor Wolf), Waltrudis Buck (Dean of Adair University), Arden Myrin (Student Mary), Daisy Prince (Elevator Voice), Peter McRobbie (Damned Man), Dan Moran (Devil), Ray Garvey (Policeman on Campus), Linda Perri (Policewoman on Campus), Tony Sirico (Policeman at Jail)

Harry, suffering from writer's block, examines the various relationships in his life, many of which wound up in his stories, much to the discomfort of the real-life principles. This film received an Oscar nomination for original screenplay.

Woody Allen, Judy Davis

Tobey Maguire

Stanley Tucci, Demi Moore

Julia Louis-Dreyfus

Woody Allen, Elisabeth Shue, Billy Crystal

Eric Lloyd, Mariel Hemingway, Woody Allen

Hazelle Goodman

Robin Williams, Julie Kavner

Kirstie Alley, Woody Allen

SCREAM 2

(DIMENSION) Producers, Cathy Konrad, Marianne Maddalena; Executive Producers, Bob Weinstein, Harvey Weinstein, Kevin Williamson; Director, Wes Craven; Screenplay, Kevin Williamson; Co-Producer, Daniel Lupi; Co-Executive Producers, Cary Granat, Richard Potter, Andrew Rona; Photography, Peter Deming; Editor, Patrick Lussier; Designer, Bob Ziembicki; Music, Marco Beltrami; *Cassandra Ari* by Danny Elfman; Costumes, Kathleen Detoro; Casting, Lisa Beach; a Konrad Pictures production in association with Craven/Maddalena Films; Distributed by Miramax Films; Dolby Digital Stereo; Panavision; Color; Rated R; 120 minutes; December release

Dewey Riley .... David Arquette
Sidney Prescott .... Neve Campbell
Gale Weathers .... Courteney Cox
Cici .... Sarah Michelle Gellar
Randy Meeks .... Jamie Kennedy
Debbie Salt .... Laurie Metcalf
Hallie .... Elise Neal
Derek .... Jerry O'Connell
Mickey .... Timothy Olyphant
Maureen .... Jada Pinkett
Cotton Weary .... Liev Schreiber
Chief Hartley .... Lewis Arquette
Joel .... Duane Martin
Sorority Sister Lois .... Rebecca Gayheart
Sorority Sister Murphy .... Portia De Rossi
Phil .... Omar Epps

and Paulette Patterson (Usher Giving out Costumes), Rasila Schroeder (Screaming Girl up Aisle), Heather Graham ("Stab" Casey), Roger L. Jackson ("The Voice"), Peter Deming (Popcorn Boy), Molly Gross (Theatre #1), Rebecca McFarland (Theatre #2), Kevin Williamson (Cotton's Interviewer), Sandy Heddings-Katulka (Girl in Dorm Hallway), Joe Washington, Angie Dillard, John Patrick, Stephanie Belt, Richard Doughty, Mark Oliver, Jennifer Weston, Shelly Benedict (Reporters), Craig Shoemaker (Artsy Teacher), Josh Jackson, Walter Franks (Film Class Guys), Nina Pertronzio (Film Class Mopey Girl), Jamie Kennedy (Randy Meeks), Marisol Nichols (Dawnie), Cornelia Kiss (Coroner at Cici's House), Lucy In (ER Doctor), Philip Pavel (Officer Andrews), Timothy T. Hillman (Captain Down), Nancy O'Dell (Tori's Interviewer), Tori Spelling (Herself), Luke Wilson ("Stab" Billy), David Warner (Drama Teacher Gus Gold), Greg Meiss (Zeus), Adam Shankman (Ghost Dancer), Jon Kriestien Andersson, Carmen M. Chavez, Anne Fletcher, Erik Hyler, Sebastan Lacause, Lance MacDonald, Sarah Christine Smith, Laurie Sposit, Ryan Lee Swanson (Dancers), Jack Baun (Tackled Cell Phoner), Corey Parker (Library Guy), Chris Doyle (Officer Richards), Jason Horgan, D.K. Arredondo, John Embry (Fraternity Brothers)

Two years after a series of killings in the town of Woodsboro, Stab, a movie based on the murders opens, prompting another killer to strike. Sequel to the 1996 Dimension/Miramax Films release Scream, with Neve Campbell, Jamie Kennedy, Courteney Cox, David Arquette, and Liev Schreiber repeating their roles.

Timothy Olyphant, Jamie Kennedy, Neve Campbell, Jerry O'Connell, Elise Neal

Leslie Nielsen, Matt Keeslar

MR. MAGOO

(WALT DISNEY PICTURES) Producer, Ben Myron; Executive Producers, Henry G. Saperstein, Andre Morgan, Robert L. Rosen; Director, Stanley Tong; Sreenplay, Pat Proft, Tom Sherohman; Based on the character from UPA Productions of America; Co-Producer, Justis Greene; Photography, Jingle Ma; Designer, John Willett; Editors, Stuart Pappé, David Rawlins, Michael R. Miller; Costumes, Tom Bronson; Music, Michael Tavera; Casting, Marcia Ross, Donna Morong; a Ben Myron production; Distributed by Buena Vista Pictures; Dolby Digital Stereo; Panavision; Eastman color; Rated PG; 87 minutes; December release

CAST

Quincy Magoo .... Leslie Nielsen
Luanne .... Kelly Lynch
Waldo .... Matt Keeslar
Bob Morgan .... Nick Chinlund
Agent Chuck Stupak .... Stephen Tobolowsky
Agent Gus Anders .... Ernie Hudson
Stacey Sampanahoditra .... Jennifer Garner
Austin Cloquet .... Malcolm McDowell
Ortega Peru .... Miguel Ferrer
Schmitt .... L. Harvey Gold
Gosha .... Art Irizawa
Hebzinski .... John Tierney
McManus .... Terence Kelly
Molinaro .... Rick Burgess
Javier .... Jerry Wasserman
Museum Curator .... Bill Dow
Ralston (Stage Manager) .... Frank C. Turner
Rosita .... Monique Rusu
Desk Clerk .... Robert Metcalfe
Tenor .... Danny Steele
Tourist .... Dolores Drake
Newswoman .... Claire Riley
Soprano .... Pat Waldron

and Michael Puttonen (Security Guard), Pamela Diaz (Tour Guide), Chancz Perry (Train Station Porter), Marke Driesschen (Radio Announcer), Brenda MacDonald (Opera Patron), Joseph Davies (TV Trainer), Shaun MacDonald (Cook Show Host), David Neale (Fix It Guy), Carrie Cain Sparks (Rosita's Dresser), Kristie Yzerman, Kelly Kay, Yvette Jackson, Tara Mead, Dan Redford, Kirk Coatte (Snowboarders), David Mylrea (Baboon Performer), Greg Burson (Animated Magoo Voice)

When a precious stolen gem inadvertently lands in his possession, bumbling millionaire Quincy Magoo becomes the center of a dastardly plot to get the jewel back.

THE APOSTLE

(OCTOBER)Producer, Rob Carliner; Executive Producer/Director/Screenplay, Robert Duvall; Photography, Barry Markowitz; Designer, Linda Burton; Editor, Steve Mack; Co-Producer, Steven Brown; Music, David Mansfield; Costumes, Douglas Hall; Casting, Renee Rousselot, Ed Johston; a Butchers Run Films Production; Dolby Stereo; CFI color; Rated PG-13; 132 minutes; December release.

CAST

Euliss "Sonny" Dewey (The Apostle E.F.) ....Robert Duvall
Jessie Dewey ....Farrah Fawcett
Tossie ....Miranda Richardson
Horace............................Todd Allen
Brother Blackwell ....John Beasley
Mrs. Dewey, Sr. ....June Carter Cash
Sam............................Walter Goggins
Joe ....Billy Joe Shaver
Troublemaker............................Billy Bob Thornton
Elmo............................Rick Dial
Mother Blackwell ....Mary Lynette Braxton
Sister Johnson ....Zelma Loyd
Sister Jewell ....Sister Jewell Jernigan
Bayou Man............................William Atlas
Sonny Supporter ....Lenore Banks
Helper ....Brett Brock
Sister Johnsons Twins ....Christopher Canady, Christian Canady
Singer............................Elizabeth Chisholm
Preacher ....Carl D. Cook
Scripture Reader............................Naomi Craig
Liquor Store Preacher ....Wayne Dehart
Texas State Trooper............................Stuart Greer
Virgil ....Emery Hopkins
Faith Healers ....Brenda B. Jakcson, Vera Kemp
12 Year Old Sonny ....Jay Robicheaux
"Amen" Men............................Terrence Rosemore
Sister Delilah............................Joyce Jolivet Starks
Jessie Jr. ....Christina Stojanovich
Bobby............................Nicholas Stojanovich

and Paul Baggett, Chili Graham, Bobby Green, Charles Johnson, Steve White, Fay Winn (Tag Team Preachers), Lenore Banks, John E. Hawkins, Jesse Walkrop (Sonny Supporters), Frank Collins, Jr., Joseph Lindsey, Melete Woods (Soloists), Hunter Hayes (Child Accordionist), Daniel Hickman (Flashback Preacher), Julie Johnson (Baptism Soloist), Sharon London (Church Woman), Fernie E. McMillan (Doctor), Jimmie J. Meaux (Church Member #2), L. Christian Mixon (The Bodyguard), Richard Nance, Graham Timbes (Church Men), Douglas Perry (LA State Trooper), Harold Portier, Sr. (Coronet George), Pat Ratliff (Accident Witness), Ronnie Stutes (Needy Receiver), Ruby Francis Terry (Choir Director), James B. Towry (Nosey Neighbor), Renee Victor (Latin Translator), Jerry H. Skelton (Organist) James Gammon

After attacking his wife's lover, Pentecostal preacher Sonny Dewey flees his Texas town, baptizes himself "The Apostle E.F." and settles down in a Louisiana bayou town to preach to the citizens. This film received an Oscar nomination for actor (Robert Duvall).

Robert Duvall

June Carter Cash, Farrah Fawcett, Christina Stojanovich

Robert Duvall, Billy Bob Thornton

The Mouse

Lee Evans, Nathan Lane

MOUSE HUNT

(DREAMWORKS) Producers, Alan Riche, Tony Ludwig, Bruce Cohen; Director, Gore Verbinski; Screenplay, Adam Rifkin; Photography, Phedon Papamichael; Designer, Linda DeScenna; Editor, Craig Wood; Costumes, Jill Ohanneson; Visual Effects Supervisor, Charles Gibson; Music, Alan Silvestri; Mouse and Cat Trainer, Boone's Animals for Hollywood; Casting, Denis Chamian; an Alan Riche/Tony Ludwig production; Dolby Digital Stereo; Technicolor; Rated PG; 97 minutes; December release

CAST

Ernie Smuntz .... Nathan Lane
Lars Smuntz .... Lee Evans
April Smuntz .... Vicki Lewis
Alexander Falko .... Maury Chaykin
The Lawyer .... Eric Christmas
Quincy Thorpe .... Michael Jeter
Ingrid .... Debra Christofferson
Hilde .... Camilla Soeberg
Auctioneer .... Ian Abercrombie
Roxanne Atkins .... Annabelle Gurwitch
The Banker .... Eric Poppick
Maury .... Ernie Sabella
Rudolf Smuntz .... Wickey Hickey
Caesar .... Christopher Walken
Mayor McKrinkle .... Cliff Emmich
Mayor's Wife .... Melanie MacQueen
Becky .... Brianna Shebby
Betty .... Danielle Shebby
Leslie Reinhart .... Leslie Upson
Zeppco Suits .... Mario Cantone, Peter Anthony Rocca
Lester Dinkus .... Steve Bean
Waitress #1 .... Suzanne Krull
Mr. Texas .... William Frankfather

and Pat Thomas (Construction Worker #1), Peter Gregory (Doctor), E.J. Callahan (Historical Clerk), Susan Blommaert (Ms. Park Avenue), Valorie Armstrong (Franklin's Wife), Michael Rae Sommers (Paramedic), Michael Ross (Cop), Jose Rey (Cuban Postal Worker), Carmen Filpi (Pallbearer#4), Harper Roisman, David Fresco (Factory Workers), Scott Smith (City Paramedic), Sarah Dampf (Crying Child), Orville Stoeber, David Weisenberg (Experts), Fred Pierce (Large Nosed Man), Clement E. Blake (Homeless Man), Saverio Carubia (Photographer), Pep Torres (Bus Boy)

Having been left a dilapidated mansion by their late father, the Smuntz brothers are delighted to find out it is an architectural masterpiece worth millions. Unfortunately, their efforts to renovate the house and sell it are waylaid by a determined mouse who refuses to vacate the premises. This was the final film of actor William Hickey who died on June 29, 1997.

Christopher Walken

Lee Evans, Nathan Lane

JACKIE BROWN

(MIRAMAX) Producer, Lawrence Bender; Executive Producers, Bob Weinstein, Harvey Weinstein, Richard N. Gladstein, Elmore Leonard; Director/Screenplay, Quentin Tarantino; Based on the novel *Rum Punch* by Elmore Leonard; Co-Producer, Paul Hellerman; Photography, Guillermo Navarro; Designer, David Wasco; Editor, Sally Menke; Costumes, Mary Claire Hannan; Casting, Jaki Brown, Robyn M. Mitchell; a Band Apart production; Dolby Digital Stereo; CFI color; Rated R; 158 minutes; December release

CAST

Jackie Brown .... Pam Grier
Ordell Robbie .... Samuel L. Jackson
Max Cherry .... Robert Forster
Melanie .... Bridget Fonda
Ray Nicolette .... Michael Keaton
Louis Gara .... Robert De Niro
Mark Dargus .... Michael Bowen
Beaumont Livingston .... Chris Tucker
Sheronda .... Lisa Gay Hamilton
Winston .... Tommy "Tiny" Lister, Jr.
Simone .... Hattie Winston
Public Defender .... Denise Crosby
Judge .... Sid Haig
Amy, Billingsley Sales Girl .... Aimee Graham
Cockatoo Bartender .... Ellis E. William
Billingsley Sales Girl #2 .... Tangie Ambrose
Raynelle, Ordell's Junkie Friend .... T'Keyah Crystal Keymah
Cabo Flight Attendant .... Venessia Valentino
Anita Lopez .... Diana Uribe
Cocktail Waitress .... Renee Kelly
Bartender at Sam's .... Elizabeth McInerney
Girl at Security Gate .... Colleen Mayne
Steakhouse Waitress .... Laura Lovelace

and Christine Lydon M.D., Julia Ervin, Juliet Lon, Michelle Berube, Gillian Ilian-Waters (Chicks Who Love Guns), Candice Briese, Gary Man (The Deputies), Jeffrey Deedrick, Roy Nesvold, Herbert Hans Wilmsen (The Sheriffs), Quentin Tarantino (Voice on Answering Machine)

Jackie Brown, a stewardess who has been smuggling money into the country for gunrunner Ordell Robbie, is confronted by the federal authorities who ask her to help them bring Ordell to justice. This film received an Oscar nomination for supporting actor (Robert Forster).

Michael Keaton, Pam Grier

Robert De Niro, Bridget Fonda

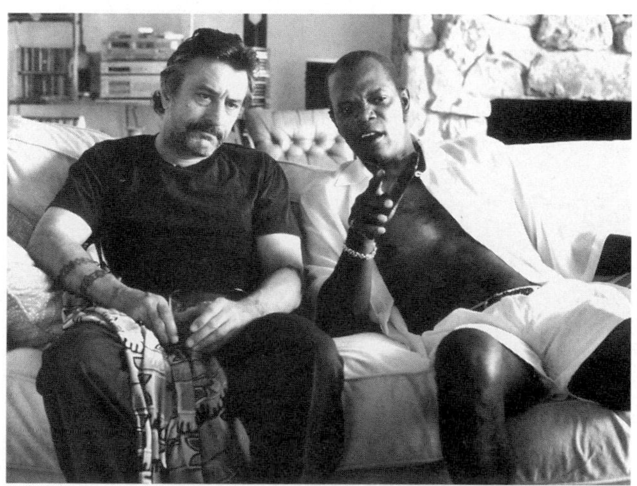

Robert De Niro, Samuel L. Jackson

Pam Grier, Robert Forster

Jack Nicholson, Helen Hunt

Helen Hunt, Greg Kinnear

Jack Nicholson, Cuba Gooding Jr., Greg Kinnear

AS GOOD AS IT GETS

(TRISTAR) formerly *Old Friends*; Producers, James L. Brooks, Bridget Johnson, Kristi Zea; Executive Producers, Richard Sakai, Laurence Mark, Laura Ziskin; Director, James L. Brooks; Screenplay, Mark Andrus, James L. Brooks; Story, Mark Andrus; Co-Producers, John D. Schofield, Richard Marks; Photography, John Bailey; Designer, Bill Brzeski; Editor, Richard Marks; Associate Producers, Aldric Porter, Maria Kavanaugh; Costumes, Molly Maginnis; Music, Hans Zimmer; Song: "Always Look on the Bright Side of Life," written by Eric Idle; Casting, Francine Maisler; a Gracie Films production; Dolby SDDS Stereo; Technicolor; Rated PG-13; 138 minutes; December release

CAST

Melvin Udall .... Jack Nicholson
Carol Connelly .... Helen Hunt
Simon Nye .... Greg Kinnear
Frank Sachs .... Cuba Gooding, Jr.
Vincent .... Skeet Ulrich
Beverly .... Shirley Knight
Jackie .... Yeardley Smith
Nora .... Lupe Ontiveros
Verdell .... Jill
Supporting Dogs .... Timer, Billy
Neighbor Woman .... Bibi Osterwald
Carl .... Ross Bleckner
Caterer .... Bernadette Balagtas
Partygoers .... Jaffe Cohen, Laurie Kilpatrick, Alice Vaughn
Handyman .... Brian Doyle-Murray
Mother at Table .... Kristi Zea
Daughter at Table .... Annie Maginnis Tippe
Cafe 24 Waitresses .... Patricia Childress, Rebekah Johnson, Missi Pyle, Leslie Stefanson, Tara Subkoff
Cafe 24 Manager .... Shane Black
Man at Table .... Peter Jacobson
Woman at Table .... Lisa Edelstein
Cafe 24 Customer .... Stan Bly
Carol's Date .... Randall Batinkoff
Spencer Connelly .... Jesse James
Street Hustlers .... Jamie Kennedy, Justin Herwick
Policewoman .... Maya Rudolph
Detective Ray .... John F. O'Donohue
Hospital Doctor .... David A. Kipper
Nurse Receptionist .... Mary Elizabeth Still
Children at Cafe 24 .... Chloe Brooks, Cooper Brooks
Passersby .... Sharon L. Alexander, Holly Denys
Dr. Green .... Lawrence Kasdan
Psychiatric Patients .... Alison Rose, Kathryn Morris
Cafe 24 Busboy .... Wood Harris
Publisher .... Linda Gehringer
Receptionist .... Julie Benz
Dr. Bettes .... Harold Ramis

Antonia Jones, (Nurse), Kaitlin Hopkins, (Woman in Lobby), Jimmy Workman, (Sean from the Bakery), Danielle Spencer, (Veterinarian), Todd Solondz, (Man on Bus), Tom McGowan (Maitre'd), Danielle Brisebois, (Singer), Matt Malloy, (Men's Store Salesman), Paul Greenberg, (Bar Waiter), Kirk Ringberg, (Food Waiter), Dave Hawthorne (Bartender)

Melvin Udall, an obsessive-compulsive romance novelist with an angry edge towards the human race, finds himself forming a bond with Carol, a single mother and waitress, and, more unexpectedly, Simon, a struggling artist whose gay lifestyle Melvin abhors. 1998 Academy Award-winner for Best Actor (Jack Nicholson) and Actress (Helen Hunt). This film received additional Oscar nominations for picture, original screenplay, supporting actor (Greg Kinnear), film editing, and original musical or comedy score.

Jack Nicholson, Greg Kinnear, Jill

Jill, Jack Nicholson

Yeardley Smith

Shirley Knight

Helen Hunt, Jack Nicholson

Greg Kinnear, Jack Nicholson, Helen Hunt

Dustin Hoffman, Anne Heche, Robert De Niro

Anne Heche, Robert De Niro, Dustin Hoffman

Robert De Niro, Dustin Hoffman

WAG THE DOG

(NEW LINE CINEMA) Producers, Jane Rosenthal, Robert De Niro, Barry Levinson; Executive Producers, Michael De Luca, Claire Rudnick Polstein, Ezra Swerdlow; Director, Barry Levinson; Screenplay, Hilary Henkin, David Mamet; Based on the book *American Hero* by Larry Beinhart; Photography, Robert Richardson; Designer, Wynn Thomas; Editor, Stu Linder; Costumes, Rita Ryack; Music, Mark Knopfler; Co-Producer, Eric McLeod; Special War & News Segments Producers, Steven Pollock, Ted Eccles; Casting, Ellen Chenoweth, Debra Zane; a Tribeca/Baltimore Pictures/Punch production; Dolby Digital Stereo; Technicolor; Rated R; 98 minutes; December release

Dustin Hoffman

CAST

Stanley Motss .... Dustin Hoffman
Conrad Brean .... Robert De Niro
Winifred Ames .... Anne Heche
Sgt. William Schumann .... Woody Harrelson
Fad King .... Denis Leary
Johnny Green .... Willie Nelson
Liz Butsky .... Andrea Martin
President .... Michael Belson
Amy Cain .... Suzanne Cryer
John Levy .... John Michael Higgins
Grace .... Suzie Plakson
Tracy Lime .... Kirsten Dunst
A.D. .... Jason Cottle
Director .... David Koechner
Pet Wrangler .... Harland Williams
Bob Richardson .... Sean Masterson
Mr. Young .... William H. Macy
Technician .... Bernard Hocke
Sharon .... Jenny Byrne
Kid with Shoes .... Maurkice Woods
Themselves .... Pops Staples, Merle Haggard, Jim Belushi, Jay Leno
Co-Pilot .... Phil Morris
Officer .... Chris Ellis
Owner .... Edwin T. Morgan
Pilot .... J. Patrick McCormack
Teenage Girl .... Jennifer Manley
Judge .... Edrie Warner
Young Man/CIA .... Richard Lawson
Gate Stewardess .... Drena De Niro
Combine Driver .... Alberto Vasquez

and Stephanie Kemp, Jack Esformes, John Cho, Michael Reid Davis (Aides), Brant Cotton (Sharon's Boyfriend), Kenneth Kern (Nashville Engineer), Michelle Levinson (Faye), Ron McCoy (Limo Driver), Derrick Morgan (CIA Agent), Garry R. Roleder (USAF Captain), George Gaynes (Senator Nole), Rick Scarry (White House Reporter), Cliff B. Howard (Ranger), Furley Lumpkin, Sean Fenton (Raking Dads), Nikki Crawford (Mom), John Franklin, Kevin Furlong (Jockeys), Lu Elrod (Southern Woman), Michael Villani (Commentator), Warren Wilson (Crossfire Interviewer), Terry Anzur (Announcer #3), Melissa Gardner (Chris Andrews Reporter), Giselle Fernandez (Press Person), Christine Devine, Richard Saxton (Chicago Newscasters), Geffrey Blake, Jerry Levine (Media Guys), Jack Shearer (Sklansky), Emmett Miller (News Break Reporter), Bill Handel (Reporter #7 - Andrew AFB), Arlene Afshangol (Albanian Girl), Hope Garber (Albanian Grandmother), Gina Menza (Press Room Reporter), Maggie Mellin (Mrs. Rose), Tom Murray (Aircraft Carrier Reporter), Shirley Prestia (Moderator Named Shirley), Ralph Tabakin (Southern Man), Marguerite Moreau (Teenage Girl in Audience), Nicole Avant, Tom Bähler, Allen Carter, Carmen Carter, Lance Eaton, Karen Geraghty, Jim Gilstrap, Jennifer Gross, Wendy Lou Halvorsen, Anthony Holiday, Brad Kalas, Billy Trudel, Mark Vieha, Julia Waters, Oren Waters, Maxine Waters ("American Dream" Singers), Craig T. Nelson

Robert De Niro, Anne Heche

Days before the election, the President of the United States is accused of making a pass at a girl scout. In order to take the media focus off of this event, a Washington troubleshooter enslists the aide of Hollywood producer Stanley Motss to create a fake "war" with Albania. This film received Oscar nominations for actor (Dustin Hoffman) and adapted screenplay.

Willie Nelson

Tulku Jamyang Kunga Tenzin, Lobsang Samten

KUNDUN

(TOUCHSTONE) Producer, Barbara De Fina; Executive Producer, Laura Fattori; Director, Martin Scorsese; Screenplay/Co-Producer, Melissa Mathison; Photography, Roger Deakins; Designer/Costumes, Dante Ferretti; Editor, Thelma Schoonmaker; Music, Philip Glass; Casting, Ellen Lewis; a Cappa/De Fina production; Distributed by Buena Vista Pictures; Dolby Digital Stereo; Super 35 Widescreen; Technicolor; Rated PG-13; 134 minutes; December release

CAST

Dalai Lama (Adult) ....Tenzin Thuthob Tsarong
Dalai Lama (Age 12) ....Gyurme Tethong
Dalai Lama (Age 5) ....Tulku Jamyang Kunga Tenzin
Dalai Lama (Age 2) ....Tenzin Yeshi Paichang
Mother...Tencho Gyalpo
Lobsang (5-10)...Tenzin Topjar
Father ....Tsewang Migyur Khangsar
Takster ....Tenzin Lodoe
Tsering Dolma..Tsering Lhamo
Lama of Sera...Geshi Yeshi Gyatso
The Messenger ....Lobsang Gyatso
Reting Rinpoche..Sonam Phuntsok
Lord Chamberlain ....Gyatso Lukhang
Master of the Kitchen ....Lobsang Samten
Taktra Rinpoche..Tsewang Jigme Tsarong
Ling Rinpoche...Tenzin Trinley
Kashag/Noblemen...............................Ngawang Dorjee, Phinsto Thonden
Layman #1 ....Chewang Tsering Ngokhang
Norbu Thundrup ....Jamyang Tenzin
Lobsang (Adult)...Tashi Dhondup
Nechung Oracle ....Jampa Lungtok
and Karma Wangchuck (Deformed Face Bodyguard), Ben Wang (General Chang Chin-Wu), Kim Chan (Second Chinese General), Henry Yuk (General Tan), Ngawang Kaldan (Prime Minister Lobsang Tashi), Jurme Wangda (Prime Minister Lukhangwa), Robert Lin (Chairman Mao), Selden Kunga (Tibetan Doctor), John Wong (Chinese Comrade), Gawa Youngdung (Old Woman), Tenzin Rampa (Tenzin Chonegyl—age 12), Vyas Ananthakrishnan (Indian Soldier)

Gyurme Tethong, Tashi Dhondup

Tenzin Thuthob Tsarong, Gyatso Lukhang

The true story of the Tibetan boy who would be declared the 14th reincarnation of the Dalai Lama. This film received Oscar nominations for art direction, cinematography, costume design, and original dramatic score.

AFTERGLOW

(SONY PICTURES CLASSICS) Producer, Robert Altman; Executive Producers, Ernst Stroh, Willi Baer; Director/Screenplay, Alan Rudolph; Co-Producer, James McLindon; Photography, Toyomichi Kurita; Editor, Suzy Elmiger; Designer, François Seguin; Costumes, Francois Barbeau; Music, Mark Isham; Associate Producer, Rebecca Morton; Casting, Lucie Robitaille; a Moonstone Entertaiment presentation of a Sandcastle 5 and Elysian Dreams production; U.S.-Canadian; Dolby Stereo; Color; Rated R; 113 minutes; December release

CAST

Lucky Mann....Nick Nolte
Phyllis Mann....Julie Christie
Marianne Byron....Lara Flynn Boyle
Jeffrey Byron....Jonny Lee Miller
Donald Duncan....Jay Underwood
Helene Pelletier....Domini Blythe
Bernard Ornay....Yves Corbeil
Count Falco/Jack Dana....Alan Fawcett
Cassie....Genevieve Bissonnette
Isabel Marino....Michele-Barbara Pelletier
Gloria Marino....France Castel
Monica Bloom....Claudia Besso
Judy the Waitress....Ellen David
The Byrons' Concierge....Don Jordan
Pedro....Bill Rowat
Frederico....Cas Anvar
Falco's Butler....David Francis
Doctor....Ivan Smith
Derelict in Park....John Dunn-Hill
Chateau Lenore Pianist....Warren "Slim" Williams
Chateau Lenore Singer....Jean-François Sauvageau
and Bernard Tanguay (Maitre D'), Dave McKeown (Security Guard), Vanya Rose (Hotel Receptionist), Mark Camacho (Ritz-Carlton Bartender), Amy Kadawaki (Chinese Restaurant Hostess), Salvatore Agostino (Restaurant Owner)

Lucky and his wife Phyllis find their already fragile marriage crumbling further apart when they become separately involved with a younger, equally unhappy couple, Marianne and her corporate-minded husband Jeffrey. This film received an Oscar nomination for actress (Julie Christie).

Nick Nolte, Julie Christie

Lara Flynn Boyle, Jonny Lee Miller

Nick Nolte, Lara Flynn Boyle

Julie Christie

Louis Gossett Jr., Nigel Hawthorne in *Inside* © *Strand Releasing*

INSIDE (Strand) Producer, Hilly Elkins; Executive Producers, Louis Gossett, Jr., Dan Paulson; Director, Arthur Penn; Screenplay, Bima Stagg; Photography, Jan Weincke; Designer, David Barkham; Editor, Suzanne Pillsbury; Music, Robert Levin; Casting, Moonyeenn Lee; a Showtime in association with Hallmark Entertainment/Elkin Entertainment and Logo Entertainment presentation; Ultra-Stereo; Color; Rated R; 94 minutes; January release. **CAST**: Eric Stoltz (Marty Strydom), Nigel Hawthorne (Col. Kruger), Louis Gossett, Jr. (Questioner), Ian Roberts (Guard Moolman), Ross Preller (Guard Potgieter), Jerry Mofokeng (Mzwaki), Louis Van Nickerk (J. Martin Strydom, Sr.), Patrick Shai (Bhambo), Janin Eser (Christie Malcolm), Joshua Lyndenberg (Guard Koos), Desmond Dube (Scabenga), Peter Suzman (Michael Radowsky), Nick Boraine (Robert Henderson), Gary Coppin (Big Policeman), Temba Indaba (Bakwana), Nandi Nyemba (Mzwaki's Wife). (Note: This film received its official premiere on Showtime in August of 1996).

SCREWED: AL GOLDSTEIN'S KINGDOM OF PORN (Cinema Village Features) Producers, Todd Phillips, Andrew Gurland; Director/Photography/Editor, Alexander Crawford; from Saint Dympna Prods.; Color; Not rated; 85 minutes; January release. Documentary on pornography mogul Al Goldstein, publisher of Screw magazine.

SPREAD THE WORD: THE PERSUASIONS (Independent) Producer/Director, Fred Parnes; No other credits available; Color; Not rated; 80 minutes; January release. Documentary of a cappella singing group The Persuasions.

KC Hall, Teri Driver in *Screwed* © St. Dympna Productions

SHADOW CONSPIRACY (Hollywood Pictures) Producer, Terry Collis; Executive Producers, Andrew G. Vajna, Buzz Feitshans IV; Director, George P. Cosmatos; Screenplay, Adi Hasak, Ric Gibbs; Photography, Buzz Feitshans IV; Designer, Joe Alves; Editor, Robert A. Ferretti; Co-Producer, Adi Hasak; Music, Bruce Broughton; Costumes, April Ferry; Casting, Karen Rae; an Andrew G. Vajna presentation of a Cinergi production; Distributed by Buena Vista Pictures; Dolby Digital Stereo; Panavision; Technicolor; Rated R; 103 minutes; January release. **CAST:** Charlie Sheen (Bobby Bishop), Linda Hamilton (Amanda Givens), Donald Sutherland (Conrad), Stephen Lang (The Agent), Sam Waterston (President), Ben Gazzara (Vice President Saxon), Henry Strozier (Treasury Secretary Murphy), Charles Cioffi (Gen. Blackburn), Stanley Anderson (Attorney Gen. Toyanbee), Nicholas Turturro (Grasso), Theodore Bikel (Prof. Pochenko), Dey Young (Janet), Reginald Davis, Johnny Newman, Antonio Todd (Basketball Players), Bobby Zajonc (Helicopter Pilot), Casey Biggs (Stokes), Richard Bauer (Grolier), Penny Fuller (Dr. Olson), Gore Vidal (Congressman Page), Tom Quinn (Reporter #1), Jonas Elmblad (Jergon), James A. Chory (Man), Paul Gleason (Blythe), Terry O'Quinn (Frank Ridell), Vicki Ross-Norris, Bob Child (News Reporters), Beverly Brigham (Cafe Waitress), Harold Surratt (Marine Colonel), Helen Carey (Tamara Yarshov), Walt MacPherson (Hickman), Scott Wesley Morgan (Agent Wyndham), F.T. Rea, James L. Byrd (Security Men), Thomas Shelton (Street Vendor), Jeffrey Thompson (Taxi Driver), Karen Bralove (First Lady), Katrina Tabori (Situation Room Assistant), Brian Smyj (Rawlings), Ralph Cosham (Driver), Ramon Estevez (Mr. Jones), Nicholas A. Puccio, Karyn V. Cody, Charles Bowen (Cabinet Members), Michael Cunningham (White House Desk Clerk), Oscar Pitts, Jr., Reginald C. Colbert, Dominick De Marco, J. Williams Midkiff, Jr. (Restaurant Patrons), Richard A. Mention III (Tech), Nick Olcott, Roy Bordon, Andreas Brandt (Secret Service), John Leisenring, Lawrence Leonard (Men in Accident), Richard Turner (Senator)

Sam Waterston, Charlie Sheen in *Shadow Conspiracy*
© Cinergi Pictures

VISITING DESIRE (Independent) Producer/Director/Photography/Screenplay, Beth B.; Editor, Melody London; Color; Not rated; 70 minutes; February release. **CAST:** Kembra Pfah, Lydia Lunch.

Lara Flynn Boyle in *Farmer and Chase* © Arrow/ J. Patrick Furden

FARMER & CHASE (Arrow) Producers, Scott Kalmbach, Julie Costanzo, Michael Seitzman; Executive Producer, Doug Humphreys; Director/Screenplay, Michael Seitzman; Photography, Michael Maley; Designer, Doug Freeman; Music, Tony Saunders; Editor, Doug Werby; Casting, Joan Marechal; a Red Sky Films presentation of a Kalmbach/Seitzman production; Color; Not rated; 97 minutes; February release. **CAST::** Ben Gazzara (Farer), Todd Field (Chase), Lara Flynn Boyle (Hillary), Ron Kael (JoJo), David Booth (Casey—FBI), Steven Anthony Jones (Ollie), George Maguire (Chet), Ted Draper (Check Cashing Clerk), Luis Oropeza (Check Cashing Guard), David Renaud (Pawn Shop Customer), Michael De Martini (Jimbo), Jack Byrne (Clarence), Pamela Dunham (Betty—Store Clerk), Yuri Lane (Steve—Store Clerk), Ira Steen (Bank Manager), Nellie Sciutto (Susan—Bank Hostage), Mike Girardin (Harold—Bank Hostage), Dixie Jenay, Leo Downey (Bank Hostages), Robert Ernst (Security Guard), Shamus Maley (Shamus), Warren White (Det. Smith), Lance Brady (Det. Bell), Denny Delk (Capt. Cornell), Jarion Moore (Detective), Danny Kovacs (Chicago Det.), Tom Dryden, Randall King (Snipers), Robert DeWalt (Taxi Driver), Walter Brown, Ed Hanson (Bank Police), Tommy Banks, Garrett Griffin, Steve Bakunas, Annie Combs (FBI Agents)

Benjamin Bratt, Steve Reevis, Calvin Levels, Jesse Borrego in *Follow Me Home* © New Millennia

FOLLOW ME HOME (New Millennia Films) Producers, Alan Renshaw, Irene Romero, Peter Bratt, Benjamin Bratt; Executive Producers, Bonnie Duran, Eduardo Duran, Jennifer Newell-Easton, Gary Rhine; Director/Screenplay, Peter Bratt; Photography, Garett Griffin; Designer, Katernia Keith; Music, Cyril Neville, Speech, Roy Finch; a Chacras Filmworks production in association with Amber Images and In Pictures; Color; Not rated; 104 minutes; February release. **CAST:** Philmore Steele (Spirit Drummer), Steve Reevis (Freddy), Jesse Borrego (Tudee), Benjamin Bratt (Abel), Calvin Levels (Kaz), Noah Verduzco (Ricky), Cynthia Tinajero (Belinda), David Carrera (Loco), Salma Hayek (Veronica), Blair Renshaw (Michael), Robert Collins (The White Man), Kim McGuire (Pat the Waitress), Alfre Woodard (Evey), Tom Towles (The Cook), Rocky McMurray (Dead Brave & D.J. Voice), David Chase (Jimmy), David Denard (Hal), Ahimsa Stone (Little Girl), John Allen Nelson (Perry), Tom Bower (Larry), Kieran Mulroney (Farmer), Lei Maa (Woman in Painting), Casey Camp (Beckoning Spirit)

Ice Cube, Elizabeth Hurley in *Dangerous Ground* © *New Line Cinema*

DANGEROUS GROUND (New Line Cinema) Producers, Gillian Gorfil, Darrell Roodt; Director, Darrell James Roodt; Screenplay, Greg Latter, Darrell Roodt; Executive Producers, Ice Cube, Pat Charbonnet; Photography, Paul Gilpin; Designer, Dimitri Repanis; Music, Stanley Clarke; Costumes, Ruy Filipe; Editor, David Heitner; a Gillian Gorfil/Darrell Roodt production; Dolby SDDS Stereo; Deluxe color; Rated R; 95 minutes; February release. **CAST:** Ice Cube (Vusi), Elizabeth Hurley (Karen), Ving Rhames (Muki), Eric "Waku" Miyeni (Steven), Sechaba Morajele (Ernest), Thokozani Nkosi (Young Vusi), Ron Smerczac (Interrogation Policeman), Wilson Dunster (Heavy Policeman), Peter Kubheka (Igqira), Roslyn Morapedi (Vusi's Mother), Mabel Mafuya (Woman), Fana Mokoena, Maimela Motubatse, Nkululeko Mabandla (Youths), Robert Whitehead (Sandton Hotel Receptionist), Gresham Phet Jaulima (Bellboy), Toni Caprari (Bar Owner), Temsie Times (Hooker), Prophets of Da City (Band in Nightclub), Helge Janssen (Crack Dealer), Anthony Bishop, Ross Preller (Thugs), Greg Latter (Sam), Ernest Ndlovu, Ike Kanupi, Simo Mogwaza, Godrey Dzingeni, Eddy Msize, Isaac Mavimbela, Peter Nkwanyana, Ernest Mbanzi, Prosperous Ban, Eric Sulu (Muki's Men), Candy Jack Lee (Chinese Girl), Robin Smith (Iron Guard), Gys De Villiers (Det. Sgt.), Veronica Mitchell (Muki's Wife)

FLIPPING (Dove Entertainment) Producers, Gene Mitchell, David Amos; Executive Producer, Michael Woods; Director/Screenplay, Gene Mitchell; Photography, Phil Parmet; Editor, Kevin Krasny; Designer, Diane Hughes; Costumes, Nadine Reimer; Casting, Pat Melton, Paul G. Bens; a Mon Frere Motion Pictures production; Dolby Stereo; Deluxe color; Not rated; 102 minutes; February release. **CAST:** David Amos (Michael Moore), David Proval (Billy White), Gene Mitchell (Shot), Shant Benjamin (Hooker), Barry Primus (Joey), Paul Klar (Dennis), Tony Burton (Chuckie), Mike Starr (C.J.), Keith David (Leo Richards), Willem Keane (Gordie), Lynn Mitchell (Careen), Christine Harte (Melanie), Kim Meredith (Jolie), Gee Thomas (Sam), David Basulto (Nick), James Howell (Marilyn the Transvestite), Christina Fonteyn, Francois Pelligan, Fabrizio (Transvestites), Nick Dimitri (Tommy Barnett), Keith Lewis (Joseph's Cafe Maitre'd), Jon Paul Jones (Bodyguard), Ara Shahbazian (Wedding Band Leader), Peter Kalos (Wedding Maitre 'd), Walt Robles (Drunk in Nightclub), Ron Gilbert (Ray-Ray), Jack Leal, Matt Gallini (Ray-Ray's Friends), Christopher Kriesa (News Reporter Voice)

Troy Sostillio in *Raising Heroes* © Phaedra

RAISING HEROES (Phaedra) Producer/Director/Screenplay/Editor, Douglas Langway; Screenplay, Douglas Langway, Henry White, Edmond Sorel; Photography, Stephen Schlueter; a Doppelganger Films production; Color; Not rated; 84 minutes; February release. **CAST:** Troy Sostillio (Josh Sullivan), Henry White (Paul McEwen), Edmond Sorel (Victor), Stewart Groves (Stephen aka Vinny), Chandra Pointer (Nicole), Robert Zolli (Claudio), Greg Bodkin (Rocco Nappi), Constantine Nikos (Vito), Julian Safavi (Micheal), Nicolas Siljee (Nicki), Susan Silijee (Susan), James Pappas (Jimmy), Victor Barbella (Gerard), Chris Ferraro (Chris), Darrell Scott Rushton (Tom), David Matwijkow (Anthony), Bonnie Perlman (Barbara), Christina Burz (Julie), Douglas Langway (Angelo), Stephen Langway (Mark), Robert Karp (Doctor), Gloria Barber (Susan's Mother), David Zayas (Deli Clerk), Lenny Finelli (Boss' Waiter)

Unforgotten © Castle Hill

UNFORGOTTEN: TWENTY-FIVE YEARS AFTER WILLOW-BROOK (Castle Hill) Producer, Danny Fisher; Executive Producer, Katie Meskell; Director, Jack Fisher; Screenplay, Stuart Warmflash; Photography, Eric Lau, Mark Kroll, Alan McPheely, Richard Mauro; Music, Hayes Greenfield; Editors, Constantine Limperis, Matthew Mallinson, Shelly Toscano; Narrator, Danny Aiello; a City Lights International presentation in association with HeartShare; Color; Not rated; 60 minutes; February release. Documentary looks at the lives of some of the survivors of the notorious Staten Island institution for the mentally retarded, Willowbrook State School, the disgraceful living conditions of which were exposed 25 years earlier by TV reporter Geraldo Rivera.

GOOD LUCK (East West Film Partners) Producers, Richard Hahn, Shirley Honickman Hahn, Andrzej Kamrowski; Executive Producers, Bob Comfort, Richard Hahn; Director, Richard Labrie; Screenplay, Bob Comfort; Photography, Maximo Munzi; Designer, Jane Ann Stewart; Editor, Neal Grieve; Music, Tim Truman; a Richard Hahn production; Dolby DTS Stereo; Color; Rated R; 98 minutes; March release. **CAST:** Gregory Hines (Bernard "Bern" Lemley), Vincent D'Onofrio (Tony "Ole" Olezniak), James Earl Jones (James Bing), Max Gail (Farmer John), Joe Theismann, Roy Firestone (Themselves), Robert O'Reilly ("Bartender"), Jack Rader ("Drag Queen"), Ramsay Midwood ("Santa Claus"), Maria O'Brien (Peggy), Sara Trigger (Heidi), Ross Huffman-Kerr (Olsen), Kathryn Howell (Doris), William C. Simmonds (Steve), Doug Mace ("Clock Hat Man"), Jerry A. Basham ("Chicken Foot Man"), Kathleen Stefano (Rhonda, the Dealer), Doug Baldwin (Owner of the Trashed Car), Maureen McVerry (Joan Redack), Heath Lourwood, James Martin (Sons), Troy Bryant (Cop in Police Car), Joe Ivy (Detective), Garwood Perkins (Buzz), Dennis Dun (Chang), Diedre Kilgore (Topless Fan), Eric Tecosky (Stadium Fan), Charles Gould Taylor (Cop on the Street), Gary Budoff, Stephen Orloff, Aaron Daniel Haber, Brad Heffler, Barry Koff (Football Fans)

Jerry A. Basham, Gregory Hines in *Good Luck*
© East-West Film Partners

RHYME AND REASON (Miramax) Producers, Charles X Block, Peter Spirer, Daniel Sollinger; Executive Producer, Helena Echegoyen; Director, Peter Spirer; Co-Producer, Richard Spero; Photography, Peter Spirer, Daniel Sollinger, George Mitas, Sean Adair, Brennan McClean, Alex Rappaport, Adam Vardy, Antonio Ponti; Music, Benedikt Brydern; Music Supervisors, Happy Walters, Andrew Shack; Executive in Charge of Production, Shannon McIntosh; Editors, Andy Robertson, David Wilson; a City Block and Aslan Pictures production; Dolby Stereo; Color; Rated R; 90 minutes; March release. Documentary on hip hop and rap, featuring Busta Rhymes, A Tribe Called Quest, Wu-Tang Clan, Pharcyde, The Fugees, The Alkoholiks, The Notorious B.I.G., Kurtis Blow and Crew, Heavy D, Grand Master Caz, Salt-N-Pepa, Speech, Biz Markie,

NAS in *Rhyme and Reason* © *Miramax Films*

Lords of the Underground, DAS EFX, Air Force Crew, Li'l Caesar, Wise Intelligent, Andre Charles, Chuck D, Erick Sermon, Craig Mack, LBC Crew, Redman, Diezzle Don, Mack 10, KRS-ONE, Cypress Hill, MC Eiht, Chaz Hays, Suave, Whodini, Guru, Spearhead, Ras Kass and Crew, Parrish Smith, Kris Kross, Xzibit, NAS, "Puffy" Combs, Paul Stewart, Sen Dog, Kid of Kid N' Play, The Luniz, Adario Strange, Keith Murray, Kool Herc, Red Alert, LL Cool J, Da Brat, Tupac, Spice 1, LV, Master P, Lost Boyz, Suga T, E-40, Too-Short, Melly Mel, Scorpio, Young MC, The Rza, Dogg Pound, Jermaine Dupri, Jay-Z, Homicide, Dr. Dre.

Spalding Gray in *Gray's Anatomy* © Northern Arts Entertainment

GRAY'S ANATOMY (Northern Arts Entertainment) Producer, John Hardy; Executive Producers, Jonathan Sehring, Caroline Kaplan, Kathleen Russo; Director, Steven Soderbergh; Screenplay, Spalding Gray; Based on his performance piece; Photography, Elliot Davis; Editor, Susan Littenberg; Music, Cliff Martinez; from Bait and Switch, Inc.; Color/Black and White; Not rated; 80 minutes; March release. A monologue by Spalding Gray.

Adrienne Shelly, Tim Guinee in *Sudden Manhattan* © Phaedra Cinema/Homegrown

SUDDEN MANHATTAN (Phaedra) Producer, Marcia Kirkley; Executive Producers, Paul D'Addario, Jeff Sine, Larry Lavine; Director/Screenplay, Adrienne Shelly; Photography, Jim Denault; Designer, Teresa Mastropierro; Costumes, Cherish Cullison; Editor, Jack Haigis; Music, Pat Irwin; a Homegrown Pictures production; Dolby Stereo; Color; Not rated; 85 minutes; March release. **CAST**: Adrienne Shelly (Donna), Tim Guinee (Adam), Roger Rees (Murphy), Louise Lasser (Dominga), Hynden Walch (Georgie), Jon Sklaroff (Alex), Paul Cassell (Ian), Chuck Montgomery (Bearded Man), David Simonds (Roses Man), Melinda Wade (Roses Woman), Pamela Gray (Bagel Business Woman), Brian Quirk (Playwright), C.C. Loveheart (Waitress), Shirl Bernheim, Elizabeth Newitt (Old Ladies), Garry Goodrow (Fainting Man), Bobby Caravella (Cop Kelly), Bill Boggs (Newscaster), Elaine Lang (Bunny Lady), Jan Leslie Harding (Crazy Diner Lady), Neil Deodhar (Convenience Guy), Trish Hunter (Georgie's Mom), Kevin Cahoon (Georgie's Brother), Emily Cutler (Georgie's Friend), Kevin Hagan (Jim), Joey Golden (Bernie), Mark Blum (Louis), Gordana Roshovich (Barbara), Hugh Palmer (Joe), Harry Bugin (Gran'pa Pete)

John Randolph in *The Hotel Manor Inn* © Manor Films

THE HOTEL MANOR INN (Manor Films) Producer/Director/Screenplay, Wayne Chesler; Executive Producers, Robert Gillings, Damon Testaverde, Wayne Chesler; Photography, Michael McCurry; Designer, Pilar Turner; Music, Alan Schwartz; Color; Not rated; 92 minutes; March release. **CAST**: John Randolph (Gus), Sam Trammell (Nolan), Burke Moses (Brian Armor), Jennifer Corby (Kathy), Fred Norris (Pete), Richard Bright (Gregor), William Preston (Charlie), Jessica Dublin (Lucille), Lawrence Vincent (Ed), Herschel Sparber (Chief Farrell), Jack William Scott (Boney), Jane Strauss (Holly), Steve Roberts (Kiki), Dory Binyon (Tara), Jerome Richards (Pat), Robert Gillings (Rob King), Zabryna Guevara (Denise), Bill London (London Luge), Michael McCurry (Preston Press), Bob Greenberg (Marty), Joseph Haddock (Camera Man), Derek Chesler (Jimmy Horn), Kali LaBorne (Sally Horn), Kevin Cottrell (D.J.), Cary Schwartz (Chief Adel), Dan Moyer (Roger Wiley), Paul Pfeifer (Hilda the Builder), Matt Ross (Coffee Man), Tom Camarda (Ladder Man), Janie Chesler (Goldie), Alex Fong (Videotape Man), David Benullo (Joe Deak)

SUZANNE FARRELL: ELUSIVE MUSE (Seahorse Films) Producer, Anne Belle; Directors, Anne Belle, Deborah Dickson; Photography, Don Lenzer, Tom Hurwitz, Wolfgang Held; Editor, Deborah Dickson; Co-Producer, Catherine Tambini; Color; Not rated; 105 minutes; March release. Documentary on ballerina Suzanne Farrell, featuring Jacques d'Amboise, Maria Calegrai, Arthur Mitchell, Heléne Alexopoulos, Paul Mejia, Maurice Béjart, Isabelle Guérin, Susan Jaffe, Peter Boal, Marie-Christine Mouis.

Suzanne Farrell in *Suzanne Farrell: Elusive Muse* © Seahorse Films

Nakia Burrise, Jason David Frank, Catherine Sutherland, Johnny Yong Bosch in *Turbo: A Power Rangers Movie* © Twentieth Century Fox

TURBO: A POWER RANGERS MOVIE (20th Century Fox) Producer, Jonathan Tzachor; Executive Producers, Haim Saban, Shuki Levy; Directors, David Winning, Shuki Levy; Screenplay, Shuki Levy, Shell Danielson; Photography, Ilan Rosenberg; Editors, Henry Richardson, B.J. Sears; Music, Shuki Levy; Designer, Yuda Ako; Costumes, Danielle Baker; a Saban Entertainment/Toei Co. production;U.S.-Japanese; Dolby Stereo; Color; Rated PG; 99 minutes; March release. **CAST**: Jason David Frank (Tommy/Red Ranger), Steve Cardenas (Rocky/Blue Ranger), Johnny Yong Bosch (Adam/Green Ranger), Catherine Sutherland (Katherine/Pink Ranger), Nakia Burrise (Tanya/Yellow Ranger), Blake Foster (Justin), Paul Schrier (Bulk), Jason Narvy (Skull), Austin St. John (Jason), Amy Jo Johnson (Kimberly), Hilary Shepard Turner (Divatox), Richard Genelle (Ernie), Jon Simanton (Lerigot), Ed Neil (Lord Zedd), Carla Pérez (Rita Repulsa), Jon Simanton (Lerigot), Gregg Bullock (Lt. Stone), Paul Schrier (Bulk)

DRUNKS (Northern Arts) Producers, Peter Cohn, Shireen Meistrich, Burtt Harris; Executive Producers, Larry Meistrich, John Hart, Tom Carouso; Director, Peter Cohn; Screenplay, Gary Lennon, based on his play *Blackout*; Photography, Peter Hawkins; Designer, Michael Shaw; Editor, Hughes Winborne; Costumes, Kim Druce; Casting, Lina Todd; a Seagoat Films and Kardana Films presentation of a Shooting Gallery production; Ultra-Stereo; Color; Rated R; 88 minutes; March release. **CAST:** Richard Lewis (Jim), Liza Harris (Melanie), Liam Ahern (Billy), George Martin (Marty), Sam Rockwell (Tony), Amanda Plummer (Shelley), Kevin Corrigan (Cam), Fanni Green (Jasmine), Parker Posey (Debbie), Dianne Wiest (Rachel), Billy Dove (Leo), Julie Halston (Carol), Faye Dunaway (Becky), Lisa Gay Hamilton (Brenda), Calista Flockhart (Helen), Annette Arnold (Kathy), Howard Rollins (Joseph), Oscar Koch (Dennis), Margaret Devine (Terry), Michael Medeiros (Charlie), Kevin Rendon (First Liquor Clerk), Burtt Harris (Harry), Laurie Taylor-Williams (Francine), Spalding Gray (Louis), Anna Thomson (Tanya), Zach Grenier (Al), Christopher Lawford (Rich), Michael Campbell (Ted), Abe Gurko (Huge Guy), David Drumgold (Chaka), Cisco Davis (Park Kid), Joey Arias (Ruby), Jonathan Cook (Freddie), Olga Merediz (Chairwoman), Judy Bauerlein (Lucy), Kevin Davis (Tom)(Note: This film made its debut on Showtime in November of 1996).

Christopher Lawford, Richard Lewis in *Drunks* © Northern Arts

Cheryl Dunye, Guinevere Turner, Lisa Marie Bronson, Valarie Walker in *The Watermelon Woman* © First Run Features

THE WATERMELON WOMAN (First Run Features) Producers, Barry Swimar, Alexandra Juhasz; Executive Producer, Michael Light; Director/Screenplay, Cheryl Dunye; Photography, Michelle Crenshaw; Co-Producer, Cate Wilson; Co-Executive Producer/Editor, Annie Taylor; Color; Not rated; 80 minutes; March release. **CAST:** Cheryl Dunye (Cheryl), Guinevere Turner (Diana), Valarie Walker (Tamara), Camille Paglia (Herself), Lisa Marie Bronson (Fae Richards), Toshi Reagon, Cheryl Clarke, Sarah Schulman.

B*A*P*S (New Line Cinema) Producers, Mark Burg, Loretha Jones; Executive Producers, Michael De Luca, Jay Stern; Director, Robert Townsend; Screenplay, Troy Beyer; Photography, Bill Dill; Designer, Keith Brian Burns; Editor, Patrick Kennedy; Costumes, Ruth Carter; Music, Stanley Clarke; Casting, Valerie McCaffrey; an Island Pictures production; Dolby Digital Stereo; Deluxe color; Rated PG-13; 90 minutes; March release. **CAST:** Halle Berry (Nisi), Martin Landau (Mr. Blakemore), Ian Richardson (Manley), Natalie Desselle (Mickey), Troy Beyer (Tracy), Luigi Amodeo (Antonio), Jonathan Fried (Isaac), Pierre (Ali), A.J. Johnson (James), Bernie Mac (Mr. Johnson), Darrel Heath

Natalie Desselle, Halle Berry in *B*A*P*S* © New Line Cinema

Cameron Foord, Sam Trammell in *Childhood's End*
© Plainview/Open City

(Terrance), Vince Cooke (Z.Z.), Faizon Love (Tiger J), Rudy Ray Moore (Nate), Darrow Igus (Bartender), Debra Wilson (Flight Attendant), Robin Van Sharner (Airline Passenger), Jessica Page (Audition Dancer), Alex Thomas (Music Store Salesman), Eric Poppick (Vincent), Downtown Julie Brown, Heavy D, Idalis DeLeon, Howard Hewitt, LL Cool J, Leon, Dennis Rodman (Themselves)

CADILLAC RANCH (Legacy) Producers, J. Todd Harris, Harvey Kahn; Executive Producers, John Davis, Stephen Nemeth, Robert William Landaas, Chip Duncan; Director, Lisa Gottlieb; Screenplay, Jennifer Cecil; Photography, Bruce Douglas Johnson; Designer, John Huke; Editor, Dan Loewenthal; Costumes, Kari Perkins; Music, Christopher Tyng; Casting, Cathy Henderson; a Davis Entertainment Classics and Water Street Pictures presentation of a J. Todd Harris/Water Street Pictures production; Panavision; CFI color; Rated R ; 104 minutes; April release. **CAST**: Christopher Lloyd (Wood Grimes), Suzy Amis (CJ Crowley), Renee Humphrey (Mary Katherine Crowley), Caroleen Feeney (Frances Crowley), Linden Ashby (Beau), Jim Metzler (Travis Crowley), Joe Stevens (Leroy), Bill Wise (Hippie Artist), Ashley Coe (Young CJ), Renee Olstead (Young Mary Katherine), Hillary Van Scoy (Young Frances), Doyle Carter (Bailiff), William Earl Ray (Judge), Robert Fieldsteel (CJ's Attorney), Barbara Lasater (Mother), Jennifer Cecil (Bridal Shower Photographer), Brad Leland (Booking Deputy), Chamblee Ferguson (Cody Nolan), Sage Schlather (Jasmine), Ray Benson (Lou), Sarah Cecil (Woman Making Out), Charles Mooneyhan, Wally Welch (Men), Gary Carter (Sgt. Polk), Richard Dillard (Capt. Steadlin), Charles Solomon (Bartender), Ken Tigar (Clown)

LICENSED TO KILL (DeepFocus Prod.) Producer/Director/Screenplay/Editor, Arthur Dong; Photography, Robert Shepard; Music, Miriam Cutler; Associate Producer, Thomas G. Miller; "Leviticus: Faggot" written and performed by Me'Shell Ndegéocello; Color; Not rated; 80 minutes; April release. Documentary looking at the experiences of several men who have murdered homosexuals.

CHILDHOOD'S END (Plainview Pictures) Producers, Jason Kliot, Joana Vicente; Director/Screenplay, Jeff Lipsky; Photography, Victoria Ford; Designer, Wing Lee; Editor, Sabine Hoffman; Costumes, Angela Wendt; Casting, Diana Jaher; Color; Not rated; 90 minutes; April release. **CAST:** Cameron Foord (Evelyn), Heather Gottlieb (Rebecca), Sam Trammell (Greg), Colleen Werthmann (Denise), Bridget White (Chloe), Reiko Aylesworth (Laurie) Philip Coccioletti (Harvey), Georgia Creighton (Saleswoman), Edie Falco (Patty), Linda Larkin (Caroline), Joe Lisi (Mr. Meyer), Keith Primi (Mark), John Rothman (Bernard), Fay Rusli (Minako), Charlie Schiff (Sid), Maureen Silliman (Mrs. Meyer), Ellen Tobie (Miranda), Cody Tucker (Virginia)

GRIND (Castle Hill) Producer, Laura Lau; Executive Producer, Tom Staub; Director, Chris Kentis; Screenplay, Laura Lau, Christ Kentis; Co-Producer, Melissa Powell; Photography, Stephen Kazmierski; Designer, Therese Deprez; Costumes, Katherine Jane Bryant; Music, Brian Kelly; Casting, Laura Lau, Melissa Powell, Cassandra Han; a Kodiak Productions L.L.C. presentation; Dolby Stereo; Color; Not rated; 96 minutes; April release. **CAST:** Billy Crudup (Eddie), Adrienne Shelley (Janey), Paul Schulze (Terry), Frank Vincent (Nick), Saul Stein (Jack), Amanda Peet (Patty), Steven Beach (Jimmy), Jason Andrews (Joey), Arthur Nascarella (John), Nick Sandow (Lenny), Tim Williams (Scott), Angela Pupello (Pam), Lydia Radzull (Liz), Tim Devlin (Scully), Joe Pallister (J.J.)

Billy Crudup in *Grind* © Castle Hill Prods. Inc.

SCHIZOPOLIS (Northern Arts) Producer, John Hardy; Director/Screenplay/Photography, Steven Soderbergh; Music, Cliff Martinez, Joseph Wilkins, Mark Mangini, Harry Garfield; Editor, Sarah Flack; Color; Not rated; 99 minutes; April release. **CAST:** Steven Soderbergh (Fletcher Munson), Betsy Brantley (Mrs. Munson/Attractive Woman #2), David Jensen (Elmo Oxygen), Eddie Jemison (Nameless Numberheadman), Scott Allen (Right Hand Man), Mike Malone (T. Azimuth Schwitters), Katherne LaNasa (Attractive Woman #1)

David Jensen in *Shizopolis*
© Northern Arts

Debra Messing, Dean Stockwell, French Stewart in *McHale's Navy*
© Universal Studios/Bubble Factory

McHALE'S NAVY (Universal) Producers, Sid Sheinberg, Bill Sheinberg, Jon Sheinberg; Executive Producers, Lance Hool, Perry Katz; Director, Bryan Spicer; Screenplay, Peter Crabbe; Story, Peter Crabbe, Andy Rose; Based on the ABC television series; Photography, Buzz Feitshans IV; Designer, Gene Rudolf; Editor, Russell Denove; Co-Producers, Tom Arnold, Conrad Hool; Costumes, Michael T. Boyd; Music, Dennis McCarthy; Casting, Lisa London, Catherine Stroud; The Bubble Factory presentation of a Sheinberg production; Dolby DTS Stereo; Eastman color; Rated PG; 109 minutes; April release. **CAST**: Tom Arnold (Lt. Cmmdr. Quinton McHale), Dean Stockwell (Capt. Wallace B. Binghampton), Debra Messing (Lt. Penelope Carpenter), David Alan Grier (Ens. Charles T. Parker), Tim Curry (Maj. Vladakov), Ernest Borgnine (Cobra), Bruce Campbell (Virgil), French Stewart (Happy), Danton Stone (Gruber), Brian Haley (Christy), Henry Cho (Willie), Anthony Jesse Cruz (Roberto), Honorato Magaloni (Castro), Guillermo Rios (Jose), Eduardo Lopez Rojas (Gonzalez), Tom Ayers (Henchman Carl), Scott Cleverdon (Henchman David), Robert Schuch (Boat Henchman), Tommy Chong (Armando/Ernesto), Paco Mauri (Doctor), Juan Rebolledo (Juan), Diego Vazquez (Rey), Lucy Moreno (Hermina), Mineko Mori (Mystic Woman), Luis Lemus (Sergeant), Alejandro Reyes (Manuel), Alex Cole (Guard), Joe Keyes (Officer), Tomas Leal (Monkey Owner), Luisa Huertas (Nurse), Joe Minjares (Pharmacist/Barber), Fima Noveck (Russian Leader), Eric Champnella (Stan), John Pyper Ferguson (Interrupting Henchman), Anthony Azizi (Bad News Henchman), Bryan Spicer (Unlucky Henchman)

Lauri Crook in *Without Air* © Phaedra Cinema

WITHOUT AIR (Phaedra Cinema) Producer, John Bick; Director/Screenplay/Photography, Neil Abramson; Editor, Suzanne Hines; Music, Kennard Ramsey; Designer, Paula Good; Black and white; Not rated; 88 minutes; April release. **CAST:** Lauri Cook (Shay), Jack May (Boyfriend), Leigh-Anne Potter (Angel), Nokie Taylor (Harry), Larry "Bait" Wiltsey (Sleazy Driver), Dennis Brockway (Donut Man), Trick Cantrell (Strip Joint DJ), Russell George (Bartender), Michelle McGlocklin, Vicky Tubbs, Angel Carpenter, Meresa Ferguson (Strip Joint Dancers), Kathy D. Bennett, Anthony R. Jackson (Arguing Couple), Christopher Rutherford (Kid), William Watson, Jimme Turner, Leon "Jelly Belly" Jeter (Men), Jimmy Ellis (Jimmy), Carrie Wilchie (Laundromat Woman), Pat Lawyer (Cajun Clyde), Vicky Alford (BBQ Counterperson), Gary Hardy (Hobo Joe), Mack Orr, Joe H. Hicks, Tony McKinney, James Bonner, Otto Carnes ("The Fieldstones")

Mary Tyler Moore, Eric Stoltz in *Keys To Tulsa*
© Gramercy Pictures

KEYS TO TULSA (Gramercy) Producers, Leslie Greif, Harley Peyton; Executive Producers, Michael Birnbaum, Peter Isacksen; Director, Leslie Greif; Screenplay, Harley Peyton; Based on the novel by Brian Fair Berkey; Line Producer, Elliot Rosenblatt; Co-Producer, Guy J. Louthan; Photography, Robert Fraisse; Music, Stephen Endelman; Designer, Derek R. Hill; Editors, Eric L. Beason, Louis F. Cioffi, Michael R. Miller; Costumes, Marie France; Casting, Fern Champion, Mark Paladini; from ITC Entertainment Group; CFI color; Rated R; 113 minutes; April release. **CAST**: Eric Stoltz (Richter Boudreau), James Spader (Ronnie Stover), Mary Tyler Moore (Cynthia Whitlow Boudreau Simpson Rawling), James Coburn (Harmon Shaw), Deborah Kara Unger (Vicky Michaels Stover), Joanna Going (Cherry), Michael Rooker (Keith Michaels), Peter Strauss (Chip Carlson), Randy Graff (Louise Brinkman), Cameron Diaz (Trudy), Dennis Letts (Preston Liddy), Josh Ridgway (Billy), Marco Perella (Bedford Shaw), George Greif (Bartender), Doran Ingrham (Tattoo Man), Alex Allen Morris (Policeman), Veron Grote (Desk Sergeant), Lauren Rochelle (Earla), Randy Stripling (Waiter), Randy Means (Victor Hill), Vicky Hutson, Lucia Reeves (News Reporters), Roger Burlage (Hills Friend), Debbie Bowman, Sanda Czapla, Marcella Mhall, Erin Swenson, Dawn Wagner (Sixty-Six Club Dancers)

NO ORDINARY LOVE (Phaedra Cinema) Producer, Eli Kabillio; Director/Screenplay, Doug Witkins; Executive Producer, Adam Fast; Photography, Armando Basulito; Music, Bob Christianson; Editor, John Orland; an Eli Kabillio production, 1995; Color; Not rated; 104 minutes; April release. **CAST:** Smith Forté (Kevin), Ericka Klein (Wendy), Robert Pecora (Andy), Mark S. Larson (Ben), Koing Kuoch (Vince), Dan Frank (Tom), Kathleen Gibson (Rona), Tymme Reitz (Ramon), Marina Palmier (Gloria), Alejandro Patino (Juan Pablo), Randy Brown (Ricky), Elizabeth Mehr (Tina), Alaina P. Pepito (Laurie), Alex Mercer (Cowboy Al), Srey Teang (Short Woman), David Vincent Holland (Transvestite), Rob Gibson

No Ordinary Love © Phaedra Cinema

(Heavy Metal Guy), Lobo Sebastian (Carlos), Fred Blanco, Jose Angel Ceja, Jesus Covarrubias, Randy Guiting (Gangbangers), Mark Solum, T.J. Paolino (Uniformed Officers), Alexandria Nicole Finkelman (Baby Patrick), Susie Spear (Rachel Kingsley), Kelly O'Brien (Officer), Gary Perez (Detective), Eli Kabillio (Interrogator)

DEAD MEN CAN'T DANCE (LIVE Entertainment) Producer, Elaine Hastings Edell; Executive Producer, Leslie Grief; Co-Producer, Frank Hildebrand; Director, Stephen M. Anderson; Screenplay, Paul Sinor, Mark Sevi, Bill Kerby; Story, Paul Sinor; Photography, Levie Isaacks; Editor, Christopher Rouse; Designer, Gary Griffin Constable; Music, Richard Marvin; Color; Rated R; 97 minutes; April release. **CAST**: Kathleen York (Capt. Victoria Elliot), Michael Biehn (Hart), Adrian Paul (Shooter), Barbara Eve Harris (Sgt. Beverly Rhodes), Kelly Jo Minter (Chrissie Brooks), Hiep Thi Le (Min Yan Chun), Jennifer Blanc (Susie Warzenak), Wendy Gazelle (Lorraine Towers), Shawnee Smith (Addy Cooper), Joel Miller (Bear Claw), Rodney Eastman (David Porter), Grace Zabriskie (Gen. Burke), Yancey Arias (Sixkiller), Mark Edward Anderson (Wayne Northrop), Paul Perri (Maj. Shelby), John Carroll Lynch (Sgt. Plonder), R. Lee Ermey (Pullman T. Fowler), Denis Forest (Dennis Larson), Greg Joung Paik (Maj. Kang), Valerie Hastings (Sgt. Tripet), Patrick Newall (Instructor)

Michael Biehn in *Dead Men Can't Dance* © LIVE Entertainment

Daisy Eagan, Monica Keena in *Ripe* ©Trimark Pictures

RIPE (Trimark) Producers, Suzy Landa, Tom Razzano; Executive Producers, Patrick Panzarella, Michael Chambers; Director/Screenplay, Mo Ogrodnik; Co-Producer, Richard Abramowitz; Photography, Wolfgang Held; Designer, Sally Petersen; Music, Anton Sanko; Editor, Sarah Durham; a C&P production; Ultra-Stereo; Color; Not rated; 93 minutes; May release. **CAST:** Monica Keena (Violet), Daisy Eagan (Rosie), Gordon Currie (Pete), Ron Brice (Ken), Karen Lynn Gorney (Janet Wuman), Vincent Laresca (Jimmy), Scott Sowers (Col. Wyman), Eric Jensen (Dave), Curtis McClarin (H), Donia Silver-Smith (Young Violet), Janna Silver-Smith (Young Rosie), Nurit Koppel (Fran), Bruce McCarty (Daniel), Candice Love (Maxine), Hollie Harper (Dell), Jennifer Chambers (Louise), Mary Leopard (Flag Lady), Zip Hannah (Drill Sergeant), Michael Chambers, Greg Bass, Jac Calabro, Matt Chiaravalle (The Phoids)

FETISHES (Cinema Village Features) Producers, Nick Broomfield, Michelle D'Acosta; Executive Producer, Sheila Nevins; Co-Producer, Jamie Ader-Brown; Director, Nick Broomfield; Photography, Christophe Lazenberg; Editors, Betty Burkhart, Nick Broomfield; Music, Jamie Muhoberac; Associate Producer, Nancy Abraham; Line Producer, S.J. Bloom; Color; Not rated; 90 minutes; May release. A look at the underground world of fetishism and sadomasochism at New York's infamous S&M parlor, Pandora's Box, featuring Mistress Natasha, Mistress Catherine, Mistress Delilah, and Mistress Raven.

Mistress Catherine (left) in *Fetishes*
© Susan Meiselas

Vincent Gallo, Kiefer Sutherland in *Truth or Consequences, N.M.*
© Triumph Films

TRUTH OR CONSEQUENCES, N.M. (Triumph) Producers, J. Paul Higgins, Kevin J. Messick, Hilary Wayne; Executive Producer, Phillip M. Goldfarb; Director, Kiefer Sutherland; Screenplay/Co-Producer, Brad Mirman; Photography, Ric Waite; Designer, Anne Stuhler; Editor, Lawrence Jordan; Costumes, Susan Bertram; Music, Jude Cole; Casting, Janet Hirshenson, Jane Jenkins; a Higgins/Messick/Wayne production; Dolby SDDS Stereo; Technicolor; Rated R; 106 minutes; May release. **CAST:** Vincent Gallo (Raymond Lembecke), Mykelti Williamson (Marcus Weans), Kiefer Sutherland (Curtis Freley), Kevin Pollak (Gordon Jacobson), Kim Dickens (Addy Monroe), Grace Phillips (Donna Moreland), James McDaniel (Frank Thompson), Rick Rossovich (Robert Boylan), John C. McGinley (Eddie Grillo), Max Perilch (Wayne), Rod Steiger (Tony Vago), Martin Sheen (Sir), Scott Christopher (Frank Pearson), Steve O'Neill (Detective), Marshall Bell (Police Lt.), Richard Clark (Don Severt), Mark Lonow (Alan Gryder), Jason Rodriguez, Jim Wilkey (Sir Men), Craig Cliver (Sheriff), Robert Peters (Market Clerk), Craig Clyde (Patrol Officer), Joan Robinson, Colin Patrick Lynch (Sheriffs), Peter Iacangelo (Wiseguy), James Verbois (Man on Hillside), Tim Parati (Cecil), Donre Sampson (Cecil's Man), Bill McIntosh, Perry Barndt, John Brimley (Warehouse Cops), Maurice Dunster (Dodge Owner), Dennis Bridwell, Richard Slaughter, Don Shanks (Vago Wiseguys), Chris Howell (Roadside Bar Fighter)

THE BLOODY CHILD (Mirage Releasing) Producer/Director/Photography, Nina Menkes; Screenplay/Editors, Nina Menkes, Tinka Menkes; a Menkesfilm production for the Independent Television Service; Color; Not rated; 85 minutes; May release. **CAST:** Tinka Menkes (Police Captain), Sherry Sibley (Murdered Wife), Russ Little (Sergeant), Robert Mueller (Murderer), Jack O'Hara (Enlisted Man)

Tina Menkes in *The Bloody Child* © Menkes Films

UNDERWORLD (Legacy) Producers, Robert Vince, William Vince; Executive Producers, Mark Amin, Michael Strange, Abra Edelman; Director, Roger Christian; Screenplay, Larry Bishop; Photography, Steven Bernstein; Designer, John Ebden; Editor, Robin Russell; Music, Anthony Marinelli; Casting, Abra Edelman, Elisa Goodman; a Keystone Pictures in association with Trimark Pictures presentation of a Robert Vince production; Color; Rated R; 95 minutes; May release. **CAST:** Denis Leary (Johnny Crown/Johnny Alt), Joe Mantegna (Frank Gavilan/Richard Essex), Annabella Sciorra (Dr. Leah), Larry Bishop (Ned Lynch), Abe Vigoda (Will Cassady), Robert Costanzo (Stan), Traci Lords (Anna), Jimmie F. Skaggs (Smilin' Phil Fox/Todd Streeb), James Otlkan (Dan "Iceberg" Eagan), Heidi Schanz (Simone/Joyce Alt), Christi Conaway (Julianne), Angela Jones (Janette), Michael David Simms (Mitch Reed), Amy Moon (Ava), Marc Baur (Leo), Michael Benyaer (Vince), Tracey Mannen (Stripper), Claudio De Victor (Bartender), Nino Caratozzolo (Billy Dax), Darcy Laurie (Buster Powell), Ken Roberts (Wild Man Palmer), Dave "Squatch" Ward (Slim Crawford), Dean Wray (Walt Clanton), Frank Ferrucci, L. Harvey Gold, Philip Granger, Sal Sortino (Villa Essex Man), Christine Anthony, Thomasina Grieve, Diana Vlaskalic (Showgirls)

Joe Mantegna, Annabella Sciorra, Denis Leary in *Underworld*
© UnderworldFilms

RUDYARD KIPLING'S THE SECOND JUNGLE BOOK: MOWGLI & BALOO (TriStar) Producer, Raju Patel; Executive Producers, Sharad Patel, Mark Damon; Co-Producer, Peter Shepherd; Co-Executive Producers, Stephen Monas, Mohammed Yusef; Director, Duncan McLachlan; Screenplay, Bayard Johnson, Matthew Horton; Based on characters from the novel *The Jungle Book* by Rudyard Kipling; Photography, Adolfo Bartoli; Designer, Errol Kelly; Music, John Scott; Editor, Marcus Manton; Casting, Don Pemrick, Dean Fronk, Jo Gilbert; an MDP Worldwide and Sharad Patel presentation of a Kiplinbook/Raju Patel production; Dolby Stereo; Technovision; Color; Rated PG; 88 minutes; May release. **CAST:** Jamie Williams (Mowgli), Bill Campbell (Harrison), Roddy McDowall (King Murphy), David Paul Francis (Chuchundra), Gulshan Grover (Buldeo), Cornelia Hayes O'Herlihy (Emily Reece), B.J. Hogg (Col. Reece), Amy Robbins (Molly Ward), Hal Fowler (Capt. Ward), Albert Moses (Conductor), Wijeratne Warakagoda (Engineer), Simon Barker (Train Official), EA Piyasena (Porter), Raja Sumanapala (Buldeo's Servant), Sunil Hettiarachchi (Rickshaw Man)

FRANK CAPRA'S AMERICAN DREAM (Columbia TriStar Television) Producer, Charles A. Duncombe, Jr.; Director/Screenplay, Kenneth Bowser; Photography, Richard Pendleton; Editor, Arnold Galssman; Music, John Hodian; Research, Richard Hutt; Presented in association with Frank Capra Prods., ZM Prods. and Sony Pictures High Definition Center; Color/Black and white; Not rated; 108 minutes; May release. Documentary on filmmaker Frank Capra, narrated by Ron Howard.

Jamie Williams, Timo in *The Second Jungle Book*
© TriStar Pictures

THE TURNING (Leo Films) formerly Home Fires Burning; Producers, William B. O'Boyle, L.A. Puopolo; Director, L.A. Puopolo; Screenplay, Chris Ceraso, L.A. Puopolo; Based on the play *Home Fires Burning* by Chris Ceraso; Photography, J. Michael McClary; Designer, Mike Moran; Costumes, Natasha Landau; Editor, Lesley Topping; Music, Herb Pilhofer; 1992; Color; Rated R; 91 minutes; May release. **CAST**: Karen Allen (Glory Lawson), Raymond J. Barry (Mark Harnish), Michael Dolan (Clifford Harnish), Tess Harper (Martha Harnish), Gillian Anderson (April Cavanaugh), Jim Simmons (Mayor), Madison Arnold (Mr. Cavanaugh), Tannis Benedict (Vivian Sinott), John Newton (Mr. Creasy), Bill O'Boyle (Pete Tarosky), Murphy Larson (Rita Smithson), Michael P. Moran (Jim McCutcheon)

JOE & JOE (Independent) Producers, Sean Patrick Brena, David Wall, David Wysocki; Director/Screenplay, David Wall; No other credits available; Color; Not rated; 80 minutes; May release. **CAST**: Sean Patrick Brennan, Tracy Griffith, David Wysocki.

Mario Yedidia, Doug Jones in *Warriors Of Virtue*
© IJL Creations/Law Bros. Ent.

WARRIORS OF VIRTUE (MGM) Producers, Dennis Law, Ronald Law, Christopher Law, Jeremy Law, Patricia Ruben; Executive Producer, Joseph Law; Director, Ronny Yu; Screenplay, Michael Vickerman, Hugh Kelley; Co-Producers, Peter Pau, Ronny Yu; Photography, Peter Pau; Editor, David Wu; Music, Don Davis; Make-up and Animatronic Character Effects, Tony Gardner & Alterian Studios; Action Choreographer, Siuming Tsui; Costumes, Shirley Chan; Visual Effects Supervisor, John Gajdecki; Line Producers, Ogden Gavanski, Hong-An Jin, Nancy Rae Stone; a Law Brothers production; Digital DTS Stereo; Panavision; Deluxe color; Rated PG; 101 minutes; May release. **CAST:** Angus Macfadyen (Komodo), Mario Yedidia (Ryan), Marley Shelton (Elysia), Chao-Li Chi (Master Chung), Jack Tate (Yun), Doug Jones (Yee), Don W. Lewis (Lai), J. Todd Adams (Chi), Adrienne Corcoran (Tsun), Michael John Anderson (Mudlap), Tom Towles (Grillo), Lee Arenberg (Mantose), Dennis Dun (Ming), Roy Ceballos (Willy Beest), Jason Hamer (Mosely), Don W. Lewis (Mayor Keena), Rickey D'Shon Collins (Chucky), Michael Dubrow (Brad), Peter Abrahamson (Chila), Stuart Kingston (Dullard), Qu Ying (Barbarotious), Gill Butler, Victoria Schoenke (Villagers), Michael Vickerman (Dragoon Commander), Warren Moon (Coach), Teryl Rothery (Kathryn), Julie Patzwald (Tracey), Kimberly Warnat (Lisa), Adam Mills (Toby), Clay McRae, Hamish Allan-Headley (Football Pals), Lian-Yi Li (Chinese Cook), Tynehead's Dog "Rush" (Bravo)

MURDER AND MURDER (Zeitgeist) Producer/Director/Screenplay, Yvonne Rainer; Photography, Stephen Kazmierski; Designer, Stephen McCabe; Costumes, Linda Gui; Music, Frank London; Casting, Heidi Griffiths; Color; Nor rated; 113 minutes; June release. **CAST:** Joanna Merlin (Doris), Kathleen Chalfant (Mildred), Catherine Kellner (Young Mildred), Isa Thomas (Jenny), Yvonne Rainer (Herself), Alice Playten, Kendal Thomas, Rod McLachlan, Jennie Moreau, Sasha Martin, Barbara Haas, Rainn Wilson

Denise Faye, Rick Negron in *The Next Step* © Phaedra Films

THE NEXT STEP (Phaedra) Producers, Aaron Reed, Hank Blumenthal; Director, Christian Faber; Screenplay, Aaron Reed; Photography, Zack Winestine; Editors, Judd Maslansky, David Codron; Music, Roni Skies, Mio Morales, Brian Otto; Choreographer, Donald Byrd; Designer, Elise Bennett; Costumes, Nancy Brous, Ivan Ingerman; Associate Producers, Taylor Nichols, Raphael Moreu; a Curb Entertainment presentation of a Wavelength production; Color; Not rated; 97 minutes; June release. **CAST**: Rick Negron (Nick), Kristin Moreu (Amy), Denise Faye (Heidi), Taylor Nichols (Peter), Gerry McIntyre (Sean), Aubrey Lynch (Steven), Michelle Pertier (Michelle), Donald Byrd (Austin), Fuschia Walker (Rolanda), Jane Edith Wilson (Greta), Barry McNabb (Owen), Yvonne Racz (Veronica), Jamie Bishton (Kevin), Michael Donaghy (Luis), Howard Wesson (Louie), Fredrick Deane (Scott), Richard Stegman (Agent), Chris Eigeman (David), Peter Reffie (Frankie), John Battista (Sal), Julio Munge (Ramon), Ted Neuhoff (Husband in Restaurant), Yvonne Trinkwater (Wife in Restaurant), Pamela Berkeley (Woman in Hotel), Mio Morales (Prem), David Turley (Beefcakes Waiter), Max Miller (Dr. Astin), Joan Ranquet (Woman in Bar), Thomas Gibson (Bartender), Star Reese (Videographer), Lisa Johnson (Dance Captain)

Rudolph Martin, Amanda De Cadenet in *Fall*
© Capella International

FALL (Capella Intl.) Producers, Eric Schaeffer, Terence Michael; Director/Screenplay, Eric Schaeffer; Photography, Joe De Salvo; Editor, Thom Zimny; Music, Amanda Kravat; a Five Minutes Before the Miracle presentation; Color; Not rated; 94 minutes; June release. **CAST**: Eric Schaeffer (Michael Shiver), Amanda DeCadenet (Sarah Easton), Rudolph Martin (Philippe), Francie Swift (Robin), Lisa Vidal (Sally), Roberta Maxwell (Joan Alterman), Jose Yenque (Scasse), Josip Kuchan (Zsarko)

TIMOTHY LEARY'S DEAD (Strand) Producers/Screenplay, Todd Easton Mills, Paul Davids; Director, Paul Davis; Photography, Paul Helling; Editors, David Wilson, Mark Deimel; Music, The Moody Blues, Ray Thomas; a Todd Easton Mills presentation; Color; Not rated; 80 minutes; June release. Documentary on former Harvard psychology professor Timothy Leary who became a guru and promoter of sixties counter-culture and psychedelic tripping; featuring Timothy Leary, Richard Alpert (Ram Dass), Frank DiPaola.

Timothy Leary in *Timothy Leary's Dead* © Strand Releasing

LATE BLOOMERS (Strand) Producers, Gretchen Dyer, Stephen Dyer, Julia Dyer; Executive Producers, Jim Jerge, Martha Little; Director, Julia Dyer; Screenplay, Gretchen Dyer; Photography, Bill Schwarz; Designer, Michael McGarty; Editors, Julia Dyer, Gretchen Dyer; Costumes, Happy Yancey, Mattie O'Neal; Music, Ted Pine; Casting, Nancy Fine; a One Mind Productions Feature, Ultra-Stereo; Color; Not rated; 104 minutes; June release. **CAST**: Connie Nelson (Dinah Groshardt), Dee Hennigan (Carly Lumpkin), Gary Carter (Rom Lumpkin), Lisa Peterson (Val Lumpkin), Esteban Powell (Jamie Hooper), Joe Nemmers (Rick Musso), T.A. Taylor (Bill Boardway)

Connie Nelson, Dee Hennigan in *Late Bloomers*
© *Strand Releasing*

THE LAST TIME I COMMITTED SUICIDE (Kushner-Locke) Producers, Edward Bates, Louise Rosner; Executive Producers, Peter Abrams, Robert F. Levy, J.P. Guerin, Peter Locke, Donald Kushner, Lawrence Mortorff; Co-Executive Producers, Estelle Lasher, Elizabeth Robinson; Director/Screenplay, Stephen Kay; Photography, Bobby Bukowski; Designer, Amy B. Ancona; Editor, Dorian Harris; Music, Tyler Bates; from Tapestry Films; Dolby Stereo; Color; Rated R; 92 minutes; June release. **CAST**: Thomas Jane (Neal), Keanu Reeves (Harry), Tom Bower (Captain), Adrien Brody (Ben), John Doe (Lew), Claire Forlani (Joan), Marg Helgenberger (Lizzy), Alexandra Holden (Vicky), Lucinda Jenny (Rosie Trickle), Pat McNamara (Father Fletcher), Gretchen Mol (Cherry Mary), Christie Rose (Mrs. Greenway), Meadow Sisto (Sarah), Amy Smart (Jeananne), Kate Williamson (Nurse). (Note: This film premiered on cable television in early 1997).

HEAD ABOVE WATER (Fine Line Features) Producers, Jim Wilson, John M. Jacobsen; Executive Producers, Guy East, Tristan Whalley; Director, Jim Wilson; Screenplay, Theresa Marie; Based on a screenplay by Geir Eriksen, Eirik Ildahl; Photography, Richard Bowen; Designer, Jeffrey Beecroft; Editor, Michael R. Miller; Music, Christopher Young; Costumes, Colleen Atwood; Casting, Elisabeth Leustig; a Tig Productions/Majestic Films production; Dolby Digital Stereo; Super 35 Widescreen; Deluxe Color; Rated PG-13; 92 minutes; June release. **CAST**: Harvey Keitel (George), Cameron Diaz (Nathalie), Craig Sheffer (Lance), Billy Zane (Kent), Shay Duffin (Policeman), Mo (Mo). (Note: This film premiered on cable television in February 1997).

Thomas Jane in *The Last Time I Committed Suicide*
© Kushner Locke Int.

Cameron Diaz, Harvey Keitel in *Head Above Water*
© Tig Productions

END OF SUMMER (JGM Enterprises) Producer/Director/Linda Yellen; Executive Produces, Ted Swanson, Karen Goodwin; Screenplay, Jonathan Platnick, Linda Yellen; Photography, David Bridges; Designer, Bob Ziembicki; Music, Patrick Seymour; a Showtime presentation in association with Hallmark Entertainment; Ultra-Stereo; Deluxe Color; Rated R; 95 minutes; June release. **CAST**: Jacqueline Bisset (Christine Van Burne), Peter Weller (Theo Remmington), Julian Sands (Basil), Amy Locane (Alice), Elizabeth Shepherd (Vera), Michael Hogan (The General), Karyn Dwyer (Jenny), Janet-Laine Green (Lucie), Dennis O'Connor (Otto), Colin Fox (Ezra), Peter James Haworth (Brother), Lynne Cormack (Sister-in-Law), Susan Coyne (Supervisor), Polly Shannon (Maid), Don Allison (Hotel Manager), June Crowley (Romantic Singer), Stan Coles (Ezra's Doctor), Emma Corosky (Helena), Barry Flatman (Mr. Anderson), Caroline Yeager (Mrs. Anderson), Nolan Jennings (Theo's Doctor), Alan Jordan (Investor), Myles Dumont (Little Boy)

Sheryl Lee, Craig Sheffer in *Bliss*
© Triumph Films

BLISS (Triumph) Producer, Allyn Stewart; Executive Producer, Matthew O'Connor; Director/Screenplay, Lance Young; Photography, Mike Molloy; Editor, Allan Lee; Music, Jan A.P. Kaczmarek; Designers, John Willettt, David Lloyd Fischer; Co-Producer, Lisa Towers; Costumes, Jori Woodman; Casting, Glenn Daniels; a Stewart Pictures production, in association with Pacific Motion Pictures Corp.; Dolby SDDS Stereo; Technicolor; Rated R; 103 minutes; June release. **CAST**: Craig Sheffer (Joseph), Sheryl Lee (Maria), Terence Stamp (Baltazar Vincenza), Casey Siemaszko (Tanner), Spalding Gray (Alfred), Leigh Taylor Young (Redhead), Lois Chiles (Eva), Blu Mankuma (Nick), Ken Camroux (Hank), Pamela Perry (Dottie), Eli Gabay (Carlos), Molly Parker (Connie), Hiro Kanagawa (Doctor), Merrilyn Gann (Motel Woman), Gillian Barber (Therapist), Peter Kelamis (Neighbor), Norman Armour (Patient), David Glyn-Jones (Priest), Quincy & Carson Welch (Boy), Serena Bodnar (Girl), Kristin Lehman (Scope/Steps Woman), Akesh Gill (Therapy Woman)

Waco: The Rules of Engagement © Somford Entertainment

WACO: THE RULES OF ENGAGEMENT (Somford Entertainment) Producers/Photography, William Gazecki, Rick Nyburg; Director/Editor, William Gazecki; Music, David Hamilton; Color; Not rated; 135 minutes; June release. Documentary on the 1993 events outside of Waco, Texas, during which four federal agents and 76 members of the Branch Davidians died. (This film received an Oscar nomination as feature-length documentary).

A LIFE APART: HASIDISM IN AMERICA (First Run Features) Producers/Directors, Menachem Daum, Oren Rudavsky; Executive Producer, Arnold Labaton; Screenplay, Menachem Daum, Bob Seidman; Photography, Oren Rudavsky; Music, Yale Strom; Editor, Ruth Schell; Narrators, Leonard Nimoy, Sarah Jessica Parker; Color; Not rated; 95 minutes; July release. Documenatary on the creation of the Hasidic communities in America following the Holocaust.

A Life Apart: Hasidism in America © First Run Features

Anthony Barrile, Nick Scotti in *Kiss Me, Guido*
© Paramount Pictures

KISS ME, GUIDO (Paramount) Producers, Ira Deutchman, Christine Vachon; Executive Producers, Jane Barclay, Tom Carouso, Sharon Harel, Christopher Lawford; Director/Screenplay, Tony Vitale; Photography, Claudia Raschke; Designer, Jeffrey Rathaus; Costumes, Victoria Farrell; Editor, Alexander Hall; Line Producer, Katie Roumel; Casting, Hopkins, Smith and Barden; a Redeemable Features production, presented in association with Kardana/Swinsky Films and Capitol Films; Color; Rated R; 86 minutes; July release. **CAST:** Nick Scotti (Frankie Zito), Anthony Barrile (Warren), Anthony DeSando (Pino Zito), Craig Chester (Terry), Domenick Lombardozzi (Joey Chips), Molly Price (Meryl), Christopher Lawford (Dakota), David Deblinger ("#"), John Tormey (Patsy Zito), Antonia Rey (Josephina Zito), Irma St. Paule (Grandma), Jennifer Esposito (Debbie), Anthony Vitale, Frankie Dellarosa (Guidos), Rebecca Waxman (Wiggy), Tony Ray Rossi (Vinny the Fish), Dwight Ewell (Usher), Marcia Firesten (Real Estate Broker), Bryan Batt (Tino), Craig Archibald (Robbie), Guinevere Turner (Indignant Lesbian), Damien Achilles, Bruce Smolanoff (Tough Guys)

Princess Odette, Jean-Bob in *The Swan Princess* © Legacy

SHOOTING PORN (Caryn Horwitz Presents) Producers, Caryn Horwitz, Doug Lindeman; Director/Creator, Ronnie Larsen; Photography, Bruce McCarthy; Editor, James Lyons; Color; Not rated; 75 minutes; July release. Documentary on the gay porn industry featuring Gino Colbert, Chi Chi LaRue (Porn Directors), Blue Blake, Bryan Kidd, Adam Rom, Hunter Scott, Rip Stone, Adam Wilde (Porn Actors), Mickey Skee, David Widmer (Porn Critics-Reviewers)

THE SWAN PRINCESS: ESCAPE FROM CASTLE MOUNTAIN (Legacy) Producers, Richard Rich, Jared F. Brown; Executive Producers, Seldon O. Young, Jared F. Brown, K. Douglas Martin; Director, Richard Rich; Screenplay, Brian Nissen; Story, Richard Rich, Brian Nissen; Editor, James D. Koford; Songs, Lex de Azevedo, Clive Romney; Music, Lex de Azevedo; Character Design, Steve E. Gordon; Storyboard Artists, Steven E. Gordon, Bruce Woodside, Frank Paur; a Nest Entertainment/Seldon O. Young, Jared F. Brown, K. Douglas Martin presentation of a Rich Animation Studios production; Color; Rated G; 71 minutes; July release. **VOICE CAST**: Michelle Nicastro (Odette), Douglas Sills (Derek), Jake Williamson (Clavius), Christy Landers (Uberta), Donald Sage MacKay (Jean-Bob), Doug Stone (Speed), Steve Vinovich (Puffin), Joseph Medrano (Lord Rogers), James Arrinton (Chamberlain), Joey Camen (Knuckles), Owen Miller (Bromley), Rosie Mann (Bridget)

Shainee Gabel, Kristin Hahn in *Anthem*
© Zeitgeist Films

ANTHEM (Zeitgeist) Producers/Directors/Screenplay, Shainee Gabel, Kristin Hahn; Executive Producer, Jo Ann Fagan; Photography, Bill Brown; Editor, Lucas Platt; a Gabel/Hahn production; Color; Not rated; 124 minutes; July release. Documentation of a 1995 road trip by Shainee Gabel and Kristin Hahn as they set out across the country to interview some of America's people, with Jim Adkisson, Miguel Algarin, Jimmy Santiago Baca, John Perry Barlow, Dorothy Betts, Rev. Marvin Lewis Booker, Douglas Brinkley, Lisa "Suckdog" Carver, Chuck D, Rita Dove, Geraldine Ferraro, Dave Foreman, Jack Healey, Wes Jackson, Winona Laduke, George McGovern, Willie Nelson, Krist Novoselic, Robert Redford, Tom Robbins, Michael Spinola, George Stephanopoulos, Michael Stipe, Studs Terkel, Hunter S. Thompson, Micah Wagner, Rebecca Walker, John Waters.

THE WINNER (LIVE Entertainment) Producer, Kenneth Schwenker; Executive Producers, Mark Damon, Rebecca DeMornay; Director, Alex Cox; Screenplay, Wendy Riss; Based on her play *A Darker Purpose*; Co-Executive Producer, Andrew Pfeffer; Photography, Denis Maloney; Designer, Cecilia Montiel; Editor, Carlos Puente; Color; Not rated; 91 minutes; July release. **CAST:** Rebecca DeMornay (Louise), Vincent D'Onforio (Philip), Richard Edson (Frankie), Saverio Guerra (Paulie), Delroy Lindo (Kingman), Michael Madsen (Wolf), Billy Bob Thornton (Jack), Frank Whaley (Joey), Luis Contreras (Guy in Couple), Ed Pansullo (Man with Broken Arm), Sy Richardson (Bartender), Craig Vincent (Man), Bigg Yeager (Philip's Father), Del Zamora (Cellmate), Roger Jennings (Croupier), Alex Cox (Gaston). (This film made its U.S. premiere earlier in the year on cable television)

Rebecca DeMornay, Michael Madsen in *The Winner*
© LIVE Entertainment

CAFE SOCIETY (Northern Arts Entertainment) Producers, Steve Alexander, Elan Sassoon; Executive Producers, Carl-Jan Colpaert, Frederic Bouin, Jim Steele; Director/Screenplay, Raymond De Felitta; Photography, Michael Mayers; Editor, Suzy Elmiger; Music, Chris Guardino; a Cineville presentation in association with Skyline Entertainment and Daylight productions; Color/Black and whitw; Not rated; 107 minutes; July release. **CAST:** Peter Gallagher (Jack Kale), Frank Whaley (Mickey Jelke), Lara Flynn Boyle (Patricia Ward), John Spencer (Ray Davioni), Anna Thompson (Erica Steele), David Patrick Kelly (J. Roland Sala), Christopher Murney (Frank Frustinsky), Paul Guilfoyle (Anthony Liebler), Richard B. Shull (Samuel Segal), Cynthia Watros (Diane Harris), Alan Manson (Judge Valente), Alan North (Frank Hogan), Kelly Bishop (Mrs. Jelke), Zach Grenier (Milton Macka), Ivy DeFelitta (Dorothy Kilgallen), Marshall Efron (Moe Persky), Robert Whaley (Marco), Joshua Whiting (Arthur), Norman Douglas (Tux), Larry Weiss (Bartender), Bill McHugh (Richard Short), Kelly Reynolds (June Short), Arnold Sherman (Greenbaum), Beth Schakatt (The Stripper), Elaina Redmond (Cora), Steve Alexander (Reporter). (This film made its U.S. premiere on cable television in 1996)

Frank Whaley, Peter Gallagher in *Cafe Society*
© Northern Arts Entertainment

BEYOND BARBED WIRE (Tribute to Freedom Foundation) Producer/Screenplay, Terri DeBono; Executive Producers, Yukio Sumida, Sherry Lapham Thomas, Charles Richard Woodson; Director/Editor/Photography, Steve Rosen; Narrator, Noriyuki "Pat" Morita; a Mac and Ava film presented in association with Sunwood Entertainment; Color/Black and white; Not raed; 88 minutes; July release. Documentary on the Japanese-Americans who fought in World War II.

Scott Thompson, Mark Metcalf, Henry Thomas in *Hijacking Hollywood*
© Broken Twig Prods.

HIJACKING HOLLYWOOD (Broken Twig Prods.) Producer/Director, Neil Mandt; Screenplay, Neil Mandt, Jim Rossow; Executive Producer, Ann Mandt; Photography, Anton Floquet; Designer, Todd Cherniawsky; Editor, Charlie Webber; Music, Erik Lundmark; a Curb Entertaiment/Broken Twig production; Ultra-Stereo; Color; Not rated; 91 minutes; July release. **CAST:** Henry Thomas (Kevin Conroy), Scott Thompson (Russell), Mark Metcalf (Michael Lawrence), Neil Mandt (Tad), Paul Hewitt (Harvey), Nicole Gian (Sarah), Art La Fleur (Eddie), Shirly Brener (Ginger), Helen Duffy (Mrs. Cohen), Mark Holton, Loren Lazerine (Officers), Hedy Popson (Sandy), J.F. Pryor (Shaft), Noella Akwiri (Receptionist), Chris Morris (Grip), Bobby Knoeral (P.A.), Steve Van Wormer (Tony), Joe Watson (Bicycler)

SOUL IN THE HOLE (Northern Arts) Producer, Lilibet Foster; Director, Danielle Gardner; Photography, Paul Gibson; Editor, Melissa Neidich; Associate Producer, Alise Allen; an Asphalt Films production; Color; Not rated; 90 minutes; August release. Documentary on the basketball street tournaments held on the playgrounds of Brooklyn, featuring Ed "Booger" Smith, Kenny Jones, Kenny's Kings.

Ed "Booger" Smith in *Soul in the Hole*
© Northern Arts

Natalie Desselle, Bill Bellamy, Mari Morrow in *How To Be A Player* © Gramercy Pictures

DEF JAM'S HOW TO BE A PLAYER (Gramercy) Producers, Mark Burg, Todd Baker, Russell Simmons, Preston Holmes; Executive Producers, Robert Newmyer, Jeffrey Silver, Stan Lathan; Co-Producers, Joanne Milter, Rose Catherine Pinkney, Carrie Morrow; Director, Lionel C. Martin; Screenplay, Mark Brown, Demetria Johnson; Story, Mark Brown; Music, Darren Floyd; Editor, William Young; Casting, Jaki Brown-Karman; a PolyGram Filmed Entertainment presentation of an Island Pictures production, in association with Outlaw Productions; Dolby Stereo; Deluxe color; Rated R; 94 minutes; August release. **CAST**: Bill Bellamy (Drayton Jackson), Natalie Desselle (Jenny Jackson), Lark Voorhies (Lisa), Mari Morrow (Katrina), Pierre (David), Jermaine "Big Hugg" Hopkins (Kilo), A.J. Johnson (Spootie), Max Julien (Uncle Fred), Beverly Johnson (Robin), Gilbert Gottfried (Tony the Doorman), Bernie Mac (Buster), Stacii Jae Johnson (Sherri), Elise Neal (Nadine), J. Anthony Brown (Uncle Snook), Amber Smith (Amber), Devika Parikh (Barbara), Bebe Drake (Mama Jackson), Gillian Iliana Waters (Shante), Tara Davis (Cute Party Girl), Marta Boyett (C.C.), Jazsmin Lewis (Pookie), Licia Shearer (Nikki), Jerod Mixon, Jamal Mixon (Kids), D.D. Rainbow (Jealous Girl), Natashia Williams (Pink Bikini Girl), Edith Grant (Peaches), Jesse Collins (D.J.), Melissa Cross (Sales Girl), Claude "Pete" Bryant (Chess Player)

THE DELTA (Strand) Producer, Margot Bridger; Director/Screenplay, Ira Sachs; Photography, Benjamin P. Speth; Designer, Bernhard Blythe; Editor, Affonso Gonçalves; Music, Michael Rohatyn; Costumes, Stevan Lazich; a Charlie Guidance production; Technicolor; Not rated; 85 minutes; August release. **CAST**: Shayne Gray (Lincoln Bloom), Thang Chan (Minh Nguyen—John), Rachel Zan Huss (Monica), Colonius Davis (Ricky Little), Larry Reynolds (Man in Park), Angelique Owens (Donut Shop Clerk), Leigh Walden (Cece Bloom), Gene Crain (Sam Bloom), Charles Ingram (Gary Bloom), Ron Gephart (Ken Bloom), Kim Newman (Denise Bloom), Polly Edelstein (Debbie Bloom), Vanita Thomas (Bernice), Randall Reinke (Danny), Melissa Dunn (Tina Clifton), Erin Grills (Jacquie Clifton), Kate Davis (Gloria Clifton), Alluring Strange (Club Band), Mark Hyman (Club Bouncer), Michael Locke (Michael—Kid on Bike), Robert Hathaway (2nd Kid on Bike), Lamar Sorrento (Ted), Richard Daggett (Pick-up Driver), Anthony Isbell (Jerry—Man in Hotel), J.R. Crumpton (Joe), Patricia A. Gill (Joe's Wife), Moses J. Peace (Policeman), Nhan Van Dang (Minh's Roommate), Bay Thi Ho (Old Vietnamese Woman), Hoang N. Pham (Minh's Friend), Mai Ballard (Pool Hall Owner)

Shayne Gray in *The Delta* © Strand Releases

Lauren Holly, Greg Kinnear in *A Smile Like Yours* © Paramount Pictures

A SMILE LIKE YOURS (Paramount) Producers, David Kirkpatrick, Tony Amatullo; Executive Producer, Robert Harling; Director, Keith Samples; Screenplay, Kevin Meyer, Keith Samples; Photography, Richard Bowen; Designer, Garreth Stover; Editor, Wayne Wahrman; Costumes, Jill Ohanneson; Music, William Ross; Title song by Diane Warren/performed by Natalie Cole; Casting, Jennifer Shull; a Rysher Entertainment presentation of a David Kirkpatrick production; Dolby Digital Stereo; Super 35 Widescreen; Deluxe color; Rated R; 99 minutes; August release. **CAST**: Greg Kinnear (Danny Robertson), Lauren Holly (Jennifer Robertson), Joan Cusack (Nancy Tellen), Jay Thomas (Steve Harris), Jill Hennessy (Lindsay Hamilton), Christopher McDonald (Richard Halstrom), Donald Moffat (Dr. Felber), France Nuyen (Dr. Chin), Marianne Muellerleile (Nurse Wheeler), Shirley MacLaine (Martha), Sheridan Samples (Holly), Barbara Larsen (Woman in Window/Woman on Plane), Tony Abou-Ganim, Nick Scoggin (Welders), Genee Nakashita (Karaoke Bar Owner), Lewis Brown, Nicholas Bearde, June Lomena, Latrice Sellers, Lynda Marie Sellers, Kirby Coleman, Dooney Jones, Bilal Muslim (Karaoke Acts), Steven Brown, Paul Ghiringhelli, Richard Thorn (Baseball Buddies), T. Michael Sutton (Pool Hall Guy), Ben Stein (Clinic Video Narrator), Meggan Kimberley, Jack Sharrar (Couple at Fertility Clinic), Nancy Carlin (Pregnant Mother), Tony Amatullo, Tim Helfet, Jeff Matloff, Brad Rivers (Surrell Board Members), Kevin Wiatt, Terri Orth-Pallavinci (Couple Entering Fertility Clinic), Craig Samples, Carol Samples, Jennifer Samples, Karen Samples, Ellen Samples (Baby Stroller Family), Michael Jang, Woody Jang, Tali Jang (Family with Camera), Ellen Hoberman, Sarah Hoberman (Mother and Daughter), Marianna Amatullo, Nicolas Amatullo (Pregnant Family), Kent Samples, Katie Samples, Brandon Samples (Reading Family), Michael Santo (Maitre D'), Jim Cranna (Guy on Plane), Charlie Holliday (Cab Driver), Marle Gaines (Perky Airline Representative), Helen Swee (Angry Flight Attendant), Joy Michiel (Woman on Plane), Jim Burke (Nancy Tellen's Groom), Christine Doherty, Kathryn Doherty, Matthew Doherty (The Robertsons' Triplets)

Kevin Sorbo in *Kull the Conqueror* © Universal Studios ,Inc.

KULL THE CONQUEROR (Universal) Producer, Raffaella De Laurentiis; Co-Producer, Hester Hargett; Director, John Nicolella; Screenplay, Charles Edward Pogue; Based on the Worlds and the Characters Created by Robert E. Howard; Photography, Rodney Charters; Designer, Benjamin Fernandez; Editor, Dallas Puett; Music, Joel Goldsmith; Costumes, Thomas Casterline, Sibylle Ulsamer; Special Effects Supervisor, Kit West; Visual Effects Supervisor, Richard Malzahn; Associate Producer, Arthur M. Lieberman; Executive Producers, Beverlee Dean, Jeff Franklin, Steve Waterman; Casting, Jeffery Passero, Elizabeth Hayden-Passero; a Raffaella De Laurentiis production; DTS Stereo; Super 35 Widescreen; Deluxe color; Rated PG-13; 95 minutes; August release. **CAST:** Kevin Sorbo (Kull), Tia Carrere (Akivasha), Thomas Ian Griffith (Taligaro), Litefoot (Ascalante), Roy Brocksmith (Tu), Harvey Fierstein (Juba), Karina Lombard (Zaretta), Edward Tudor-Pole (Enaros), Douglas Henshall (Ducalon), Joe Shaw (Dalgar), Sven Ole Thorsen (King Borna), Terry O'Neill (Ship Captain), Pat Roach (Zuleki), John Hallam (Mandara), Peter Petruna, Boris Bacik (Slaves), Paul Kynman, Paul Weston (Dragon Legion Guards)

BUTCH CAMP (Billingsgate Prod.) Producers, Timothy E. Sabo, Steven Gellman; Executive Producer, Gary Metzger; Director/Screenplay, Alessandro De Gaetano; Photography, C. Brett Webster; Editors, Amy Harvey, Jeanne Bonansinga; Music, Conrad Pope; Color; Not rated; 103 minutes; August release. **CAST:** Judy Tenuta (Samantha Rottweiler), Paul Denniston (Matt Grabowski), Jason Terisi (Rod Cazzone), Jordan Roberts (Janet), Bill Ingraham (Danny), Duane Sharp, Joel Himelhoch, Richard Henzel, John Kimilcko, Sean Solan, Stephanie Ferrell.

Vincent Kartheiser, Patrick Stewart in *Masterminds* © Columbia Pictures Industries, Inc.

MASTERMINDS (Columbia) Producers, Robert Dudelson, Floyd Byars; Executive Producers, Matthew O'Connor, David Saunders; Director, Roger Christian; Screenplay, Floyd Byars; Story, Floyd Byars, Alex Siskin, Chris Black; Co-Executive Producer, Richard M. Heller; Photography, Nic Morris; Designer, Douglas Higgins; Editor, Robin Russell; Costumes, Monique Sanchez, Derek J. Baskerville; Music, Anthony Marinelli; Associate Producers, Patti Allen, T. Michael O'Connor; Casting, Andrea Stone; a Pacific Motion Pictures production; a Byars/Duddelson production; Dolby SDDS Stereo; Super 35 Widescreen; Deluxe color; Rated PG-13; 106 minutes; August release. **CAST:** Patrick Stewart (Rafe Bentley), Vincent Kartheiser (Ozzie Paxton), Brenda Fricker (Principal Claire Maloney), Brad Whitford (Miles Lawrence), Matt Craven (Jake Paxton), Annabelle Gurwitch (Helen Paxton), Jon Abrahams (K-Dog), Katie Stuart (Melissa Randall), Michael MacRae (Foster Deroy), Callum Keith Rennie (Ollie), Earl Pastko (Capt. Jankel), Jason Schombing (Marvin), Michael David Simms (Col. Duke), David Paul Grove (Ferret), Akiko Morison (Janet), Teryl Rothery (Ms. Saunders), Vanessa Morley (Gabby), Douglas Arthurs, Phillip Granger, Andrew Kavadas, Lauro Chartrand, Charles Andre, Alan Van Sprang, Nino Caratozzolo (Happy Boys), Bruce Pinard (Happy Boy Guard), April Telek (Sexy Girl), Steve Makaj (Capt. Majors), Jay Brazeau (Eliot), Douglas Newell (Science Teacher), Frank Cassini (Cop), Kimberly Unger (Flight Attendant), Pamela Martin, Merrett Green (TV Reporters), Andrew Wheeler (Bank Officer), Michael Benyaer (Taxi Driver)

Matthew Hennessey, Lee Holmes, Steve Parlavecchio, Kevin Corrigan in *Bandwagon* © CFP Distribution

BANDWAGON (CFP) Producers, Alyson Poole, John Schultz; Co-Producer, Michael Shevloff; Director/Screenplay, John Schultz; Photography, Shawn Maurer; Editor, John Pace; Music, Greg Kendall; a Lakeshore Entertainment and Pamlico Pictures presentation; Dolby Stereo; Color; Not rated; 99 minutes; September release. **CAST:** Kevin Corrigan (Wynn Knapp), Lee Holmes (Tony Ridge), Matthew Hennessey (Charlie Flagg), Steve Parlavecchio (Eric Ellwood), Doug MacMillan (Linus Tate)

CRACKING UP (Phaedra Cinema) Producer/Director/Editor, Matt Mitler; Screenplay, Matt Mitler, Theodore P. Lorusso; Photography, Mark Traver; Music, Arthur Rosen; Co-Producer, Lilli Mitler; Associate Producers, Robert Prichard, Jennifer Prichard, William Otterson; a Foolish Mortal Films production; Color; Not rated; 93 minutes; September release. **CAST**: Matt Mitler (Danny Gold), Carolyn McDermott (Carolyn Davis), Kevin Brown (Dack Waterbone), Kimberly Flynn (Kimberly Lane), Debra Wilson (Alliandra Burrel), Jason Brill (Jake Weinberg), Jeff Eyres (Cosmo), David Wells (Alan Malcolm), Jonathan Powers (Mr. Strong), Frank Senger (Mr. Kansy), Cynthia Rector (Head Shaved Girl), Chuck Montgomery (M.C. Lucky Jackson), Sherry Anderson, John Augustine (Philanthropic Couple), Todd Alcott, Gail Dennison (Themselves)

James Woods, Kevin Corrigan in
Kicked in the Head © October Films

KICKED IN THE HEAD (October Films) Producer, Barbara De Fina; Executive Producer, Martin Scorsese; Director, Matthew Harrison; Screenplay, Kevin Corrigan, Matthew Harrison; Photography, John Thomas, Howard Krupa; Editor, Michael Berenbaum; Music, Stephen Endelman; Designer, Kevin Thompson; Costumes, Nina Canter; Casting, Sheila Jaffe, Georgianne Walken; a De Fina/Cappa Production; Dolby Stereo; Color; Rated R; 88 minutes; September release. **CAST**: Kevin Corrigan (Redmond), Linda Fiorentino (Megan), Michael Rapaport (Stretch), James Woods (Uncle Sam), Burt Young (Jack), Lili Taylor (Happy), Olek Krupa (Borko), Elliot Cuker (Sheldon), David Deblinger (Escalator Man), Alan Davidson (Subway Gunman), Bianca Bakija (Pearl), Sol Frieder (Elderly Man), Matthew Harrison (Luau Man), Gary Perez (Dean), John Ventimiglia (Man at Party), Royale Watkins (Chicky), Lawton Paseka (Pilot), George Odom (Door Person), Nicole Baptiste (Cop)

Pamela Stewart, Tara Bellando in
100 Proof

100 PROOF (Independent-Film Forum) Producer/Editor, George Maranville; Executive Producer, Jay Faires; Director/Screenplay, Jeremy Horton; Photography, Harold Jarboe; Costumes, Peggy Watts; Designer, Patrick McNeese; Music, Michael Mossier; Color; Not rated; 94 minutes; September release. **CAST:** Pamela Stewart (Rae), Tara Bellando (Carla), Jack Stubblefield Johnson (Arco), Minnie Bates Yancy (Sissy), Larry Brown (Eddie), Kevin Hardesty (Roger), Jim Varney (Rae's Father), Loren Crawford (Trudy), Joe Ventura (Ted), Warren Ray (Tommy), Jeff Lycan (R.T.), Bobby Simmons (Toby), Peter Smith (Fryman), Buck Finley (Chester), Joe Gatton (Owen), Nick Ewan, Josh Barrett (Boys), Clint Voight, Brad K. Ingram (Policemen), Archie Borders, Evelyn Blythe (Yuppies), Ed Desiato (Chappy), Ben Daughtrey (Parkette Cook), Peggy Watts (Liquor Customer)

THE TOILERS AND THE WAYFARERS (Outsider Enterprises) Producers, Karen Manion, Ralf Schirg, Keith Froelich; Executive Producer, Marc Huestis; Director/Screenplay, Keith Froelich; Photography, Jim Tittle; Editors, Robb Harriss, Keith Froelich; Music, Chan Poling; Casting, Jessica Nelson; 1995; Black and White; Not rated; 75 minutes; September release. **CAST:** Matt Klemp (Dieter), Ralf Schirg (Udo), Andrew Woodhouse (Phillip), Jerome Samuelson (Helmut), Joan Wheeler (Anna), Michael Glen (Lt. Scallon), Ralph Jacobus (Carl)

Macky Alston, George DeGrafenreid
in *Family Name* © Opelika Pictures

FAMILY NAME (Opelika Pictures) Producer, Selina Lewis; Executive Producer, Nicholas Gottlieb; Director, Macky Alston; Narration Written by Macky Alston, Kay Gayner; Photography, Eliot Rockett; Editors, Sandra Marie Christie, Christopher White; Music, Camara Kambon; Color; Not rated; 89 minutes; September release. Filmmaker Macky Alston traces his lineage, discovering that his forebearers were North Carolina slaveholders.

JULIAN PO (Fine Line Features) Producers, Joseph Pierson, Jon Glascoe; Executive Producers, Allan Mindel, Denise Shaw; Director/Screenplay, Alan Wade; Photography, Bernd Heinl; Designer, Stephen McCabe; Editor, Jeffrey Wolf; Costumes, Juliet Polcsa; Music, Patrick Williams; Casting, Todd Thaler; Dolby Stereo; Color; Rated PG-13; 84 minutes; September release. **CAST:** Christian Slater (Julian Po), Robin Tunney (Sarah), Michael Parks (Vern), Cherry Jones (Lucy), Frankie R. Faison (Sheriff), Harve Presnell (Mayor), Allison Janney (Lilah), LaTanya Richardson (Darlene), Dina Spybey (Dee), Bruce Bohne (Pastor Bean), Roy Cooper (Tobias), Zeljko Ivanek (Potter), Io Tillett Wright (Walter)

Christian Slater, Robin Tunney in
Julian Po © Fine Line Features

Tony Tucci, Michael Parducci, Thomas Brandise, Tom Malloy in *Gravesend*
© Island Digital Media

GRAVESEND (Island Digital Media) Producer/Director/Screenplay, Salvatore Stabile; Executive Producers, Toni Ross, Mark Ross, Daniel Edelman; Photography, Joseph Dell'Olio; Editors, Miranda Devin, Salvatore Stabile; Music, Bill Laswell; Presented by Oliver Stone; Dolby Stereo; Color; Rated R; 85 minutes; September release. **CAST**: Tony Tucci (Zane), Michael Parducci (Ray), Tom Malloy (Chicken), Thomas Brandise (Mikey), Macky Aquilino (JoJo the Junkie)

DELINQUENT (Beyond Films/Big Bad Prods.) Producer/Director/Screenplay, Peter Hall; Photography, Todd Crockett; Music, Gang of Four; Editor, Thom Zimny; Color; Not rated; 84 minutes; September release. **CAST:** Desmond Devenish (Tim), Shawn Batten (Tracy DeLors), Jeff Paul (Ben), Marisa Townshend (Mrs. Richman), Ian Eaton (Eddie), Melissa Chalsma, Donald Christopher, Maraya Chase, Olga Matlin, Peter Hall, Meg Myles, Ruby Mitchell.

Tom Gilroy, Neal Jones in *Ratchet*
© Phaedra Cinema

RATCHET (Phaedra Cinema) Producers, George Belshaw, John S. Johnson; Executive Producer, Hank Blumenthal; Director/Screenplay, John S. Johnson; Photography, Joaquin Baca-Asay; Designer, Debbie Devilla; Costumes, Jana Rosenblatt; Music, Paul Schwartz; Editors, James Lyons, Keith Reamer; Casting, Susan Shopmaker; from Ratchet Productions LLC in association with Altar Rocks Films Inc.; Ultra-Stereo; Color; Not rated; 114 minutes; September release. **CAST:** Tom Gilroy (Elliott Callahan), Margaret Welsh (Catherine Ripley), Mitchell Lichtenstein (Tim Greenleaf), Murit Koppel (Julia Webb), Matthew Dixon (Henry Carver), Neal Jones (Sam O'Leary), Robert Whaley (Ed Deputy), John A. Mackay (Chief Groves), David Dossey (Man in Airplane), Isabelle Fortea (Kitty Webb), Anthony Greenleaf (Photographer), Timothy Britton Parker (Jeffrey Kahn), Shari-Lyn Safir (Margaret Dickson)

LATIN BOYS GO TO HELL (Strand) Producer, Jurgen Bruning; Executive Producer, Steve Gallagher; Co-Producers, Fernando Colomo P.C., Beatriz de la Gandara; Director, Ela Troyano; Screenplay, Andre Salas, Ela Troyano; Additional Soap Dialog, Carmelita Tropicana; Based on the novel by Andre Salas; Photography, James Carman; Art Director, Uzi Parnes; Editor, Brian A. Kates; Music, John Zorn; from Stance Company/GM Films; Color; Not rated; 86 minutes; September release. **CAST:** Irwin Ossa (Justin), John Bryant Davila (Angel), Jenifer Lee Simard (Andrea), Alexis Artiles (Braulio), Mike Ruiz (Carlos), Annie Lobst (Monica), Dashia (Jackie), Norma Maldonado (Mrs. Vega), Jehad Nga (Sylvano), Guinevere Turner (Sombra), Rebecca Bugos (Luz), Umberto Gonzalez (Rodrigo), Yvonne Washington (Gladys), Reynier Molenaar (Eduardo), Iris Prado Salas (Braulio's Mom), J.R. Valdes, William Gonzalez (Bartenders), Adrian Sanchez (Italian Guy), Fil Fernandez (Cashier), Ari Gold (Trash Popstar), Pepper Burns, Veronica Fox (Gender Illusionists), Jose Munoz (Mr. Bully), Carmelita Tropicana (Mrs. Bully)

Mike Ruiz in *Latin Boys Go To Hell*
© Strand Releasing

RIDING THE RAILS (Artistic License) Producers/Directors/Screenplay, Michael Uys, Lexy Lovell; Photography, Samuel Henriques; Editor, Howard Sharp; Music, Jay Sherman-Godfrey; an Out of the Blue/American History Project production; DuArt color; Not rated; 72 minutes; September release. Documentary on teenage freight-train riders during the Great Depression, featuring Clarence Lee, Bob "Guitar Whitey" Symmonds, John Fawcett, Jim Mitchell, Charley Bull, Rene Champion, Peggy De Hart.

Riding the Rails © National Archives

Robert Englund, Kane Hodder, Tony Todd in *Wishmaster* © Live Entertainment

WISHMASTER (LIVE Entertainment) Producers, Pierre David, Clark Peterson, Noel A. Zanitsch; Executive Producer, Wes Craven; Director, Robert Kurtzman; Screenplay, Peter Atkins; Photography, Jacques Haitkin; Designers, Dorian Vernaccio, Deborah Raymond; Music, Harry Manfredini; Co-Producer, David Tripet; Editor, David Handman; Line Producer, Russ Markowitz; Costumes, Karyn Wagner; Visual Effects Supervisor, Thomas C. Rainone; Special Make-Up Effects, Robert Kurtzman, Greg Nicotero, Howard Berger; Casting, Cathy Henderson-Martin, Dori Zuckerman; a Pierre David production; Dolby Digital Stereo; Eastman color; Rated R; 90 minutes; September release. **CAST:** Tammy Lauren (Alexandra Amberson), Andrew Divoff (The Djinn/Nathaniel Demarest), Robert Englund (Raymond Beaumont), Tony Todd (Johnny Valentine), Wendy Benson (Shannon Amberson), Tony Crane (Josh Aickman), Chris Lemmon (Nick Merritt), Jenny O'Hara (Wendy Derlith), Angus Scrimm (Narrator), Ari Barak (Zoroaster), Jake McKinnon (Skeleton Man), Greg Funk (Snake Man), Richard Assad (Persian King), Ted Raimi (Ed Finney), Danny Hicks (Customs Official), Josef Pilato (Mickey Torelli), Tom Kendall (Etchison), John Byner (Doug Clegg), Ashley Power (Sierra), Verne Troyer, Walter Phelan (Creature Stages), Ricco Ross (Lt. Nathanson), Buck Flower (Homeless Man), Reggie Banister (Pharmacist), Peter Liapis, Frank Nicotero (Pharmacy Customers), Brian Klugman (Medical Student), Gretchen Palmer (Ariella), Jean St. James (Customer), Azita Azar (Student with Mask), Joe Svezia (Uniformed Cop), Kane Hodder (Merritt's Guard), Dennis Hayden (Security Guard), Betty McGuire (Mrs. Merritt), Renee Faia (Insurance Assistant), Cyndi Pass (Glass Woman), Howard Berger, Robert Jacob (Party Guards), Brad Mead (Cop at Blackwood)

Toshiya Nagasawa, Eugene Nomura, Nick Feyz in *Sleepy Heads* © Phaedra Cinema

THE LAY OF THE LAND (Northern Arts) Producers, Jonathan D. Krane, Sally Kellerman; Executive Producers, Edward Oleschak, Ralph Clemente; Director, Larry Arrick; Screenplay, Mel Shapiro; Co-Producer, Mary Hinton; Photography, Frederic Goodich; Designer, Clare Brown; Editor, Richard Brummer; Costumes, Judy B. Schwartz, Beverly Safire; Music, Jeff Lass; Casting, Carol Lefko; a JKG Production presentation of a Jonathan D. Krane production; Color; Rated R; 94 minutes; September release. **CAST**: Sally Kellerman (M.J. Dankworth), Ed Begley, Jr. (Harvey Dankworth), Sandra Taylor (Muriel Johanson), Stuart Margolin (Carmine Ficcone), Tyne Daly (Dr. Guttmacher), Rance Howard (Dr. Brown), Avery Schreiber (Dean Bill Whittier), April Shawhan (Erma Whittier), Tom Nowicki (Bob Chambers), Elisabeth Redford (Blanche Cafferty), Timothy McLoughlin (Gordon Dimitri), Patrick Desmond (Dr. Smith), Avis-Marie Barnes (Secretary), Riley Gelwicks (Jack Dankworth), Jesse Zeigler (Timmy Dankworth), David Sollberg (Leslie), Cyndi Vicino (Gunshop Saleslady), Richard Bassett (Bookshop Salesman), Bobbi Spencer (Landlady), Frank Eugene Matthews Jr., Dennis Wood (Janitors), Suzanne Shepherd (Alice), Claire Kellerman, Densi Van Gerena, Scott Graham, Mikki McKeever (Students)

James Belushi, Dennis Quaid, Tupac Shakur in *Gang Related* © MGM DistributingCo.

SLEEPY HEADS (Phaedra Cinema) Producers, Yuko Yoshikawa, Shunji Okada, Yoshifumi Hosoya; Director/Photography, Yoshifumi Hosoya; Screenplay, Yoshifumi Hosoya, Nick Feyz, Christo Assefi, Edwin Baker; Editor, Keiko Deguchi; Designer, Mark Helmuth; Music, Joshua Stone; an Elephant Studio/Zazou Productions presentation; Dolby; Color; Not rated; 86 minutes; September release. **CAST**: Eugene Nomura (Hiro), Toshiya Nagasawa (Ken), Takahiro "Engin" Fujita (Akira), Nick Feyz (B.J.), Sayuri Higuchi Emerson (Akiko), Snakey Mao (Shun), Mariko H. Fusillo (Haruka), Yuki Nishida (Keiko), Masayuki Nakanishi (Daisuke), Ron Contawe (Gang Leader)

GANG RELATED (Orion) Producers, Brad Krevoy, Steve Stabler, John Bertolli; Executive Producer, Lynn Bigelow-Kouf; Director/Screenplay, Jim Kouf; Photography, Brian J. Reynolds; Designer, Charles Breen; Costumes, Shari Feldman; Editor, Todd Ramsay; Music, Mickey Hart; Co-Producer, Jeffrey D. Ivers; Line Producer, Jeffrey Downer; Casting, Carol Lewis; a Brad Krevoy & Steve Stabler production; Super 35 Widescreen; DTS Stereo; Deluxe color; Rated R; 112 minutes; October release. **CAST**: James Belushi (Divinci), Tupac Shakur (Rodriguez), Lela Rochon (Cynthia), Dennis Quaid (William), James Earl Jones (Arthur Baylor), David Paymer (Elliot Goff), Wendy Crewson (Helen Eden), Gary Cole (Richard Simms), T.C. Carson (Manny Ladrew), Brad Greenquist (Richard Stein), James Handy (Capt. Henderson), Kool Moe Dee (Lionel Hudd), Victor Love (Hooper), Robert LaSardo (Sarkasian), Perry Anzilotti (Vic), Gregory Scott Cummins (Clyde), Tiny Lister Jr. (Cutless Supreme), Thomas Mills (Patrolman Mahoney), Rick LaFond (Desk Officer), Anthony C. Hall (James), Catero Colbert (Cortez), Steve Wilcox (Dave), Alexander Folk (Reverend), Paul Gold (Lineup Suspect), Douglas Bennet

(Guard), David Weisenberg (Doctor), Will Jeffries (Dunner Attorney), Jason Bagby (Young Man), Chris Hendrie (Judge Weinberg), Bob Apisa (Dunner Bailiff), Terrance Ellis (Gun Seller), Todd Patrick Breaugh (Steven J. Allen), Yuri Ogawa (Jury Foreperson), Joseph Hieu (Asian Man), Deborah Rennard (Caroline Divinci), Edward Edwards (Sgt. Gardner), Fred Ornstein (Officer), Taylor Anderson (Butler), Tom Ormeny (Nathan McCall), Tony Perez (Judge Pine), Ron Cummins (Bailiff), Elizabeth Maynard (Newscaster), Charlene Simpson (Manny's Secretary), Jimmie F. Skaggs (Duncan), Leonard O. Turner (Guard at Cynthia's Jail), Andrea C. Robinson, Dafidd McCracken, Nellie Sciutto (Reporters), Donald Craig (Sinclair), Lisa Dinkins (Nurse), Teddy Lane Jr. (Guard at County), Reginald W. Miller, George Christy, Jesse J. Donnelly (Detectives), Peter Navy Tuiasosopo (Bob the Bouncer), Myles DeRussy III (Officer)

KISS AND TELL (FilmWorks) Producer, David R. Kappes; Executive Producers, Mitchell Galin, Richard P. Rubinstein; Director, Andy Wolk; Screenplay/Story, David Birke; Photography, Paul Maibaumn; Designer, Michael Helmy; Editor, Lauren A. Schaffer; Music, Tim Truman; Color; Not rated; 90 minutes; October release. **CAST:** Cheryl Ladd (Jean McAvoy), John Terry (Eric McAvoy), Derin Altay (Arlane), John Bedford Lloyd (Dan Turman), C.K. Bibby (Dr. Hayes), Michael Burgess (E.R. Doctor), Barry Corbin (George Reed), Diana De Garmo (Cindy), Aubrey Dollar (Candy Stripper), David Forrester (Cop), Randell Haynes (Psychiatrist), J. Michael Hunter (Ted Wallace), Gen. Fermon Judd, Jr. (Bartender), Chuck Kinlaw (Father), Lorri Lindberg (Molly), Leslie Riley (Sue), Francie Swift (Kelly Krieger), Nello Tare (Tour Guide), Marty Terry (Elderly Lady), Caitlin Clarke, Jack Gilpin

Keelin Curnuck in *Wonderland*
© Fox Lorber

PLAN B (Puny But Loud Prods.) Producer, Lulu Baskins-Leva; Executive Producers, Elizabeth Joslin, Burr Joslin, Shelly Leva; Director/Screenplay, Gary Leva; Photography, Yoram Astrakhan; Music, Andrew Rose; Designer, Carol Strober; Editor, Jane Allison Fleck; Dolby Stereo; Color; Rated R; 102 minutes; October release. **CAST:** Jon Cryer (Stuart Winer), Lisa Darr (Clare Sadler), Lance Guest (Jack Sadler), Mark Matheisen (Ricky Stone), Sara Mornell (Gina Ferris), Clauda Carey (Marie), Donna Wieczorkowski (Liz), Staey Katzin, Ilia Volokh, John Kozeluh, Annie Grindlay, Candace DeSarro, Justin Ross, Nicole Chamberlain, Christine Mitges, Jose Heredia, Heather Harris, Roger La Page.

WONDERLAND (Fox Lorber) Producer/Director/Photography/Editor, John O'Hagan; Executive Producers, Ted Hope, James Schamus, David Linde; Associate Producers, Sheri Bylander, Gabrielle Kelly, Anne Carey; Co-Producer, Mary Janes Skalski; DuArt color; Not rated; 80 minutes; October release. Documentary celebrating the 50th Anniversary of America's first mass-produced, planned suburb, Levittown, New York; featuring Eddie Money, Bill Griffith, Keelin Curnuck, and various residents of Levittown past and present.

Director Jim Jarmusch, Neil Young in
Year Of The Horse © October Films

YEAR OF THE HORSE (October) Producer, L.A. Johnson; Executive Producers, Bernard Shakey, Elliot Rabinowitz; Director, Jim Jarmusch; Photography, L.A. Johnson, Jim Jarmusch; Editor, Jay Rabinowitz; Music, Neil Young & Crazy Horse; a Shakey Pictures production; Dolby Digital Stereo; Color; Rated R; 107 minutes; October release. Documentary on Neil Young and his band Crazy Horse in concert, featuring Ralph Molina, Frank "Poncho" Sampedro, Billy Talbot, Neil Young.

THE TWILIGHT OF THE GOLDS (Avalanche) Producers, Paul Colichman, Mark R. Harris, John Davimos; Executive Producer, Garry Marshall; Director, Ross Marks; Screenplay, Jonathan Tolins, Seth Bass; Based upon the play by Jonathan Tolins; Co-Producer/Casting, Valorie Massalas; Line Producers, John Schouweiler, Lisa Levy; Photography, Tom Richmond; Music, Lee Holdridge; Editor, Dana Congdon; a Showtime presentation of a Regent Entertainment/Below the Belt productions and Hallmark Entertainment; Color; Rated PG-13; 93 minutes; October release. **CAST:** Jennifer Beals (Suzanne Stein), Jon Tenney (Rob Stein), Faye Dunaway (Phyllis Gold), Brendan Fraser (David Gold), Garry Marshall (Walter Gold), Rosie O'Donnell (Jackie), Sean O'Bryan (Steven), Patrick Bristow (Brandon), John Schlesinger (Adrian Lodge), Phil Reeves (Suzanne's Doctor), Lucas Richman (Brik), Robert Barry Fleming (Randy), Kathleen Marshall (Debby Klein), Mark Medoff (Mr. Klein). (This film originally premiered on the Showtime Cable Network in March of 1997.)

Garry Marshall, Brendan Fraser in
The Twilight of the Golds © Avalanche/ CFD

Harland Williams, Raven in *Rocketman* © Disney Enterprises

ROCKETMAN (Walt Disney Pictures) Producer, Roger Birnbaum; Director, Stuart Gillard; Screenplay, Craig Mazin, Greg Erb; Story, Oren Aviv, Craig Mazin, Greg Erb; Photography, Steven Poster; Designer, Roy Forge Smith; Editor, William D. Gordean; Costumes, Daniel Orlandi; Executive Producers, Jon Turteltaub, Oren Aviv, Jonathan Glickman; Co-Executive Producer, Richard H. Prince; Co-Producers, Jamie Masada, Peter Safran; Music, Michael Tavera; Casting, Rick Montgomery, Dan Parada; a Roger Birnbaum/Gold/Miller production, presented in association with Caravan Pictures; Distributed by Buena Vista Pictures; Dolby Digital Stereo; Eastman color; Rated PG; 93 minutes; October release. **CAST:** Harland Williams (Fred Z. Randall), Jessica Lundy (Julie Ford), William Sadler ("Wild Bill" Overbeck), Jeffrey DeMunn (Paul Wick), James Pickens, Jr. (Ben Stevens), Beau Bridges (Bud Nesbitt), Peter Onorati (Gary Hackman), Don Lake (Flight Surgeon), William Arthur Jenkins, Ken Farmer (Mission Controllers), Blake Boyd (Gordon A. Peacock), Brandon Kaplan (Young Fred), Paxton Whitehead (British Reporter), Don Armstrong (Anchorman), Pamela West, Marjorie Carroll (Nuns), Claire Birnbaum (School Kid #1), Sean Tweedley (NASA Lab Tech), Cindy Hogan, Felicia Griffin (Reporters), Lidia Porto (Gary's Nurse), Richard Dillard (The President), Gil Glasgow (Bartender), Raven (Ulysses), Shelley Duvall (Fred's Mom)

LOVE ALWAYS (Legacy) Producer, Isaac Artenstein; Executive Producers, Ken Branson, Coop Cooprider; Director, Jude Pauline Eberhard; Screenplay, Jude Pauline Eberhard, Sharlene Baker; Based on the novel Finding Signs by Sharlene Baker; Photography, Xavier Perez Grobet; Editor, Joel Goodman; Music, Jamie Valle, Anton Sanko; a Persistence of Vision Films presentation of an Isaac Artenstein production. Color; Rated R; 93 minutes; October release. **CAST:** Marisa Ryan (Julia Bradshaw), Moon Zappa (Mary Ellen), Beverly D'Angelo (Miranda), Michael Reilly Burke (Mark Righetti), Mick Murray, Tracy Fraim, Beth Grant, Doug Hutchison, Jerry O'Donnell, Vareli Arizmendi.

Nick Sutton, Jacob Reynolds in *Gummo* © Fine Line Features

GUMMO (Fine Line Features) Producer, Cary Woods; Director/Screenplay, Harmony Korine; Co-Producers, Robin O'Hara, Scott Macaulay; Photography, Jean Yves Escoffier; Editor, Christopher Tellefsen; Designer, Dave Doernberg; Costumes, Chloe Sevigny; an Independent Pictures production; Dolby Stereo; Color; Rated R; 95 minutes; October release. **CAST:** Jacob Reynolds (Solomon), Nick Sutton (Tummler), Jacob Sewell (Bunny Boy), Darby Dougherty (Darby), Chloe Sevigny (Dot), Carisa Bara (Helen), Linda Manz (Solomon's Mom), Max Perlich (Cole)

THE LOVEMASTER (Rocket Pictures) Producer, Tom Coleman; Executive Producers, Alan David, Mark Breen; Co-Producer, Holly MacConkey; Director, Michael Goldberg; Screenplay, Craig Shoemaker, Michael Goldberg; Based on a story by Craig Shoemaker; Photography, Phil Parmet, Jeff Zimmerman; Editors, Richard Currie, Jeremy Kasten; Music, Michael Skloff, Giorgio Bertuccelli; Designer, Gary Randall; Costumes, Maud Kersnowski; Casting, Robyn Ray; Foto-Kem color; Rated R; 84 minutes; October release. **CAST:** Craig Schoemaker (Craig), Farrah Fawcett (The Date), Courtney Thorne-Smith (Deb Memet), Harley Jane Kozak (Karen), Esther Auerbach (Nana), Karen Witter (Marie), Kurt Rambis (Kurt), George Wendt (Therapist), Robert Steinberg (Steiny)

Dan Haggerty, Dylan Haggerty in *Grizzly Mountain* © Mega Comm., Inc.

TIMELESS (Phaedra Cinema) Producer, Patricia Bice; Director/Screenplay/Editor, Chris Hart; Co-Producer, Joe Hart; Photography, Chris Norr; Music, Joseph Hart, Sr.; Color; Not rated; 90 minutes; October release. **CAST:** Peter Byrne (Terry), Melissa Duge (Lyrica), Michael Griffiths (Tommy), Joe Hart (Flood), Thomas Grube (Bill), Jim Cronin (Dix), Larry Robinson (Max), Marilise Tronto (Grace), Tony Kruk (Manny Gould), Arnold Merkitch (Bartender), Ann Parker (Manny Gould's Secretary), Frank McMahon (Max's Friend), Robin Farbman, Jodi Salmond (Couple Shopping), Marta Bukowski (Flood's Girl), Jerry Kocka (Mickie the Bartender), Joseph Tudisco (Trucker Driver), Gerald Del Sol (Shop Foreman), Robert Van Lindt (Bill's Boss), Clinton Lee Reeves (Man in Bar)

GRIZZLY MOUNTAIN (Legacy) Producers, Anthony Dalesandro, Peter White; Executive Producers, Eric Parkinson, Nicholas Konstant, George Furla; Executive in Charge of Production, Michael Slifkin; Director, Jeremy Haft; Screenplay, Jeremy Haft, Peter White; Story, Eric Parkinson; Photography, Andy Parke; Music, Jon McCallum; Editors, Richard Westover, Anthony Dalesandro; a Mega Communications, Inc. in association with Napor Kids presentation of a Parkinson/Konstant/Furla production; Ultra-Stereo; Color; Rated G; 96 minutes; October release. **CAST:** Dan Haggerty (Jeremiah), Dylan Haggerty (Dylan), Nicole Lund (Nicole), Kim Morgan Greene (Betty), Perry Stephens (Boss Man/Burts), Robert Patteri (Roscoe), Andrew Craig (Bailey), Robert Budaska (Jones),

E.E. "Ed" Bell (Mayor), Martin Kove (Marshall Jackson), Don Borza (Bill Marks), Marguerite Hickey (Karen Marks), Megan Haggerty (Megan Marks), Gil Revilla (Chief), Mark Abbott (Tukayoo)

THE DELI (Golden Monkey Pictures) Producers, Sylvia Caminer, John Dorrian; Director, John Andrew Gallagher; Screenplay, John Dorrian, John Andrew Gallagher; Photography, Bob Lechterman; Designer, Lisa Frantz; Costumes, Melissa Toth; Music, Ernie Mannix; Editor, Sue Blainey; Color; Not rated; 96 minutes; November release. **CAST**: Mike Starr (Johnny), Matt Keeslar (Andy), Judith Malina (Vincenza Amico), Brian Vincent (Pinky), Michael Badalucco (Eric), Heavy D (Bo), Ice-T (Phil), Iman (Avocado Lady), Michael Imperioli (Matty), David Johansen (The Cabbie), Heather Matarazzo (Sabrina), Debi Mazar (Teresa), William McNamara (Kevin), Gretchen Mol (Mary), Christopher Noth (Sal), Tony Sirico (Tony), Jerry Stiller (Petey), Frank Vincent (Tommy), Burt Young (J.C.)

Michael Imperioli, Mike Starr in *The Deli* © Golden Monkey Pictures

HABIT (Glass Eye Pix/Passport Cinemas) Producer, Dayton Taylor; Director/Screenplay/Editor, Larry Fessenden; Photography, Frank DeMarco; Associate Producer, Susan A. Stover; Costumes, Loren Bevans; Music, Geoffrey Kidde; Color; Not rated; 112 minutes; November release. **CAST**: Larry Fessenden (Sam), Meredith Snaider (Anna), Aaron Beall (Nick), Patricia Coleman (Rae), Heather Woodbury (Liza), Jesse Hartman (Lenny), Marcus A. Miranda (Segundo), Herb Rogers (Slimma), Hart Fessenden (Sam's Dad), Lon Waterford (Mr. Lyons), Alan Bandit (Norman in Bridgehampton), Dale Cameron (Sandy in Bridgehampton), Whitney Alexandra McGann (Kid in Bridgehampton), Helene Weintraub (Liza's Nosy Neighbor), Michael Buscemi (Liza's Friend Dave), Rebecca Moore (Liza's Friend Susan), Jack Dingas (Harry at the Party), Kelly Reichardt (Partygirl on Phone), Cain Berlinger (Carrot Man), Ginny Hack (What's with That Guy Patron), Tom Hale (Record Executive on Cellular Phone), Derek Davis (Kid Hurt in Accident), Erc Vesbit (Halloween Delivery Man), Danilo Randjic Coleman (Devil Boy), Beverly Washington (Segundo's Wife), Christopher Reyes (Segundo's Son), Jain V. Alonso (Segundo's Daughter), John Gaddy (Departing Tenant at Liza's)

NEVER MET PICASSO (Turbulent Arts) Producers, Patrick Cunningham, Stephen Kijak; Executive Producer, Jennifer Ryan; Director/Screenplay, Stephen Kijak; Photography, David Tames; Designers, Humberto Cordero, Julie Lupien; Costumes, Kathleen Chisholm; Editor, Angelica Brisk; Music, Kristin Hersh, Bill Lee; a Mighty Reel production; Color; Not rated; 90 minutes; November release. **CAST**: Alexis Arquette (Andrew Magnus), Georgia Ragsdale (Lucy), Margot Kidder (Genna Magnus), Don McKellar (Jerry), Keith David (Larry), Alvin Epstein (Uncle Alfred), Omewenne (Ingrid), Diane Beckett (Mailwoman), Craig Hickman (Poetry Slammer), David Levine (Jack), John O'Callaghan (Paul), Jody O'Neil (Marc), Eddie Rutkowski (Young David/Mailperson), Ursula Ryan (Nurse), Richard Snee (Thomas Magnus), Adrienne Starrs (Diane), Suzanne Crosby, Lanie Fischera (Art Critics), Lakia Norwood, Verna Turbulence, Stephanie Whyte (Drag Queens)

Meredith Snaider, Larry Fessenden in *Habit* © GlassEys/ Passport

COLD AROUND THE HEART (20th Century Fox) Producers, Craig Baumgarten, Dean Halsted, Adam Merims; Executive Producer, Richard Rutowski; Director/Screenplay, John Ridley; Photography, Malik Hassan Sayeed; Designer, Kara Lindstrom; Music, Mason Daring; Costumes, Sara Jane Slotnick; Editor, Eric L. Beason; a Baumgarten-Prophet Entertainment/Illusion Entertainment/Kushner-Locke productions; Super 35 Wiidescreen; Color; Rated R; 96 minutes; November release. **CAST**: David Caruso (Ned Tash), Kelly Lynch (Jude), Stacey Dash (Bec Rosenberg), Christopher Noth (T), John Spencer (Uncle Mike), Pruitt Taylor Vince (Johnny "Cokebottles" Costello), Richard Kind (Nabbish), Kirk Baltz (Detective Argan), Jennifer Jostyn (Inez), Tom McGowan (Gun Store Man), Mark Boone Junior (Angry Man), Jack Brind (Motel Man), Tracey Ross (Nurse Woman), Gareth Williams (Car Dealer Man), Richard Arquette (Gas Station Man), Jack Wallace (Police Captain Man), Viggis Knittridge (Himself)

Nicole Prescott, Kevin Thigpen in *Tar* © Mongrel Films

TAR (Mongrel Movies) Producer, Abigail Hunt; Director, Goetz Grossmann; Screenplay, Goetz Grossmann, James A. Pearson, Gilbert Giles; Photography, Lloyd Handwerker; Designer, Pavel Salek; Costumes, Robin Newland; Editor, Sabine Krayenbuhl; Music, John Hill, Billy Bourne; Casting, Caroline Sinclair; Color; Not rated; 90 minutes; November release. **CAST:** Kevin Thigpen (Curtis), Nicole Prescott (Tracy), Seth Gilliam (Tyrone), Ron Brice (Jamal), Frank Minucci (Hank), Chris McKinney, Tracie Jade, Bo Rucker, Danny Johnson, John Henry Cox, Robert Colston, Ernestine Johnson, John Carter, Achilles Lavidis, Ann Gartland, Charlie Smith, Kieve Gitlin, Kesean Gardner, Evan Parke, David Maxwell

John Savage in *The Mouse*
© Strand Releasing

Peter Greene, Darling Narita in *Bang*
© Panorama Entertainment

THE MOUSE (Strand) Producers, Hank Blumenthal, Harris Tulchin, John Savage; Co-Producer, Matt Janes; Director/Screenplay, Daniel Adams; Executive Producers, Richard Segedin, Charlie Irish, Jimmy Walter; Photography, Denise Brassard; Designer, Gay Studebaker; Editor, Victoria Street; Costumes, Deborah Newhall; Music, Jonathon Edwards; Casting, Sheila Jaffe, Georgianne Walken; an Early Morning Films presentation; Color; Not rated; 98 minutes; November release. **CAST:** John Savage (Bruce "The Mouse" Strauss), Angelica Torn (Mary Lou Strauss), Rip Torn (Trucker - God), Charles Bailey-Gates (Joe), Irina Cashen (Jamie Strauss), Tim Williams (Frank "Gator" Lux), Edward Lynch (Ron "Butcher" Stander), Rhasaan Orange, Gary Galone, Danny Venezia (Shamsters), Burt Young, Randall "Tex" Cobb, Vinny Pazienza, Sean O'Grady, Danny Campbell, Jim Tunney, Kip Diggs, Dick Ryan (Themselves), Ray "Boom Boom" Mancini (Larry), Richard Segedin (Sammy), Vito Antuofermo (Trainer), Tommy Makem (Commissioner Adams), Dominic Chianese (Al the Trainer), Keena Keel (Ann), Gerald Orange (Pete), Verdell Smith (Marty McCormick), Jack Celli (Flashback Promoter), Mario Cianfione (Lopez), John Nacco (Bernie), Ed Begine (Don the Promoter), Steve Brito (Dead Boxer), Frank Gio (Commissioner Brennan), Charlie Irisih (Drunk), Michael A. Biase (Ear Doctor), George Van Voorhis (Dead Boxer Trainer), Frank "The Gator" Lux (Lopez Newscaster), Ron "The Butcher" Stander (Bar Patron), Bruce "The Mouse" Strauss (Angelo), Rebecca Rae Adams (Ginny), Mitch Fennel (Ryan Trainer), Daniel Welch (Flashback), Susan Youngs, Michael Campbell, Edward Biggine (McCormick Hecklers), Randy Gordon (Fan), Guy Strauss (Finger Referee), Richard Pitts-Wiley (McCormick Referee), Nick Hasomeris (Flasback Referee), Bill Galvin, Tim Miller, James Paul Ludwig (Lopez Reporters), Wendy Adams, Tonya Jeria (Round Card Girls), Tom Kemp (Commissioner Collins), Lance Norris (Bear Bartender), Burke Carroll (Bear), William J. Devany (McCormick Trainer), Bernie Barry (Lopez Referee)

NICK AND JANE (Avalanche) Producer, Bill McCutchen III; Co-Producer/Director, Rich Mauro; Screenplay, Rich Mauro, Peter Quigley, Neil William Alumkal; Photography, Chris Norr; Music, Mark Suozzo; Editors, Wendey Stanzler, Rich Mauro; Line Producer, Kirsten Bates-Renaud; Casting, Eve Battaglia; a Prophecy Pictures Inc. presentation of an Emeralde Productions in association with Mira Vista Films and Cobalt Films production; Dolby Stereo; Color; Rated R; 96 minutes; November release. **CAST:** Dana Wheeler-Nicholson (Jane), James McCaffrey (Nick), Dave Johansen (Carter), Gedde Watanabe (Enzo), John Dossett (John), Lisa Gay Hamilton (Vick), Saundra Santiago (Stephanie), Clinton Leupp (Miss CoCo), George Coe (Mr. Morgan), Siobhan Fallon (Julie), Dianne Brill (Celine), Ron Parady (Mr. Phillips), Jim Bigwood (Prof. Garrett), Jin Kameno (Restaurant Manager)

BANG (Panorama Entertainment) Producers, Daniel M. Berger, Ladd Vance; Executive Producers, Tomy E. Drissi, Ziggi Golding, Sean B. Kelly, Jude Narita; Director/Screenplay, Ash; Photography, Dave Gasperik; Designer, Daniel M. Berger; Editors, Ash, Daniel M. Berger; an Eagle Eye Films Inc. presentation; Ultra-Stereo; Color; Not rated; 98 minutes; November release. **CAST:** Darling Narita (The Girl), Peter Greene (Adam), Michael Newland (Officer Rattler), Eric Schrody (Pimp), Michael Arturo (Officer Trotter), James Sharpe (Officer Ham), Luis Guizar (Jesus), Art Cruz (Juan), David Allen Graff (The Producer), Stanley Herman (Landlord), Donald "Notorious" D (O.G. on Rooftop), Noble James (Rooftop Dealer), Eric Kirkpatrick (Tucker), Wandi Herman (Piwi on Roof), David Conner (Ivan), Stephanie Martini (Joy), Jason Pepper (Newscaster/TV Cop), Lucy Lui (Hooker), David Preston (Cook), Paul Saucido (Drive by Cholo), Tom Prisco (Addict), Claudia Kareem (Waitress), Daniel Berger (Man on Bus), Pamela Tomasetti (Housewife), Roberta Rodman (Audition Model), Rowen Kerr (Golfer), Darren Lane (Businessman), Juanita Salinas (Latina Woman),

Dana Wheeler-Nicholson, James McCaffrey in *Nick and Jane* © CFP

RonReaco Lee, Deanna Davis in *How I Spent My Summer Vacation* © Cinema Guild

Robin Shou, Sandra Hess, Irina Pantaeva,
Lynn Red Williams in *Mortal Kombat : Annihilation*
© New Line Cinema Inc.

Molly Gross, Marisa Ryan, Claudia Rossi,
Natasha La Ferriere in *Slaves To The Underground*
© Overseas Filmgroup

HOW I SPENT MY SUMMER VACATION (Cinema Guild) Producers, Alan James Gay, Christopher Mills; Director/Screenplay, John Fisher; Photography, Charles Mills; Art Director, Tim Dempsey; Music, Johnny Barrow; Editors, Norman Todd, Alan James Gay; Costumes, D'Carol Randle, Wayne Van Nuygen; Casting, Shay Bentley-Griffin; a Castleway Entertainment presentation of an Alan James Gay production; Color; Not rated; 75 minutes; November release. **CAST:** RonReaco Lee (Perry), Deanna Davis (Stephanie), E. Roger Mitchell (Joseph), Mike Ngaujah (D'Angelo), Jade Janise Dixon (Tammy), Darren Law (Nolan), Maude Bond (Monica), T'Erica Jenks (Kim), Angela Thigpen (Rachel), Parish German (Young Lady in Parking Lot), Kee McKinney (Donna), Deborah Duke (Mace Lady), Nevaina Graves (Tina), Amil Gibbs (Rude Guy), Derrell Keith Lester (Buster), Maisha Dyson (Rhonda), Felice Monteith (Helen), John Fisher (Voice Over Questioning Stephanie)

MORTAL KOMBAT: ANNIHILATION (New Line Cinema) Producer, Lawrence Kasanoff; Executive Producers, Alison Savitch, Carla Fry, Brian Witten; Director, John R. Leonetti; Screenplay, Brent V. Friedman, Bruce Zabel; Story, Lawrence Kasanoff, Joshua Wexler, John Tobias; Based on the videogame created by Ed Boon & John Tobias; Co-Producer, Kevin Reidy; Photography, Matthew F. Leonetti; Designer, Charles Wood; Editor, Peck Prior; Music, George S. Clinton; Costumes, Jennifer J. Parsons; Visual Effects Supervisors, Chuck Comisky, Alison Savitch; Stunts, Pat Johnson, Eddie Stacey; Fight Choreographer, Robin Shou; Casting, Fern Champion, Mark Paladini; a Lawrence Kasanoff/Threshold Entertainment production; Dolby SDDS Stereo; Fotokem color; Rated PG-13; 93 minutes; November release. **CAST:** Robin Shou (Liu Kang), Talisa Soto (Kitana), James Remar (Rayden), Sandra Hess (Sonya Blade), Lynn Red Williams (Jax), Brian Thompson (Shao-Kahn), Reiner Schoene (Shinnok), Musetta Vander (Sindel), Irina Pantaeva (Jade), Deron McBee (Motaro), Marjean Holden (Sheeva), Litefoot (Nightwolf), Chris Conrad (Johnny Cage), John Medlen (Ermac), J.J. Perry (Cyrax/Scorpion), Tyrone Wiggins (Rain), Dennis Keiffer (Baraka), Ridley Tsui Po Wah (Smoke), Keith Cooke Hirabayashi (Sub-Zero), Lance LeGault, Carolyn Seymour (Elder Gods), Dana Hee (Mileena)

ILL GOTTEN GAINS (Spats Films) Director/Screenplay, Joel B. Marsden; Photography, Ben Kufrin; Designer, Stacie B. London; Music, Mike Baum; Editor, David Schaufele; Color; Rated R; 101 minutes; November release. **CAST:** Djimon Hounsou (Fyah), Akosua Busia (Fey), De'aundre Bonds (Pop), Eartha Kitt (The Wood), Reg E. Cathey (Nassor), Tom Fitzpatrick (Jeremiah), Mario Gardner (Barc), Clabe Hartley (Skinner), Jamillah Nicole (Fa), Tom Taglang (Cowlie), Tony Torn (The Vet), Peter Navy Tuiasosopo (Cooper), Claudia Robinson (Femi)

SLAVES TO THE UNDERGROUND (First Look Pictures) Producers, Kristine Peterson, Bill Cody, Raquel Caballes Maxwell; Executive Producers, Joel Soisson, Jeffrey Thal, Judy Friend; Director, Kristine Peterson; Screenplay, Bill Cody; Photography, Zoran Hochstatter; Designer, Michael Moran; Editor, Eric Vizents; Music, Mike Martt; a Neo Motion Pictures production; Dolby Stereo; Color; Rated R; 94 minutes; November release. **CAST**: Molly Gross (Shelly), Marisa Ryan (Suzy), Jason Bortz (Jimmy), Bob Neuwirth (Big Phil), Natacha La Ferriere (Zoe), Claudia Rossi (Brenda), James Garver (Brian), Peter Szumlas (Dale)

THE SELLER (Proletariat Pictures) Producers, Craig Schlattman, Juliet Bashore; Director/Screenplay, Craig Schlattman; Photography, Wes Llewellyn, Bubba Bukowski; Eidtors, Lester Fatt, Victor Livingston; Music, Garic Cargi; Art Director, J. Lyons; Dolby; Color; Not rated; 113 minutes; December release. **CAST**: Brian Brophy (Bartholomew Trust), Kathy Morozova (Melissa Barnstead), Arthur Roberts (Derrick Murdock), Adam Paul (Dwight Lately), Andre Marquis (Quinton Bendick), Mink Stole (Aunt Betty), David Alexander (Jimbo Carvelton), Jeffrey von Meyer (Robert Barnstead), Nancy van Iderstine (Carla Barnstead Normack), T.J. Castronovo (Herman), Craig Schlattman (Bartender), Jim Boyce (TV Announcer), Bob Van Rossum (Cowboy), Dan Frank (Don), John Smith, Franklin Youri (Valets)

DOGS: THE RISE AND FALL OF AN ALL-GIRL BOOKIE JOINT (Phaedra Cinema) Executive Producer, Marcia Kirkley; Director/Screenplay, Eve Annenberg; Co-Producers, Heather D'Adamo, Eve Annenberg; Photography, Joe Foley, Wolfgang Held; Designer, Miro Bazac; Editor, Jack Haigis; Music, John Gunter, Richard Thompson; Color; Not rated; 80 minutes; December release. CAST: Toby Huss (Sammy Cybernowski), Pam Columbus (Leila), Pam Gray (Stephanie), Leo Marks (Arnie), Amadeo D'Adamo (Bruce), Melody Beale (Amina), Eve Annenberg (Gypsy)

Melody Beal, Pamela Gray, Eve Annenberg
in *Dogs* © Phaedra Cinema

Anthony Crivello, David Norona in *Twisted* © Leisure Time Features

TWISTED (Leisure Time Features) Producer, Adrian Agromonte; Executive Producers, Bernard Arbit, Barry Witz, Mark Weiner; Director/Screenplay, Seth Michael Donsky; Photography, Hernan Toro; Editors, Tom McArdle, Seth Michael Donsky; Designer, Scott Bailey; Music, Q Lazzarus, Danny Z; Costumes, Rosemary Ponzo; a Dons Quixote Production in association with Miravista Films; Color; Not rated; 100 minutes; December release. CAST: David Norona (Angel), Keiven McNeil Graves (Lee), William Hickey (Andre), Anthony Crivello (Eddie), Jean Loup (Fine Art), Billy Porter (Shiniqua), Elizabeth Franz (Social Worker), Ray Aranha (Can Man)

RUNNING TIME (Panoramic Pictures) Producers, Josh Becker, Jane Goe; Director/Screenplay, Josh Becker; Story, Peter Y. Choi; Photography, Kurt Rauf; Music, Joseph LoDuca; Editor, Kaye Davis; Black and white; Not rated; 79 minutes; December release. **CAST:** Bruce Campbell (Carl), Jeremy Roberts (Patrick), Anita Barone (Janie), Stan Davis (Buzz), Gordon Jennison (Donny), Art LaFleur (Warden), Dana Craig (Mr. Mueller), Bidget Hoffman (Receptionist)

HOME ALONE 3 (20th Century Fox) Producers, John Hughes, Hilton Green; Executive Producer, Ricardo Mestres; Director, Raja Gosnell; Screenplay, John Hughes; Photography, Julio Macat; Designer, Henry Bumstead; Music, Nick Glennie-Smith; Costumes, Jodie Tillen; Editors, Bruce Green, Malcolm Campbell, David Rennie; Casting, Billy Hopkins, Suzanne Smith, Kerry Barden, Jennifer McNamara; a John Hughes production; Dolby Digital Stereo; Deluxe color; Rated PG; 102 minutes; December release. **CAST:** Alex D. Linz (Alex), Olek Krupa (Beaupre), Rya Kihlstedt (Alice), Lenny Von Dohlen (Jernigan), David Thornton (Unger), Haviland Morris (Karen), Kevin Kilner (Jack), Marian Seldes (Mrs. Hess), Seth Smith (Stan), Scarlett Johansson (Molly), Christopher Curry (Agent Stuckey), Baxter Harris (Police Captain), James Saito (Chinese Mob Boss), Kevin Gudahl (Techie), Richard Hamilton (Cab Driver), Freeman Coffey (Recruiting Officer), Krista Lally (Dispatcher), Neil Flynn, Tony Mockus Jr., James L. Chisem (Police Officers), Pat Healy (Agent Rogers), Darwin L. Harris (Photographer), Adrianne Duncan (Flight Attendant), Sharon Sachs (Annoying Woman), Joseph L. Caballero (Security Guard), Larry C. Tankson (Cart Driver), Jennifer Daley (Police Photographer #2), Darren T. Knaus (Voice of Parrot)

Olek Krupa, Alex D. Linz in *Home Alone 3* © Twentieth Century Fox

Sean Penn, Malcolm McDowell in *Hugo Pool* © BMG / Northern Arts

HUGO POOL (Northern Arts/BMG Independents) Producer, Barbara Ligeti; Executive Producers, Douglas Berquist, Michael Frislev, Chad Oakes, Iren Koster, Lawrence Steven Meyers; Director, Robert Downey; Screenplay, Robert Downey, Laura Downey; Photography, Joseph Montgomery; Editor, Joe D'Augustine; Music, Danilo Perez; Designer, Lauren Gabor; Costumes, Jocelyn F. Wright; a Nomadic Pictures presentation of a Downey/Ligeti production; Dolby Stereo; Color; Rated R; 93 minutes; December release. **CAST**: Patrick Dempsey (Floyd Gaylen), Robert Downey, Jr. (Franz Mazur), Richard Lewis (Chic Chicalini), Malcolm McDowell (Henry Dugay), Alyssa Milano (Hugo Dugay), Cathy Moriarty (Minerva), Sean Penn (The Leprechaun), Mark Boone Junior (Pool Supply Man), Brendan B. Dawson (Man with Truck), Sean Glenn (Andy), Bert Remsen (Sad Old Man), Kevin Dornan (Bad Advice Father), Michael Mazzola (Kid), Chuck Barris (Irwin), Jim Shield (Lifeguard), Ann Magnuson (Drowning Matron), Eddie Perez (Gardener), Lora Gomez Eastwood, Pablo Ferro, Helen Hewitt Garb (Merengue Dancers), Domingo Ambriz (Spanish Husband), Paul Herman (Rabbi), Joanne Dearing (Extra's Mother), Michael Goldman (Extra's Father), Michael Bolger (One Man Band), Aaron Cuhr, Jacob James Hanft, N. Dylan Pfeifer (Party Waiters), Larry Kaplan (Man at Track), Brian David Zola (Guard at Track), Barbara Ligeti (Radio Newscaster) (Cable premiere: 11/97)

OFFICE KILLER (Strand) Producers, Christine Vachon, Pamela Koffler; Executive Producers, Tom Carouso, John Hart, Ted Hope, James Schamus; Director, Cindy Sherman; Screenplay, Elise MacAdam, Tom Kalin; Story, Cindy Sherman, Elise MacAdam; Additional Dialogue, Todd Haynes; Photography, Russell Fine; Editor, Merril Stern; Designer, Kevin Thompson; Music, Evan Lurie; Special Effects Makeup, Rob Benevides; Casting, Billy Hopkins, Suzanne Smith, Kerry Barden; a prresentation in association with Good Machine and Kardana/Swinsky Films of a Good Fear film; Color; Not rated; 81 minutes; December release. **CAST**: Carol Kane (Dorine Douglas), Molly Ringwald (Kim Poole), Jeanne Tripplehorn (Norah Reed), Barbara Sukowa (Virginia Wingate), Michael Imperioli (Daniel Birch), David Thornton (Gary Michaels), Mike Hodge (Mr. Landau), Alice Drummond (Carlotta Douglas), Florina Rodov (Receptionist), Jason Brill (Delivery Man), Eddie Malavarca (Brian the Mailboy), Doug Barron (Ted), Linda Powell (Naomi), Albert Macklin (Brad), Michelle Hurst (Kate), Paula Cale (Paula), Harvey Kaplan (Steve), Marla Sucharetza (Mrs. Gary Michaels), Rachel Aviva (Young Dorine), Marceline Hugot (Young Carlotta), Wayne Maxwell (Jimmy the Homeless

Man), Julia McIlvaine (Linda the Girl Scout), Cleopatra St. John (Girl Scout #2), Danny Morgenstern (Ted's Secretary), Timothy D. Stikney, Christopher Tracy (Paramedics)

THE EDUCATION OF LITTLE TREE (Paramount) Producer, Jake Eberts; Director/Screenplay, Richard Friedenberg; Based on the novel by Forrest Carter; Co-Producers, Lenny Young, Louise Gendron; Photography, Anastas Michos; Designer, Dan Bishop; Editor, Wayne Wahrman; Music, Mark Isham; Costumes, Renée April; Casting, Vera Miller, René Haynes; a Jake Eberts production, presented in association with Allied Films/Lightmotive; Color; Rated PG; 117 minutes; December release. **CAST**: James Cromwell (Granpa), Tantoo Cardinal (Granma), Joseph Ashton (Little Tree), Graham Green (Willow John), Leni Parker (Martha), Rebecca Dewey (Dolly), William Rowat (Henry), Robert Daviau (Ralph), Christopher Heyerdahl (Pine Billy), Norris Domingue (Mr. Jenkins), Mika Boorem (Little Girl), Mark Jeffrey Miller (Preacher), Gordon Masten (Politician), Howard Rosenstein (Calf's Owner), Teddy-Lee Dillon, James Rae, Alain Goulem (Revenuers), Griffith Brewer (Church Man), Dawn Ford (Church Woman), Lisa Bronwyn Moore (Elizabeth), Larry Day (Mr. Lane), Dean Hagopian (Joe Taylor), Jonathan Stark (Girl's Father), Pauline Little (Mrs. Higgenbotham), Peter Colvey (Proctor #1), Michel Perron (Headmaster), Chris Fennell (Wilburn), Victoria Barkoff (Teacher), Karentiio Phillips (Older Boy), Pierre Boudreau (Pilgrim), Richard Jutras (Indian), Jeff Jeffcoat (Voice of Older Little Tree)

Jeanne Tripplehorn in *Office Killer*
© Strand Releasing

VEGAS VACATION (Jerry Weintraub Productions) Producer, Jerry Weintraub; Executive Producers, Matty Simmons, Susan Ekins; Director, Stephen Kessler; Screenplay, Elisa Bell; Story, Elisa Bell, Bob Ducsay; Photography, William A. Fraker; Designer, David L. Snyder; Editor, Seth Flaum; Music, Joel McNeely; Distributed by WB; Dolby; Technicolor; Rated PG-13; 95 minutes; February release. **CAST**: Chevy Chase (Clark Griswold), Beverly D'Angelo (Ellen Griswold), Randy Quaid (Cousin Eddie), Ethan Embry (Rusty Griswold), Marisol Nichols (Audrey Griswold), Miriam Flynn (Cousin Catherine), Shae D'Lyn (Cousin Vickie), Wayne Newton (Himself), Siegfried and Roy (Themselves), Wallace Shawn (Marty), Sid Caesar (Old Guy), Julio Oscar Mechoso (Limo Driver), Sly Smith (Mirage Security Guard), Julia Sweeney (Mirage Reception Person), Corinna Harney Jones (Girl at Blackjack Table), Joe Armeno (Roulette Stickman), Christie Brinkley (Woman in Ferrari), Juliette Brewer (Cousin Ruby-Sue), Zach Moyes (Cousin Denny), John Finnegan (Hoover Dam Guide), Seth Walker (Bellman), Howard Platt (Maitre 'd), Elizabeth Illia (Woman at Concert), Wayne Brown, Gary Devaney (Croupiers), Maria Cina (Mirage Cashier), Wendy Kaufman (Wendy), Joe LaCoco (Riviera Bartender), David L. Garoutte (Riviera Security Guard), C.C. Costigan (Kelli), Peter George (Marcus), Frank Mendonga (Kurt), Daniel Steven Lopez (Kyle), Shannah Laumeister (Mariah), Aki (Aki), Bud Ekins (O'Shea's Security Guard), Jerry Weintraub (Jilly), Bernie Yuman (Doc Sandy), Paul Kessler (Silent Al), S.A. Griffin (Pit Boss), Lou DiMaggio (Casino Host), Ruth Gillis (Saleswoman), Samuel J. Marber (Painter), Antonio Mitchell (Larry), Jason Stuart (Buffet Guy), Nick Mazzola (War Dealer), Jim Migliore (Rock Paper Scissors Dealer), Reno Nichols (Coin Tosser), Frank Washko, Jr. (Guess Which Hand Dealer), Ken Michelman (Pick a Number Dealer), Clinton Brandhagen (Valet), Hayley Mortison (Girl in Hot Tub), Gene Ellison Jones (Mirage Guard at Party), Steve "Biscuit" Walker (Bouncer), Rusty Meyers (Club Manager), Roxy Swaney (Keno Caller), Billy Morrissette, Sharon Mendel (Paramedics), Larry Hankin (Preacher)

ROSEWOOD (Peters Entertainment) Producer, Jon Peters; Executive Producer, Tracy Barone; Director, John Singleton; Screenplay, Gregory Poirier; Photography, Johnny E. Jensen; Designer, Paul Sylbert; Editor, Bruce Cannon; Co-Producer, Penelope L. Foster; Music, John Williams; Costumes, Ruth E. Carter; Casting, Marion Dougherty; a Peters Entertainment production in association with New Deal Productions; Distributed by WB; Dolby; Panavision; Technicolor; Rated R; 142 minutes; February release. **CAST:** Jon Voight (John Wright), Ving Rhames (Mann), Don Cheadle (Sylvester), Bruce McGill (Duke Purdy), Loren Dean (James Taylor), Esther Rolle (Aunt Sarah), Elise Neal (Scrappie), Robert Patrick (Lover), Michael Rooker (Sheriff Walker), Catherine Kellner (Fanny Taylor), Akosua Busia (Jewel), Paul Benjamin (James Carrier), Kevin Jackson (Sam Carter), Mark Boone Junior (Poly), Muse Watson (Henry Andrews), Badja Djola (John Bradley), Kathryn Meisle (Mary Wright), Jaimz Woolvett (Deputy Earl), James Edward Coleman II (Arnett), Tristan Hook (Emmett Purdy), Benea Ousley (Philomena), Isabell Monk (Emma), Bridgid Coulter (Gertrude), Gabie Chavis (Minnie), Vanessa Baden (Lee Ruth), Marcus Barrington (Denny), Matthew Davison (Timothy), Brett Rice (William Bryce), Ric Reitz (John Bryce), Ken Sagoes (Big Baby), Phil Moore (Aaron Carrier), Lowell Fenner (Judge Johnson), Andrew "J.R." Tarver (Preacher), Harold G. Crawford (Clevus), Marc Macaulay (Bobby), Clarence Thomas (Lemuel), Blaine Farmer (Michael Wright), Valerie Herald, Susan Gallagher (Women), Steven Tyler (Little Ronnie), Danny Hanemann (White Brother), Eldrid Foye (Blackman), Michael Galloway (Cracker #2), Macon McCalman (Governor Hardee), Tom Schuster (Kid's Redneck Dad), Peggy Sheffield (Mrs. Ellis Walker), Steve Raulerson (Sheriff of Bronson), Henry Laurence (Man #2)

SELENA (Q Productions Inc.—Esparza/Katz Prod.) Producers, Moctesuma Esparza, Robert Katz; Executive Producer, Abraham Quintanilla; Co-Executive Producer, David Wisnievitz; Co-Producer, Peter Lopez; Director/Screenplay, Gregory Nava; Photography, Edward Lachman; Designer, Cary White; Editor, Nancy Richardson; Music, Dave Grusin; Costumes, Elisabetta Beraldo; Casting, Roger Mussenden; Distributed by WB; Dolby; Super 35 Widescreen; Technicolor; Rated PG; 130 minutes; March release. **CAST**: Jennifer Lopez (Selena Quintanilla), Edward James Olmos (Abraham Quintanilla), Jon Seda (Chris Perez), Constance Marie (Marcella Quintanilla), Jacob Vargas (Abie Quintanilla),

Graham Greene, Joseph Ashton in
The Education of Little Tree © Paramount Pictures

Lupe Ontiveros (Yolanda Saldivar), Jackie Guerra (Suzette Quintanilla), Alexandra Meneses (Sara), Peter Astrudillo, Ricky Vela (Themselves), Ruben Gonzalez (Joe Ojeda), Don Shelton (Stage Dancer), Richard Emanuele (Concert Reporter), Panchito Gomez (Young Abraham—Dinos 1961), Richard Coca (Bobby—Dinos 1961), George Perez (Seff—Dinos 1961), Brian Fallteen (Club Owner), Carmen Martinez, Elisabeth Gonzalez, Richard Iglesias (Irate Club Goers), Everett Sifuentes (Lerma's Club Owner), Gil Glasgow (Police Officer—1961), Rebecca Lee Meza (Young Selena), Victoria Elena Flores (Young Suzette), Rafael Tamayo (Young Abie), Carl William Holler (Neighbor), Bel Hernandez (Dolores Quintanilla), Gail Cronauer (Customer), Elia Ortiz (Waitress), Fernando Cubillas (Eddie Quintanilla), Sal Lopez (Juan Luis), Richard Williams Hughes (MC), Erick Carrillo, Frank Mendez (Cholos), Seidy Lopez (Deborah), Francisco J. De La Fuente, Keith Kaslow (Hotel Managers), Don Cass (Security Guard), Peter P. Montejano, Michael Guerrero, Ronald Gonzales, Chris Doughten (Chris' Friends), Leon Singer (Concert Promoter), Martha Flores, Terry Elena Ordaz (Monterrey Reporters), Marcos Padilla (Concert Official), Valerio Longoria, Sr. (Accordian Player), Philip Raybourn (Bungie Jump Attendant), Mark Carrillo (Manuel), Darline Tigrett (Mexico City Reporter), Donnie Neubauer (Record Executive), John Verea (Jose Behar), Joe Stevens (Record Producer), Marika Baca, Michelle McManus (Pedicurists), Barbara Petricini-Buxton (Saleslady), Leonardo Martinez (Boutique Worker), Molly Moroney (Store Manager), Desi McGill (Blonde Teenager), Tom Christopher (Grammy Presenter), Cora Cardona (Head Seamstress), Amin Mery (Paramedic)

CATS DON'T DANCE (Turner Feature Animation) Producers, David Kirschner, Paul Gertz; Executive Producers, David Steinberg, Charles L. Richardson, Sandy Russell Gartin; Director, Mark Dindal; Screenplay, Roberts Gannaway, Cliff Ruby, Elana Lesser, Theresa Pettengill; Story, Rick Schneider, Robert Lence, Mark Dindal, Brian McEntee, David Womersley, Kelvin Yasuda; Co-Producers, Jim Katz, Barry Weiss; Art Director, Brian McEntee; Music, Steve Goldstein; Songs, Randy Newman; Editor, Dan Molina; Casting, Judy Taylor, Lynda Gordon; Storyboard, Rich Schneider, Mark Dindal; Layout, David Womersley; Background, Jim Hickey; Clean-Up, Don Parmele; Effects and Computer Graphics Imagery, Mark Myer; a David Kirschner production; Distributed by WB; Dolby; Color; Rated G; 75 minutes; March release. **VOICE CAST**: Scott Bakula (Danny), Jasmine Guy (Sawyer—speaking), Natalie Cole (Sawyer—singing), Ashley Peldon (Darla Dimple—speaking), Lindsay Ridgeway (Darla Dimple—singing), Kathy Najimy (Tillie), John Rhys-Davies (Woolie), George Kennedy (L.B. Mammoth), Rene Auberjonois (Flanigan), Hal Holbrook (Cranston), Don Knotts (T.W.), Betty Lou Gerson (Francis), Matthew Herried (Pudge), Frank Welker (Farley Wink), David Johansen (Bus Driver), Mark Dindal (Max)

MURDER AT 1600 (Regency Enterprises) Producers, Arnold Kopelson, Arnon Milchan; Executive Producers, Anne Kopelson, Michael Nathanson, Stephen Brown; Director, Dwight Little; Screenplay, Wayne Beach, David Hodgin; Co-Producer, Ralph S. Singleton; Photography, Steven Bernstein; Designer, Nelson Coates; Editors, Billy Weber, Leslie Jones; Music, Christopher Young; Costumes, Denise Cronenberg; Casting, Amanda Mackey Johnson, Cathy Sandrich; an Arnold Kopelson production; Presented in association with Regency Enterprises; Distributed by WB; Dolby; Technicolor; Rated R; 107 minutes; April release. **CAST:** Wesley Snipes (Det. Regis), Diane Lane (Nina Chance), Daniel Benzali (Spikings), Dennis Miller (Det. Stengel), Alan Alda (Jordan), Ronny Cox (Pres. Jack Neil), Diane Baker (Kitty Neil), Tate Donovan (Kyle Neil), Harris Yulin (Gen. Clark Tully), Nicholas Pryor (Paul Moran), Charles Rocket (Jeffrey), Nigel Bennett (Burton Cash), Tamara Gorski (Young Woman in Bar), Douglas O'Keeffe (Assassin—John Kerry), Tony Nappo (Luchessi), Mary Moore (Carla Town), George R. Robertson (Mack Falls), Ho Chow (Tepper), James Millington (Lt. Marty Dill), John Bourgeois (Capt. Farr), Peter James Haworth, Aron Tager (Treasury Guards), David Gardner (Speaker of the House), Cliff McMullen (Sniper—Carl), Keith Williams (Lawyer Randy Queeg), Grace Armas (Screaming Cleaning Woman), David Fraser (Brack Electronics), George Sperdakos (Reporter—Last Press), Sandra Caldwell (Mrs. Wallace), Frank Moore (Capt. Ford Gibbs), Richard Blackburn (Coroner Jimmy Foley), James Gallanders (Law Student), Victor Ertmanis (Cop Bartender), Richard Fitzpatrick (Law Professor), Michael Ricupero (Landlord), Chris Gillett (V.P. Gordon Dylan), J. Craig Sandy (FBI Agent #1), Robert Bidaman (V.P. Aide), Carol Anderson (Capt. Farr's Asst.), Christopher Kennedy (Techy), Mike Kinney (Reporter—Jail), Michael Hambrick, Dan Duran, Sandi Stahlbrand (CNN Reporters), Jackie Bensen, Maureen Bunyan, Kathryn Klvana (TV Reporters), Sheldon Turcott (CNN Newscaster #1), Tom Urich (CNN News Anchor), Tino Monte (Local Newscaster), Raven Dauda (Waitress), Michael Dyson (Treasury Drone), Doris E. McMillon, Lewis Grenville (Network Reporters), Moe Kelso (Gorgeous Woman), Junior Williams (Medic), Howard Hoover, Bryan Renfro, Markus Parilo, Leight E. Brinkman, Len Wagner, Peter Ellery, Ray Paisley, Brian King (Suits), Donald Jones (Reporter C), Marco Bianco, Matt Birman, Eric Bryson, Walter Masko, Branko Racki, Mike Shute, Anton Tyukodi (Secret Service)

LEO TOLSTOY'S ANNA KARENINA (Icon Prod.) Producer, Bruce Davey; Executive Producer, Stephen McEveety; Director/Screenplay, Bernard Rose; Based on the novel by Leo Tolstoy; Photography, Daryn Okada; Designer, John Myhre; Editor, Victor Du Bois; Costumes, Maurizio Millenotti; Casting, Marion Dougherty; Distributed by WB; Dolby Stereo; Panavision; Technicolor; Rated R; 108 minutes; April release. **CAST**: Sophie Marceau (Anna Karenina), Sean Bean (Vronsky), Alfred Molina (Levin), Mia Kirshner (Kitty), James Fox (Karenin), Fiona Shaw (Lydia), Danny Huston (Stiva), Phyllida Law (Vronskaya), David Schofield (Nikolai), Saskia Wickham (Dolly), Jennifer Hall (Betsy), Anna Calder Marshall (Shcherbatskaya), Valerie Braddell (Ambassador's Wife), Niall Buggy (Doctor), Anthony Calf (Serpuhovsky), Vernon Dobtcheff (Pestov), Hamish Falconer (Seriozha), Stefan Gryff (Korsunsky), Barbara Horne (Miss Edwards), Larissa Kousnetsova (Agatha), Jeremy Sheffield (Boris), Justine Waddell (Nordston), Mikail Hmelev (Mahotin), Ksenia Rappoport (Maria), Peter Sholohov (Kapitonich), Julia Krasnova (Annushka), Ludmila Kurepova (Sorokina), German Maximov (Priest), Tatiana Zaharova (Midwife), Sergei Scherbina (Korney), Gelena Ivleva (Lizaveta), Father Vadim Sadovnikov (Inn Priest), Sergei Parshin (Doctor's Doorman), Valery Kukhareshen (Specialist Doctor), Nora Griakalova (Myagkaya), Oleg Kosminsky (Titus), Victor Guiranov, Leonty Varenstov (Peasants), Igor Efimov (Servant), Konstantin Lukashov (Moscow Railway Worker), Alexandra Lavrova (Young Anna)

FATHERS' DAY (Silver Pictures) Producers, Joel Silver, Ivan Reitman; Executive Producers, Joe Medjuck, Daniel Goldberg, Francis Veber; Director, Ivan Reitman; Screenplay, Lowell Ganz, Babaloo Mandel; Based on the film Les Comperes by Francis Veber; Photography, Stephen H. Burum; Designer, Thomas Sanders; Editors, Sheldon Kahn, Wendy Greene Bricmont; Co-Producers, Gordon Webb, Karyn Fields; Music, James Newton Howard; Songs "Young Boy" and "The World Tonight" written and performed by Paul McCartney; Costumes, Rita Ryack; Casting, Bonnie Timmermann, Michael Chinich; a Silver Pictures production in association with Northern Lights Entertainment; Distributed by WB; Dolby; Panavision; Technicolor; Rated PG-13; 98 minutes; May release. **CAST:** Robin Williams (Dale Putley), Billy Crystal (Jack Lawrence), Julia Louis-Dreyfus (Carrie Lawrence), Nastassja Kinski (Collette Andrews), Charlie Hofheimer (Scott Andrews), Bruce Greenwood (Bob Andrews), Dennis Burkley (Calvin), Haylie Johnson (Nikki), Charles Rocket (Russ Trainor), Patti D'Arbanville (Shirley Trainor), Jared Harris (Lee), Louis Lombardi (Matt), Mark McGrath, Craig Bullock, Charles Stan Frazier, Matthew Murphy Karges, Rodney Sheppard (Sugar Ray Band), Alan Berger (Rex), Tom Verica (Peter), Jennifer Crystal (Rose), David Ripley, Ryan "Rhino" Michaels (Roadies), Jason Reitman (Wrong Kid in Alley), William Hall (Hotel Clerk), Ricky Harris (Bellhop), Paul Herman (Mr. Barmore), Christopher Jaymes (Gas Station Guy), Catherine Reitman (Victoria), Claudette Wells (Ms. Tweesbury), Susan Traylor (Flight Attendant), Dana Gould (Room Service Waiter), Meagen Fay (Megan), Mary Gillis (Slot Machine Lady), Mindy Seeger (Nurse), Jennifer Echols (Ball Park Vendor), Marc Glimcher (Cashier), Geoffrey Infeld (Mime), Harry E. Northup (Cop—Reno Jail), Tamara Zook (Waitress—Francene), Frank Medrano (Mechanic), Elston Ridgle (Security Guard), Kim Shattuck, Ronnie Barnett, Roy McDonald (The Muffs), Caroline Reitman (Lost Girl), Lee Weaver (Airline Passenger), Jose "Esau" Pena (Boat Painter), Andre Zotoff (Doorman), Kay Ford (Woman in Lobby), Jasmine Rose (Nosering Girl), Mel Gibson (Pierced Guy)

ADDICTED TO LOVE (Outlaw Production/Miramax) Producers, Jeffrey Silver, Bobby Newmyer; Executive Producers, Bob Weinstein, Harvey Weinstein; Director, Griffin Dunne; Screenplay, Robert Gordon; Photography, Andrew Dunn; Designer, Robin Standefer; Editor, Elizabeth Kling; Co-Producers, Caroline Baron, Johanna Demetrakas; Music, Rachel Portman; Costumes, Renee Ehrlich Kalfus; Casting, Amanda Mackey Johnson, Cathy Sandrich; Distributed by WB; Dolby; Technicolor; Rated R; 100 minutes; May release. **CAST:** Meg Ryan (Maggie), Matthew Broderick (Sam), Kelly Preston (Linda), Tcheky Karyo (Anton), Maureen Stapleton (Nana), Nesbitt Blaisdell (Ed Green), Remak Ramsay (Prof. Wells), Lee Wilkof (Carl), Dominick Dunne (Matheson), Susan Forristal (Cecile), Larry Pine (Street Comic), Debbon Ayer (Gwen), Maurizio Benazzo (Euro-Chic Man), Paolo Calamari (French Bartender), Helmar Augustus Cooper (Bus Driver), Tom Forrest (Astronomer), Shoshanna Gleich (School Teacher), Jacqueline Heinze (Bald Girl), Mike Hodge (Linda's Doorman), Daniel Dae Kim (Undergrad Assist.), Bill Kux (Desk Clerk), Steve McAuliff (Business Man), Conrad McLaren (Motorcycle Man), Bill Timoney (Restaurant Patron)

BATMAN & ROBIN (Joel Schumacher Film) Producer, Peter MacGregor-Scott; Executive Producers, Benjamin Melniker, Michael E. Uslan; Director, Joel Schumacher; Screenplay, Akiva Goldsman; Based upon Batman characters created by Bob Kane and published by DC Comics; Photography, Stephen Goldblatt; Designer, Barbara Ling; Editor, Dennis Virkler; Visual Effects, John Dykstra; Music, Elliot Goldenthal; Costumes, Ingrid Ferrin, Robert Turturice; Co-Producer, William M. Elvin; Casting, Mali Finn; Distributed by WB; Dolby; Technicolor; Rated PG-13; 130 minutes; June release. **CAST:** Arnold Schwarzenegger (Mr. Freeze/Dr. Victor Fries), George Clooney (Batman/Bruce Wayne), Chris O'Donnell (Robin/Dick Grayson), Uma Thurman (Poison Ivy/Dr. Pamela Isley), Alicia Silverstone (Batgirl/Barbara Wilson), Michael Gough (Alfred Pennyworth), Pat Hingle (Commissioner Gordon), John Glover (Dr. Jason Woodrue), Elle MacPherson (Julie Madison), Vivica A. Fox (Ms. B. Haven), Vendela K. Thommessen (Nora Fries), Jeep Swenson (Bane), Elizabeth Sanders (Gossip Gerty), John Fink (Aztec Museum Guard), Michael Reid MacKay (Antonio Diego), Eric Lloyd (Young Bruce Wayne), Jon Simmons (Young Alfred), Christian Boeving, Stogie Kenyatta, Andy LaCombe (Snowy Cones Thugs), Joe Sabatino (Frosty), Michael Paul Chan (Observatory Scientist), Kimberly Scott (Observatory Associate), Jay Luchs, Roger Nehls (Observatory Reporters), Anthony E. Cantrell (Observatory Press), Alex Daniels, Peter Navy Tuiasosopo (Observatory Guards), Harry Van Gorkum (M.C.), Sandra Taylor, Elizabeth Guber (Debutantes), Jack Betts, Marc Glimcher, Mark P. Leahy, Jim McMullan (Party Guests), Senator Patrick Leahy (Himself), Jesse Ventura, Ralf Moeller (Arkham Asylum Guards), Doug Hutchison (Golum), Tobias Jelinek, Greg Lauren, Dean Cochran (Motorcycle Gang), Coolio (Banker), Nicky Katt (Spike), Lucas Berman (Tough Boy Biker), Uzi Gal, Howard Velasco (Cops), Bruce Roberts (Handsome Cop), John Ingle (Doctor), Azikiwee Anderson, Michael Bernardo, Steve Blalock, Steve Boyles, Dave Cardoza, Christopher Caso, Mark Chadwick, Danny Costa, Stephan Desjardins, Todd Grossman, James Hardy, Steven Ito, Dennis Keiffer, James Kim, Simon Kim, Dennis Lefevre, Jean Luc Martin, Cory M. Miller, Chris Mitchell, Christopher Nelson, Jim Palmer, Jeff Podgurski, Robert Powell, Chris Sayour, Don Sinnar, Paul Sklar, Takis Triggelis (Ice Thugs)

WILD AMERICA (Morgan Creek Prod.) Producers, James G. Robinson, Irby Smith, Mark Stouffer; Executive Producers, Gary Barber, Steve Tisch, Bill Todman, Jr.; Director, William Dear; Screenplay, David Michael Wieger; Photography, David Burr; Designer, Steven Jordan; Editor, O. Nicholas Brown; Music, Joel McNeely; Costumes, Mary McLeod; Casting, Pam Dixon Mickelson; a James G. Robinson presentation of a Morgan Creek production in association with the Steve Tisch Company; Dolby; Clairmont-Scope; Color; Rated PG; 106 minutes; July release. **CAST**: Jonathan Taylor Thomas (Marshall), Devon Sawa (Mark), Scott Bairstow (Marty), Frances Fisher (Agnes), Jamie Sheridan (Marty Sr.), Tracey Walter (Leon), Don Stroud (Stango), Zack Ward (D.C.), Claudia Stedelin (Annie), Anastasia Spivey (Donna Jo), Leighanne Wallace (Tanna), Amy Lee Douglas (Julie Anne), Sonny Shroyer (Bud), Rachel Fowler (Sarah), Jennifer Crumbley (Betsy), Maggie Blackkettle (Old Native Woman), Larry Reese (Dr. Pierce), Susan Dear (Donna Pierce), Nadine Browning (Woman at Gravesite), Norman Taber (D.C. Gang Member), Devon Dear, Jennifer Mikelson, Emily Messmer (Swoon Girls), Danny Glover (Mountain Man)

CONTACT (South Side Amusement Co.) Producers, Robert Zemeckis, Steve Starkey; Executive Producers, Joan Bradshaw, Lynda Obst; Director, Robert Zemeckis; Screenplay, James V. Hart, Michael Goldenberg; Based on the novel by Carl Sagan; Co-Producers/Based on the story by Carl Sagan, Ann Druyan; Photography, Don Burgess; Designer, Ed Verreaux; Editor, Arthur Schmidt; Music, Alan Silvestri; Costumes, Joanna Johnston; Senior Visual Effects Supervisor, Ken Ralston; Casting, Victoria Burrows; Distributed by WB; Dolby; Panavision; Technicolor; Rated PG; 150 minutes; July release. **CAST:** Jodie Foster (Ellie Arroway), Matthew McConaughey (Palmer Joss), James Woods (Michael Kitz), John Hurt (S.R. Hadden), Tom Skerritt (David Drumlin), Angela Bassett (Rachel Constantine), Jena Malone (Young Ellie), David Morse (Ted Arroway), Rob Lowe (Richard Rank), Jake Busey (Joseph), Geoffrey Blake (Fisher), William Fichtner (Kent), SaMi Chester (Vernon), Timothy McNeil (Davio), Laura Elena Surillo (Cantina Woman), Henry Strozier (Minister), Michael Chaban (Hadden Suit), Maximilian Martini (Willie), Thomas Garner (Ian Broderick), Conroy Chino (KOB—TV Reporter), Dan Gifford (Jeremy Roth), Vance Valencia (Senator Valencia), Behrooz Afrakhan (Middle Eastern Anchor), Saemi Nakamura (Japanese Anchor), Maria Celeste Arraras (Latina Anchor), Ian Whitcomb (British Anchor), Michael Albala (Decryption Hacker), Ned Netterville (Decryption Expert), Leo Lee (Major Domo), William Jordan (Chairman of Joint Chiefs), David St. James (Joint Chief), Haynes Brooke (Drumlin Aid), Steven Ford (Major Russell), Alex Zemeckis (Major Russell's Son), Janie Peterson (Major Russell's Daughter), Phillip Bergeron (French Committee Member), Jennifer Balgobin (Dr. Patel), Anthony Fife Hamilton (British Committee Member), Rebecca T. Beucler (NASA Public Relations), Marc Macaulay (NASA Technician), Pamela Wilsey (Voice of NASA), Tucker Smallwood (Mission Director), Jeff Johnson (Mechanical), Yuji Okumoto (Electrical), Gerry Griffin, Kristoffer Ryan Winters (Dynamics), Brian Alston (Communications), Rob Elk (Pad Leader), Mark Thomason (Security), José Rey (Controller #8), Todd Patrick Breaugh (New VLA Technician), Alex Veadov (Russian Cosmonaut), Alice Kushida (Scientist), Robin Gammell (Project Official), Richardson Morse (Mission Doctor), Seiji Okamura (Japanese Ensign), Mak Takano, Tom Tanaka (Japanese Techs), Catherine Dao (Life Support), Valorie Armstrong (Senator), Jim Hild, Bill Thomas (Reporters), Diego Montoya (School Boy), Larry King, Donna J. Kelley, Leon Harris, Claire Shipman, Tabitha Soren, Geraldo Rivera, Jay Leno, Natalie Allen, Robert D. Novak, Geraldine A. Ferraro, Ann Druyan, Kathleen Kennedy, Jill Dougherty, John Holliman, Bobbie Battista, Dee Dee Myers, Bryant Gumbel, Linden Soles, Bernard Shaw (Themselves)

CONSPIRACY THEORY (Silver Pictures) Producers, Joel Silver, Richard Donner; Executive Producer, Jim Van Wyck; Director, Richard Donner; Screenplay, Brian Helgeland; Photography, John Schwartzman; Designer, Paul Sylbert; Editors, Frank J. Urioste, Kevin Stitt; Co-Producers, Dan Cracchiolo, J. Mills Goodloe, Rick Solomon; Music, Carter Burwell; Costumes, Ha Nguyen; Casting, Marion Dougherty; a Silver Pictures production in association with Shuler Donner/Donner productions; Distributed by WB; Dolby; Panavision; Technicolor; Rated R; 135 minutes; August release. **CAST:** Mel Gibson (Jerry Fletcher), Julia Roberts (Alice Sutton), Patrick Stewart (Dr. Jonas), Cylk Cozart (Agent Lowry), Stephen Kahan (Wilson), Terry Alexander (Flip), Alex McArthur (Cynic), Rod McLachlan, Michael Potts, Jim Sterling (Justice Guards), Rich Hebert (Public Works Man), Brian J. Williams (Clarke), G.A. Aguilar (Piper), Cece Neber Labao (Finch's Secretary), Saxon Trainor (Alice's Secretary), Claudia Stedelin (Wilson's Secretary), Leonard Jackson (Old Man—Bookstore), Donal Gibson (Doctor—Roosevelt Hospital), Joanna Sanchez (Nurse—Roosevelt Hospital), Michael Shamus Wiles, Mik Scriba (Cops—Roosevelt Hospital), Patrick Wild (Intern in Jerry's Room), Mushond Lee, Kevin Kindlin, Troy Garity (Interns), J. Mills Goodloe (Jonas' Aide), Michael Kurtz (Well Dressed Man), Pete Koch (Fire Captain), Kevin Jackson, Nick Kusenko, Karl Makinen (CIA Agents), Darren Peel (Geronimo Cleet), Marian Collier (Geronimo Cook), John Harms (Agent Murphy), Christine Toy Johnson (Bookstore Clerk), David Koch, Danny Smith, Juan Riojas (Techs), Paul Tuerpé Dean Winters (Cleets), Jose Ramon Rosario, Louis Cantarini (Angry Vendors), Sean

Patrick Thomas, Peter Jacobson (Surveillance Operators), Edita Brychta (Finch's Receptionist), Sage Allen (Grouchy Nurse), Thomas McCarthy (Helicopter Spotter), K.T. Vogt (Woman in Mental Hospital), Joshua Fardon (Hospital Guard), Joan Lunden (TV Announcer), Charles McDaniel (Bureaucrat), Matte Osian, David Hamilton Simonds (Operatives), Rick Hoffman (Night Security—Federal Building), Edward J. Rosen (Old Man—Diner), Bert Remsen (Alice's Father), Lincoln Simonds (Cop by Laundry Chute), Bill Henderson (Hospital Security), Jay Fiondella (Patient), James Louis Oliver (Man in Justice Department), Kerry Palmisano, Victory Grace Palmisano, Kate Bayley (Nurses' Aides), Irene Hilleary (Justice Department Receptionist), Stephen Liska (Hospital Orderly), Don Stanley (Justice Department Guard), Lorna R. Millen (Charge Nurse), Brad Rea, Jim Van Wyck, Jayson Merrill, Dan Cracchiolo (Spotters), John Schwartzman (Sniper), Raymond King, Jared Crawford (Bucket Drummers), Jeremy A. Graham, Chad Santiago (Rappers), Christo Morse (Taxi Patron), H. Clay Dear, Daniel Nugent (Traffic Cops), Andrew Lauren, Tom Schanley, Kenneth Tigar, Judy Woodbury (Lawyers), Maureen Lauder (Lady with Dog)

FREE WILLY 3: THE RESCUE (Regency Enterprises) Producer, Jennie Lew Tugend; Executive Producers, Lauren Shuler Donner, Richard Donner, Arnon Milchan; Director, Sam Pillsbury; Screenplay, John Mattson; Photography, Tobias Schliessler; Designer, Brent Thomas; Editor, Margie Goodspeed; Music, Cliff Eidelman; Co-Producers, Douglas C. Merrifield, Mark Marshall; Costumes, Maya Mani; Casting, Judy Taylor, Lynne Carrow; a Shuler Donner/Donner production presented in association with Regency Enterprises; Distributed by WB; Dolby; Clairmont-scope; Technicolor; Rated PG; 86 minutes; August release. **CAST:** Jason James Richter (Jesse), August Schellenberg (Randolph), Annie Corley (Drew), Vincent Berry (Max), Patrick Kilpatrick (Wesley), Tasha Simms (Mary), Peter Lacroix (1st Mate Sanderson), Stephen E. Miller (Dineen), Ian Tracey (Kron), Matthew Walker (Capt. Drake), Roger R. Cross (1st Mate Stevens), Rick Burgess (Smiley), Roman Danylo (Pizza Kid)

FIRE DOWN BELOW (Seagal/Nasso Production) Producers, Steven Seagal, Julius R. Nasso; Executive Producers, William S. Gilmore, Jeb Stuart; Director, Felix Enriquez Alcalá; Screenplay, Jeb Stuart, Philip Morton; Story, Jeb Stuart; Co-Producer, Ronald G. Smith; Photography, Tom Houghton; Music, Nick Glennie-Smith; Designer, Joe Alves; Editor, Robert A. Ferretti; Costumes, Rosanna Norton; Casting, Shari Rhodes, Joseph Middleton; Distributed by WB; Dolby; Technicolor; Rated R; 105 minutes; September release. **CAST:** Steven Seagal (Jack Taggert), Marg Helgenberger (Sarah Kellogg), Stephen Lang (Earl), Brad Hunt (Orin, Jr.), Kris Kristofferson (Orin, Sr.), Harry Dean Stanton (Cotton), Levon Helm (Rev. Goodall), Mark Collie (Hatch), Alex Harvey (Sims), Ed Bruce (Lloyd), Amelia Neighbors (Edie), Richard Masur (Pratt), Newell Alexander, Michael Krawic (FBI Agents), Clay Jeter (Walter), Yvonne Pollard (Mother), Peggy Lynn (Betsy Hamill), Patsy Lynn (Patsy Hamill), John Diehl (Frank Elkins), Michael Mattison (Walter's Father), Dennis Letts (Dr. Schultz), Melodie Past (Store Clerk), Petrice Jordan (Natalie), Ellaraino (Judge), John Prosky, Dan O'Donahue (Aides), Gina Mari (Darlene), Scott L. Schwartz (Pimple), Rick Johnson, Joe Basile, Brian Leckner (Security), Andy Stahl (EPA Agent), Robert Ridgely (Simon), Lana Vassie (Amber), Randy Travis (Ken Adams), Ernie Lively (Todd), Lisa Coles (Beauty), David Brisbin (Lawyer), Blue Deckert (Chick Larsen), James Mathers (Marshal), Michelle von Flotow (Waitress), Charley J. Epling (Alberta), Ginger Carroll (Receptionist), Dan Beene (Dilbert/Grocer), Kimberly Cole, Brett Mellon, Randall R. Roberts, Kennita Collins, Benjamin Mays, LeAndra Arrowood, Ben Greer (Townspeople), Marty Stuart, Travis Tritt (Themselves), Julius R. Nasso (Actor), Aaron Chadwick, Michael Crosby, Jan Eddy (Pot Growers), John R. Gulino (Joey Chips), Nicky Julius (Casino Patron), Bruce Benson (Helicopter Pilot), Wililam H. Greer (Choir Minister), Julie Dawn Mullins (Christine), Lonnie Duran Tackett, Mackie Richerson (Minors)

L.A. CONFIDENTIAL (Regency Enterprises) Producers, Arnon Milchan, Curtis Hanson, Michael Nathanson; Executive Producers, David L. Wolper, Dan Kolsrud; Director, Curtis Hanson; Screenplay, Brian Helgeland, Curtis Hanson; Based on the novel by James Ellroy; Photography, Dante Spinotti; Designer, Jeannine Oppewall; Editor, Peter Honess; Co-Producer, Brian Helgeland; Costumes, Ruth Myers; Music, Jerry Goldsmith; Casting, Mali Finn; a Regency Enterprises presentation of an Arnon Milchan/David L. Wolper production; Dolby; Super 35 Widescreen; Technicolor; Rated R; 136 minutes; September release. CAST: Kevin Spacey (Jack Vincennes), Russell Crowe (Bud White), Guy Pearce (Ed Exley), James Cromwell (Dudley Smith), Kim Basinger (Lynn Bracken), Danny DeVito (Sid Hudgens), David Strathairn (Pierce Patchett), Ron Rifkin (D.A. Ellis Loew), Matt McCoy ("Badge of Honor" Star Brett Chase), Paul Guilfoyle (Mickey Cohen), Paolo Seganti (Johnny Stompanato), Elisabeth Granli, Sandra Taylor (Mickey Cohen's Mambo Partners), Steve Rankin (Officer Arresting Mickey Cohen), Graham Beckel (Dick Stensland), Allan Graf (Wife Beater), Precious Chong (Wife), Symba Smith (Jack's Dancing Partner), Bob Clendenin (Reporter at Hollywood Station), Lennie Loftin (Photographer at Hollywood Station), Will Zahrn (Liquor Store Owner), Amber Smith (Susan Lefferts), Darrell Sandeen (Buzz Meeks), Michael Warwick (Sid's Assistant), Simon Baker Denny (Matt Reynolds), Shawnee Free Jones (Tammy Jordan), Matthew Allen Bretz (Officer Escorting Mexicans), Thomas Rosales, Jr. (First Mexican), Shane Dixon, Norman Howell, Brian Lally, Don Pulford, Chris Short (Officers/Detectives at Hollywood Station), John Mahon (Police Chief), Tomas Arana (Breuning), Michael McCleery (Carlisle), George Yager (Gangster at Victory Motel), Jack Conley (Vice Captain), Ginger Slaughter (Secretary in Vice), Jack Knight (Detective at Detective Bureau), John H. Evans (Patrolman at Nite Owl Cafe), Gene Wolande (Forensic Chief), Brian Bossetta (Forensic Officer), Michael Chieffo (Coroner), Gwenda Deacon (Mrs. Lefferts), Mike Kennedy (Bud's Rejected Partner), Ingo Neuhaus (Jack's Rejected Partner), Robert Harrison (Pierce Patchett's Bodyguard), Jim Metzler (City Councilman), Robert Barry Fleming (Boxer), Jeremiah Birkett (Ray Collins), Salim Grant (Louis Fontaine), Karreem Washington (Ty Jones), Noel Evangelisti (Stenographer), Marisol Padilla Sanchez (Inez Soto—Rape Victim), Jeff Sanders (Sylvester Fitch), Steve Lambert (Roland Navarette), Jordan Marder (Officer at Detective Bureau), Gregory White (Mayor), April Breneman, Lisa Worthy (Look-Alike Dancers), Beverly Sharpe (Witness on "Badge of Honor"), Colin Mitchell (Reporter at Hospital), John Slade (Photographer at Hospital), Brenda Bakke (Lana Turner), Kevin Maloney (Frolic Room Bartender), Patrice Walters, Rebecca Jane Klingler (Police File Clerks), Irene Roseen (D.A. Ellis Loew's Secretary), Scott Eberlein (West Hollywood Sheriff's Deputy), David St. James (Detective at Hush-Hush Office), Bodie Newcomb (Officer at Hush-Hush Office), Jeff Austin, Henry Meyers, Robert Foster, Michael Ossman, Kevin Kelly, Dick Stilwell, Henry Marder, Jess Thomas, Monty McKee, Samuel Thompson, Jody Wood (Detectives)

THE DEVIL'S ADVOCATE (Regency Enterprises) Producers, Arnon Milchan, Arnold Kopelson, Anne Kopelson; Executive Producers, Taylor Hackford, Michael Tadross, Erwin Stoff, Barry Bernardi, Steve White; Director, Taylor Hackford; Screenplay, Jonathan Lemkin, Tony Gilroy; Based on the novel by Andrew Neiderman; Photography, Andrzej Bartkowiak; Designer, Bruno Rubeo; Editor, Mark Warner; Music, James Newton Howard; Demons Designer/Creator, Rick Baker; Visual Effects, Richard Greenberg; Costumes, Judianna Makovsky; Casting, Nancy Klopper, Mary Colquhoun; a Kopelson Entertaiment production in association with Regency Enterprises; Distributed by WB; Dolby; Panavision; Technicolor; Rated R; 144 minutes; October release. **CAST:** Keanu Reeves (Kevin Lomax), Al Pacino (John Milton), Charlize Theron (Mary Ann Lomax), Jeffrey Jones (Eddie Barzoon), Judith Ivey (Mrs. Lomax), Connie Nielsen (Christabella), Craig T. Nelson (Alexander Cullen), Tamara Tunie (Jackie Heath), Ruben Santiago-Hudson (Leamon Heath), Debra Monk (Pam Garrety), Vyto Ruginis (Weaver), Laura Harrington (Melissa Black), Pamela Gray (Diana Barzoon), George Wyner (Meisel), Christopher Bauer (Gettys), Connie Embesi (Mrs. Gettys), Jonathan Cavallary (Gettys' Son), Heather Matarazzo (Barbara), Murphy Guyer

(Barbara's Father), Leo Burmester (Florida Prosecutor), Bill Moor (Florida Judge), Neal Jones (Florida Reporter), Eddie Aldridge (Florida Bailiff), Mark Deakins (Florida Lawyer #1), Rony Clanton (Junkie), George Gore II (Boy), Alan Manson (Judge Sklar), Brian Poteat (Pie Face), Daniel Oreskes (Metro D.A.), Kim Chan (Chinese Man), Caprice Benedetti (Menage a Trois Woman), Don King (Himself), Ray Garvey, Rocco Musacchia (Fight Fans), Susan Kellermann (Joyce Rensaleer), James Saito (Takaori Osumi), Harsh Nayyar (Parvathi Resh), M.B. Ghaffari (Bashir Toabal), Nicki Cochrane (Multi-Lingual Party Guest), Fenja Klaus (Female #1), Gino Lucci (Limo Driver), Novella Nelson (Botanica Woman), Vincent Laresca, Benny Nieves (Big Guys), Franci Leary (Babs Coleman), Gloria L. Henry (Tiffany), Jorge Navarro (Spanish Restaurant Manager), Jose Fernandes Torres (Flamenco Guitarist), Antonio Vargas Cortes (Flamenco Singer), Elena Camunez Andujar (Flamenco Dancer), Monica Keena (Allesandra), Linda Atkinson (Therapist), William Hill (Feeney), Juan Hernandez (Paparazzi), Wei Mei (Gizelle), E. Katherine Kerr (Judge), Liza Harris, Bill Boggs, Bo Rucker (Reporters), Michael Lombard (Judge Poe), Marc Manfro, J. Nester (Bailiffs), John Rothman (Broygo), George Sperdakos (Technician), Hollis Granville, Edward Seamon (Old Men), Patrick Joseph Byrnes, Gregory Lichtenson (Joggers), Socorro Santiago, Marcia DeBonis (Nurses), Marie Stuart Vassallo (Patient Marie), Tom Riis Farrell (Priest), Harold Surratt (Orderly #1), Senator Alfonse D'Amato, Ambassador Charles Gagano, Lou Rudin, Ernie Grunseld, Alan Grubman (Themselves), Cadillac Moon (Band), Delroy Lindo (Animal Sacrifice Practioner)

MAD CITY (Arnold Kopelson Production) Producers, Arnold Kopelson, Anne Kopelson; Director, Costa Gavras; Screenplay, Tom Matthews; Story, Tom Matthews, Eric Williams; Executive Producers, Wolfgang Glattes, Stephen Brown, Jonathan D. Krane; Photography, Patrick Blossier; Designer, Catherine Hardwicke; Editor, Francoise Bonnot; Music, Thomas Newman; Costumes, Deborah Nadoolman; Casting, Amanda Mackey Johnson, Cathy Sandrich; an Arnold Kopelson production in association with Punch Productions; Distributed by WB; Dolby; Super 35 Widescreen; Technicolor; Rated PG-13; 114 minutes; November release. **CAST**: John Travolta (Sam), Dustin Hoffman (Brackett), Mia Kirshner (Laurie), Alan Alda (Hollander), Robert Prosky (Lou Potts), Blythe Danner (Mrs. Banks), William Atherton (Dohlen), Ted Levine (Lemke), Tammy Lauren (Miss Rose), William O'Leary (CTN Junior Executive), Raymond J. Barry (Dobbins), Lucinda Jenney (Jenny), Akosua Busia (Diane), Ebbe Roe Smith (Bartholomew), Bingwa (Nat Jackson), Chris Byrne (KXBD Cameraman), Bobby Brewer, Max Becker, Philip David Robinson, Milton Davis Jr., Jeremy Espinoza, Nicole Fellows, Victoria Gregson, Molly Hager, Sarah Haney, Kyla Pratt, Paige Tamada, Hannah Vaughan (The Kids), Dyllan Christopher (Sam's Son), Kiersten Nally (Cliff's Daughter), Sylvia Short (Mrs. Baily), Scanlon Gail (Bob), Charlie Holliday (Banker), Kevin Cooney (Principal), John Landis (Doctor), Susan Segal (Tabloid Reporter), Jenna Byrne (Reporter KMUR), Jason Cottle (Hollander's Assistant), Randall Batinkoff (CTN Junior Executive), Julian Wall (British Reporter), Laura Davis (Hollander's Producer), Nick Scoggin (Statz), Julio Oscar Mechoso (Air Force Sergeant), Rueben Grundy (Reporter Reuben), David Clennon (Street Preacher), Jay Leno (Himself), Stephen E. Kaufman (Hollander's Lawyer), Richard Portnow (Brackett's Agent), Bill Rafferty (Bill Gottsegen), Kurt Johnson (Macho Parent), Susan Burig (Stage Manager), Pastor D. Seifert (Minister), J.P. Bumstead (Fisherman), Sean O'Kane (Lemke's Assistant), Donal O'Sullivan (Policeman), Lee Ann Manley (Rachel's Mother), Velina Brown (Bonnie's Mother), Michelle Pelletier (Max's Mother), Patricia Smith (Jenny's Mother), Adina Goldman (Lou's Assistant), Roger Shamas (Hollander's Driver), Stephen Brown (Hollander's Associate), Richard Gross (FBI Agent), Adam M. Koppekin (Assistant), Aaron Lucich (Sniper), Caryn Matchinga (Mother), Tom Fridley (Young Man), Christopher Michael Moore, Dirk Blocker (Bowlers), Pamela S. Laws, John Halbleib, Shannon L. Linke (Folk Singers), Eric Wycoff, Norman Berry, Chad Russell, Steven Lazaneo, Omar Lima (Rap Singers), Bill Nunn

THE MAN WHO KNEW TOO LITTLE (Regency Enterprises) Producers, Arnon Milchan, Michael Nathanson, Mark Tarlov; Executive Producers, Elisabeth Robinson, Joe Caracciolo, Jr.; Director, Jon Amiel; Screenplay, Robert Farrar, Howard Franklin; Based on the novel Watch *That Man* by Robert Farrar; Photography, Robert Stevens; Designer, Jim Clay; Editor, Pamela Power; Music, Chris Young; Co-Producer, Madeline Warren; Costumes, Janty Yates; Casting, Michelle Guish, Hopkins Smith & Barden; a Regency Enterprises presentation of an Arnon Milchan/Polar production; Distributed by WB; Dolby; Color; Rated PG-13; 94 minutes; November release. **CAST**: Bill Murray (Wallace Ritchie), Peter Gallagher (James Ritchie), Joanne Whalley (Lori), Alfred Molina (Boris), Richard Wilson (Daggenhurst), John Standing (Embleton), Simon Chandler (Hawkins), Geraldine James (Dr. Ludmilla Kropotkin), Anna Chancellor (Barbara Ritchie), Nicholas Woodeson (Sergei), Cliff Parisi (Uri), John Thomson (Dimitri), Janet Henfrey (Ms. Goldstein), Terry O'Neill (Spenser), Isabel Hernandez (Consuela), Donald Pickering (Sir Duncan), Venetia Barrett (Sir Duncan's Wife, Felicity), Terence Harvey (Herr Schuster), Cate Fowler (Frau Schuster), Richard Dixon (Rupert), Sarah Crowden (Sylvia/Fiona), Barnaby Kay (Swat Team Leader/PC in James), David Hounslow (Wilkie), Adam Fogerty (Newman), Jacqueline Phillips (Annabel), Inday Ba (Des), Dexter Fletcher (Otto), Josephine Gradwell (WPC—Wendy), Linda Broughton (Middle-Aged Woman), David Boyce (Middle-Aged Man), Jo Dow (Hotel Manager), Bob Holmes (Husband in Hotel Room), Paul Shearer (TV Reporter), Yoshinori Yamamoto (Japanese Man), Toshie Ogura (Japanese Woman), Charles Simon (Aged Desk/Night Clerk), Roger Morlidge (PC Cochrane), Ashley Gunstock (2nd Policeman in Car), Judith Dawson (TV Newscaster), David Michaels (MI5 Agent), Damian Myerscough (Stage Manager), Jason Round (Policeman), Andrew Woodall (Det. Sgt. Malloy), Malcolm Storry (Chief Ins. Cockburn), Eddie Marsan, Tat Whalley (Muggers), Fred Whitham (Toastmaster), Daryll Kay, Linzi Lazlo-Carr (Liveried Children), Richard Cubison (Immigration Officer), Sarah Greene, Mike Smith (TV Presenters), Je Freeman (CIA Man), Maxwell Caulfield (British Agent), Mike Justus (Waiter)

MIDNIGHT IN THE GARDEN OF GOOD AND EVIL (Malpaso/Silver Pictures) Producers, Clint Eastwood, Arnold Stiefel; Director, Clint Eastwood; Executive Producer, Anita Zuckerman; Screenplay, John Lee Hancock; Based on the book by John Berendt; Co-Producer, Tom Rooker; Photography, Jack N. Green; Designer, Henry Bumstead; Music, Lennie Niehaus; Editor, Joel Cox; Casting, Phyllis Huffman; Distributed by WB; Dolby; Panavision; Technicolor; Rated R; 155 minutes; November release. **CAST**: John Cusack (John Kelso), Kevin Spacey (Jim Williams), Jack Thompson (Sonny Seiler), Irma P. Hall (Minerva), Jude Law (Billy Hanson), Alison Eastwood (Mandy Nicholls), Paul Hipp (Joe Odom), The Lady Chablis (Chablis Deveau), Dorothy Loudon (Serena Dawes), Anne Haney (Margaret Williams), Kim Hunter (Betty Harty), Geoffrey Lewis (Luther Driggers), Richard Herd (Henry Skerridge), Leon Rippy (Det. Boone), Bob Gunton (Finley Largent), Michael O'Hagan (Geza von Habsburg), Gary Anthony Williams (Bus Driver), Tim Black (Jeff Braswell), Muriel Moore (Mrs. Baxter), Sonny Seiler (Judge White), Terry Rhoads (Assistant D.A.), Victor Brandt (Bailiff), Patricia Herd (Juror #1), Nick Gillie (Juror #20), Patrika Darbo (Sara Warren), J. Patrick McCormack (Doctor), Emma Kelly (Herself), Tyrone Lee Weaver (Ellis), Gregory Goossen (Prison Cell Lunatic), Shannon Eubanks (Mrs. Hamilton), Virginia Duncan, Rhoda Griffis, Judith Robinson (Card Club Women), JoAnn Pflug (Cynthia Vaughn), James Moody (Mr. Glover), John Duncan (Gentleman in Park), Bess S. Thompson (Pretty Girl), Jin Hi Soucy (Receptionist), Michael Rosenbaum (George Tucker), Dan Biggers (Harry Cram), Georgia Allen (Lucille Wright), Collin Wilcox Paxton (Woman at Party), Charles Black (Alpha), Aleta Mitchell (Alphabette), Michael "Kevin" Harry (Phillip), Dorothy Kingery (Jim Williams' Sister), Amanda Kingery (Jim Williams' Nice Amanda), Susan Kingery (Jim Williams' Niece Susan), Ted Manson (Passer-by), Margaret R. Davis (Ruth), Danny Nelson (Senator), Bree Luck (Woman at Club), Ann Cusack (Delivery Woman), Jerry Spence (Hair Dresser)

STEEL (Quincy Jones-David Salzman Entertainment) Producers, Quincy Jones, David Salzman, Joel Simon; Executive Producers, Shaquille O'Neal, Leonard Armato, Bruce Binkow; Director/Screenplay, Kenneth Johnson; Based upon characters published by DC Comics; "Steel" created by Louise Simonson, Jon Bogdanove; Photography, Mark Irwin; Designer, Gary Wissner; Editor, John F. Link; Co-Producer, Mark Allan; Music, Mervyn Warren; Steel's Suit by Greg Cannom; Costumes, Catherine Adair; Casting, Shana Landsburg, Laura Adler; Distributed by WB; Dolby; Clairmont Scope; Technicolor; Rated PG-13; 97 minutes; August release. **CAST:** Shaquille O'Neal (John Henry Irons), Annabeth Gish (Sparky), Judd Nelson (Nathaniel Burke), Richard Roundtree (Uncle Joe), Irma P. Hall (Grandma Odessa), Ray J. (Martin), Charles Napier (Col. David), Kerrie Keane (Senator), Eric Pierpoint (Major), Tembi Locke (Norma), Thom Barry (Senior Cop), Gary Graham (Detective), Eric Saiet (Young Cop), Hill Harper (Slats), George Lemore (Cutter), Joseph Palmer (Holdecker), Eric Poppick (Mr Hunt "Mugging Victim"), Rutanya Alda (Mrs. Hunt), John Hawkes (Mugger), Steve Mattila (Big Willy Daniels), Claire Stansfield (Duvray), Kevin Grevioux (Singer), Tim deZarn, Michael Shamus Wiles (Skinheads), Kamau Holloway, Norris Young (Skins), Maurice Chasse (French Mercenary), Josh Cruze (Columbian), Harvey Silver (Lamont), Nancy Wolfe (American Overlord), Danny Hartigan (Chauffer), Rick Worthy (Swat Man), Marabina Jaimes (Swat Woman), Scotch Ellis Loring (Swat Officer), Ben Martin (District Attorney), Dirk Wallace Craft (Officer Craft), Jacquelyn Houston (Soldier), John F. O'Donohue (Federal Reserve Guard), Patrick Hayes, Manner "Mooky" Washington (Pre-Teens), Cyd Strittmatter (Lieutenant), John Donohue (Crewman #1), Jody Fasanella (Matronly Secretary), Kevin Sifuentes (Reef Driver), Joe Wandell (Reef Gunman), Joshua G. Adams, Zane Graham (Basketball Kids)

ONE EIGHT SEVEN (Icon Prod.) Producers, Bruce Davey, Stephen McEveety; Director, Kevin Reynolds; Screenplay, Scott Yagemann; Photography, Ericson Core; Designer, Stephen Storer; Editor, Stephen Semel; Costumes, Darryle Johnson; Music Supervisor, Chris Douridas; Casting, Marion Dougherty; an Icon Production; Distributed by WB; Dolby; Deluxe color; Rated R; 119 minutes; July release. **CAST:** Samuel L. Jackson (Trevor Garfield), John Heard (Dave Childress), Kelly Rowan (Ellen Henry), Clifton Gonzalez Gonzalez (Cesar), Tony Plana (Garcia), Karina Arroyave (Rita), Lobo Sebastian (Benny), Jack Kehler (Hyland), Jonah Rooney (Stevie), Demetrius Navarro (Paco), Ebony Monique Solomon (Lakesia), Yannis Borgis (Barsek), Dominic Hoffman (Victor), Martha Velez (Mrs. Chacon), Method Man (Dennis Broadway), Sage Allen (Teacher), Kathryn Leigh Scott (Anglo Woman), Donal Gibson (Animal Regulation Officer), Liza Del Mundo (Asian Girl), Vic Polizos (Asst. Coroner), Leonard L. Thomas (N.Y. Asst. Principal), Antwon Tanner (Augie), Gannon Brown (Tywan), Larry Costales (Hispanic Man), David Reyes (Investigator), Joanna Sanchez (Iris), Richard Riehle (Walter), Harry James (Librarian), Esther Scott (Mrs. Ford), Esther "Tita" Mercado (Mrs. Santana), Chase A. Garland (Struggling Student), Guy Torry (Voice in Crowd), Anthony Aguilar (Chicano Tagger)

THE POSTMAN (Tig Prod.) Producers, Jim Wilson, Steve Tisch, Kevin Costner; Director, Kevin Costner; Screenplay, Eric Roth, Brian Helgeland; Based on the novel by David Brin; Photography, Stephen Windon; Designer, Ida Random; Editor, Peter Boyle; Music, James Newton Howard; Song: "You Didn't Have to Be So Nice" by John Sebastian and Steve Boone/performed by Amy Grant and Kevin Costner; Costumes, John Bloomfield; Casting, Mindy Marin; a Tig Production; Distributed by WB; Dolby; Panavision; Technicolor; Rated R; 177 minutes; December release. **CAST:** Kevin Costner (The Postman), Will Patton (Bethlehem), Larenz Tate (Ford), Olivia Williams (Abby), James Russo (Idaho), Daniel von Bargen (Sheriff Briscoe), Tom Petty (Bridge City Mayor), Scott Bairstow (Luke), Giovanni Ribisi (Bandit #20), Roberta Maxwell (Irene March), Joe Santos (Getty), Ron McLarty (Old George), Peggy Lipton (Ellen March), Brian Anthony Wilson (Woody), Todd Allen (Gibbs), Rex Linn (Mercer), Shawn Hatosy (Billy), Ryan Hurst (Eddie), Charles Esten (Michael), Anne Costner (Ponytail), Ty O'Neal (Drew), Kirk Fox (Gangly Recruit), Ken Linhart (Disappointed Conscript), Korey Scott Pollard (Thin Recruit), Kayla Lambert (Shakespeare Girl), Austin Howard Early (Shakespeare Boy), Ellen Geer (Mrs. Thompson), Randle Mell (Village Mayor), Cooper Taylor (Tony), Dylan Haggerty (Slow Recruit), Michael Milgrom (Holnist Projectionist), Keith C. Howell (Holnist Scout), H.P. Evetts (Holnist Soldier), Jeff Johnson, Jeff McGrail (Rope Bridge Soldiers), Lily Costner (Lily March), Gregory Avellone (Pineview Man), Susan Brightbill, Elisa Daniel, Jenny Buchanan, Ann Manning (Pineview Women), Andy Garrison (Pineview Sentry), Rusty Hendrickson (Pineview Minister), Marvin Winton (Pineview Old Man), Jono Manson, John J. Coinman, Veron T. Williams, Mark Clark, Blair Forward, Robyn Pruitt-Hamm, Michelle Ramminger (Pineview Band), Tom Novak, Richard Joel (Benning Gatekeepers), George Wyner (Benning Mayor), Brooke Becker, Eva Gayle Six (Benning Women), Todd Lewis (Benning Man), Joe Costner (Letter Boy), Kathi Sheehan (Mother of Letter Boy), Amy Weinstein, Betty Moyer (Elvis Women), Joseph McKenna (Holnist Captain), Neal Preston Coon (Bridge City Boy), Rick Wadkins (Bridge City Man), Shiree Porter (Bridge City Woman), Anthony Guidera (Bridge City Guard), Jade Herrera (Carrier), Greg Serano (California Carrier), Derk Cheetwood (Carrier Twelve), Mark Thomason (Adult Letter Boy), Mary Stuart Masterson (Hope—Grown-up)

Kate Winslet, Leonardo DiCaprio

Titanic © Paramount Pictures/ Twentieth Century Fox

Leonardo DiCaprio, Kate Winslet

Kathy Bates, Frances Fisher

Bill Paxton, Gloria Stuart, Suzy Amis

TITANIC

(PARAMOUNT/20TH CENTURY FOX) Producers, James Cameron, Jon Landau; Executive Producer, Rae Sanchini; Director/Screenplay, James Cameron; Photography, Russell Carpenter; Designer, Peter Lamont; Editors, Conrad Buff, James Cameron, Richard A. Harris; Costumes, Deborah L. Scott; Visual Effects Supervisor, Robert Legato; Music, James Horner; Song: "My Heart Will Go On" by James Horner (music) and Will Jennings (lyric)/performed by Celine Dion; Co-Producers, Al Giddings, Grant Hill, Sharon Mann; Casting, Mali Finn; a Lightstorm Entertainment production; Dolby Digital Stereo; Panavision; Deluxe color; Rated PG-13; 193 minutes; December release

CAST

Jack Dawson ... Leonardo DiCaprio
Rose DeWitt Bukater ... Kate Winslet
Cal Hockley ... Billy Zane
Molly Brown ... Kathy Bates
Ruth DeWitt Bukater ... Frances Fisher
Old Rose ... Gloria Stuart
Brock Lovett ... Bill Paxton
Captain E.J. Smith ... Bernard Hill
Spicer Lovejoy ... David Warner
Thomas Andrews ... Victor Garber
Bruce Ismay ... Jonathan Hyde
Lizzy Calvert ... Suzy Amis
Lewis Bodine ... Lewis Abernathy
Bobby Buell ... Nicholas Cascone
Anatoly Milkailavich ... Dr. Anatoly M. Sagalevitch
Fabrizio ... Danny Nucci
Tommy Ryan ... Jason Barry
1st Officer Murdoch ... Ewan Stewart
Fifth Officer Lowe ... Ioan Gruffudd
2nd Officer Lightoller ... Johnny Phillips
Chief Officer Wilde ... Mark Lindsay Chapman
Quartermaster Rowe ... Richard Graham
Quartermaster Hichens ... Paul Brightwell
Master at Arms ... Ron Donachie
John Jacob Astor ... Eric Braeden
Madeleine Astor ... Charlotte Chatton
Col. Archibald Gracie ... Bernard Fox

and Michael Ensign (Benjamin Guggenheim), Fannie Brett (Madame Aubert), Jenette Goldstein (Irish Mommy), Camilla Overbye Roos (Helga Dahl), Linda Kerns (3rd Class Woman), Amy Gaipa (Trudy Bolt), Martin Jarvis (Sir Duff Gordon), Rosalind Ayres (Lady Duff Gordon), Rochelle Rose (Countess of Rothes), Jonathan Evans-Jones (Wallace Hartley), Brian Walsh (Irish Man), Rocky Taylor (Bert Cartmell), Alexandre Owens (Cora Cartmell), Simon Crane (4th Officer Boxhall), Edward Fletcher (6th Officer Moody), Scott G. Anderson (Frederick Fleet), Martin East (Lookout Lee), Craig Kelly (Harold Bride), Gregory Cooke (Jack Phillips), Liam Tuohy (Chief Baker Joughin), James Lancaster (Father Byles), Elsa Raven (Ida Straus), Lew Palter (Isidor Straus), Reece P. Thompson III (Irish Little Boy), Laramie Landis (Irish Little Girl), Amber and Alison Waddell (Cal's Crying Girl), Mark Rafael Truitt (Yaley), John Walcutt (1st Class Husband), Terry Forrestal (Chief Engineer Bell), Derek Lea (Leading Stoker Barrett), Richard Ashton (Carpenter John Hutchinson), Sean M. Nepita (Elevator Operator), Brendan Connolly (Scotland Road Steward), David Cronnelly (Crewman), Garth Wilton (1st Class Waiter), Martin Laing (Promenade Deck Steward), Richard Fox, Nick Meaney, Kevin Owers, Mark Capri (Stewards), Marc Cass, Paul Herbert (Hold Stewards), Emmett James (1st Class Steward), Christopher Byrne (Stairwell Steward), Oliver Page (Steward Barnes), James Garrett (Titanic Porter), Erik Holland (Olaf Dahl), Jari Kinnunen (Bjorn Gunderson), Anders Falk (Olaus Gunderson), Martin Hub (Slovakian Father), Seth Adkins (Slovakian 3 Year Old Boy), Barry Dennen (Praying Man), Vern Urich (Man in Water), Rebecca Jane Klingler (Mother at Stern), Tricia O'Neil (Woman), Kathleen Dunn (Woman in Water), Romeo Francis (Syrian Man), Mandana Marino (Syrian Woman), Van Ling (Chinese Man), Bjørn (Olaf), Dan Pettersson (Sven), Shay Duffin (Pubkeeper), Greg Ellis (Carpathia Steward), Diana Morgan (News Reporter), I Salonisti (Titanic Orchestra), Gaelic Storm (Steerage Band)

(Clockwise from bottom left) Leonardo DiCaprio, Rochelle Rose, Jonathan Hyde, Bernard Fox, Fannie Brett, Michael Ensign, Rosalind Ayres, Martin Jarvis, Billy Zane, Kate Winslet, Victor Garber, Kathy Bates

Billy Zane, Kate Winslet

After a drawing of her is found in the wreckage of the Titanic, one-hundred-year-old Rose recounts the story of how she fell in love with steerage passenger Jack Dawson aboard the ill-fated vessel on its maiden voyage in 1912. 1998 Academy Award-winner for Best Picture, Director, Cinematography, Art Direction, Costume Design, Film Editing, Original Dramatic Score, Song ("My Heart Will Go"), Sound, Sound Effects Editing, and Visual Effects. This film received additional Oscar nominations for actress (Kate Winslet), supporting actress (Gloria Stuart), and makeup. Its eleven awards tied it with Ben-Hur (MGM, 1959) for the Academy record, as had its fourteen nominations that tied it with All About Eve (20th Century Fox, 1950). This film became the biggest box office hit of 1997 and the highest grossing motion picture of all time. Previous films on the Titanic include Titanic (20th Century Fox, 1953), starring Clifton Webb and Barbara Stanwyck; and A Night to Remember (1958), starring Kenneth More.

Kate Winslet, Leonardo DiCaprio

JACK NICHOLSON
in *As Good As It Gets*
© TriStar Pictures
ACADEMY AWARD FOR BEST ACTOR OF 1997

HELEN HUNT
in *As Good As It Gets*
© TriStar Pictures
ACADEMY AWARD FOR BEST ACTRESS OF 1997

ROBIN WILLIAMS
in *Good Will Hunting*
© Miramax Films
ACADEMY AWARD FOR BEST SUPPORTING ACTOR OF 1997

KIM BASINGER
for *L.A. Confidential*
ACADEMY AWARD FOR BEST SUPPORTING ACTRESS OF 1997

ACADEMY AWARD NOMINEES FOR BEST ACTOR

Matt Damon in *Good Will Hunting*

Robert Duvall in *The Apostle*

Peter Fonda in *Uiee's Gold*

Dustin Hoffman in *Wag the Dog*

ACADEMY AWARD NOMINEES FOR BEST ACTRESS

Helena Bonham Carter in *The Wings of the Dove*

Julie Christie in *Afterglow*

Judi Dench in *Mrs. Brown*

Kate Winslet in *Titanic*

ACADEMY AWARD NOMINEES FOR BEST SUPPORTING ACTOR

Robert Forster in *Jackie Brown*

Anthony Hopkins in *Amistad*

Greg Kinnear in *As Good As It Gets*

Burt Reynolds in *Boogie Nights*

ACADEMY AWARD NOMINEES FOR BEST SUPPORTING ACTRESS

Joan Cusack in *In & Out*

Minnie Driver in *Good Will Hunting*

Julianne Moore in *Boogie Nights*

Gloria Stuart in *Titanic*

Jan Decleir

Fedja van Huet, Betty Schuurman

Fedja van Huet, Victor Low, Tamar van de Dop

CHARACTER

(SONY PICTURE CLASSICS) Producer, Laurens Geels; Director, Mike van Diem; Screenplay, Mike van Diem, Laurens Geels, Rund van Megen; Photography, Rogier Stoffers; Art Directors, Jelier & Schief; Editor, Jessica de Kooning; Music, Het Paleis van Boem; Casting, Jeannette Snik; Netherlands; Dolby Stereo; Color; Rated R; 125 minutes; March 1998 release

CAST

Katadreuffe ....Fedja van Huet
Deverhaven ....Jan Decleir
Joba...Betty Schuurman
De Gankelaar ....Victor Low
Lorna te George...Tamar van de Dop
Jan Maan..Hans Kesting
Retenstein ....Lou Landre
Stroomkoning ....Bernhard Droog
De Bree ....Frans Vortsman
Schuwagt...Fred Goessens

A young lawyer, arrested for the murder of Rotterdam's most feared bailiff, proclaims his innocence and recounts the series of ecents in his life leading up to the time od the crime.

Fedja van Huet, Victow Low

ACADEMY AWARD WINNER FOR BEST FOREIGN LANGUAGE FILM

PROMISING NEW ACTORS OF 1997

Joey Lauren Adams
(Chasing Amy)

Ben Affleck
(Chasing Amy, Going All the Way, Good Will Hunting)

Aaron Eckhart
(In the Company of Men)

Stacy Edwards
(In the Company of Men)

Lee Evans
(Mouse Hunt, The Fifth Element)

Jennifer Lopez
(Blood and Wine, Selena, Anaconda, U Turn)

Debbi Morgan
(Eve's Bayou)

Jude Law
(Gattaca; I Love You, I Love You Not; Midnight in the Garden of Good and Evil)

Tobey Maguire
(The Ice Storm, Deconstructing Harry)

Sarah Polley
(The Sweet Hereafter)

Angelina Jolie
(Playing God)

Freddie Prinze, Jr.
(The House of Yes, I Know What You Did Last Summer)

TOP 100 BOX OFFICE FILMS OF 1997

1. Titanic (Par-20th/Dec) $600,770,000
2. Men in Black (Col/Jul) $250,100,000
3. The Lost World: Jurassic Park (Univ/May) $229,100,000
4. Liar Liar (Univ/Mar) $181,420,000
5. Air Force One (Col/Jul) $172,630,000
6. As Good As It Gets (TriS/Dec) $147,660,000
7. Good Will Hunting (Mir/Dec) $138,410,000
8. Star Wars (reissue) (20th/Jan) $138,200,000
9. My Best Friend's Wedding (TriS/Jun) $126,710,000
10. Tomorrow Never Dies (MGM-UA/Dec) $124,690,000

Leonardo DiCaprio, Kate Winslet in *Titanic*
© Paramount Pictures/Twentieth Century Fox

11. Face/Off (Par/Jun) $112,300,000
12. Batman and Robin (Jun) $107,310,000
13. George of the Jungle (BV/Jul) $105,200,000
14. Con Air (BV/Jun) $101,100,000
15. Contact (Jul) $100,900,000
16. Scream 2 (Mir/Dec) $100,320,000
17. Hercules (BV/Jun) $99,100,000
18. Flubber (BV/Nov) $92,830,000
19. Conspiracy Theory (Aug) $76,100,000
20. I Know What You Did Last Summer (Col/Oct) $72,240,000

Gary Oldman in *Air Force One*
© Columbia Pictures Industries, Inc.

21. The Empire Strikes Back (reissue) (20th/Feb) $67,600,000
22. Dante's Peak (Univ/Feb) $67,200,000
23. Anaconda(Col/Apr) $65,900,000
24. L.A. Confidential (Sept) $64,430,000
25. The Fifth Element (Col/May) $63,800,000
26. In & Out(Par/Sep) $63,100,000
27. Mouse Hunt (DW/Dec) $61,850,000
26. The Saint(Par/Apr) $61,400,000
29. The Devil's Advocate (Oct) $60,800,000
30. Kiss the Girls (Par/Oct) $60,160,000
31. Jungle 2 Jungle (BV/Mar) $59,900,000
32. Anastasia(20th/Nov) $58,300,000
33. Spawn (NLC/Aug) $55,100,000
34. The Jackal (Univ/Nov) $54,700,000
35. Starship Troopers (TriS/Nov) $54,200,000
36. Austin Powers: Intl. Man of Mystery (NLC/May) $53,900,000
37. Breakdown (Par/May) $50,150,000
38. Absolute Power (Col/Feb) $50,110,000

Hercules, Pegasus in *Hercules*
© Disney Enterprises, Inc.

39. The Game (Poly/Sep) $48,300,000
40. G.I. Jane(BV/Aug) $48,200,000
41. Speed 2: Cruise Control (20th/Jun) $47,600,000
42. Alien Resurrection (20th/Nov) $47,540,000
43. Volcano (20th/Apr) $47,500,000
44. The Full Monty (Fox S/Aug) $45,890,000
45. John Grisham's The Rainmaker (Par/Nov) $45,820,000
46. Return of the Jedi (reissue) (20th/Mar) $45,500,000
47. Bean (Gram/Nov) $44,910,000
48. Cop Land(Mir/Aug) $44,900,000
49. Nothing to Lose (BV/Jul) $44,500,000
50. Soul Food (20th/Sep) $43,600,000

51. Amistad (DW/Dec) $43,270,000
52. Wag the Dog (NLC/Dec) $42,980,000
53. The Devil's Own (Col/Mar) $42,900,000
54. Donnie Brasco (TriS/Feb)..$42,100,000
55. The Peacemaker (DW/Sep) $41,300,000
56. Private Parts (Par/Mar) $41,200,000
57. Money Talks (NLC/Aug)...$41,100,000
58. Jackie Brown (Mir/Dec) $39,480,000
59. Seven Years in Tibet (TriS/Oct)...$37,870,000
60. Vegas Vacation (Feb) $36,500,000
61. Mortal Kombat: Annihilation (NLC/Nov)..............................$35,900,000
62. Selena (Mar) $35,500,000
63. Addicted to Love(May) $34,700,000
64. The Relic (Par/Jan) $33,900,000
65. Metro (BV/Jan)...$32,100,000

Freddie Prinze Jr., Jennifer Love Hewitt in
I Know What You Did Last Summer
© Mandalay Entertainment

66. For Richer or Poorer (Univ/Dec)..$31,540,000
67. Beverly Hills Ninja (TriS/Jan)..$31,500,000
68. Picture Perfect (20th/Aug)...$31,400,000
69. Fools Rush In (Col/Feb) $29,500,000
70. Home Alone 3 (20th/Dec) $29,390,000
71. Romy & Michele's High School Reunion (BV/Apr).......$29,220,000
72. Out to Sea (20th/Jul)...$29,100,000
73. Fathers' Day (May)..$28,900,000
74. Grosse Pointe Blank (BV/Apr)...$28,100,000
75. The Edge (20th/Sep) $27,800,000
76. Boogie Nights (NLC/Oct) $26,330,000
77. An American Werewolf in Paris (BV/Dec) $26,320,000
78. Murder at 1600 (Apr) $25,800,000
79. Mimic (Mir/Aug)..$25,430,000
80. Midnight in the Garden of Good & Evil (Nov) $24,680,000

Vivica A. Fox, Vanessa L. Williams, Nia Long in *Soul Food*
© Twentieth Century Fox

81. Air Bud (BV/Aug) $24,610,000
82. Hoodlum (MGM/Aug)..$23,300,000
83. Good Burger (Par/Jul) $22,860,000
84. Red Corner (MGM/Oct) $21,870,000
85. Mr. Magoo (BV/Dec) $21,280,000
86. The Apostle (Oct/Dec)...$20,720,000
87. Booty Call (Col/Feb) $19,490,000
88. Gone Fishin' (BV/May)...$19,270,000
89. Event Horizon (Par/Aug)..$17,800,000
90. That Darn Cat (BV/Feb)...$17,100,000
91. That Old Feeling (Univ/Apr)..$15,810,000
92. Fire Down Below (Sep)...$15,800,000
93. Rocketman (BV/Oct)...$15,100,000
94. Eve's Bayou (Tri/Nov) $14,840,000
95. The Sixth Man (BV/Apr)...$14,730,000

Johnny Depp in *Donnie Brasco*
© Mandalay Entertainment

96. The Postman (Dec) $14,300,000
97. Excess Baggage (Col/Aug)..$14,100,000
98. Def Jam's How to Be a Player (Gram/Aug)..........................$13,870,000
99. Wishmaster (Tri/Sep)..$13,730,000
100. The Wings of the Dove (Mir/Nov) $13,670,000

Sergei Bodrov, Jr.

Oleg Menshikov

Susanna Mekhralieva

PRISONER OF THE MOUNTAINS

(ORION CLASSICS) Producers, Boris Giller, Sergei Bodrov; Director, Sergei Bodrov; Screenplay, Arif Aliev, Sergei Bodrov, Boris Giller; Photography, Pavel Lebeshev; Editors, Olga Grinshpun, Vera Kruglova, Alan Baril; Art Director, Valery Kostrin; Music, Leonid Desyatnikov; a Caravan Co. and BG Production with the Russian State Film Commission; Russian, 1996; Dolby Stereo; Color; Rated R; 99 minutes; January release

CAST

Sacha....................Oleg Menshikov
Vania....................Sergei Bodrov, Jr.
Abdoul-Mourat....................Djemal Sikharulidze
Dina....................Susanna Mekhralieva
The Captain....................Alexei Jharkov
The Mother....................Valentina Fedotova

Abdoul-Mourat captures two Russian soldiers and holds them for ransom in his isolated Muslim community. This film was nominated for an Oscar in the foreign-lanuage film category for 1996.

Djemal Sikharulidze

JACKIE CHAN'S FIRST STRIKE

(NEW LINE CINEMA) Producer, Barbie Tung; Executive Producer, Leonard Ho; Director, Stanley Tong; Screenplay, Stanley Tong, Nick Tramontane, Greg Mellott, Elliot Tong; Photography, Jingle Ma; Designer, Oliver Wong; Editors, Peter Cheung, Chi Wai Yau; Music, J. Peter Robinson; Hong Kong 1996; a Raymond Chow/Golden Harvest production; Dolby Stereo; Technovision; Color; Rated PG-13; 110 minutes; January release

CAST

Jackie ....Jackie Chan
Tsui ....Jackson Lou
Annie ....Chen Chun Wu
Uncle Bill ....Bill Tung
Col. Gregor Yegorov..Jouri Petrov
Natasha ....Grishajeva Nonna
Mark ....John Eaves
Uncle Seven ....Terry Woo
Commander Korda ....Kristoff Kaczmarek
and Ailen Sit, Chan Man Ching, Rocky Lai, Chan Wai To (Golden Dragon Club Members), Brett Arthur, Mark French, Damien Gates, Mark Gilks, Nathan Jones, Mathew Walker Kininmonth, John Langmead, Steve Livingstone, Steve Morris (Hit Men), Brenton Heeren, Steve Jones (Snipers), Jennifer Hung, Doris Lam, Shirley Mak, Wella Shieh (Annie's Relatives), Symantha Liu (Channel 7 Reporter), Gary Wilkinson (News Anchorman), Low Houi Kang (H.K. Policeman), Esmond Ren, Jim Hsin (C.I.A. Members), Igro Guleen (USS Agent), N. Leshcinkov (Gen. Gudanov), Rusean Scripnik (Strike Force Leader), Alexander Ustichenko (Major Majenko)

A Hong Kong police officer is contracted by both the CIA and Russian intelligence in hopes that he can locate a stolen Ukranian nuclear warhead.

Jackie Chan

ULYSSES' GAZE

(FOX LORBER) Producer/Director, Theo Angelopoulos; Screenplay, Theo Angelopoulos, Tonino Guerra, Petros Markaris; Photography, Yorgos Arvanitis; Editor, Yannis Tsitsopoulos; Music, Eleni Karaindrou; Designer, Yorgos Patsas, Mile Nicolic; Costumes, Yorgos Ziakas; a Theo Angelopoulos Films Prods.-Greek Film Center (Athens)/Paradis Films-La Generale d'Images-La Sept Cinema (Paris)/Basic Cinematografica-Istituto Luce-RAI (Rome) co-production in association with Tele Munchen, Concorde Films, Channel 4; Greek-French-Italian, 1995; Dolby Stereo; Color; Not rated; 177 minutes; January release

CAST

A ....Harvey Keitel
Naomi Levy and the "Wives"......................................Maïa Morgenstern
Library Curator ....Erland Josephson
Taxi Driver..Thanassis Vengos
Nikos ....Yorgos Michalakopoulos
Old Woman ....Dora Volanaki
and Mania Papadimitriou, Angel Ivanof, Ljuba Tadic, Gert Llanaj, Agni Vlahou, Giannis Zavradinos, Vangelis Kazan

A movie director returns to Greece after a 35-year absence to make a documentary about a family of pioneering filmmakers.

Harvey Keitel

Jacqueline McKenzie, John Lynch

John Lynch, Jacqueline McKenzie

John Lynch, Colin Friels

ANGEL BABY

(CFP) Producers, Timothy White, Jonathan Shteinman; Director/Screenplay, Michael Rymer; Photography, Ellery Ryan; Designer, Chris Kennedy; Editor, Danny Cooper; Costumes, Kerri Mazzocco; Casting, Alison Barrett Casting, Trish McAskill; a Stamen/Meridian Films production; a presentation of the Australian Film Finance Corporation; Australian 1995; Dolby Stereo; Color; Not rated; 105 minutes; January release

CAST

Harry .... John Lynch
Kate .... Jacqueline McKenzie
Morris .... Colin Friels
Louise .... Deborra-Lee Furness
Sam .... Daniel Daperis
Dave .... David Argue
Rowan .... Geoff Brooks
Frank .... Humphry Bower

Harry, a young man troubled by periods of psychosis, meets and falls in love with the similarly disturbed Kate at one of his group therapy sessions.

MARGARET'S MUSEUM

(CFP) Producers, Mort Ransen, Christopher Zimmer, Claudio Luca, Steve Clark-Hall; Director, Mort Ransen; Screenplay, Gerald Wexler, Mort Ransen; Based on The Glace Bay Miner's Museum and other stories by Sheldon Currie; Photography, Vic Sarin; Editor, Rita Roy; Designers, William Fleming, David McHenry; Costumes, Nicoletta Massone; Music, Milan Kymlicka; Casting, Stuart Aikins, Anne Tait; a Cabin Fever Entertainment presentation/a Malofilm Communications presentation of a Ranfilm/Imagex/Télé-Action/Skyline production; Canadian-1995; Color; Rated R; 118 minutes; February release

CAST

Margaret MacNeil .... Helena Bonham Carter
Neil Currie .... Clive Russell
Jimmy .... Craig Olejnik
Catherine .... Kate Nelligan
Angus .... Kenneth Welsh
Marilyn .... Andrea Morris
Grandfather .... Peter Boretski
Mr. Campbell .... Barry Dunn
Mrs. Campbell .... Norma Dell'Agnese
and Glenn Wadman (Willy), Elizabeth Richardson (Sister), Ida Donovan (Sarah), Gordon Joe (Hum Sing), Wayne Reynolds (Fraser), Murdoch MacDonald (Clerk), Yow Wah Chee (Chinese Cook), Terry O'Keefe (Miner), Liam Hussey (Peter), Mary Alvena Poole (Woman), Carol Kennedy (Tourist Woman), Bruce MacLeod (Mountie), Peter Maclean, Malcolm "Maxi" MacNeil, Alec MacDougall, Alan MacLeod (Old Men), Emma Fahey (Alma McLaren), Sam White (Young Man), Amy Jo Lamb (Young Margaret), Ian Mugford, Billy Fraser (Little Boys), David B. Lamb (Roddie MacKenzie), Aaron Schneider (Tourist Man), Peter Marinker (Hiring Man), Paul Young, Sean Hewitt, Matt Zimmerman (Doctors)

In a mining town in 1940s Nova Scotia, Margaret MacNeil, who relishes being an outcast and has sworn she will not marry, finds herself falling in love with a charismatic roustabout, Neil Currie.

Helena Bonham Carter, Clive Russell

Kate Nelligan

Michael Urwin, Andrew Ableson, Darren Petrucci

BOYFRIENDS

(FIRST RUN FEATURES) Producers/Directors/Screenplay, Neil Hunter, Tom Hunsinger; Photography, Richard Tisdall; Editor, John Trumper; Art Director, James Dearlove; an Essex Features presentation; British, 1996; Color; Not rated; 82 minutes; February release

CAST

Paul .... James Dreyfus
Matt .... Michael Urwin
Will .... David Coffey
Ben .... Mark Sands
Owen .... Andrew Ableson
Adam .... Darren Petrucci
James .... Michael McGrath

Three gay couples spend a weekend in the country where they examine the status of their relationships.

SMILLA'S SENSE OF SNOW

(FOX SEARCHLIGHT) Producers, Bernd Eichinger, Martin Moszkowicz; Director, Bille August; Screenplay, Ann Biderman; Based on the novel Miss Smilla's Feeling for Snow by Peter Hoeg; Photography, Jorgen Persson; Designer, Anna Asp; Editor, Janus Billeskov Jansen; Costumes, Barbara Baum; Music, Hans Zimmer, Harry Gregson Williams; a Bernd Eichinger production; British-German-Swedish-Danish; Dolby Digital Stereo; Panavision; Color; Rated R; 121 minutes; February release

Julia Ormond

CAST

Smilla Jaspersen .... Julia Ormond
The Mechanic .... Gabriel Byrne
Tork Hviid .... Richard Harris
Elsa Lubing .... Vanessa Redgrave
Moritz Jaspersen .... Robert Loggia
Lagermann .... Jim Broadbent
Sigmund Lukas .... Mario Adorf
Ravn .... Bob Peck
Dr. Loye .... Tom Wilkinson
Benja .... Emma Croft
Lander .... Peter Capaldi
Jakkelsen .... Jürgen Vogel
Isaiah .... Clipper Miano
Juliane .... Agga Olsen
Hansen .... Erik Holmey
and Claire Skinner

Smilla Jaspersen, convinced that an Inuit boy's fall from a rooftop was not accidental, begins an investigation that uncovers a link to a powerful mining company.

Richard Harris

Gabriel Byrne, Julia Ormond

KAMA SUTRA: A TALE OF LOVE

(TRIMARK) Producers, Mira Nair, Lydia Dean Pilcher; Executive Producer, Michiyo Yoshizaki; Director, Mira Nair; Screenplay, Helena Kriel, Mira Nair; Co-Producer, Caroline Baron; Photography, Declan Quinn; Designer, Mark Friedberg; Editor, Kristina Boden; Costumes, Eduardo Castro; Music, Mychael Danna; an NDF International Ltd., Pony Canyon Inc., and Pandora Films, in association with Channel Four Films presentation of a Mirabai Production; Indian-British 1996; Dolby Stereo; Color; Not rated; 115 minutes; February release

CAST

Maya .... Indira Varma
Tara .... Sarita Choudhury
Jai Kumar .... Ramon Tikaram
Raj Singh .... Naveen Andrews
Rasa Devi .... Rekha
Biki .... Khalik Tyabji
Annabi .... Arundhati Rao
Young Maya .... Surabhi Bhansali
Young Tara .... Garima Dhup
Maham Anga .... Pearl Padamsee
Dilki .... Kusum Haidar
Doctor Mani .... Harish Patel
Babu .... Ranjit Chowdhry
Rupa .... Achla Sachdev
Bashir .... Arjun Sajnani
Vazir .... Avijit Dutt

and Anjum Rajabali (Madho Singh), Anand Kumar (Prem. Siddharth), Debi Basu (Dance Teacher), Rahul Vohra (Royal Messenger), Manize Boga (Aunt Laila), Prabeen Singh (Praveen), Sinia Jain (Begum Para), Urvashi Nair (Rich Friend), Bhanumathi Rao (Old Woman), Vasudeo Bhatt (Astrologer), Moneeka Misra Tanvir (Madame), Shubha Mudgal (Singer)

During the 16th century Tara, a princess, and Maya, her servant, approach sexuality in a variety of different ways, using the teachings of "The Kama Sutra."

Naveen Andrews, Indira Varma

Pascal Duquenne, Daniel Auteuil

Pascal Duquenne, Daniel Auteuil

THE EIGHTH DAY

(GRAMERCY) Producer, Philippe Godeau; Director/Screenplay, Jaco Van Dormael; Photography, Walther Vanden Ende; Set Deisnger, Hubert Pouille; Costumes, Yan Tax; Editor, Susana Rossberg; Music, Pierre Van Dormael; a PolyGram Filmed Entertainment presentation of a co-production of Pan-Européenne production, Homemade Films, TF1 Films production, RTL TV1, Working Title and D.A. Films; French-Belgian, 1996; Dolby Digital Stereo; Super 35 Widescreen; Color; Not rated; 114 minutes; March release

CAST

Harry .... Daniel Auteuil
Georges .... Pascal Duquenne
Julie .... Miou-Miou
Georges' Mother .... Isabelle Sadoyan
Company Director .... Henri Garcin
Nathalie .... Michèle Maes
Luis Mariano .... Laszlo Harmati
Julie's Mother .... Hélène Roussel
Fabienne .... Fabienne Loriaux
Fabienne's Husband .... Didier De Neck

A salesman whose personal life has fallen to ruin befriends a young man named Georges who is challenged with Down's Syndrome.

CRASH

(FINE LINE FEATURES) Producer/Director/Screenplay, David Cronenberg; Based on the book by J.G. Ballard; Executive Producers, Jeremy Thomas, Robert Lantos; Co-Executive Producers, Andras Hamori, Chris Auty; Co-Producers, Stephane Reichel, Marilyn Stonehouse; Photography, Peter Suschitzky; Designer, Carol Spier; Costumes, Denise Cronenberg; Editor, Ronald Sanders; Music, Howard Shore; Casting, Deirdre Bowen; a Robert Lantos and Jeremy Thomas presentation of an Alliance Communications production; Canadian, 1996; Dolby Stereo; Color; Rated NC-17; 98 minutes; March release

Deborah Unger, James Spader

CAST

James Ballard .... James Spader
Helen Remington .... Holly Hunter
Vaughan .... Elias Koteas
Catherine Ballard .... Deborah Unger
Gabrielle .... Rosanna Arquette
Colin Seagrave .... Peter MacNeill
Airport Hooker .... Yolande Julian
Vera Seagrave .... Cheryl Swarts
Salesman .... Judah Katz
Tattooist .... Nicky Guadagni
A.D. .... Ronn Sarosiak
Grip .... Boyd Banks
Man in Hanger .... Markus Parilo
Camera Girl .... Alice Poon
Trask .... John Stoneham, Jr.

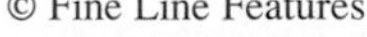

TV producer James Ballard and Dr. Helen Remington find themselves becoming involved in a bizarre cult in which people get erotic thrills through car crashes.

Elias Koteas

James Spader, Deborah Unger

James Spader, Holly Hunter

THE QUIET ROOM

(FINE LINE FEATURES) Producers, Domenico Procacci, Rolf de Heer; Co-Producers, Giuseppe Pedersoli, Sharon Jackson, Fiona Paterson; Director/Screenplay, Rolf de Heer; Photography, Tony Clark; Editor, Tania Nehme; Music, Graham Tardif; Designer, Fiona Paterson; a Vertigo/Fandango production, presented in association with Domenico Procacci; Australian, 1996; Dolby Stereo; Color; Rated PG; 91 minutes; March release

CAST

Mother ....Celine O'Leary
Father ....Paul Blackwell
Girl (Age 7)....................Chloe Ferguson
Girl (Age 3) ....Phoebe Ferguson
Babysitter ....Kate Greetham
Workman ....Todd Telford
Carpet Cleaners ....Peter Ferris, Peter Green

In response to her parents' growing marital difficulties, a 7-year-old girl stops talking altogether.

Chloe Ferguson, Paul Blackwell, Celine O'Leary

Frances O'Connor, Radha Mitchell, Matthew Dyktynski, Matt Day, Alice Garner

LOVE AND OTHER CATASTROPHES

(FOX SEARCHLIGHT) Producer, Stavros Andonis Efthymiou; Director, Emma-Kate Croghan; Screenplay, Yael Bergman, Emma-Kate Croghan, Helen Bandis; Story, Stavros Andonis Efthymiou; Photography, Justin Brickle; Editor, Ken Sallows; Co-Producers, Helen Bandis, Yael Bergman; Music, Oleh Witer, Daryl McKenzie; a Beyond Films presentation; Australian, 1996; Dolby Stereo; Color; Rated R; 76 minutes; March release

CAST

Alice ....Alice Garner
Mia....................Frances O'Connor
Ari....................Matthew Dyktynski
Michael....................Matt Day
Danni ....Radha Mitchell
Savita....................Suzi Dougherty
Professor Leach....................Kim Gyngell
Dr. Russell ....Suzanne Dowling
Toby....................Torquil Neilson
Susan....................Christine Stephen-Daly
Zac....................Dominic McDonald
Alvin ....Alvin Chong
Myles ....Myles Collins
Tony ....Anthony Neate
Brigid ....Brigid Kelly
Emma ....Emma de Clario
Shanti....................Shanti Gudgeon
and Maurie Annese (Computer Geek), Nicholas Crawford Smith (Nick), Adrian Martin (Himself), Leroy Ryan (Nazi), Sanjot Kaur Sekhon (Sanjot), Caroline Lloyd (Carol), Kate Croghan (Office Worker), Joyce Yuen (Lecturer), Paul Harris (Professor Novak)

Comedy follows a day in the life of five university students.

GENTLEMEN DON'T EAT POETS

(LIVE ENTERTAINMENT) aka *The Grotesque*, and *Grave Indiscretions;* Producer, Trudie Styler; Executive Producer, Stephen Evans; Director, John-Paul Davidson; Screenplay, Patrick McGrath, John Paul-Davidson; Based on the novel *The Grotesque* by Patrick McGrath; Photography, Andrew Dunn; Designer, Jan Roelfs; Associate Producer, Anita Sumner; Costumes, Colleen Atwood, Graham Churchyard; Editor, Tariq Anwar; Music, Anne Dudley; Casting, Joyce Nettles; a Trudie Styler production, presented in association with J&M Entertainment and Xingu Films; British, 1995; Dolby Stereo; Color; Rated R; 97 minutes; March release

CAST

Sir Hugo Coal .... Alan Bates
Lady Harriet Coal .... Theresa Russell
Fledge .... Sting
Sir Edward Cleghorn .... John Mills
Cleo Coal .... Lena Headey
Mrs. Giblet .... Anna Massey
Sidney Giblet .... Steven Mackintosh
George Lecky .... Jim Carter
Lavinia Freebody .... Maria Aitken
Inspector Limp .... James Fleet
Doris Fledge .... Trudie Styler
John Lecky .... Chris Barnes
Harbottle .... Timothy Kightley
Sykes-Herring .... Richard Durden
Hubert Cleggie .... Nick Lucas
Connie Babblehump .... Annette Badland
Freddy Hough .... David Henry
and Bob Goody (Father Pin), Edward Jewesbury (Sir Edward Tome), David Killick (Sir Humphrey Stoker), Geoffrey Freshwater (Jury Foreman), Jeffry Wickham (Justice Congreve), Michael Cronin (Dr. Walter Dendrite), Eleanor Church (Nurse)

A conniving butler takes a job at the Coal estate and proceeds to seduce most of the household members. Sting and Trudie Styler are real-life husband and wife.

Alan Bates, Sting

HOLLOW REED

(CFP) Producer, Elizabeth Karlsen; Executive Producers, Nik Powell, Stephen Woolley; Director, Angela Pope; Screenplay, Paula Milne; Photography, Remi Adefarasin; Designer, Stuart Walker; Editor, Sue Wyatt; Music, Anne Dudley; Co-Executive Producers, Andres Vicente Gomez, Finola Dwyer, Neville Bolt, Hanno Huth; Costumes, Pam Downe; Casting, Susie Figgis; a Scala, Senator Films and Channel Four Films presentation; British-German, 1996; Dolby Stereo; Color; Not rated; 106 minutes; April release

CAST

Martyn Wyatt .... Martin Donovan
Hannah Wyatt .... Joely Richardson
Tom Dixon .... Ian Hart
Frank Donally .... Jason Flemyng
Oliver Wyatt .... Sam Bould
Doctor Razmu .... Shaheen Khan
Jamie's Mother .... Kelly Hunter
Site Foreman .... Tim Crouch
Record Shop Girl .... Jane Hill
Unemployed Youth .... Glen Hammond
Mr. Bugler .... Simon Chandler
School Nurse .... Dilys Hamlett
Doctor Ian Slater .... Andy Rashleigh
Martyn's Lawyer .... David Calder
Sgt. Curtis .... Maeve Murphy
Court Welfare Officer .... Victoria Scarborough
Hannah's Lawyer .... Roger Lloyd Pack
High Court Welfare Officer .... Kenneth Anderson
Martyn's Barrister .... Annette Badland
Hannah's Barrister .... Douglas Hodge
High Court Judge .... Edward Hardwicke

Having left his wife for another man, Martyn Wyatt now fights to get his son away from his ex-wife's abusive boyfriend.

Martin Donovan, Ian Hart

PARADISE ROAD

Glenn Close, Julianna Margulies

(FOX SEARCHLIGHT) Producers, Sue Milliken, Greg Coote; Executive Producers, Andrew Yap, Graham Burke; Director/Screenplay, Bruce Beresford; Based on a story by David Giles, Martin Meader; Photography, Peter James; Designer, Herbert Pinter; Editor, Tim Wellburn; Music, Ross Edwards; Costumes, Terry Ryan; a Village Roadshow Pictures/YTC Pictures production, in association with Planet Pictures; Australian-U.S.; Dolby Stereo; Panavision; Color; Rated R; 115 minutes; April release

CAST

Adrienne Pargiter	Glenn Close
Margaret Drummond	Pauline Collins
Susan Macarthy	Cate Blanchett
Dr. Verstak	Frances McDormand
Topsy Merritt	Julianna Margulies
Rosemary Leighton-Jones	Jennifer Ehle
Mrs. Roberts	Elizabeth Spriggs
Sister Wilhelminia	Joanna Ter Steege
Mrs. Dickson	Wendy Hughes
Mrs. Tippler	Pamela Rabe
Edna	Lisa Hensley
Mrs. Pike	Penne Hackforth-Jones
Wing	Pauline Chan
Celia Roberts	Tessa Humphries
Bett	Anita Hegh
Oggi	Susie Porter
Helen Van Praagh	Marta Dusseldorp
Mrs. O'Riorden	Lia Scallon
Mrs. Cronje	Marijke Mann
The Snake	Clyde Kusatsu
Colonel Hiroyo	Sab Shimono
Captain Tanaka	Stan Egi
Interpreter	David Chung
Singer at Raffles	Julie Anthony
Bill Seary	Aden Young
Dennis	Paul Bishop
William Pargiter	Stephen O'Rourke
Mr. Dickson	Vincent Ball
Marty Merritt	Nicholas Hammond
Robbie Rober	Noel Ferrier
Major-General Downes	Robert Grubb
Westmacott	Steven Grives

Glenn Close, Pauline Collins

During World War II a disparate group of women survive the bombing of their ship as it flees Singapore only to be captured by the Japanese and placed in a prison camp.

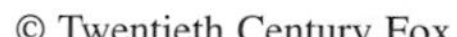

Frances McDormand, Cate Blanchett

Tessa Humphries, Elizabeth Spriggs, Julianna Margulies, Anita Hegh, Jennifer Ehle

KISSED

(GOLDWYN) Producers, Dean English, Lynne Stopkewich; Executive Producer, John Pozer; Director, Lynne Stopkewich; Screenplay, Angus Fraser, Lynne Stopkewich; Based on the short story "We So Seldom Look on Love" by Barbara Gowdy; Photography, Gregory Middleton; Editors, John Pozer, Peter Roeck, Lynne Stopkewich; Designer, Eric McNab; Music, Don MacDonald; Casting, Wendy O'Brien Livingstone; a Boneyard Film Company production, produced in association with British Columbia Film; Canadian, 1996; Dolby Stereo; Color; Not rated; 73 minutes; April release

CAST

Sandra Larson ....Molly Parker
Matt...Peter Outerbridge
Mr. Wallis..Jay Brazeau
Young Sandra...Natasha Morley
Carol ....Jessie Winter Mudie
Jan..James Timmons
Biology Teacher ....Joe Maffei
Detective ....Robert Thurston
Mother Larson ....Annabel Kershaw
Father Larson ....Tim Dixon
Lisa Brown..Amber Warnat
Minister ....Bill Finck
Mourner ....Janet Craig
Embalming Professor ....Edward Davey
and Hamish Wilson (Gurney Goner), Valerie Boeke (Cancer Corpse), Jeff Richards (Tony the Torso), Noel Boulanger (Prep Room Demo), Debra L. Huntley (Dead Madonna), John Pozer (Class Carcass), Raul Inglis (Lucky Stiff), Andrew Guy (Coffin Deceased), David Lone (Long Gone)

Sandra's childhood obsession with dead animals develops into a bizarre desire to make love to the corpses at the funeral home where she works.

Peter Outerbridge, Molly Parker

James Frain, Ian Hart

NOTHING PERSONAL

(TRIMARK) Producers, Jonathan Cavendish, Tracy Seaward; Executive Producer, James Mitchell; Director, Thaddeus O'Sullivan; Screenplay, Daniel Mornin, based on his novel All Our Fault; Photography, Dick Pope; Designer, Mark Geraghty; Editor, Michael Parker; Costumes, Consolata Boyle; Music, Philip Appleby; Casting, Ros & John Hubbard; a Channel Four Films with the participation of Bord Scannan na hEireann—The Irish Film Board—British Screen and Little Bird Productios; Irish; Dolby Digital Stereo; Color; Not rated; 86 minutes; April release

CAST

Ginger...Ian Hart
Liam...John Lynch
Kenny ....James Frain
Leonard...Michael Gambon
Eddie ....Gary Lydon
Tommy ....Ruaidhri Conroy
Ann ....Maria Doyle Kennedy
Kathleen ....Jeni Courtney
Cecil...Gerard McSorley
Michael ....Gareth O'Hare
Young Liam ....Ciaran Fitzgerald
Malachy ....Antony Brophy
Jake..BJ Hogg
Billy ....Jim Duran
Lizzie...Cathy White
Gloria ....Lynne James
Joe ....Joe Rea
Susan ....Amanda Maguire
and Robbie Doolin (Drunk Fella), Oliver Maguire (Marty), Andrew Roddy (Lizzie's Husband), Frank McCusker (1st Man), Seamus Ball (Jimmy), Danny McElhinney (Pub Bomber), Janet Moran (Waitress), Lydia Courtney (Penelope), Noah Eli Davis (Scruffy Young Man), Alan Burke (Ginger's Brother), Colm O'Brien (Young Kenny)

Kenny, a vengeful Protestant Loyalist squad leader, is stunned by the orders of a cease fire between the Protestants and the Catholics and the wishes of his superior that Kenny kill his violent friend Ginger as a sort of peace offering to the enemy.

A CHEF IN LOVE

(SONY PICTURES CLASSICS) Producer, Marc Ruscart; Director, Nana Djordjadze; Screenplay, Irakli Kvirikadze; Adaptation, Andre Grall; Photography, Guiorgui Beridze; Designer, Vakhtang Rouroua, Teimour Chmaladze; Music, Goran Bregovic; Editors, Vessela Martschewski, Guili Grigoriani; a Les Films du Rivage, Studios Adam et Eve, La Sept Cinema, Studio Babelsberg, CMC, Sotra, Innova co-production; French-Georgian, 1996; Dolby Stereo; Color; Rated PG-13; 100 minutes; April release

CAST

Pascal Ichac....Pierre Richard
Marcelle Ichac....Micheline Presle
Cecilia Abachidze....Nino Kirtadze
Zigmund Gogoladze....Teimour Kahmhadze
Anton Gogoladze....Jean-Yves Gautier
and Ramaz Tchkhikvadze

In 1995 Paris a painter is given a manuscript which describes his mother's relationship with a famous French chef. This film received an Oscar nomination in the foreign-language film category for 1996.

© Sony Pictures Entertainment

Nino Kirtadze, Pierre Richard

Maggie Cheung

IRMA VEP

(ZEITGEIST) Producer, Georges Benayoun; Executive Producer, Françoise Guglielmi; Director/Screenplay, Olivier Assayas; Photography, Eric Gautier; Designer, Francoise-Renaud Labarthe; Editor, Luc Barnier; Costumes, Francoise Clavel, Jessica Doyle; a Dacia Films production; French, 1996; Color; Not rated; 96 minutes; April release

CAST

Maggie....Maggie Cheung
Rene Vidal....Jean-Pierre Leaud
Zoe....Nathalie Richard
Mireille....Bulle Ogier
Jose Murano....Lou Castel
American Woman....Arsinee Khanjian
Journalist....Antonie Basler
Laure....Nathalie Boutefeu
Desormeaux....Alex Descas
Maite....Dominique Faysse
Markus....Bernard Nissile
Ferdinand/Moreno....Olivier Torres

Hong Kong action star Maggie Cheung comes to France to appear as "Irma Vep," the head of a band of vampires, in director Rene Vidal's remake of the silent seral "Les Vampires."

© Zeitgeist Films

FLAMENCO

(NEW YORKER) Producer, Juan Lebrón; Director, Carlos Saura; Executive Producer, José López Rodero; Photography, Vittorio Storaro; Designers, José Lopéz, Carlos Regidor; Costumes, Rafael Palmero; Editor, Pablo del Amo; Music Producer and Director, Isidro Muñoz; Spanish, 1995; Color; Not rated; 100 minutes; April release. Documentary on the variations of the flamenco dance featuring Paco de Lucía, Manolo Sanlúcar, Lole y Manuel, Joaquín Cortés, Farruco, Farruquito, Mario Maya, Matilde Coral, Enrique Morente, José Mercé, José Menese, Merche Esmeralda, Manuela Carrasco, La Paquera de Jerez, Carmen Linares, Paco Toronjo, Fernanda de Utrera, Chocolate, Paco Del Gastor.

© New Yorker Films

CHILDREN OF THE REVOLUTION

(MIRAMAX) Producer, Tristram Miall; Director/Screenplay, Peter Duncan; Photography, Martin McGrath; Designer, Roger Ford; Editor, Simon Martin, Music, Nigel Westlake; Costumes, Terry Ryan; Associate Producer, Greg Ricketson; a presentation of the Australian Film Finance Corporation; Australian, 1996; Dolby Digital Stereo; Color; Rated R; 101 minutes; May release

CAST

Joan Fraser....................Judy Davis
Nine....................Sam Neill
Josef Stalin....................F. Murray Abraham
Joe....................Richard Roxburgh
Anna....................Rachel Griffiths
Welch....................Geoffrey Rush
Barry....................Russell Kiefel
Dr. Wilf Wilke....................John Gaden
Young Joe....................Ben McIvor
Brendan Shaw....................Marshall Napier
Bernard Shaw....................Ken Radley
Mavis....................Fiona Press
Yuri....................Alex Menglet
Colin Slansky....................Rowan Woods
Police Commissioner....................Harold Hopkins
Mrs. Savage....................Heather Mitchell
Beria....................Paul Livingstone
Malenkov....................Stephen Abbott
Khrushchev....................Dennis Watkins
Allan Miles....................Ron Haddrick
Ted....................Barry Langrishe
Minister....................Robbie McGregor
Police Sergeant....................Roy Billing

Communist Joan Fraser looks back on how her infatuation with Josef Stalin led to her having his child.

F. Murray Abraham, Judy Davis

Judy Davis, Geoffrey Rush

Aleksandra Vujcic, Madeline McNamara, Marton Csokas, Rade Serbedzija, Elizabeth Mavric

BROKEN ENGLISH

(SONY CLASSICS) Producer, Robin Scholes; Executive Producer, Timothy White; Director, Gregor Nicholas; Screenplay, Gregor Nicholas, Johanna Pigott, Jim Salter; Photography, John Toon; Editor, David Coulson; Music, Murray Grindlay, Murray McNabb; Designer, Michael Kane; Casting, Fiona Edgar; a Village Roadshow Pictures Worldwide presentation of a Communicado Production in association with the New Zealand Film Commission and New Zealand on Air; New Zealand, 1996; Dolby Stereo; Color; Rated NC-17; 90 minutes; May release

CAST

Ivan....................Rade Serbedzija
Nina....................Aleksandra Vujcic
Eddie....................Julian Arahanga
Darko....................Marton Csokas
Mira....................Madeline McNamara
Vanya....................Elizabeth Mavric
Clara....................Jing Zhao
Wu....................Yang Li

Nina, having fled with her family to New Zealand from war-torn Croatia, finds herself falling in love with a handsome Maori boy much to the displeasure of her overly-protective father.

THE DESIGNATED MOURNER

(FIRST LOOK PICTURES) Producers, Donna Grey, David Hare; Executive Producers, Mark Shivas, Simon Curtis; Director, David Hare; Screenplay, Wallace Shawn, based on his play; Photography, Oliver Stapleton; Designer, Bob Crowley; Music, Richard Hartley; Editor, George Akers; a BBC Films presentation of a Greenpoint Film; British; Dolby Stereo; Color; Rated R; 93 minutes; May release

CAST

Jack .... Mike Nichols
Judy .... Miranda Richardson
Howard .... David de Keyser

Jack, mourning the passing of his stepfather, a famous poet, reflects on the death of intellectualism and compassion. Director Mike Nichols makes his theatrical film debut as an actor.

© First Line Pictures

Jérémie Renier

DIARY OF A SEDUCER

(LEISURE TIME FEATURES) Producer, Philippe Saal; Executive Producer, Paulo Branco; Director/Screenplay, Daniele Dubroux; Photography, Laurent Machuel; Editor, Jean-Francois Naudon; Music, Jean-Marie Senia; Art Director, Patrick Durand; Costumes, Anne Schotte; a production of Gemini Films with the participation of the National Center of Cinematography and Canal+; French; Color; Not rated; 95 minutes; May release

CAST

Claire Conti .... Chiara Mastroianni
Gregoire Moreau .... Melvil Poupaud
Hubert Markus .... Hubert Saint Macary
Sebastien .... Mathieu Amalric
Anne, Claire's Mother .... Daniele Dubroux
Hugo .... Jean-Pierre Leaud
Diane .... Micheline Presle
Robert .... Serge Merlin
Charlotte .... Karen Viard

A copy of Kierkegaard's Diary of a Seducer turns anyone who comes into contact with the book into a romantic fool.

© Leisure Time Features

Miranda Richardson, Mike Nichols

LA PROMESSE

(NEW YORKER) Producers, Luc Dardenne, Hassen Daldoul; Directors/Screenplay, Jean-Pierre Dardenne, Luc Dardenne; Photography, Alain Marcoen, Benoit Dervaux; Associate Producers, Jacqueline Pierreux, Claude Waringo; Set Designer, Igor Gabriel; Costumes, Monic Parelle; Editor, Marie-Helene Dozo; Music, Jean-Marie Billy, Denis M'Punga; a presentation of Luc and Jean-Pierre Dardenne—Les Films du Fleuve—Hassen Daldoul—Touza Productions & Touza Films—Claude Waringo—Samsa Film—Jacqueline Pierreux—RTBF (Belgian Television); French-Belgian-Luxembourgian-Tunisian, 1996; Dolby Digital Stereo; Color; Not rated; 93 minutes; May release

CAST

Igor .... Jérémie Renier
Roger .... Olivier Gourmet
Assita .... Assita Ouedraogo
Hamidou .... RasmanéOuedraogo
Ibrahim .... R. Amrani
Nicolai .... I. Tanaru

15 year-old Igor is forced to accept his father's illegal way of making a living by exploiting illegal immigrants until a young African laborer is killed on the job, causing Igor to try to help the man's widow

© New Yorker Films

Jean-Pierre Leaud, Chiara Mastroianni

THE FIFTH ELEMENT

Bruce Willis

(COLUMBIA) Producer, Patrice Ledoux; Director/Story, Luc Besson; Screenplay, Luc Besson, Robert Mark Kamen; Photography, Thierry Arbogast; Designer, Dan Weil; Editor, Sylvie Landra; Co-Producer, Iain Smith; Special Visual Effects Supervisor, Mark Stetson; Costumes, Jean-Paul Gaultier; Music, Eric Serra; Stunts, Marc Boyle; Casting, Lucinda Syson; a Gaumont Production; French; Dolby SDDS Stereo; Super 35 Widescreen; Eastman color; Rated PG-13; 127 minutes; May release

Chris Tucker

CAST

Korben Dallas .... Bruce Willis
Zorg .... Gary Oldman
Cornelius .... Ian Holm
Leeloo .... Milla Jovovich
Ruby Rhod .... Chris Tucker
Billy .... Luke Perry
General Munro .... Brion James
President Lindberg .... Tommy "Tiny" Lister, Jr.
Fog .... Lee Evans
David .... Charlie Creed Miles
Right Arm .... Tricky
General Staedert .... John Neville
Professor Pacoli .... John Bluthal
Mugger .... Mathieu Kassovitz
Mactilburgh .... Christopher Fairbank
Thai .... Kim Chan
Neighbor .... Richard Leaf
Major Iceborg .... Julie T. Wallace
General Tudor .... Al Matthews
Diva .... Maïwenn Le Besco
Priest .... John Bennett
Left Arm .... Ivan Heng
President's Aide .... Sonita Henry
Scientist's Aide .... Tim McMullan
Munro's Captain .... Hon Ping Tang
Head Scientist .... George Khan
Head of Military .... John Hughes
Omar .... Roberto Bryce
Aziz .... Said Talidi

and Justin Lee Burrows, Richard Ashton, Jerome Blake, Kevin Molloy (Mondoshawan), Bill Reimbold (Mactilburgh's Assistant), Colin Brooks (Staedert's Captain), Anthony Chinn (Mactilburgh's Technicians), Sam Douglas (Chief NY Cop), Derek Ezenagu (NY Cop), David Kennedy, David Barrass, Roger Monk, Mac McDonald, Mark Seaton, Jean Luc Caron, Riz Meedin, Jerry Ezekiel (Flying Cops), Indra Ove, Nicole Merry, Stacey McKenzie (VIP Stewardesses), Rachel Willis, Genevieve Maylam, Josie Perez, Natasha Brice (Stewardesses), Sophia Goth (Check In Attendant), Martin McDougall (Warship Captain), Peter Dunwell (Diva's Manager), Paul Priestley, Jason Salkey (Cops), Stewart Harvey Wilson, Dave Fishley, Carlton Chance (Ruby Rhod Assistants), Gin Clarke (Diva's Assistant), Vladimir McCrary (Human Aknot), Clifton Lloyd Bryan (Mangalore Aknot/Airport Guard), Aron Paramor (Mangalore Akanit), Alan Ruscoe (Mangalore Kino), Christopher Adamson (Airport Cop), Eve Salvail (Tawdry Girl), Kaleem Janjua (Shuttle Pilot), Tyrone Tyrell (Shuttle Co-Pilot), Kevin Brewerton (Shuttle Mechanic), Kevin Molloy, Vince Pellegrino (Ground Crew), Ian Beckett (Baby Ray), Sonny Caldinez (Emperor Kodar Japhet), Zeta Graff (Princess Achen), Eddie Ellwood (Roy Von Bacon), Yui, Laura DePalma (Fhloston Hostesses), Michael Culkin (Hefty Man), Lenny McLean (Police Chief), Robert Oates (Fhloston Commander), John Sharian (Fhloston Captain), Fred Williams (Hotel Manager), Sibyl Buck (Zorg's Secretary), Sarah Carrington, Grant James, Ali Yassine, Sean Buckley (Scientists), Dane Messam, Roger Monk, Nathan Hamlett, Cecil Cheng (Military Technicians), Scott Woods, Leon Dekker (Lab Guards), David Garvey, Stanley Kowalski, Omar Hibbert Williams (Staedert's Technicians), Robert Clapperton (Robot Barman), Robert Alexander (Warship Technician), Mia Frye (TV Stewardess), Leo Williams, Keith Martin (Power Operators), J.D. Dawodu, Patrick Nicholls, Shaun Davis, Roy Garcia Singh, Alex Georgijev (Zorg's Men), Marie Guillard, Renee Montemayor, Stina Richardson (Burger Assistants)

Tiny Lister, Jr. (c)

In 23rd Century New York cab driver Korben Dallas rescues Leeloo, a strange being who is the key element needed to save the earth from cosmic anti-life forces. This film received an Oscar nomination for sound effects editing.

Maïwenn LeBesco

Gary Oldman

Charlie Creed Miles, Milla Jovovich, Ian Holm

PONETTE

(ARROW) Producer, Alain Sarde; Director/Screenplay, Jacques Doillon; Photography, Caroline Champetier; Costumes, Astrid Traissac; Set Designer, Henri Berthon; Editor, Jacqueline Fano (Leconte); Music, Philippe Sarde; Co-Produced by Les Films Alain Sarde, Rhone-Alpes Cinema with the participation of La Region Rhone Alpes, Centre National de la Cinematographie and Canal+; French, 1996; Dolby Stereo; Color; Not rated; 97 minutes; May release

CAST

Ponette........Victoire Thivisol
Ponette's Cousins........Matiaz Bureau, Delphine Schiltz
The Mother........Marie Trintignant
The Father........Xavier Beauvois
The Aunt........Claire Nebout
Aurélie........Aurelie Verillon
Ada........Leopoldine Serre
The Teacher........Henri Berthon
Carla........Carla Ibled
Luce........Luckie Royer
Antoine........Antoine Du Merle
Marianne........Marianne Favre

Surviving a car crash which has killed her mother, 4-year-old Ponette deals with the tragedy by clinging to the notion that her mother will somehow come back to her.

Victoire Thivisol

Xavier Beauvois, Victoire Thivisol

Om Puri (left)

Pavan Malhotra

BROTHERS IN TROUBLE

(FIRST RUN FEATURES) Producer/Screenplay, Robert Buckler; Executive Producer, George Faber; Director, Udayan Prasad; Photography, Alan Almond; Designer, Chris Townsend; Editor, Barrie Vince; Music, Stephen Warbeck; Casting, Lucinda Syson; a BBC Film presentation of a Renegade Films production, in association with Kinowelt Film Produktion and Mikado Film; British, 1995; Dolby Digital Stereo; Color; Not rated; 102 minutes; May release

CAST

Hussein Shah........Om Puri
Mary........Angeline Ball
Amir........Pavan Malhotra
Sakib........Pravesh Kumar
Irshad........Ahsen Bhatti
Old Ram........Badi Uzzaman
Gholam........Bhasker
The Agent........Kulvinder Ghir
Prostitute........Lesley Clare O'Neill

Amir smuggles himself into England only to find that living and working conditions for himself and seventeen other illegal Pakistani immigrants with whom he resides, is no easier than it was back home.

BRASSED OFF

(MIRAMAX) Producer, Steve Abbott; Co-Producer, Olivia Stewart; Director/Screenplay, Mark Herman; Photography, Andy Collins; Designer, Don Taylor; Editor, Mike Ellis; Costumes, Amy Roberts; Music, Trevor Jones; Brass Music Performed by The Grimethorpe Colliery Band; Casting, Priscilla John, Julia Duff; a Channel Four Films presentation of a Steve Abbott/Prominent Features production; British, 1996; Dolby Stereo; Color; Rated R; 101 minutes; May release

Ewan McGregor, Tara Fitzgerald, Pete Postlethwaite

CAST

Danny....Pete Postlethwaite
Gloria....Tara Fitzgerald
Andy....Ewan McGregor
Phil....Stephen Tompkinson
Harry....Jim Carter
Jim....Philip Jackson
Ernie....Peter Martin
Vera....Sue Johnston
Ida....Mary Healey
Rita....Lill Roughley
Sandra....Melanie Hill
Simmo....Peter Gunn
McKenzie....Stephen Moore
Greasley....Ken Colley
Mrs. Foggan....Olga Grahame
Gary....Toni Garlacki
Kylie....Sky Ingram
Shane....Luke McGann
Craig....Christopher Tetlow
Chapman....Bernard Wrigley
Heavies....Ken Kitson, Adrian Hood
Ward Sister....Sally Adams
Bus Driver....Tubby Andrews
Nurse....Katherine Dow Beyton

and Adam Fogerty (Miner), Jacqueline Naylor, Vanessa Know-Mawer (Mothers), Sally Ann Matthews (Waitress), Bob Rodgers (Halifax Judge), Max Smith (Night Watchman), Ronnie Stevens (Albert Hall Judge), Peter Wallis (Elderly Man)

Tara Fitzgerald, Ewan McGregor

In the Yorkshire village of Grimley, the town's brass band tries to concentrate on rehearsing for the National Championships while facing the almost certain closure of the mine and the resulting loss of employment for all the band's members.

Pete Postlethwaite

Stephen Tompkinson, Pete Postlethwaite

THE VAN

(FOX SEARCHLIGHT) Producer, Lynda Miles; Executive Producer, Mark Shivas; Co-Producer/Screenplay, Roddy Doyle, based on his novel; Director, Stephen Frears; Photography, Oliver Stapleton; Designer, Mark Geraghty; Costumes, Consolata Boyle; Editor, Mick Audsley; Music, Eric Clapton, Richard Hartley; Presented in association with BBC Films; a Deadly Films production in association with Beacon Pictures; British, 1996; Dolby Stereo; Color; Rated R; 105 minutes; May release

CAST

Larry ....Colm Meaney
Bimbo ....Donal O'Kelly
Maggie ....Ger Ryan
Mary ....Caroline Rothwell
Diane ....Neili Conroy
Kevin ....Ruaidhri Conroy
Weslie ....Brendan O'Carroll
Sam..Stuart Dunne

Bimbo, favoring unemployment after being fired from his bakery job, hits on the idea of running a fast-food truck with his friend Larry as his business partner.

Yoshi Oida

Ewan McGregor, Vivian Wu

Ger Ryan, Colm Meaney, Ruaidhri Conroy

THE PILLOW BOOK

(CFP) Producer, Kees Kasander; Executive Producers, Terry Glinwood, Jean Louis Piel, Denis Wigman; Director/Screenplay, Peter Greenaway; Photography, Sacha Vierny; Designers, Wilbert van Dorp, Andree Putnam, Emi Wada; Costumes, Dien van Straalen, Koji Tatsuno, Martin Margiela, Emi Wada; Editors, Chris Wyatt, Peter Greenaway; Calligraphy, Brody Neuenschwander, Yukki Yaura; from Channel Four Films/Studio Canal+/Delux Productions, with the support of The Eurimages Fund of the Council of Europe/Nederlands Fonds Voor de Film; British-Netherlands-French, 1996; Dolby Stereo; Super 35 Widescreen; Color; Not rated; 126 minutes; June release

CAST

Nagiko ....Vivian Wu
The Publisher..Yoshi Oida
The Father ....Ken Ogata
The Aunt & The Maid ....Hideko Yoshida
Jerome..Ewan McGregor
The Mother ....Judy Ongg
The Husband..Ken Mitsuishi
Hoki ....Yutaka Honda
Jerome's Mothe ....Barbara Lott
The Book of the Innocent ....Wichert Dromkert
The Book of the Idiot..Martin Tukker
The Book of Old Age..Wu Mei
The Book of the Exhibitionist ....Tom Kane
The Book of the Seducer ....Kheim Lam
The Book of Youth ....Daishi Hori
The Book of Secrets ....Kinya Tsuruyama
The Book of the Betrayer..Eiichi Tanaka
The Book of Silence ....Rick Waney
The Book of Birth & Beginnings....................................Masaru Matsuda
The Book of the Dead..Wataru Murofush
and Miwako Kawai, Chizurur Ohnishi, Shiho Takmatsu, Aki Ishimaru (Young Nagikos), Hisashi Hidaka, Dehong Chen, Ham Cham Luong, Akihiro Nishida, Kentaro Matsuo, Nguyen Duc Nhan, Augusto Aristotle, Roger To Thanh Hien, Chris Bearne (Calligraphers), Ronald Guttman (Lecturer), Ryuko Azuma (Grandmother), Seitaro Koyama, Tatsuya Kimura (Nephew), Yoshihiko Nagata, Atsushi Miura (Husband's Friends), Kazushi Ishimaru (Baby Nagiko), Hikari Abe (Nagiko's Baby), Ai Kanafuji, Yoshino Yoshioka, Yuki Nou, Masami Nishio, Satomi Kimura, Michiko Matsuo (Nagiko's Friends), Arnita Swanson (Edele), Jim Adhi Limas (Man in Lift), Miho Tanaka, Fabienne De Marco, Tania De Jaeger (Model Friends at Cafe Typo), Lu Jinhua (Wife of Calligrapher), Tien Sing Wang, Chau, See Wah Leung, Kha (Intruders), Kumi Komino (Elderly Secretary), Yuki Hayashi, Maskai Taketani (Young Secretaries), Mr. and Mrs. Lo (Old Servant and Wife), See Yan Leung (Bookshop Manager), Francois Van Den Bergen (Book of Seducer)

Having been painted on by her father for each birthday, Nagiko searches for a lover to fulfill her fetish for being drawn on.

WHEN THE CAT'S AWAY

(SONY CLASSICS) Producers, Aissa Djabri, Farid Lahouassa, Manuel Munz; Director/Screenplay, Cédric Klapisch; Photography, Benoit Delhomme; Editor, Francine Sandberg; Costumes, Pierre Yves Gayraud; Designer, Francois Emmanuelli; a co-production of Vertigo Productions and France2 Cinema with the participation of Canal+; French; Dolby Stereo; Color; Rated R; 95 minutes; June release

CAST

Chloé....Garance Clavel
Jamel....Zinedine Soualem
Madame Renée....Renée Le Calm
Michel....Olivier Py
Gris-Gris....Arapimou
Rambo....Rambo
Drummer....Romain Duris
Photographer's Assistant....Nicolas Koretzky
Madame Dubois....Andrée Damant
Flo the Hair Stylist....Estelle Larrivaz
Victoire....Camille Japy
Stylist....Marina Tomé
Models....Marine Delterme, Helene De Fougerolles, Liane Leroy, Jane Bradbury
Publicist....Marie Riva
Photographer....Frederic Aufray
Assistant Stylist....Philippe Garcia
Carlos....Simon Abkarian
Drunk Guy....Antoine Chappey
Madame Henriette....Jacqueline Jehanneuf
Woman Who Gets Lost....Madeleine Marie
Baker....Coraly Zahonero
African Worker....Eriq Ebouaney
Bartender....Aurélia Petit
Bouncer....Jean-Marc Truong
Agressive Guys....Francis Renaud, Franck Bussi
Michel's First Boyfriend....Michel Glasko
Michel's Second Boyfriend....Franck Manzoni
Eleven of Spades Militant....Eric Savin
Mover/Painter....Pascal Chardin
Bel Canto, the Painter....Joel Brisse
Denis....Denis Falgoux

and Danielle Hoisnard (Madame Verligodin), Suzanne Plasson (Odile), Marcelle Dupuy (Pipelette), Marthe Fouquet (Madame Vilchenu), Aline Chantal (Madame Doubrowsky), Gisele Laquit (Gisele), Olympe Brugeille (Madame Brugeille), Jean-Marie and Lila (Owners of the Bar des Taillandiers), Felipe Moya (Troude), P'Tit Louis (Homeless Guy), Kristelle (Kristelle), Paola Ramirez, Carlos Donoso (Salsa Dancers), Marilyne Canto (Cop)

When Chloé returns from vacation she discovers that the absent-minded Madame Renée, entrusted with watching her cat, has lost the animal, leading the two on a picaresque series of misaventures as they search for the missing feline.

Garance Clavel

Garance Clavel, Arapimou

Zinedine Soualem, Renée Le Calm, Garance Clavel

TEMPTRESS MOON

(MIRAMAX) Producers, Tong Cunlin, Hsu Feng; Executive Producer, Sunday Sun; Director, Chen Kaige; Screenplay, Shu Kei; Story, Chen Kaige, Wang Anyi; Photography, Christopher Doyle; Art Director, Huang Qiagui; Costumes, William Chang Suk-ping, Chen Changmin; Music, Zhao Jiping; Editor, Pei Xiaonan; Hong Kong, 1996; Color; Rated R; 115 minutes; June release

CAST

Yu Zhongliang ...... Leslie Cheung
Pang Ruyi ...... Gong Li
Pang Duanwu ...... Kevin Lin
Yu Xiuyi (Zhongliang's Sister) ...... He Saifei
Li Niangjiu ...... Zhang Shi
Pang An ...... Lin Lianqun
Elder Qi ...... Ge Xiangting
Boss ...... Xie Tian
Jingyun ...... David Wu
"The Woman of Heavenly Lane" ...... Zhou Jie
Pang Zhengda ...... Zhou Yemang
Yu Zhongliang (Child) ...... Ren Lei
Pang Ruyi (Child) ...... Wang Ying
Pang Duanwu (Child) ...... Ge Lin

Young Zhongliang, raised as a servant at the decadent Pang family estate, grows up and ventures to pre-Communist era Shanghai where he becomes a gigolo.

Gong Li

THE INNOCENT SLEEP

(CASTLE HILL) Producers, Scott Michell, Matthew Vaughn; Executive Producer, Rod Mitchell; Director, Scott Michell; Screenplay, Ray Villis, Derek Trigg; Photography, Alan Dunlop; Editor, Derek Trigg; Costumes, Stephanie Collie; Designer, Eve Mavrakis; Music, Mark Ayres; Casting, Simone Ireland; British, 1996; Dolby Stereo; Super 35 Widescreen; Color; Rated R; 90 minutes; June release

CAST

Alan Terry ...... Rupert Graves
Billie Hayman ...... Annabella Sciorra
Matheson ...... Michael Gambon
Cavani ...... Franco Nero
James ...... John Hannah
George ...... Graham Crowden
Lusano ...... Oliver Cotton
Thorn ...... Tony Bluto
Pelham ...... Paul Brightwell
Mac ...... Campbell Morrison
Sheila Terry ...... Hilary Crowson
Police Constable ...... Sean Gilder
Police Sergeant ...... Biran Lipson
Willie ...... Dermot Kerrigan

and Kieran Smith (Newspaper Vendor), Dermot Keaney (Driver), Alex Richardson, Chris Chering (Thugs), Chris Jury (News Photographer), Laura Berkeley (Glamorous Blonde), Hugh Walters (Lewis), Crispin Redman (Simon, C.I.D.), Katy Carr (Alice), Chris Armstrong (C.I.D. Man), Lehla Eldridge (Morgue Attendant), Struan Rodger (Peter Samson), Stephen Yardley (Drago), Ken Ratcliffe (Stephens), Carmen de Venere (Cavani's Aide), Paul Gregory (Newsreader), Robert James (Hopkin), Susan Gilmore (News Programme Presenter), Peter Cartwright (Gerald Phillips), Julian Rivett (Bike Courier), Patrick Duggan (Landlord), Hilary Waters, Riz Abbasi, Martin Biltcliffe, James Peck (Journalists), Peter Howell (Sir Frank), Ben de Saumserez (Assassin)

Alan Terry, a homeless man living on the streets of London, fears for his life after witnessing the brutal murder of a high-profile businessman.

Rupert Graves

Annabella Sciorra

EAST SIDE STORY

(KINO) Producer, Andrew Horn; Director, Dana Ranga; Screenplay, Dana Ranga, Andrew Horn; Translations, Sergei Grimalschi, Irina Goldstein, Karin Beck; Photography, Mark Daniels; Editor, Guido Krajewski; Costumes, Suse Brown; Produced by ANDA Films/WDR/DocStar/Canal+; German-French; Color/Black and White; Not rated; 77 minutes; June release. A look at the socialist movie musicals made behind the Iron Curtain during Communist rule; featuring Andrea Schmidt, Brit Kruger, Barbara Harnisch (Communist Party Girls); interviews with Karin Schröder, Brigitte Ulbrich, Helmut Hanke, Hans-Joachim Wallstein, Maya Turorskaya, Maragarita Andrushkevitch, Chris Doerk, Frank Schöbel. Featuring musicals numbers from the films Hard Work, Happy Holiday (GDR, 1950), The Antique Coin (Bulgaria/GDR, 1965), Adventure in Marienstadt (Poland, 1954), A Handful of Notes (GDR, 1962), New Year's Punch (GDR, 1960), Vacation on the Black Sea (Romania, 1963), I Don't Want to Marry (Romania, 1961), The Jolly Fellows (USSR, 1934), Volga Volga (USSR, 1938), The Swineherd and the Shepherd (USSR, 1941), Tractor Drivers (USSR, 1939), Cossacks of the Kuban River (USSR, 1946), The Bright Path (USSR, 1940), At 6PM at the End of the War (USSR, 1944), Ernest Thalmann—Class Leader (GDR, 1955), My Wife Wants to Sing (GDR, 1958), Midnight Revue (GDR, 1962), The Lovable White Mouse (GDR, 1964), Hot Summer (GDR, 1968), No Cheating Darling (GDR, 1973), Woman on the Rails (Czechoslovakia, 1965), Carnvial Night (USSR, 1957)

Shaghayegh Djodat

GABBEH

(NEW YORKER) Producers, Khalil Doroudt-Chi, Khalil Mahmoudi; Executive Producer, Mustafa Mirza-Khani; Director/Screenplay/Art Director/Editor, Mohsen Makhmalbaf; Photography, Mahmoud Kalari; Music, Hossein Alizadeh; a co-production of Sanayeh Dasti of Iran and MK2 (France); Iranian-French, 1996; Color; Not rated; 75 minutes; June release

CAST

Gabbeh .... Shaghayegh Djodat
The Uncle .... Abbas Sayahi
The Old Man .... Hossein Moharami
The Old Woman .... Roghieh Moharami

A woman named Gabbeh arises from a carpet to tell an old woman and her husband the story of how she is being pursued by a horseman who wishes to marry her.

FOR ROSEANNA

(FINE LINE FEATURES) formerly *Roseanna's Grave*; Producers, Paul Trijbits, Alison Owen, Dario Poloni; Executive Producers Ruth Vitale, Mark Ordesky, Jonathan Weisgel, Miles Donnelly; Director, Paul Weiland; Screenplay, Paul Tureltaub; Line Producer, Chris Thompson; Photography, Henry Brahm; Designer, Rod McLean; Editor, Martin Walsh; Music, Trevor Jones; Costumes, Annie Hardinge; Casting, Nina Gold; Presented in association with Spelling FIlms, of a Hungry Eye Trijbits/Worrell production; British-Italian; Dolby SDDS Stereo; Panavision; Technicolor, Rated PG-13; 98 minutes; June release

CAST

Marcello .... Jean Reno
Roseanna .... Mercedes Ruehl
Cecilia .... Polly Walker
Antonio .... Mark Frankel
Father Bramilla .... Giuseppe Cederna
Dr. Benvenuto .... Renato Scarpa
Capestro .... Luigi Dilberti
Rossi .... Roberto Della Casa
Iaccoponi .... Trevor Peacock
Francesca .... Fay Ripley
Sgt. Baggio .... George Rossi
Umberto .... Romano Ghinin
Enzo .... Giovanni Pallavicino
Salvatore .... Jorge Krimer
Nunzio .... Daniele Ferretti
Pavone .... Paul Müller
Gianna .... Lucia Guzzardi

and Lidia Biondi (Signora Aprea), Anna Mazzotti (Claudia), Giuseppe Paplia (Dino), Luis C. Garcia (Pasquale), Mario Donatone (Old Gaurd), Peter Gunn, Pietro Bontempo (Cops), Alfred Varelli (Shoe Shop Owner), Gisella Mathews (Sister), Franco Odoardi (Patient), Julia Hine (Secretary), Luciana De Falco (Gigi), Stefani Stella (Hooker), Francesco Gabrielle (Maristrate), Zita Perczel (Old Woman in Court)

Marcello, determined to fulfill his dying wife Roseanna's wish that she be buried in one of the few remaining plots in the village cemetary, goes out of his way to make sure that nobody in town dies before her.

Mercedes Ruehl, Jean Reno

Jean Reno

Mirtha Ibarra

GUANTANAMERA!

(CFP) Producer, Gerardo Herrer; Executive Producer, Camilo Vives; Directors, Tomás Gutiérrez Alea, Juan Carlos Tabio; Screenplay, Eliseo Alberto Diego, Tomás Gutiérrez Alea, Juan Carlos Tabio; Photography, Hans Burmann; Art Director, Onelia Larralde; Music, José Nieto; Editor, Carmen Frias; Cuban; Dolby Digital Stereo; Color; Not rated; 101 minutes; July release

CAST

Adolfo .... Carlos Cruz
Georgina .... Mirtha Ibarra
Candido .... Raúl Eguren
Mariano .... Jorge Perugorria
Ramon .... Pedro Fernández
Tony .... Luis Alberto Garcia Novoa
Aunt Yoyita .... Conchita Brando
Iku .... Suset Pérez Malberti

Returning to the town of Guantanamera after a fifty year absence, Yoyita finds herself reunited with her former lover, Candido.

ALIVE AND KICKING

(FIRST LOOK PICTURES) a.k.a. *Indian Summer*; Producer, Martin Pope; Director, Nancy Meckler; Screenplay, Martin Sherman; Photography, Chris Seager; Designer, Cecelia Brereton; Editor, Rodney Holland; Music, Peter Salem; Associate Producer, Lorraine Goodman; Costumes, Monica Howe; Choreographer, Liz Ranken; Casting, Janey Fothergill; a Channel Four Films presentation of an M-P production; British; Dolby Stereo; Color; Rated R; 100 minutes; July release

CAST

Tonio .... Jason Flemyng
Jack .... Antony Sher
Luna .... Dorothy Tutin
Ramon .... Anthony Higgins
Tristan .... Bill Nighy
Duncan .... Philip Voss
Millie .... Diane Parish
Vincent .... Aiden Waters
Catherine .... Natalie Roles
Luke .... Freddy Douglas
Howard .... Kenneth Tharp
Alan .... Michael Keegan-Dolan
Night Nurse .... Ruth Lass
Doctor .... Linda Bassett
Nurse .... Hilary Reynolds
Muggers .... Dickon Tolson

and David Ashton, Annabel Leventon (Paris Mourners), David Phelan (Mourner), Dugald Bruce Lockhart (Man at Club), Ian Abbey (T-Shirt Man), John Baxter (Man at Bar), Jason Cheater (Smoking Man), Ellen Van Schuylenburch (Dance Teacher), Marty Cruickshank (Woman at Party), Allan Corduner (Therapist), Richard Hope (Karaoke Doctor), Martin Sherman (Man at Pub), Sakuntala Ramanee (Hospital Doctor), Frank Boyce (Man in Park), Frank Bock, Odette Hughes, Michelle Levi, Ulala Yamamoto, Stephen Houghton (Dancers)

Tonio, a narcissistic dancer, and Jack, a therapist, begin an unlikely romance.

Jason Flemyng, Antony Sher

Anthony Higgins, Jason Flemyng

Jason Flemyng

Dorothy Tutin

Koji Yakusho

SHALL WE DANCE?

(MIRAMAX) Producers, Yasuyoshi Tokuma, Shoji Masui, Yuji Ogata; Executive Producers, Hiroyuki Kato, Seiji Urushido, Shigeru Ohno, Kazuhiro Igarashi, Testuya Ikeda; Director/Screenplay, Masayuki Suo; Photography, Naoki Kayano; Designer, Kyoko Heya; Music, Yoshikazu Suo; Shall We Dance? performed by Taeko Ohnuki; Editor, Junichi Kikuchi; a Daiea, NTV, Hakuhodo and Nippan presentation of an Altamira Pictures production; Japanese, 1996; Dolby Stereo; Super 35 Widescreen; Color; Rated PG; 118 minutes; July release

CAST

Shohei Sugiyama....Koji Yakusho
Mai Kishikawa....Tamiyo Kusakari
Tomio Aoki....Naoto Takenaka
Toyoko Takahashi....Eriko Watanabe
Toru Miwa....Akira Emoto
Tokichi Hattori....Yu Tokui
Masahiro Tanaka....Hiromasa Taguchi
Tamako Tamura....Reiko Kusamura
Masako Sugiyama....Hideko Hara
Ryou Kishikawa....Syuichiro Moriyama
Hiromasa Kimoto....Masahiro Motoki
Natsuko....Misa Shimizu

An average middle-aged businessman finds his life changing for the better when he signs up for a ballroom dancing class.

Tamiyo Kusakari, Koji Yakusho

Reiko Kusamura, Yu Tokui, Hiromasa Taguchi, Koji Yakusho

Hideko Hara, Koji Yakusho

Tamiyo Kusakari

Koji Yakusho, Tamiyo Kusakari, Reiko Kusamura

Billy Connolly, Judi Dench

Judi Dench, Billy Connolly

Billy Connolly, Judi Dench

Judi Dench

MRS. BROWN

(MIRAMAX) Producer, Sarah Curtis; Executive Producers, Douglas Rae, Andrea Calderwood, Rebecca Eaton, Nigel Warren-Green; Director, John Madden; Screenplay, Jeremy Brock; Photography, Richard Greatrex; Designer, Martin Childs; Music, Stephen Warbeck; Costumes, Deirdre Clancy; Editor, Robin Sales; Make Up Designer, Lisa Westcott; Associate Producer, Paul Sarony; Casting, Michelle Guish; a BBC Films and WGBH/Mobil Masterpiece Theatre in association with Irish Screen presentation of an Ecosse Films production; British-Irish; Dolby Stereo; Color; Rated PG; 103 minutes; July release

Billy Connolly, Judi Dench

CAST

Queen Victoria ....Judi Dench
John Brown ....Billy Connolly
Henry Ponsonby ....Geoffrey Palmer
Benjamin Disrael ....Antony Sher
Archie Brown ....Gerard Butler
Doctor Jenner ....Richard Pasco
Bertie, Prince of Wales..David Westhead
Lady Ely ....Bridget McConnel
Lady Churchill..Georgie Glen
Lady in Waiting ....Catherine O'Donnell
Princess Alexandria..Sara Stewart
Princess Helena ....Finty Williams
Princess Louise ....Clair Nicolson
Princess Alice..Hattie Ladburty
Prince Alfred ....Oliver Kent
Prince Arthur..Alex Menzies
Prince Leopold ....Simon McKerrell
Bertie's Valet..Rupert Farley
Mrs. Grant ....Elaine Collins
Mr. Grant..Jimmy Chisholm
Lord Stanley ....Jason Morell
Assistant Dresser ....Rebecca Charles
Mary Ann Disraeli..Cherith Mellor
Speaker of the House..George Hall
Commons Counter ....Robin Marchal
Dean of Windsor ....Oliver Ford Davies
and Patrick Hannaway, John Ramsay (Journalists), Delia Lindsay (Society Lady), James Vaughan (Sir Charles Dilke), Brendan O'Hea (Barney), Theo Steele (Footman)

Antony Sher, Judi Dench

Still overcome by grief three years after the death of her husband, Queen Victoria places herself in self-exile until Scotsman John Brown coaxes her back into the world. This film received Oscar nominations for actress (Judi Dench) and makeup.

Judi Dench, Billy Connolly

Billy Connolly

OPERATION CONDOR

(DIMENSION) formerly *Armour of God II: Operation Condor*; Producer, Leonard Ho; Executive Producer, Raymond Chow; Director, Jackie Chan; Screenplay, Jackie Chan, Edward Tang; English Dialogue, Maggie Dickie; Photography, Wong Ngok Tai; Art Directors, Oliver Wong, Eddie Ma, Lo Ka Yiu; Music, Stephen Endelman; Editor, Cheung Yiu Chung; Special Effects, Cinefax Workshop Co. Ltd., Unlimited Effects (HK) Ltd.; a Media Asia Distribution presentation 1991; Distributed by Miramax Films; Dolby SDDS Stereo; Technovision; Color; Rated PG-13; 92 minutes; July release

CAST

Jackie (Condor)....Jackie Chan
Ada....Carol Cheng
Elsa....Eva Cobo De Garcia
Momoko....Shoko Ikeda
Adolf....Alfred Brel Sanchez
Tasza....Jonathan Isgar
Amon....Daniel Mintz
Duke Scapio....Bozidar Smiljanic
and Ken Goodman, Gregory Tartaglia, Lyn Percival, Bruce Fontaine, Archer Wayne, Brandon Charles, Low Houi Kang, Peter Klimenko, Christian Perrochaud (Adolf's Guards), Mark King, Bryan Baker (Duke's Guards), Charles Yeomans (Man with Stolen Clothes)

The United Nations sends secret agent Condor to stop a group of international terrorists who have discovered the whereabouts of a fortune in stolen gold that they plan to use for evil means.

Jackie Chan, Carol Cheng

PAPERBACK ROMANCE

(GOLDWYN) Producer, Bob Weis; Director/Screenplay, Ben Lewin; Co-Producer, Judi Levine; Photography, Vince Monton; Editor, Peter Carrodus; Designer, Peta Lawson; Costumes, Anna Borghesi; Music, Paul Grabowsky; Casting, Liz Mulinar Consultants; an Australian Film Finance Corporation in association with Generation Films, Lewin Films and Pandora Cinema presentation; Australian, 1994; Dolby Digital Stereo; Color; Rated R; 89 minutes; August release

CAST

Sophie....Gia Carides
Eddie....Anthony LaPaglia
Gloria....Rebecca Gibney
Yuri....Jacek Koman
Kate....Sioban Tuke
Bruce Wrightman....Lewis Fiander
Anne-Marie LePine....Robyn Nevin
George LePine....Marshall Napier
Myra....Mary-Anne Fahey
Benny....Michael Edward-Stevens
Nicholas....Steady Eddy
Det. Sgt. Scott....Michael Vietch
Det. Tyrone....Russell Fletcher
Sophie's Doctor....Nicholas Bell
Ernst....Kurt Ludescher
Diamond Cutter....Max Bruch
Library Clerk....Lynda Gibson
and David Watson (Professor-type at Party), Kirk Alexander (Celebrant), Paul Karo (Defence Lawyer), Terry Norris (Judge), Alvin Chong (Chinese Doctor), Ernie Grey (Doctor at Wedding), Agnieszka Perepeczko (Woman at Wedding), Carolyn Bock (Hotel Hospitality Lady), Maggie Stevens (Mrs. Wrightman), Cliff Ellen (Airline Porter), Alexandra Lewin (Music Student), Paul Wishart (Courier), Mandy Bowden (Marjorie), Alan Levy (Wrong Man at Party), Geoff Lipton (Taxi Driver), Suzanne Chamberlain (Woman in Hotel Lobby), Petru Gheorghiu (Party Host), Phillipa Lee (Woman at Party), Teresa Blake (Woman on Greek Island), Pandora Finch (Madelaine), Eli Yanay (Man on Greek Island), Karen Davitt (Artist), Tasilimn Emiabata (Artist's Model), Teresa Blake (Catburglar)

Sophie, a romance novelist, is overheard spinning the erotic details of her latest work by Eddie, a jewelry dealer, who finds himself drawn to her sexual tastes.

Anthony LaPaglia, Rebecca Gibney

Anthony LaPaglia, Gia Carides

TROJAN EDDIE

(CASTLE HILL) Producer, Emma Burge; Executive Producers, Rod Stoneman, Alan J. Wands, Kevin Menton, Nigel Warren-Green; Director, Gillies MacKinnon; Screenplay, Billy Roche; Co-Producer, Seamus Byrne; Photography, John deBorman; Designer, Frank Conway; Costumes, Consolata Boyle; Editor, Scott Thomas; Music, John Keane; Casting, Hubbard Casting; a Channel Four Films presentation with the participation of Bord Scannan na hEireann/The Irish Film Board; an Initial Films production in association with Irish Screen; British-Irish, 1996; Dolby Stereo; Color; Not rated; 105 minutes; August release

CAST

Trojan Eddie	Stephen Rea
John Power	Richard Harris
Dermot	Stuart Townsend
Kathleen	Aislin McGuckin
Ginger	Brendan Gleeson
Raymie	Sean McGinley
Shirley	Angeline Ball
Carol	Angela O'Driscoll
Betty	Brid Brennan
Patsy McDonagh	Jason Gilroy
Rosy	Maria McDermottroe
Gerry	Sean Lawlor
Lady Cash	Britta Smith
Matt	Pat Laffan
Reg	Jimmy Keogh
Eddie's Mother	Gladys Sheehan
Arthur	Noel Donovan

and Aoife MacEoin (Landlady), Pecker Dunne (Traveller), Linda Quinn (Travelling Woman), Dolores Keane (Red-Haired Traveller), Orla Charlton (Young Woman), Billy Roche (Man), Des Cave (Priest), Michael Collins (Second Traveller), Aisling O'Flanagan (Daughter #1—Jenny), Roisin O'Flanagan (Daughter #2—Rebecca), Eugene O'Brien (Lady Cash's Son), Charlotte Bradley (Farmer's Wife)

Eddie, just released from prison, sets up a business selling items from the back of a van with partner Dermot, the son of the head of a band of Gaelic gypsies who covets the same woman as Dermot.

Dominique Valadié, Anouk Grinberg

Richard Harris, Aislin McGuckin

Stephen Rea

MON HOMME

(ARTIFICIAL EYE) Producer, Alain Sarde; Director/Screenplay, Bertrand Blier; Photography, Pierre Lhomme; Set Designer, Willy Holt, Georges Glon; Editor, Claudine Merlin; Costumes, Christian Gasc; Music, Barry White, Henryk Mikolaji Gorecki; Casting, Gérard Moulévrier; Produced by Les Films Alain Sarde—Plateau A—Studio Images 2, with the participation of Canal+; French, 1996; Dolby Digital Stereo; Panavision; Color; Not rated; 95 minutes; August release

CAST

Marie	Anouk Grinberg
Jeannot	Gérard Lanvin
Sanguine	Valéria Bruni Tedeschi
Jean-François	Olivier Martinez
Bérangère	Sabine Azéma
Gilberte	Dominique Valadié
First Client	Mathieu Kassovitz
Second Client	Jacques François
Third Client	Michel Galabru
Mélissa	Dominique Lollia
Personnel Director	Bernard Fresson
Inspecteur Marvier	Bernard Le Coq
Monsieur Claude	Jean-Pierre Léaud

Marie, a good-hearted prostitute, takes in Jeannot, a homeless man, who becomes her lover and her pimp.

THE FULL MONTY

(FOX SEARCHLIGHT) Producer, Uberto Pasolini; Director, Peter Cattaneo; Screenplay, Simon Beaufoy; Photography, John de Borman; Designer, Max Gottlieb; Costumes, Jill Taylor; Co-Producers, Polly Leys, Paul Bucknor; Associate Producer, Lesley Stewart; Music, Anne Dudley; Choreographer, Suzanne Grand; Casting, Susie Figgis; a Redwave Films production; British; Dolby Stereo; Metrocolour London; Rated R; 95 minutes; August release

CAST

Gaz....Robert Carlyle
Gerald....Tom Wilkinson
Dave....Mark Addy
Jean....Lesley Sharp
Mandy....Emily Woof
Lomper....Steve Huison
Horse....Paul Barber
Guy....Hugo Speer
Linda....Deirdre Costello
Reg....Bruce Jones
Nathan....William Snape
Barry....Paul Butterworth
Alan....Dave Hill
Terry....Andrew Livingstone
Sharon....Vinny Dhillon
Bee....Kate Layden
Sheryl....Joanna Swain
Louise....Diane Lane
Dole Clerk....Kate Rutter
Lomper's Mum....June Broughton
Police Inspector....Glenn Cunningham
Duty Sergeant....Chris Brailsford
Policeman....Steve Garti
Job Club Manager....Malcolm Pitt
Director....Dennis Blanch
Social Worker....Daryl Fishwick
Repossession Man....David Lonsdale
Horse's Mum....Muriel Hunt
Beryl....Fiona Watts
Horse's Sisters....Theresa Maduemezia, Fiona Nelson
Brass Band....The British Steel Stocksbridge Band

A group of men, unable to find work since the closing of their steelmill, hit upon the outrageous idea of earning money by starting a striptease act. 1997 Academy Award winner for Best Original Musical or Comedy Score. This film received additional Oscar nominations for picture, director, and screenplay.

Paul Barber

Hugo Speer

William Snape, Robert Carlyle

Robert Carlyle

Tom Wilkinson, Hugo Speer, Paul Barber, Robert Carlyle

Tom Wilkinson, William Snape, Robert Carlyle, Steve Huison, Hugo Speer, Paul Barber, Mark Addy

William Snape, Mark Addy, Robert Carlyle, Steve Huison, Tom Wilkinson

Mark Benton, Lynda Steadman

Katrin Cartlidge, Joe Tucker

Lynda Steadman, Katrin Cartlidge

CAREER GIRLS

(OCTOBER) Producer, Simon Channing-Williams; Director/Screenplay, Mike Leigh; Photography, Dick Pope; Music, Marianne Jean-Baptiste, Tony Remy; Editor, Robin Sales; Designer, Eve Stewart; a Channel Four Films presentation of a Thin Man production; British; Dolby Stereo; Color; Rated R: 87 minutes; August release

CAST

Hannah ....Katrin Cartlidge
Annie ....Lynda Steadman
Claire ....Kate Byers
Ricky ....Mark Benton
Mr. Evans ....Andy Serkis
Adrian ....Joe Tucker
Ricky's Nan ....Margo Stanley
Lecturer..Michael Healy

Annie and Hannah, who have not seen each other in the six years since they attended University, reunite for a weekend together, one that results in a re-evaluation of their friendship.

Katrin Cartlidge

Katrin Cartlidge, Lynda Steadman

LOVE SERENADE

(MIRAMAX) Producer, Jan Chapman; Director/Screenplay, Shirley Barrett; Photography, Mandy Walker; Designer, Steven Jones-Eveans; Costumes, Anna Borghesi; Editor, Denise Haratzis; Casting, Alison Barrett; Presented in association with Australian Film Finance Corporation; Australian, 1996; Dolby Stereo; Super 35 Widescreen; Color; Rated R; 101 minutes; August release

CAST

Dimity Hurley........Miranda Otto
Vicki-Ann Hurley........Rebecca Frith
Ken Sherry........George Shevtsov
Albert Lee........John Alansu
Deborah........Jessica Napier
Curler Victim........Jill McWilliam
Boy on Ride........Ryan Jackson
Beautiful Baby........Sabrina Norris

In a small Australian town a pair of sisters, both of whom feel that life is passing them by, set their sights on a newly arrived disc jockey, causing a rift between them.

Rebecca Frith, Miranda Otto

Max von Sydow, Ernst Jacobi

HAMSUN

(FIRST RUN FEATURES) Producer, Erik Crone; Director/Photography, Jan Troell; Screenplay, Per Olov Enquist; Based on the book *Processen mod Hamsun* by Thorkild Hansen; Editors, Ghita Beckendorff, Jan Troell; Music, Arvo Part, Johann Strauss, Richard Wagner; Swedish-Danish-Norwegian-German, 1996; Color; Not rated; 160 minutes; August release

CAST

Knut Hamsun........Max von Sydow
Marie Hamsun........Ghita Nørby
Ellinor Hamsun........Anette Hoff
Cecilia Hamsun........Asa Söderling
Arild Hamsun........Gard B. Eidsvold
Tore Hamsun........Eindride Eidsvold
Vidkun Quisling........Sverre Anker Ousdal
Adolf Hitler........Ernst Jacobi
Psychiatrist........Erik Hivju

The true story of how Noble Prize-winning Norwegian novelist Knut Hamsun fell from his position of fame and power after blindly supporting the Nazi cause during World War II.

FIRE

(ZEITGEIST) Producers, Bobby Bedi, Deepa Mehta; Executive Producers, Suresh Bhalla, David Hamilton; Director/Screenplay, Deepa Mehta; Photography, Giles Nuttgens; Editor, Barry Farrell; Designer, Aradhana Seth; Music, A.R. Rahman; Line Producer, Anne Masson; Canadian-Indian, 1996; Ultra-Stereo; Color; Not rated; 104 minutes; August release

CAST

Radha........Shabana Azmi
Sita........Nandita Das
Ashok........Kulbushan Kharbanda
Jatin........Jaaved Jaaferi
Mundu........Ranjit Chowdhry
Biji........Kushal Rekhi

Radha, an obedient New Delhi housewife, finds solace from her loveless marriage when her brother-in-law's new wife, Sita becomes part of the household.

Shabana Azmi, Ranjit Chowdhry

THE DISAPPEARANCE OF GARCIA LORCA

(TRIUMPH) formerly *Death in Granada*; Producer, Marcos Zurinaga, Enrique Cerezo; Executive Producers, Moctesuma Esparza, Robert Katz; Director, Marcos Zurinaga; Screenplay, Marcos Zurinaga, Juan Antonio Ramos, Neil Cohen; Based on the books *The Assassination of Federico Garcia Lorca* and *Federico Garcia Lorca: A Life* by Ian Gibson; Photography, Juan Ruiz Anchia; Editor, Carole Kravetz; Designer, Gil Parrondo; Costumes, Leon Revuelta; Associate Producers, Carolyn Caldera, Palmy Carballido; a Miramar Films-Esparza/Katz co-production with Enrique Cerezo, P.C.; Spanish-Puerto Rican-U.S.; Dolby Stereo; Panavision; Color; Rated R; 114 minutes; September release

CAST

Federico Garcia Lorca ....Andy Garcia
Ricardo ....Esai Morales
Lozano ....Edward James Olmos
Colonel Aguirre...Jeroen Krabbe
Taxi ....Giancarlo Giannini
Centeno ....Miguel Ferrer
Maria Eugenia ....Marcela Walerstein
Vicente Fernandez ....Eusebio Lazaro
Nacha Montero ....Marina Saura
Mercedes..Teresa Jose Berganza
Clotilde ....Azucena De La Fuente
Gabino ....Emilio Munoz
and Naim Thomas (Ricardo—14 years old), Gonzalo Penche (Jorge Aguirre), Alicia Borrachero (Lydia), Jose Coronado (Nestor Gonzalez), Ivonne Coll (Angelina Gonzalez), Miriam Tubert (Gonzalez's Mother), Jill Ramez (Carlota), Willie Marquez (Lorca's Father), Carmen Zapata (Lorca's Mother), Palmy Carballido (Concha Garcia Lorca), Simon Andreu (General Velez), Lara Dominguez (Lydia—11 years old), Ellea Ratier (Maria Eugenia—11 years old), Blaki (Aguirre's Servant), Perico Duran (Concierge), Concha Gomez Conde (Concierge's Wife), Gelian Cotto (Ricardo's Daughter), George Lian Cotto (Ricardo's Son), Jesus Daniel, Luis Gutierrez, Freddie De Arce, John Garcia (Thugs)

Ricardo, a journalist settled in San Juan, decides to investigate the mysterious events around the murder of his idol, poet Federico Garcia Lorca.

Mathieu Kassovitz, Anouk Grinberg

Andy Garcia

A SELF MADE HERO

(STRAND) Producer, Patrick Godeau; Director, Jacques Audiard; Screenplay, Alain Le Henry, Jacques Audiard; Based on the novel by Jean-François Deniau; Photography, Jean-Marc Fabre; Designer, Michel Vandestien; Costumes, Caroline De Vivaise; Editor, Juliette Welfling; Music, Alexandre Desplat; Presented in association with Alicelo - Lumiere - France 3 Cinema - M6 Films - Initial Groupe co-production with Cofimage 7 - Studio Images 2 - Canal+ - The Centre National de la Cinematographie and the support of Procirep; French; Dolby Stereo; Color; Not rated; 105 minutes; September release

CAST

Albert Dehousse...Mathieu Kassovitz
Servane...Anouk Grinberg
Yvette ....Sandrine Kiberlain
Dionnet...Albert Dupontel
Older Albert ....Jean-Louis Trintignant
Madame Louvier/Madame Revuz/The Général's Wife.......Nadia Barentin
Ernst ....Bernard Bloch
Louvier...François Chattot
Caron ....Philippe Duclos
Man "English Girls"......................................Armand de Baudry D'Asson
Nervoix...Wilfred Benaiche
Monsieur Jo...François Berleand
Leguen...Philippe Berodot
and Gilles Del Frate (The Partisan), Stéfan Elbaum, Christophe Kourotchkine ("Little Versailles" Men), Marc Ernotte (De Vaincourt), Jérôme Floch (Etienne), Isabelle Gruault (Lutétia Young Woman), Donatien Guillot (Knickerbocker), Philippe Harel (Information Officer), Philippe Lehembre (Maître Becquard), François Levantal (Delavelle), Patrick Ligardes (Malbert), Clotilde Mollet (Odette), Philippe Mahon (The Général), Yann Pradal (FF1 1), Bruno Putzulu (Meyer), Georges Siatidis (Bauchamps), Laurent Vacher (Maldoror Man), Yves Verhoeven (Boutin), David Fernandes (Albert, child), Xavier Arcache (Jean Caron, child), Eléonore Godeau (Little Girl at Kiosk), Thomas Vindevogel (Lout)

Albert Dehousse, a life-long liar, creates a past for himself as a member of the French Resistance during World War II.

DIFFERENT FOR GIRLS

(FIRST LOOK PICTURES) Producer, John Chapman; Executive Producers, George Faber, Laura Gregory; Director, Richard Spence; Screenplay, Tony Marchant; Line Producer, Barney Reisz; Photography, Sean Van Hales; Designer, Grenville Horner; Editor, David Gamble; Music, Stephen Warbeck; Costumes, Susannah Buxton; Make-Up Designer, Fae Hammond; a BBC Films in association with CiBy Sales Limited and Maurice Marciano/Great Guns presentation of an X Pictures Film; British; Dolby Stereo; Color; Rated R; 92 minutes; September release

Rupert Graves, Steven Mackintosh

CAST

Paul Prentice .... Rupert Graves
Kim Foyle .... Steven Mackintosh
Pamela .... Miriam Margolyes
Jean .... Saskia Reeves
Alison .... Charlotte Coleman
Neil .... Neil Dudgeon
Angela .... Nisha K. Nayar
Defense Solicitor .... Lia Williams
Recovery Agent .... Ian Dury
DS Cole .... Robert Pugh
Taxi Driver .... Philip Davis
PC Ken .... Rick Warden
PC Alan .... Kevin Allen
Sergeant Harry .... Gerard Horan
Prosecuting Solicitor .... Edward Tudor-Pole
Mike Rendell .... Adrian Rawlins
Barry Stapleton .... Peter-Hugo Daly
Biker Jim .... Shend

and Llewella Gideon (Receptionist), Charles De'Ath (Young Man at Gig), Robert Demeger (Magistrate), Malcolm Shields (Soldier), Graham Fellows (Dispatch Manager), Ruth Sheen (Nosey Woman), Christie Jennings (Waitress), Stephen Walker (Karl Foyle), Blake Ritson (Young Prentice), James D. White (Finer), Colin Ridgewell (Shrimp), Jamie Leyser (Matthew Payne)

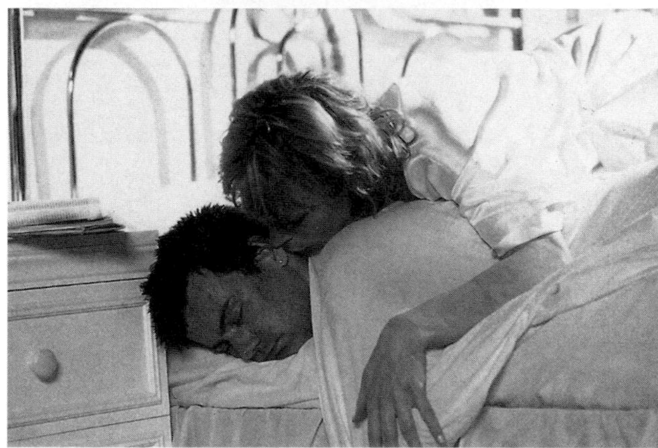

Rupert Graves, Steven Mackintosh

Paul Prentice, an aging London bike messenger, meets up with Kim Foyle who, prior to her sex change operation, had been Paul's taunted schoolmate, Karl.

Rupert Graves

Nisha K. Nayar, Rupert Graves

INTIMATE RELATIONS

(FOX SEARCHLIGHT) Producers, Angela Hart, Lisa Hope, Jon Slan; Executive Producer, Gareth Jones; Director/Screenplay, Philip Goodhew; Line Producers, Simon Hardy, Simon Scotland; Photography, Andrés Garréton; Designer, Caroline Greville-Morris; Music, Lawrence Shragge; Editor, Pia Di Ciaula; Casting, Susan Forrest, Maximilian Boxer; a Handmade Films presentation of a Boxer Films and Paragon Entertainment Corporation production; British-Canadian, 1996; Dolby Stereo; Color; Rated R; 102 minutes; September release

CAST

Marjorie Beasley.......Julie Walters
Harold Guppy.......Rupert Graves
Stanley Beasley.......Matthew Walker
Joyce Beasley.......Laura Sadler
Deirdre.......Holly Aird
Maurice Guppy.......Les Dennis
Iris Guppy.......Elizabeth McKechnie
George.......James Aidan
Mr. Pugh.......Michael Bertenshaw
Mrs. Fox-Davies.......Judy Clifton
Deirdre's Baby.......Christopher Cook
Pauline.......Candace Hallinan

and Charles Hart (Hotel Receptionist), George Hart (Car Vendor), Amanda Holden (Pamela), Nicholas Hoult (Bobby), Annie Keller (Jean), Elsie Kelly (Enid), Max (Princess Margaret), Gary Meredith (Mr. Jarvis), Sarah-Jane McKechnie (Mrs. Latimer), Lucy Rivers (Valerie), Sonya Sadler (Mrs. Clitherow), Leanne Summers (Girl at Swimming Pool)

In a small town in 1954 England, Marjorie Beasley, a seemingly content housewife in her early fifties, makes it her goal to seduce the younger man who has moved into her family's home as a lodger.

Rupert Graves, Julie Walters

Julie Walters, Rupert Graves

Julie Walters, Rupert Graves, Laura Sadler

CAPITAINE CONAN

(KINO) Producers, Alain Sarde, Frederic Bourboulon; Director, Bertrand Tavernier; Screenplay, Bertrand Tavernier, Jean Cosmos; Based on the novel by Roger Vercel; Photography, Alain Choquart; Art Director, Guy-Claude Francois; Editors, Luce Grunenwaldt, Laure Blancherie, Khadicha Bariha-Simsolo; Costumes, Jacqueline Moreau, Agnes Evein; Music, Oswald D'Andrea; Produced by Les Films Alain Sarde/Little Bear Films/TF1 Films Production, with the participation of Canal+ and Studio Images 2; French, 1996;Widescreen; Color; Not rated; 132 minutes; September release

CAST

Conan .... Philippe Torreton
Norbert .... Samuel Le Bihan
De Scève .... Bernard Le Coq
Beuillard .... Laurent Schilling
Rouzic .... Jean-Yves Roan
Grenais .... Phillipe Helies
Caboulet .... Tonio Descanville
Corporal Armurier .... Eric Savin
Mahut .... Olivier Loustau
Lethore .... Jean-Marie Juan
Madeline Erlane .... Catherine Rich
Commandant Bouvier .... Francois Berleand
General Pitard de Lauzier .... Claude Rich

and Andre Falcon (Colonel Voirin), Claude Brosset (Pere Dubreuil), Crina Muresan (Ilyana), Cecile Vassort (Georgette), Francois Levantal (Forgeol), Pierre Val (Jean Erlane), Roger Knobelspiess (Major Cuypene), Frederic Pierrot (Train Officer), Jean-Claude Calon (Officer Greffier Loisy)

Following World War I, Capitaine Conan and his troops are ordered to stay behind in the Balkans to act as border patrol, an assignment that leads to the arrest of two of the soldiers in connection to the murder of two women.

© Kino International

Philippe Torreton

Gregoire Colin

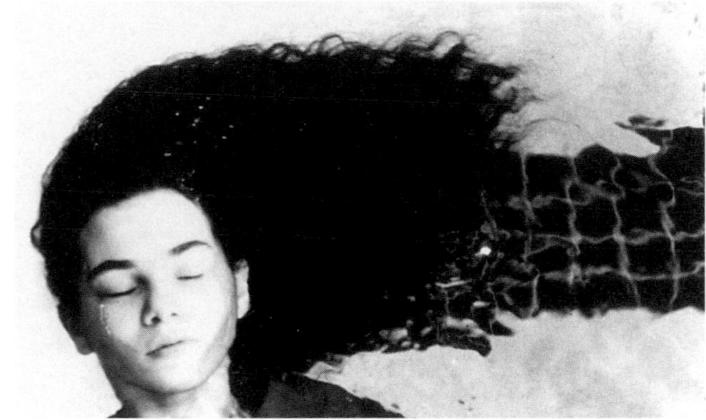

Alice Houri

NENETTE AND BONI

(STRAND) Producer, Georges Benayoun; Executive Producer, Francoise Guglielmi; Director, Claire Denis; Screenplay, Jean-Pol Fargeau, Claire Denis; Photography, Agnes Godard; Set Designer, Arnaud de Moleron; Costumes, Elisabeth Tavernier; Editor, Yann Dedet; Music, Tindersticks; French, 1996; Dolby Stereo; Color; Not rated; 103 minutes; October release

CAST

Boni .... Gregoire Colin
Nenette .... Alice Houri
The Baker Woman .... Valeria Bruni-Tedeschi
The Baker .... Vincent Gallo
Mr. Luminaire .... Jacques Nolot
The Uncle .... Gerard Meylan
The Gynecologist .... Alex Descas
The Wise Woman .... Jamila Farah

and Sebastien Pons, Mounir Aissa, Christophe Carmona, Djellali El'Ouzeri, Malek Sultan (Boni's Friends)

Boni, a lonely young man who works as a pizza maker, finds his life disrupted by the arrival of his pregnant fifteen-year-old sister Nenette.

© Strand Releasing

A LIFE LESS ORDINARY

Cameron Diaz, Ewan McGregor

(20TH CENTURY FOX) Producer, Andrew MacDonald; Director, Danny Boyle; Screenplay, John Hodge; Photography, Brian Tufano; Designer, Kave Quinn; Editor, Masahiro Hirakubo; Costumes, Rachael Fleming; Music Supervisor, Randall Poster; Line Producer, Margaret Hilliard; Choreographer, Adam Shankman; Casting, Donna Isaacson; Music, David Arnold; a Figment Film, developed and supported by Channel 4 Films; British; Dolby Digital Stereo; Super 35 Widescreen; Deluxe color; Rated R; 103 minutes; October release

CAST

Robert	Ewan McGregor
Celine	Cameron Diaz
O'Reilly	Holly Hunter
Jackson	Delroy Lindo
Mr. Naville	Ian Holm
Mayhew	Ian McNeice
Elliot	Stanley Tucci
Al	Tony Shalhoub
Gabriel	Dan Hedaya
Ted	Frank Kanig
Frank	Mel Winkler
Ms. Gesteten	Anne Cullimore Decker
Lily	K.K. Dodds
Walt	Christopher Gorham
Tod	Maury Chaykin
Hiker	Timothy Olyphant
Karaoke Cowboy	Robert Kellogg
Felix	David Stifel
Attendant	Duane Stephens
Cashier	Jayceen Craven
Bank Tellers	Crystal Martinez, Kitty Brunson
Customer	Jan Hanks
Bank Daughter	Mary-Cristina Schaub
Client	Chuck Gowdy
Celine's Mom	Judith Ivey
Secretary	Toni Lynn Byrd

Delroy Lindo, Holly Hunter

Bored and beautiful Celine is delighted when Robert, one of her father's disgruntled employees, decides to kidnap her and hold her for ransom.

Ewan Mc Gregor, Cameron Diaz

Cameron Diaz

I LOVE YOU, I LOVE YOU NOT

(AVALANCHE) Producers, Joe Caracciolo Jr., John Fiedler, Mark Tarlov; Executive Producers, Cameron McCracken, Bob Weinstein, Harvey Weinstein; Co-Producer, Frank Henschke, Pierre Novat; Director, Billy Hopkins; Screenplay Wendy Kesselman; Photography, Maryse Alberti; Designers, Bill Barclay, Gudrun Roscher; Editors, Paul Karasick, Jim Clark; Costumes, Sabine Boebbis, Candice Donnelly; a Polar Enterainment/Die Hauskunst & Romb/Chrysalis Films Intl/Canal+/Filmstifung North Phine Westphalia production; French-German-British-U.S. 1996; Color; Not rated; 89 minutes; October release

CAST

Daisy .... Claire Danes
Nana .... Jeanne Moreau
Ethan Wells .... Jude Law
Mr. Gilman .... Jerry Tanklow
Jane .... Carrie Slaza
Chris .... Josiah A. Mayo
Jessica .... Emily Burkes-Nossiter
Hope .... Natasha Wolff
Tony .... James Van Der Beek
Seth .... Kris Park
Alison .... Lauren Fox
Angel of Death .... Robert Sean Leonard

Daisy, a shy intelligent teenager who feels alienated from her classmates, find sanctuary in her weekend visits to her grandmother, a Holocaust survivor with whom she shares a deep bond.

Jude Law, Claire Danes

Claire Danes, Jeanne Moreau

Danny Gilmore, Jason Cadieux

Danny Gilmore, Jason Cadieux

LILIES

(TURBULENT ARTS) Producers, Anna Stratton, Robin Cass, Arnie Gelbart; Director, John Greyson; Screenplay, Michel Marc Bouchard; Photography, Daniel Jobin; Designer, Sandra Kybartas; Costumes, Linda Muir; Editor, Andre Corriveau; Music, Mychael Danna; a Triptych Media Inc./Galafilm Inc. co-production; Canadian, 1996; Color; Not rated; 95 minutes; October release

CAST

The Countess .... Brent Carver
The Bishop .... Marcel Sabourin
Older Simon .... Aubert Pallascio
Simon .... Jason Cadieux
Vallier .... Danny Gilmore
Young Bilodeau .... Matthew Ferguson
Lydie-Anne .... Alexander Chapman
The Baroness .... Remy Girard
The Baron .... Robert Lalonde
Chaplain/Father St. Michael .... Ian D. Clark
Timothee .... Gary Farmer

The prisoners at a federal penitentiary kidnap a visiting Catholic bishop and force him to watch a reenactment of an event that took place between him and one of the inmates forty years earlier.

THE WIND IN THE WILLOWS

Nicol Williamson, Steve Coogan, Eric Idle

(COLUMBIA) Producers, John Goldstone, Jake Eberts; Director/Screenplay, Terry Jones; Based on the novel by Kenneth Grahame; Photography, David Tattersall; Designer/Costumes, James Acheson; Music/Songs, John Du Prez, Terry Jones, Andre Jacquemin, Dave Howman; Music, John Du Prez; Editor, Julian Doyle; Make-Up Design, Jan Sewell; Casting, Irene Lamb; Choreographer, Arlene Phillips; Visual Effects, Peter Chiang, Peter Hutchinson; an Allied Filmmakers presentation of a John Goldstone production; British; Color; Rated PG; 83 minutes; October release

CAST

Mole .... Steve Coogan
Rat .... Eric Idle
Toad .... Terry Jones
Chief Weasel .... Antony Sher
Badger .... Nicol Williamson
Mr. Toad's Lawyer .... John Cleese
Judge .... Stephen Fry
Engine Driver .... Bernard Hill
The Sun .... Michael Palin
Car Salesman .... Nigel Planer
Jailer's Daughter .... Julia Sawalha
Tea-Lady .... Victoria Wood
St. John Weasel .... Robert Bathurst
Sentry .... Don Henderson
Geoffrey Weasel/Mole's Clock .... Richard James
Clarence Weasel .... Keith Lee Castle
Prosecution Counsel .... Roger Ashton-Griffiths
Clerk of the Court .... Bernard Padden
Samantha .... Sarah Crowden
Justi .... Hugo Blick
Policeman .... William Lawrance
Guard .... Richard Ridings
Detectives .... Peter Whitfield, John Levitt
Elderly Gentleman .... John Boswall
Booking Clerk .... David Hatton
Drunken Weasel .... Graham McTavish

Terry Jones

The peaceful riverside animals find their land being seized by the Wild Wood weasels who intend to build a factory and slaughterhouse. The novel was previously featured as part of the animated Walt Disney film The Adventures of Ichabod and Mr. Toad (1949).

John Cleese

Eric Idle, Steve Coogan

HAPPY TOGETHER

(KINO) Producer/Director/Screenplay, Wong Kar-Wai; Executive Producer, Chan Ye-Cheng; Photography, Christopher Doyle; Associate Producers, Hiroko Shinohara, T.J. Chung, Christophe Tseng Ching-Chao; Designer, William Chang Suk-Ping; Editors, William Chang Suk-Ping, Wong Ming-Lam; Music, Danny Chung; a Block 2 Pictures Inc. in association with Prenom H Co., Ltd., a Seowoo Film Col. Ltd. presentation of a Jet Tone Production; Hong Kong/Chinese; Dolby Stereo; Color/Black and White; Not rated; 97 minutes; October release

CAST

Lai Yiu-Fai ....Tony Leung Chiu-Wai
Ho Po-Wing ....Leslie Cheung Kwok-Wing
Chang...Chang Chen

Believing it will help their floundering relationship, Ho Po-Wing and his lover Lai Yiu-Fai move to Buenos Aires, only to find themselves breaking up.

Leslie Cheung, Tony Leung

Matt Day, Frances O'Connor

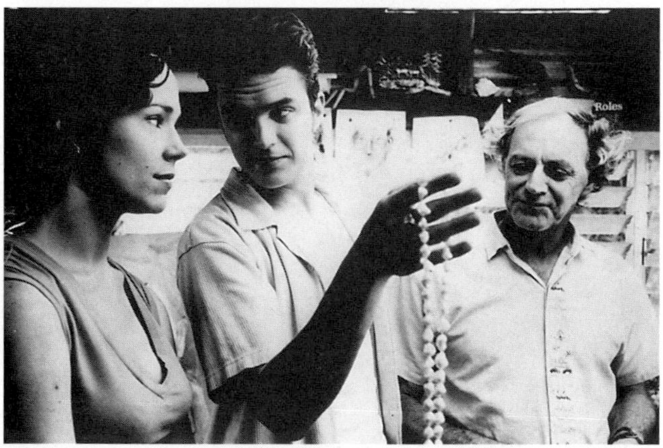

Frances O'Connor, Matt Day, Barry Otto

Matt Day, Frances O'Connor

KISS OR KILL

(OCTOBER) Producers, Bill Bennett, Jennifer Bennett; Co-Producer, Corrie Soeterboek; Executive Producers, Mikael Borglund, Gary Hamilton; Director/Screenplay, Bill Bennett; Photography, Malcolm McCulloch; Designer, Andrew Plumer; Editor, Henry Dangar; a Bill Bennett Production in association with the Australian Film Finance Corporation; Australian; Dolby Stereo; Color; Rated R; 93 minutes; November release

CAST

Nikki ....Frances O'Connor
Al..Matt Day
Hummer ....Chris Haywood
Adler Jones...Barry Otto
Crean..Andrew S. Gilbert
Zipper Doyle ....Barry Langrishe
Stan..Max Cullen
Bel...Jennifer Bennett

Nikki and Al, a pair of grifters who make their money by robbing businessmen, are forced to flee when one of the men accidentally dies leaving them with a suitcase containing an incriminating video tape.

BEAN

(GRAMERCY) Producers, Peter Bennett-Jones, Eric Fellner, Tim Bevan; Executive Producer, Richard Curtis; Director, Mel Smith; Screenplay, Richard Curtis, Robin Driscoll; Based on the character devised by Rowan Atkinson and Richard Curtis; Co-Producer, Rebecca O'Brien; Photography, Francis Kenny; Designer, Peter Larkin; Editor, Christopher Blunden; Costumes, Hope Hanafin; Music, Howard Goodall; Casting, Ronnie Yeskel, John and Ros Hubbard; a PolyGram Filmed Entertainment presentation of a Working Title production in association with Tiger Aspect Films; British; Dolby Stereo; Technicolor; Rated PG-13; 90 minutes; November release

Rowan Atkinson, Peter MacNicol

CAST

Mr. Bean ....Rowan Atkinson
David Langley...Peter MacNicol
Alison Langley ....Pamela Reed
George Grierson..Harris Yulin
General Newton ....Burt Reynolds
Stingo Wheelie ....Johnny Galecki
Kevin Langley...Andrew J. Lawrence
Jennifer Langley ....Tricia Vessey
Lord Walton ....Peter Egan
Chairman ....Sir John Mills
Gareth ....Peter Capaldi
Delilah...June Brown
Dr. Rosenblum...Peter James
Dr. Cutler ....Clive Corner
Dick Journo ....Rob Brownstein
Phyllis Quill ....Julia Pearlstein
Elmer ....Larry Drake
Walter Merchandise ....Tom McGowan
Bernice Schimmel ....Sandra Oh
Stewardess Nicely...Alison Goldie
Passenger Tucker ....Dakin Matthews
Timmy Pewker, Jr. ....Scott Charles
Officer Stubbles ....Thomas Mills
Mrs. Goodwoman..Ronnie Yeskel
Lieutenant Brutus...Richard Gant

and Chris Ellis (Detective Butler), Priscilla Shanks (Sylvia Grierson), Richard Hicks (Kart Pusherman), Danny Goldring (Security Buck), Gigi Fields (Nurse Desking), Lela Ivey (Nurse Pots), David Doty (Dr. Jacobson), Robert Curtis-Brown (Doctor Frowning), April Grace (Nurse Pans), Perry Anzilotti (Dr. Squeaking), Janni Brenn (Nurse Dyper), Annette Helde (Nurse Gripes)

Rowan Atkinson

Mr. Bean, a bumbling employee of London's National Art Gallery, is sent to America to accompany the masterpiece Whistler's Mother, which is to be exhibited in Los Angeles.

Andrew Lawrence, Peter MacNicol, Tricia Vessey, Pamela Reed, Rowan Atkinson

Peter MacNicol, Rowan Atkinson

BENT

(GOLDWYN) Producers, Michael Solinger, Dixie Linder; Executive Producers, Sarah Radclyffe, Hisami Kuroiwa; Director, Sean Mathias; Screenplay, Martin Sherman, based on his play; Photography, Yorgos Arvanitis; Designer, Stephen Brimson Lewis; Co-Producers, Sean Mathias, Martin Sherman; Editor, Isabel Lorente; Music, Philip Glass; Costumes, Stewart Meachem; Casting, Andy Pryor; a Channel Four Films and Goldwyn Entertainment Company presentation in association with NDF Inc., Ask Kodansha Co. Ltd. and the Arts Council of England; Distributed by MGM Distribution Co.; British; Dolby Stereo; Rank color; Rated NC-17; 105 minutes; November release

Clive Owen, Lothaire Bluteau

CAST

Horst .... Lothaire Bluteau
Max .... Clive Owen
Rudy .... Brian Webber
Uncle Freddie .... Ian McKellen
Greta .... Mick Jagger
Wolf .... Nikolaj Waldau
Stormtrooper .... Jude Law
Waiter .... Gresby Nash
Half-Woman, Half-Man .... Suzanne Bertish
Gestapo Man .... David Meyer
SS Captain .... Stefan Marling
SS Guards .... Richard Laing, Crispian Belfrage
Muttering Woman .... Johanna Kirby
Fluff in Park .... David Phelan
Officer on Train .... Rupert Graves
Guards on Train .... David Stark, Charlie Watts
Girl on Train .... Holly Davidson
Guard on Road .... Rupert Penry Jones
Corporal .... Paul Kynman
Captain .... Paul Bettany

and Claire Cunningham, Shira Haviv, Filip Van Huffel, Sacha Lee, Ben Maher, Jane Mason (Random Dance Company), Nat (Flame Throwing Man), Packer (Happy Sad Man), Ernesto (Leaping Man), Myer Taub (Rudy's Dresser), Geraldine Sherman, Rachel Weisz (Prostitutes), Mary Davidson, Sadie Frost, Lou Gish, Simon Hammerstein, Johan Johnstone, Chris Karlitz, Mark Misauer, Howard Sacks, Mandy Stone, William Stone, Daisy de Villeneuve, Poppy de Villeneuve, Jane de Villeneuve, Helen Whitehouse, Zed (Max's Friends)

Mick Jagger

Max's promiscuous Berlin nightlife is dispruted when the SS decides to wipe out Germany's gay community, sending Max and his lover Rudy on the run. Ian McKellen, who plays Uncle Rudy, appeared as Max in the original 1979 London production.

Brian Webber, Clive Owen

Clive Owen, Ian McKellen

Alison Elliott, Alex Jennings, Helena Bonham Carter

Charlotte Rampling, Helena Bonham Carter

Linus Roache, Alison Elliott

Alison Elliott, Helena Bonham Carter, Linus Roache

THE WINGS OF THE DOVE

(MIRAMAX) Producers, Stephen Evans, David Parfitt; Executive Producers, Bob Weinstein, Harvey Weinstein, Paul Feldsher; Director, Iain Softley; Screenplay, Hossein Amini; Based on the novel by Henry James; Photography, Eduardo Serra; Designer, John Beard; Editor, Tariq Anwar; Music, Ed Shearmur; Costumes, Sandy Powell; Casting, Michelle Guish; a Renaissance Films production; British; Dolby Digital Stereo; Super 35 Widescreen; Fujicolor; Rated R; 101 minutes; November release

CAST

Kate Croy ....Helena Bonham Carter
Merton Densher..Linus Roache
Millie Theale...Alison Elliott
Aunt Maude ....Charlotte Rampling
Susan..Elizabeth McGovern
Kate's Father ....Michael Gambon
Lord Mark...Alex Jennings
Journalists ....Ben Miles, Philip Wright
Butler...Alexander John
Opium Den Lady ....Shirley Chantrell
Merton's Party Companion...Diana Kent
Eugenio...Georgio Serafini
Concierge...Rachele Crisafulli

Told she will be disinherited if she continues her relationship with journalist Merton Densher, Kate Croy plots to have Merton romance and wed the fatally ill heiress Millie Theale. This film received Oscar nominations for actress (Helena Bonham Carter), cinematography, costume design, and adapted screenplay.

Helena Bonham Carter, Linus Roache

Alison Elliott, Linus Roache, Helena Bonham Carter

Linus Roache, Helena Bonham Carter

Alison Elliott, Linus Roache, Helena Bonham Carter

Stephen Dillane, Woody Harrelson

Marisa Tomei

Emira Nusevic, Stephen Dillane

WELCOME TO SARAJEVO

(MIRAMAX) Producers, Graham Broadbent, Damian Jones; Director, Michael Winterbottom; Screenplay, Frank Cottrell Boyce; Based on the book *Natasha's Story* by Michael Nicholson; Photography, Daf Hobson; Designer, Mark Geraghty; Costumes, Janty Yates; Editor, Trevor Waite; Music, Adrian Johnston; Line Producer, Paul Sarony; Casting, Simone Ireland, Vanessa Pereira; a Channel Four Films presentation of a Dragon Pictures production; British; Dolby Digital Stereo; Super 35 Widescreen; Color; Rated R; 100 minutes; November release

CAST

Michael Henderson .... Stephen Dillane
Flynn .... Woody Harrelson
Nina .... Marisa Tomei
Emira .... Emira Nusevic
Jane Carson .... Kerry Fox
Risto .... Goran Visnjic
Gregg .... James Nesbitt
Annie McGee .... Emily Lloyd
Jacket .... Igor Dzambazov
Mrs. Savic .... Gordana Gadzic
Helen Henderson .... Juliet Aubrey
Zeljko .... Drazen Sivak
Munira .... Vesna Orel
Dragan .... Davor Janjic
Emira's Uncle .... Vladimir Jokanovic
Lucky Strike .... Izudina Brutus
Sanja .... Labina Mitevska
Alma .... Sanja Buric
Altar Boy .... Haris Secic
UN Convoy Official .... Kerry Shale
Baker .... Majda Tusar
Baker's Husband .... Miralem Zupcevic
UN V.I.P. .... Peter Kelly
Nina Co-Worker .... Dijana Bolanca
Zivko .... Nino Levi
Road Runner .... Berina Salijevic
Christopher Henderson .... Frank Dillane
Jane Henderson .... Paige Brogan-Smith

and Petar Arsovski (Joey), Viktorija Peceva (Ajsha), Nikolina Kujaca (Bride), Joana Popovska (Bride's Mother), Natali Rajinovska (Bride's Sister), Brankica Jankoska (Hairdresser), Dragan Marinkovic (Chetnik Leader), Senad Basic (Black Marketeer Leader), Ines Hadzovic (Hospital Girl), Cesir Adi (Child on Bus), Milan Plistina (Beauty Contest Compere), Ines Fancovic (Woman Shouting at Bread Queue), Haris Sarvan, Pejdah Dzevad (Black Marketeers)

British news correspondent Michael Henderson is sent to cover the 1992 siege in Sarajevo where he hopes to bring attention to the plight of the orphans left behind by the carnage.

Stephen Dillane, Dragan Marinkovic

THE SWEET HEREAFTER

(FINE LINE FEATURES) Producers, Atom Egoyan, Camelia Frieberg; Director/Screenplay, Atom Egoyan; Based on the novel by Russell Banks; Executive Producers, Robert Lantos, Andras Hamori; Photography, Paul Sarossy; Designer, Phillip Barker; Costumes, Beth Pasternak; Editor, Susan Shipton; Music, Mychael Danna; Associate Producer, David Webb; Line Producer, Sandra Cunningham; an Alliance Communications presentation of an Ego Film Arts production; Canadian; Dolby Digital Stereo; Panavision; Eastman color; Rated R; 110 minutes; November release

Earl Pastko, Arsinée Khanjian

CAST

Mitchell Stephens....Ian Holm
Nicole Burnell....Sarah Polley
Billy Ansell....Bruce Greenwood
Sam Burnell....Tom McCamus
Dolores Driscoll....Gabrielle Rose
Wanda Otto....Arsinée Khanjian
Risa Walker....Alberta Watson
Wendell Walker....Maury Chaykin
Mary Burnell....Brooke Johnson
Hartley Otto....Earl Pastko
Abbott Driscoll....David Hemblen
Alison....Stephanie Morgenstern
Zoe Stephens....Caerthan Banks
Stewardess....Kirsten Kieferle
Bear....Simon Baker
Jessica....Sarah Rosen Fruitman
Mason....Marc Donato
Sea....Devon Finn
Klara....Fides Krucker
Young Zoe....Magdalena Sokoloski
Young Mitchell....James D. Watts
Jenny....Allegra Denton
Schwartz....Peter Donaldson
Dr. Robeson....Russell Banks

Attorney Mitchell Stephens arrives in a remote town in British Columbia to investigate the details behind a devestating school bus accident in which nearly two dozen children were killed. The film received Oscar nominations for director and adapted screenplay.

Ian Holm

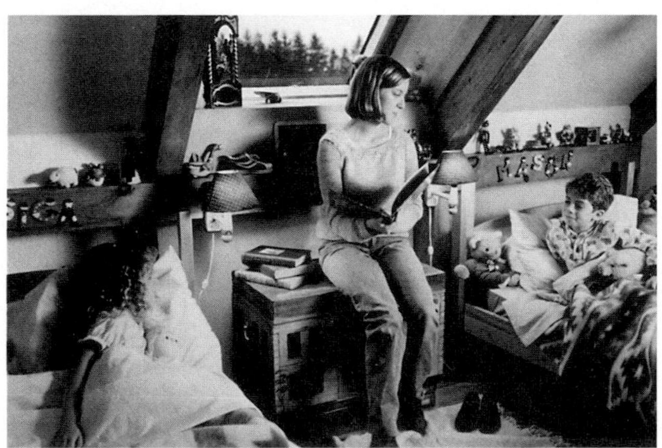

Sarah Rosen Fruitman, Sarah Polley, Marc Donato

Alberta Watson, Bruce Greenwood

THE TANGO LESSON

(SONY PICTURES CLASSICS) Producer, Christopher Sheppard; Co-Producers, Oscar Kramer, Christian Keller Sarmiento (Argentina), Simona Benzakein (France); Director/Screenplay/Music, Sally Potter; Photography, Robby Müller; Designer, Carlos Conti; Costumes, Paul Minter; Editor, Herve Schneid; Choreographer, Pablo Veron; Casting, Irene Lamb; an Adventure Pictures presentation; Argentinian-French; Dolby Digital Stereo; Black and white/color; Rated PG; 101 minutes; November release

CAST

Sally....Sally Potter
Pablo....Pablo Veron
Red Model....Morgane Maugran
Yellow Model....Geraldine Maillet
Blue Model....Katernia Mechera
Fashion Designer....David Toole
Photographer....George Yiasoumi
Pablo's Partner....Carolina Iotti
Man at Tea Dance....Howard Lee
Builder....Heathcoat Williams
Waiter....Juan Jose Czalkin
Gustavo....Gustavo Naveira
Fabian....Fabian Salas
Carlos....Carlos Copello
Olga....Olga Besio

and Michele Parent, Claudine Mavros, Monique Couturier (Seamstresses), Matthew Hawkins, Simon Worgan (Bodyguards), Zobeida, Orazio Massaro, Anne Fassio, Guillaume Gallienne, Michel Andre, Flaminio Corcos (Pablo's Friends), Horacio Marassi (Shoe Man), David Derman, Oscar Dante Lorenzo, Omar Vega (Salon Dancers), Cantilo Pena (Hotel Porter), Maria Noel, Fabian Stratas, Gregory Dayton (Movie Executives), Peter Eyre (English Tango Fan), Emmanuelle Tertipis (Woman in Dressing Room), Ruben Orlando Di Napoli (Master of Ceremonies), Tito Haas (Taxi Driver), Alicia Monti (Carlos' Partner), Maria Fernanda Lorences (Woman Opening Door), Luis Sturla, Amanda Beita (Couple Opening Door), Marcos Woinski (Man Opening Door), Eduardo Rojo (Janitor), Oscar Arribas (Man at Synagogue)

A filmmaker, having trouble with her next script, becomes the pupil of an Argentinian tango dancer under the condition that he star in her next film.

Sally Potter, Pablo Veron

Pablo Veron, Carolina Iotti

WILL IT SNOW FOR CHRISTMAS?

(ZEITGEIST) Producer, Humbert Balsan; Director/Screenplay, Sandrine Veysset; Photography, Hélène Louvart; Art Director, Jack Dubus; Editor, Nelly Quettier; Costumes, Nathalie Raoul; a production of Ognon Pictures with the participation of the Centre National de la Cinématographie and Canal+ and the participation of the Caisse Centrale D'Activités Sociales du Personnel des Industries Électrique et Gazière; French, 1996; Dolby Stereo; Color; Not rated; 90 minutes; December release

CAST

Mother....Dominique Reymond
Father....Daniel Duval
Jeanne....Jessica Martinez
Bruno....Alexandre Roger
Pierrot....Xavier Colonna
Marie....Fanny Rochetin
Blandine....Flavia Chimènes
Paul....Jérémy Chaix
Rémi....Guillaume Mathonnet

and Éric Huyard (Yvan), Leys Cappatti (Bernard), Marcel Guilloux-Delaunay (Schoolteacher), Bouaza Annab, Bouziane Bouakline (Arab Workers), Julie Peysson, Irène Galitzine (Students)

A young mother, living in a stone farmhouse in southern France, tries to fill the lives of her seven illegitimate children with hope and small pleasures

Dominique Reymond

Phyllida Law, Emma Thompson

THE WINTER GUEST

(FINE LINE FEATURES) Producers, Ken Lipper, Edward R. Pressman; Executive Producers, Ruth Vitale, Jonathan Weisgal, Emma Clarke; Co-Producer, Steve Clark-Hall; Director, Alan Rickman; Screenplay, Sharman MacDonald, Alan Rickman; Adapated from the play by Sharman MacDonald; Photography, Seamus McGarvey; Editor, Scott Thomas; Costumes, Joan Bergin; Music, Michael Kamen; Designer, Robin Cameron Don; Visual Effects Supervisor, Steve Rundell; Associate Producer, Alan J. Wands; Casting, Joyce Nettles; a Pressman Lipper production presented in association with Capitol Films, Channel Four Films and the Scottish Arts Council National Lottery Fund; British; Dolby Stereo; Technicolor; Rated R; 110 minutes; December release

CAST

Elspeth .... Phyllida Law
Frances .... Emma Thompson
Lily .... Sheila Reid
Chloe .... Sandra Voe
Nita .... Arlene Cockburn
Alex .... Gary Hollywood
Tom .... Sean Biggerstaff
Sam .... Douglas Murphy
Minister .... Tom Watson
Cafe Proprietor .... Jan Shand
Passer-by .... Sandy Neilson
Bus Driver .... Billy McElhaney
Woman in Tea Shop .... Helen Devon
Boy in Tea Shop .... Harry Welsh
Young Man in Church .... Christian Zanone
Jamie .... Ross Lewis

In a seaside Scottish town on the coldest day of winter, Elspeth decides to visit her daughter Frances who is still suffering from the recent loss of her husband. This marked the directorial and screenwriting debut of actor Alan Rickman. Law and Thompson are real-life mother and daughter.

Emma Thompson

Phyllida Law, Sean Biggerstaff

Pierce Brosnan, Michelle Yeoh

Pierce Brosnan, Michelle Yeoh

Desmond Llewelyn, Pierce Brosnan

Pierce Brosnan

Michelle Yeoh, Jonathan Pryce, Götz Otto

Michelle Yeoh

TOMORROW NEVER DIES

Pierce Brosnan

(UNITED ARTISTS) Producers, Michael G. Wilson, Barbara Broccoli; Director, Roger Spottiswoode; Screenplay, Bruce Feirstein; Photography, Robert Elswit; Designer, Allan Cameron; Music, David Arnold; Title song by Sheryl Crow and Mitchell Froom/performed by Sheryl Crow; Editors, Dominique Fortin, Michel Arcand; Costumes, Lindy Hemming; Special Effects Supervisor, Chris Corbould; Main Title Designer, Daniel Kleinman; Line Producer, Anthony Waye; Stunts/2nd Unit Director, Vic Armstrong; Casting, Debbie McWilliams; an Albert R. Broccoli's Eon Productions Limited presentation; Distributed by MGM Distribution Co.; Dolby DTS Stereo; Panavision; Deluxe color; Rated PG-13; 119 minutes; December release

CAST

James Bond .... Pierce Brosnan
Elliot Carver .... Jonathan Pryce
Wai Lin .... Michelle Yeoh
Paris Carver .... Teri Hatcher
Henry Gupta .... Ricky Jay
Stamper .... Götz Otto
Wade .... Joe Don Baker
Dr. Kaufman .... Vincent Schiavelli
M .... Judi Dench
Q .... Desmond Llewelyn
Moneypenny .... Samantha Bond
Robinson .... Colin Salmon
Admiral Roebuck .... Geoffrey Palmer
Minister of Defence .... Julian Fellowes
General Bukharin .... Terence Rigby
Professor Inga Bergstrom .... Cecilie Thomsen
Tamara Steel .... Nina Young
PR Lady .... Daphne Deckers
Dr. Dave Greenwalt .... Colin Stinton
Master Sergeant 3 .... Al Matthews
Stealth Boat Captain .... Mark Spalding

and HMS Chester: Bruce Alexander (Captain), Anthony Green (Firing Officer); HMS Devonshire: Christopher Bowen (Commander Richard Day), Andrew Hawkins (Lt. Commander Peter Hume), Dominic Shaun (Lt. Commander), Julian Rhind-Tutt (Yeoman), Gerard Butler (Leading Seaman), Adam Barker (Sonar); HMS Bedford: Michael Byrne (Admiral Kelly), Pip Torrens (Captain), Hugh Bonneville (Air Warfare Officer), Jason Watkins (Principal Warfare Officer), Eoin McCarthy (Yeoman), Brendan Coyle (Leading Seaman); and David Ashton (First Sea Lord), William Scott-Masson, Laura Brattan (Staff Officers), Nadia Cameron (Beth Davidson), Liza Ross (Mary Golson), Hugo Napier (Jeff Hobbs), Rolf Saxon (Philip Jones), Vincent Wang (Mig Pilot), Philip Kwok (General Chang)

Michelle Yeoh

James Bond tries to stop a power-hungry media billionaire who plots domination of the world's news bureaus by manufacturing his own series of crises. This marks the 18th official installment of the James Bond series from United Artists, the second featuring Brosnan (Bond), Judi Dench (M), and Samantha Bond (Moneypenny) and the sixteenth for Desmond Llewelyn (Q).

Pierce Brosnan, Michelle Yeoh

Teri Hatcher

AN AMERICAN WEREWOLF IN PARIS

(HOLLYWOOD PICTURES) Producer, Richard Claus; Executive Producer/Director, Anthony Waller; Screenplay, Tim Burns, Tom Stern, Anthony Waller; Based on characters created by John Landis in the film An American Werewolf in London; Co-Producer, Alexander Buchman; Photography, Egon Werdin; Designer, Matthias Kammermeier; Editor, Peter R. Adam; Music, Wilbert Hirsch; Visual Effects, Santa Barbara Studios; Line Producer, Patricia McMahon; Visual Effects Supervisors, John Grower, Bruce Walters; Werewolf Design/Visual Effects Art Director, Peter Lloyd; Costumes, Maria Schicker; Animatronic and Prosthetic Effects Creators, Magicon & Crawley Creatures; Animatronic and Prosthetic Effects Supervisors, Joachim Grueninger, Jez Harris; Casting, Gail Levin; a Richard Claus production; Presented in association with Cometstone Pictures and J&M Entertainment; Distributed by Buena Vista Pictures; British-Dutch-Luxembourgian-U.S.-French; Dolby Digital Stereo; Widescreen; Color; Rated R; 97 minutes; December release

CAST

Andy McDermott .... Tom Everett Scott
Serafine .... Julie Delpy
Brad .... Vince Vieluf
Chris .... Phil Buckman
Amy .... Julie Bowen
Claude .... Pierre Cosso
Dr. Pigot .... Thierry Lhermitte
Inspector Leduc .... Tom Novembre
Chief Bonnet .... Maria Machado
Detective Ben Bou .... Ben Salem Bouabdallah
Officer with Flashlight .... Serge Basso
Bouncer .... Charles Maquignon
First Lycanthrope .... Jochen Schneider
Second Lycanthrope .... Alan McKenna
Third Lycanthrope .... Herve Sogne
Fourth Lycanthrope .... Edgar Kohn
Professor Martin .... Jean-Claude Deret
Serafine's Mother .... Isabelle Costantini
Nightclub Visitor .... Davis Freeman
Surgeon .... Chris Bearne

and Pierre Bodry (Waiter on Train), Peter Riemens (Waiter in Restaurant), Emile Cappachione (Bodybuilder), Serge Hugel (French Car Driver), John Waller (British Car Driver), Anthony Waller (Metro Driver)

Andy, an American college student on vacation in Paris, meets a mysterious woman who happens to be a werewolf. A follow-up to the 1981 Universal release An American Werewolf in London which starred David Naughton and Jenny Agutter.

Julie Delpy, Tom Everett Scott

Tom Everett Scott, Julie Delpy

Phil Buckman, Vince Vieluf, Tom Everett Scott

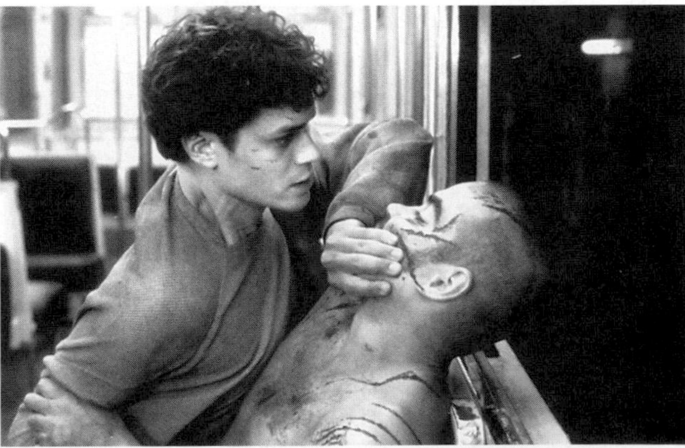

Tom Everett Scott, Pierre Cosso

MA VIE EN ROSE (MY LIFE IN PINK)

(SONY PICTURES CLASSICS) Producer, Carole Scotta; Director, Alain Berliner; Screenplay, Chris vander Stappen, Alain Berliner; Photography, Yves Cape; Set Designer, Veronique Melery; Costumes, Karen Muller Serreau; Editor, Sandrine Deegen; Special Effects, Sparx; Make-up, Kaatje Van Damme; Co-Producers, John McGrath, Jacqueline Pierraux; Co-produced by WFE, RTBF (Belgium), Haut et Court, La Sept Cinema, TF1 Film production (France), Freeway Films (U.K.), with the participation of Belgique European, Coproduction Fund and Eurimages, Canal+, Cofimage 8, Avance Surrecettes/CNC, Centre du Cinema et de l'Audiovisual de la Communaute Francaise; Belgian-French-British; Dolby Stereo; Color; Rated R; 88 minutes; December release

CAST

Ludovic....Georges Du Fresne
Hanna....Michèle Laroque
Pierre....Jean-Philippe Ecoffey
Elisabeth....Hélène Vincent
Jerome....Julien Riviere
Zoe....Cristina Barget
Thom....Gregory Diallo
Jean....Erik Cazals De Fabel
Albert....Daniel Hanssens
Lisette....Laurence Bibot
Jeannot....Jean-Francois Gallotte
Monique....Caroline Baehr
Schoolteacher....Anne Cossens
Chris....Raphaelle Santini
Chid Psychologist....Marie Bunel

Seven-year-old Ludovic sends his family into an uproar when the boy announces that he is one day destined to be a girl.

Georges Du Fresne, Jean-Philippe Ecoffey, Cristina Barget, Michèle Laroque

Hélène Vincent, Georges Du Fresne, Michèle Laroque

Julien Riviere, Georges Du Fresne

Georges Du Fresne

THE BOXER

(UNIVERSAL) Producers, Jim Sheridan, Arthur Lappin; Director, Jim Sheridan; Screenplay, Jim Sheridan, Terry George; Photography, Chris Menges; Designer, Brian Morris; Editor, Gerry Hambling; Music, Gavin Friday, Maurice Seezer; Associate Producer, Nye Heron; Boxing Consultant, Barry McGuigan; Costumes, Joan Bergin; Casting, Nuala Moiselle; a Hell's Kitchen production; Irish; Dolby DTS Stereo; Technicolor; Rated R; 107 minutes; December release

CAST

Danny Flynn ....Daniel Day-Lewis
Maggie ....Emily Watson
Joe Hamill ....Brian Cox
Ike Weir ....Ken Stott
Harry ....Gerard McSorley
Patsy ....Eleanor Methven
Liam ....Ciaran Fitzgerald
Matt Maguire ....Kenneth Cranham
Prison Officers ....Daragh Donnelly, Frank Coughlan, Sean Kearns
Bride ....Lorraine Pilkington
Groom ....Niall Shanahan
Priest ....Father John Wall
Betty ....Maria McDermottro
Prison Governor ....Oliver Maguire
Sean ....David McBlain
Cake Decorator ....Sandra Corbally
Pianist ....Tess Sheridan
Joe Hamill's Aide ....David Hayman
Singer ....Josie Doherty
Agnes' Son ....Joseph Rea
Agnes ....Joan Sheehy
Peter Mallon ....Peter Sheridan
Old Man in Shelter ....Larry Byrne
Car Bomb Driver ....Joe Gallagher
Boy on Bicycle ....Sean Brunett
Bomb Victim ....James Hayes
Sean's Helper ....Richie Piggott
Soldier on Roof ....Jack Waters
Doorman at Gym ....Padraic O'Neill
Old Men in Gym ....Mark Mulholland, John Cowley, Don Foley
Caretaker of Gym ....Tim McDonnell
Boxer on Pads ....Philip Sutcliffe
Mrs. Boots ....Britta Smith
Bootsy ....Gavin Kennedy

and Eamon Brown (Referee-1st Fight), Martin Lynch (Journalist), Gavin Brown Liam's Opponent), Noel O'Donovan (Timekeeper-1st Fight), Joe Colgan (Danny's Cornerman), Damien Denny (Eddie Carrol), Nye Heron (Eddi's Trainer), Paul Ronan (Eddie's Corneman), Carol Scanlan, Kate Perry, Andrea Irvine, Joan McGarry, Theresa McComb, Catherine Dunne, Kerrie Duggan, Sharon Dunne, Derbhla McClelland (Wedding Guests), Paul Sheridan, John Sheridan, Pat Mulryan, Peter O'Donoghue, Martin Dunne, Tommy O'Neil (IRA Men), Liam Carney (Mr. Walsh), Veronica Duffy (Mrs. Walsh), Des Braiden (Mr. Orr), Joan Brosnan Walsh (Mrs. Orr), Sean Donaghy (Mickey), Brian Milligan (Ned), Vinny Murphy, Mick Nolan, Berts Folan (Danny's Supporters), Juliet Cronin (Cardgirl-1st Fight), Kirsten Sheridan (Girl with Drinks), Mickey Tohill (Billy Patterson), Ian McElhinney (Reggie Bell), Conor Bradford (TV Announcer), Anna Meegan (Woman at 2nd Fight), Al Morris (Referee —2nd Fight), Ian Thompson (Child at 2nd Fight), Paul Wesley (Danny's Sparring Partner), Michael James Ford (Head Waiter), John Cooke (Toastmaster), Cornelius Carr, Norman Kelly (London Fighters), Gerry Storey (Cornerman), Fred Tiedt (Referee—London Fight), Clayon Stewart (Akim), Jery O'Leary (Timekeeper—London Fight), Jules Kingelesi, Dennis Mika (Akim's Corner), David Heap (Maitre D'), John Hewitt (Ike's Drinking Buddy), Janine McGuinness (Cardgirl—London Fight), Tom Maguire (Policeman at Checkpoint)

Danny Flynn, a former IRA member, released from a fourteen year stint in prison, begins an affair with Maggie, the wife of a currently imprisoned organization member, much to the disapproval of the IRA.

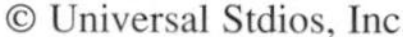

Daniel Day-Lewis, Emily Watson

Ciaran Fitzgerald, Emily Watson

Brian Cox, Emily Watson

Cate Blanchett, Ralph Fiennes

Ralph Fiennes

Cate Blanchett, Ralph Fiennes

Cate Blanchett

OSCAR AND LUCINDA

(FOX SEARCHLIGHT) Producers, Robin Dalton, Timothy White; Director, Gillian Armstrong; Screenplay, Laura Jones; Based on the novel by Peter Carey; Photography, Geoffrey Simpson; Designer, Luciana Arrighi; Music, Thomas Newman; Editor, Nicholas Beauman; Associate Producer, Mark Turnbull; Costumes, Janet Patterson; Casting, Alison Barrett, Kathleen Mackie; a Dalton Films production, presented in association with the Australian Film Finance Corporation and the New South Wales Film and Television Office; Australian; Color; Panavision; Rated R; 132 minutes; December release

CAST

Oscar Hopkins....................Ralph Fiennes
Lucinda Leplastrier....................Cate Blanchett
Reverend Dennis Hasset....................Ciaran Hinds
Hugh Stratton....................Tom Wilkinson
Mr. Jeffris....................Richard Roxburgh
Theophilus....................Clive Russell
Percy Smith....................Bille Brown
Miriam Chadwick....................Josephine Byrnes
Wardley-Fish....................Barnaby Kay
Jimmy D'Abbs....................Barry Otto
Betty Stratton....................Linda Bassett
Narrator....................Geoffrey Rush
Young Lucinda....................Polly Cheshire
Elizabeth Leplastrier....................Gillian Jones
Abel Leplastrier....................Robert Menzies
Young Oscar....................Adam Hayes
13-year-old Oscar....................James Tingey
Mrs. Williams....................Matyelok Gibs
Fanny Drabble....................Sonia Ritter

and Will Barton, Jonathan Markwood, Nicholas Tennant, Sam Newman, Nicholas Fordham (College Students), Peter Whitford (Mr. Ahearn), Lynette Curran (Mrs. Ahearn), Ron Blanchard (Steamer Captain), Colin Taylor (Frazer), Michelle Doake (Hotel Maid), Karen Vickey, Elspeth MacTavish (Society Gossips) Andrea Moore (Miss Shaddock), Leverne McDonnell (Miss Malcolm), Geoff Morrell (Charley Fig), Christian Manon (Mr. Tomasetti)

Oscar, a somewhat emotionally unbalanced minister with a penchant for picking winning race horses, finds himself joining forces with Lucinda, a wealthy Australian who owns a glass works in Sydney. This film received an Oscar nomination for costume design.

Julie Epstein, Max Epstein, Willie Epstein in *A Tickle in the Heart*
© Kino International

A TICKLE IN THE HEART (Kino) Producers, Edward Rosenstein, Martin Hagemann, Thomas Kufus; Director, Stefan Schwietert; Based on an idea by Joel Rubin, Rita Ottens; Photography, Robert Richman; Editor, Arpad Bondy; Music, The Epstein Brothers; Produced by Zero Film/Ö Film/Neapel Film; German, 1996; Black and white; Not rated; 84 minutes; January release. Documentary about the Kings of Klezmer, Max, Willie and Julie Epstein, featuring Peter Solokow, Harriet Goldstein Darr, Pat Merola, Harry Kolstein, Joel Rubin.

THE JEW (First Run Features) Producer, Antonio da Cunha Telles; Director, Jom Tob Azulay; Screenplay, Millor Fernandes, Geraldo Carneiro, Gilvan Pereira; Photography, Eduardo Serra; Music, Rui Luis Pereira; Editors, José Manuel Lopes, Pedro Ribeiro, Ruy Guerra; Portuguese-Brazilian, 1995; Color; Not rated; 85 minutes; January release. **CAST:** Felipe Pinheiro (António José da Silva), Dina Sfat (Lourença Coutinho), Mário Viegas (King João V), Edwin Luisi (Alexandre), JoséNeto (Priest)

ANGEL DUST (Northern Arts) Producers, Taro Maki, Kenzo Horikoshi, Eiji Izumi; Director, Sogo Ishii; Screenplay, Yorozu Ikuta, Sogo Ishii; Photography, Norimichi Kasamatsu; Music, Hiroyuki Nagashima; Editors, Hiroshi Matsuo, Sogo Ishii; a Twins Japan Inc./Euro Space production; Japanese, 1994; Dolby Stereo; Color; Not rated; 116 minutes; January release. **CAST:** Kaho Minami (Setsuko Suma), Takeshi Wakamatsu (Rei Aku), Etsushi Toyokawa (Tomoo), Ryoko Takizawa (Yuki Takei)

Kaho Minami in *Angel Dust*
© Northern Arts

Johnny Peterson (c) in *Saint Clara*
© *Kino International*

OUT OF THE PRESENT (Independent) Director, Andrei Ujica; No other credits available; Russian; Color; Not rated; 96 minutes; January release. Documentary using footage from four different space missions to the Mir space station.

SAINT CLARA (Kino) Producers, Marek Rozenbaum, Uri Sabag; Directors/Screenplay, Ari Folman, Ori Sivan; Based on the novel by Pavel Kohout; Original Story, Jelena Machinova; Photography, Valentin Belanogov; Designer, Ariel Glaser; Music, Barry Saharov; Israeli, 1996; Color; Not rated; 85 minutes; January release. **CAST**: Lucy Dubinchik (Clara Chanov), Halil Elohev (Eddie Tikel), Johnny Peterson (Rosy Rosenthal), Maya Mayron (Libby), Israel Damidov (Elvis Chanov), Yigal Naor (Headmaster Tissona), Maya De Fries (Eleanor Galash), Tal Feignboim (Galit Biron), Tal Ben Bina (Tikel's Mother), Menashe Noy (Tikel's Father), Jenia Doudina (Clara's Mother), Ronald Hairlovsky (Clara's Father), Joseph El Dror (Teacher Mounitz), Orly Zilberschatz-Banai (TV Reporter), Ronny Bachar (Vered Rosenthal), Tomer Patlock (Asthma), Divan Sivan (Baby Chanov), Helena Zoubtov (Seismographic Engineer)

RATS IN THE RANKS (Film Australia/Arundel Films) Producers/Directors, Bob Connolly, Robin Anderson; Executive Producer, Chris Oliver; Photography, Bob Connolly; Editors, Ray Thomas, Bob Connolly; Produced in association with the Australian Broadcasting Corporation, Channel Four and La Sept ARTE; Australian; Color; Not rated; 98 minutes; February release. **CAST:** Larry Hand (Himself)

Larry Hand in *Rats in the Ranks*
© Film Australia

Simon Bossell, Saffron Burrows, Aden Young in *Hotel de Love*

HOTEL DE LOVE (LIVE Entertainment) Producers, Michael Lake, David Parker; Director/Screenplay, Craig Rosenberg; Executive Producers, Peter Heller, Alex Waislitz, Heloise Waislitz; Photography, Stephen Windon; Editor, Bill Murphy; Music, Brett Rosenberg; Designer, Simon Dobbin; Costumes, Bruce Finlayson; Casting, Maura Fay & Associates, Lou Mitchell; a Village Roadshow Pictures and Pratt Films production; Australian; Dolby Stereo; Color; Rated R; 95 minutes; February release. **CAST:** Aden Young (Rick Dunne), Saffron Burrows (Melissa Morrison), Simon Bossell (Stephen Dunne), Pippa Grandison (Alison Leigh), Ray Barrett (Jack Dunne), Julia Blake (Edith Dunne), Peter O'Brien (Norman), Belinda McClory (Janet), Caleb Cluff (Bruce), Cassandra Magrath (Suzy), Andrew Bibby (Matt), Alan Hopgood (Ronnie), Raelee Hill (Emma Andrews), Margaret Hoctor (Bridesmaid), Bayard Templin (Melissa's Father), Robert Lowe (Priest), Leo Faust (Brett), Alan Stone (Minister), Sally Lightfoot (Maid), Barbara Burder (Mrs. Fielding), Robert Tuttleby (Mr. Fielding), Craig Gillespie (Young Man), Madonna Munasinha (Young Woman—Eleanor), Michelle Twigden (Young Girl—Nail Biter), Cameron Nugent (Young Man She Kisses), Paul Crossley (Handsome Guy), Bettina Petrone (Handsome Guy's Girlfriend), Stephanie Turner, Andrew Russell (Lovers)

SALUT COUSIN! (Seventh Art) Producer, Jacques Bidou; Director, Merzak Allouache; Screenplay, Merzak Allouache, Caroline Thivel; Photography, Pierre Aim; Editor, Pierre Abela; Music, Safy Boutella; French-Algerian, 1996; Color; Not rated; 102 minutes; February release. **CAST:** Gad Elmaleh (Alilo), Mess Hattou (Mok), Magaly Berdy (Fatoumata), Ann Gisel Glass (Laurence), Jean Benguigui (Maurice), Xavier Maly (Claude), Cheik Doukoure (Voisin Ivoirien), Dalia Renauault (Malika), Fatiha Cheriguene (The Aunt), Malek Kates (Uncle), Mohamed Ourdach (Rachid), Mostefa Djadam (Said), Arno Chevrier (Gonrand), Mosefa Stiti (Father of the Bride), Isaac Sharry (Isaac the Actor)

Ann Gisel Glass, Mess Hattou in *Salut Cousin!*

Ulf Friberg, Max von Sydow in *Jerusalem*

JERUSALEM (First Look Pictures) Producer, Ingrid Dahlberg; Director/Screenplay, Bille August; Based on the novel by Selma Lagerlöf; Photography, Jörgen Persson; Editor, Janus Billeskov-Jansen; Music, Stefan Nilsson; Designer, Anna Asp; Costumes, Ann-Margret Fyregård; Swedish-Danish, 1996; Dolby Stereo; Color; Not rated; 166 minutes; March release. **CAST:** Ulf Friberg (Ingmar), Maria Bonnevie (Gertrud), Pernilla August (Karin), Reine Brynolfsson (Tim), Lena Endre (Barbro), Jan Mybrand (Gabriel), Sven-Bertil Taube (Hellgum), Björn Granath (Storm), Viveka Seldahl (Stina), Mona Malm (Eva Gunnarsdotter), Hans Alfredson (Mats Hök), Torsten Sjöholm (Gunnar Hok), Max von Sydow (The Vicar), Olympia Dukakis (Mrs. Gordon), Annika Borg (Gunhild), Johan Rabaeus (Eljas), Sven Wollter (Big Ingmar), Mats Dahlbäck (Hans Berger), Anders Nyström (Sven Persson), Douglas Johansson (Lars Tipers), Nils Eklund (The Landlord), Lars Engstrom (The Doctor), Viktor Friberg (The Sawmilworker), Stina von Sydow (The Maid), André Beinö (Young Ingmar), Stina Wargert (Young Gertrud), Amanda Steen (Greta), Jan Sjödin (Gabriel's Father), Eva Stellby (Gabriel's Mother), Michael Nyqvist, Lasse Almebäck (Carpenters), Rolf Jenner, Christer Flodin (Big Men), John Gunnarsson ("Jesus"), Claes Esphagen (Forest Administrator), Fredrik Ohlsson (The Lawyer), Mel Cobb, Sydnee Blake, Katherne Kjellgren (Americans)

TANGO FEROZ (Tara) Producers, Claudio Pustelnik, Katrina Bayonas; Director, Marcelo Piñeyro; Screenplay, Aida Bortnik, Marcelo Piñeyro; Photography, Alfredo F. Mayo; Editor, Miguel Perez; Art Director, Jorge Ferrari; Argentinian; Dolby Stereo; Color; Not rated; 125 minutes; March release. **CAST:** Hector Alterio (Lobo), Imanol Arias (Angel), Cecilia Dopazo (Mariana), Fernan Miras (Tango)

Fernan Miras, Cecilia Dopazo in *Tango Feroz*

Barry Otto, Toni Cotllette, Paul Chubb in *Cosi*
© Miramax Films

A MONGOLIAN TALE (New Yorker) Producer, Ma Fung-kwok, Wellington Fung; Executive Producer, Jin Ji-wu, Du Yong-ling; Director, Xie Fei; Screenplay, Zhang Cheng-zhi, based on his novel *Black Steed*; Photography, Fu Jing-sheng; Editors, Xie Fei, Zhao Xiu-qin; Music, Tengger; a Media Asia Films and Beijing Youth Film Studio presentation; Mongolian, 1995; Color; Not rated; 103 minutes; April release. **CAST:** Tengger (Beiyinpalica), Naranhua (Someyer), Dalarsurong (Nai Nai)

COSI (Miramax) Producers, Richard Brennan, Timothy White; Executive Producer, Phaedon Vass; Director, Mark Joffe; Screenplay, Louis Nowra; Photography, Ellery Ryan; Designer, Chris Kennedy; Editor, Nicholas Beuman; Associate Producer, Lynn Gailey; Casting, Alison Barret; Australian, 1996;; Color; Rated R; 100 minutes; April release. **CAST:** Ben Mendelsohn (Lewis), Toni Collette (Julie), Barry Otto (Roy), Pamela Rabe (Ruth), Jacki Weaver (Cherry), Colin Hay (Zac), David Wenham (Doug), Paul Chubb (Henry), Colin Friels (Errol), Rachel Griffiths (Lucy), Aden Young (Nick), Tony Llewellyn-Jones (Kirner), Kerry Walker (Sandra), Robin Ramsay (Minister for Health), Henry Maas (Bernard Goldman), Raymond Walsh (Air Wrestler), Lawrence Woodward (Electrician), Brian Ellison (Rigger), Tamara Kuldin (Seamstress), Dennis Allard (Carpenter), Toni Moran (Painter), David Anthony (Knucklehead), Skye Wansey (Ms. Spock), Samantha McDeed (Pink Lady)

TO HAVE (OR NOT) (Cinema Parallel) Producers, Francois Cuel, George Benayoun; Director/Screenplay, Laetitia Masson; Photography, Caroline Champetier; Editor, Yann Dedet; Music, Marianne Faithfull, Nick Drake, Cheb Mami; a co-production of CLP-Dacia Films/National Center for Cinematography et Canal+ presented in association with Fabiano Canosa; French; Color; Not rated; 90 minutes; April release. **CAST:** Sandrine Kiberlain (Alice), Arnaud Giovaninetti (Bruno), Roschdy Zem (Night Porter)

Russell Crowe, Bridget Fonda in *Rough Magic*
© Rysher Entertainment

Michael Muller, Susanne Birkemose Konsgaard in *Portland*
© Zentropa

THE SADNESS OF SEX (Tara) Director, Rupert Wainwright; Screenplay, Barry Yourgrau, based on his book; Photography, AndréPienaar; Music, Tomandandy (Tom Hajdu, Andy Milburn); Designer, Franco De Cotiis; Costumes, Mariska M. Nicholson; Editor, Brian Berdan; from Skyvision Partners; Canadian, 1995; Ultra-Stereo; Color; Not rated; 87 minutes; April release. **CAST**: Barry Yourgrau (The Host), Peta Wilson (Girl of His Dreams), Mark Benesh (Son), Richard Bulley (Dad), Dianne Zeust (Mom)

PORTLAND (Zentropa) Producer, Peter Aalbaek Jensen; Director/Screenplay, Niels Arden Oplev; Photography, Henrik Jongdahl; Editor, Henrik Fleischer; Music, Sons of Cain; Danish, 1996; Color; Not rated; 103 minutes; May release. **CAST:** Anders Wodskou Berthelsen (Janus), Michael Muller (Jakob), Ulrich Thomsen (Lasse), Iben Hjejle (Eva), Birthe Neumann (Mother), Baard Owe (Kaj), Edith Thrane (Mrs. Eriksen), Helle Charotte Dolleris (Irene), Susanne Birkemose Konsgaard (Minna), Karsten Geisnæs (Kenneth), Preben Raunsbjerg (Johny), René Johnsen (Peter), Allan Johansen (Hans), Peter Heidemann Jørgensen (Jens), Jens Albinus (Carsten), Hans Henrik Voetmann (Suicide)

ROUGH MAGIC (Goldwyn) Producers, Laurie Parker, Declan Baldwin; Executive Producers, Yves Attal, Jonathan Taplin, Andrew Karsch; Director, Clare Peploe; Screenplay, Robert Mundy, William Brookfield, Clare Peploe; Based upon the novel *Miss Shumway Waves a Wand* by James Hadley Chase; Photography, John J. Campbell; Designer, Waldemar Kalinowski; Editor, Suzanne Fenn; Music, Richard Hartley; Costumes, Richard Hornung; Casting, Elisabeth Leustig; a UGC Images and Recorded Picture Company presentation in association with Martin Scorsese; French-British, 1995; Dolby Stereo; Foto-Kem color; Rated PG-13; 104 minutes; May release. **CAST:** Bridget Fonda (Myra Shumway), Russell Crowe (Alex Ross), Jim Broadbent (Doc Ansell), D.W. Moffett (Cliff Wyatt), Kenneth Mars (Magician), Paul Rodriguez (Diego), Andy Romano (Clayton), Richard Schiff (Wiggins), Euva Anderson (Diego's Wife/Tojola), Michael Ensign (Powerbroker), Gabriel Pingarron (Telegraph Man), Santos Morales, Rene Pereyra (Policemen), Gregory Avellone (Burly Usher), Mark Del Castillo (Clayton's Assistant), Chris Otto (Mechanic), Jose Escandon (Waiter), Ana Cristina Vasquez (Maid), Barkley (Dog)

MONDO (Shadow Distribution/Upstate Films) Producer, Michèle Ray-Gavras; Director/Screenplay, Tony Gatliff; Story, J.M.G. Le Clezio; Photography, Eric Guichard; Editor, Nicole D.V. Berckmans; a production of K.G. Productions with the participation of Canal+ and the Centre National de Cinemtographie; French; Color; Not rated; 80 minutes; May release. **CAST**: Ovidiu Balan (Mondo), Philippe Petit (The Magician), Pierette Fesch (Thi-Chin), Schahla Aalam (The Magician's Companion), Jerry Smith (Dadi), Maurice Maurin (Giordan the Fisherman), Catherine Brun (Church Solist/The Woman in the Elevator)

Llyr Evans, Rhys Ifans in *Twin Town*
© Gramercy Pictures

TWIN TOWN (Gramercy) Producer, Peter McAleese; Executive Producers, Andrew MacDonald, Danny Boyle; Director, Kevin Allen; Screenplay, Kevin Allen, Paul Durden; Photography, John Mathieson; Designer, Pat Campbell; Music, Mark Thomas; Editor, Oral Norrie Ottey; Costumes, Rachel Fleming; Casting, Nina Gold; a PolyGram Filmed Entertainment presentation of a Figment Films production in association with Agenda; British; Dolby Digital Stereo; Color; Not rated; 99 minutes; May release. **CAST**: Llyr Evans (Julian), Rhys Ifans (Jeremy), Dorien Thomas (Greyo), Dougray Scott (Terry), Biddug Williams (Mrs. Mort), Ronnie Williams (Mr. Mort), Huw Ceredig (Fatty), Rachel Scorgie (Adie), Di Botcher (Jean), Mary Allen (Olive), Paul Durden (Taxi Driver), David Hayman (Dodgy), Kevin Allen (TV Presenter), Brian Hibbard (Dai Rees), Morgan Hopkins (Chip), Sion Tudor Owen (Dewi), William Thomas (Bryn), Denny Durden (Kazoo Player), Jenny Evans (Bonny), Helen Griffith (Lynette), Royston John (Ivor), Julie Davies (Madeline), Gillian Elise (Pat), Steffan Rhodri (Hunky), Nicholas McGaughey (Chunky), Brian Hancock (Drunk in Toilet), Martin Ace (Rocking Sikh), Bhasker Patel (Renjit), Michael Cunningham (Mr. Waldron), Boyd Clack (Vicar), Keith Allen (Emrya), Charlie (Cantona), Snowy (Fergie)

GAMERA: GUARDIAN OF THE UNIVERSE (A.D. Vision) Producer, Yasuyoshi Tokuma; Director, Shusuke Kaneko; Screenplay, Kazunori Ito; Photography, Junichi Tozawa, Kenji Takama; Music, Koh Ohtani; Special Effects, Shinji Higuchi; Japanese, 1995; Dolby Stereo; Color; Not rated; 92 minutes; April release. **CAST:** Tsuyosi Ihara (Yoshinari Yonemori), Akira Onodera (Naoya Kusanagi), Ayako Fujitani (Asagi Kusanagi), Shinobu Nakayama (Mayumi Nagamine)

Gayaos, Gamera in *Gamera: Gaurdian of the Universe*

Tetsuo II: Body Hammer © Manga Entertainment

CHRONICLE OF A DISAPPEARANCE (Intl. Film Circuit) Producer, Elia Suleiman, Dhat Productions; Director/Screenplay, Elia Suleiman; Photography, Marc Andre Batigne; Editor, Anna Ruiz; Music, Alla, Abed Azrie, Leonard Cohen, Natacha Atlas; Casting, Ula Tabari; Palestine, 1996; Dolby Stereo; Color; Not rated; 88 minutes; May release. **CAST:** Elia Suleiman (E.S.), Ula Tabari (Adan), Nazira Suleiman (Mother), Fuad Suleiman (Father), Jamal Daher (Owner of the Holyland Shop)

TETSUO II: BODY HAMMER (Manga) Producers, Fuminori Shishido, Fumio Kurokawa, Nobuo Takeuchi, Hiromi Aihara; Executive Producers, Hiroshi Koizumi, Shinya Tsukamoto; Director/Screenplay/Photography/Art Director/Editor, Shinya Tsukamoto; Music, Chu Ishikawa, Tomoyasu Hotei; Special Make-up & Effects, Takashi Oda, Kan Takahama, Akira Fukaya; Japanese, 1991; Stereo; Color; Not rated; 83 minutes; June release. **CAST:** Tomoroh Taguchi (Tomoo Taniguchi), Nobu Kanaoka (Kana), Shinya Tsukamoto (Guy), Sujin Kim (Taniguchi's Father), Hideaki Tezuka (Punk—Big Brother), Nobuo Asada (Punk—Young Brother), Toraemon Utazawa (Dr. Arita), Min Iwata (Taniguchi's Mother)

DUST OF LIFE (Swift) Producer, Jean Brehat; Executive Producer, Charles Wang; Director, Rachid Bouchareb; Screenplay, Bernard Gesbert, Rachid Bouchareb; Adapted from the book *Fanta Hill* by Duyen Anh; Photography, Youcef Sahraoui; Music, Safy Boutella; Editor, Hélène Ducret; from 3B Productions; French-Algerian, 1994; Color; Widescreen; Not rated; 87 minutes; June release. **CAST:** Daniel Guyant (Son), Gilles Chitlaphone (Bob), Leon Outtrabady (Shrimp), Jéhan Pagès (Little Hai), Eric Nguyen (One-Two), Siu Lin Lam (Greaser), Yann Roussel (Steel Muscles), William Low (Commander)

Gilles Chitlaphone, Daniel Guyant, Leon Outtrabady in
Dust of Life © *Swift*

Ghalia Lacroix in *For Ever Mozart*
© New Yorker Films

Yondejunai, Tseded in *Molom*
© Lung Ta-Compagnie Des Films

FOR EVER MOZART (New Yorker) Producers, Ruth Waldburger, Alain Sarde; Executive Producer/Director, Jean-Luc Godard; Photography, Christophe Pollack; Designer, Ivan Niclass; Music, David Darling, Ketil Bjornstad, Ben Harper, Gyorgi Kurtag; Produced by Vega Film/Aventura Films/Périphéria/ECM; Swiss-French, 1996; Color; Not rated; 85 minutes; July release. **CAST:** Madeleine Assas, Ghalia Lacroix, Bérangère Allaux, Vicky Messica, Frédéric Pierrot.

LOVE'S DEBRIS (In Pictures) Producers, Wieland Schultz-Keil, Jean-Pierre Bailly, Christoph Meyer-Wiel; Director, Werner Schroeter; Based on an idea by Werner Schroeter, Claire Alby; Photography, Elfi Mikesch; Editor, Juliane Lorez; Designer/Costumes, Alberte Bersaqc; an MC4 and Imalyre/VTCOM production; German-French; Dolby Stereo; Color; Not rated; 120 minutes; July release. A documentary on opera, featuring Carole Bouquet, Isabelle Huppert, Anita Cerquetti, Martha Modl, Rita Gorr, Katherine and Kristine Ciesinski, Laurence Dale, Jenny Drivala, Gail Gilmore, Sergueï Larin, Trudeliese Schmidt.

BRILLIANT LIES (Castle Hill) Producers, Richard Franklin, Sue Farrelly; Director, Richard Franklin; Screenplay, Peter Fitzpatrick, Richard Franklin; Photography, Geoff Burton; Designer, Tracy Watt; Editor, David Pulbrook; Costumes, Roger Kirk; Casting, Greg Apps; Australian, 1996; Dolby Stereo; Color; Not rated; 93 minutes; July release. **CAST:** Gia Carides (Susy Connor), Anthony La Paglia (Gary Fitzgerald), Zoe Carides (Katy Connor), Ray Barrett (Brian Connor), Michael Veitch (Paul Connor), Catherine Wilkin (Marion Lee), Neil Melville (Vince Williams), Jennifer Jarman Walker (Ruth Miller), Grant Tilly (Steve Lovett), Beverley Dunn (President), Brad Lindsay (Registrar), Barry Friedlander (Mr. Buxton), Iain Murton (Mr. Hall), Tim Elston (Young Brian), Nathalie Gauchi (Young Katy), Emily-Jane Romig (Young Susy), Daniel Holten (Young Paul), Lisa Aldenhoven (Stephanie Fitzgerald)

CONSPIRATORS OF PLEASURE (Zeitgeist) Producers, Jaromir Kallista, Jan Svankmajer; Co-Producer, P. Assouline, Keith Griffiths; Director/Screenplay/Costumes/Set Designer, Jan Svankmajer; Photography, Miroslav Spala; Puppet Designer, Eva Svankmajer; Animation, Bedrich Glaser, Martin Kublak; Editor, Marie Zemanova; Czech-British; Dolby Stereo; Color; Not rated; 83 minutes; August release. CAST: Petr Meissel, Anna Wetlinska, Gabriela Wilhelmova, Jiri Labus, Barbora Hrzanova, Pavel Novy

MOLOM: A LEGEND OF MONGOLIA (Norkat Company) Executive Producer, Fabien Quaki; Producer/Director/Screenplay, Marie Jaoul De Poncheville; Music, John McLaughlin, Trilok Gurtu; Photography, Jacques Besse; Editor, Danielle Anezin; Line Producer, Vincent Roget; a Lung Ta production with the participation of Canal+/France 2/Centre National de la Cinematographie/Ministre de la Culture de la Francophonie/Foundation Elf/Foundation Gan pour le Cinema; Mongolian-French; Color; Not rated; 93 minutes; August release. **CAST:** Tseded (Molom), Yondejunai (Yonden)

LISBON STORY (Fox Lorber) Producers, Ulrich Felsberg, Paulo Branco, Wim Wenders; Executive Producer, Joao Canijo; Director/Screenplay, Wim Wenders; Photography, Liza Rinzler; Designer, ZéBranco; Editors, Peter Przygodda, Anne Schnee; a Road Movies Filmproduktion/Madragoa Films, in collaboration with LISBOA 94 and WDR; Portuguese, 1995; Dolby Stereo; Color; Not rated; 100 minutes; August release. **CAST**: Rudiger Vogler (Phillip Winter), Patrick Bauchau (Friedrich Monroe), Vasco Sequeira (The Van Driver), Canto E. Castro (The Barber), Viriato JoséDa Silva (The Cobbler), Joao Canijo (The Swindler), Ricardo Colares (Ricardo), Joel Ferreira (Zé), Sofia Bénard De Costa (Sofia), Vera Cunha Rocha (Vera), Elisabete Cunha Rocha (Beta)

PIPPI LONGSTOCKING (Legacy) Producers, Hasmi Giakoumis, Merle-Anne Ridley; Executive Producers, Michael Hirsch, Patrick Loubert, Clive Smith; Co-Executive Producer, David Ferguson; Director, Clive Smith; Art Director, Clive Powsey; Animation Directors, Robin Budd, Bill Giggie; Screenplay, Catharina Stackelberg, Susie Snooks, Ken Sobol, Frank Nissen, Clive Smith; Based on the books by Astrid Lindgren; Character Design, Frank Nissen; Design Supervisors, Paul Riley, Dermot Walshe; Editor, Noda Tsamardos; a co-production of AB Svensk Filmindustri, Idunafilm, Trickompany and Nelvana; Canadian-Swedish-German; Dolby Stereo; Color; Rated G; 75 minutes; August release. **VOICE CAST:** Melissa Altro (Pippi Longstocking), Catherine O'Hara (Mrs. Prysselius), Carole Pope (The Teacher), Dave Thomas (Thunder-Karlsson), Gordon Pinsent (Captain Longstocking)

Pippi Longstocking © Idvna/TFC/Nelvana/SF

Lou Castel, Johanna Ter Steege in *The Birth of Love*
© Courtesy Noon Pictures

AARON'S MAGIC VILLAGE (CFP) Producers, Dora Benousilio, Peter Volkle; Director, Albert Hanan Kaminski; Screenplay, Albert Hanan Kaminski, Jacqueline Galia Benousilio; Adapted from Isaac Bashevis Singer's Stories for Children; Music, Michel Legrand; Songs, Michel Legrand, Sheldon Harnick; an Albert Kaminski Film and a Benousilio-Volkle production; French-German, 1995; Color; Rated G; 80 minutes; September release. **VOICE CAST:** Fyvush Finkel (Narrator), Tommy Michaels (Aaron), Tovah Feldshuh (Aunt Sarah/Zlateth the Goat/The Matchmaker), Ronn Carroll (Uncle Shlemiel), Harry Goz (Gronam Ox), Steve Newman (The Sorcerer), Ivy Austin (The Lantuch), Lee Wilkof, Chip Zien, Lewis J. Stadlen

THE BIRTH OF LOVE (Noon Pictures) Producers, Christian Paumier, Martine Cassinelli, Cyrille Bragnier, Rossella Ragazzi, Pierre-Alain Schatzmann, Claudia Sontheim; Director, Philippe Garrel; Screenplay, Philippe Garrel, Marc Cholodenko, Muriel Cerf; Photography, Raoul Coutard; Music, John Cale; Editors, Sophie Coussein, Yann Dedet, Nathalie Hubert, Alexandra Strauss; French, 1993; Black and white; Not rated; 94 minutes; September release. **CAST:** Lou Castel (Paul), Jean-Pierre Leaud (Marcus), Johanna Ter Steege (Ulrika), Domonique Reymond (Helene), Marie-Paule Laval (Fanchon)

MY SEX LIFE ... OR HOW I GOT INTO AN ARGUMENT (Zeitgeist) Producers, Pascal Caucheteux, Gregoire Sorlet; Director, Arnaud Desplechin; Screenplay, Arnaud Desplechin, Emmanuel Bourdieu; Photography, Eric Gautier, Stéphane Fontaine, Dominique Perrier-Royer; Designer, Antoine Platteau; Music, Krishna Lévy; Costumes, Claire Gérard-Hirne, Delphine Hayat; Editors, François Gédigier, Laurence Briaud; French, 1996; Not rated; 178 minutes; September release. **CAST:** Mathieu Amalric (Paul), Emmanuelle Devos (Esther), Emmanuel Salinger (Nathan), Marianne Denicourt (Sylvia), Jeanne Balibar (Valérie), Chiara Mastroianni (Patricia), Thibault de Montalembert (Bob), Denis Podalydès (Jean-Jacques), Fabrice Desplechin (Ivan), Michel Vuillermoz (Frédéric Rabier), Hélène Lapiower (Le Mérou), Roland Amstutz (Chernov), Marion Cotillard (Student Ivan), Solenn Jarniou (Pascale), Philippe Duclos (Spiritual Guide), Elisabeth Maby ("Tatie"), Paule Annen (Madame Chernov), Anne-Katerine Normant (Esther's Friend), Vincent Nemeth (Friend), David Gabison (Representative of the Diocese)

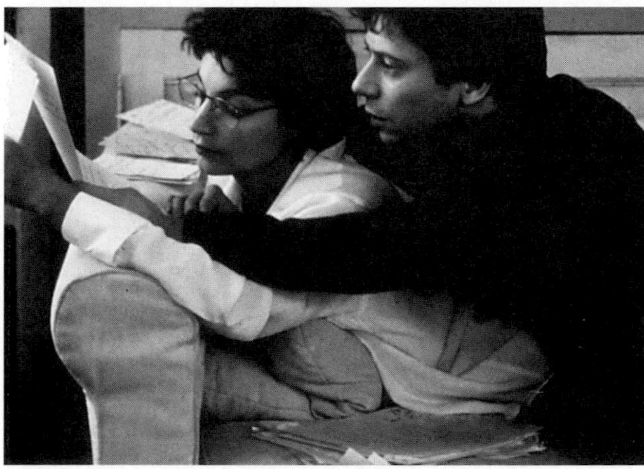

Jeanne Balibar, Mathieu Amalric in
My Sex Life , or How I Got into an Argument © Zeitgeist Films

Thierry Lhermite, Philippe Noiret in *Ripoux Contre Ripoux*
© Interama

RIPOUX CONTRE RIPOUX (MY NEW PARTNER AT THE RACES) (Interama) Producers, Bertrand de la Fontaine, Claude Zidi; Director, Claude Zidi; Screenplay, Simon Michael, Claude Zidi; Photography, Jean-Jacques Tarbes; Editor, Nicole Saunier; Music, Frances Lai; a Films 7 - Orly Films -Sedif - TF1 Films production; French, 1989; Color; Not rated; 107 minutes; September release. **CAST:** Philippe Noiret (René, Thierry Lhermite (Francois), Guy Marchand (Inspector Brisson), Line Renaud (Simone), Grace De Capitani (Natacha), Michel Aumont (Commissaire Bloret), Jean-Pierre Castaldi (Inspector Portal), Jean-Claude Brialy (Le Banquier), Jean Benguigui (Cesarini), Christian Bouillette (Le Bijoutier), Roger Jendly (Albert le Fourgue), Georges Montillier (Le Marchand de Fringues), RenéMorard (Fernand), Alain Mottet (Le Préfet), Bernard Freyd (Guichard), Tadie Huene (Le Marabout), Patricia Karim (La Boutiquiére), Michel Cremades (Le Braquerur)

MOUTH TO MOUTH (BOCA A BOCA) (Miramax) Producers, César Benítez, Joaquín Oristrell, Manuel Gómez Pereira; Director, Manuel Gomez Pereira; Screenplay, Joaquín Oristrell, Juan Luis Iborra, Naomi Wise, Manuel Gómez Pereira; Executive Producers, César Benítez, Fernando Garcillán; Photography, Juan Amorós; Music, Bernardo Bonezzi; Editor, Guillermo Represa; Costumes, Nereida Bonmatí; for Sogetel/Bocaboca Proucciones, S.A./Star Line Productions, S.L.; Spanish, 1996; Dolby Digital Stereo; Color; Rated R; 105 minutes; September release. **CAST**: Javier Bardem (Victor), Josep María Flotats (Ricardo), Aitana Sánchez-Gijón (Amanda), María Barranco (Angela), Myriam Mézières (Sheila), Jordi Bosch (Thug), Sam Makenzie (Oswaldo), Fernando Guillén-Cuervo (Raul), Amparo Baró (Margot), Candela Peña (Tanya)

MY MOTHER'S COURAGE (National Center for Jewish Film) Producer/Director/Screenplay, Michael Verhoeven; Based on the novel by George Tabori; Photography, Michael Epp, Theo Bierkens; Music, Juliann Nott, Simon Verhoeven; Editor, David Freeman; Designer, Wolfgang Hundhammer; German-British, 1995; Dolby Stereo; Cinemascope; Color; Not rated; 88 minutes; September release. **CAST:** George Tabori (Himself), Pauline Collins (Elsa Tabori), Ulrich Tukur (SS Officer), Natalie Morse (Maria), Robert Giggenbach (Cornelius Tabori), Heribert Sasse (Kelemen), Günter Bothur ("Moustache"), Simon Verhoeven

Javier Bardem, Aitana Sanchez-Gijon in *Mouth to Mouth*
© Miramax Films

(Young SS Man), Buddy Elias (Rabbi), Peter Radtke (German Teacher "Wireless"), Otto Grünmandl (Julius), Hana Frejkova (Martha), Jens Harzer (Young Man in Pyjamas), Tatjana Vilhelmova (Olga), Istvan Iglodi (Usicky), Eddi Arent (Klapka), Wolfgang Gasser (Igoldi), Johanna Mertinz (Tram Conductor), Jindrich Bonaventura (Greenshirt with Chalk), Jiri Knot (German Bookkeeper)

YO SOY, DEL SON A LA SALSA (RMM FilmWorks) Producer/Director, Rigoberto Lopez; Screenplay, Rigoberto Lopez, Leonardo Padura; Photography, Luis Garcia, Jose M. Riera; Editor, Miriam Talavera; Cuban; Color; Not rated; 100 minutes; September release. Documentary on Caribbean dance music with Celia Cruz, Tito Puente, Oscar D'Leon, Cheo Feliciano, Fania All-Stars, Eddie Palmieri, Johnny Pacheco, El Gran Combo, Marc Anthony, Andy Montanez, Gilberto Santa Rosa, Larry Harlow, Issac Delgado, Tito Gomez, Papo Lucca, Dave Valentin, Tite Curet Alonso, Israel Loperz "Cachao", Joe Cuba, Chucho Valdes, Los Van Van, Adalberto Alvarez, Yoruba Andabo, Grupo Changui, Lazaro Herrera , Rudy Calzado.

STAG (CFP) Producers, John Duning, Michael Paseornek; Executive Producers, Gabrielle Kelly, Jeff Sackman, Andre Link; Director, Gavin Wilding; Screenplay, Evan Tylor, Pat Bermel; Story, Jason Schombing; Photography, Maryse Alberti; Editor, Mark Sanders; Music, Paul J. Zaza; Designer, Phyllis Cedar; Costumes, Ane Crabtree; Casting, Tom McSweeney; a Rampage Entertainment production; Color; Not rated; 92 minutes; September release. **CAST:** Andrew McCarthy (Peter), John Stockwell (Victor), Kevin Dillon (Dan), Taylor Dayne (Serena), Mario Van Peebles (Michael), Ben Gazzara (Frank), Mark Blum, Gerald Anthony, William McNamara, John Henson, Gregalan Williams, Jennifer Miller, William Prael, Jerry Stiller. (This film made its U.S. debut on HBO in June of 1997).

TAXI LISBOA (Wolf Gauditz) Producer/Director/Screenplay, Wolf Gauditz; Photography, Claus Langer, Rodger Hinrichs; Editor, André Bendocchi-Alves; Music, Gert Wilden, Jr.; a Solofilm/München, in coproduction with BR, München/SR, Saarbrücken; Portuguese-German-Italian; Dolby Stereo; Color; Not rated; 86 minutes; October release. **CAST**: Augusto Macedo, Antonio Torchiaro, Josefina Lind, Leonore Mau, Ana-Teresa Sousa, Gerard Samaan.

DANCEHALL QUEEN (Island Digital Media) Producers, Carolyn Pfeiffer, Carl Bradshaw; Executive Producers, Chris Blackwell, Dan Genetti; Directors, Don Letts, Rick Elgood; Screenplay, Suzanne Fenn, Ed Wallace, Don Letts; Based on an idea by Ed Wallace, Carl Bradshaw; Photography, Louis Mulvey; Editor, Suzanne Fenn; an Island Jamaica Films presentation in association with Hawk's Nest productions; Color; Not rated; 94 minutes; October release. **CAST**: Audrey Reid (Marcia), Carl Davis ("Uncle" Larry), Paul Campbell (Priest), Pauline Stone-Myrie (Mrs. Gordon), Cherine Anderson, Mark Danvers, Patrice Harrison, Anika Grason, Donald Thompson, Henry Brown, Carl Bradshaw, Michael London, Beenie Man, Lady Saw, Anthony B, Chevelle Franklyn.

Pauline Collins, Natalie Morse in *My Mother's Courage*

PRETTY VILLAGE, PRETTY FLAME (Fox Lorber) Producers, Goran Bjelogrlic, Dragan Bjelogrlic, Nikola Kojo; Executive Producer, Milko Josifov; Director, Srdjan Dragojevic; Screenplay, Vanja Bulic, Srdjan Dragojevic, Nikola Pejakovic; Photography, Dusan Joksimovic; Editor, Petar Markovic; Music, Laza Ristovski; a Cobra Film Department presentation in association with MCRS and RTS; Yugoslav, 1996; Color; Not rated; 125 minutes; October release. **CAST**: Dragan Bjelogrlic (Milan), Nikola Kojo (Velja), Velimir-Bata Zivojinovic (Gvozden), Dragan Maksimovic (Petar), Zoran Cvijanovic (Brzi), Nikola Pejakovic (Halil), Dragan Petrovic (Laza), Milorad Mandic (Gavra)

LIKE A BRIDE (Atara Releasing) Executive Producer, Tita Lombardo; Director, Guita Schyfter; Screenplay, Hugo Hiriart; Based on the book by Rosa Nissan; Photography, Toni Kuhn; Editor, Carlos Bolado; Art Director, Tere Pecanins; Music, Joaquin Guitierrez; Mexican, 1993; Color; Not rated; 115 minutes; October release. **CAST:** Claudette Maille (Oshinica Mataraso), Angelica Aragon (Sara), Maya Mishalska (Rifke Groman), Ernesto Laguardia (Saavedra)

FOREIGN LAND (Riofilme/Videofilmes) Executive Producer, Flávio R. Tambellini; Directors, Walter Salles, Daniela Thomas; Screenplay, Daniela Thomas, Marcos Bernstein, Walter Salles, Millôr Fernandes; Photography, Walter Carvalho; Art Director, Daniela Thomas; Editors, Walter Salles, Felipe Lagerda; Music, Jose Miguel Wisnik; Costumes, Cristina Camargo; Portuguese; Color; Not rated; 100 minutes; October release. **CAST**: Fernanda Torres (Alex), Fernando Alves Pinto (Paco), Luis Melo (Igor), Alexandre Borges (Miguel), Laura Cardoso (Manuela), João Lagarto (Pedro), Tcheky Karyo (Kraft)

Dragan Bjelogrlic in *Pretty Village, Pretty Flame*
© Fox Lorber

BEAUMARCHAIS THE SCOUNDREL (New Yorker) Producer, Charles Gassot; Director, Edouard Molinaro; Screenplay, Edouard Molinaro, Jean-Claude Brisville; Inspired by an unpublished work by Sacha Guitry; Photography, Michael Epp; Executive Producer, Dominique Brunner; Editor, Veronique Parnet; Costumes, Sylvie De Segonzac; Set Designer, Jean-Marc Kerdelhue; Music, Jean-Claude Petit; a co-production of Téléma, Le Studio Canal+, France 2 Cinema, France 3 Cinema, with the participation of Canal+ and the assistance of Procirep/Investimage 4/Sofiarp 2; French, 1996; Panavision; Color; Not rated; 100 minutes; October release. **CAST**: Fabrice Luchini (Beaumarchais), Manuel Blanc (Gudin), Sandrine Kiberlain (Marie-Therese), Michel Serrault (Louis XV), Jacques Weber (Duc de Chaulnes), Michel Piccoli (Prince de Conti), Jean-François Balmer (Sartine), Florence Thomassin (Marion Menard), Isabelle Carré (Rosine), Claire Nebout (The Knight of Éon), Jean Yanne (Goezman), Martin Lamotte (Comte De La Blache), Jean-Claude Brialy (The Abbot), Dominique Besnehard (Louis XVI), Axelle Laffont (Mariette Lejay), Murray Head (Lord Rochford), Patrick Bouchitey (Monsieur Lejay), José Garcia (Figaro), François Morel (Peasant at Court), Alain Chabat (Courtier at Versailles), Pierre Gérard (Comte De Provence), Judith Godrèche (Marie-Antoinette), Evelyne Bouix (Madame Vigee-Lebrun), Michel Aumont (Baron De Breteuil), Jean-Marc Besset (Desfontaines), Roland Blanche (Thevenot De Morande), Jeff Nuttall (Benjamin Franklin)

DEEP CRIMSON (New Yorker) Producers, Miguel Necoechea, Paolo Barbachano; Executive Producer, Tita Lombardo; Director, Arturo Ripstein; Screenplay, Paz Alicia Garciadiego; Photography, Guillermo Granillo; Designers, Macarena Folache, Marisa Pecanins, Monica Chirinos; Editor, Rafael Castanedo; Music, David Mansfield; a co-production of Ivania Films/MK2/Wanda Films/Institute Mexicano de Cinematographia/TVE; Mexican-French-Spanish, 1996; Color; Not rated; 109 minutes; October release. **CAST:** Regina Orozco (Coral Fabre), Daniel Gimenez Cacho (Nicolas Estrella), Marisa Paredes (Irene Gallardo), Patricia Reyes Espindola (The Widow Ruelas), Juanita Norton (Julieta Egurrola), Rosa Furman (The Widow Morrison), Veronica Merchant (Rebecca San Pedro), Sherlyn Gonzales (Teresa), Giovanni Florido (Carlitos), Bianca Flordio (Mercedes)

THE KNOWLEDGE OF HEALING (In Pictures) Producer, Marcel Hoehn; Director/Screenplay, Franz Reichle; Photography, Pio Corradi; Editors, Myriam Flury, Franz Reichle; a T&C Film AG production; Tibetan; Color; Not rated; 90 minutes; November release. Documentary on Tibetan medicine featuring H.H. Tenzin Gyatso XIV Dalai Lama of Tibet, Tenzin Choedrak, Chimit-Dorzhi Dugarov, Karl Lutz, Alfred Hassig, Herbert Schwabl, Herbert Klima, Alexander P. Nechunayev, Dashinima D. Ayusheyev, Isaac Ginsburg, Lobsang Dolker, Tenzin Choedon, Nikita B. Maglayev, Viktoria Tsyrengarmayeva, Dolgor B. Linkovoin, Fritz Sterki.

A COUCH IN NEW YORK (Northern Arts) Producers, Régine Konckier, Jean-Luc Ormieres; Executive Producer, Robin O'Hara; Director, Chantal Akerman; Screenplay, Chantal Akerman, Jean-Louis Benoit; Photography, Dietrich Lohmann; Editor, Claire Atherton; Music, Paolo Conte, Sonia Atherton; Designer, Christian Marti; a Les Films Balengicaga, France 2 Cinema M6 Films (Paris)/Paradise Films, RTBF-Television Belge (Brussels)/Babelsberg Film Produktion (Berlin) production, with the participation of Canal+, Film Board Berlin Brandenburg; French-Belgian-German, 1996; Dolby Stereo; Color; Not rated; 109 minutes; November release. **CAST:** William Hurt (Henry Harriston), Juliette Binoche (Béatrice Saulnier), Paul Guilfoyle (Dennis), Stephanie Buttle (Anne), Richard Jenkins (Campton), Kent Broadhurst (Tim), Henry Bean (Stein), Barbara Garrick (Lisbeth Honeywell), Bernard Breuse (Jerome), Matthew Burton (Wood), Henry Burton (Stein), Bernard Breuse (Jérome), Adam LeFevre (Patron), Tiffany Frazer (Julie), Wendy Way (Airport Employee), Jean-Baptiste Filleau (Julien), Lysako Karunga (Martin), Blaise Chakir (Thomas). (This film made its U.S. debut on cable television in July of 1996).

BUGIS STREET (Margin Films) Produced by Jaytex Prods.; Director, Fan Yon; Screenplay, Yuo Chan, Fan Yon; Photography, Jacky Tang; Editor, Ma Kam; Singapore-Cantonese, 1994; Color; Not rated; 100 minutes; November release. **CAST**: Michael Lam, Hiep Thi Le. No other credits available.

Birdo Lucci, Napoleon in *Napoleon*
© MGM Distribution

NAPOLEON (Goldwyn) Producers, Michael Bourchier, Mario Andreacchio; Director, Mario Andreacchio; Screenplay, Michael Bourchier, Mario Andreacchio, Mark Saltzman; Executive Producers, Masato Hara, Ron Saunders; Producer for Herald Ace, Naonori Kawamura; Producer for the Samuel Goldwyn Company, Mark Saltzman; Photography, Roger Dowling; Designer, Vicki Niehus; Music, Bill Conti; Editor, Edward McQueen-Mason; Line Producer, John Wild; Dog & Bird Handler/Trainer, The Cuong Truong; a Herald Ace Inc. presentation in association with Nippon Herald Films/Fuji Television & Pony Canyon of a Film Australia/Herald Ace and Furry Feature Films production; Distributed by MGM Distribution; Australian; Dolby Digital; Color; Rated G; 82 minutes; October release. **VOICE CAST:** Jamie Croft (Napoleon), Philip Quast (Birdo), Susan Lyons (Napoleon's Mom/Wallaby), Coralie Sawade (Kid's Mother), Brenton Whittle (Owl/Frog/Wombat/Wallaby/Desert Mouse), Anne Lambert (Spider/Earless Wallaby), Carole Skinner (Cat), Catherine Lambert, Tracey Canini, Annabel Sims, Neusa Timms, Debbie Horn (Lorikeets/Rabbits), Lucia Mastrantone (Lone Lorikeet), Frank Whitton (Koala), Fiona Press (Wallaby/Mother Dingo), Steven Vidler (Snake/Desert Mouse/Turtle), David Argue (Frill Necked Lizard), Edward McQueen-Mason (Echidna), Stuart Pankin (Perenti Lizard/Father Penguin), Mignon Kent (Nancy), Michael Wilkop (Sid), Barry Humphries (Kangaroo), Casey Siemaszko (Conan), Joan Rivers (Mother Penguin), Stuart Zagnit, Carolyn Sloan (Penguins)

Fabrice Luchini, Sandrine Kiberlain in *Beaumarchais the Scoundrel*
© New Yorker Films

Daniel Gimenez Cacho, Regina Orozco in *Deep Crimson*
© New Yorker Films

Bryan Brown in *Dead Heart*
© Fox Lorber

DEAD HEART (Fox Lorber) Producers, Bryan Brown, Helen Watts; Director/Screenplay, Nicholas Parsons; Photography, James Bartle; Designer, Brian Edmonds; Costumes, Edie Kurzer; Australian; Color; Not rated; 106 minutes; November release. **CAST:** Bryan Brown (Ray), Ernie Dingo (David), Angie Milliken (Kate), Aaron Pedersen (Tony), Gnarnay Yarrahe Waitaire (Poppy), Lewis Fitzgerald (Les), Anne Tenney (Sarah), John Jarratt (Charlie), Lafe Charlton (Billy), Djunawong Stanley Mirindo (Tjulpu), Peter Francis (Mannga)

THE WITMAN BOYS (Bunyik Entertainment) Producer, Ferenc Kardos; Director, Janos Szasz; Screenplay, Geza Csath, Janos Szasz; Photography, Tibor Mathe; Editor, Anna Kornis; Designer, Jozsef Romvary; a Budapest Filmstudio-MTM Kommunikacios-47eme Parallele-StudioFilmowe Zebra-Mafilm co-production; Hungarian-French-Polish; Color; Not rated; 92 minutes; November release. **CAST:** Alpar Fogarassi (Janos Witman), Szaboles Gergely (Erno Witman), Maia Morgenstern (Mrs. Witman), Dominika Ostalowska (Iren), Peter Andorai (Talloi), Lajos Kovacs (Denes Witman)

O AMOR NATURAL (First Run Features/Icarus) Producer, Pieter van Huystee; Director/Screenplay, Heddy Honigmann; Editor, Marc Nolens; a Pieter van Huystee Film & TV/NPS TV production; Dutch-Portuguese; Color; Not rated; 76 minutes; December release. Documentary celebrating the erotic poetry of Brazil's Carlos Drummond.

WE FREE KINGS (I Magi Randagi) (Independent) Producer, Francesco Torelli; Director/Screenplay, Sergio Citti; Photography, Franco Di Giacomo; Music, Ennio Morricone; Art Director, Danilo Donati; Editor, Ugo De Rossi; a co-production of I.P.S. S.r.l. (Rome)—Journal Film (Berlin)—Films Sans Frontieres (Paris); Italian-French-German; Color; Not rated; 94 minutes; December release. **CAST**: Silvio Orlando, Patrick Bauchau, Rolf Zacher, David Grieco, Michele Salimbeni, Nanni Tamma, Laura Betti, Franco Citti, Ninetto Davoli, Gastone Moschin.

LA RENCONTRE (Artistic License) Conceived and Directed by Alain Cavalier; from Les Films de l'Astrophone; French, 1996; Not rated; 76 minutes; December release. The filmmaker's visual diary of objects that remind him of a woman he loved.

GUY (Gramercy) Producers, Vincent D'Onofrio, Warren Robert Jason, Renee Missel; Director, Michael Lindsay-Hogg; Screenplay, Kirby Dick; Photography, Arturo Smith; Music, Geoffrey Beal; Editor, Dody Dorn; produced by KRRWH Inc. aka GUY Prods./North Rhine Westfalia Filmfund/Pandora Film/PolyGram Filmed Entertainment; British-German, 1996; Color; Rated R; 91 minutes; December release. **CAST:** Vincent D'Onofrio (Guy), Hope Davis, Kimber Riddle

Juliette Binoche, William Hurt in *A Couch in New York*
© Northern Arts

Silvio Orlando, Patrick Bauchau, Rolf Zacher in *We Free Kings*

Danny Aiello

Jennifer Aniston

Dan Aykroyd

Kevin Bacon

Biographical Data

(Name, real name, place and date of birth, school attended)

AAMES, WILLIE (William Upton): Los Angeles, CA, July 15, 1960.
AARON, CAROLINE: Richmond, VA, Aug. 7, 1954. Catholic U.
ABBOTT, DIAHNNE: NYC, 1945.
ABBOTT, JOHN: London, June 5, 1905.
ABRAHAM, F. MURRAY: Pittsburgh, PA, Oct. 24, 1939. UTx.
ACKLAND, JOSS: London, Feb. 29, 1928.
ADAMS, BROOKE: NYC, Feb. 8, 1949. Dalton.
ADAMS, CATLIN: Los Angeles, Oct. 11, 1950.
ADAMS, DON: NYC, Apr. 13, 1926.
ADAMS, EDIE (Elizabeth Edith Enke): Kingston, PA, Apr. 16, 1927. Juilliard, Columbia.
ADAMS, JULIE (Betty May): Waterloo, IA, Oct. 17, 1926. Little Rock, Jr. College.
ADAMS, MASON: NYC, Feb. 26, 1919. UWi.
ADAMS, MAUD (Maud Wikstrom): Lulea, Sweden, Feb. 12, 1945.
ADJANI, ISABELLE: Germany, June 27, 1955.
AFFLECK, BEN: Berkeley, CA, Aug. 15, 1972.
AGAR, JOHN: Chicago, IL, Jan. 31, 1921.
AGUTTER, JENNY: Taunton, England, Dec. 20, 1952.
AIELLO, DANNY: NYC, June 20, 1933.
AIMEE, ANOUK (Dreyfus): Paris, France, Apr. 27, 1934. Bauer-Therond.
AKERS, KAREN: NYC, Oct. 13, 1945, Hunter College.
ALBERGHETTI, ANNA MARIA: Pesaro, Italy, May 15, 1936.
ALBERT, EDDIE (Eddie Albert Heimberger): Rock Island, IL, Apr. 22, 1908. U of Minn.
ALBERT, EDWARD: Los Angeles, Feb. 20. 1951. UCLA.
ALBRIGHT, LOLA: Akron, OH, July 20, 1925.
ALDA, ALAN: NYC, Jan. 28, 1936. Fordham.
ALEANDRO, NORMA: Buenos Aires, Dec. 6, 1936.
ALEJANDRO, MIGUEL: NYC, Feb. 21, 1958.
ALEXANDER, JANE (Quigley): Boston, MA, Oct. 28, 1939. Sarah Lawrence.
ALEXANDER, JASON (Jay Greenspan): Newark, NJ, Sept. 23, 1959. Boston U.
ALICE, MARY: Indianola, MS, Dec. 3, 1941.
ALLEN, DEBBIE (Deborah): Houston, TX, Jan. 16, 1950. Howard U.
ALLEN, JOAN: Rochelle, IL, Aug. 20, 1956. EastIllU.
ALLEN, KAREN: Carrollton, IL, Oct. 5, 1951. UMd.
ALLEN, NANCY: NYC, June 24, 1950.
ALLEN, REX: Wilcox, AZ, Dec. 31, 1922.
ALLEN, STEVE: NYC, Dec. 26, 1921.
ALLEN, TIM: Denver, CO, June 13, 1953. W. MI. Univ.
ALLEN, WOODY (Allan Stewart Konigsberg): Brooklyn, Dec. 1, 1935.
ALLEY, KIRSTIE: Wichita, KS, Jan. 12, 1955.
ALLYSON, JUNE (Ella Geisman): Westchester, NY, Oct. 7, 1917.
ALONSO, MARIA CONCHITA: Cuba, June 29, 1957.
ALT, CAROL: Queens, NY, Dec. 1, 1960. HofstraU.
ALVARADO, TRINI: NYC, Jan. 10, 1967.
AMIS, SUZY: Oklahoma City, OK, Jan. 5, 1958. Actors Studio.
AMOS, JOHN: Newark, NJ, Dec. 27, 1940. Colo. U.
ANDERSON, KEVIN: Waukeegan, IL, Jan. 13, 1960.
ANDERSON, LONI: St. Paul, MN, Aug. 5, 1946.
ANDERSON, MELISSA SUE: Berkeley, CA, Sept. 26, 1962.
ANDERSON, MELODY: Edmonton, Canada, 1955. Carlton U.
ANDERSON, MICHAEL, JR.: London, England, Aug. 6, 1943.
ANDERSON, RICHARD DEAN: Minneapolis, MN, Jan. 23, 1950.
ANDERSSON, BIBI: Stockholm, Sweden, Nov. 11, 1935. Royal Dramatic Sch.
ANDES, KEITH: Ocean City, NJ, July 12, 1920. Temple U., Oxford.
ANDRESS, URSULA: Bern, Switzerland, Mar. 19, 1936.
ANDREWS, ANTHONY: London, Dec. 1, 1948.
ANDREWS, JULIE (Julia Elizabeth Wells): Surrey, England, Oct. 1, 1935.
ANGLIM, PHILIP: San Francisco, CA, Feb. 11, 1953.
ANISTON, JENNIFER: Sherman Oaks, CA, Feb. 11, 1969.
ANN-MARGRET (Olsson): Valsjobyn, Sweden, Apr. 28, 1941. Northwestern U.
ANSARA, MICHAEL: Lowell, MA, Apr. 15, 1922. Pasadena Playhouse.
ANSPACH, SUSAN: NYC, Nov. 23, 1945.
ANTHONY, LYSETTE: London, 1963.
ANTHONY, TONY: Clarksburg, WV, Oct. 16, 1937. Carnegie Tech.
ANTON, SUSAN: Yucaipa, CA, Oct. 12, 1950. Bemardino College.
ANTONELLI, LAURA: Pola, Italy, Nov. 28, 1941.
ANWAR, GABRIELLE: Lalehaam, England, Feb. 4, 1970
APPLEGATE, CHRISTINA: Hollywood CA, Nov. 25, 1972.
ARCHER, ANNE: Los Angeles, Aug. 25, 1947.
ARCHER, JOHN (Ralph Bowman): Osceola, NB, May 8, 1915. USC.
ARDANT, FANNY: Monte Carlo, Mar 22, 1949
ARKIN, ADAM: Brooklyn, NY, Aug. 19, 1956.
ARKIN, ALAN: NYC, Mar. 26, 1934. LACC.

Scott Bakula

ARMSTRONG, BESS: Baltimore, MD, Dec. 11, 1953.
ARNAZ, DESI, JR.: Los Angeles, Jan. 19, 1953.
ARNAZ, LUCIE: Hollywood, July 17, 1951.
ARNESS, JAMES (Aurness): Minneapolis, MN, May 26, 1923. Beloit College.
ARQUETTE, DAVID: Sept. 8, 1971.
ARQUETTE, PATRICIA: NYC, Apr. 8, 1968.
ARQUETTE, ROSANNA: NYC, Aug. 10, 1959.
ARTHUR, BEATRICE (Frankel): NYC, May 13, 1924. New School.
ASHER, JANE: London, Apr. 5, 1946.
ASHLEY, ELIZABETH (Elizabeth Ann Cole): Ocala, FL, Aug. 30, 1939.
ASHTON, JOHN: Springfield, MA, Feb. 22, 1948. USC.
ASNER, EDWARD: Kansas City, KS, Nov. 15, 1929.
ASSANTE, ARMAND: NYC, Oct. 4, 1949. AADA.
ASTIN, JOHN: Baltimore, MD, Mar. 30, 1930. U Minn.
ASTIN, MacKENZIE: Los Angeles, May 12, 1973.
ASTIN, SEAN: Santa Monica, Feb. 25, 1971.
ATHERTON, WILLIAM: Orange, CT, July 30, 1947. Carnegie Tech.
ATKINS, CHRISTOPHER: Rye, NY, Feb. 21, 1961.
ATKINS, EILEEN: London, June 16, 1934.

Alec Baldwin

ATKINSON, ROWAN: England, Jan. 6, 1955. Oxford.
ATTENBOROUGH, RICHARD: Cambridge, England, Aug. 29, 1923. RADA.
AUBERJONOIS, RENE: NYC, June 1, 1940. Carnegie Tech.
AUDRAN, STEPHANE: Versailles, France, Nov. 8, 1932.
AUGER, CLAUDINE: Paris, France, Apr. 26, 1942. Dramatic Cons.
AULIN, EWA: Stockholm, Sweden, Feb. 14, 1950.
AUMONT, JEAN PIERRE: Paris, France, Jan. 5, 1909. French Nat'l School of Drama.
AUTRY, GENE: Tioga, TX, Sept. 29, 1907.
AVALON, FRANKIE (Francis Thomas Avallone): Philadelphia, PA, Sept. 18, 1939.
AYKROYD, DAN: Ottawa, Canada, July 1, 1952.
AZNAVOUR, CHARLES (Varenagh Aznourian): Paris, France, May 22, 1924.
AZZARA, CANDICE: Brooklyn, NY, May 18, 1947.
BACH, CATHERINE: Warren, OH, Mar. 1, 1954.
BACALL, LAUREN (Betty Perske): NYC, Sept. 16, 1924. AADA.
BACH, BARBARA: Queens, NY, Aug. 27, 1946.
BACKER, BRIAN: NYC, Dec. 5, 1956. Neighborhood Playhouse.
BACON, KEVIN: Philadelphia, PA, July 8, 1958.
BAIN, BARBARA: Chicago, IL, Sept. 13, 1934. U Ill.
BAIO, SCOTT: Brooklyn, NY, Sept. 22, 1961.
BAKER, BLANCHE: NYC, Dec. 20, 1956.
BAKER, CARROLL: Johnstown, PA, May 28, 1931. St. Petersburg, Jr. College.
BAKER, DIANE: Hollywood, CA, Feb. 25, 1938. USC.
BAKER, JOE DON: Groesbeck, TX, Feb.12, 1936.
BAKER, KATHY: Midland, TX, June 8, 1950. UC Berkley.
BAKULA, SCOTT: St. Louis, MO, Oct. 9, 1955. KansasU.
BALABAN, BOB: Chicago, IL, Aug. 16, 1945. Colgate.
BALDWIN, ADAM: Chicago, IL, Feb. 27, 1962.
BALDWIN, ALEC: Massapequa, NY, Apr. 3, 1958. NYU.
BALDWIN, STEPHEN: Long Island, NY, 1966.
BALDWIN, WILLIAM: Massapequa, NY, Feb. 21, 1963.
BALE, CHRISTIAN: Pembrokeshire, West Wales, Jan. 30, 1974.
BALLARD, KAYE: Cleveland, OH, Nov. 20, 1926.
BANCROFT, ANNE (Anna Maria Italiano): Bronx, NY, Sept. 17, 1931. AADA.
BANDERAS, ANTONIO: Malaga, Spain, Aug. 10, 1960.
BANERJEE, VICTOR: Calcutta, India, Oct. 15, 1946.
BANES, LISA: Chagrin Falls, OH, July 9, 1955. Juilliard.
BANNEN, IAN: Airdrie, Scotland, June 29, 1928.
BARANSKI, CHRISTINE: Buffalo, NY, May 2, 1952. Juilliard.
BARBEAU, ADRIENNE: Sacramento, CA, June 11, 1945. Foothill College.

William Baldwin

BARDOT, BRIGITTE: Paris, France, Sept. 28, 1934.
BARKIN, ELLEN: Bronx, NY, Apr. 16, 1954. Hunter College.
BARNES, BINNIE (Gitelle Enoyce Barnes): London, Mar. 25, 1906.
BARNES, CHRISTOPHER DANIEL: Portland, ME, Nov. 7, 1972.
BARR, JEAN-MARC: San Diego, CA, Sept. 1960.
BARRAULT, JEAN-LOUIS: Vesinet, France, Sept. 8, 1910.
BARRAULT, MARIE-CHRISTINE: Paris, France, Mar. 21, 1944.
BARREN, KEITH: Mexborough, England, Aug. 8, 1936. Sheffield Playhouse.
BARRETT, MAJEL (Hudec): Columbus, OH, Feb. 23. Western Reserve U.
BARRIE, BARBARA: Chicago, IL, May 23, 1931.
BARRY, GENE (Eugene Klass): NYC, June 14, 1919.
BARRY, NEILL: NYC, Nov. 29, 1965.
BARRYMORE, DREW: Los Angeles, Feb. 22, 1975.
BARRYMORE, JOHN DREW: Beverly Hills, CA, June 4, 1932. St. John's Military Academy.
BARTEL, PAUL: Brooklyn, NY, Aug. 6, 1938. UCLA.
BARTY, BILLY: (William John Bertanzetti) Millsboro, PA, Oct. 25, 1924.

Jacqueline Bisset

BARYSHNIKOV, MIKHAIL: Riga, Latvia, Jan. 27, 1948.
BASINGER, KIM: Athens, GA, Dec. 8, 1953. Neighborhood Playhouse.
BASSETT, ANGELA: NYC, Aug. 16, 1958.
BATEMAN, JASON: Rye, NY, Jan. 14, 1969.
BATEMAN, JUSTINE: Rye, NY, Feb. 19, 1966.
BATES, ALAN: Allestree, Derbyshire, England, Feb. 17, 1934. RADA.
BATES, JEANNE: San Francisco, CA, May 21, 1918. RADA.
BATES, KATHY: Memphis, TN, June 28, 1948. S. Methodist U.
BAUER, STEVEN (Steven Rocky Echevarria): Havana, Cuba, Dec. 2, 1956. U Miami.
BAXTER, KEITH: South Wales, England, Apr. 29, 1933. RADA.
BAXTER, MEREDITH: Los Angeles, June 21, 1947. Intelochen Acad.
BAYE, NATHALIE: Mainevile, France, July 6, 1948
BEACHAM, STEPHANIE: Casablanca, Morocco, Feb. 28, 1947.
BEALS, JENNIFER: Chicago, IL, Dec. 19, 1963.
BEAN, ORSON (Dallas Burrows): Burlington, VT, July 22, 1928.
BEAN, SEAN: Sheffield, Yorkshire, England, Apr. 17, 1958.
BEART, EMMANUELLE: Gassin, France, Aug. 14, 1965.
BEATTY, NED: Louisville, KY, July 6, 1937.
BEATTY, WARREN: Richmond, VA, Mar. 30, 1937.
BECK, JOHN: Chicago, IL, Jan. 28, 1943.
BECK, MICHAEL: Memphis, TN, Feb. 4, 1949. Millsap College.
BECKINSALE, KATE: England, July 26, 1974.
BEDELIA, BONNIE: NYC, Mar. 25, 1946. Hunter College.
BEGLEY, ED, JR.: NYC, Sept. 16, 1949.
BELAFONTE, HARRY: NYC, Mar. 1, 1927.
BEL GEDDES, BARBARA: NYC, Oct. 31, 1922.
BELL, TOM: Liverpool, England, 1932.
BELLER, KATHLEEN: NYC, Feb. 10, 1957.
BELLWOOD, PAMELA (King): Scarsdale, NY, June 26, 1951.
BELMONDO, JEAN PAUL: Paris, France, Apr. 9, 1933.
BELUSHI, JAMES: Chicago, IL, June 15, 1954.
BELZER, RICHARD: Bridgeport, CT, Aug. 4, 1944.
BENEDICT, DIRK (Niewoehner): White Sulphur Springs, MT, March 1, 1945. Whitman College.
BENEDICT, PAUL: Silver City, NM, Sept. 17, 1938.
BENIGNI, ROBERTO: Tuscany, Italy, Oct. 27, 1952.
BENING, ANNETTE: Topeka, KS, May 29, 1958. SFSt. U.
BENJAMIN, RICHARD: NYC, May 22, 1938. Northwestern U.
BENNENT, DAVID: Lausanne, Sept. 9, 1966.
BENNETT, ALAN: Leeds, England, May 9, 1934. Oxford.
BENNETT, BRUCE (Herman Brix): Tacoma, WA, May 19, 1909. U Wash.

Ruben Blades

Diahann Carroll

Cher

BENNETT, HYWEL: Garnant, So. Wales, Apr. 8, 1944.
BENSON, ROBBY: Dallas, TX, Jan. 21, 1957.
BERENGER, TOM: Chicago, IL, May 31, 1950, U Mo.
BERENSON, MARISA: NYC, Feb. 15, 1947.
BERG, PETER: NYC, 1964. Malcalester College.
BERGEN, CANDICE: Los Angeles, May 9, 1946. U PA.
BERGEN, POLLY: Knoxville, TN, July 14, 1930. Compton, Jr. College.
BERGER, HELMUT: Salzburg, Austria, May 29, 1942.
BERGER, SENTA: Vienna, Austria, May 13, 1941. Vienna Sch. of Acting.
BERGER, WILLIAM: Austria, Jan. 20, 1928. Columbia.
BERGERAC, JACQUES: Biarritz, France, May 26, 1927. Paris U.
BERGIN, PATRICK: Dublin, Feb. 4, 1951.
BERKLEY, ELIZABETH: Detroit, MI, July 28, 1972.
BERKOFF, STEVEN: London, England, Aug. 3, 1937.
BERLE, MILTON (Berlinger): NYC, July 12, 1908.
BERLIN, JEANNIE: Los Angeles, Nov. 1, 1949.
BERLINGER, WARREN: Brooklyn, Aug. 31, 1937. Columbia.
BERNHARD, SANDRA: Flint, MI, June 6, 1955.
BERNSEN, CORBIN: Los Angeles, Sept. 7, 1954. UCLA.
BERRI, CLAUDE (Langmann): Paris, France, July 1, 1934.
BERRIDGE, ELIZABETH: Westchester, NY, May 2, 1962. Strasberg Inst.
BERRY, HALLE: Cleveland, OH, Aug. 14, 1968.
BERRY, KEN: Moline, IL, Nov. 3, 1933.
BERTINELLI, VALERIE: Wilmington, DE, Apr. 23, 1960.
BEST, JAMES: Corydon, IN, July 26, 1926.
BETTGER, LYLE: Philadelphia, PA, Feb. 13, 1915. AADA.
BEY, TURHAN: Vienna, Austria, Mar. 30, 1921.
BEYMER, RICHARD: Avoca, IA, Feb. 21, 1939.
BIALIK, MAYIM: San Diego, CA, Dec. 12, 1975.
BIEHN, MICHAEL: Anniston, AL, July 31, 1956.
BIKEL, THEODORE: Vienna, May 2, 1924. RADA.
BILLINGSLEY, PETER: NYC, Apr. 16, 1972.
BINOCHE, JULIETTE: Paris, France, Mar. 9, 1964.
BIRKIN, JANE: London, Dec. 14, 1947
BIRNEY, DAVID: Washington, DC, Apr. 23, 1939. Dartmouth, UCLA.
BIRNEY, REED: Alexandria, VA, Sept. 11, 1954. Boston U.
BISHOP, JOEY (Joseph Abraham Gotllieb): Bronx, NY, Feb. 3, 1918.
BISHOP, JULIE (Jacqueline Wells): Denver, CO, Aug. 30, 1917. Westlake School.
BISSET, JACQUELINE: Waybridge, England, Sept. 13, 1944.
BLACK, KAREN (Ziegler): Park Ridge, IL, July 1, 1942. Northwestern.

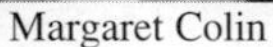

Margaret Colin

Robbie Coltrane

Sean Connery

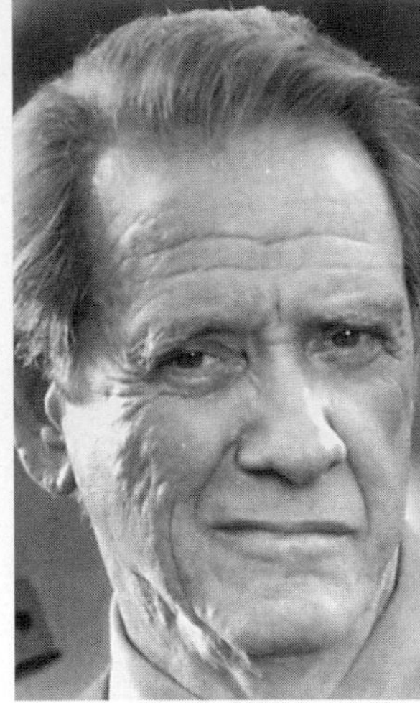

Richard Crenna

BLACKMAN, HONOR: London, Aug. 22, 1926.
BLADES, RUBEN: Panama City, July 16, 1948. Harvard.
BLAIR, BETSY (Betsy Boger): NYC, Dec. 11, 1923.
BLAIR, JANET (Martha Jane Lafferty): Blair, PA, Apr. 23, 1921.
BLAIR, LINDA: Westport, CT, Jan. 22, 1959.
BLAKE, ROBERT (Michael Gubitosi): Nutley, NJ, Sept. 18, 1933.
BLAKELY, SUSAN: Frankfurt, Germany, Sept. 7, 1950. U TX.
BLAKLEY, RONEE: Stanley, ID, 1946. Stanford U.
BLETHYN, BRENDA: Ramsgate, Kent, Eng., Feb. 20, 1946.
BLOOM, CLAIRE: London, Feb. 15, 1931. Badminton School.
BLOOM, VERNA: Lynn, MA, Aug. 7, 1939. Boston U.
BLOUNT, LISA: Fayettville, AK, July 1, 1957. UAk.
BLUM, MARK: Newark, NJ, May 14, 1950. UMinn.
BLYTH, ANN: Mt. Kisco, NY, Aug. 16, 1928. New Waybum Dramatic School.
BOCHNER, HART: Toronto, Canada, Oct. 3, 1956. U San Diego.
BOCHNER, LLOYD: Toronto, Canada, July 29, 1924.
BOGARDE, DIRK: London, Mar. 28, 1921. Glasgow & Univ. College.
BOGOSIAN, ERIC: Woburn, MA, Apr. 24, 1953. Oberlin College.
BOHRINGER, RICHARD: Paris, France, Jan. 16, 1941.
BOLKAN, FLORINDA (Florinda Soares Bulcao): Ceara, Brazil, Feb. 15, 1941.
BOLOGNA, JOSEPH: Brooklyn, NY, Dec. 30, 1938. Brown U.
BOND, DEREK: Glasgow, Scotland, Jan. 26, 1920. Askes School.
BONET, LISA: San Francisco, CA, Nov. 16, 1967.
BONHAM-CARTER, HELENA: London, England, May 26, 1966.
BONO, SONNY (Salvatore): Detroit, MI, Feb. 16, 1935.
BOONE, PAT: Jacksonville, FL, June 1, 1934. Columbia U.
BOOTHE, JAMES: Croydon, England, Dec.19, 1930
BOOTHE, POWERS: Snyder, TX, June 1, 1949. So. Methodist U.
BORGNINE, ERNEST (Borgnino): Hamden, CT, Jan. 24, 1917. Randall School.
BOSCO, PHILIP: Jersey City, NJ, Sept. 26, 1930. CatholicU.
BOSLEY, TOM: Chicago, IL, Oct. 1, 1927. DePaul U.
BOSTWICK, BARRY: San Mateo, CA, Feb. 24, 1945. NYU.
BOTTOMS, JOSEPH: Santa Barbara, CA, Aug. 30, 1954.
BOTTOMS, SAM: Santa Barbara, CA, Oct. 17, 1955.
BOTTOMS, TIMOTHY: Santa Barbara, CA, Aug. 30, 1951.
BOULTING, INGRID: Transvaal, So. Africa, 1947.
BOUTSIKARIS, DENNIS: Newark, NJ, Dec. 21, 1952. CatholicU.
BOWIE, DAVID (David Robert Jones): Brixton, South London, England, Jan. 8, 1947.
BOWKER, JUDI: Shawford, England, Apr. 6, 1954.
BOXLEITNER, BRUCE: Elgin, IL, May 12, 1950.
BOYLE, LARA FLYNN: Davenport, IA, Mar. 24, 1970.
BOYLE, PETER: Philadelphia, PA, Oct. 18, 1933. LaSalle College.
BRACCO, LORRAINE: Brooklyn, NY, 1955.
BRACKEN, EDDIE: NYC, Feb. 7, 1920. Professional Children's School.
BRAEDEN, ERIC (Hans Gudegast): Kiel, Germany, Apr. 3, 1942.
BRAGA, SONIA: Maringa, Brazil, June 8, 1950.
BRANAGH, KENNETH: Belfast, No. Ireland, Dec. 10, 1960.
BRANDAUER, KLAUS MARIA: Altaussee, Austria, June 22, 1944.
BRANDIS, JONATHAN: CT, Apr. 13, 1976.
BRANDO, JOCELYN: San Francisco, Nov. 18, 1919. Lake Forest College, AADA.
BRANDO, MARLON: Omaha, NB, Apr. 3, 1924. New School.
BRANDON, CLARK: NYC, Dec. 13, 1958.
BRANDON, MICHAEL (Feldman): Brooklyn, NY.
BRANTLEY, BETSY: Rutherfordton, NC, Sept. 20, 1955. London Central Sch. of Drama.
BRENNAN, EILEEN: Los Angeles, CA, Sept. 3, 1935. AADA.
BRIALY, JEAN-CLAUDE: Aumale, Algeria, 1933. Strasbourg Cons.
BRIDGES, BEAU: Los Angeles, Dec. 9, 1941. UCLA.
BRIDGES, JEFF: Los Angeles, Dec. 4, 1949.
BRIDGES, LLOYD: San Leandro, CA, Jan. 15, 1913.
BRIMLEY, WILFORD: Salt Lake City, UT, Sept. 27, 1934.
BRINKLEY, CHRISTIE: Malibu, CA, Feb. 2, 1954.
BRITT, MAY (Maybritt Wilkins): Sweden, Mar. 22, 1936.
BRITTANY, MORGAN (Suzanne Cupito): Los Angeles, Dec. 5, 1950.
BRITTON, TONY: Birmingham, England, June 9, 1924.
BRODERICK, MATTHEW: NYC, Mar. 21, 1962.
BROLIN, JAMES: Los Angeles, July 18, 1940. UCLA.
BROMFIELD, JOHN (Farron Bromfield): South Bend, IN, June 11, 1922. St. Mary's College.
BRON, ELEANOR: Stanmore, England, 1934.
BRONSON, CHARLES (Buchinsky): Ehrenfield, PA, Nov. 3, 1920.
BROOKES, JACQUELINE: Montclair, NJ, July 24, 1930. RADA.
BROOKS, ALBERT (Einstein): Los Angeles, July 22, 1947.
BROOKS, MEL (Melvyn Kaminski): Brooklyn, NY, June 28, 1926.
BROSNAN, PIERCE: County Meath, Ireland. May 16, 1952.
BROWN, BLAIR: Washington, DC, Apr. 23, 1947. Pine Manor.

Alan Cumming

John Cusack

Tim Daly

Judy Davis

BROWN, BRYAN: Panania, Australia, June 23, 1947.
BROWN, GARY (Christian Brando): Hollywood, CA, 1958.
BROWN, GEORG STANFORD: Havana, Cuba, June 24, 1943. AMDA.
BROWN, JAMES: Desdemona, TX, Mar. 22, 1920. Baylor U.
BROWN, JIM: St. Simons Island, NY, Feb. 17, 1935. Syracuse U.
BROWNE, LESLIE: NYC, 1958.
BROWNE, ROSCOE LEE: Woodbury, NJ, May 2, 1925.
BUCHHOLZ, HORST: Berlin, Germany, Dec. 4, 1933. Ludwig Dramatic School.
BUCKLEY, BETTY: Big Spring, TX, July 3, 1947. TxCU.
BUJOLD, GENEVIEVE: Montreal, Canada, July 1, 1942.
BULLOCK, SANDRA: Arlington, VA, July 26, 1964.
BURGHOFF, GARY: Bristol, CT, May 24, 1943.
BURGI, RICHARD: Montclair, NJ, July 30, 1958.
BURKE, PAUL: New Orleans, July 21, 1926. Pasadena Playhouse.
BURNETT, CAROL: San Antonio, TX, Apr. 26, 1933. UCLA.
BURNS, CATHERINE: NYC, Sept. 25, 1945. AADA.
BURNS, EDWARD: Valley Stream, NY, Jan. 28, 1969.
BURROWS, DARREN E.: Winfield, KS, Sept. 12, 1966
BURSTYN, ELLEN (Edna Rae Gillhooly): Detroit, MI, Dec. 7, 1932.
BURTON, LeVAR: Los Angeles, CA, Feb. 16, 1958. UCLA.
BUSCEMI, STEVE: Brooklyn, NY, Dec. 13, 1957.
BUSEY, GARY: Goose Creek, TX, June 29, 1944.
BUSFIELD, TIMOTHY: Lansing, MI, June 12, 1957. E. Tenn. St. U.
BUTTONS, RED (Aaron Chwatt): NYC, Feb. 5, 1919.
BUZZI, RUTH: Westerly, RI, July 24, 1936. Pasadena Playhouse.
BYGRAVES, MAX: London, Oct. 16, 1922. St. Joseph's School.
BYRNE, DAVID: Dumbarton, Scotland, May 14, 1952.
BYRNE, GABRIEL: Dublin, Ireland, May 12, 1950.
BYRNES, EDD: NYC, July 30, 1933.
CAAN, JAMES: Bronx, NY, Mar. 26,1939.
CAESAR, SID: Yonkers, NY, Sept. 8, 1922.
CAGE, NICOLAS (Coppola): Long Beach, CA, Jan.7, 1964.
CAINE, MICHAEL (Maurice Micklewhite): London, Mar. 14, 1933.
CAINE, SHAKIRA (Baksh): Guyana, Feb. 23, 1947. Indian Trust College.
CALHOUN, RORY (Francis Timothy Durgin): Los Angeles, Aug. 8, 1922.
CALLAN, MICHAEL (Martin Calinieff): Philadelphia, Nov. 22, 1935.
CALLOW, SIMON: London, June 15, 1949. Queens U.
CALVERT, PHYLLIS: London, Feb. 18, 1917. Margaret Morris School.
CALVET, CORRINE (Corinne Dibos): Paris, France, Apr. 30, 1925. U Paris.
CAMERON, KIRK: Panorama City, CA, Oct. 12, 1970.
CAMP, COLLEEN: San Francisco, CA, 1953.
CAMPBELL, BILL: Chicago, IL, July 7, 1959.
CAMPBELL, GLEN: Delight, AR, Apr. 22, 1935.
CAMPBELL, NEVE: Guelph, Ontario, Canada, Oct. 3, 1973.
CAMPBELL, TISHA: Oklahoma City, OK, Oct. 13, 1968.
CANALE, GIANNA MARIA: Reggio Calabria, Italy, Sept. 12, 1927.
CANNON, DYAN (Samille Diane Friesen): Tacoma, WA, Jan. 4, 1937.
CAPERS, VIRGINIA: Sumter, SC, Sept. 25, 1925. Juilliard.
CAPSHAW, KATE: Ft. Worth, TX, Nov. 3, 1953. UMo.
CARA, IRENE: NYC, Mar. 18, 1958.
CARDINALE, CLAUDIA: Tunis, N. Africa. Apr. 15, 1939. College Paul Cambon.
CAREY, HARRY, JR.: Saugus, CA, May 16, 1921. Black Fox Military Academy.
CAREY, PHILIP: Hackensack, NJ, July 15, 1925. U Miami.
CARIOU, LEN: Winnipeg, Canada, Sept. 30, 1939.
CARLIN, GEORGE: NYC, May 12, 1938.
CARLYLE, ROBERT: Glasgow, Scotland, Apr. 14, 1961.
CARMEN, JULIE: Mt. Vernon, NY, Apr. 4, 1954.
CARMICHAEL, IAN: Hull, England, June 18, 1920. Scarborough College.
CARNE, JUDY (Joyce Botterill): Northampton, England, 1939. Bush-Davis Theatre School.
CARNEY, ART: Mt. Vernon, NY, Nov. 4, 1918.
CARON, LESLIE: Paris, France, July 1, 1931. Nat'l Conservatory, Paris.
CARPENTER, CARLETON: Bennington, VT, July 10, 1926. Northwestern.
CARRADINE, DAVID: Hollywood, Dec. 8, 1936. San Francisco State.
CARRADINE, KEITH: San Mateo, CA, Aug. 8, 1950. Colo. State U.
CARRADINE, ROBERT: San Mateo, CA, Mar. 24, 1954.
CARREL, DANY: Tourane, Indochina, Sept. 20, 1936. Marseilles Cons.
CARRERA, BARBARA: Managua, Nicaragua, Dec. 31, 1945.
CARREY, JIM: Jacksons Point, Ontario, Canada, Jan. 17, 1962.
CARRIERE, MATHIEU: Hannover, West Germany, Aug. 2, 1950.
CARROLL, DIAHANN (Johnson): NYC, July 17, 1935. NYU.
CARROLL, PAT: Shreveport, LA, May 5, 1927. Catholic U.
CARSON, JOHN DAVID: California, Mar. 6, 1952. Valley College.
CARSON, JOHNNY: Corning, IA, Oct. 23, 1925. U of Neb.
CARSTEN, PETER (Ransenthaler): Weissenberg, Bavaria, Apr. 30, 1929. Munich Akademie.
CARTER, NELL: Birmingham, AL, Sept. 13, 1948.

Julie Delpy

Leonardo DiCaprio

Matt Dillon

CARTWRIGHT, VERONICA: Bristol, England, Apr 20, 1949.
CARUSO, DAVID: Forest Hills, NY, Jan. 7, 1956.
CARVEY, DANA: Missoula, MT, Apr. 2, 1955. SFST.Col.
CASELLA, MAX: Washington D.C, June 6, 1967
CASEY, BERNIE: Wyco, WV, June 8, 1939.
CASS, PEGGY (Mary Margaret Cass): Boston, MA, May 21, 1924.
CASSAVETES, NICK: NYC, 1959, Syracuse U, AADA.
CASSEL, JEAN-PIERRE: Paris, France, Oct. 27, 1932.
CASSEL, SEYMOUR: Detroit, MI, Jan. 22, 1935.
CASSIDY, DAVID: NYC, Apr. 12, 1950.
CASSIDY, JOANNA: Camden, NJ, Aug. 2, 1944. Syracuse U.
CASSIDY, PATRICK: Los Angeles, CA, Jan. 4, 1961.
CATES, PHOEBE: NYC, July 16, 1962.
CATTRALL, KIM: Liverpool, England, Aug. 21, 1956. AADA.
CAULFIELD, MAXWELL: Glasgow, Scotland, Nov. 23, 1959.
CAVANI, LILIANA: Bologna, Italy, Jan. 12, 1937. U Bologna.
CAVETT, DICK: Gibbon, NE, Nov. 19, 1936.
CHAKIRIS, GEORGE: Norwood, OH, Sept. 16, 1933.
CHAMBERLAIN, RICHARD: Beverly Hills, CA, March 31, 1935. Pomona.
CHAMPION, MARGE (Marjorie Belcher): Los Angeles, Sept. 2, 1923.
CHAN, JACKIE: Hong Kong, Apr. 7, 1954
CHANNING, CAROL: Seattle, WA, Jan. 31, 1921. Bennington.
CHANNING, STOCKARD (Susan Stockard): NYC, Feb. 13, 1944. Radcliffe.
CHAPIN, MILES: NYC, Dec. 6, 1954. HB Studio.
CHAPLIN, GERALDINE: Santa Monica, CA, July 31, 1944. Royal Ballet.
CHAPLIN, SYDNEY: Los Angeles, Mar. 31, 1926. Lawrenceville.
CHARISSE, CYD (Tula Ellice Finklea): Amarillo, TX, Mar. 3, 1922. Hollywood Professional School.
CHARLES, WALTER: East Strousburg, PA, Apr. 4, 1945. Boston U.
CHASE, CHEVY (Cornelius Crane Chase): NYC, Oct. 8, 1943.
CHAVES, RICHARD: Jacksonville, FL, Oct. 9, 1951. Occidental College.
CHAYKIN, MAURY: Canada, July 27, 1954
CHEN, JOAN (Chen Chung): Shanghai, Apr. 26, 1961. CalState.
CHER (Cherilyn Sarkisian): El Centro, CA, May 20, 1946.
CHILES, LOIS: Alice, TX, Apr. 15, 1947.
CHONG, RAE DAWN: Vancouver, Canada, Feb. 28, 1962.
CHONG, THOMAS: Edmonton, Alberta, Canada, May 24, 1938.
CHRISTIAN, LINDA (Blanca Rosa Welter): Tampico, Mexico, Nov. 13, 1923.
CHRISTIE, JULIE: Chukua, Assam, India, Apr. 14, 1941.
CHRISTOPHER, DENNIS (Carrelli): Philadelphia, PA, Dec. 2, 1955. Temple U.
CHRISTOPHER, JORDAN: Youngstown, OH, Oct. 23, 1940. Kent State.
CILENTO, DIANE: Queensland, Australia, Oct. 5, 1933. AADA.
CLAPTON, ERIC: London, Mar. 30, 1945.
CLARK, CANDY: Norman, OK, June 20, 1947.
CLARK, DANE: NYC, Feb. 18, 1915. Cornell, Johns Hopkins U.
CLARK, DICK: Mt. Vernon, NY, Nov. 30, 1929. Syracuse U.
CLARK, MATT: Washington, DC, Nov. 25, 1936.
CLARK, PETULA: Epsom, England, Nov. 15, 1932.
CLARK, SUSAN: Sarnid, Ont., Canada, Mar. 8, 1943. RADA.
CLAY, ANDREW DICE (Andrew Silverstein): Brooklyn, NY, Sept. 29, 1957, Kingsborough College.
CLAYBURGH, JILL: NYC, Apr. 30, 1944. Sarah Lawrence.
CLEESE, JOHN: Weston-Super-Mare, England, Oct. 27, 1939, Cambridge.
CLOONEY, ROSEMARY: Maysville, KY, May 23, 1928.
CLOSE, GLENN: Greenwich, CT, Mar. 19, 1947. William & Mary College.
COBURN, JAMES: Laurel, NB, Aug. 31, 1928. LACC.
COCA, IMOGENE: Philadelphia, Nov. 18, 1908.
CODY, KATHLEEN: Bronx, NY, Oct. 30, 1953.
COFFEY, SCOTT: HI, May 1, 1967.
COLE, GEORGE: London, Apr. 22, 1925.
COLEMAN, GARY: Zion, IL, Feb. 8, 1968.
COLEMAN, DABNEY: Austin, TX, Jan. 3, 1932.
COLEMAN, JACK: Easton, PA, Feb. 21, 1958. Duke U.
COLIN, MARGARET: NYC, May 26, 1957.
COLLET, CHRISTOPHER: NYC, Mar. 13, 1968. Strasberg Inst.
COLLINS, JOAN: London, May 21, 1933. Francis Holland School.
COLLINS, PAULINE: Devon, England, Sept. 3, 1940.
COLLINS, STEPHEN: Des Moines, IA, Oct. 1, 1947. Amherst.
COLON, MIRIAM: Ponce, PR., 1945. UPR.
COLTRANE, ROBBIE: Ruthergien, Scotland, Mar. 30, 1950.
COMER, ANJANETTE: Dawson, TX, Aug. 7, 1942. Baylor, Tex. U.
CONANT, OLIVER: NYC, Nov. 15, 1955. Dalton.
CONAWAY, JEFF: NYC, Oct. 5, 1950. NYU.
CONNELLY, JENNIFER: NYC, Dec. 12, 1970
CONNERY, SEAN: Edinburgh, Scotland, Aug. 25, 1930.
CONNERY, JASON: London, Jan. 11, 1963.
CONNICK, HARRY, JR.: New Orleans, LA, Sept. 11, 1967.
CONNOLLY, BILLY: Glasgow, Scotland, Nov. 24, 1942.
CONNORS, MIKE (Krekor Ohanian): Fresno, CA, Aug. 15, 1925. UCLA.
CONRAD, ROBERT (Conrad Robert Falk): Chicago, IL, Mar. 1, 1935. Northwestern U.
CONSTANTINE, MICHAEL: Reading, PA, May 22, 1927.
CONTI, TOM: Paisley, Scotland, Nov. 22, 1941.
CONVERSE, FRANK: St. Louis, MO, May 22, 1938. Carnegie Tech.

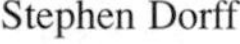
Stephen Dorff

Robert Downey, Jr.

Richard Dreyfuss

Minnie Driver

CONWAY, GARY: Boston, Feb. 4, 1936.
CONWAY, KEVIN: NYC, May 29, 1942.
CONWAY, TIM (Thomas Daniel): Willoughby, OH, Dec. 15, 1933. Bowling Green State.
COOGAN, KEITH (Keith Mitchell Franklin): Palm Springs, CA, Jan. 13, 1970.
COOPER, BEN: Hartford, CT, Sept. 30, 1930. Columbia U.
COOPER, CHRIS: Kansas City, MO, July 9, 1951. UMo.
COOPER, JACKIE: Los Angeles, Sept. 15, 1921.
COPELAND, JOAN: NYC, June 1, 1922. Brooklyn College, RADA.
CORBETT, GRETCHEN: Portland, OR, Aug. 13, 1947. Carnegie Tech.
CORBIN, BARRY: Dawson County, TX, Oct. 16, 1940. Texas Tech. U.
CORBY, ELLEN (Hansen): Racine, WI, June 13, 1913.
CORCORAN, DONNA: Quincy, MA, Sept. 29, 1942.
CORD, ALEX (Viespi): Floral Park, NY, Aug. 3, 1931. NYU, Actors Studio.
CORDAY, MARA (Marilyn Watts): Santa Monica, CA, Jan. 3, 1932.
COREY, JEFF: NYC, Aug. 10, 1914. Fagin School.
CORNTHWAITE, ROBERT: St. Helens, OR, Apr. 28, 1917. USC.
CORRI, ADRIENNE: Glasgow, Scot., Nov. 13, 1933. RADA.
CORT, BUD (Walter Edward Cox): New Rochelle, NY, Mar. 29, 1950. NYU.
CORTESA, VALENTINA: Milan, Italy, Jan. 1, 1924.
COSBY, BILL: Philadelphia, PA, July 12, 1937. Temple U.
COSTER, NICOLAS: London, Dec. 3, 1934. Neighborhood Playhouse.
COSTNER, KEVIN: Lynwood, CA, Jan. 18, 1955. CalStaU.
COURTENAY, TOM: Hull, England, Feb. 25, 1937. RADA.
COURTLAND, JEROME: Knoxville, TN, Dec. 27, 1926.
COX, BRIAN: Dundee, Scotland, June 1, 1946. LAMDA.
COX, COURTENEY: Birmingham, AL, June 15, 1964.
COX, RONNY: Cloudcroft, NM, Aug. 23, 1938.
COYOTE, PETER (Cohon): NYC, Oct. 10, 1941.
CRAIG, MICHAEL: Poona, India, Jan. 27, 1929.
CRAIN, JEANNE: Barstow, CA, May 25, 1925.
CRAVEN, GEMMA: Dublin, Ireland, June 1, 1950.
CRAWFORD, MICHAEL (Dumbel-Smith): Salisbury, England, Jan. 19, 1942.
CREMER, BRUNO: Paris, France, 1929.
CRENNA, RICHARD: Los Angeles, Nov. 30, 1926. USC.
CRISTAL, LINDA (Victoria Moya): Buenos Aires, Feb. 25, 1934.
CROMWELL, JAMES: Los Angeles, CA, Jan. 27, 1940.
CRONYN, HUME (Blake): Ontario, Canada, July 18, 1911.
CROSBY, DENISE: Hollywood, CA, Nov. 24, 1957.
CROSBY, HARRY: Los Angeles, CA, Aug. 8, 1958.
CROSBY, MARY FRANCES: Los Angeles, CA, Sept. 14, 1959.
CROSS, BEN: London, Dec. 16, 1947. RADA.
CROSS, MURPHY (Mary Jane): Laurelton, MD, June 22, 1950.
CROUSE, LINDSAY: NYC, May 12, 1948. Radcliffe.
CROWE, RUSSELL: New Zealand, Apr. 7, 1964.
CROWLEY, PAT: Olyphant, PA, Sept. 17, 1932.
CRUISE, TOM (T. C. Mapother, IV): July 3, 1962, Syracuse, NY.
CRYER, JON: NYC, Apr. 16, 1965, RADA.
CRYSTAL, BILLY: Long Beach, NY, Mar. 14, 1947. Marshall U.
CULKIN, MACAULAY: NYC, Aug. 26, 1980.
CULLUM, JOHN: Knoxville, TN, Mar. 2, 1930. U Tenn.
CULLUM, JOHN DAVID: NYC, Mar. 1, 1966.
CULP, ROBERT: Oakland, CA, Aug. 16, 1930. U Wash.
CUMMING, ALAN: Perthshire, Scotland, 1964.
CUMMINGS, CONSTANCE: Seattle, WA, May 15, 1910.
CUMMINGS, QUINN: Hollywood, Aug. 13, 1967.
CUMMINS, PEGGY: Prestatyn, N. Wales, Dec. 18, 1926. Alexandra School.
CURRY, TIM: Cheshire, England, Apr. 19, 1946. Birmingham U.
CURTIN, JANE: Cambridge, MA, Sept. 6, 1947.
CURTIS, JAMIE LEE: Los Angeles, CA, Nov. 22, 1958.
CURTIS, KEENE: Salt Lake City, UT, Feb. 15, 1925. U Utah.
CURTIS, TONY (Bernard Schwartz): NYC, June 3, 1924.
CUSACK, JOAN: Evanston, IL, Oct. 11, 1962.
CUSACK, JOHN: Chicago, IL, June 28, 1966.
CUSACK, SINEAD: Dalkey, Ireland, Feb. 18, 1948
DAFOE, WILLEM: Appleton, WI, July 22, 1955.
DAHL, ARLENE: Minneapolis, Aug. 11, 1928. U Minn.
DALE, JIM: Rothwell, England, Aug. 15, 1935.
DALLESANDRO, JOE: Pensacola, FL, Dec. 31, 1948.
DALTON, TIMOTHY: Colwyn Bay, Wales, Mar. 21, 1946. RADA.
DALTREY, ROGER: London, Mar. 1, 1944.
DALY, TIM: NYC, Mar. 1, 1956. Bennington College.
DALY, TYNE: Madison, WI, Feb. 21, 1947. AMDA.

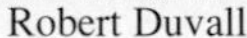
Robert Duvall

Ethan Embry

Rupert Everett

Dennis Farina

DAMON, MATT: Cambridge, MA, Oct. 8, 1970.
DAMONE, VIC (Vito Farinola): Brooklyn, NY, June 12, 1928.
DANCE, CHARLES: Plymouth, England, Oct. 10, 1946.
DANES, CLAIRE: New York, NY, Apr. 12, 1979.
D'ANGELO, BEVERLY: Columbus, OH, Nov. 15, 1953.
DANGERFIELD, RODNEY (Jacob Cohen): Babylon, NY, Nov. 22, 1921.
DANIELS, JEFF: Athens, GA, Feb. 19, 1955. EMichSt.
DANIELS, WILLIAM: Brooklyn, NY, Mar. 31, 1927. Northwestern.
DANNER, BLYTHE: Philadelphia, PA, Feb. 3, 1944. Bard College.
DANNING, SYBIL (Sybille Johanna Danninger): Vienna, Austria, May 4, 1949.
DANSON, TED: San Diego, CA, Dec. 29, 1947. Stanford, Carnegie Tech.
DANTE, MICHAEL (Ralph Vitti): Stamford, CT, 1935. U Miami.
DANZA, TONY: Brooklyn, NY, Apr. 21, 1951. UDubuque.
D'ARBANVILLE-QUINN, PATTI: NYC, 1951.
DARBY, KIM (Deborah Zerby): North Hollywood, CA, July 8, 1948.
DARCEL, DENISE (Denise Billecard): Paris, France, Sept. 8, 1925. U Dijon.
DARREN, JAMES: Philadelphia, PA, June 8, 1936. Stella Adler School.
DARRIEUX, DANIELLE: Bordeaux, France, May 1, 1917. Lycee LaTour.
DAVENPORT, NIGEL: Cambridge, England, May 23, 1928. Trinity College.
DAVID, KEITH: NYC, June 4, 1954. Juilliard.
DAVIDOVICH, LOLITA: Toronto, Ontario, Canada, July 15, 1961.
DAVIDSON, JAYE: Riverside, CA, 1968.
DAVIDSON, JOHN: Pittsburgh, Dec. 13, 1941. Denison U.
DAVIS, CLIFTON: Chicago, IL, Oct. 4, 1945. Oakwood College.
DAVIS, GEENA: Wareham, MA, Jan. 21, 1957.
DAVIS, JUDY: Perth, Australia, Apr. 23, 1955.
DAVIS, MAC: Lubbock, TX, Jan. 21,1942.
DAVIS, NANCY (Anne Frances Robbins): NYC, July 6, 1921. Smith College.
DAVIS, OSSIE: Cogdell, GA, Dec. 18, 1917. Howard U.
DAVIS, SAMMI: Kidderminster, Worcestershire, England, June 21, 1964.
DAVISON, BRUCE: Philadelphia, PA, June 28, 1946.
DAWBER, PAM: Detroit, MI, Oct. 18, 1954.
DAY, DORIS (Doris Kappelhoff): Cincinnati, Apr. 3, 1924.
DAY, LARAINE (Johnson): Roosevelt, UT, Oct. 13, 1917.
DAY LEWIS, DANIEL: London, Apr. 29, 1957. Bristol Old Vic.
DAYAN, ASSI: Israel, Nov. 23, 1945. U Jerusalem.
DEAKINS, LUCY: NYC, 1971.
DEAN, JIMMY: Plainview, TX, Aug. 10, 1928.
DEAN, LOREN: Las Vegas, NV, July 31, 1969.
DeCAMP, ROSEMARY: Prescott, AZ, Nov. 14, 1913.
DeCARLO, YVONNE (Peggy Yvonne Middleton): Vancouver, B.C., Canada, Sept. 1, 1922. Vancouver School of Drama.
DEE, FRANCES: Los Angeles, Nov. 26, 1907. Chicago U.
DEE, JOEY (Joseph Di Nicola): Passaic, NJ, June 11, 1940. Patterson State College.
DEE, RUBY: Cleveland, OH, Oct. 27, 1924. Hunter College.
DEE, SANDRA (Alexandra Zuck): Bayonne, NJ, Apr. 23, 1942.
DeHAVEN, GLORIA: Los Angeles, July 23, 1923.
DeHAVILLAND, OLIVIA: Tokyo, Japan, July 1, 1916. Notre Dame Convent School.
DELAIR, SUZY (Suzanne Delaire): Paris, France, Dec. 31, 1916.
DELANY, DANA: NYC, March 13, 1956. Wesleyan U.
DELPY, JULIE: Paris. Dec, 21, 1969.
DELON, ALAIN: Sceaux, France, Nov. 8, 1935.
DELORME, DANIELE: Paris, France, Oct. 9, 1926. Sorbonne.
DeLUISE, DOM: Brooklyn, NY, Aug. 1, 1933. Tufts College.
DeLUISE, PETER: NYC, Nov. 6, 1966.
DEMONGEOT, MYLENE: Nice, France, Sept. 29, 1938.
DeMORNAY, REBECCA: Los Angeles, Aug. 29, 1962. Strasberg Inst.
DEMPSEY, PATRICK: Lewiston, ME, Jan. 13, 1966.
DeMUNN, JEFFREY: Buffalo, NY, Apr. 25, 1947. Union College.
DENCH, JUDI: York, England, Dec. 9, 1934.
DENEUVE, CATHERINE: Paris, France, Oct. 22, 1943.
DeNIRO, ROBERT: NYC, Aug. 17, 1943. Stella Adler.
DENISON, MICHAEL: Doncaster, York, England, Nov. 1, 1915. Oxford.
DENNEHY, BRIAN: Bridgeport, CT, Jul. 9, 1938. Columbia.
DENVER, BOB: New Rochelle, NY, Jan. 9, 1935.
DEPARDIEU, GERARD: Chateauroux, France, Dec. 27, 1948.
DEPP, JOHNNY: Owensboro, KY, June 9, 1963.
DEREK, BO (Mary Cathleen Collins): Long Beach, CA, Nov. 20, 1956.
DEREK, JOHN: Hollywood, Aug. 12, 1926.
DERN, BRUCE: Chicago, IL, June 4, 1936. UPA.
DERN, LAURA: Los Angeles, Feb. 10, 1967.
DeSALVO, ANNE: Philadelphia, Apr. 3.
DEVANE, WILLIAM: Albany, NY, Sept. 5, 1939.
DeVITO, DANNY: Asbury Park, NJ, Nov. 17, 1944.
DEXTER, ANTHONY (Walter Reinhold Alfred Fleischmann): Talmadge, NB, Jan. 19, 1919. U Iowa.
DEY, SUSAN: Pekin, IL, Dec. 10, 1953.
DeYOUNG, CLIFF: Los Angeles, CA, Feb. 12, 1945. Cal State.
DIAMOND, NEIL: NYC, Jan. 24, 1941. NYU.
DIAZ, CAMERON: Long Beach, CA, Aug. 30, 1972.
DiCAPRIO, LEONARDO: Hollywood, CA, Nov.11, 1974.

DICKINSON, ANGIE (Angeline Brown): Kulm, ND, Sept. 30, 1932. Glendale College.
DILLER, PHYLLIS (Driver): Lima, OH, July 17, 1917. Bluffton College.
DILLMAN, BRADFORD: San Francisco, Apr. 14, 1930. Yale.
DILLON, KEVIN: Mamaroneck, NY, Aug. 19, 1965.
DILLON, MATT: Larchmont, NY, Feb. 18, 1964. AADA.
DILLON, MELINDA: Hope, AR, Oct. 13, 1939. Goodman Theatre School.
DIXON, DONNA: Alexandria, VA, July 20, 1957.
DOBSON, KEVIN: NYC, Mar. 18, 1944.
DOBSON, TAMARA: Baltimore, MD, May 14, 1947. MD Inst. of Art.
DOHERTY, SHANNEN: Memphis, TN, Apr. 12, 1971.
DOLAN, MICHAEL: Oklahoma City, OK, June 21, 1965.
DOMERGUE, FAITH: New Orleans, June 16, 1925.
DONAHUE, TROY (Merle Johnson): NYC, Jan. 27, 1937. Columbia U.
DONAT, PETER: Nova Scotia, Jan. 20, 1928. Yale.
DONNELLY, DONAL: Bradford, England, July 6, 1931.
D'ONOFRIO, VINCENT: Brooklyn, NY, June 30, 1959.
DONOHOE, AMANDA: London, June 29 1962.
DONOVAN, TATE: NYC, Sept. 25, 1963.
DOOHAN, JAMES: Vancouver, BC, Mar. 3, 1920. Neighborhood Playhouse.
DOOLEY, PAUL: Parkersburg WV, Feb. 22, 1928. U WV.
DORFF, STEPHEN: CA, July 29, 1973.
DOUGLAS, DONNA (Dorothy Bourgeois). Baywood, LA, Sept. 26, 1935.
DOUGLAS, ILLEANA: MA, July 25, 1965.
DOUGLAS, KIRK (Issur Danielovitch): Amsterdam, NY, Dec. 9, 1916. St. Lawrence U.
DOUGLAS, MICHAEL: New Brunswick, NJ, Sept. 25, 1944. U Cal.
DOUGLASS, ROBYN: Sendai, Japan, June 21, 1953. UCDavis.
DOURIF, BRAD: Huntington, WV, Mar. 18, 1950. Marshall U.
DOWN, LESLEY-ANN: London, Mar. 17, 1954.
DOWNEY, ROBERT, JR.: NYC, Apr. 4, 1965.
DRAKE, BETSY: Paris, France, Sept. 11, 1923.
DRESCHER, FRAN: Queens, NY, Sept. 30, 1957.
DREW, ELLEN (formerly Terry Ray): Kansas City, MO, Nov. 23, 1915.
DREYFUSS, RICHARD: Brooklyn, NY, Oct. 19, 1947.
DRILLINGER, BRIAN: Brooklyn, NY, June 27, 1960. SUNY/Purchase.
DRIVER, MINNIE (Amelia Driver): London, Jan. 31, 1971.
DUCHOVNY, DAVID: NYC, Aug. 7, 1960. Yale.
DUDIKOFF, MICHAEL: Torrance, CA, Oct. 8, 1954.
DUGAN, DENNIS: Wheaton, IL, Sept. 5, 1946.
DUKAKIS, OLYMPIA: Lowell, MA, June 20, 1931.
DUKE, BILL: Poughkeepsie, NY, Feb. 26, 1943. NYU.

Sally Field

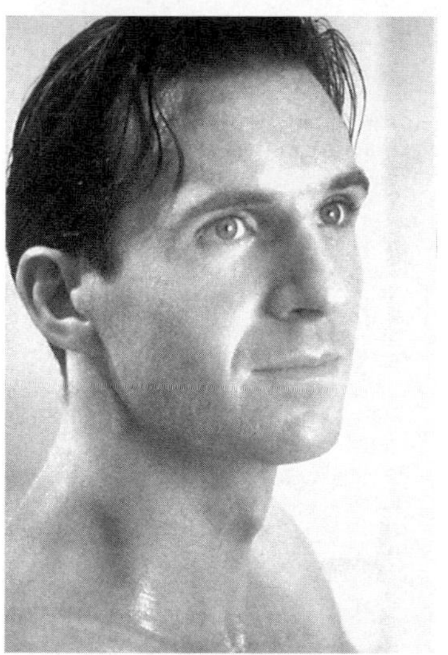
Ralph Fiennes

Linda Fiorentino

DUKE, PATTY (Anna Marie): NYC, Dec. 14, 1946.
DUKES, DAVID: San Francisco, June 6, 1945.
DULLEA, KEIR: Cleveland, NJ, May 30, 1936. SF State College.
DUNAWAY, FAYE: Bascom, FL, Jan. 14, 1941, Fla. U.
DUNCAN, SANDY: Henderson, TX, Feb. 20, 1946. Len Morris College.
DUNNE, GRIFFIN: NYC, June 8, 1955. Neighborhood Playhouse.
DUPEREY, ANNY: Paris, France, 1947.
DURBIN, DEANNA (Edna): Winnipeg, Canada, Dec. 4, 1921.
DURNING, CHARLES S. : Highland Falls, NY, Feb. 28, 1923. NYU.
DUSSOLLIER, ANDRE: Annecy, France, Feb. 17, 1946.
DUTTON, CHARLES: Baltimore, MD, Jan. 30, 1951. Yale.
DUVALL, ROBERT: San Diego, CA, Jan. 5, 1931. Principia College.
DUVALL, SHELLEY: Houston, TX, July 7, 1949.
DYSART, RICHARD: Brighton, ME, Mar. 30, 1929.
DZUNDZA, GEORGE: Rosenheim, Germ., July 19, 1945.
EASTON, ROBERT: Milwaukee, WI, Nov. 23, 1930. U Texas.
EASTWOOD, CLINT: San Francisco, May 31, 1931. LACC.
EATON, SHIRLEY: London, 1937. Aida Foster School.
EBSEN, BUDDY (Christian, Jr.): Belleville, IL, Apr. 2, 1910. U Fla.
ECKEMYR, AGNETA: Karlsborg, Sweden, July 2. Actors Studio.
EDELMAN, GREGG: Chicago, IL, Sept. 12, 1958. Northwestern U.
EDEN, BARBARA (Huffman): Tucson, AZ, Aug. 23, 1934.
EDWARDS, ANTHONY: Santa Barbara, CA, July 19, 1962. RADA.
EGGAR, SAMANTHA: London, Mar. 5, 1939.
EICHHORN, LISA: Reading, PA, Feb. 4, 1952. Queens Ont. U RADA.
EIKENBERRY, JILL: New Haven, CT, Jan. 21, 1947.
EILBER, JANET: Detroit, MI, July 27, 1951. Juilliard.
EKBERG, ANITA: Malmo, Sweden, Sept. 29, 1931.
EKLAND, BRITT: Stockholm, Sweden, Oct. 6, 1942.
ELDARD, RON: Long Island, NY, Feb. 20, 1965.
ELIZONDO, HECTOR: NYC, Dec. 22, 1936.
ELLIOTT, CHRIS: NYC, May 31, 1960.
ELLIOTT, PATRICIA: Gunnison, CO, July 21, 1942. UCol.
ELLIOTT, SAM: Sacramento, CA, Aug. 9, 1944. U Ore.
ELWES, CARY: London, Oct. 26, 1962.
ELY, RON (Ronald Pierce): Hereford, TX, June 21, 1938.
EMBRY, ETHAN (Ethan Randall): Huntington Beach, CA, June 13, 1978.
ENGLUND, ROBERT: Glendale, CA, June 6, 1949.
ERDMAN, RICHARD: Enid, OK, June 1, 1925.
ERICSON, JOHN: Dusseldorf, Ger., Sept. 25, 1926. AADA.

ERMEY, R. LEE (Ronald): Emporia, KS, Mar. 24, 1944
ESMOND, CARL (Willy Eichberger): Vienna, June 14, 1906. U Vienna.
ESPOSITO, GIANCARLO: Copenhagen, Denmark, Apr. 26, 1958.
ESTEVEZ, EMILIO: NYC, May 12, 1962.
ESTRADA, ERIK: NYC, Mar. 16, 1949.
EVANS, DALE (Francis Smith): Uvalde, TX, Oct. 31, 1912.
EVANS, GENE: Holbrook, AZ, July 11, 1922.
EVANS, JOSH: NYC, Jan. 16, 1971.
EVANS, LINDA (Evanstad): Hartford, CT, Nov. 18, 1942.
EVERETT, CHAD (Ray Cramton): South Bend, IN, June 11, 1936.
EVERETT, RUPERT: Norfolk, England, 1959.
EVIGAN, GREG: South Amboy, NJ, Oct. 14, 1953.
FABARES, SHELLEY: Los Angeles, Jan. 19, 1944.
FABIAN (Fabian Forte): Philadelphia, Feb. 6, 1943.
FABRAY, NANETTE (Ruby Nanette Fabares): San Diego, Oct. 27, 1920.
FAHEY, JEFF: Olean, NY, Nov. 29, 1956.
FAIRBANKS, DOUGLAS, JR.: NYC, Dec. 9, 1907. Collegiate School.
FAIRCHILD, MORGAN (Patsy McClenny): Dallas, TX, Feb. 3, 1950. UCLA.
FALK, PETER: NYC, Sept. 16, 1927. New School.
FARENTINO, JAMES: Brooklyn, NY, Feb. 24, 1938. AADA.
FARGAS, ANTONIO: Bronx, NY, Aug. 14, 1946.
FARINA, DENNIS: Chicago, IL, Feb. 29, 1944.
FARINA, SANDY (Sandra Feldman): Newark, NJ, 1955.
FARNSWORTH, RICHARD: Los Angeles, Sept. 1, 1920.
FARR, FELICIA: Westchester, NY, Oct. 4. 1932. Penn State College.
FARROW, MIA (Maria): Los Angeles, Feb. 9, 1945.
FAULKNER, GRAHAM: London, Sept. 26, 1947. Webber-Douglas.
FAWCETT, FARRAH: Corpus Christie, TX, Feb. 2, 1947. TexU.
FAYE, ALICE (Ann Leppert): NYC, May 5, 1912.
FEINSTEIN, ALAN: NYC, Sept. 8, 1941.
FELDMAN, COREY: Encino, CA, July 16, 1971.
FELDON, BARBARA (Hall): Pittsburgh, Mar. 12, 1941. Carnegie Tech.
FELDSHUH, TOVAH: NYC, Dec. 27, 1953, Sarah Lawrence College.
FELL, NORMAN: Philadelphia, PA, Mar. 24, 1924.
FELLOWS, EDITH: Boston, May 20, 1923.
FENN, SHERILYN: Detroit, MI, Feb. 1, 1965.
FERRELL, CONCHATA: Charleston, WV, Mar. 28, 1943. Marshall U.
FERRER, MEL: Elbeton, NJ, Aug. 25, 1912. Princeton U.
FERRER, MIGUEL: Santa Monica, CA, Feb. 7, 1954.
FERRIS, BARBARA: London, 1943.
FIEDLER, JOHN: Plateville, WI, Feb. 3, 1925.
FIELD, SALLY: Pasadena, CA, Nov. 6, 1946.
FIELD, SHIRLEY-ANNE: London, June 27, 1938.
FIENNES, RALPH: Suffolk, England, Dec. 22, 1962. RADA.
FIERSTEIN, HARVEY: Brooklyn, NY, June 6, 1954. Pratt Inst.
FINCH, JON: Caterham, England, Mar. 2, 1941.
FINLAY, FRANK: Farnworth, England, Aug. 6, 1926.
FINNEY, ALBERT: Salford, Lancashire, England, May 9, 1936. RADA.
FIORENTINO, LINDA: Philadelphia, PA, Mar. 9, 1960.
FIRTH, COLIN: Grayshott, Hampshire, England, Sept. 10, 1960.
FIRTH, PETER: Bradford, England, Oct. 27, 1953.
FISHBURNE, LAURENCE: Augusta, GA, July 30, 1961.
FISHER, CARRIE: Los Angeles, CA, Oct. 21, 1956. London Central School of Drama.
FISHER, EDDIE: Philadelphia, PA, Aug. 10, 1928.
FISHER, FRANCES: Orange, TX, 1952.
FITZGERALD, TARA: London, Sept. 17, 1968.
FITZGERALD, GERALDINE: Dublin, Ireland, Nov. 24, 1914. Dublin Art School.
FLAGG, FANNIE: Birmingham, AL, Sept. 21, 1944. UAl.
FLANNERY, SUSAN: Jersey City, NJ, July 31, 1943.
FLEMING, RHONDA (Marilyn Louis): Los Angeles, Aug. 10, 1922.
FLEMYNG, ROBERT: Liverpool, England, Jan. 3, 1912. Haileybury College.
FLETCHER, LOUISE: Birmingham, AL, July 22 1934.
FOCH, NINA: Leyden, Holland, Apr. 20, 1924.
FOLLOWS, MEGAN: Toronto, Canada, Mar. 14, 1968.
FONDA, BRIDGET: Los Angeles, Jan. 27, 1964.
FONDA, JANE: NYC, Dec. 21, 1937. Vassar.
FONDA, PETER: NYC, Feb. 23, 1939. U Omaha.
FONTAINE, JOAN: Tokyo, Japan, Oct. 22, 1917.
FOOTE, HALLIE: NYC, 1953. UNH.
FORD, GLENN (Gwyllyn Samuel Newton Ford): Quebec, Canada, May 1, 1916.
FORD, HARRISON: Chicago, IL, July 13, 1942. Ripon College.
FOREST, MARK (Lou Degni): Brooklyn, NY, Jan. 1933.
FORREST, FREDERIC: Waxahachie, TX, Dec. 23, 1936.
FORREST, STEVE: Huntsville, TX, Sept. 29, 1924. UCLA.
FORSLUND, CONNIE: San Diego, CA, June 19, 1950. NYU.
FORSTER, ROBERT (Foster, Jr.): Rochester, NY, July 13, 1941. Rochester U.
FORSYTHE, JOHN (Freund): Penn's Grove, NJ, Jan. 29, 1918.
FORSYTHE,WILLIAM: Brooklyn, NY, June 7, 1955
FOSSEY, BRIGITTE: Tourcoing, France, Mar. 11, 1947.

Laurence Fishburne

Richard Gere

Danny Glover

Cuba Gooding, Jr.

David Marshall Grant

Andy Griffith

Linda Hamilton

Ed Harris

FOSTER, JODIE (Ariane Munker): Bronx, NY, Nov. 19, 1962. Yale.
FOSTER, MEG: Reading, PA, May 14, 1948.
FOX, EDWARD: London, Apr. 13, 1937. RADA.
FOX, JAMES: London, May 19, 1939.
FOX, MICHAEL J.: Vancouver, BC, June 9, 1961.
FOXWORTH, ROBERT: Houston, TX, Nov. 1, 1941. Carnegie Tech.
FRAKES, JONATHAN: Bethlehem, PA, Aug. 19, 1952. Harvard.
FRANCIOSA, ANTHONY (Papaleo): NYC, Oct. 25, 1928.
FRANCIS, ANNE: Ossining, NY, Sept. 16, 1932.
FRANCIS, ARLENE (Arlene Kazanjian): Boston, Oct. 20, 1908. Finch School.
FRANCIS, CONNIE (Constance Franconero): Newark, NJ, Dec. 12, 1938.
FRANCKS, DON: Vancouver, Canada, Feb. 28, 1932.
FRANKLIN, PAMELA: Tokyo, Feb. 4, 1950.
FRANZ, ARTHUR: Perth Amboy, NJ, Feb. 29, 1920. Blue Ridge College.
FRANZ, DENNIS: Chicago, IL, Oct. 28, 1944.
FRASER, BRENDAN: Indianapolis, IN, Dec. 3, 1968.
FRAZIER, SHEILA: NYC, Nov. 13, 1948.
FRECHETTE, PETER: Warwick, RI, Oct. 1956. URI.
FREEMAN, AL, JR.: San Antonio, TX, Mar. 21, 1934. CCLA.
FREEMAN, KATHLEEN: Chicago, IL, Feb. 17, 1919.
FREEMAN, MONA: Baltimore, MD, June 9, 1926.
FREEMAN, MORGAN: Memphis, TN, June 1, 1937. LACC.
FREWER, MATT: Washington, DC, Jan. 4, 1958, Old Vic.
FRICKER, BRENDA: Dublin, Ireland, Feb. 17, 1945.
FRIELS, COLIN: Glasgow, Sept. 25, 1952.
FRY, STEPHEN: Hampstead, London, Eng., Aug. 24, 1957.
FULLER, PENNY: Durham, NC, 1940. Northwestern U.
FUNICELLO, ANNETTE: Utica, NY, Oct. 22, 1942.
FURLONG, EDWARD: Glendale, CA, Aug. 2, 1977.
FURNEAUX, YVONNE: Lille, France, 1928. Oxford U.
GABLE, JOHN CLARK: Los Angeles, Mar. 20, 1961. Santa Monica College.
GABOR, ZSA ZSA (Sari Gabor): Budapest, Hungary, Feb. 6, 1918.
GAIL, MAX: Derfoil, MI, Apr. 5, 1943.
GAINES, BOYD: Atlanta, GA, May 11, 1953. Juilliard.
GALLAGHER, PETER: NYC, Aug. 19, 1955. Tufts U.
GALLIGAN, ZACH: NYC, Feb. 14, 1963. ColumbiaU.
GAM, RITA: Pittsburgh, PA, Apr. 2, 1928.
GAMBON, MICHAEL: Dublin, Ireland, Oct. 19, 1940.
GANZ, BRUNO: Zurich, Switzerland, Mar. 22, 1941.
GARBER, VICTOR: Montreal, Canada, Mar. 16, 1949.
GARCIA, ANDY: Havana, Cuba, Apr. 12, 1956. FlaInt.
GARFIELD, ALLEN (Allen Goorwitz): Newark, NJ, Nov. 22, 1939. Actors Studio.
GARFUNKEL, ART: NYC, Nov. 5, 1941.
GARLAND, BEVERLY: Santa Cruz, CA, Oct. 17, 1926. Glendale College.
GARNER, JAMES (James Baumgarner): Norman, OK, Apr. 7, 1928. Okla. U.
GAROFALO, JANEANE: Newton, NJ, Sept. 28, 1964.
GARR, TERI: Lakewood, OH, Dec. 11, 1949.
GARRETT, BETTY: St. Joseph, MO, May 23, 1919. Annie Wright Seminary.
GARRISON, SEAN: NYC, Oct. 19, 1937.
GARY, LORRAINE: NYC, Aug. 16, 1937.
GASSMAN, VITTORIO: Genoa, Italy, Sept. 1,1922. Rome Academy of Dramatic Art.
GAVIN, JOHN: Los Angeles, Apr. 8, 1935. Stanford U.
GAYLORD, MITCH: Van Nuys, CA, Mar. 10, 1961. UCLA.
GAYNOR, MITZI (Francesca Marlene Von Gerber): Chicago, IL, Sept. 4, 1930.
GAZZARA, BEN: NYC, Aug. 28, 1930. Actors Studio.
GEARY, ANTHONY: Coalsville, UT, May 29, 1947. UUt.
GEDRICK, JASON: Chicago, IL, Feb. 7, 1965. Drake U.
GEESON, JUDY: Arundel, England, Sept. 10, 1948. Corona.
GEOFFREYS, STEPHEN: Cincinnati, OH, Nov. 22, 1964. NYU.
GEORGE, SUSAN: West London, England, July 26, 1950.
GERARD, GIL: Little Rock, AR, Jan. 23, 1940.
GERE, RICHARD: Philadelphia, PA, Aug. 29, 1949. U Mass.
GERROLL, DANIEL: London, Oct. 16, 1951. Central.
GERTZ, JAMI: Chicago, IL, Oct. 28, 1965.
GETTY, BALTHAZAR: Los Angeles, CA, Jan. 22, 1975.
GETTY, ESTELLE: NYC, July 25, 1923. New School.
GHOLSON, JULIE: Birmingham, AL, June 4, 1958.
GHOSTLEY, ALICE: Eve, MO, Aug. 14, 1926. Okla U.
GIANNINI, GIANCARLO: Spezia, Italy, Aug. 1, 1942. Rome Acad. of Drama.
GIBB, CYNTHIA: Bennington, VT, Dec. 14, 1963.
GIBSON, HENRY: Germantown, PA, Sept. 21, 1935.
GIBSON, MEL: Peekskill, NY, Jan. 3, 1956. NIDA.
GIELGUD, JOHN: London, Apr. 14, 1904. RADA.
GIFT, ROLAND: Birmingham, England, May 28 1962.
GILBERT, MELISSA: Los Angeles, CA, May 8, 1964.
GILES, NANCY: NYC, July 17, 1960, Oberlin College.
GILLETTE, ANITA: Baltimore, MD, Aug. 16, 1938.
GILLIAM, TERRY: Minneapolis, MN, Nov. 22, 1940.
GILLIS, ANN (Alma O'Connor): Little Rock, AR, Feb. 12, 1927.
GINTY, ROBERT: NYC, Nov. 14, 1948. Yale.

Ethan Hawke

GIRARDOT, ANNIE: Paris, France, Oct. 25, 1931.
GISH, ANNABETH: Albuquerque, NM, Mar. 13, 1971. DukeU.
GIVENS, ROBIN: NYC, Nov. 27, 1964.
GLASER, PAUL MICHAEL: Boston, MA, Mar. 25, 1943. Boston U.
GLASS, RON: Evansville, IN, July 10, 1945.
GLEASON, JOANNA: Winnipeg, Canada, June 2, 1950. UCLA.
GLEASON, PAUL: Jersey City, NJ, May 4, 1944.
GLENN, SCOTT: Pittsburgh, PA, Jan. 26, 1942. William and Mary College.
GLOVER, CRISPIN: NYC, Sept 20, 1964.
GLOVER, DANNY: San Francisco, CA, July 22, 1947. SFStateCol.
GLOVER, JOHN: Kingston, NY, Aug. 7, 1944.
GLYNN,CARLIN: Cleveland, Oh, Feb. 19, 1940. Actors Studio.
GOLDBERG, WHOOPI (Caryn Johnson): NYC, Nov. 13, 1949.
GOLDBLUM, JEFF: Pittsburgh, PA, Oct. 22, 1952. Neighborhood Playhouse.
GOLDEN, ANNIE: Brooklyn, NY, Oct. 19, 1951.
GOLDSTEIN, JENETTE: Beverly Hills, CA, 1960.

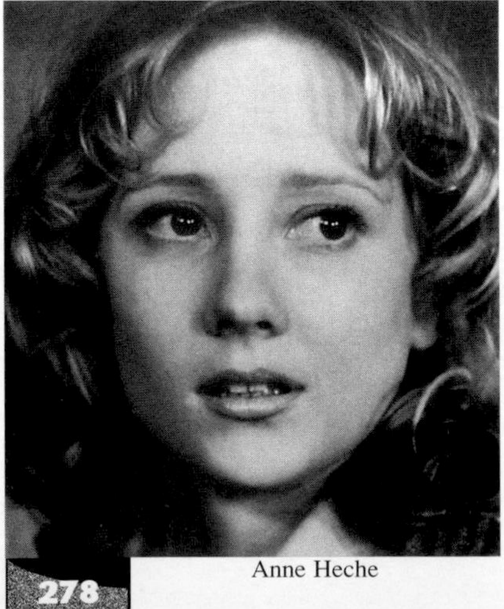
Anne Heche

GOLDTHWAIT, BOB: Syracuse, NY, May 1, 1962.
GOLDWYN, TONY: Los Angeles, May 20, 1960. LAMDA.
GOLINO, VALERIA: Naples, Italy, Oct. 22, 1966.
GONZALEZ, CORDELIA: Aug. 11, 1958, San Juan, PR. UPR.
GONZALES-GONZALEZ, PEDRO: Aguilares, TX, Dec. 21, 1926.
GOODALL, CAROLINE: London, Nov. 13, 1959. BristolU.
GOODING, CUBA, JR.: Bronx, N.Y., Jan. 2, 1968.
GOODMAN, DODY: Columbus, OH, Oct. 28, 1915.
GOODMAN, JOHN: St. Louis, MO, June 20, 1952.
GORDON, KEITH: NYC, Feb. 3, 1961.
GORMAN, CLIFF: Jamaica, NY, Oct. 13, 1936. NYU.
GORSHIN, FRANK: Pittsburgh, PA, Apr. 5, 1933.
GORTNER, MARJOE: Long Beach, CA, Jan. 14, 1944.
GOSSETT, LOUIS, JR.: Brooklyn, NY, May 27, 1936. NYU.
GOULD, ELLIOTT (Goldstein): Brooklyn, NY, Aug. 29, 1938. Columbia U.
GOULD, HAROLD: Schenectady, NY, Dec. 10, 1923. Cornell.
GOULD, JASON: NYC, Dec. 29, 1966.
GOULET, ROBERT: Lawrence, MA, Nov. 26, 1933. Edmonton.
GRAF, DAVID: Lancaster, OH, Apr. 16, 1950. OhStateU.
GRAFF, TODD: NYC, Oct. 22, 1959. SUNY/ Purchase.
GRAHAM, HEATHER: Milwauke, WI, Jan. 29, 1970.
GRANGER, FARLEY: San Jose, CA, July 1, 1925.
GRANT, DAVID MARSHALL: Westport, CT, June 21, 1955. Yale.
GRANT, HUGH: London, Sept. 9, 1960. Oxford.
GRANT, KATHRYN (Olive Grandstaff): Houston, TX, Nov. 25, 1933. UCLA.
GRANT, LEE: NYC, Oct. 31, 1927. Juilliard.
GRANT, RICHARD E: Mbabane, Swaziland, May 5, 1957. Cape Town U.
GRAVES, PETER (Aurness): Minneapolis, Mar. 18, 1926. U Minn.
GRAVES, RUPERT: Weston-Super-Mare, England, June 30, 1963.
GRAY, CHARLES: Bournemouth, England, 1928.
GRAY, COLEEN (Doris Jensen): Staplehurst, NB, Oct. 23, 1922. Hamline.
GRAY, LINDA: Santa Monica, CA, Sept. 12, 1940.
GRAY, SPALDING: Barrington, RI, June 5, 1941.
GRAYSON, KATHRYN (Zelma Hedrick): Winston-Salem, NC, Feb. 9, 1922.
GREEN, KERRI: Fort Lee, NJ, Jan. 14, 1967. Vassar.
GREENE, ELLEN: NYC, Feb. 22, 1950. Ryder College.
GREENE, GRAHAM: Six Nations Reserve, Ontario, June 22, 1952
GREER, JANE: Washington, DC, Sept. 9, 1924.

Samuel L.Jackson

GREER, MICHAEL: Galesburg, IL, Apr. 20, 1943.
GREIST, KIM: Stamford, CT, May 12, 1958.
GREY, JENNIFER: NYC, Mar. 26, 1960.
GREY, JOEL (Katz): Cleveland, OH, Apr. 11, 1932.
GREY, VIRGINIA: Los Angeles, Mar. 22, 1917.
GRIECO, RICHARD: Watertown, NY, Mar. 23, 1965.
GRIEM, HELMUT: Hamburg, Germany, Apr. 6, 1932. HamburgU.
GRIER, DAVID ALAN: Detroit, MI, June 30, 1955. Yale.
GRIER, PAM: Winston-Salem, NC, May 26, 1949.
GRIFFITH, ANDY: Mt. Airy, NC, June 1, 1926. UNC.
GRIFFITH, MELANIE: NYC, Aug. 9, 1957. Pierce College.
GRIMES, GARY: San Francisco, June 2, 1955.
GRIMES, SCOTT: Lowell, MA, July 9, 1971.
GRIMES, TAMMY: Lynn, MA, Jan. 30, 1934. Stephens College.
GRIZZARD, GEORGE: Roanoke Rapids, NC, Apr. 1, 1928. UNC.
GRODIN, CHARLES: Pittsburgh, PA, Apr. 21, 1935.

James Earl Jones

Nicole Kidman

GROH, DAVID: NYC, May 21, 1939. Brown U, LAMDA.
GROSS, MARY: Chicago, IL, Mar. 25, 1953.
GROSS, MICHAEL: Chicago, IL, June 21, 1947.
GUEST, CHRISTOPHER: NYC, Feb. 5, 1948.
GUEST, LANCE: Saratoga, CA, July 21, 1960. UCLA.
GUILLAUME, ROBERT (Williams): St. Louis, MO, Nov. 30, 1937.
GUINNESS, ALEC: London, Apr. 2, 1914. Pembroke Lodge School.
GULAGER, CLU: Holdenville, OK, Nov. 16 1928.
GUTTENBERG, STEVE: Massapequa, NY, Aug. 24, 1958. UCLA.
GUY, JASMINE: Boston, Mar. 10, 1964.
HAAS, LUKAS: West Hollywood, CA, Apr. 16, 1976.
HACK, SHELLEY: Greenwich, CT, July 6, 1952.
HACKETT, BUDDY (Leonard Hacker): Brooklyn, NY, Aug. 31, 1924.
HACKMAN, GENE: San Bernardino, CA, Jan. 30, 1930.
HAGERTY, JULIE: Cincinnati, OH, June 15, 1955. Juilliard.

Harvey Keitel

HAGMAN, LARRY (Hageman): Weatherford, TX, Sept. 21, 1931. Bard.
HAID, CHARLES: San Francisco, June 2, 1943. CarnegieTech.
HAIM, COREY: Toronto, Canada, Dec. 23, 1972.
HALE, BARBARA: DeKalb, IL, Apr. 18, 1922. Chicago Academy of Fine Arts.
HALEY, JACKIE EARLE: Northridge, CA, July 14, 1961.
HALL, ALBERT: Boothton, AL, Nov. 10, 1937. Columbia.
HALL, ANTHONY MICHAEL: Boston, MA, Apr. 14, 1968.
HALL, ARSENIO: Cleveland, OH, Feb. 12, 1959.
HALL, HUNTZ: Boston, MA, Aug. 15, 1920.
HAMEL, VERONICA: Philadelphia, PA, Nov. 20, 1943.
HAMILL, MARK: Oakland, CA, Sept. 25, 1952. LACC.
HAMILTON, CARRIE: NYC, Dec. 5, 1963.
HAMILTON, GEORGE: Memphis, TN, Aug. 12, 1939. Hackley.
HAMILTON, LINDA: Salisbury, MD, Sept. 26, 1956.
HAMLIN, HARRY: Pasadena, CA, Oct. 30, 1951.
HAMPSHIRE, SUSAN: London, May 12, 1941.
HAMPTON, JAMES: Oklahoma City, OK, July 9, 1936. NTexasStU.
HAN, MAGGIE: Providence, RI, 1959.
HANDLER, EVAN: NYC, Jan. 10, 1961. Juillard.
HANKS, TOM: Concord, CA, Jul. 9, 1956. CalStateU.
HANNAH, DARYL: Chicago, IL, Dec. 3, 1960. UCLA.
HANNAH, PAGE: Chicago, IL, Apr. 13, 1964.
HARDIN, TY (Orison Whipple Hungerford, II): NYC, June 1, 1930.
HAREWOOD, DORIAN: Dayton, OH, Aug. 6, 1950. U Cinn.
HARMON, MARK: Los Angeles, CA, Sept. 2, 1951. UCLA.
HARPER, JESSICA: Chicago, IL, Oct. 10, 1949.
HARPER, TESS: Mammoth Spring, AK, 1952. SWMoState.
HARPER, VALERIE: Suffern, NY, Aug. 22, 1940.
HARRELSON, WOODY: Midland, TX, July 23, 1961. Hanover College.
HARRINGTON, PAT: NYC, Aug. 13, 1929. Fordham U.
HARRIS, BARBARA (Sandra Markowitz): Evanston, IL, July 25, 1935.
HARRIS, ED: Tenafly, NJ, Nov. 28, 1950. Columbia.
HARRIS, JULIE: Grosse Point, MI, Dec. 2, 1925. Yale Drama School.
HARRIS, MEL (Mary Ellen): Bethlehem, PA, 1957. Columbia.
HARRIS, RICHARD: Limerick, Ireland, Oct. 1, 1930. London Acad.
HARRIS, ROSEMARY: Ashby, England, Sept. 19, 1930. RADA.
HARRISON, GEORGE: Liverpool, England, Feb. 25, 1943.
HARRISON, GREGORY: Catalina Island, CA, May 31, 1950. Actors Studio.
HARRISON, NOEL: London, Jan. 29, 1936.

Natassja Kinski

HARROLD, KATHRYN: Tazewell, VA, Aug. 2, 1950. Mills College.
HARRY, DEBORAH: Miami, IL, July 1, 1945.
HART, ROXANNE: Trenton, NJ, 1952, Princeton.
HARTLEY, MARIETTE: NYC, June 21, 1941.
HARTMAN, DAVID: Pawtucket, RI, May 19, 1935. Duke U.
HARTMAN, PHIL: Ontario, Canada, Sept. 24, 1948.
HASSETT, MARILYN: Los Angeles, CA, Dec. 17, 1947.
HATCHER, TERI: Sunnyvale, CA, Dec. 8, 1964.
HAUER, RUTGER: Amsterdam, Holland, Jan. 23, 1944.
HAVER, JUNE: Rock Island, IL, June 10, 1926.
HAVOC, JUNE (Hovick): Seattle, WA, Nov. 8, 1916.
HAWKE, ETHAN: Austin, TX, Nov. 6, 1970.
HAWN, GOLDIE: Washington, DC, Nov. 21, 1945.
HAWTHORNE, NIGEL: Coventry, Eng., Apr. 5, 1929.
HAYEK, SALMA: Coatzacoalcos, Veracruz, Mexico, Sept. 2, 1968.

Kevin Kline

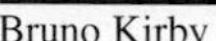

Bruno Kirby

Nathan Lane

John Leguizamo

Robert Sean Leonard

HAYES, ISAAC: Covington, TN, Aug. 20, 1942.
HAYS, ROBERT: Bethesda, MD, July 24, 1947, SD State College.
HEADLY, GLENNE: New London, CT, Mar. 13, 1955. AmCollege.
HEALD, ANTHONY: New Rochelle, NY, Aug. 25, 1944. MIStateU.
HEARD, JOHN: Washington, DC, Mar. 7, 1946. Clark U.
HEATHERTON, JOEY: NYC, Sept. 14, 1944.
HECHE, ANNE: Aurora, OH, May 25, 1969.
HECKART, EILEEN: Columbus, OH, Mar. 29, 1919. Ohio State U.
HEDAYA, DAN: Brooklyn, NY, July 24, 1940.
HEDISON, DAVID: Providence, RI, May 20, 1929. Brown U.
HEDREN, TIPPI (Natalie): Lafayette, MN, Jan. 19, 1931.
HEGYES, ROBERT: Metuchen, NJ, May 7, 1951.
HELMOND, KATHERINE: Galveston, TX, July 5, 1934.
HEMINGWAY, MARIEL: Ketchum, ID, Nov. 22, 1961.
HEMMINGS, DAVID: Guilford, England, Nov. 18, 1941.
HEMSLEY, SHERMAN: Philadelphia, PA, Feb. 1, 1938.
HENDERSON, FLORENCE: Dale, IN, Feb. 14, 1934.
HENDRY, GLORIA: Jacksonville, FL, 1949.
HENNER, MARILU: Chicago, IL, Apr. 6, 1952.
HENRIKSEN, LANCE: NYC, May 5, 1940.
HENRY, BUCK (Henry Zuckerman): NYC, Dec. 9, 1930. Dartmouth.
HENRY, JUSTIN: Rye, NY, May 25, 1971.
HEPBURN, KATHARINE: Hartford, CT, May 12, 1907. Bryn Mawr.
HERMAN, PEE-WEE (Paul Reubenfeld): Peekskill, NY, Aug. 27, 1952.
HERRMANN, EDWARD: Washington, DC, July 21, 1943. Bucknell, LAMDA.
HERSHEY, BARBARA (Herzstein): Hollywood, CA, Feb. 5, 1948.
HESSEMAN. HOWARD: Lebanon, OR, Feb. 27, 1940.
HESTON, CHARLTON: Evanston, IL, Oct. 4, 1922. Northwestern U.
HEWITT, JENNIFER LOVE: Waco, TX, Feb. 21, 1979.
HEWITT, MARTIN: Claremont, CA, Feb. 19, 1958. AADA.
HEYWOOD, ANNE (Violet Pretty): Birmingham, England, Dec. 11, 1932.
HICKMAN, DARRYL: Hollywood, CA, July 28, 1933. Loyola U.
HICKMAN, DWAYNE: Los Angeles, May 18, 1934. Loyola U.
HICKS, CATHERINE: NYC, Aug. 6, 1951. Notre Dame.
HIGGINS, ANTHONY (Corlan): Cork City, Ireland, May 9, 1947. Birmingham Sch. of Dramatic Arts.
HIGGINS, MICHAEL: Brooklyn, NY, Jan. 20, 1926. AmThWing.
HILL, ARTHUR: Saskatchewan, Canada, Aug. 1, 1922. U Brit. College.
HILL, BERNARD: Manchester, England, Dec. 17, 1944.
HILL, STEVEN: Seattle, WA, Feb. 24, 1922. U Wash.
HILL, TERRENCE (Mario Girotti): Venice, Italy, Mar. 29, 1941. U Rome.
HILLER, WENDY: Bramhall, Cheshire, England, Aug. 15, 1912. Winceby House School.
HILLERMAN, JOHN: Denison, TX, Dec. 20, 1932.
HINES, GREGORY: NYC, Feb.14, 1946.
HINGLE, PAT: Denver, CO, July 19, 1923. Tex. U.
HIRSCH, JUDD: NYC, Mar. 15, 1935. AADA.
HOBEL, MARA: NYC, June 18, 1971.
HODGE, PATRICIA: Lincolnshire, England, Sept. 29, 1946. LAMDA.
HOFFMAN, DUSTIN: Los Angeles, Aug. 8, 1937. Pasadena Playhouse.
HOGAN, JONATHAN: Chicago, IL, June 13, 1951.
HOGAN, PAUL: Lightning Ridge, Australia, Oct. 8, 1939.
HOLBROOK, HAL (Harold): Cleveland, OH, Feb. 17, 1925. Denison.
HOLLIMAN, EARL: Tennesas Swamp, Delhi, LA, Sept. 11, 1928. UCLA.
HOLM, CELESTE: NYC, Apr. 29, 1919.
HOLM, IAN: Ilford, Essex, England, Sept. 12, 1931. RADA.
HOMEIER, SKIP (George Vincent Homeier): Chicago, IL, Oct. 5, 1930. UCLA.
HOOKS, ROBERT: Washington, DC, Apr. 18, 1937. Temple.
HOPE, BOB (Leslie Townes Hope): London, May 26, 1903.
HOPKINS, ANTHONY: Port Talbot, So. Wales, Dec. 31, 1937. RADA.
HOPPER, DENNIS: Dodge City, KS, May 17, 1936.
HORNE, LENA: Brooklyn, NY, June 30, 1917.
HORSLEY, LEE: Muleshoe, TX, May 15, 1955.
HORTON, ROBERT: Los Angeles, July 29, 1924. UCLA.
HOSKINS, BOB: Bury St. Edmunds, England, Oct. 26, 1942.
HOUGHTON, KATHARINE: Hartford, CT, Mar. 10, 1945. Sarah Lawrence.
HOUSER, JERRY: Los Angeles, July 14, 1952. Valley, Jr. College.
HOWARD, ARLISS: Independence, MO, 1955. Columbia College.
HOWARD, KEN: El Centro, CA, Mar. 28, 1944. Yale.
HOWARD, RON: Duncan, OK, Mar. 1, 1954. USC.
HOWARD, RONALD: Norwood, England, Apr. 7, 1918. Jesus College.
HOWELL, C. THOMAS: Los Angeles, Dec. 7, 1966.
HOWELLS, URSULA: London, Sept. 17, 1922.
HOWES, SALLY ANN: London, July 20, 1930.
HOWLAND, BETH: Boston, MA, May 28, 1941.
HUBLEY, SEASON: NYC, May 14, 1951.
HUDDLESTON, DAVID: Vinton, VA, Sept. 17, 1930.

HUDSON, ERNIE: Benton Harbor, MI, Dec. 17, 1945.
HUGHES, BARNARD: Bedford Hills, NY, July 16, 1915. Manhattan College.
HUGHES, KATHLEEN (Betty von Gerkan): Hollywood, CA, Nov. 14, 1928. UCLA.
HULCE, TOM: Plymouth, MI, Dec. 6, 1953. N.C. Sch. of Arts.
HUNNICUT, GAYLE: Ft. Worth, TX, Feb. 6, 1943. UCLA.
HUNT, HELEN: Los Angeles, June 15, 1963.
HUNT, LINDA: Morristown, NJ, Apr. 1945. Goodman Theatre.
HUNT, MARSHA: Chicago, IL, Oct. 17, 1917.
HUNTER, HOLLY: Atlanta, GA, Mar. 20, 1958. Carnegie-Mellon.
HUNTER, KIM (Janet Cole): Detroit, Nov. 12, 1922.
HUNTER, TAB (Arthur Gelien): NYC, July 11, 1931.
HUPPERT, ISABELLE: Paris, France, Mar. 16, 1955.
HURLEY, ELIZABETH: Hampshire, Eng., June 10, 1965.
HURT, JOHN: Lincolnshire, England, Jan. 22, 1940.
HURT, MARY BETH (Supinger): Marshalltown, IA, Sept. 26, 1948. NYU.
HURT, WILLIAM: Washington, DC, Mar. 20, 1950. Tufts, Juilliard.
HUSSEY, RUTH: Providence, RI, Oct. 30, 1917. U Mich.
HUSTON, ANJELICA: Santa Monica, CA, July 9, 1951.
HUTTON, BETTY (Betty Thornberg): Battle Creek, MI, Feb. 26, 1921.
HUTTON, LAUREN (Mary): Charleston, SC, Nov. 17, 1943. Newcomb College.
HUTTON, TIMOTHY: Malibu, CA, Aug. 16, 1960.
HYER, MARTHA: Fort Worth, TX, Aug. 10, 1924. Northwestern U.
ICE CUBE (O'Shea Jackson): Los Angeles, June 15, 1969.
IDLE, ERIC: South Shields, Durham, England, Mar. 29, 1943. Cambridge.
INGELS, MARTY: Brooklyn, NY, Mar. 9, 1936.
IRELAND, KATHY: Santa Barbara, CA, Mar. 8, 1963.
IRONS, JEREMY: Cowes, England, Sept. 19, 1948. Old Vic.
IRVING, AMY: Palo Alto, CA, Sept. 10, 1953. LADA.
IRWIN, BILL: Santa Monica, CA, Apr. 11, 1950.
ISAAK, CHRIS: Stockton, CA, June 26, 1956. UofPacific.
IVANEK, ZELJKO: Lujubljana, Yugo., Aug. 15, 1957. Yale, LAMDA.
IVEY, JUDITH: El Paso, TX, Sept. 4, 1951.
JACKSON, ANNE: Alleghany, PA, Sept. 3, 1926. Neighborhood Playhouse.
JACKSON, GLENDA: Hoylake, Cheshire, England, May 9, 1936. RADA.
JACKSON, JANET: Gary, IN, May 16, 1966.
JACKSON, KATE: Birmingham, AL, Oct. 29, 1948. AADA.
JACKSON, MICHAEL: Gary, IN, Aug. 29, 1958.
JACKSON, SAMUELL.: Atlanta, Dec. 21, 1948.
JACKSON, VICTORIA: Miami, FL, Aug. 2, 1958.
JACOBI, DEREK: Leytonstone, London, Oct. 22, 1938. Cambridge.
JACOBI, LOU: Toronto, Canada, Dec. 28, 1913.
JACOBS, LAWRENCE-HILTON: Virgin Islands, Sept. 14, 1953.
JACOBY, SCOTT: Chicago, IL, Nov. 19, 1956.
JAGGER, MICK: Dartford, Kent, England, July 26, 1943.
JAMES, CLIFTON: NYC, May 29, 1921. Ore. U.
JARMAN, CLAUDE, JR.: Nashville, TN, Sept. 27, 1934.
JASON, RICK: NYC, May 21, 1926. AADA.
JEAN, GLORIA (Gloria Jean Schoonover): Buffalo, NY, Apr. 14, 1927.
JEFFREYS, ANNE (Carmichael): Goldsboro, NC, Jan. 26, 1923. Anderson College.
JEFFRIES, LIONEL: London, June 10, 1926. RADA.
JERGENS, ADELE: Brooklyn, NY, Nov. 26, 1922.
JETER, MICHAEL: Lawrenceburg, TN, Aug. 26, 1952. Memphis St.U.
JILLIAN, ANN (Nauseda): Cambridge, MA, Jan. 29, 1951.
JOHANSEN, DAVID: Staten Island, NY, Jan. 9, 1950.
JOHN, ELTON (Reginald Dwight): Middlesex, England, Mar. 25, 1947. RAM.
JOHNS, GLYNIS: Durban, S. Africa, Oct. 5, 1923.
JOHNSON, DON: Galena, MO, Dec. 15, 1950. UKan.
JOHNSON, PAGE: Welch, WV, Aug. 25, 1930. Ithaca.
JOHNSON, RAFER: Hillsboro, TX, Aug. 18, 1935. UCLA.
JOHNSON, RICHARD: Essex, England, July 30, 1927. RADA.
JOHNSON, ROBIN: Brooklyn, NY, May 29, 1964.
JOHNSON, VAN: Newport, RI, Aug. 28, 1916.
JONES, CHRISTOPHER: Jackson, TN, Aug. 18, 1941. Actors Studio.
JONES, DEAN: Decatur, AL, Jan. 25, 1931. Actors Studio.
JONES, GRACE: Spanishtown, Jamaica, May 19, 1952.
JONES, JACK: Bel-Air, CA, Jan. 14, 1938.
JONES, JAMES EARL: Arkabutla, MS, Jan. 17, 1931. U Mich.
JONES, JEFFREY: Buffalo, NY, Sept. 28, 1947. LAMDA.
JONES, JENNIFER (Phyllis Isley): Tulsa, OK, Mar. 2, 1919. AADA.
JONES, L.Q. (Justice Ellis McQueen): Aug 19, 1927.
JONES, SAM J.: Chicago, IL, Aug. 12, 1954.
JONES, SHIRLEY: Smithton, PA, March 31, 1934.
JONES, TERRY: Colwyn Bay, Wales, Feb. 1, 1942.
JONES, TOMMY LEE: San Saba, TX, Sept. 15, 1946. Harvard.

Laura Linney

Michael Madsen

Stephen Mailer

Dylan McDermott

JOURDAN, LOUIS: Marseilles, France, June 19, 1920.
JOY, ROBERT: Montreal, Canada, Aug. 17, 1951. Oxford.
JUDD, ASHLEY: Los Angeles, CA, Apr. 19, 1968.
JURADO, KATY (Maria Christina Jurado Garcia): Guadalajara, Mex., Jan. 16, 1927.
KACZMAREK, JANE: Milwaukee, WI, Dec. 21, 1955.
KAHN, MADELINE: Boston, MA, Sept. 29, 1942. Hofstra U.
KANE, CAROL: Cleveland, OH, June 18, 1952.
KAPLAN, MARVIN: Brooklyn, NY, Jan. 24, 1924.
KAPOOR, SHASHI: Calcutta, India, Mar. 18, 1938.
KAPRISKY, VALERIE (Cheres): Paris, France, Aug. 19, 1962.
KARRAS, ALEX: Gary, IN, July 15, 1935.
KATT, WILLIAM: Los Angeles, CA, Feb. 16, 1955.
KAUFMANN, CHRISTINE: Lansdorf, Graz, Austria, Jan. 11, 1945.
KAVNER, JULIE: Burbank, CA, Sept. 7, 1951. UCLA.
KAZAN, LAINIE (Levine): Brooklyn, NY, May 15, 1942.
KAZURINSKY, TIM: Johnstown, PA, March 3, 1950.
KEACH, STACY: Savannah, GA, June 2, 1941. U Cal., Yale.
KEATON, DIANE (Hall): Los Angeles, CA, Jan. 5, 1946. Neighborhood Playhouse.
KEATON, MICHAEL: Coraopolis, PA, Sept. 9, 1951. KentStateU.
KEDROVA, LILA: Leningrad, 1918.
KEEL, HOWARD (Harold Leek): Gillespie, IL, Apr. 13, 1919.
KEITEL, HARVEY: Brooklyn, NY, May 13, 1939.
KEITH, DAVID: Knoxville, TN, May 8, 1954. UTN.
KELLER, MARTHE: Basel, Switzerland, 1945. Munich Stanislavsky Sch.
KELLERMAN, SALLY: Long Beach, CA, June 2, 1936. Actors Studio West.
KELLEY, DeFOREST: Atlanta, GA, Jan. 20, 1920.
KEMP, JEREMY (Wacker): Chesterfield, England, Feb. 3, 1935. Central Sch.
KENNEDY, GEORGE: NYC, Feb. 18, 1925.
KENNEDY, LEON ISAAC: Cleveland, OH, 1949.
KENSIT, PATSY: London, Mar. 4, 1968.
KERR, DEBORAH: Helensburg, Scotland, Sept. 30, 1921. Smale Ballet School.
KERR, JOHN: NYC, Nov. 15, 1931. Harvard, Columbia.
KERWIN, BRIAN: Chicago, IL, Oct. 25, 1949.
KEYES, EVELYN: Port Arthur, TX, Nov. 20, 1919.
KHAMBATTA, PERSIS: Bombay, Oct. 2, 1950.
KIDDER, MARGOT: Yellow Knife, Canada, Oct. 17, 1948. UBC.
KIDMAN, NICOLE: Hawaii, June 20, 1967.
KIEL, RICHARD: Detroit, MI, Sept. 13, 1939.
KIER, UDO: Koeln, Germany, Oct. 14, 1944.
KILEY, RICHARD: Chicago, IL, Mar. 31, 1922. Loyola.

Bette Midler

Julianne Moore

Rob Morrow

KILMER, VAL: Los Angeles, Dec. 31, 1959. Juilliard.
KINCAID, ARON (Norman Neale Williams, III): Los Angeles, June 15, 1943. UCLA.
KING, ALAN (Irwin Kniberg): Brooklyn, NY, Dec. 26, 1927.
KING, PERRY: Alliance, OH, Apr. 30, 1948. Yale.
KINGSLEY, BEN (Krishna Bhanji): Snaiton, Yorkshire, England, Dec. 31, 1943.
KINNEAR, GREG: Logansport, IN, June 17, 1963.
KINSKI, NASTASSJA: Berlin, Ger., Jan. 24, 1960.
KIRBY, BRUNO: NYC, Apr. 28, 1949.
KIRK, TOMMY: Louisville, KY, Dec.10 1941.
KIRKLAND, SALLY: NYC, Oct. 31, 1944. Actors Studio.
KITT, EARTHA: North, SC, Jan. 26, 1928.
KLEIN, ROBERT: NYC, Feb. 8, 1942. Alfred U.
KLEMPERER, WERNER: Cologne, Mar. 22, 1920.
KLINE, KEVIN: St. Louis, MO, Oct. 24, 1947. Juilliard.
KLUGMAN, JACK: Philadelphia, PA, Apr. 27, 1922. Carnegie Tech.
KNIGHT, MICHAEL E.: Princeton, NJ, May 7, 1959.
KNIGHT, SHIRLEY: Goessel, KS, July 5, 1937. Wichita U.
KNOX, ELYSE: Hartford, CT, Dec. 14, 1917. Traphagen School.
KOENIG, WALTER: Chicago, IL, Sept. 14, 1936. UCLA.
KOHNER, SUSAN: Los Angeles, Nov. 11, 1936. U Calif.
KORMAN, HARVEY: Chicago, IL, Feb. 15, 1927. Goodman.
KORSMO, CHARLIE: Minneapolis, MN, July, 1978.
KORVIN, CHARLES (Geza Korvin Karpathi): Czechoslovakia, Nov. 21, 1907. Sorbonne.
KOTEAS, ELIAS: Montreal, Quebec, Canada, 1961. AADA.
KOTTO, YAPHET: NYC, Nov. 15, 1937.
KOZAK, HARLEY JANE: Wilkes-Barre, PA, Jan. 28, 1957. NYU.
KRABBE, JEROEN: Amsterdam, The Netherlands, Dec. 5, 1944.
KREUGER, KURT: St. Moritz, Switzerland, July 23, 1917. U London.
KRIGE, ALICE: Upington, So. Africa, June 28, 1955.
KRISTEL, SYLVIA: Amsterdam, The Netherlands, Sept. 28, 1952.
KRISTOFFERSON, KRIS: Brownsville, TX, June 22, 1936, Pomona College.
KRUGER, HARDY: Berlin, Germany, April 12, 1928.
KUDROW, LISA: Encino, CA, July 30, 1963.
KURTZ, SWOOSIE: Omaha, NE, Sept. 6, 1944.
KWAN, NANCY: Hong Kong, May 19, 1939. Royal Ballet.
LaBELLE, PATTI: Philadelphia, PA, May 24, 1944.
LACY, JERRY: Sioux City, IA, Mar. 27, 1936. LACC.
LADD, CHERYL (Stoppelmoor): Huron, SD. July 12, 1951.
LADD, DIANE (Ladner): Meridian, MS, Nov. 29, 1932. Tulane U.

Viggo Mortensen

LAHTI, CHRISTINE: Detroit, MI, Apr. 4, 1950. U Mich.
LAKE, RICKI: NYC, Sept. 21, 1968.
LAMARR, HEDY (Hedwig Kiesler): Vienna, Sept. 11, 1913.
LAMAS, LORENZO: Los Angeles, Jan. 28, 1958.
LAMBERT, CHRISTOPHER: NYC, Mar. 29, 1958.
LANDAU, MARTIN: Brooklyn, NY, June 20, 1931. Actors Studio.
LANDRUM, TERI: Enid, OK, 1960.
LANE, ABBE: Brooklyn, NY, Dec. 14, 1935.
LANE, DIANE: NYC, Jan. 22, 1963.
LANE, NATHAN: Jersey City, NJ, Feb. 3, 1956.
LANG, STEPHEN: NYC, July 11, 1952. Swarthmore College.
LANGE, HOPE: Redding Ridge, CT, Nov. 28, 1931. Reed College.
LANGE, JESSICA: Cloquet, MN, Apr. 20, 1949. U Minn.
LANGELLA, FRANK: Bayonne, NJ, Jan. 1, 1940. SyracuseU.
LANSBURY, ANGELA: London, Oct. 16, 1925. London Academy of Music.
LaPAGLIA, ANTHONY: Adelaide, Australia. Jan 31, 1959.
LARROQUETTE, JOHN: New Orleans, LA, Nov. 25, 1947.

Joe Morton

LASSER, LOUISE: NYC, Apr. 11, 1939. Brandeis U.
LATIFAH, QUEEN (Dana Owens): East Orange, NJ, 1970.
LAUGHLIN, JOHN: Memphis, TN, Apr. 3.
LAUGHLIN, TOM: Minneapolis, MN, 1938.
LAUPER, CYNDI: Astoria, Queens, NYC, June 20, 1953.
LAURE, CAROLE: Montreal, Canada, Aug. 5, 1951.
LAURIE, HUGH: Oxford, Eng., June 11, 1959.
LAURIE, PIPER (Rosetta Jacobs): Detroit, MI, Jan. 22, 1932.
LAUTER, ED: Long Beach, NY, Oct. 30, 1940.
LAVIN, LINDA: Portland, ME, Oct. 15 1939.
LAW, JOHN PHILLIP: Hollywood, CA, Sept. 7, 1937. Neighborhood Playhouse, U Hawaii.
LAW, JUDE: Lewisham, Eng., Dec. 29, 1972.
LAWRENCE, BARBARA: Carnegie, OK, Feb. 24, 1930. UCLA.
LAWRENCE, CAROL (Laraia): Melrose Park, IL, Sept. 5, 1935.
LAWRENCE, VICKI: Inglewood, CA, Mar. 26, 1949.
LAWRENCE, MARTIN: Frankfurt, Germany, Apr. 16, 1965.
LAWSON, LEIGH: Atherston, England, July 21, 1945. RADA.
LEACHMAN, CLORIS: Des Moines, IA, Apr. 30, 1930. Northwestern U.
LEARY, DENIS: Boston, MA, Aug. 18, 1957.
LEAUD, JEAN-PIERRE: Paris, France, May 5, 1944.
LeBLANC, MATT: Newton, MA, July 25, 1967.
LEDERER, FRANCIS: Karlin, Prague, Czech., Nov. 6, 1906.
LEE, CHRISTOPHER: London, May 27, 1922. Wellington College.
LEE, MARK: Australia, 1958.
LEE, MICHELE (Dusiak): Los Angeles, June 24, 1942. LACC.
LEE, PEGGY (Norma Delores Egstrom): Jamestown, ND, May 26, 1920.
LEE, SPIKE (Shelton Lee): Atlanta, GA, Mar. 20, 1957.
LEGROS, JAMES: Minneapolis, MN, Apr. 27, 1962.
LEGUIZAMO, JOHN: Columbia, July 22, 1965. NYU.
LEIBMAN, RON: NYC, Oct. 11, 1937. Ohio Wesleyan.
LEIGH, JANET (Jeanette Helen Morrison): Merced, CA, July 6, 1926. ColofPacific.
LEIGH, JENNIFER JASON: Los Angeles, Feb. 5, 1962.
LeMAT, PAUL: Rahway, NJ, Sept. 22, 1945.
LEMMON, CHRIS: Los Angeles, Jan. 22, 1954.
LEMMON, JACK: Boston, Feb. 8, 1925. Harvard.
LENO, JAY: New Rochelle, NY, Apr. 28, 1950. Emerson College.
LENZ, KAY: Los Angeles, Mar. 4, 1953.
LENZ, RICK: Springfield, IL, Nov. 21, 1939. U Mich.
LEONARD, ROBERT SEAN: Westwood, NJ, Feb. 28, 1969.
LERNER, MICHAEL: Brooklyn, NY, June 22, 1941.
LESLIE, BETHEL: NYC, Aug. 3, 1929. Brearley School.

Armin Mueller-Stahl

LESLIE, JOAN (Joan Brodell): Detroit, Jan. 26, 1925. St. Benedict's.
LESTER, MARK: Oxford, England, July 11, 1958.
LEVELS, CALVIN: Cleveland. OH, Sept. 30, 1954. CCC.
LEVIN, RACHEL: NYC, 1954. Goddard College.
LEVINE, JERRY: New Brunswick, NJ, Mar. 12, 1957, Boston U.
LEVY, EUGENE: Hamilton, Canada, Dec. 17, 1946. McMasterU.
LEWIS, CHARLOTTE: London, Aug.7, 1967.
LEWIS, GEOFFREY: San Diego, CA, Jan. 1, 1935.
LEWIS, JERRY (Joseph Levitch): Newark, NJ, Mar. 16, 1926.
LEWIS, JULIETTE: Los Angeles CA, June 21, 1973.
LIGON, TOM: New Orleans, LA, Sept. 10, 1945.
LINCOLN, ABBEY (Anna Marie Woolridge): Chicago, IL, Aug. 6, 1930.
LINDEN, HAL: Bronx, NY, Mar. 20, 1931. City College of NY.
LINDSAY, ROBERT: Ilketson, Derbyshire, England, Dec. 13, 1951, RADA.
LINN-BAKER, MARK: St. Louis, MO, June 17, 1954, Yale.

Dermot Mulroney

LINNEY, LAURA: New York, NY, Feb. 5, 1964.
LIOTTA, RAY: Newark, NJ, Dec. 18, 1955. UMiami.
LISI, VIRNA: Rome, Nov. 8, 1937.
LITHGOW, JOHN: Rochester, NY, Oct. 19, 1945. Harvard.
LLOYD, CHRISTOPHER: Stamford, CT, Oct. 22, 1938.
LLOYD, EMILY: London, Sept. 29, 1970.
LOCKE, SONDRA: Shelbyville, TN, May, 28, 1947.
LOCKHART, JUNE: NYC, June 25, 1925. Westlake School.
LOCKWOOD, GARY: Van Nuys, CA, Feb. 21, 1937.
LOGGIA, ROBERT: Staten Island, NY, Jan. 3, 1930. UMo.
LOLLOBRIGIDA, GINA: Subiaco, Italy, July 4, 1927. Rome Academy of Fine Arts.
LOM, HERBERT: Prague, Czechoslovakia, Jan. 9, 1917. Prague U.
LOMEZ, CELINE: Montreal, Canada, May 11, 1953.
LONDON, JULIE (Julie Peck): Santa Rosa, CA, Sept. 26, 1926.
LONE, JOHN: Hong Kong, Oct 13, 1952. AADA.
LONG, SHELLEY: Ft. Wayne, IN, Aug. 23, 1949. Northwestem U.
LOPEZ, JENNIFER: Bronx, NY, July 24, 1970.
LOPEZ, PERRY: NYC, July 22, 1931. NYU.
LORD, JACK (John Joseph Ryan): NYC, Dec. 30, 1928. NYU.
LOREN, SOPHIA (Sophia Scicolone): Rome, Italy, Sept. 20, 1934.
LOUIS-DREYFUS, JULIA: NYC, Jan. 13, 1961.
LOUISE, TINA (Blacker): NYC, Feb. 11, 1934, Miami U.
LOVE, COURTNEY (Love Michelle Harrison): San Francisco, July 9, 1965.
LOVETT, LYLE: Klein, TX, Nov. 1, 1957.
LOVITZ, JON: Tarzana, CA, July 21, 1957.
LOWE, CHAD: Dayton, OH, Jan. 15, 1968.
LOWE, ROB: Charlottesville, VA, Mar. 17, 1964.
LOWITSCH, KLAUS: Berlin, Apr. 8, 1936, Vienna Academy.
LUCAS, LISA: Arizona, 1961.
LUCKINBILL, LAURENCE: Fort Smith, AK, Nov. 21, 1934.
LUFT, LORNA: Los Angeles, Nov. 21, 1952.
LULU (Marie Lawrie): Glasgow, Scotland, Nov. 3, 1948.
LUNA, BARBARA: NYC, Mar. 2, 1939.
LUNDGREN, DOLPH: Stockolm, Sweden, Nov. 3, 1959. Royal Inst.
LuPONE, PATTI: Northport, NY, Apr. 21, 1949, Juilliard.
LYDON, JAMES: Harrington Park, NJ, May 30, 1923.
LYNCH, KELLY: Minneapolis, MN, Jan. 31, 1959.
LYNLEY, CAROL (Jones): NYC, Feb. 13, 1942.
LYON, SUE: Davenport, IA, July 10, 1946.
MacARTHUR, JAMES: Los Angeles, Dec. 8, 1937. Harvard.
MACCHIO, RALPH: Huntington, NY, Nov. 4, 1961.
MacCORKINDALE, SIMON: Cambridge, England, Feb. 12, 1953.
MacDOWELL, ANDIE (Rose Anderson MacDowell): Gaffney, SC, Apr. 21, 1958.
MacGINNIS, NIALL: Dublin, Ireland, Mar. 29, 1913. Dublin U.
MacGRAW, ALI: NYC, Apr. 1, 1938. Wellesley.
MacLACHLAN, KYLE: Yakima, WA, Feb. 22, 1959. UWa.
MacLAINE, SHIRLEY (Beaty): Richmond, VA, Apr. 24, 1934.
MacLEOD, GAVIN: Mt. Kisco, NY, Feb. 28, 1931.
MacNAUGHTON, ROBERT: NYC, Dec. 19, 1966.
MACNEE, PATRICK: London, Feb. 1922.
MacNICOL, PETER: Dallas, TX, Apr. 10, 1954. UMN.
MacPHERSON, ELLE: Sydney, Australia, 1965.
MACY, W. H. (William): Miami, FL, Mar. 13, 1950. Goddard College.
MADIGAN, AMY: Chicago, IL, Sept. 11, 1950. Marquette U.
MADONNA (Madonna Louise Veronica Cicone): Bay City, MI, Aug. 16, 1958. UMi.
MADSEN, MICHAEL: Chicago, IL, Sept. 25, 1958.
MADSEN, VIRGINIA: Winnetka, IL, Sept. 11, 1963.
MAGNUSON, ANN: Charleston, WV, Jan. 4, 1956.
MAGUIRE, TOBEY: Santa Monica, CA, June 27, 1975.
MAHARIS, GEORGE: Astoria, NY, Sept. 1, 1928. Actors Studio.
MAHONEY, JOHN: Manchester, England, June 20, 1940, WUIll.
MAILER, STEPHEN: NYC, Mar. 10, 1966. NYU.
MAJORS, LEE: Wyandotte, MI, Apr. 23, 1940. E. Ky. State College.
MAKEPEACE, CHRIS: Toronto, Canada, Apr. 22, 1964.
MAKO (Mako Iwamatsu): Kobe, Japan, Dec. 10, 1933. Pratt.
MALDEN, KARL (Mladen Sekulovich): Gary, IN, Mar. 22, 1914.
MALKOVICH, JOHN: Christopher, IL, Dec. 9, 1953, IllStateU.
MALONE, DOROTHY: Chicago, IL, Jan. 30, 1925.
MANN, TERRENCE: KY, 1945. NCSchl Arts.
MANOFF, DINAH: NYC, Jan. 25, 1958. CalArts.
MANTEGNA, JOE: Chicago, IL, Nov. 13, 1947. Goodman Theatre.
MANZ, LINDA: NYC, 1961.
MARAIS, JEAN: Cherbourg, France, Dec. 11, 1913, St. Germain.
MARCHAND, NANCY: Buffalo, NY, June 19, 1928.
MARCOVICCI, ANDREA: NYC, Nov. 18, 1948.
MARIN, CHEECH (Richard): Los Angeles, July 13, 1946.
MARIN, JACQUES: Paris, France, Sept. 9, 1919. Conservatoire National.
MARINARO, ED: NYC, Mar. 31, 1950. Cornell.
MARS, KENNETH: Chicago, IL, 1936.
MARSH, JEAN: London, England, July 1, 1934.
MARSHALL, E. G.: Owatonna, MN, June 18, 1910. U Minn.
MARSHALL, KEN: NYC, 1953. Juilliard.
MARSHALL, PENNY: Bronx, NY, Oct. 15, 1942. UN. Mex.
MARSHALL, WILLIAM: Gary, IN, Aug. 19, 1924. NYU.
MARTIN, ANDREA: Portland, ME, Jan. 15, 1947.
MARTIN, DICK: Battle Creek, MI Jan. 30, 1923.
MARTIN, GEORGE N.: NYC, Aug. 15, 1929.
MARTIN, MILLICENT: Romford, England, June 8, 1934.
MARTIN, PAMELA SUE: Westport, CT, Jan. 15, 1953.
MARTIN, STEVE: Waco, TX, Aug. 14, 1945. UCLA.
MARTIN, TONY (Alfred Norris): Oakland, CA, Dec. 25, 1913. St. Mary's College.
MASON, MARSHA: St. Louis, MO, Apr. 3, 1942. Webster College.
MASSEN, OSA: Copenhagen, Denmark, Jan. 13, 1916.
MASSEY, DANIEL: London, Oct. 10, 1933. Eton and King's Coll.
MASTERS, BEN: Corvallis, OR, May 6, 1947. UOr.
MASTERSON, MARY STUART: Los Angeles, June 28, 1966, NYU.
MASTERSON, PETER: Angleton, TX, June 1, 1934. Rice U.
MASTRANTONIO, MARY ELIZABETH: Chicago, IL, Nov. 17, 1958. UIll.
MASUR, RICHARD: NYC, Nov. 20, 1948.
MATHESON, TIM: Glendale, CA, Dec. 31, 1947. CalState.
MATHIS, SAMANTHA: NYC, May 12, 1970.
MATLIN, MARLEE: Morton Grove, IL, Aug. 24, 1965.
MATTHAU, WALTER (Matuschanskayasky): NYC, Oct. 1, 1920.
MATTHEWS, BRIAN: Philadelphia, Jan. 24. 1953. St. Olaf.
MATURE, VICTOR: Louisville, KY, Jan. 29, 1915.
MAY, ELAINE (Berlin): Philadelphia, Apr. 21, 1932.
MAYO, VIRGINIA (Virginia Clara Jones): St. Louis, MO, Nov. 30, 1920.
MAYRON, MELANIE: Philadelphia, PA, Oct. 20, 1952. AADA.
MAZURSKY, PAUL: Brooklyn, NY, Apr. 25, 1930. Bklyn College.
MAZZELLO, JOSEPH: Rhinebeck, NY, Sept. 21, 1983.
McCALLUM, DAVID: Scotland, Sept. 19, 1933. Chapman College.
McCAMBRIDGE, MERCEDES: Jolliet, IL, Mar. 17, 1918. Mundelein College.
McCARTHY, ANDREW: NYC, Nov. 29, 1962, NYU.
McCARTHY, KEVIN: Seattle, WA, Feb. 15, 1914. Minn. U.
McCARTNEY, PAUL: Liverpool, Eng- land, June 18, 1942.
McCLANAHAN, RUE: Healdton, OK, Feb. 21, 1934.
McCLORY, SEAN: Dublin, Ireland, Mar. 8, 1924. U Galway.
McCLURE, MARC: San Mateo, CA, Mar. 31, 1957.
McCLURG, EDIE: Kansas City, MO, July 23, 1950.
McCOWEN, ALEC: Tunbridge Wells, England, May 26, 1925. RADA.

Liam Neeson

Leslie Nielsen

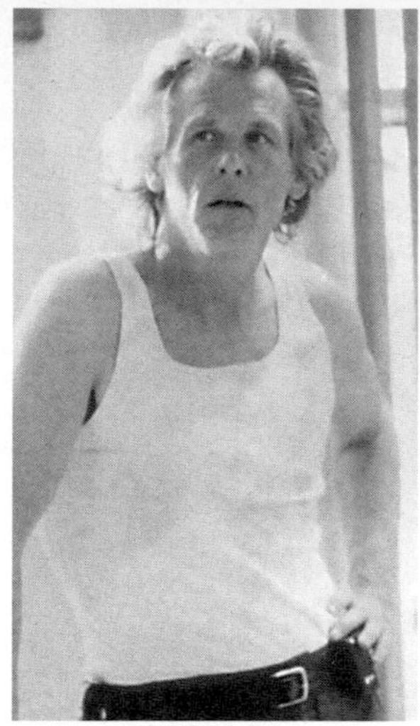
Nick Nolte

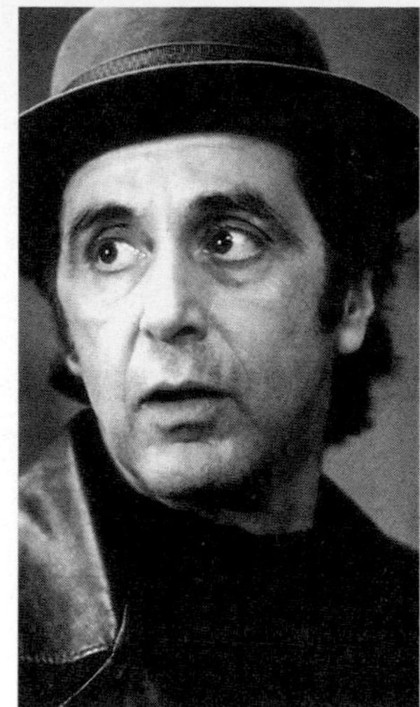
Al Pacino

McCRANE, PAUL: Philadelphia, PA, Jan. 19. 1961.
McCRARY, DARIUS: Walnut, CA, May 1, 1976.
McDERMOTT, DYLAN: Waterbury, CT, Oct. 26, 1962. Neighborhood Playhouse.
McDONNELL, MARY: Wilkes Barre, PA, Apr. 28, 1952.
McDORMAND, FRANCES: Illinois, June 23, 1957.
McDOWALL, RODDY: London, Sept. 17, 1928. St. Joseph's.
McDOWELL, MALCOLM (Taylor): Leeds, England, June 19, 1943. LAMDA.
McENERY, PETER: Walsall, England, Feb. 21, 1940.
McENTIRE, REBA: McAlester, OK, Mar. 28, 1955. SoutheasternStU.
McGAVIN, DARREN: Spokane, WA, May 7, 1922. College of Pacific.
McGILL, EVERETT: Miami Beach, FL, Oct. 21, 1945.
McGILLIS, KELLY: Newport Beach, CA, July 9, 1957. Juilliard.
McGINLEY, JOHN C.: NYC, Aug. 3, 1959. NYU.
McGOOHAN, PATRICK: NYC, Mar. 19, 1928.
McGOVERN, ELIZABETH: Evanston, IL. July 18, 1961. Juilliard.
McGOVERN, MAUREEN: Youngstown, OH, July 27, 1949.
McGREGOR, EWAN: Perth, Scotland, March 31, 1971
McGUIRE, BIFF: New Haven, CT, Oct. 25. 1926. Mass. Stale College.
McGUIRE, DOROTHY: Omaha, NE, June 14, 1918.
McHATTIE, STEPHEN: Antigonish, NS, Feb. 3. Acadia U AADA.
McKAY, GARDNER: NYC, June 10, 1932. Comell.
McKEAN, MICHAEL: NYC, Oct. 17, 1947.
McKEE, LONETTE: Detroit, MI, July 22, 1955.
McKELLEN, IAN: Burnley, England, May 25, 1939.
McKENNA, VIRGINIA: London, June 7, 1931.
McKEON, DOUG: Pompton Plains, NJ, June 10, 1966.
McKERN, LEO: Sydney, Australia, Mar. 16, 1920.
McKUEN, ROD: Oakland, CA, Apr. 29, 1933.
McLERIE, ALLYN ANN: Grand Mere, Canada, Dec. 1, 1926.
McMAHON, ED: Detroit, MI, Mar. 6, 1923.
McNAIR, BARBARA: Chicago, IL, Mar. 4, 1939. UCLA.
McNAMARA, WILLIAM: Dallas, TX, Mar. 31, 1965.
McNICHOL, KRISTY: Los Angeles. CA, Sept. 11, 1962.
McQUEEN, ARMELIA: North Carolina, Jan. 6, 1952. Bklyn Consv.
McQUEEN, CHAD: Los Angeles, CA, Dec. 28, 1960. Actors Studio.
McRANEY, GERALD: Collins, MS, Aug. 19, 1948.
McSHANE, IAN: Blackburn, England, Sept. 29, 1942. RADA.
MEADOWS, JAYNE (formerly Jayne Cotter): Wuchang, China, Sept. 27, 1924. St. Margaret's.
MEARA, ANNE: Brooklyn, NY, Sept. 20, 1929.
MEAT LOAF (Marvin Lee Aday): Dallas, TX, Sept. 27, 1947.
MEDWIN, MICHAEL: London, 1925. Instut Fischer.
MEKKA, EDDIE: Worcester, MA, June 14, 1952. Boston Cons.
MELATO, MARIANGELA: Milan, Italy, 1941. Milan Theatre Acad.
MEREDITH, LEE (Judi Lee Sauls): Oct. 22, 1947. AADA.
MERKERSON, S. EPATHA: Saganaw, MI, Nov. 28, 1952. Wayne St. Univ.
MERRILL, DINA (Nedinia Hutton): NYC, Dec. 29, 1925. AADA.
METCALF, LAURIE: Edwardsville, IL, June 16, 1955., IIIStU.
METZLER, JIM: Oneonda, NY, June 23. Dartmouth.
MICHELL, KEITH: Adelaide, Australia, Dec. 1, 1926.
MIDLER, BETTE: Honolulu, HI, Dec. 1, 1945.
MILANO, ALYSSA: Brooklyn, NY, Dec. 19, 1972.
MILES, JOANNA: Nice, France, Mar. 6, 1940.
MILES, SARAH: Ingatestone, England, Dec. 31, 1941. RADA.
MILES, SYLVIA: NYC, Sept. 9, 1934. Actors Studio.
MILES, VERA (Ralston): Boise City, OK, Aug. 23, 1929. UCLA.
MILLER, ANN (Lucille Ann Collier): Chireno, TX, Apr. 12, 1919. Lawler Professional School.
MILLER, BARRY: Los Angeles, CA, Feb. 6, 1958.
MILLER, DICK: NYC, Dec. 25, 1928.
MILLER, JASON: Long Island City, NY, Apr. 22, 1939. Catholic U.
MILLER, LINDA: NYC, Sept. 16, 1942. Catholic U.
MILLER, PENELOPE ANN: Santa Monica, CA, Jan. 13, 1964.
MILLER, REBECCA: Roxbury, CT, 1962. Yale.
MILLS, DONNA: Chicago, IL, Dec. 11, 1945. UIl.
MILLS, HAYLEY: London, Apr. 18, 1946. Elmhurst School.
MILLS, JOHN: Suffolk, England, Feb. 22, 1908.
MILLS, JULIET: London, Nov. 21, 1941.
MILNER, MARTIN: Detroit, MI, Dec. 28, 1931.
MIMIEUX, YVETTE: Los Angeles, Jan. 8, 1941. Hollywood High.
MINNELLI, LIZA: Los Angeles, Mar. 19, l946.
MIOU-MIOU (Sylvette Henry): Paris, France, Feb. 22, 1950.
MIRREN, HELEN (Ilynea Mironoff): London, July 26, 1946.
MITCHELL, JAMES: Sacramento, CA, Feb. 29, 1920. LACC.
MITCHELL, JOHN CAMERON: El Paso, TX, Apr. 21, 1963. NorthwesternU.
MITCHUM, JAMES: Los Angeles, CA, May 8, 1941.
MODINE, MATTHEW: Loma Linda, CA, Mar. 22, 1959.

Gwyneth Paltrow

David Paymer

Sean Penn

Ryan Phillippe

MOFFAT, DONALD: Plymouth, England, Dec. 26, 1930. RADA.
MOFFETT, D. W.: Highland Park, IL, Oct. 26, 1954. Stanford U.
MOHR, JAY: New Jersey, Aug. 23, 1971.
MOKAE, ZAKES: Johannesburg, So. Africa, Aug. 5, 1935. RADA.
MOLINA, ALFRED: London, May 24, 1953. Guildhall.
MOLL, RICHARD: Pasadena, CA, Jan. 13, 1943.
MONTALBAN, RICARDO: Mexico City, Nov. 25, 1920.
MONTGOMERY, BELINDA: Winnipeg, Canada, July 23, 1950.
MONTGOMERY, GEORGE (George Letz): Brady, MT, Aug. 29, 1916. U Mont.
MOODY, RON: London, Jan. 8, 1924. London U.
MOOR, BILL: Toledo, OH, July 13, 1931. Northwestern.
MOORE, CONSTANCE: Sioux City, IA, Jan. 18, 1919.
MOORE, DEMI (Guines): Roswell, NM, Nov. 11, 1962.
MOORE, DICK: Los Angeles, Sept. 12, 1925.
MOORE, DUDLEY: Dagenham, Essex, England, Apr. 19, 1935.
MOORE, JULIANNE (Julie Anne Smith): Fayetteville, NC, Dec. 30, 1960.
MOORE, KIERON: County Cork, Ireland, 1925. St. Mary's College.
MOORE, MARY TYLER: Brooklyn, NY, Dec. 29, 1936.
MOORE, ROGER: London, Oct. 14, 1927. RADA.
MOORE, TERRY (Helen Koford): Los Angeles, Jan. 7, 1929.
MORALES, ESAI: Brooklyn, NY, Oct. 1, 1962.
MORANIS, RICK: Toronto, Canada, Apr. 18, 1954.
MOREAU, JEANNE: Paris, France, Jan. 23, 1928.
MORENO, RITA (Rosita Alverio): Humacao, P.R., Dec. 11, 1931.
MORGAN, HARRY (HENRY) (Harry Bratsburg): Detroit, Apr. 10, 1915. U Chicago.
MORGAN, MICHELE (Simone Roussel): Paris, France, Feb. 29, 1920. Paris Dramatic School.
MORIARTY, CATHY: Bronx, NY, Nov. 29, 1960.
MORIARTY, MICHAEL: Detroit, MI, Apr. 5, 1941. Dartmouth.
MORISON, PATRICIA: NYC, Mar. 19, 1915.
MORITA, NORIYUKI "PAT": Isleton, CA, June 28, 1932.
MORRIS, GARRETT: New Orleans, LA, Feb. 1, 1937.
MORRIS, HOWARD: NYC, Sept. 4, 1919. NYU.
MORROW, ROB: New Rochelle, NY, Sept. 21, 1962.
MORSE, DAVID: Hamilton, MA, Oct. 11, 1953.
MORSE, ROBERT: Newton, MA, May 18, 1931.
MORTENSEN, VIGGO: New York, NY, 1958.
MORTON, JOE: NYC, Oct. 18, 1947. Hofstra U.
MOSES, WILLIAM: Los Angeles, Nov. 17, 1959.
MOSTEL, JOSH: NYC, Dec. 21, 1946. Brandeis U.
MOUCHET, CATHERINE: Paris, France, 1959. Ntl. Consv.
MUELLER-STAHL, ARMIN: Tilsit, East Prussia, Dec. 17, 1930.
MULDAUR, DIANA: NYC, Aug. 19, 1938. Sweet Briar College.
MULGREW, KATE: Dubuque, IA, Apr. 29, 1955. NYU.
MULHERN, MATT: Philadelphia, PA, July 21, 1960. Rutgers Univ.
MULL, MARTIN: N. Ridgefield, OH, Aug. 18, 1941. RISch. of Design.
MULLIGAN, RICHARD: NYC, Nov. 13, 1932.
MULRONEY, DERMOT: Alexandria, VA, Oct. 31, 1963. Northwestern.
MUMY, BILL (Charles William Mumy, Jr.): San Gabriel, CA, Feb. 1, 1954.
MURPHY, EDDIE: Brooklyn, NY, Apr. 3, 1961.
MURPHY, MICHAEL: Los Angeles, CA, May 5, 1938. UAz.
MURRAY, BILL: Wilmette, IL, Sept. 21, 1950. Regis College.
MURRAY, DON: Hollywood, CA, July 31, 1929.
MUSANTE, TONY: Bridgeport, CT, June 30, 1936. Oberlin College.
MYERS, MIKE: Scarborough, Canada, May 25, 1963.
NABORS, JIM: Sylacauga, GA, June 12, 1932.
NADER, GEORGE: Pasadena, CA, Oct. 19, 1921. Occidental College.
NADER, MICHAEL: Los Angeles, CA, 1945.
NAMATH, JOE: Beaver Falls, PA, May 31, 1943. UAla.
NAUGHTON, DAVID: Hartford, CT, Feb. 13, 1951.
NAUGHTON, JAMES: Middletown, CT, Dec. 6, 1945.
NEAL, PATRICIA: Packard, KY, Jan. 20, 1926. Northwestern U.
NEESOM, LIAM: Ballymena, Northern Ireland, June 7, 1952.
NEFF, HILDEGARDE (Hildegard Knef): Ulm, Germany, Dec. 28, 1925. Berlin Art Acad.
NEILL, SAM: No. Ireland, Sept. 14, 1947. U Canterbury.
NELL, NATHALIE: Paris, France, Oct. 1950.
NELLIGAN, KATE: London, Ont., Canada, Mar. 16, 1951. U Toronto.
NELSON, BARRY (Robert Nielsen): Oakland, CA, Apr. 16, 1920.
NELSON, CRAIG T.: Spokane, WA, Apr. 4, 1946.
NELSON, DAVID: NYC, Oct. 24, 1936. USC.
NELSON, JUDD: Portland, ME, Nov. 28, 1959, Haverford College.
NELSON, LORI (Dixie Kay Nelson): Santa Fe, NM, Aug. 15, 1933.
NELSON, TRACY: Santa Monica, CA, Oct. 25, 1963.
NELSON, WILLIE: Abbott, TX, Apr. 30, 1933.
NEMEC, CORIN: Little Rock, AK, Nov. 5, 1971.
NERO, FRANCO (Francisco Spartanero): Parma, Italy, Nov. 23, 1941.
NESMITH, MICHAEL: Houston, TX, Dec. 30, 1942.
NETTLETON, LOIS: Oak Park, IL, 1931. Actors Studio.
NEWHART, BOB: Chicago, IL, Sept. 5, 1929. Loyola U.
NEWLEY, ANTHONY: Hackney, London, Sept. 24, 1931.

Lou Diamond Phillips

Brad Pitt

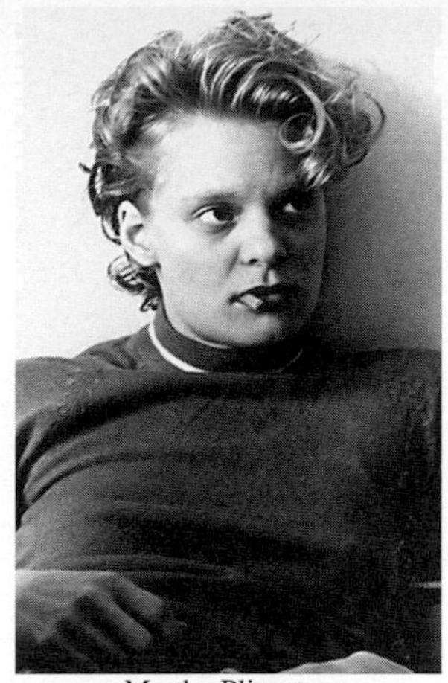
Martha Plimpton

Parker Posey

NEWMAN, BARRY: Boston, MA, Nov. 7, 1938. Brandeis U.
NEWMAN, LARAINE: Los Angeles, Mar. 2, 1952.
NEWMAN, NANETTE: Northampton, England, 1934.
NEWMAN, PAUL: Cleveland, OH, Jan. 26, 1925. Yale.
NEWMAR, JULIE (Newmeyer): Los Angeles, Aug. 16, 1933.
NEWTON-JOHN, OLIVIA: Cambridge, England, Sept. 26, 1948.
NGUYEN, DUSTIN: Saigon, Vietnam, Sept. 17, 1962.
NICHOLAS, DENISE: Detroit, MI, July 12, 1945.
NICHOLAS, PAUL: London, 1945.
NICHOLS, NICHELLE: Robbins, IL, Dec. 28, 1933.
NICHOLSON, JACK: Neptune, NJ, Apr. 22, 1937.
NICKERSON, DENISE: NYC, 1959.
NICOL, ALEX: Ossining, NY, Jan. 20, 1919. Actors Studio.
NIELSEN, BRIGITTE: Denmark, July 15, 1963.
NIELSEN, LESLIE: Regina, Saskatchewan. Canada, Feb. 11, 1926. Neighborhood Playhouse.
NIMOY, LEONARD: Boston, MA, Mar. 26, 1931. Boston College, Antioch College.
NIXON, CYNTHIA: NYC, Apr. 9, 1966. Columbia U.
NOBLE, JAMES: Dallas, TX, Mar. 5, 1922, SMU.
NOIRET, PHILIPPE: Lille, France, Oct. 1, 1930.
NOLAN, KATHLEEN: St. Louis, MO, Sept. 27, 1933. Neighborhood Playhouse.
NOLTE, NICK: Omaha, NE, Feb. 8, 1940. Pasadena City College.
NORRIS, CHRISTOPHER: NYC, Oct. 7, 1943. Lincoln Square Acad.
NORRIS, CHUCK (Carlos Ray): Ryan, OK,Mar. 10, 1940.
NORTH, HEATHER: Pasadena, CA, Dec. 13, 1950. Actors Workshop.
NORTH, SHEREE (Dawn Bethel): Los Angeles. Jan. 17, 1933. Hollywood High.
NORTHAM, JEREMY: Cambridge, Eng., Dec. 1, 1961.
NORTON, EDWARD: Boston, MA, Aug. 18, 1969.
NORTON, KEN: Jacksonville, Il, Aug. 9, 1945.
NOURI, MICHAEL: Washington, DC, Dec. 9, 1945.
NOVAK, KIM (Marilyn Novak): Chicago, IL, Feb. 13, 1933. LACC.
NOVELLO, DON: Ashtabula, OH, Jan. 1, 1943. UDayton.
NUYEN, FRANCE (Vannga): Marseilles, France, July 31, 1939. Beaux Arts School.
O'BRIAN, HUGH (Hugh J. Krampe): Rochester, N,. Apr. 19, 1928. Cincinnati U.
O'BRIEN, CLAY: Ray, AZ, May 6, 1961.
O'BRIEN, MARGARET (Angela Maxine O'Brien): Los Angeles, Jan. 15, 1937.
O'BRIEN, VIRGINIA: Los Angeles, Apr. 18, 1919.
O'CONNELL, JERRY (Jeremiah O'Connell): New York, NY, Feb. 17, 1974.
O'CONNOR, CARROLL: Bronx, NY, Aug. 2, 1924. Dublin National Univ.
O'CONNOR, DONALD: Chicago, IL, Aug. 28, 1925.
O'CONNOR, GLYNNIS: NYC, Nov. 19, 1955. NYSU.
O'DONNELL, CHRIS: Winetka, IL, June 27, 1970.
O'DONNELL, ROSIE: Commack, NY, March 21, 1961.
O'HARA, CATHERINE: Toronto, Canada, Mar. 4, 1954.
O'HARA, MAUREEN (Maureen Fitz-Simons): Dublin, Ireland, Aug. 17, 1920.
O'HERLIHY, DAN: Wexford, Ireland, May 1, 1919. National U.
O'KEEFE, MICHAEL: Larchmont, NY, Apr. 24, 1955. NYU, AADA.
OLDMAN, GARY: New Cross, South London, England, Mar. 21, 1958.
OLIN, KEN: Chicago, IL, July 30, 1954. UPa.
OLIN, LENA: Stockholm, Sweden, Mar. 22, 1955.
OLMOS, EDWARD JAMES: Los Angeles, Feb. 24, 1947. CSLA.
O'LOUGHLIN, GERALD S.: NYC, Dec. 23, 1921. U Rochester.
OLSON, JAMES: Evanston, IL, Oct. 8, 1930.
OLSON, NANCY: Milwaukee, WI, July 14, 1928. UCLA.
O'NEAL, GRIFFIN: Los Angeles, 1965.
O'NEAL, RON: Utica, NY, Sept. 1, 1937. Ohio State.
O'NEAL, RYAN: Los Angeles, Apr. 20, 1941.
O'NEAL, TATUM: Los Angeles, Nov. 5, 1963.
O'NEIL, TRICIA: Shreveport, LA, Mar. 11, 1945. Baylor U.
O'NEILL, ED: Youngstown, OH, Apr. 12, 1946.
O'NEILL, JENNIFER: Rio de Janeiro, Feb. 20, 1949. Neighborhood Playhouse.
ONTKEAN, MICHAEL: Vancouver, B.C., Canada, Jan. 24, 1946.
O'QUINN, TERRY: Newbury, MI, July 15, 1952.
ORBACH, JERRY: Bronx, NY, Oct. 20, 1935.
O'SHEA, MILO: Dublin, Ireland, June 2, 1926.
O'SULLIVAN, MAUREEN: Byle, Ireland, May 17, 1911. Sacred Heart Convent.
O'TOOLE, ANNETTE (Toole): Houston, TX, Apr. 1, 1953. UCLA.
O'TOOLE, PETER: Connemara, Ireland, Aug. 2, 1932. RADA.
OVERALL, PARK: Nashville, TN, Mar. 15, 1957. Tusculum College.
OZ, FRANK (Oznowicz): Hereford, England, May 25, 1944.
PACINO, AL: NYC, Apr. 25, 1940.
PACULA, JOANNA: Tamaszow Lubelski, Poland, Jan. 2, 1957. Polish Natl. Theatre Sch.
PAGET, DEBRA (Debralee Griffin): Denver, Aug. 19, 1933.
PAIGE, JANIS (Donna Mae Jaden): Tacoma, WA, Sept. 16, 1922.
PALANCE, JACK (Walter Palanuik): Lattimer, PA, Feb. 18, 1920. UNC.
PALIN, MICHAEL: Sheffield, Yorkshire, England, May 5, 1943, Oxford.
PALMER, BETSY: East Chicago, IN, Nov. 1, 1926. DePaul U.
PALMER, GREGG (Palmer Lee): San Francisco, Jan. 25, 1927. U Utah.
PALMINTERI, CHAZZ (Calogero Lorenzo Palminteri): New York, NY, May 15, 1952.
PAMPANINI, SILVANA: Rome, Sept. 25, 1925.
PANEBIANCO, RICHARD: NYC, 1971.
PANKIN, STUART: Philadelphia, Apr. 8, 1946.

PANTOLIANO, JOE: Jersey City, NJ, Sept. 12, 1954.
PAPAS, IRENE: Chiliomodion, Greece, Mar. 9, 1929.
PAQUIN, ANNA: Winnipeg, Manitoba, Canada, July, 24, 1982.
PARE, MICHAEL: Brooklyn, NY, Oct. 9, 1959.
PARKER, COREY: NYC, July 8, 1965. NYU.
PARKER, ELEANOR: Cedarville, OH, June 26, 1922. Pasadena Playhouse.
PARKER, FESS: Fort Worth, TX, Aug. 16, 1925. USC.
PARKER, JAMESON: Baltimore, MD, Nov. l8, 1947. Beloit College.
PARKER, JEAN (Mae Green): Deer Lodge, MT, Aug. 11, 1912.
PARKER, MARY-LOUISE: Ft. Jackson, SC, Aug. 2, 1964. Bard College.
PARKER, NATHANIEL: London, 1963.
PARKER, SARAH JESSICA: Nelsonville, OH, Mar. 25, 1965.
PARKER, SUZY (Cecelia Parker): San Antonio, TX, Oct. 28, 1933.
PARKER, TREY: Auburn, AL, May 30, 1972.
PARKINS, BARBARA: Vancouver, Canada, May 22, 1943.
PARKS, MICHAEL: Corona, CA, Apr. 4, 1938.
PARSONS, ESTELLE: Lynn, MA, Nov. 20, 1927. Boston U.
PARTON, DOLLY: Sevierville, TN, Jan. 19, 1946.
PATINKIN, MANDY: Chicago, IL, Nov. 30, 1952. Juilliard.
PATRIC, JASON: NYC, June 17, 1966.
PATRICK, DENNIS: Philadelphia, Mar. 14, 1918.
PATTERSON, LEE: Vancouver, Canada, Mar. 31, 1929. Ontario College.
PATTON, WILL: Charleston, SC, June 14, 1954.
PAULIK, JOHAN: Prague, Czech., 1975.
PAVAN, MARISA (Marisa Pierangeli): Cagliari, Sardinia, June 19, 1932. Torquado Tasso College.
PAXTON, BILL: Fort Worth, TX, May. 17, 1955.
PAYMER, DAVID: Long Island, NY, Aug. 30, 1954.
PAYS, AMANDA: Berkshire, England, June 6, 1959.
PEACH, MARY: Durban, S. Africa, 1934.
PEARCE, GUY: England, Oct. 5, 1967.
PEARSON, BEATRICE: Dennison, TX, July 27, 1920.
PECK, GREGORY: La Jolla, CA, Apr. 5, 1916. U Calif.
PEÑA, ELIZABETH: Cuba, Sept. 23, 1961.
PENDLETON, AUSTIN: Warren, OH, Mar. 27, 1940. Yale U.
PENHALL, BRUCE: Balboa, CA, Aug. 17, 1960.
PENN, SEAN: Burbank, CA, Aug. 17, 1960.
PEREZ, JOSE: NYC, 1940.
PEREZ, ROSIE: Brooklyn, NY, Sept. 6, 1964.
PERKINS, ELIZABETH: Queens, NY, Nov. 18, 1960. Goodman School.
PERKINS, MILLIE: Passaic, NJ, May 12, 1938.
PERLMAN, RHEA: Brooklyn, NY, Mar. 31, 1948.

Jonathan Pryce

Bill Pullman

Kathleen Quinlan

PERLMAN, RON: NYC, Apr. 13, 1950. UMn.
PERREAU, GIGI (Ghislaine): Los Angeles, Feb. 6, 1941.
PERRINE, VALERIE: Galveston, TX, Sept. 3, 1943. U Ariz.
PERRY, LUKE (Coy Luther Perry, III): Fredricktown, OH, Oct. 11, 1966.
PESCI, JOE: Newark, NJ. Feb. 9, 1943.
PESCOW, DONNA: Brooklyn, NY, Mar. 24, 1954.
PETERS, BERNADETTE (Lazzara): Jamaica, NY, Feb. 28, 1948.
PETERS, BROCK: NYC, July 2, 1927. CCNY.
PETERS. JEAN (Elizabeth): Caton, OH, Oct. 15, 1926. Ohio State U.
PETERSEN, PAUL: Glendale, CA, Sept. 23, 1945. Valley College.
PETERSEN, WILLIAM: Chicago, IL, Feb. 21, 1953.
PETERSON, CASSANDRA: Colorado Springs, CO, Sept. 17, 1951.
PETTET, JOANNA: London, Nov. 16, 1944. Neighborhood Playhouse.
PETTY, LORI: Chattanooga, TN, 1964.
PFEIFFER, MICHELLE: Santa Ana, CA, Apr. 29, 1958.
PHILLIPPE, RYAN (Matthew Phillippe): New Castle, DE, Sept. 10, 1975.
PHILLIPS, LOU DIAMOND: Phillipines, Feb. 17, 1962, UTx.
PHILLIPS, MacKENZIE: Alexandria, VA, Nov. 10, 1959.
PHILLIPS, MICHELLE (Holly Gilliam): Long Beach, CA, June 4, 1944.
PHILLIPS, SIAN: Bettws, Wales, May 14, 1934. UWales.
PHOENIX, JOAQUIN: Puerto Rico, Oct. 28, 1974.
PICARDO, ROBERT: Philadelphia, PA, Oct. 27, 1953. Yale.
PICERNI, PAUL: NYC, Dec. 1, 1922. Loyola U.
PIGOTT-SMITH, TIM: Rugby, England, May 13, 1946.
PINCHOT, BRONSON: NYC, May 20, 1959. Yale.
PINE, PHILLIP: Hanford, CA, July 16, 1920. Actors' Lab.
PISCOPO, JOE: Passaic. NJ, June 17, 1951.
PISIER, MARIE-FRANCE: Vietnam, May 10, 1944. U Paris.
PITILLO, MARIA: Mahwah, NJ, 1965.
PITT, BRAD (William Bradley Pitt): Shawnee, OK, Dec. 18, 1963.
PIVEN, JEREMY: NYC, July 26, 1965.
PLACE, MARY KAY: Tulsa OK, Sept. 23, 1947. U Tulsa.
PLAYTEN, ALICE: NYC, Aug. 28, 1947. NYU.
PLESHETTE, SUZANNE: NYC, Jan. 31, 1937. Syracuse U.
PLIMPTON, MARTHA: NYC, Nov. 16, 1970.
PLOWRIGHT, JOAN: Scunthorpe, Brigg, Lincolnshire, England, Oct. 28, 1929. Old Vic.
PLUMB, EVE: Burbank, CA, Apr. 29, 1958.
PLUMMER, AMANDA: NYC, Mar. 23, 1957. Middlebury College.
PLUMMER, CHRISTOPHER: Toronto, Canada, Dec. 13, 1927.
PODESTA, ROSSANA: Tripoli, June 20, 1934.

POITIER, SIDNEY: Miami, FL, Feb. 27, 1927.
POLANSKI, ROMAN: Paris, France, Aug. 18, 1933.
POLITO, JON: Philadelphia, PA, Dec. 29, 1950. Villanova U.
POLITO, LINA: Naples, Italy, Aug. 11, 1954.
POLLACK, SYDNEY: South Bend, IN, July 1, 1934.
POLLAK, KEVIN: San Francisco, Oct. 30, 1958.
POLLAN, TRACY: NYC, June 22, 1960.
POLLARD, MICHAEL J.: Passaic, NJ, May 30, 1939.
POSEY, PARKER: Baltimore, MD, Nov. 8, 1968.
POSTLETHWAITE, PETE: London, Feb. 7, 1945.
POTTS, ANNIE: Nashville, TN, Oct. 28, 1952. Stephens College.
POWELL, JANE (Suzanne Burce): Port-land, OR, Apr. 1, 1928.
POWELL, ROBERT: Salford, England, June 1, 1944. Manchester U.
POWER, TARYN: Los Angeles, CA, Sept. 13, 1953.
POWER, TYRONE, IV: Los Angeles, CA, Jan. 22, 1959.
POWERS, MALA (Mary Ellen): San Francisco, CA, Dec. 29, 1921. UCLA.
POWERS, STEFANIE (Federkiewicz): Hollywood, CA, Oct. 12, 1942.
PRENTISS, PAULA (Paula Ragusa): San Antonio, TX, Mar. 4, 1939. Northwestern U.
PRESLE, MICHELINE (Micheline Chassagne): Paris, France, Aug. 22, 1922. Rouleau Drama School.
PRESLEY, PRISCILLA: Brooklyn, NY, May 24, 1945.
PRESNELL, HARVE: Modesto, CA, Sept. 14, 1933. USC.
PRESTON, KELLY: Honolulu, HI, Oct. 13, 1962. USC.
PRESTON, WILLIAM: Columbia, PA, Aug. 26, 1921. PaStateU.
PRICE, LONNY: NYC, Mar. 9, 1959. Juilliard.
PRIESTLEY, JASON: Vancouver, Canada, Aug, 28, 1969.
PRIMUS, BARRY: NYC, Feb. 16, 1938. CCNY.
PRINCE (P. Rogers Nelson): Minneapolis, MN, June 7, 1958.
PRINCIPAL, VICTORIA: Fukuoka, Japan, Jan. 3, 1945. Dade, Jr. College.
PROCHNOW, JURGEN: Berlin, June 10, 1941.
PROSKY, ROBERT: Philadelphia, PA, Dec. 13, 1930.
PROVAL, DAVID: Brooklyn, NY, May 20, 1942.
PROVINE, DOROTHY: Deadwood, SD, Jan. 20, 1937. U Wash.
PRYCE, JONATHAN: Wales, UK, June 1, 1947, RADA.
PRYOR, RICHARD: Peoria, IL, Dec. 1, 1940.
PULLMAN, BILL: Delphi, NY, Dec. 17, 1954. SUNY/Oneonta, UMass.
PURCELL, LEE: Cherry Point, NC, June 15, 1947. Stephens.
PURDOM, EDMUND: Welwyn Garden City, England, Dec. 19, 1924. St. Ignatius College.
QUAID, DENNIS: Houston, TX, Apr. 9, 1954.

Vanessa Redgrave

Burt Reynolds

Christina Ricci

QUAID, RANDY: Houston, TX, Oct. 1, 1950. UHouston.
QUINLAN, KATHLEEN: Mill Valley, CA, Nov. 19, 1954.
QUINN, AIDAN: Chicago, IL, Mar. 8, 1959.
QUINN, ANTHONY: Chihuahua, Mex., Apr. 21, 1915.
RAFFERTY, FRANCES: Sioux City, IA, June 16, 1922. UCLA.
RAFFIN, DEBORAH: Los Angeles, Mar. 13, 1953. Valley College.
RAGSDALE, WILLIAM: El Dorado, AK, Jan. 19, 1961. Hendrix College.
RAILSBACK, STEVE: Dallas, TX, 1948.
RAINER, LUISE: Vienna, Austria, Jan. 12, 1910.
RALSTON, VERA (Vera Helena Hruba): Prague, Czech., July 12, 1919.
RAMIS, HAROLD: Chicago, IL, Nov. 21, 1944. WashingtonU.
RAMPLING, CHARLOTTE: Surmer, England, Feb. 5, 1946. U Madrid.
RAMSEY, LOGAN: Long Beach, CA, Mar. 21, 1921. St. Joseph.
RANDALL, TONY (Leonard Rosenberg): Tulsa, OK, Feb. 26, 1920. Northwestern U.
RANDELL, RON: Sydney, Australia, Oct. 8, 1920. St. Mary's College.
RAPP, ANTHONY: Chicago, Oct. 26, 1971.
RASCHE, DAVID: St. Louis, MO, Aug. 7, 1944.
RAYMOND, GENE (Raymond Guion): NYC, Aug. 13, 1908.
REA, STEPHEN: Belfast, No. Ireland, Oct. 31, 1949.
REAGAN, RONALD: Tampico, IL, Feb. 6, 1911. Eureka College.
REASON, REX: Berlin, Ger., Nov. 30, 1928. Pasadena Playhouse.
REDDY, HELEN: Melbourne, Australia, Oct. 25, 1942.
REDFORD, ROBERT: Santa Monica, CA, Aug. 18, 1937. AADA.
REDGRAVE, CORIN: London, July 16, 1939.
REDGRAVE, LYNN: London, Mar. 8, 1943.
REDGRAVE, VANESSA: London, Jan. 30, 1937.
REDMAN, JOYCE: County Mayo, Ireland, 1919. RADA.
REED, OLIVER: Wimbledon, England, Feb. 13, 1938.
REED, PAMELA: Tacoma, WA, Apr. 2, 1949.
REEMS, HARRY (Herbert Streicher): Bronx, NY, 1947. U Pittsburgh.
REES, ROGER: Aberystwyth, Wales, May 5, 1944.
REESE, DELLA: Detroit, MI, July 6, 1932.
REEVE, CHRISTOPHER: NYC, Sept. 25, 1952. Cornell, Juilliard.
REEVES, KEANU: Beiruit, Lebanon, Sept. 2, 1964.
REEVES, STEVE: Glasgow, MT, Jan. 21, 1926.
REGEHR, DUNCAN: Lethbridge, Canada, Oct. 5, 1952.
REID, ELLIOTT: NYC, Jan. 16, 1920.
REID, TIM: Norfolk, VA, Dec, 19, 1944.
REILLY, CHARLES NELSON: NYC, Jan. 13, 1931. UCt.
REINER, CARL: NYC, Mar. 20, 1922. Georgetown.
REINER, ROB: NYC, Mar. 6, 1947. UCLA.

James Russo

Greta Scacchi

Annabella Sciorra

Kyra Sedgwick

REINHOLD, JUDGE (Edward Ernest, Jr.): Wilmington, DE, May 21, 1957. NCSchool of Arts.
REINKING, ANN: Seattle, WA, Nov. 10, 1949.
REISER, PAUL: NYC, Mar. 30, 1957.
REMAR, JAMES: Boston, MA, Dec. 31, 1953. Neighborhood Playhouse.
REMSEN, BERT: Glen Cove, NY, Feb. 25, 1925. Ithaca.
RENFRO, BRAD: Knoxville, TN, July 25, 1982.
RENO, JEAN (Juan Moreno): Casablanca, Morocco, July 30, 1948.
REVILL, CLIVE: Wellington, NZ, Apr. 18, 1930.
REY, ANTONIA: Havana, Cuba, Oct. 12, 1927.
REYNOLDS, BURT: Waycross, GA, Feb. 11, 1935. Fla. State U.
REYNOLDS, DEBBIE (Mary Frances Reynolds): El Paso, TX, Apr. 1, 1932.
RHOADES, BARBARA: Poughkeepsie, NY, Mar. 23, 1947.
RHODES, CYNTHIA: Nashville, TN, Nov. 21, 1956.
RHYS-DAVIES, JOHN: Salisbury, England, May 5, 1944.
RIBISI, GIOVANNI: Los Angeles, CA, Mar. 31, 1976.
RICCI, CHRISTINA: Santa Monica, CA, Feb. 12, 1980.
RICHARD, CLIFF (Harry Webb)**:** India, Oct. 14, 1940.
RICHARDS, MICHAEL: Culver City, CA, July 14, 1949.
RICHARDSON, JOELY: London, Jan. 9, 1965.
RICHARDSON, LEE: Chicago, IL, Sept. 11, 1926.
RICHARDSON, MIRANDA: Southport, England, Mar. 3, 1958.
RICHARDSON, NATASHA: London, May 11, 1963.
RICKLES, DON: NYC, May 8, 1926. AADA.
RICKMAN, ALAN: Hammersmith, England, Feb. 21, 1946.
RIEGERT, PETER: NYC, Apr. 11, 1947. U Buffalo.
RIFKIN, RON: NYC, Oct. 31, 1939.
RIGG, DIANA: Doncaster, England, July 20, 1938. RADA.
RINGWALD, MOLLY: Rosewood, CA, Feb. 16, 1968.
RITTER, JOHN: Burbank, CA, Sept. 17, 1948. US. Cal.
RIVERS, JOAN (Molinsky): Brooklyn, NY, NY, June 8, 1933.
ROBARDS, JASON: Chicago, IL, July 26, 1922. AADA.
ROBARDS, SAM: NYC, Dec. 16, 1963.
ROBBINS, TIM: NYC, Oct. 16, 1958. UCLA.
ROBERTS, ERIC: Biloxi, MS, Apr. 18, 1956. RADA.
ROBERTS, JULIA: Atlanta, GA, Oct. 28, 1967.
ROBERTS, RALPH: Salisbury, NC, Aug. 17, 1922. UNC.
ROBERTS, TANYA (Leigh): Bronx, NY, Oct. 15, 1954.
ROBERTS, TONY: NYC, Oct. 22, 1939. Northwestern U.
ROBERTSON, CLIFF: La Jolla, CA, Sept. 9, 1925. Antioch College.
ROBERTSON, DALE: Oklahoma City, July 14, 1923.
ROBINSON, CHRIS: West Palm Beach, FL, Nov. 5, 1938. LACC.
ROBINSON, JAY: NYC, Apr. 14, 1930.
ROBINSON, ROGER: Seattle, WA, May 2, 1940. USC.
ROCHEFORT, JEAN: Paris, France, 1930.
ROCK, CHRIS: Brooklyn, NY, Feb. 7, 1966.
ROGERS, CHARLES "BUDDY": Olathe, KS, Aug. 13, 1904. U Kan.
ROGERS, MIMI: Coral Gables, FL, Jan. 27, 1956.
ROGERS, ROY (Leonard Slye): Cincinnati, Nov. 5, 1912.
ROGERS, WAYNE: Birmingham, AL, Apr. 7, 1933. Princeton.
ROLLE, ESTHER: Pompano Beach, FL, Nov. 8, 1922.
ROMAN, RUTH: Boston, Dec. 23, 1922. Bishop Lee Dramatic School.
RONSTADT, LINDA: Tucson, AZ, July 15, 1946.
ROOKER, MICHAEL: Jasper, AL, Apr. 6, 1955.
ROONEY, MICKEY (Joe Yule, Jr.): Brooklyn, NY, Sept. 23, 1920.
ROSE, REVA: Chicago, IL, July 30, 1940. Goodman.
ROSEANNE (Barr): Salt Lake City, UT, Nov. 3, 1952.
ROSS, DIANA: Detroit, MI, Mar. 26, 1944.
ROSS, JUSTIN: Brooklyn, NY, Dec. 15, 1954.
ROSS, KATHARINE: Hollywood, Jan. 29, 1943. Santa Rosa College.
ROSSELLINI, ISABELLA: Rome, June 18, 1952.
ROSSOVICH, RICK: Palo Alto, CA, Aug. 28, 1957.
ROTH, TIM: London, May 14, 1961.
ROUNDTREE, RICHARD: New Rochelle, NY, Sept. 7, 1942. Southern Ill.
ROURKE, MICKEY (Philip Andre Rourke, Jr.): Schenectady, NY, Sept. 16, 1956.
ROWE, NICHOLAS: London, Nov. 22, 1966, Eton.
ROWLANDS, GENA: Cambria, WI, June 19, 1934.
RUBIN, ANDREW: New Bedford, MA, June 22, 1946. AADA.
RUBINEK, SAUL: Fohrenwold, Germany, July 2, 1948.
RUBINSTEIN, JOHN: Los Angeles, CA, Dec. 8, 1946. UCLA.
RUCKER, BO: Tampa, FL, Aug. 17, 1948.
RUDD, PAUL: Boston, MA, May 15, 1940.
RUDD, PAUL: Passaic, NJ, Apr. 6, 1969.
RUDNER, RITA: Miami, FL, Sept. 17, 1955.
RUEHL, MERCEDES: Queens, NY, Feb. 28, 1948.

RULE, JANICE: Cincinnati, OH, Aug. 15, 1931.
RUPERT, MICHAEL: Denver, CO, Oct. 23, 1951. Pasadena Playhouse.
RUSH, BARBARA: Denver, CO, Jan. 4, 1927. U Calif.
RUSH, GEOFFREY: Toowoomba, Queensland, Australia, July 6, 1951. Univ. of Queensland.
RUSSELL, JANE: Bemidji, MI, June 21, 1921. Max Reinhardt School.
RUSSELL, KURT: Springfield, MA, Mar. 17, 1951.
RUSSELL, THERESA (Paup): San Diego, CA, Mar. 20, 1957.
RUSSO, JAMES: NYC, Apr. 23, 1953.
RUTHERFORD, ANN: Toronto, Canada, Nov. 2, 1920.
RYAN, JOHN P.: NYC, July 30, 1936. CCNY.
RYAN, MEG: Fairfield, CT, Nov. 19, 1961. NYU.
RYAN, TIM (Meineslschmidt): Staten Island, NY, 1958. Rutgers U.
RYDER, WINONA (Horowitz)**:** Winona, MN, Oct. 29, 1971.
SACCHI, ROBERT: Bronx, NY, 1941. NYU.
SÄGEBRECHT, MARIANNE: Starnberg, Bavaria, Aug. 27, 1945.
SAINT, EVA MARIE: Newark, NJ, July 4, 1924. Bowling Green State U.
SAINT JAMES, SUSAN (Suzie Jane Miller): Los Angeles, Aug. 14, 1946. Conn. College.
ST. JOHN, BETTA: Hawthorne, CA, Nov. 26, 1929.
ST. JOHN, JILL (Jill Oppenheim): Los Angeles, Aug. 19, 1940.
SALA, JOHN: Los Angeles, CA, Oct. 5, 1962.
SALDANA, THERESA: Brooklyn, NY, Aug. 20, 1954.
SALINGER, MATT: Windsor, VT, Feb. 13, 1960. Princeton, Columbia.
SALT, JENNIFER: Los Angeles, Sept. 4, 1944. Sarah Lawrence College.
SAMMS, EMMA: London, Aug. 28, 1960.
SAN GIACOMO, LAURA: Orange, NJ, Nov. 14, 1961.
SANDERS, JAY O.: Austin, TX, Apr. 16, 1953.
SANDLER, ADAM: Bronx, NY, Sept. 9, 1966.
SANDS, JULIAN: Yorkshire, England, Jan 15, 1958.
SANDS, TOMMY: Chicago, IL, Aug. 27, 1937.
SAN JUAN, OLGA: NYC, Mar. 16, 1927.
SARA, MIA (Sarapocciello)**:** Brooklyn, NY, June 19, 1967.
SARANDON, CHRIS: Beckley, WV, July 24, 1942. U WVa., Catholic U.
SARANDON, SUSAN (Tomalin): NYC, Oct. 4, 1946. Catholic U.
SARRAZIN, MICHAEL: Quebec City, Canada, May 22, 1940.
SAVAGE, FRED: Highland Park, IL, July 9, 1976.
SAVAGE, JOHN (Youngs): Long Island, NY, Aug. 25, 1949. AADA.
SAVIOLA, CAMILLE: Bronx, NY, July 16, 1950.
SAVOY, TERESA ANN: London, July 18, 1955.
SAXON, JOHN (Carmen Orrico): Brooklyn, NY, Aug. 5, 1935.
SBARGE, RAPHAEL: NYC, Feb. 12, 1964.
SCACCHI, GRETA: Milan, Italy, Feb. 18, 1960.
SCALIA, JACK: Brooklyn, NY, Nov. 10, 1951.
SCARWID, DIANA: Savannah, GA, Aug. 27, 1955, AADA. Pace U.
SCHEIDER, ROY: Orange, NJ, Nov. 10, 1932. Franklin-Marshall.
SCHEINE, RAYNOR: Emporia, VA, Nov. 10. VaCommonwealthU.
SCHELL, MARIA: Vienna, Jan. 15, 1926.
SCHELL, MAXIMILIAN: Vienna, Dec. 8, 1930.
SCHLATTER, CHARLIE: Englewood, NJ, May 1, 1966. Ithaca College.
SCHNEIDER, JOHN: Mt. Kisco, NY, Apr. 8, 1960.
SCHNEIDER, MARIA: Paris, France, Mar. 27, 1952.
SCHREIBER, LIEV: San Francisco, CA, Oct. 4, 1967.
SCHRODER, RICK: Staten Island, NY, Apr. 13, 1970.
SCHUCK, JOHN: Boston, MA, Feb. 4, 1940.
SCHULTZ, DWIGHT: Milwaukee, WI, Nov. 10, 1938. MarquetteU.
SCHWARZENEGGER, ARNOLD: Austria, July 30, 1947.
SCHWIMMER, DAVID: Queens, NY, Nov. 12, 1966.
SCHYGULLA, HANNA: Katlowitz, Germany, Dec. 25, 1943.
SCIORRA, ANNABELLA: NYC, Mar. 24, 1964.
SCOFIELD, PAUL: Hurstpierpoint, England, Jan. 21, 1922. London Mask Theatre School.
SCOGGINS, TRACY: Galveston, TX, Nov. 13, 1959.
SCOLARI, PETER: Scarsdale, NY, Sept. 12, 1956. NYCC.
SCOTT,CAMPBELL: South Salem, NY, July 19, 1962. Lawrence.
SCOTT, DEBRALEE: Elizabeth, NJ, Apr. 2, 1953
SCOTT, GEORGE C.: Wise, VA, Oct. 18, 1927. U Mo.
SCOTT, GORDON (Gordon M. Werschkul): Portland, OR, Aug. 3, 1927. Oregon U.
SCOTT, LIZABETH (Emma Matso): Scranton, PA, Sept. 29, 1922.
SCOTT, MARTHA: Jamesport, MO, Sept. 22, 1914. U Mich.
SCOTT THOMAS, KRISTIN: Redruth, Cornwall, Eng., May 24, 1960.
SEAGAL, STEVEN: Detroit, MI, Apr. 10, 1951.
SEARS, HEATHER: London, Sept. 28, 1935.
SECOMBE, HARRY: Swansea, Wales, Sept. 8, 1921.
SEDGWICK, KYRA: NYC, Aug. 19, 1965. USC.
SEGAL, GEORGE: NYC, Feb. 13, 1934. Columbia.
SELBY, DAVID: Morganstown, WV, Feb. 5, 1941. UWV.
SELLARS, ELIZABETH: Glasgow, Scotland, May 6, 1923.
SELLECK, TOM: Detroit, MI, Jan. 29, 1945. USCal.
SERNAS, JACQUES: Lithuania, July 30, 1925.
SERRAULT, MICHEL: Brunoy, France. Jan. 24, 1928. Paris Consv.
SETH, ROSHAN: New Delhi, India. 1942.

Rufus Sewell

Charlie Sheen

Craig Sheffer

SEWELL, RUFUS: Twickenham, Eng., Oct. 29, 1967.
SEYMOUR, JANE (Joyce Frankenberg): Hillingdon, England, Feb. 15, 1952.
SHALHOUB, TONY: Oct. 7, 1953.
SHARIF, OMAR (Michel Shalhoub): Alexandria, Egypt, Apr. 10, 1932. Victoria College.
SHANDLING, GARRY: Chicago, IL, Nov. 29, 1949.
SHATNER, WILLIAM: Montreal, Canada, Mar. 22, 1931. McGill U.
SHAVER, HELEN: St. Thomas, Ontario, Canada, Feb. 24, 1951.
SHAW, STAN: Chicago, IL, 1952.
SHAWN, WALLACE: NYC, Nov. 12, 1943. Harvard.
SHEA, JOHN: North Conway, NH, Apr. 14, 1949. Bates, Yale.
SHEARER, HARRY: Los Angeles, Dec. 23, 1943. UCLA.
SHEARER, MOIRA: Dunfermline, Scotland, Jan. 17, 1926. London Theatre School.
SHEEDY, ALLY: NYC, June 13, 1962. USC.
SHEEN, CHARLIE (Carlos Irwin Estevez): Santa Monica, CA, Sept. 3, 1965.
SHEEN, MARTIN (Ramon Estevez): Dayton, OH, Aug. 3, 1940.
SHEFFER, CRAIG: York, PA, Apr. 23, 1960. E. StroudsbergU.
SHEFFIELD, JOHN: Pasadena, CA, Apr. 11, 1931. UCLA.
SHELLEY, CAROL: London, England, Aug. 16, 1939.
SHEPARD, SAM (Rogers): Ft. Sheridan, IL, Nov. 5, 1943.
SHEPHERD, CYBILL: Memphis, TN, Feb. 18, 1950. Hunter, NYU.
SHER, ANTONY: England, June 14, 1949.
SHERIDAN, JAMEY: Pasadena, CA, July 12, 1951.
SHIELDS, BROOKE: NYC, May 31, 1965.
SHIRE, TALIA: Lake Success, NY, Apr. 25, 1946. Yale.
SHORT, MARTIN: Toronto, Canada, Mar. 26, 1950. McMasterU.
SHOWALTER, MAX (formerly Casey Adams): Caldwell, KS, June 2, 1917. Pasadena Playhouse.
SHUE, ELISABETH: S. Orange, NJ, Oct. 6, 1963. Harvard.
SHULL, RICHARD B.: Evanston, IL, Feb. 24, 1929.
SIDNEY, SYLVIA: NYC, Aug. 8, 1910. Theatre Guild School.
SIEMASZKO, CASEY: Chicago, IL, March 17, 1961.
SIKKING, JAMES B.: Los Angeles, Mar. 5, 1934.
SILVA, HENRY: Brooklyn, NY, 1928.
SILVER, RON: NYC, July 2, 1946. SUNY.
SILVERMAN, JONATHAN: Los Angeles, CA, Aug. 5, 1966. USC.
SIMMONS, JEAN: London, Jan. 31, 1929. Aida Foster School.
SIMON, PAUL: Newark. NJ, Nov. 5, 1942.
SIMON, SIMONE: Bethune, France, Apr. 23, 1910.
SIMPSON, O. J. (Orenthal James): San Francisco, CA, July 9, 1947. UCLA.
SINATRA, FRANK: Hoboken, NJ, Dec. 12, 1915.
SINBAD (David Adkins): Benton Harbor, MI, Nov. 10, 1956.
SINCLAIR, JOHN (Gianluigi Loffredo): Rome, Italy, 1946.
SINDEN, DONALD: Plymouth, England, Oct. 9, 1923. Webber-Douglas.
SINGER, LORI: Corpus Christi, TX, May 6, 1962. Juilliard.
SINISE, GARY: Chicago, Mar. 17. 1955.
SKARSGÅRD, STELLAN: Gothenburg, Vastergotland, Sweden, June 13, 1951.
SKERRITT, TOM: Detroit, MI, Aug. 25, 1933. Wayne State U.
SKYE, IONE (Leitch): London, England, Sept. 4, 1971.
SLATER, CHRISTIAN: NYC, Aug. 18, 1969.
SLATER, HELEN: NYC, Dec. 15, 1965.
SMITH, CHARLES MARTIN: Los Angeles, CA, Oct. 30, 1953. CalState U.
SMITH, JACLYN: Houston, TX, Oct. 26, 1947.
SMITH, JADA PINKETT: Baltimore, MD, Sept. 18, 1971.
SMITH, KEVIN: Red Bank, NJ, Aug. 2, 1970.
SMITH, KURTWOOD: New Lisbon, WI, Jul. 3, 1942.
SMITH, LANE: Memphis, TN, Apr. 29, 1936.
SMITH, LEWIS: Chattanooga, TN, 1958. Actors Studio.
SMITH, LOIS: Topeka, KS, Nov. 3, 1930. U Wash.
SMITH, MAGGIE: Ilford, England, Dec. 28, 1934.
SMITH, ROGER: South Gate, CA, Dec. 18, 1932. U Ariz.
SMITH, WILL: Philadelphia, PA, Sept. 25, 1968.
SMITHERS, WILLIAM: Richmond, VA, July 10, 1927. Catholic U.
SMITS, JIMMY: Brooklyn, NY, July 9, 1955. Cornell U.
SNIPES, WESLEY: NYC, July 31, 1963. SUNY/Purchase.
SNODGRESS, CARRIE: Chicago, IL, Oct. 27, 1946. UNI.
SOLOMON, BRUCE: NYC, 1944. U Miami, Wayne State U.
SOMERS, SUZANNE (Mahoney): San Bruno, CA, Oct. 16, 1946. Lone Mt. College.
SOMMER, ELKE (Schletz): Berlin, Germany, Nov. 5, 1940.
SOMMER, JOSEF: Greifswald, Germany, June 26, 1934.
SORDI, ALBERTO: Rome, Italy, June 15, 1920.
SORVINO, MIRA: Tenafly, NJ, Sept. 28, 1967.
SORVINO, PAUL: NYC, Apr. 13, 1939. AMDA.
SOTHERN, ANN (Harriet Lake): Valley City, ND, Jan. 22, 1909.
SOTO, TALISA (Miriam Soto): Brooklyn, NY, Mar. 27, 1967.
SOUL, DAVID: Chicago, IL, Aug. 28, 1943.
SPACEK, SISSY: Quitman, TX, Dec. 25, 1949. Actors Studio.
SPACEY, KEVIN: So. Orange, NJ, July 26, 1959. Juilliard.
SPADE, DAVID: Birmingham, MS, July 22, 1964.
SPADER, JAMES: Buzzards Bay, MA, Feb. 7, 1960.
SPANO, VINCENT: Brooklyn, NY, Oct. 18, 1962.
SPENSER, JEREMY: Ceylon, 1937.
SPRINGFIELD, RICK (Richard Spring Thorpe): Sydney, Australia, Aug. 23, 1949.

Elisabeth Shue

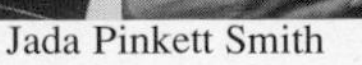
Jada Pinkett Smith

Mira Sorvino

Kevin Spacey

Mary Steenburgen

Madeleine Stowe

Meryl Streep

Sharon Stone

STACK, ROBERT: Los Angeles, Jan. 13, 1919. USC.
STADLEN, LEWIS J.: Brooklyn, NY, Mar. 7, 1947. Neighborhood Playhouse.
STAHL, NICK: Dallas, TX, Dec. 5, 1979.
STALLONE, FRANK: NYC, July 30, 1950.
STALLONE, SYLVESTER: NYC, July 6, 1946. U Miami.
STAMP, TERENCE: London, July 23, 1939.
STANG, ARNOLD: Chelsea, MA, Sept. 28, 1925.
STANLEY, KIM (Patricia Reid): Tularosa, NM, Feb. 11, 1925. U Tex.
STANTON, HARRY DEAN: Lexington, KY, July 14, 1926.
STAPLETON, JEAN: NYC, Jan. 19, 1923.
STAPLETON, MAUREEN: Troy, NY, June 21, 1925.
STARR, RINGO (Richard Starkey): Liverpool, England, July 7, 1940.
STEEL, ANTHONY: London, May 21, 1920. Cambridge.
STEELE,BARBARA: England, Dec. 29, 1937.
STEELE, TOMMY: London, Dec. 17, 1936.
STEENBURGEN, MARY: Newport, AR, 1953. Neighborhood Playhouse.
STEIGER, ROD: Westhampton, NY, Apr. 14, 1925.
STERLING, JAN (Jane Sterling Adriance): NYC, Apr. 3, 1923. Fay Compton School.
STERLING, ROBERT (William Sterling Hart): Newcastle, PA, Nov. 13, 1917. UPittsburgh.
STERN, DANIEL: Bethesda, MD, Aug. 28, 1957.
STERNHAGEN, FRANCES: Washington, DC, Jan. 13, 1932.
STEVENS, ANDREW: Memphis, TN, June 10, 1955.
STEVENS, CONNIE (Concetta Ann Ingolia): Brooklyn, NY, Aug. 8, 1938. Hollywood Professional School.
STEVENS, FISHER: Chicago, IL, Nov. 27, 1963. NYU.
STEVENS, STELLA (Estelle Eggleston): Hot Coffee, MS, Oct. 1, 1936.
STEVENSON, PARKER: Philadelphia, PA, June 4, 1953. Princeton.
STEWART, ALEXANDRA: Montreal, Canada, June 10, 1939. Louvre.
STEWART, ELAINE (Elsy Steinberg): Montclair, NJ, May 31, 1929.
STEWART, MARTHA (Martha Haworth): Bardwell, KY, Oct. 7, 1922.
STEWART, PATRICK: Mirfield, England, July 13, 1940.
STIERS, DAVID OGDEN: Peoria, IL, Oct. 31, 1942.
STILLER, BEN: NYC, Nov. 30, 1965.
STILLER, JERRY: NYC, June 8, 1931.
STING (Gordon Matthew Sumner): Wallsend, England, Oct. 2, 1951.
STOCKWELL, DEAN: Hollywood, Mar. 5, 1935.
STOCKWELL, JOHN (John Samuels, IV): Galveston, TX, Mar. 25, 1961. Harvard.
STOLER, SHIRLEY: Brooklyn, NY, Mar. 30, 1929.
STOLTZ, ERIC: Whittier, CA, Sept. 30, 1961. USC.
STONE, DEE WALLACE (Deanna Bowers): Kansas City, MO, Dec. 14, 1948. UKS.
STORM, GALE (Josephine Cottle): Bloomington, TX, Apr. 5, 1922.
STOWE, MADELEINE: Eagle Rock, CA, Aug. 18, 1958.
STRAIGHT, BEATRICE: Old Westbury, NY, Aug. 2, 1916. Dartington Hall.
STRASBERG, SUSAN: NYC, May 22, 1938.
STRASSMAN, MARCIA: New Jersey, Apr. 28, 1948.
STRATHAIRN, DAVID: San Francisco, Jan. 26, 1949.
STRAUSS, PETER: NYC, Feb. 20, 1947.
STREEP, MERYL (Mary Louise): Summit, NJ, June 22, 1949. Vassar, Yale.
STREISAND, BARBRA: Brooklyn, NY, Apr. 24, 1942.
STRITCH, ELAINE: Detroit, MI, Feb. 2, 1925. Drama Workshop.
STROUD, DON: Honolulu, HI, Sept. 1, 1937.
STRUTHERS, SALLY: Portland, OR, July 28, 1948. Pasadena Playhouse.
SUMMER, DONNA (LaDonna Gaines): Boston, MA, Dec. 31, 1948.
SUTHERLAND, DONALD: St. John, New Brunswick, Canada, July 17, 1935. U Toronto.
SUTHERLAND, KIEFER: Los Angeles, CA, Dec. 18, 1966.
SVENSON, BO: Goreborg, Sweden, Feb. 13, 1941. UCLA.
SWAYZE, PATRICK: Houston, TX, Aug. 18, 1952.
SWEENEY, D. B. (Daniel Bernard Sweeney): Shoreham, NY, Nov. 14, 1961.
SWINBURNE, NORA (Elinore Johnson): Bath, England, July 24, 1902. RADA.
SWIT, LORETTA: Passaic, NJ, Nov. 4, 1937, AADA.
SYLVESTER, WILLIAM: Oakland, CA, Jan. 31, 1922. RADA.
SYMONDS, ROBERT: Bistow, AK, Dec. 1, 1926. TexU.
SYMS, SYLVIA: London, June 1, 1934. Convent School.
SZARABAJKA, KEITH: Oak Park, IL, Dec. 2, 1952. UChicago.
T, MR. (Lawrence Tero): Chicago, IL, May 21, 1952.
TABORI, KRISTOFFER (Siegel): Los Angeles, Aug. 4, 1952.
TAKEI, GEORGE: Los Angeles, CA, Apr. 20, 1939. UCLA.
TALBOT, NITA: NYC, Aug. 8, 1930. Irvine Studio School.
TAMBLYN, RUSS: Los Angeles, Dec. 30, 1934.
TARANTINO, QUENTIN: Knoxville, TN, Mar. 27, 1963.
TATE, LARENZ: Chicago, IL, Sept. 8, 1975.
TAYLOR, DON: Freeport, PA, Dec. 13, 1920. Penn State U.
TAYLOR, ELIZABETH: London, Feb. 27, 1932. Byron House School.
TAYLOR, LILI: Glencoe, IL, Feb. 20, 1967.
TAYLOR, RENEE: NYC, Mar. 19, 1935.
TAYLOR, ROD (Robert): Sydney, Aust., Jan. 11, 1929.
TAYLOR-YOUNG, LEIGH: Washington, DC, Jan. 25, 1945. Northwestern.
TEEFY, MAUREEN: Minneapolis, MN, 1954, Juilliard.
TEMPLE, SHIRLEY: Santa Monica, CA, Apr. 23, 1927.
TENNANT, VICTORIA: London, England, Sept. 30, 1950.

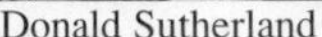
Donald Sutherland

Quentin Tarentino

Lili Taylor

Henry Thomas

TERZIEFF, LAURENT: Paris, France, June 25, 1935.
TEWES, LAUREN: Braddock, PA, Oct. 26, 1954.
THACKER, RUSS: Washington, DC, June 23, 1946. Montgomery College.
THAXTER, PHYLLIS: Portland, ME, Nov. 20, 1921. St. Genevieve.
THELEN, JODI: St. Cloud, MN, 1963.
THERON, CHARLIZE: Benoni, So. Africa, Aug. 7, 1975.
THEWLIS, DAVID: Blackpool, Eng., 1963.
THOMAS, HENRY: San Antonio, TX, Sept. 8, 1971.
THOMAS, JAY: New Orleans, July 12, 1948.
THOMAS, MARLO (Margaret): Detroit, Nov. 21, 1938. USC.
THOMAS, PHILIP MICHAEL: Columbus, OH, May 26, 1949. Oakwood College.
THOMAS, RICHARD: NYC, June 13, 1951. Columbia.
THOMPSON, EMMA: London, England, Apr.15, 1959. Cambridge.
THOMPSON, FRED DALTON: Laurenceberg, TN, Aug. 19, 1942
THOMPSON, JACK (John Payne): Sydney, Australia, Aug. 31, 1940.
THOMPSON, LEA: Rochester, MN, May 31, 1961.
THOMPSON, REX: NYC, Dec. 14, 1942.
THOMPSON, SADA: Des Moines, IA, Sept. 27, 1929. Carnegie Tech.
THORNTON, BILLY BOB: Hot Spring, AR, Aug. 4, 1955.
THORSON, LINDA: Toronto, Canada, June 18, 1947. RADA.
THULIN, INGRID: Solleftea, Sweden, Jan. 27, 1929. Royal Drama Theatre.
THURMAN, UMA: Boston, MA, Apr. 29, 1970.
TICOTIN, RACHEL: Bronx, NY, Nov. 1, 1958.
TIERNEY, LAWRENCE: Brooklyn, NY, Mar. 15, 1919. Manhattan College.
TIFFIN, PAMELA (Wonso): Oklahoma City, OK, Oct. 13, 1942.
TIGHE, KEVIN: Los Angeles, Aug. 13, 1944.
TILLY, JENNIFER: Los Angeles, CA, Sept. 16, 1958.
TILLY, MEG: Texada, Canada, Feb. 14, 1960.
TOBOLOWSKY, STEPHEN: Dallas, Tx, May 30, 1951. So. Methodist U.
TODD, BEVERLY: Chicago, IL, July 1, 1946.
TODD, RICHARD: Dublin, Ireland, June 11, 1919. Shrewsbury School.
TOLKAN, JAMES: Calumet, MI, June 20, 1931.
TOMEI, MARISA: Brooklyn, NY, Dec. 4, 1964. NYU.
TOMLIN, LILY: Detroit, MI, Sept. 1, 1939. Wayne State U.
TOPOL (Chaim Topol): Tel-Aviv, Israel, Sept. 9, 1935.
TORN, RIP: Temple, TX, Feb. 6, 1931. UTex.
TORRES, LIZ: NYC, Sept. 27, 1947. NYU.
TOTTER, AUDREY: Joliet, IL, Dec. 20, 1918.
TOWSEND, ROBERT: Chicago, IL, Feb. 6, 1957.
TRAVANTI, DANIEL J.: Kenosha, WI, Mar. 7, 1940.
TRAVIS, NANCY: Astoria, NY, Sept. 21, 1961.
TRAVOLTA, JOEY: Englewood, NJ, 1952.
TRAVOLTA, JOHN: Englewood, NJ, Feb. 18, 1954.
TREMAYNE, LES: London, Apr. 16, 1913. Northwestern, Columbia, UCLA.
TREVOR, CLAIRE (Wemlinger): NYC, March 8, 1909.
TRINTIGNANT, JEAN-LOUIS: Pont-St. Esprit, France, Dec. 11, 1930. DullinBalachova Drama School.
TSOPEI, CORINNA: Athens, Greece, June 21, 1944.
TUBB, BARRY: Snyder, TX, 1963. AmConsv Th.
TUCCI, STANLEY: Katonah, NY, Jan. 11, 1960.
TUCKER, MICHAEL: Baltimore, MD, Feb. 6, 1944.
TUNE, TOMMY: Wichita Falls, TX, Feb. 28, 1939.
TURNER, JANINE (Gauntt): Lincoln, NE, Dec. 6, 1963.
TURNER, KATHLEEN: Springfield, MO, June 19, 1954. UMd.
TURNER, TINA (Anna Mae Bullock): Nutbush, TN, Nov. 26, 1938.
TURTURRO, JOHN: Brooklyn, NY, Feb. 28, 1957. Yale.
TUSHINGHAM, RITA: Liverpool, England, Mar. 14, 1940.
TUTIN, DOROTHY: London, Apr. 8, 1930.
TWIGGY (Lesley Hornby): London, Sept. 19, 1949.
TWOMEY, ANNE: Boston, MA, June 7, 1951. Temple U.
TYLER, BEVERLY (Beverly Jean Saul): Scranton, PA, July 5, 1928.
TYLER, LIV: Portland, ME, July 1, 1977.
TYRRELL, SUSAN: San Francisco, 1946.
TYSON, CATHY: Liverpool, England, June 12, 1965. Royal Shake. Co.
TYSON, CICELY: NYC, Dec. 19, 1933. NYU.
UGGAMS, LESLIE: NYC, May 25, 1943. Juilliard.
ULLMAN, TRACEY: Slough, England, Dec. 30, 1959.
ULLMANN, LIV: Tokyo, Dec. 10, 1938. Webber-Douglas Acad.
ULRICH, SKEET (Bryan Ray Ulrich): North Carolina, Jan. 20, 1969.
UMEKI, MIYOSHI: Otaru, Hokaido, Japan, Apr. 3, 1929.
UNDERWOOD, BLAIR: Tacoma, WA, Aug. 25, 1964. Carnegie-Mellon U.
URICH, ROBERT: Toronto, Canada, Dec. 19, 1946.
USTINOV, PETER: London, Apr. 16, 1921. Westminster School.
VACCARO, BRENDA: Brooklyn, NY, Nov. 18, 1939. Neighborhood Playhouse.
VALANDREY, CHARLOTTE (Anne Charlone Pascal): Paris, France, 1968.
VALLI, ALIDA: Pola, Italy, May 31, 1921. Academy of Drama.
VALLONE, RAF: Riogio, Italy, Feb. 17, 1916. Turin U.
VAN ARK, JOAN: NYC, June 16, 1943. Yale.
VAN DAMME, JEAN-CLAUDE (J-C Vorenberg): Brussels, Belgium, Apr. 1, 1960.
VAN DE VEN, MONIQUE: Netherlands, 1952.
VAN DEVERE, TRISH (Patricia Dressel): Englewood Cliffs, NJ, Mar. 9, 1945. Ohio Wesleyan.
VAN DOREN, MAMIE (Joan Lucile Olander): Rowena SD, Feb. 6, 1933.
VAN DYKE, DICK: West Plains, MO, Dec. 13, 1925.
VANITY (Denise Katrina Smith): Niagara, Ont., Can, Jan. 4, 1959.
VAN PALLANDT, NINA: Copenhagen, Denmark, July 15, 1932.

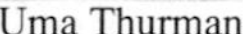
Uma Thurman

Marisa Tomei

Christopher Walken

Denzel Washington

VAN PATTEN, DICK: NYC, Dec. 9, 1928.
VAN PATTEN, JOYCE: NYC, Mar. 9, 1934.
VAN PEEBLES, MARIO: NYC, Jan. 15, 1958. Columbia U.
VAN PEEBLES, MELVIN: Chicago, IL, Aug. 21, 1932.
VANCE, COURTNEY B.: Detroit, MI, Mar. 12, 1960.
VARNEY, JIM: Lexington, KY, June 15, 1949.
VAUGHN, ROBERT: NYC, Nov. 22, 1932. USC.
VAUGHN, VINCE: Minneapolis, MN, Mar. 28, 1970.
VEGA, ISELA: Mexico, 1940.
VELJOHNSON, REGINALD: NYC, Aug. 16, 1952.
VENNERA, CHICK: Herkimer, NY, Mar. 27, 1952. Pasadena Playhouse.
VENORA, DIANE: Hartford, CT, 1952. Juilliard.
VERDON, GWEN: Culver City, CA, Jan. 13, 1925.
VERNON, JOHN: Montreal, Canada, Feb. 24, 1932.

Sigourney Weaver

VEREEN, BEN: Miami, FL, Oct. 10, 1946.
VICTOR, JAMES (Lincoln Rafael Peralta Diaz): Santiago, D.R., July 27, 1939. Haaren HS/NYC.
VINCENT, JAN-MICHAEL: Denver, CO, July 15, 1944. Ventura.
VIOLET, ULTRA (Isabelle Collin-Dufresne): Grenoble, France, 1935.
VITALE, MILLY: Rome, Italy, July 16, 1928. Lycee Chateaubriand.
VOHS, JOAN: St. Albans, NY, July 30, 1931.
VOIGHT, JON: Yonkers, NY, Dec. 29, 1938. Catholic U.
VON DOHLEN, LENNY: Augusta, GA, Dec. 22, 1958. UTex.
VON SYDOW, MAX: Lund, Sweden, July 10, 1929. Royal Drama Theatre.
WAGNER, LINDSAY: Los Angeles, June 22. 1949.
WAGNER, NATASHA GREGSON: Los Angeles, CA, Sept. 29, 1970.
WAGNER, ROBERT: Detroit, Feb. 10, 1930.
WAHL, KEN: Chicago, IL, Feb. 14, 1953.
WAITE, GENEVIEVE: South Africa, 1949.
WAITE, RALPH: White Plains, NY, June 22, 1929. Yale.
WAITS, TOM: Pomona, CA, Dec. 7, 1949.
WALKEN, CHRISTOPHER: Astoria, NY, Mar. 31, 1943. Hofstra.
WALKER, CLINT: Hartfold, IL, May 30, 1927. USC.
WALLACH, ELI: Brooklyn, NY, Dec. 7, 1915. CCNY, U Tex.
WALLACH, ROBERTA: NYC, Aug. 2, 1955.
WALLIS, SHANI: London, Apr. 5, 1941.
WALSH, J.T.: San Francisco,. CA. Sept. 28, 1943.
WALSH, M. EMMET: Ogdensburg, NY, Mar. 22, 1935. Clarkson College, AADA.
WALSTON, RAY: New Orleans, Nov. 22, 1917. Cleveland Playhouse.
WALTER, JESSICA: Brooklyn, NY, Jan. 31, 1944 Neighborhood Playhouse.
WALTER, TRACEY: Jersey City, NJ, Nov. 25, 1942.
WALTERS, JULIE: London, Feb. 22, 1950.
WALTON, EMMA: London, Nov. 1962. Brown U.
WARD, BURT (Gervis): Los Angeles, July 6, 1945.
WARD, FRED: San Diego, CA, Dec. 30, 1942.

WARD, RACHEL: London, Sept. 12, 1957.
WARD, SELA: Meridian, MS, July 11, 1956.
WARD, SIMON: London, Oct. 19, 1941.
WARDEN, JACK (Lebzelter): Newark, NJ, Sept. 18, 1920.
WARNER, DAVID: Manchester, England, July 29, 1941. RADA.
WARNER, MALCOLM-JAMAL: Jersey City, NJ, Aug. 18, 1970.
WARREN, JENNIFER: NYC, Aug. 12, 1941. U Wisc.
WARREN, LESLEY ANN: NYC, Aug. 16, 1946.
WARREN, MICHAEL: South Bend, IN, Mar. 5, 1946. UCLA.
WARRICK, RUTH: St. Joseph, MO, June 29, 1915. U Mo.
WASHINGTON, DENZEL: Mt. Vernon, NY, Dec. 28, 1954. Fordham.
WASSON, CRAIG: Ontario, OR, Mar. 15, 1954. UOre.
WATERSTON, SAM: Cambridge, MA, Nov. 15, 1940. Yale.
WATLING, JACK: London, Jan. 13, 1923. Italia Conti School.

Michael York

WATSON, EMILY: London, Jan. 14, 1967.
WAYANS, DAMON: NYC, Sept. 4, 1960.
WAYANS, KEENEN, IVORY: NYC, June 8, 1958. Tuskegee Inst.
WAYNE, PATRICK: Los Angeles, July 15, 1939. Loyola.
WEATHERS, CARL: New Orleans, LA, Jan. 14, 1948. Long Beach CC.
WEAVER, DENNIS: Joplin, MO, June 4, 1924. U Okla.
WEAVER, FRITZ: Pittsburgh, PA, Jan. 19, 1926.
WEAVER, SIGOURNEY (Susan): NYC, Oct. 8, 1949. Stanford, Yale.
WEBER, STEVEN: March 4, 1961.
WEDGEWORTH, ANN: Abilene, TX, Jan. 21, 1935. U Tex.
WELCH, RAQUEL (Tejada): Chicago, IL, Sept. 5, 1940.
WELD, TUESDAY (Susan): NYC, Aug. 27, 1943. Hollywood Professional School.
WELDON, JOAN: San Francisco, Aug. 5, 1933. San Francisco Conservatory.
WELLER, PETER: Stevens Point, WI, June 24, 1947. AmThWing.
WENDT, GEORGE: Chicago, IL, Oct. 17, 1948.
WEST, ADAM (William Anderson): Walla Walla, WA, Sept. 19, 1929.
WETTIG, PATRICIA: Cincinatti, OH, Dec. 4, 1951. TempleU.
WHALEY, FRANK: Syracuse, NY, July 20, 1963. SUNY/Albany.
WHALLEY-KILMER, JOANNE: Manchester, England, Aug. 25, 1964.
WHEATON, WIL: Burbank, CA, July 29, 1972.
WHITAKER, FOREST: Longview, TX, July 15, 1961.
WHITAKER, JOHNNY: Van Nuys, CA, Dec. 13, 1959.
WHITE, BETTY: Oak Park, IL, Jan. 17, 1922.
WHITE, CHARLES: Perth Amboy, NJ, Aug. 29, 1920. Rutgers U.
WHITELAW, BILLIE: Coventry, England, June 6, 1932.
WHITMAN, STUART: San Francisco, Feb. 1, 1929. CCLA.
WHITMORE, JAMES: White Plains, NY, Oct. 1, 1921. Yale.
WHITNEY, GRACE LEE: Detroit, MI, Apr. 1, 1930.
WHITTON, MARGARET: Philadelphia, PA, Nov, 30, 1950.
WIDDOES, KATHLEEN: Wilmington, DE, Mar. 21, 1939.
WIDMARK, RICHARD: Sunrise, MN, Dec. 26, 1914. Lake Forest.
WIEST, DIANNE: Kansas City, MO, Mar. 28, 1948. UMd.
WILBY. JAMES: Burma, Feb. 20, 1958.
WILCOX, COLIN: Highlands, NC, Feb. 4, 1937. U Tenn.
WILDER, GENE (Jerome Silberman): Milwaukee, WI, June 11, 1935. UIowa.
WILLIAMS, BILLY DEE: NYC, Apr. 6, 1937.
WILLIAMS, CARA (Bernice Kamiat): Brooklyn, NY, June 29, 1925.
WILLIAMS, CINDY: Van Nuys, CA, Aug. 22, 1947. KACC.
WILLIAMS, CLARENCE, III: NYC, Aug. 21, 1939.
WILLIAMS, ESTHER: Los Angeles, Aug. 8, 1921.
WILLIAMS, JOBETH: Houston, TX, Dec 6, 1948. Brown U.
WILLIAMS, PAUL: Omaha, NE, Sept. 19, 1940.
WILLIAMS, ROBIN: Chicago, IL, July 21, 1951. Juilliard.
WILLIAMS, TREAT (Richard): Rowayton, CT, Dec. 1, 1951.
WILLIAMS, VANESSA L.: Tarrytown, NY, Mar. 18, 1963.
WILLIAMSON, FRED: Gary, IN, Mar. 5, 1938. Northwestern.
WILLIAMSON, NICOL: Hamilton, Scotland, Sept. 14, 1938.
WILLIS, BRUCE: Penns Grove, NJ, Mar. 19, 1955.
WILLISON, WALTER: Monterey Park, CA, June 24, 1947.
WILSON, DEMOND: NYC, Oct. 13, 1946. Hunter College.
WILSON, ELIZABETH: Grand Rapids, MI, Apr. 4, 1925.
WILSON, FLIP (Clerow Wilson): Jersey City, NJ, Dec. 8, 1933.
WILSON, LAMBERT: Paris, France, 1959.
WILSON, SCOTT: Atlanta, GA, 1942.
WINCOTT, JEFF: Toronto, Canada, May 8, 1957.
WINCOTT, MICHAEL: Toronto, Canada, Jan. 6, 1959. Juilliard.
WINDE, BEATRICE: Chicago, IL, Jan. 6.
WINDOM, WILLIAM: NYC, Sept. 28, 1923. Williams College.
WINDSOR, MARIE (Emily Marie Bertelson): Marysvale, UT, Dec. 11, 1924. Brigham Young U.
WINFIELD, PAUL: Los Angeles, May 22, 1940. UCLA.
WINFREY, OPRAH: Kosciusko, MS, Jan. 29, 1954. TnStateU.
WINGER, DEBRA: Cleveland, OH, May 17, 1955. Cal State.
WINKLER, HENRY: NYC, Oct. 30, 1945. Yale.
WINN, KITTY: Washington, D.C., Feb, 21, 1944. Boston U.
WINNINGHAM, MARE: Phoenix, AZ, May 6, 1959.
WINSLET, KATE: Reading, Eng., Oct. 5, 1975.
WINSLOW, MICHAEL: Spokane, WA, Sept. 6, 1960.
WINTER, ALEX: London, July 17, 1965. NYU.
WINTERS, JONATHAN: Dayton, OH, Nov. 11, 1925. Kenyon College.
WINTERS, SHELLEY (Shirley Schrift): St. Louis, Aug. 18, 1922. Wayne U.
WITHERS, GOOGIE: Karachi, India, Mar. 12, 1917. Italia Conti.
WITHERS, JANE: Atlanta, GA, Apr. 12, 1926.
WITHERSPOON, REESE (Laura Jean Reese Witherspoon): Nashville, TN, Mar. 22, 1976.
WONG, B.D.: San Francisco, Oct. 24,1962.
WONG, RUSSELL: Troy, NY, 1963. SantaMonica College.
WOOD, ELIJAH: Cedar Rapids, IA, Jan 28, 1981.
WOODARD, ALFRE: Tulsa, OK, Nov. 2, 1953. Boston U.
WOODLAWN, HOLLY (Harold Ajzen-berg): Juana Diaz, PR, 1947.
WOODS, JAMES: Vernal, UT, Apr. 18, 1947. MIT.
WOODWARD, EDWARD: Croyden, Surrey, England, June 1, 1930.
WOODWARD, JOANNE: Thomasville, GA, Feb. 27, 1930. Neighborhood Playhouse.
WORONOV, MARY: Brooklyn, NY, Dec. 8, 1946. Cornell.
WORTH, IRENE (Hattie Abrams): Nebraska, June 23, 1916. UCLA.
WRAY, FAY: Alberta, Canada, Sept. 15, 1907.
WRIGHT, AMY: Chicago, IL, Apr. 15, 1950.
WRIGHT, MAX: Detroit, MI, Aug. 2, 1943. WayneStateU.
WRIGHT, ROBIN: Dallas, TX, Apr. 8, 1966.
WRIGHT, TERESA: NYC, Oct. 27, 1918.
WUHL, ROBERT: Union City, NJ, Oct. 9, 1951. UHouston.
WYATT, JANE: NYC, Aug. 10, 1910. Barnard College.
WYMAN, JANE (Sarah Jane Fulks): St. Joseph, MO, Jan. 4, 1914.
WYMORE, PATRICE: Miltonvale, KS, Dec. 17, 1926.
WYNN, MAY (Donna Lee Hickey): NYC, Jan. 8, 1930.
WYNTER, DANA (Dagmar): London, June 8. 1927. Rhodes U.
YORK, MICHAEL: Fulmer, England, Mar. 27, 1942. Oxford.
YORK, SUSANNAH: London, Jan. 9, 1941. RADA.
YOUNG, ALAN (Angus): North Shield, England, Nov. 19, 1919.
YOUNG, BURT: Queens, NY, Apr. 30, 1940.
YOUNG, CHRIS: Chambersburg, PA, Apr. 28, 1971.
YOUNG, LORETTA (Gretchen): Salt Lake City, UT, Jan. 6, 1912. Immaculate Heart College.
YOUNG, ROBERT: Chicago, IL, Feb. 22, 1907.
YOUNG, SEAN: Louisville, KY, Nov. 20, 1959. Interlochen.
ZACHARIAS, ANN: Stockholm, Sweden, Sweden, 1956.
ZADORA, PIA: Hoboken, NJ, 1954.
ZELLWEGER, RENEE: Katy, TX, Apr. 25, 1969.
ZERBE, ANTHONY: Long Beach, CA, May 20, 1939.
ZIMBALIST, EFREM, JR.: NYC, Nov.30, 1918. Yale.
ZUNIGA, DAPHNE: Berkeley, CA, Oct. 28, 1963. UCLA.

OBITUARIES

HY AVERBACK, 76, former actor-turned-director died on Oct. 14, 1997 in Los Angeles following heart surgery. His credits as a director include *Chamber of Horrors, Where Were You When the Lights Went Out?, I Love You Alice B. Toklas, The Great Bank Robbery, Suppose They Gave a War and Nobody Came,* and *Where the Boys Are* (1984). Survived by his wife, two sons, a daughter, a sister, and a grandson.

JOHN BEAL (James Alexander Bliedung), 87, Missouri-born film, theatre and television actor died on April 26, 1997 in Santa Cruz, CA. He came to Hollywood in 1933 to repeat his stage role in *Another Language,* and was thereafter seen in such movies as *Hat Coat and Glove, The Little Minister, Les Miserables* (1935), *Laddie, Break of Hearts, M'Liss, Border Cafe, Double Wedding, Madame X* (1937), *Port of Seven Seas, The Arkansas Traveler, The Cat and the Canary, Ellery Queen and the Perfect Crime, Atlantic Convoy, Edge of Darkness, So Dear to My Heart, Song of Surrender, Chicago Deadline, My Six Convicts, Remains to Be Seen, The Vampire, The Sound and the Fury, Ten Who Dared,* and *The Firm.* He is survived by two daughters and two grandsons.

John Beal

Thelma Carpenter

SALLY BLANE (Elizabeth Jane Young), 87, Colorado-born screen actress died at her home in Los Angeles on Aug. 27, 1997. Debuting as a child in the 1917 film *Sirens of the Sea,* her many other credits include *Casey at the Bat, The Vagabaond Lover, Little Accident, Once a Sinner, Ten Cents a Dance, Night of Terror, I Am a Fugitive from a Chain Gang, Advice to the Lovelorn, One Mile from Heaven, Charlie Chan at Treasure Island* (which was directed by her husband, Norman Foster), *The Story of Alexander Graham Bell* (in which she appeared with sisters Polly and Loretta Young, and her half-sister Gretchen Young) and *A Bullet for Joey.* She is survived by Loretta Young, her son, and her daughter.

THELMA CARPENTER, 77, Brooklyn-born singer-actress was found dead in her Manhattan apartment on May 15, 1997. She was seen in such movies as *Hellzapoppin, The Wiz,* and *The Cotton Club.* No reported survivors.

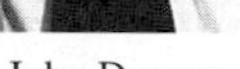

John Denver

David Doyle

ADRIANA CASELOTTI, 80, Connecticut-born singer who supplied the voice of Snow White in Walt Disney's classic 1937 animated feature *Snow White and the Seven Dwarfs,* died of cancer on Jan. 19, 1997 at her home in Los Angeles.

JOHN DENVER (Henry John Deutschendorf, Jr.), 53, New Mexico-born singer whose hit singles include "Annie's Song," "Rocky Mountain High," and "Thank God I'm a Country Boy" was killed in a plane crash in Monterey Bay, CA, on Oct. 11, 1997. He starred in the 1977 film *Oh God!* and narrated the documentary *Fire and Ice.* Survived by three children.

DAVID DOYLE, 67, character actor best known for co-starring in the hit television series "Charley's Angels," died of a heart attack on Feb. 28, 1997 in Los Angeles. His movie credits include *No Way to Treat a Lady, Paper Lion, Coogan's Bluff, Vigilante Force, Lady Liberty, The Comeback,* and *Capricorn One.* No reported survivors.

CHRIS FARLEY, 33, Wisconsin-born comedian was found dead of a drug overdose in his Chicago apartment on Dec. 18, 1997. A cast member of the series "Saturday Night Live" he appeared in the movies *Wayne's World, Coneheads, Wayne's World 2, Airheads, Billy Madison, Tommy Boy, Black Sheep, Beverly Hills Ninja,* and, released posthumously, *Almost Heroes,* and *Dirty Work.* Survived by his parents, three borthers, and a sister.

GEORGE FENNEMAN, 77, Beijing-born announcer and actor, best known as the affable sidekick of Groucho Marx on the hit game show "You Bet Your Life," died of emphysema on May 29, 1997 at his home in Los Angeles. He was also seen in the movies *The Thing from Another World* and *How to Succeed in Business Without Really Trying.* He is survived by his wife, son, and two daughters.

SAMUEL FULLER, 85, Massachusetts-born cult director-writer of such movies as *The Naked Kiss* and *Shock Corridor,* died of unspecified causes on Oct. 30, 1997 at his home in the Hollywood Hills. He received his first credit in 1949 on the western *I Shot Jesse James,* after which he directed such films as *The Baron of Arizona, The Steel Helmet, Fixed Bayonets, Pickup on South Street, House of Bamboo, Run of the Arrow, Forty Guns, Verboten, The Crimson Kimono, Underworld USA, Merrill's Marauders, The Big Red One,* and *White Dog.* He also appeared as an actor in such movies as *The American Friend, Somebody to Love,* and *The End of Violence.* Survived by his wife and a daughter.

Chris Farley

Tamara Geva

TAMARA GEVA, 91, Russian ballet dancer and actress died at her Manhattan home on Dec. 9, 1997. She was seen in such movies as *Their Big Moment, Manhattan Merry-Go-Round,* and *Orchestra Wives.* No immediate survivors.

BRIAN GLOVER, 63, British character actor died from complications from a brain tumor on July 24, 1997 in London. His movie credits include *Kes, Mister Quilp, Jabberwocky, The Great Train Robbery* (1979), *An American Werewolf in London, Britannia Hospital, The Company of Wolves, Kafka, Leon the Pig Farmer,* and *Alien3.* Survived by his wife, two children, and four grandchildren.

GEORGES GUETARY, 82, French singer-actor (born in Egypt to Greek parents), best known to American audiences for singing "I'll Build a Stairway to Paradise" in the 1951 Oscar-winning film *An American in Paris,* died on Sept. 13, 1997 in Mougins, France, of undisclosed causes. He is survived by his wife and two children.

Brian Glover

William Hickey

WILLIAM HICKEY, 69, Brooklyn-born character actor of screen, stage and television, who received an Oscar nomination for playing the decrepit Mafia don in *Prizzi's Honor,* died on June 29, 1997 in Manhattan from complications of emphysema and bronchitis. Among his movie credits are *A Hatful of Rain, The Producers, The Boston Strangler, Little Big Man, A New Leaf, Wise Blood, The Name of the Rose, Bright Lights Big City, Sea of Love, My Blue Heaven, Tales from the Darkside: The Movie, Puppet Master, Forget Paris,* and his last, *Mouse Hunt,* released posthumously. Survivors include his sister.

JUZO ITAMI (Yoshihiro Ikeuchi), 64, Japanese director of the noted film *Tampopo* lept to his death from a rooftop in Tokyo on Dec. 20, 1997. His other credits include *The Funeral* (1984), *A Taxing Woman,* and *A Taxing Woman's Return.* Survived by his wife, actress Nobuko Miyamoto, and his two sons.

Juzo Itami

Richard Jaeckel

RICHARD JAECKEL, 70, New York-born character player who went from working in the mailroom at 20th Century-Fox to becoming a character actor in dozens of movies, died on June 14, 1997 of cancer in Woodland Hills, CA. Following his 1943 debut in *Guadalcanal Diary* he was seen in such movies as *Wing and a Prayer, City Across the River, Battleground, Sands of Iwo Jima, The Gunfighter, My Son John, Come Back Little Sheba, The Big Leaguer, The Violent Men, Attack!, 3:10 to Yuma, The Naked and the Dead, Platinum High School, Town Without Pity, Four for Texas, The Dirty Dozen, The Devil's Brigade, The Green Slime, Chisum, Sometimes a Great Notion* (for which he received an Oscar nomination), *Ulzana's Raid, Pat Garrett and Billy and Kid, Chosen Survivors, The Drowning Pool, Grizzly, Twilight's Last Gleaming, Herbie Goes Bananas, ...All the Marbles, Starman,* and *Black Moon Rising.* He is survived by his wife, a sister, and two sons.

PAUL JARRICO, 82, Los Angeles-born producer-writer was killed in a car accident on his way home from a ceremony honoring blacklisted writers on Oct. 28, 1997 in California. His credits include *Beauty for the Asking, The Face Behind the Mask, Tom Dick and Harry* (for which he received an Oscar nomination), *Thousands Cheer, Song of Russia, The Search, The White Tower,* and *The Day the Hot Line Got Hot.* He served as producer on *Salt of the Earth,* and wrote, but was not credited due to his blacklisting status, *Five Branded Women* and *Treasure of the Aztecs.* Survived by his wife and his son.

Stubby Kaye

Sheldon Leonard

STUBBY KAYE, 79, Bronx-born screen and stage performer, best remembered for his rendition of "Sit Down, You're Rockin' the Boat" in the original Broadway production and 1955 screen version of *Guys and Dolls,* died of undisclosed causes on Dec. 14, 1997 in Rancho Mirage, CA. His other movies include *Li'l Abner* (repeating his stage role of "Marryin' Sam"), *40 Pounds of Trouble, Cat Ballou* (in which he sang the title song with Nat King Cole), *Sweet Charity, Can Hieronymus Merkin Ever Forget Mercy Humppe and Find True Happiness?,* and *Who Framed Roger Rabbit.* No reported survivors.

BRIAN KEITH, 75, New Jersey-born screen, stage and television actor who went from character parts to stardom in several Disney films and on television, was found dead on June 24, 1997 at his home in Malibu, CA, of a self-inflicted gunshot wound. He had been suffering from cancer. The son of character actor Robert Keith he had made his movie debut at the age of three but did not start his film career officially until the 1950s. From that point on his was seen in such motion pictures as *Arrowhead, Alaska Seas, The Violent Men, Five Against the House, Storm Center, Run of the Arrow, Chicago Confidential, Dino, Fort Dobbs, The Young Philadelphians, Ten Who Dared, The Deadly Companions, The Parent Trap, Moon Pilot, Savage Sam, The Pleasure Seekers, A Tiger Walks, Those Calloways, The Hallelujah Trail, The Rare Breed, Nevada Smith, The Russians Are Coming the Russians Are Coming, Reflections in a Golden Eye, With Six You Get Eggroll, Krakatoa: East of Java, Gaily Gaily, Suppose They Gave a War and Nobody Came, Scandalous John, The McKenzie Break, The Yakuza, The Wind and the Lion, Nickelodeon, Hooper, Meteor, Mountain Men, Sharky's Machine, Young Guns,* and *Welcome Home.* Survived by his wife, actress Victoria Young.

Brian Keith

Burgess Meredith

DOROTHY KINGSLEY, 87, New York City-born screenwriter, noted for her scripts of several MGM musicals including *Kiss Me Kate* and *Seven Brides for Seven Brothers,* died in Monterey, CA, on Sept. 26, 1997. Her other credits include *The Skipper Surprised His Wife, Bathing Beauty, Easy to Wed, On an Island With You, Look Who's Laughing, A Date With Judy, Neptune's Daughter, Two Weeks With Love, Angels in the Outfield* (1951), *Texas Carnival, It's a Big Country, Small Town Girl* (1953), *Dangerous When Wet, Jupiter's Darling, Don't Go Near the Water, Pal Joey, Green Mansions, Can-Can, Pepe, Valley of the Dolls,* and *Half a Sixpence.* Survived by two sons, two daughters, and nine grandchildren.

BURTON LANE (Burton Levy), 84, New York City-born composer whose scores included *Finian's Rainbow* and *On a Clear Day You Can See Forever,* died at his home in Manhattan on Jan. 5, 1997. His songs were heard in such motion pictures as *Dancing Lady, Kid Millions, Folies Bergere, Reckless* (1935), *College Holiday, Swing High Swing Low, Cafe Society, Las Vegas Nights, Babes on Braodway* (receiving an Oscar nomination for "How About You?"), *Panama Hattie, DuBarry Was a Lady, Presenting Lily Mars, Hollywood Canteen, Royal Wedding* (Oscar nomination for "Too Late Now"), *Give a Girl a Break, Jupiter's Darling,* and *Heidi's Song.* Survived by his wife, a daughter, and three stepdaughters.

Toshiro Mifune

Edward Mulhare

ROSINA LAWRENCE (Rosina Marchisio-McCabe), 84, dancer-actress died on June 23, 1997 in Manhattan. Her film credits include *Ten Dollar Raise, Paramount on Parade, A Connecticut Yankee, Disorderly Conduct, Music is Magic, Reckless* (1935), *The Great Ziegfeld* (as Marilyn Miller), and *Pick a Star.* She retired from films in 1939 following marriage. She is survived by her second husband, writer John McCabe, two daughters, a son, and five grandchildren.

SHELDON LEONARD (Sheldon Leonard Bershad), 89, New York City-born character actor who specialized in tough guy types and later went on to a successful career as a television producer-director, died at his home in Beverly Hills on January 10, 1997. Among his acting credits on film are *Another Thin Man, Buy Me That Town, Rise and Shine, Week-End in Havana, Tortilla Flat, Born to Sing, Lucky Jordan, Tennessee Johnson, Hit the Ice, City Without Men, Taxi Mister, To Have and Have Not, The Falcon in Hollywood, Zombies on Broadway, Captain Kidd, Bowery Bombshell, The Gentleman Bisbehaves, It's a Wonderful Life, Sinbad the Sailor, The Gangster, Jinx Money, My Dream is Yours, Abbott and Costello Meet the Invisible Man, Come Fill the Cup, Young Man With Ideas, Stop You're Killing Me, Money from Home, Guys and Dolls, Pocketful of Miracles,* and *The Brinks' Job.* On television he won two Emmy Awards for directing "The Danny Thomas Show" and one for producing "My World and Welcome to It." He is survived by his wife, a son, a daughter, and four grandchildren.

Don Porter

Denver Pyle

ROBERT LEWIS, 88, actor,director and founder of the Actors Studio, died of a heart attack on a Manhattan street on Nov. 23, 1997. He acted in such movies as *Dragon Seed, Son of Lassie, Ziegfeld Follies,* and *Monsieur Verdoux,* and was the director of the 1956 remake of *Anything Goes.* On Broadway he directed such works as *Brigadoon, The Teahouse of the August Moon, Witness for the Prosecution,* and *On a Clear Day You Can See Forever.* Survived by his sister.

JEAN LOUIS, 89, Paris-born costume designer died on April 20, 1997 at his home in Palm Springs, CA. His many motion picture credits include *Thousand and One Nights, Gilda, Tomorrow is Forever, The Jolson Story, Dead Reckoning, Down to Earth, The Lady from Shanghai, The Loves of Carmen, Jolson Sings Again, Knock on Any Door, In a Lonely Place, Born Yesterday, The Marrying Kind, Affair in Trinidad, The Big Heat, Miss Sadie Thompson, From Here to Eternity, Salome, Phffft, It Should Happen to You, A Star is Born* (1954), *Picnic, Queen Bee, The Eddy Duchin Story, The Solid Gold Cadillac* (for which he won an Academy Award), *Pal Joey, Bell Book and Candle, Pillow Talk, The Last Angry Man, Suddenly Last Summer, Judgment at Nuremberg, Send Me No Flowers, Ship of Fools, Guess Who's Coming to Dinner, Thoroughly Modern Millie,* and *Waterloo.* Survived by his wife, actress Loretta Young, and his brother.

Marjorie Reynolds

Alexander Salkind

CATHERINE McLEOD, 75, screen and television actress died of pneumonia on May 11, 1997 in Encino, CA. Her film credits include *I've Always Loved You, Courage of Lassie, That's My Man, The Fabulous Texan, So Young So Bad, My Wife's Best Friend,* and *Ride the Wild Surf.* She is survived by her husband, actor Don Keefer, three sons, and a sister.

Robert Mitchum

James Stewart

BURGESS MEREDITH (Oliver Burgess Meredith), 89, versatile Ohio-born screen, stage and television actor whose notable roles included playing George in the 1939 version of *Of Mice and Men* and the fight trainer Mickey in *Rocky* (for which he received an Oscar nomination), died on Sept. 9, 1997 at his home in Malibu, CA. He made his Hollywood debut in 1936 repeating his Broadway role in *Winterset,* and then went on to appear in such films as *Spring Madness, Idiot's Delight, Castle on the Hudson, Second Chorus* (opposite Paulette Goddard who became his third wife), *That Uncertain Feeling, Tom Dick and Harry, The Story of G.I. Joe, Diary of a Chambermaid, Magnificent Doll, On Our Merry Way, Mine Own Executioner, The Man on the Eiffel Tower* (which he also directed), *Joe Butterfly, Advise and Consent, The Cardinal, A Big Hand for the Little Lady, Batman* (as the Penguin, a role he played on the tv series), *Hurry Sundown, Stay Away Joe, Skidoo, There Was a Crooked Man, Such Good Friends, The Day of the Locust* (Oscar nomination), *The Hindenburg, Burnt Offerings, The Sentinel, Magic, Foul Play, The Great Bank Hoax, When Time Ran Out..., True Confessions, Clash of the Titans, Santa Claus, Full Moon in Blue Water, State of Grace, Grumpy Old Men,* and *Grumpier Old Men.* He is survived by his fourth wife, a son, a daughter, and a granddaughter.

TOSHIRO MIFUNE, 77, Japan's leading motion picture actor who became an international star via his work with director Akira Kurosawa in *Rashomon, Yojimbo,* and *Seven Samurai,* among others, died of organ failure on Dec. 24, 1997 at his home in Tokyo. Among his many other films are *Drunken Angel, The Silent Duel, The Lower Depths, Throne of Blood, The Hidden Fortress, Sanjuro, The Legacy of the Five Hundred Thousand* (which he also directed), *Red Beard, Grand Prix, Hell in the Pacific, Red Sun, Paper Tiger, Midway, The Bushido Blade, 1941, Winter Kils, Inchon,* and *The Challenge.*

ROBERT MITCHUM, 79, Connecticut-born screen and television actor, a major star for more than fifty years via his work in such movies as *The Story of G.I. Joe* (for which he earned an Oscar nomination), *Out of the Past, The Night of the Hunter, Heaven Knows Mr. Allison, The Sundowners, Cape Fear* (1962), and *Ryan's Daughter,* died at his home in Santa Barbara, CA, on July 1, 1997. Earlier in the year he had been diagnosed with lung cancer. Among his many other motion pictures are *Border Patrol, The Human Comedy, Bar 20, Thirty Seconds Over Tokyo, Till the End of Time, Undercurrent, Pursued, Crossfire, Rachel and the Stranger, Blood on the Moon, The Red Pony, The Big Steal, Holiday Affair, His Kind of Woman, Macao, The Lusty Men, Second Chance, River of No Return, Track of the Cat, Not as a Stranger, Bandido, Fire Down Below, The Enemy Below, Thunder Road, The Wonderful Country, Home from the Hill, The Grass is Greener, The Last Time I Saw Archie, The Longest Day, Two for the Seesaw, Rampage, What a Way to Go!, Mister Moses, The Way West, El Dorado, Villa Rides!, Five Card Stud, The Wrath of God, The Friends of Eddie Coyle, Farewell My Lovely, Midway, The Last Tycoon, The Big Sleep* (1978), *That Championship Season, Maria's Lovers, Mr. North, Scrooged, Cape Fear* (1991), and *Dead Man.* Survived by his wife of 57 years, two sons, actors James and Christopher Mitchum, a daughter, a brother, and two sisters.

ALVY MOORE, 75, screen and television character actor, perhaps best known for playing Mr. Kimball on the sitcom "Green Acres," died on May 4, 1997 in Palm Desert, CA. His movies include *Susan Slept Here, Five Against the House, Screaming Eagles, The Wackiest Ship in the Army, The Brotherhood of Satan* (which he also produced), *The Witchmaker, Herbie Rides Again,* and *A Boy and His Dog* (also producer). No reported survivors.

EDWARD MULHARE, 74, Irish screen, stage and tv actor, best known in America for following Rex Harrison in the role of Henry Higgins in the Broadway musical *My Fair Lady* and in the television adaptation of *The Ghost and Mrs. Muir,* died of lung cancer on May 24, 1997 at his home in Van Nuys, CA. His movies include *Signpost to Murder, Von Ryan's Express, Our Man Flint, Eye of the Devil, Caprice, Megaforce,* and *Out to Sea.* Survived by two brothers.

DON PORTER, 84, Oklahoma-born character actor, best known for his roles on the tv series "Private Secretary" and "Gidget," died at his home in Beverly Hills on Feb. 11, 1997. He was seen in such films as *Top Sergeant, 711 Ocean Drive, Because You're Mine, The Racket, Our Miss Brooks, Bachelor in Paradise, Gidget Goes to Rome, Youngblood Hawke, The Candidate, Forty Carats,* and *White Line Fever.* Survived by his wife, actress Peggy Converse, a daughter, and a son.

Red Skelton

DENVER PYLE, 77, Colorado-born screen and television actor, who played the sheriff who ambushed *Bonnie and Clyde* in the 1967 film classic, died on Dec. 25, 1997 in Burbank, CA. He had been suffering from lung cancer. Among his other movies are *The Guilt of Janet Ames, The Man from Colorado, Flame of Youth, Rough Riders of Durango, Oklahoma Annie, The Lusty Men, Texas Bad Man, Canyon Ambush, The Boy from Oklahoma, To Hell and Back, Run for Cover, Please Murder Me, I Killed Wild Bill Hickok, The Lonely Man, The Left-Handed Gun, Fort Massacre, The Party Crashers, The Horse Soldiers, The Alamo, Home from the Hill, The Man Who Shot Liberty Valance, Cheyenne Autumn, Shenandoah, Bandolero!, Cahill U.S. Marshal,* and *Escape to Witch Mountain.* On television he became well known for his role on the series "The Dukes of Hazzard." He survived by his wife and two sons.

Jesse White

Fred Zinnemann

MARJORIE REYNOLDS (Marjorie Goodspeed), 79, Idaho-born screen and television actress, best remembered for starring opposite Bing Crosby and Fred Astaire in the classic musical *Holiday Inn* died at her home in Manhattan Beach, CA, on Feb. 1, 1997. Among her other films are *College Humor* (billed as Marjorie Moore), *Overland Express, Streets of New York, Mr. Wong in Chinatown, Robin Hood of the Pecos, Cyclone on Horseback, Dixie, Ministry of Fear, Up in Mabel's Room, Bring on the Girls, Duffy's Tavern, Monsieur Beaucaire, The Time of Their Lives, Bad Men of Tombstone, That Midnight Kiss, The Great Jewel Robbery, His Kind of Woman,* and *Juke Box Rhythm.* On television she starred opposite William Bendix on "The Life of Riley." She is survived by her daughter.

WILLIAM REYNOLDS, 87, film editor who won Academy Awards for his work on *The Sound of Music* and *The Sting,* died of cancer on July 16, 1997 in South Pasadena, CA. He received additional nominations for *Fanny, The Sand Pebbles, Hello Dolly!, The Godfather,* and *The Turning Point.* He also co-produced the 1957 film *Time Limit.* No reported survivors.

ROBERT RIDGELY, 65, New Jersey-born screen and stage character actor died of cancer on Feb. 8, 1997 at his home in Toluca Lake, CA. His movies include *Blazing Saddles, Melvin and Howard, Beverly Hills Cop II, Robin Hood: Men in Tights, The Ref,* and *Boogie Nights.* Survived by his wife and a brother.

ALEXANDER SALKIND, 75, European producer, best known for the 1978 production of *Superman,* died on March 8, 1997 in Neuilly outside of Paris of unspecified causes. His other films include *The Three Musketeers* (1974), *The Four Musketeers* (1975), *Superman II, Superman III, Santa Claus,* and *Christopher Columbus: The Discovery.* He is survived by his son and co-producer Ilya Salkind, his wife and five grandchildren.

RED SKELTON (Richard Skelton), 84, Indiana-born screen and television comedian known for his mix or slapstick and pantomime, died on Sept . 17, 1997 in Rancho Mirage, CA. Following his 1938 debut in *Having Wonderful Time* he was seen in such motion pictures as *The People vs. Dr. Kildare, Lady Be Good, Whistling in the Dark, Panama Hattie, Ship Ahoy, DuBarry Was a Lady, I Dood It, Thousands Cheer, Bathing Beauty, Ziegfeld Follies, The Show-Off, Merton of the Movies, A Southern Yankee, The Fuller Brush Man, Neptune's Daughter, The Yellow Cab Man, Three Little Words, Duchess of Idaho, Watch the Birdie, Excuse My Dust, Lovely to Look At, The Clown, Half a Hero, Around the World in 80 Days,* and *Those Magnificent Men in Their Flying Machines.* His variety series "The Red Skelton Show" ran on CBS for nineteen seasons. Survived by his wife, his daughter, and a grandddaughter.

DAWN STEEL, 51, Hollywood producer and the first woman to head a major movie studio, died on Dec. 20, 1997 in Los Angeles, after suffering from a brain tumor. From 1987 to 1991 she headed Columbia Pictures. Afterwards she served as producer on *Honey I Blew Up the Kid, Cool Runnings, Sister Act 2: Back in the Habit, Fallen,* and *City of Angels.* Survived by her husband, daughter, and brother.

DON STEELE, 61, radio disk jockey , died of lung cancer on Aug. 5, 1997 at his home in Los Angeles. He appeared in such movies as *Rock' n' Roll High School, Death Race 2000, Gremlins, Eating Raoul,* and *Bordello of Blood.* Survived by his wife.

JAMES STEWART, 89, Pennsylvania-born screen, stage and television actor, one of the most popular and beloved of all Hollywood performers, who won the 1940 Academy Award for *The Philadelphia Story* and earned addtional nominations for *Mr. Smith Goes to Washington, It's a Wonderful Life, Harvey,* and *Anatomy of a Murder*, died at his home in Beverly Hills, CA, on July 2, 1997 from a blood clot in his lung. His other movies are *Murder Man* (1935 debut), *Rose Marie* (1936), *Next Time We Love, Wife vs. Secretary, Small Town Girl* (1936), *Speed, The Gorgeous Hussy, Born to Dance, After the Thin Man, Seventh Heaven* (1937), *The Last Gangster, Navy Blue and Gold, Of Human Hearts, Vivacious Lady, The Shopworn Angel* (1938), *You Can't Take It With You, Made for Each Other* (1933), *Ice Follies of 1939, It's a Wonderful World, Destry Rides Again, The Shop Around the Corner, The Mortal Storm, No Time for Comedy, Come Live With Me, Pot o' Gold, Ziegfeld Girl, Magic Town, Call Northside 777, On Our Merry Way, Rope, You Gotta Stay Happy, The Stratton Story, Malaya, Winchester 73, Broken Arrow* (1950), *The Jackpot, No Highway in the Sky, The Greatest Show on Earth, Bend of the River, Carbine Williams, The Naked Spur, Thunder Bay, The Glenn Miller Story, Rear Window, The Far Country, Strategic Air Command, The Man from Laramie, The Man Who Knew Too Much* (1956), *The Spirit of St. Louis, Night Passage, Vertigo, Bell Book and Candle, The FBI Story, The Mountain Road, Two Rode Together, The Man Who Shot Liberty Valance, Mr. Hobbs Takes a Vacation, How the West Was Won, Take Her She's Mine, Cheyenne Autumn, Dear Brigitte, Shenandoah, The Flight of the Phoenix, The Rare Breed, Firecreek, Bandolero!, The Cheyne Social Club, Fools' Parade, The Shootist, The Big Sleep* (1978), *The Magic of Lassie, The Green Horizon/Afurika Monogatari,* and *An American Tail: Fievel Goes West* (voice). His many honors include the Kennedy Center Honors, the American Film Institute Life Achievement Award, the Presidential Medal of Freedom, and a special Academy Award in 1984. He is survived by his stepson and two daughters.

TOMOYUKI TANAKA, 86, Japanese film producer best known for the series of "Godzilla" films starting with *Godzilla King of the Monsters* in 1954 (1956 in America), died in Tokyo on Apr. 2, 1998. Survived by his wife and three sons.

JESSE WHITE, 79, Buffalo-born screen, stage and tv character actor who first came to prominence playing gruff orderly Wilson in the Broadway and film versions of *Harvey,* died on Jan. 9, 1997 in Los Angeles following complications of surgery. Among his other movies are *Death of a Salesman, Bedtime for Bonzo, Francis Goes to the Races, Million Dollar Mermaid, Forever Female, Hell's Half Acre, The Girl Rush, Designing Woman, Country Music Holiday, Marjorie Morningstar, The Rise and Fall of Legs Diamond, On the Double, Sail a Crooked Ship, It's Only Money, It's a Mad Mad Mad Mad World, Pajama Party, A House is Not a Home, Dear Brigitte, The Spirit is Willing, The Ghost in the Invisible Bikini, The Reluctant Astronaut, Bless the Beasts and Children, The Cat from Outer Space,* and *Matinee*. Television viewers knew him best as the Maytag repair from a series of commercials that ran for over twenty years. Survived by his wife, two daughters, a son, five sisters, two brothers, and three grandchildren.

BO WIDERBERG, 66, Swedish director, best known for the 1967 film *Elvira Madigan*, died of an unspecified illness on May 1, 1997 in Angelholm, Sweden. His other credits include *All Things Fair* (which was nominated for an Oscar for foreign-language film), *Adalen '31, Raven's End,* and *Joe Hill.* No reported survivors.

MAX YOUNGSTEIN, 84, Hollywood executive and producer, died at his Los Angeles home on July 8, 1997. He was head of production at United Artists from 1951 to 1962. Later he served as producer on such movies as *Fail Safe, The Money Trap,* and *Welcome to Hard Times.* Survivors include his wife, four daughters, and a son.

FRED ZINNEMANN, 89, Austria-born Hollywood director who won Academy Awards for his work on *From Here to Eternity* and *A Man for All Seasons* (also winning a second Oscar for producing) died on Mar. 14, 1997 at his home in London. He received additional nominations for *The Search, High Noon, The Nun's Story, The Sundowners,* and *Julia.* His other credits include *Kid Glove Killer* (his debut in 1942), *Eyes in the Night, The Seventh Cross, My Brother Talks to Horses, The Men, Teresa, The Member of the Wedding, Oklahoma!, A Hatful of Rain, Behold a Pale Horse, The Day of the Jackal,* and *Five Days One Summer.* Survived by his wife, a son, and four grandchildren.

INDEX